Musings of an Infovore

*

The Essays

of

Raymond R. A. Burke

Geek, Batman cosplayer, and wannabe Iceland explorer - Raymond Burke is a British-born author. His background includes a teenaged life in Canada and the US, his twenties in the British Army as an aircraft technician, his thirties as a mature archaeology student with BSc and MSc degrees from University College London, and from his forties a sci-fi author. He is also a member of The Mars Society.

Raymond cunningly lives without a fridge, satellite TV, iPods, and he also can't drive. And while he has taken up 3D printing, he's a self-confessed 21st century caveman - and loves it!

Through all, he has been a keen writer. He lives in London.

ACKNOWLEDGMENTS

I would like to say a big thank you to Helium.com, the writing site which gave me the opportunity to express my thoughts and ideas during a downturn in my life. To Mark Ranalli, President & CEO of Helium for creating such a great site and to all the senior staff who helped me along the way, listened to ideas, and had the belief in me to manage the Arts & Humanities Channel. To the stewards I managed and who made life at Helium fun and informative. And of course to my fellow Helium writers who enlightened and entertained me.

My writing wasn't formed in a vacuum, nor just from my time writing essays at university, but mostly from my formative years at schools and experiences growing up in other countries and in various employments. So a big thank you to my teachers, supervisors, colleagues, fellow students, and friends who inspired me along my writing journey.

My sincerest gratitude to those who have allowed me to contribute their correspondence to this work: Dr Paul Halpern; to The Gatsby Charitable Foundation for Lord Sainsbury's permission; Bruno Comby – President of the Environmentalists for Nuclear Energy, and to the Mayor of London Office.

Cover design by Ennel John Espanola and Janet Dado (DPI Printing Solutions).

Formatting by Catherine Entero.

To

My parents

CONTENTS

INTRODUCTION

I suppose this book is part autobiography as seen through the eyes of my essays and subsequent updated thoughts. To begin with, way back for a time in 2007-08, I was unemployed for roughly eight months, having completed my MSc in Archaeology in 2006 and left my job in the security industry the following year. While I lazily looked for new work, I somehow came across and joined an online writing site, Helium.com, in early December 2007. There you could publish your articles on a variety of subjects, rate other articles, participate in debates, make money, and for the right third-party publisher get paid even more.

I had already started writing my first sci-fi novel (almost 30 years in the making and then some), written essays and dissertations at university, plus created songs and poems in my spare time. But I hadn't considered writing articles with the hope of earning money. So, here was my chance.

From that time onward, I wrote over 230 articles on a multitude of subjects. It was a very creative time for me even after I started working again. I finished my sci-fi novel in 2010 (self-published in 2012) and continued to write articles for the website until 2011, when I decided to call it quits due to my growing work commitments.

Because of my superlative writing skills (as most of my ancient history articles were edited essays from uni) and my archaeological background, in March 2008, I was recruited by a member of the Channel-level Stewards for the Arts and Humanities Channel. I became a channel steward for the Ancient History sub-channel.

My duties as a sub-channel steward were to police the site making sure articles were up to scratch, ensure the site rules were obeyed, and encourage writers. This included going through and vetting articles for writing standards and article length (as there was a prescribed minimum limit), off-topic or title interpretation issues, tidying up duplicate titles, flagging articles for plagiarism, editing or deleting of non-compliant articles, infractions of personal details, and applauding creative and outstanding works. There was also a duty to rate other writers' articles. In that way, articles rose and fell on their merit and that progression up the ranks was how one got paid. Payments were small, but stacked up and once at a certain threshold funds were released to your preferred account.

Other than writing articles and earning money for well-rated articles, writers could also make more money by having their articles chosen by third-party partners (usually from their sponsored titles or debates) and published in their own magazines or websites. I sold a few articles, which I'm very proud of and which also led to a short-lived volunteer writing/editing gig in a start-up online sci-fi magazine.

In April 2009, I took over as the Arts and Humanities Channel Manager from the outgoing manager with the job of wrangling stewards of the sub-channels Dance, History, Language, Literature, Museums & Galleries, Philosophy, Theater & Drama, Visual Arts, Writing, and Arts and Humanities (other). The other Channels such as Science, Politics, Business, Culture, etc, had similar relevant sub-channel breakdowns. While hard work it was a pleasure. My duties included creating contests titles and overseeing quality of articles. My role also saw me vet and hire new stewards for various sub-channels, brief them on their role expectations, send out monthly 'stew brews' newsletters on the state of affairs of the channel and also an end of year report.

I also helped to shape the Arts and Humanities channel by successfully suggesting new topics and taxonomies like Canadian History and new Asian, African and Middle East History sub-channels, as the hierarchy were slow to change and create new channels without valid reasons. But such changes helped writers present their articles within clear, defined channels.

When Helium branched out with their latest brainwave called Beta Zones, where common articles and themes could be collected together like a webpage, I created the Mars Beta Zone for articles solely about the planet Mars. It was accompanied by the group I set up: We are the Martians, a forum for Mars-centric authors.

Along the way, I also suggested new ideas to the management team to grow the website beyond its online presence such as creating physical book volumes in the same vein as New Scientist magazine had published books made up of their favourite question and answer sessions at the back of their magazines. But while that did not come to fruition, over the years, I started thinking about collecting my own articles together into a single book-length volume.

You have to remember that most of this time period was before the prolific rise of social media and the rampant rise of vitriol and echo chambers and where everyone is a content provider for free. I rather enjoyed the simpler long-form version of reasoned critique and creation.

Further to my role and desire to grow the website, I also reached out to other businesses on behalf of the website's marketing and publicity campaigns seeking out partnerships. Helium's programme was designed for writers to write for charities and non-profit organisations. This allowed the partners to sponsor and create topics for the writers and to increase their publicity, membership, and participation for both the writing site and the partner company.

During 2008, I came up with some crazy and hopefully innovative ideas for the hierarchy such as online business cards for the channel managers, physical books (as mentioned), expanding the brand of the company with physical products, conferences to bring together the dispersed writer community, a Milestone series to celebrate those who had written 50/100/200 articles, etc, or to celebrate membership anniversaries, or who had earned a certain amount. But my Best Article of the Year idea gained the attention of the Director of Content and Community who turned it into The Best of Helium Zone. I also wanted vouchers for stewards and channel managers to reward them for their hard and voluntary work, though we were gifted company T-Shirts.

I'd like to think I ran a tight ship and entertained others with my articles and management style in progressing the Arts and Humanities channel. But in January 2011, I decided to step away from the online writing/channel manager roles, and focus on my paying job after I had been promoted. While it was hard to leave, it was the right choice. However, it didn't stop me from writing and there are a few articles included in this book, some uncompleted, which I felt they should be included as they represent my thoughts during that period of time.

While this book focuses on the articles and essays, a second volume will concentrate on the entertainment essays, songs, poems, projects, and proposed TV shows I created before and after this same time period. Though that creative spirit hasn't left me, these volumes of work mostly centered between 2007-2011 were lifelines during darker times and I'm proud to share them here. Not included are a few short stories I had written for Helium and others submitted to publishers.

In 2014, Helium disappeared, closing down at the end of the year as new leaner and meaner writing websites rose and other fortunes waned. But now they are back having reinvented themselves as a freelance writing network with a more professional-writing ethic. I wish them luck.

A note on the essays and articles I have written. Unlike other writers who lost their articles when the website closed in 2014, I had saved copies on my hard drive or as printed copies and have a complete collection. Each article will appear, unedited from their original form, with the date of the article, the Channel it was written for, the sub-channel they were under(if remembered or noted), and for some a brief

2020 vision update or summary of why they were written and other random thoughts. Though the articles are over ten years old, a great many still offer relevant talking points for today. Food for thought in these difficult times.

Although on the writing platform the Channel of Arts and Humanities encompassed dance, history, language, literature and writing, museums and galleries, philosophy, theater and drama, and visual arts, I have separated out history and philosophy to form their owns sections as they have larger bodies of work in themselves.

Lastly, I hope you enjoy the articles. Some may be controversial. We all have differing views on subjects, especially on politics and religion. I'm not an expert on many of the issues, these being my honest and inner thoughts put to paper and are my legacy for good or bad. Whether you agree or disagree, I hope they offer some challenging debates, or fun, and maybe inspire you to write your own articles or book. Oh, and if you want to know what an Infovore is, then read on...

Raymond R.A. Burke
October 2020

Arts & Humanities

10/Apr/2008

Arts & Humanities – Literary Themes & Ideas
Favorite Books

My Favourite Books

2020 vision

Gosh, for one of these books, I became a fan-boy writing to the authors, scientists no less, to give them my take on the universe's origins. I was pleasantly surprised to get a reply and have included the brief correspondence at the end of the article.

If I had to add three more books to complete a top ten since I wrote this article then I would add *The Shock Doctrine*, by Naomi Klein (2007), which broadened my world view and added an unexpected author to my favourite's list. *Decoding the Heavens* by Jo Marchant (2008) documenting the recovery and understanding of the fascinating Antikythera mechanism, one of my favourite 'history mystery' subjects. Plus I had my original hardback autographed by Jo Marchant at a New Scientist event where she had given a talk. And, lastly *Tesla vs Edison*, by Nigel Cawthorne (2016), an excellent depiction of the work, rivalry, and lives of the two geniuses. There are a few other books which inspired me, but these are my absolute favourites.

There are many books and authors that I love and admire, but some have truly stood out in my own personal library. They would constitute a bibliography of my life in that they have inspired me and led my life in directions I would never have imagined as a young boy, whether in academics, professionally or personally. Some books are permanent and timeless fixtures, while others are permeable and reflect the changing times, though are no less important. Here are my Top Seven Books:

The Illiad:

Homer, no not that one, but the original Greek poet set the Classical Greek mythology book club afire with his tale of The Trojan War. Paris steals Helen away from husband Agamemnon, so he and his brother build their coalition army, enlist the canny, horse-building Odysseus, entice Achilles to fight for them, and head for Troy. Meanwhile, Paris' family prepare for war, Cassandra sees it all, but no one believes her. On the other side you have the Gods who choose sides and secretly wage war.

The battles scenes are epic, with whole chapters on who's who, their lineage, their life and how they died. It is a master class in tale weaving passed down through the generations and as real in your imagination as it is in the ruins of a small, obscure Turkish village.

The Hobbit:
J.R.R. Tolkien's masterpiece is such a tale of adventure that it is 'unputdownable'. To me it eclipses the later Ring Trilogy, because of its simpleness, pace and characters. I cannot wait for Guillermo del Toro to work his magic on this as Peter Jackson did the 'Lord of the Rings' books. Of course this is pre-Frodo and centres on his uncle Bilbo Baggins and his battle against Smaug the dragon for treasure, through which he finds the fateful Ring. It is Beowulf for Middle Earth and the Anglo-Saxon myth-like narration makes it seem so real. It is a must read and surely the epitome of any book professing to entertain adults and children about myth, magic and adventure.

Brave New Universe:
Paul Halpern and Paul Wesson are the newest to my list; this physics book really described to me the universe in a new light, even after reading copious and well-written books about the cosmos. It is the only book I have ever emailed the authors to praise them. Does that make me a physics groupie? Explaining Olber's and Fermi's Paradoxes, describing a Hypersphere, discussing dark matter, and much more elegant theories behind the secrets of the universe, Brave New Universe finally opened my eyes to understand the universe, such as it is.

Fingerprints of the Gods:
Graham Hancock wrote the book that for me started off the New Age Archaeology trend. I was in the Army at the time and posted in Belize, when I first read this book. I was close enough to visit some sites in Mexico and then had leave in Peru, so I investigated more. It prompted me to want to study archaeology and though I later learned that such material was frowned upon by the established academics, it nevertheless taught me to think differently about history and that science and experts

do not have all the answers. This is still the stand-out book in that field and now that New Age material has faded somewhat, it will probably remain a nostalgic, yet distinguished shelf filler.

Moondust:
Andrew Smith went in search of the men who fell to Earth and interviewed all the surviving Moonwalkers. If anyone really doubts the reality of the moon missions or for those who want to know more about these heroes, then this is the book for you. Smith's writing is impeccable; you can hear the astronauts' voices as they reflect upon their lives, it is so clear that they blasted off into the stark abyss and upon their return, they either left something behind, or the moon took it. These men are not the same; they are not normal in that for a body with little gravity, the moon exerted a cosmic weight upon their shoulders. While they are greater for it, there is such an inexpressible nature about them. The moon still grips them, like a shadow, like moondust within their souls.

The Arctic Grail:
Pierre Berton has written a book about Arctic exploration from its beginnings that at once is an epic of harrowing tragedy and overwhelming triumph. It takes you into the freezing hell that is the Arctic, makes you trek with the heroes and foolhardy, and then threatens to leave you in an ice-bound state. With men, dressed in little more than their naval uniforms, they braved -40° weather, dragging hundreds of tons of supplies over hundreds of miles. This was done in the name of exploration for the British Realm, to find the fabled North West Passage and then the North Pole. But most of all, it was done for survival. These were intrepid explorers, the likes of which we will never see again, maybe, until Martian exploration.

The Case For Mars:
Robert Zubrin has written the definitive book on how we will get to Mars. There have been many books since and many more technological advances, but in Zubrin there is also the facilitator, the organiser and the communicator. NASA is listening, but it will be the politicians that will make the decisions. The book was important in laying out past problems in going to Mars in regards to expense, technology and manning issues. There is a more 'sustainable' way to go to Mars and 'live off the land' making fuel, water, air and materials to survive. As rovers and satellites

gather more information over years, which would take a human weeks or months, it becomes important that the resources and training that have been established because of this book make the case for Mars, a foregone conclusion.

These are the books that have inspired me thus far, there are potentially more, but I have yet to read them. Explore your own book world, see how they have influenced you and remember the thrill of reading them.

***

My letter to scientists Paul Halpern and Paul Wesson. My thanks to Dr. Halpern for giving his permission to reproduce our correspondence.

27.01.2007

to: Paul Halpern,
Subject: Brave New Universe

Dear Professors Halpern and Wesson,

I am emailing to express my gratification after reading your book 'Brave New Universe'. After reading it I found myself understanding the complexities of the cosmos much more (even hyperspheres, after having read a lot of other physics books.)

My Background is in archaeology, but I like looking into the deeper past, the future and 'out there'. I was inspired and in reading the chapters about higher and curled dimensions and hypersurfaces, I wondered if there was a simpler way to look at at the universe.

In discussing M-Theory and superstring theory with 11 dimensions (p. 184-5), I imagined that we we already know what all the dimensions are and what they do. I do not know if this has been put forward before, but to me the known and extra dimensions are:

1. Length
2. breadth/width
3. depth
4. time (entropic field)
5. mass (higgs-boson field)
6. Gravity (gravitons)
7. strong force
8. weak force
9. electromagnetic force
10. dark matter (solitons/axions)
11. dark energy

These 11 dimensions represent branes, whose surfaces mesh tightly together to form an interwoven fabric that is the universal plane.

The 5th Dimension is the extra large dimension containing mass (p. 205), which I assume to be a hyperfield of Higgs-bosons.

Dimensions, 6·11 are the tightly woven Kaluza-Klein spaces. Their spaces are so tightly curled that they become almost fluidic in nature and can leak through the other larger branes in varying concentrations On passing through the 5th dimension, they gain their mass or loop quantum/string qualities before appearing in dimensions1-3. This could suggest a hierarchy among dimensions in that 'particles' pass from one brane to another in such an order as to give rise to the universe we see.

This suggests a direction in space and time, the 4th dimension seen as an entropic field, which causes a scalar flow across the branes, manifested as cause and effect.

Could this M-Theory (M for Mesh) work?

I remain inspired by your work and I thank you for reading this. I look forward to finding out more about our universe.

Regards,

Raymond Burke

Dr. Halpern responded later the same day.

27.01.2007

Dear Ray

Thank for your kind letter. It is interesting to hear about your idea for the significance of the higher dimensions. It will be curious to see if extra dimensions turn up in experiments.

Since your background is in archaeology, perhaps you have an interest in "hidden layers' beneath the surface of what can be seen. Archeology and cosmology are both fascinating ways to reveal the past and place the present day in the context of a deeper history.

Best wishes and good luck with your research,

Paul Halpern

11/Apr/2008

Arts & Humanities - Literary Themes & Ideas
Best picture books including photographs, illustrations, and graphics

Ten Great Photographic Books to Read and Why

2020 vision

When I was leaving the British Army in 1997, I chose to do a resettlement course to help find work after my discharge. At first, I had started driving lessons, but I didn't really like it (and still don't drive), plus everyone told me I could take lessons at any time and to choose something I could turn into a profession. So, as I liked photography and acted as my unit's unofficial photographer taking pics of events and travels, I elected to learn more about photography. I took the City and Guilds Media Photography, Part 1 in July 1997 at The Media Training Centre, Worcester, where I gained distinction and credit Awards.

After, I looked for work when I had moved back to London, whether in studios or freelance. With one agency I had called, I did have an opportunity to be part of an online library by taking pics of London transport (i.e. buses, trains, taxis, etc) but as it was getting on to late September/early October time and a bit chillier, I declined to take on the job and shortly after when I got work in security, that put paid to my photography career.

I still love photography and see it as a great visual journey of my life. However, I'm wary of digital photos and posting everything online. I miss the almost romantic nostalgia and texture of photo albums. One day the virtual cloud may dissipate and all our treasured pictorial collections could be lost down the digital drain, forever.

There are a great many books with photographs, illustrations, graphics or works of art in them covering many subjects; pictures that will remain etched in one's mind or inspire one to write, draw, photograph or travel to the origins of that picture. In no particular order, here is my top 10 list of such books:

1. The Past From Above:
Georg Gerster has captured glorious archaeological sites from the air, spanning a period of over 40 years. There really are some breathtaking images and some of the rarest taken over China, Israel, Iran, Iraq, and Egypt before their airspaces became more restricted. It is a weighty tome, an artefact of images that does justice to its subjects. You will never find a more global and glory-filled collection of aerial shots of ancient cities, brought to life by a camera.

2. With Scott to the Pole:
This is a fantastic, over-sized book, charting the 1912 Terra Nova Expedition to the South Pole by Captain Robert Falcon Scott. The Photographs are by Herbert Ponting and are stunning to say the least. You see and feel the raw beauty of the Antarctic, get a sense of winter life in a wooden hut, isolated against the winds and ice, share in the scientific work and also see the haunted look in many an eye as the season wears on. It is a great record and tribute to both Scott and Ponting.

3. South With Endurance:
This is the companion book to 'With Scott to the Pole', this time with Frank Hurley's incredible photos following Sir Ernest Shackleton's Antarctic Expedition in 1914-17. As with Ponting, Hurley has captured the spellbinding nature of the voyage, the loss of the Endurance, and the heroic and desperate voyage in the James Caird to South Georgia Island. There are some amazing portraits of the crew, which serve to remind us of their poignant ordeals and are not eulogy to their deaths.

4. Full Moon:
Michael Light has two books in this list, the first being a revisit to the moon to celebrate the 30th anniversary of the moon landing. The pictures convey the extraordinary blackness of space, printed on specially designed black paper to achieve this effect. NASA generously allowed Light access to their archive and he has produced an outstanding narration of the Apollo missions through oft seen and rare photos. These visions of the greatest journey ever made by man were originally captured in pure essence by the Moonwalkers themselves, but now they have resurfaced triumphantly into the light.

5. 100 Suns:
Michael Light's follow up was a strange subject and though nuclear tests were controversial, they were never seen other than by the scientists and the soldiers sent to set the tests up around the world. As Light states, this is not a celebration of nuclear testing, but 'an unprecedented historical document' and 'profoundly disconcerting as a spectacle'. This is a chronology of nuclear testing and a show of the awesome destructiveness of such weapons. There are also amazing little snaps of history in the captions, of nuclear clouds narrowly missing cities, and of John Wayne, and many cast and crew from a particular film, who may have developed their cancers from filming in an area heavily tested within. The images are absolutely captivating, whether in black and white or glaring Technicolor, like explosive artwork, until you remember the purpose and viciousness of such weapons. It is an astonishing book and hopefully the last and only time you will see such a weapon in full bloom.

6. Magnificent Mars:
Ken Croswell's book is for me the most complete book about Mars with telescopic, orbital and rover pictures, capturing and aiding in the story of Mars through its life and its relationship between the elements Earth, Air, Fire and Water. The images sift through Martian history with sweeping panoramic views, foldout pages and stand alone photos of truly magnificent Martian scenery. Mars is the only other planet that can be photographed to the degree that Earth is, with spectacular locations to die for. How long before we can visit them in person?

7. An Extraordinary Gathering of Angels:
This little gem of a book, by Margaret Barker, I found in the St. Paul's Cathedral Gift shop. It is, as it says, an extraordinary collection of over 170 pictures of Angels from Jewish and Christian tradition, including paintings, icons and sculptures. There is a history of Angels, how they have manifested themselves and changed over the millennia. If ever you wanted a definitive 'bible' to the Angels, then this is it!

8. The Book of Cities:
A revelation of a book I picked up from an eclectic gift shop. Philip Dodd and Ben Donald take in 250 cities, starting from the Greenwich Meridian and working their way west, presenting each city in longitudinal order. This innovative travelogue then delights the reader as you realize

that some countries stretch several longitudes and its cities pop up in between cities from other countries. Some of the descriptions may be out of date (as I was reliably informed by a friend from Accra), but the book is an essential pictorial guide around the world. Enjoy!

9. The Modern Antiquarian:

Julian Cope has compiled a most exhaustive and unique history of standing stones and circles in the UK, and along with the sequel 'The Megalithic European' (a sneaky inclusion) constitute a major and updated archaeological encyclopedia on the great lithic building traditions that still fascinate us today. Colour coded sections denote the various regions within Great Britain, so searching for your favourite standing stone is made easier. The sheer scale of this task is brilliant and would be much appreciated by anyone who wanted to follow in the footsteps of any ancient ancestors.

10. 30,000 Years of Art:

Okay, I am cheating here, I do not actually own this book, nor have I read it, but any book that can cover the art of humanity in over 1000 fabulous pages deserves its place in this list on reputation alone. Phaidon Editors should be congratulated on such a daunting task, having to decide which representative one thousand pieces of art would best encapsulate the best of mankind. The exceptional achievement of a book would have pride of place in any library, ancient or modern. It is in a class of its own and superbly illustrates the reason for this and any other list regarding visual spectacle. What will take our fancy in another 30,000 years?

25/Jun/2008

Arts & Humanities - Language
Origins of last names

What's in a Country Surname?

2020 vision
I'll admit, so lame was this article that one reviewer just proclaimed 'No, no, no!' So that good then? But then I rewrote it slightly for a 21/Jul/2010 title. It's still bad as it's inaccurate in detail, but hopefully thoughtful in some respects. I won't bore you with the other version of the article.

It is well documented that surnames have their origins in types of trades or occupations (e.g. Thatcher, Butcher, Potter, etc), familial relationships (e.g. son/daughter of, Simonsson, Godinsdottir, van/von, etc) and geographic denominatives (e.g. Forrest, Norman, Saxon, etc). But there are more sources for surnames that go beyond trades, family, geography, and nicknames. And it seems mostly confined to the English-speaking world.

Some people in Britain can often have surnames of countries (with spelling variations) whether Mr. England, Mr. Briton, Scott, Scotland, Welsh, Ireland, etc (not forgetting the female variations too) and foreign country surnames as well. Is this just a quirk of the English language? And why should this be so? This is different to geographical denominative names as it encompasses the whole country, is a later development, may not reflect the origins of the person, and seems to appear only in the English-speaking world in general.

For example: whether on the European continent or not, we have surnames like Mr. Brittan (Brittany), Franck, Frank, French; or Mr. Holland or Denmark. But while some country names do appear others seem absent. Is there a Mr. Swede or Sweden, Mr. Iceland, Messrs Norway, Finland or Greenland? We have Mr. Poll, but Mr. Poland. Where are the Messrs Greek, Germany, Deutsche, or Hungary. There are cases of Messrs. Espana, German, Israel, and maybe a few Mr. Turks. There are plenty of Mr. Jordans, but in Jordan? Will mother

Russia have a few sons and daughters named Mr. or Mrs. Russia? There are Mr. Cechs, but are there any Mr. Czechs or Slovaks? Europe seems to reside in Britain in this peculiar custom.

Heading out to Asia we have the Chinese. Some of their surnames seem based on their country's name like Mr. Chin, a variation of Qin or Ch'in? But would their citizens be surnamed after other countries? Does Japan have a Mr. Nippon or are there Messrs Korea, Thailand, Nepal, Tibet, Burma or Malay? When Genghis Khan left this world he had hundreds of offspring, but do any Mr. Mongols or Mongolias exist or would any of his far-flung descendants now be called Mr. England? And while India may be a girl's forename does the same ring true as a surname? With billions of Indians and Chinese the chance of possessing a foreign country surname may exist.

In Africa, is there a Mr. or Mrs. Ghana, Nigeria, Zambia, Algeria or Malawi? Will Mr. Congo shake hands with Messrs. Kenya, Burundi, Uganda, Libya or Sudan? However, as most African countries were created or named by Colonialists would such a surname be an advantage or detrimental? Do the inhabitants name themselves with traditional surnames that refer to their country? Or are there ancient surnames from past empires such as the Songay, Benin (Dahomey or Fon), or Mali down in Timbuktu? Would such names have filtered in through imperialism or recent migration?

From Canada to Tierra del Fuego, from Hawaii to Brazil, and all parts in between are there any surnames that match their countries. Mr Amerigo (Vespucci) may have inspired the naming of America, but are there any Messrs. Amerigos or Americas in the Americas? Columbus prompted Columbia and Simon Bolivar liberated Bolivia, but do any of those countries' citizens share in their countries' names? Does Mr. Peru know a Mr. Mexico, or Guatemala, Belize, Nicaragua, Venezuela, Panama or Chile? Will there be any silver linings in discovering Mr. Argentina? Mr. Brazil, a famous Scottish footballer, sounds familiar, but are there any Mr Brasílias in Brazil? Are we missing something in the translation? Are there native Spanish or Portuguese variations on these surnames?

Mr. Tasman had a devil of a time discovering Tasmania, but Mr. Australia has yet to emerge. New or not, Mr. Zealand would find his roots in Holland. Will we find a Mr. Sumatra, Borneo or Timor? From the Philippines to Papua New Guinea, Tahiti to Rapa Nui, does Oceania have a different tradition concerning surnames or will there be similarities?

What is different or inherent in the English-speaking world in the choosing and appropriation of surnames from their own or other countries? Maybe the history of the English-speaking world through their language, or patriotism or shared culture lends itself to making up new words and rules and creating surnames from anything distinctive, even a country's name. Like nominative determinism (such as Mr. Baker who's a baker or Mr. Seaman who's a sea man) do such country surnames reflect origins or a presence to belonging to a country? Even now, after the Empire, the British-speaking world still likes to acquire foreign possessions, right down to their names. In any case, the choice of a 'geo-nominative' surname is distinctive and culturally identifiable, but let's hope there are other such surname quirks around the world.

12/Jul/2008

Reflections: What architecture means to me

Regaining Our Sense of Architecture

2020 vision
Besides the structure I helped build as described below in the article, during the Institute of Archaeology's annual PrimTech course (an introduction course for first-year students in the arts of primary technologies), I had also helped build a rudimentary 3-man log lean-to in the jungles of Belize while on an Army tour in 1996. It took the three of us quite a few hours to chop down enough trees, avoiding the ones with sap which could squirt out the trunk and blind you and those with sharp spikes on their trunks, plus trying to avoid high branches dropping down on you. One branch hit me just below my eye. I was lucky it missed the eyeball and to this day people still say they can see a slight dint just below my left eye. The hazards of building a primitive shelter.

Anyway, the three of us put the frame together and topped it off with branches and large leaves just as it got dark. We lit a large fire to keep animals away (though in the morning we were told by our guide there had been a jaguar in the area), but it attracted the insects, with some sounding like they had twin engines on them. However, the fire was intoxicating, like a primitive TV. We watched in silence as it crackled and told us stories in its flames. We were knackered and appreciated the effort it took just to get something like this simple structure built.

I love buildings, from humble houses to the highest of skyscrapers. While studying archaeology I often pondered the questions of who had first thought of building a shelter with sticks and branches, mammoth tusks, mud, mud brick, and stones; with wattle and daub walls, thatched roofs, and fur-lined interiors. There is so much that goes into architecture, aspects that the layman cannot see or imagine or has forgotten.

Structure:
On an experimental archaeology course, I helped to reconstruct a simple branch structure with thatched roof. All we had to go on was post-hole evidence and the rest was up to us to interpret how the building looked

and was constructed. It usually ended up taking on a square shape, with interweaving or twine-tied branches for sturdiness and a sloping thatched roof.

Fast forward a few millennia and the same could be true of today, except we have wood, brick, slate, glass, steel and high tech composites. Technology has enabled us to build a better house of sticks, whether it is round, square or polygonal. Our basic need for shelter still sees us housed in utilitarian boxes, no matter how fancy the outside is. We may feel our modern age has seen innovative building techniques in design, cladding, and size, but an archaeologist from the future will interpret from our foundations that we continued the tradition of our ancestors, but with different materials. We are still cavemen, but with better tools and toys.

Aesthetics:
There is something so gratifying in the symmetry and solidness of a finely constructed building, no matter its age or function. It is why we have ancient and modern wonders of the world. They appeal to our sense of aesthetics and our world is built upon heritage and landmarks. In this globalising world, buildings take on a similar look, but with local variations from New York to Dubai, to Kuala Lumpur to Shanghai, the skyscraper may look the same, but the nod toward traditional aesthetics is unmistakable. We love buildings that have beauty and character.

The Greeks first hit upon the formula for harmonic proportions, which was continued during the Roman era and then again through the Renaissance. Such eye pleasing monuments are a tribute to our ancestors who knew what would please the Gods and man; from the Pyramids to the Taj Mahal, London's Swiss Re to the Empire State Building, there is a part of our brain that rejoices in symmetry, harmony, beauty, and integrity. A building has to look great; it has to make you feel something inside; make you want to touch it, maybe own it; and appeal to your sense(s) of cosmic order. That is a building with heart and it makes your own beat faster in wondrous admiration.

Location:
Even in the middle of a congested city, some buildings stand out. In combination with the structure and the aesthetics, the location of a building can mean its survival as an icon or its forgotten isolation leading to dereliction. The skyline of London has changed dramatically

31

over the past two decades with the development of Canary Wharf, the Square Mile and around St. Paul's Cathedral, which often sees battles between developers and those who want to maintain traditional sight lines to and from the Cathedral. These sight lines are remnants of traditions that existed between henges and causeways, and lines of sight to particular important places. It's our connection to the past, reassuring our faith that the world we now perceive still stands.

Some houses used to be built facing east toward the rising, life-giving sun with the back of the house receiving the sunset of the dead. Houses could face the prevailing wind to cool the interior or to stoke the hearth. The house was a part of the environment then, so was man, now architects and designers bring the environment inside with aircon, waterwalls, and hanging plants. However, all is not lost, we might not realise it, but we still maintain our relationship to the past through architecture.

Ritual:
As a lecturer once told us, even though we might not think we appreciate architecture, or feel anything for a building, or notice the location of where we live or work; we do, but we have internalised our reactions and emotions. There are probably parts of a building a person likes the most or feels more comfortable in. They have a preferred desk or chair, and a choice location to hang out. Where I've worked, staff members brought in personal guests to see where they worked. No doubt, they then looked out the window from their privileged perch on the umpteenth floor and admired the view.

Without realising it, they've reverted to their past ancestors in remotely analysing the structures around them and comparing them with their own edifice; they're noting which other buildings on the horizon catch their eye or in which direction they live; and they are appreciating the layout of the city and how the building blocks of a city centre are aligned. Without being conscious of it, the average person is still concerned about the structure, aesthetics and location of architecture, through their own personal habits and mores; it has just been repressed by modern life.

So when out and about in the city or country, take a good look at the buildings; consider their structure, location and aesthetics. Try to get a feel for the building, imagine its character, and contemplate it and the surrounding environment. Once you can contextualise a building, architecture becomes a whole new and meaningful experience. Our past is a clear reflection of the future, and architecture can still teach us a lot about ourselves and our environment.

04/Feb/2009

Art & Humanities – Language
The best known fictional languages

Fictional Languages: Kryptonian

2020 vision

It must be a real art to create a fictional language standing up to the scrutiny of linguistic adherents. But isn't it strange we have never heard Superman speak his native tongue? He's been around for over 80 years and the spoken language is still a mystery, though we have seen the strange pictorial symbols written down. Maybe that will change soon with the proliferation of Supergirl and Superman depictions on TV and film. The links near the end were still active as of September 2020.

What does the language of Superman sound like? Have you ever heard the Man of Steel utter a word of it? In the TV show Smallville, we have come closest to finding out more about the culture of Krypton, but still while we have an alphabet of Kryptonian symbols, the oral content is somewhat lacking.

We have heard the Klingon tongue, designed by Marc Okrand, and you can study it at university or even read the Klingon dictionary. We have heard Vulcan, Romulan, and countless other Star Trek languages spoken. Star Wars thrived on foreign stellar languages even if one character Nien Nunb (Lando's co-pilot in Star Wars –Return of the Jedi) was actually speaking Haya, a Kenyan language. In fact, most other languages from Star Wars were actually existing Earth languages. Even the Hobbits from JRR Tolkien's Lord of the Rings have their own language. While each of these has had some kind of public verbal outing, Kryptonian has remained silent.

In the comic book 'Superman/Batman', when the latest version of Supergirl landed, the word bubbles had her spouting some form of language with strange non-alphabetic geometric symbols connected by lines, like a flowchart or a machine language, though Batman could decipher it. Was Kryptonian so advanced that they spoke like computers? Was the language so advanced that maybe it's more telepathic than oral? Is Kryptonian the language of love or a scientific language? Is it guttural, a flowing singsong sound or of clicks and chirps? How did it evolve? Why have we never heard the language of one of the most superior races in the universe? Would future Xeno-linguists be able to decipher a language as alien as Kryptonian? No comic book page can convey the sound of an alien lingo. We need to hear it in order to understand its meaning and gain depth into the character of the speaker.

Attempts to rationalise the language through different sources from TV shows and comic book reboots have only muddied the waters a bit since differing versions have occurred. First, the language originally appeared in Superman comics as 'alien' squiggles. There was also a version that had 118 symbols invented by Al Turniansky and used by DC Comics in 2000. This was the latest canonical version, until Smallville entered the scene with its own new Kryptonian language. But why should the new Kryptonian alphabet match ours and have 26 letters and a corresponding series of numbers. In the latest development, Darren Doyle has produced a more cohesive history, interpretation, and lexicon of the Kryptonian language with The Kryptonese Language Project.

But have we had a breakthrough in our hunt for spoken Kryptonian? In Smallville Series 7, episode 9, 'Gemini' there was a character who was heard to whisper Kryptonian, so Clark/Bizarro claimed. Not much could be heard, except a low kind of chant. There are claims that Lionel Luthor spoke Kryptonian in Series 5, but recollections have him just scribbling a lot of Kryptonian symbols. As the series progresses, will more of the elusive language of Krypton come to light? Will we see Kryptonese-to-English language books and dictionaries? Shouldn't Jor-El be teaching Kal-El these simple things instead of encouraging his son to speak American English like an unabashed first-generation immigrant? Kryptonian should be out and proud.

Recently, the chemical characteristics of the mineral Kryptonite have been revealed, from a mineral found in a Serbian mine. So how long until other Kryptonian secrets come to the surface? Unlike many Earth languages, at least Kryptonian is being rescued from being an extinct language. But how long will it be until we hear Krypton's greatest export actually speak his native tongue. Come on Superman, spare us few words and declare yourself in Kryptonian.

26/Apr/2009

Arts & Humanities

The Benefits of Journaling

2020 vision

I kept diaries during my time in the army, but found the small daily spaces too confining. Even with the most exciting events, there's not enough room to tell the story. Only while I was at university as an archaeology student, travelling and working in Peru, did I see the real benefit of starting a journal. And I haven't stopped since.

In 2000, I bought a close friend a blank-paged, 6"x 4", copper-embossed journal for her birthday, which she loved, and which then inspired me to get one of my own. From working and travelling around Peru, I was able to dedicate as much space as I wanted to about any subject. I wrote about excavation work, the hotels, how I relaxed, friends I made, even the day my sister told me I had a brand new nephew. There are ticket stubs from buses, planes, and trains, tourist pamphlets, drawings, maps, postcards, my week-long trip to Bolivia, and even a small Peruvian flag bulging out from the ring-binding. It was a six-week trip of a lifetime embodied within the pages of one journal. I never looked back; it was journals all the way.

After having such a great journal experience, I have continued in that vein with different blank-paged journals, some with ornate copper-covered designs or others with normal hard-back covers with elastic wrap-around page markers. I even have one special shop I purchase from as they have a great selection of hand made journals, an advantage over less hardier diaries.

Journals give one a chance to be expressive in a free space, without the need for a daily entry. It is kind of like a personal off-line blog, all the best (or worse) bits of your life as it happens. Tickets to concerts and cinemas; invitations or guest passes to parties, lectures, museums, conferences, and other events; business cards from people and restaurants; folded menus and bills/receipts from memorable meetings; foreign stamps; train tickets to unfamiliar places; even an unused ticket to a Superbowl party (due to freak snow storm) are in the journal. There is also a materialistic streak when I note special items I have bought – usually books. I especially log -in red ink or with a red star- articles, stories or book details, TV programme ideas, and at the end of each month, I tot up my Helium articles, their rank and how many written so I can keep a monthly tally myself. At the end of the year I have a 'retro' page, where I have a retrospective look at the year past in point form; all the highlights that stood out. Having a journal is a great way to condense the outstanding moments of one's life on paper.

In the future, I will get a 7"x 5" sized journal, slightly bigger than my current journal. This would be for when I go travelling and fill it with 'old fashioned' print photos with more room to write all about my adventures. Journals jog your memory and are the perfect basis for a biography or memoir as they are more substantial than diaries, having a more quantifiable identity. A journal is a more conscious undertaking, something to be cherished and kept for posterity. Every year my diaries are replaced, any relevant material going into the journal. Diaries may not cost a lot, but a journal would last longer, being able to pack in multiple years. Or even if a small journal covered just one event like a trip of a lifetime –you would have all the space and time to write in one volume. Journals are more cost-effective. Journals are for keeps and could be left on the shelf in volumes, if wanted.

Journals transcend the calendar year, they are timeless. You can put a title year on the front of a journal, but more often than not, a journal will cover more than a year's worth of experience. A diary restricts your creativity and entries. A diary confines you to the man-made year, while a journal offers freedom of managing your own agenda and period of journaling. For me, New Year's Day does not necessarily re-set my year. For instance, I commemorate my years from personal events. My life has been a cycle of roughly 5, 6, or 11 years –very weird- but changes seem to happen in my life, not usually by my own design, over those time scales. I am now in a post-unemployment phase, following my 'year of hell' in 2007/8, the brightest point being discovering Helium while online looking for work. Without that, I would never have discovered Helium and my life and journals would be the poorer for it.

Journals are for life – really the journey of your life. While diaries can be important in one's life, they rein in one's ability to create a long-term and adaptable narrative. You have a daily, monthly, or yearly chronicle only. A journal offers greater scope for reflection and writing on a grander scale. Go for the journal; go write your life.

26/Apr/2009

Art & Humanities - Museums and Galleries
Imagine that you have decided to launch a new museum …
what type of museum would you establish and why?

The Elemental Museum

Before the atomic age, we had the four perceived elements of Earth, Air, Wind, and Fire. Everything stemmed from and was built with these gifts from the Gods. We now take them for granted, but our ancient forbearers depended upon them, nay, prayed for them, for their lives. So, what better way to remember our ancestors than to commemorate those ancient elements with their own museum with the art, sculpture, crafts, other artefacts, even the building itself, all made from those elemental building blocks.

Earth:
The art work would be of earth-related materials, painted by plant-based paints (all plants and wood are from the earth and grown with wind and water and nurtured by the great ball of fire in the sky or from the nutrients of charcoal in the ground). Natural colouring from mineral pigments like ochre, cinnabar, haematite, or gems and semi-precious stones could decorate the art work. Artists would have an infinite of natural ingredients from which to work from. The power of stone, the finesse of clay, and the versatility of wood would be displayed in their awesome states. In small surrounding galleries, visitors would be encouraged to work clay, sculpt stone or knap flint, and carve wood, to create their own portable art, a memory of the 'living' natural museum. In other galleries would be examples of minerals and elements in their raw state. Earth provides the building stuff of life and is the most familiar element seen in museums.

Water:
Water is poetry in motion, flowing art that eddies through life –water is life. The museum would be surrounded and infiltrated by flowing water in carefully designed and gradated streams. Pools of fish, foot pools, and bubbling brooks would soothe and cool the visitors and museum, respectively. In another gallery would stand the 'water-seum', where

samples of every river, lake, sea, and ocean would be collected in large sealed transparent jars in order to preserve a piece of what was once pristine water and how it has changed over time. Such 'water-seums' may be the only thing left of many rivers and lakes, once global warming has affected many bodies of water a few decades from now. Fountains would pervade the grounds to entertain and demonstrate the mechanics of water motion. The highlight would be a water wall, falling through the air into a pebble stone pool; a refreshing sight and sound of nature.

The Museum:
The museum itself would be built in the form of large roundhouses in small village-like pods. Each pod, with its own natural element theme, would have stone foundations with wattle and daub walls and thatched roofs. Stone walls would ring the pods and separate exhibits. The museum would be a synergy of the natural elements, using each to highlight their characteristics. Modern technology would be absent (except in the need of health and safety situations) so that the true nature and rawness of the elements could be appreciated. The visitors' café would have traditional hand-cooked rustic foods, the gift shop would offer natural man-made crafts, and the low-tech approach would continue with the museum being run on sustainable energy like wind or water power.

Fire:
Each roundhouse would be heated by central hearths managed by attendants using small bellows, and whose wispy smoke would escape through the open 'chimney' above. Fire, with the use of kilns, could be shown in use to harden earth/clay for pots, bricks and tablets or to make metal from 'stone' like copper, tin, and antimony. How to make fire from striking flint, how to harness fire, and how to make art from fire could be taught in more side galleries. Fire was the first TV set. Sitting around a camp fire watching the wood burn and crackle, leap and make sparks, and twist and bend in the wind, would have added a mesmerising atmosphere to night time stories, dances, and meetings. Such fire shows would be a feature of the fire pod galleries where performers would bring to life the ancient magic of fire.

Air:
Air is music, the rushing of the wind sings to everyone. Controlled air, via bellows, fans, and windmills would be the principle source of the

museum's lighting and other energy needs. Within the roundhouses, flutes, pan pipes, horns, didgeridoos, and stone or wood chimes would bring the sound of air alive. Air is fuel and its power would be felt and heard throughout the museum. The wind scatters seeds and pollen, controls water currents, stokes the fire, and enforces sea, air and land storms. Air is the distributor of life. Within an air gallery would be large tubes of colourful water and sand, through which air would be pumped. The tubes would be layered and represent the force and nature of air from the stratosphere down to the oceans. Air is constantly present and the air galleries would help to capture some of its life.

The fifth elements:
Are there fifth elements? Some people say that love or magic are the fifth elements. Could these be represented in such a museum? Could the four basic elements create aspects of love and/or magic? Love can unite people and make people believe they can do anything, especially with Earth, Air, Wind, and Fire. Love is an emotional element, inspired by or inspiring acts of creation from the four elements. Magic is the result of a piece of clay becoming a pot, a statue appearing from a lump of stone, a symbol carved on a piece of wood. Magic mystifies, inspires, and weaves together the other elements, as the spiritual element. Magic is the spirit of the mind, that intellectual spark that comes from knowledge of the physical and emotional elements. Love and Magic would already be captured within the art, surrounding the visitor, encouraging them to create their own art, seek out more art, and imbue themselves with the spirit of art.

The elemental museum would be an eclectic collection of art, combining the four elements to bring life into the museum, for visitors to participate and create their own elemental wonders. The roundhouses made of natural materials would necessarily have to change and grow, be repaired and rebuilt, as a living piece of art in itself. The four elements are not static creatures, but dynamic forces, and the elemental museum would reflect this.

27/Apr/2009

Arts & Humanities
Thor Heyerdahl: His amazing voyages

Thor Heyerdahl: Explorer or Showman

2020 vision

I had never heard of Tucume before, until a friend told me about it. We visited it together while on a break from a dig in Peru in 2000. It's the biggest pyramid complex in South America, but as outsiders thought the area looked like a series of natural mounds the site remained unheralded and under-studied until Thor Heyerdahl took an interest in the 1980s.

Norwegian adventurer Thor Heyerdahl's experimental sea voyages in traditionally-built papyrus reed or balsa wood boats were not to prove that ancient man had crossed the oceans of the world, but that they had the capability to do so. His views on colonisation by way of the oceans are still often misunderstood. Heyerdahl was usually lumped in with the new age writers even though he scorned that discipline for their misuse and abuse of archaeology while at the same time often criticising academics for not reaching out beyond their scientific paradigms.

Heyerdahl was an anthropologist and explorer. Born in Larvik, Norway, 1914, he first came to fame when in 1947, he and a group of men sailed from Peru to Polynesia in the balsa-wood raft called Kon-Tiki. He had wanted to investigate whether Polynesian myths about settlers from the East were true. The Kon-Tiki did make it westward to Polynesia, but whether or not ancient Peruvians did sail there would need further archaeological examination. Next, in 1969, Heyerdahl contested the fact that traditional reed boats could only sail on rivers. From Morocco, he used the papyrus-reed boat Ra I to keep him afloat in the ocean for months, rather than the days or weeks that the experts had predicted. In the following year, he sailed in Ra II from Morocco to Barbados. Again, while proving the concept that ancient boats could have crossed the Atlantic, the jury was still out on whether they did. Such voyages gave ammunition to his detractors that he was trying to prove that Egyptians had crossed the ocean and taught the New Worldwide how to build pyramids. This was far from the truth, though Heyerdahl did believe that the reed boat was important in spreading ancient culture.

Heyerdahl expeditions to Easter Island and the Galapagos in the 1950s found evidence that pre-Polynesian and per-Inca societies, respectively, had at least landed on these islands. One of Heyerdahl lesser known projects had been his work at Tucume from 1988-1993. Tucume, in northern Peru, is a complex of twenty-six pyramids, the biggest in South America. Heyerdahl helped investigate and uncover the history of the Pr-Inca site including the fact that they had sailing technology and had contact with Easter Island. Heyerdahl theories, excavations, and voyages could prove that the Pacific and Atlantic were indeed highways for culture for much longer than generally thought.

The Foundation for Exploration on Cultural Origins (FERCO), which Heyerdahl was a part of, was set up to investigate 'the climatic and cultural changes around 3000 BC'. During that time Mesopotamia, Egypt, the Mayans and Hindu among others all either started upon the road to civilization or their calendars began at that time. It is an attempt at trying to piece together a history of man relating to specific environmental periods. Heyerdahl was certainly no showboating New Alger. He wanted to spark debate and understand ancient man and his technology. Heyerdahl work, over the years, had also taken him to The Maldives, the Tigris River, and the Canary Islands, among other places, all in the pursuit of knowledge about ancient man's technological and exploration capabilities. Thor Heyerdahl died, aged 87, in 2002, the Norwegian government honouring him with a State Funeral.

Thor Heyerdahl was a showman in a way, popularizing ancient history, but it was also to highlight and discover important aspects of ancient life. There are not many adventurers or explorers in his mold today. Nowadays, anyone attempting to do what he did or some other grandiose expedition would be accompanied by a whole film crew and be filmed like a reality TV programmer for self-promotion. Heyerdahl was a practical explorer and anthropologist willing to answer his own questions and physically pull it off. We may never encounter his like again.

Source:

Heyerdahl, T. 2000. *In The Footsteps of Adam*. London: Little, Brown & Company.

Heyerdahl, T., Sandweiss, D.H. & Narvaez, A.1995. Pyramids of Tucume. London: Thames and Hudson.

16/Jun/2009

Arts & Humanities - Music
Band reviews: Opeth

Opeth

2020 vision
What can I say? I'm a metalhead and I love this band. Since this article they have produced four more albums and experimented with their sound, not all to the liking of some of their fans. But to me not a single bad album has been made. They've grown and become more expansive and accomplished in their orchestrations.

I've had the pleasure of seeing them live twice when they toured in London. The first time was at the iconic Roundhouse in Camden, October 2014. In standing section near the stage, I inadvertently found myself in the middle of a melee with people throwing themselves around tilt-a-whirl. I thought there was a riot starting, until I realized I was standing at the edge of the mosh pit. Like others, I held my ground ignoring them to enjoy the music. The next concert was at the SSE Arena, Wembley in November 2016. I took a seat that time to enjoy the music from the safety of the upper tier...

Opeth is a Swedish heavy metal band formed in 1990. However, while Opeth is part of the death metal family, they have also fashioned their own sound, dubbed Progressive Death Metal, by integrating progressive, folk, blues, and jazz into their music. After several personnel changes, the band now consists of Mikael Akerfeldt (the oldest serving member and musical genius behind the latest incarnation, on vocals and guitars), Martin Mendez (bass guitars), Fredrik Akesson (rhythm and lead guitars), Per Wiberg (mellotrons, organs and pianos), and Martin 'Axe' Axenrot (drums and percussion).

Opeth are not your normal metal band. There is a poetic quality to their music with simply, beautifully constructed songs and contemplative music within the 'traditional' metal chords. Akerfeldt switches between clear voice and gruff singing, each change seamlessly taking you on a journey from one melodic field to another. Each song is texturally layered with surging styles mixed together in a non-clashing way with dynamic, acoustic soul-piercing guitars, clean playing, traditional heavy strains, racing drums, ethereal flutes, haunting pianos, lofty strings and woodwinds. These are orchestral arrangements that could legitimately grace the Proms.

In days gone by, such groups as Metallica, Slayer, Megadeath, and Entombed were personal favourites, but in Opeth, with their music scaled to epic proportions, there was an instant realization that something had been missing from the select group of metal behemoths. Opeth have stories in the music, the pathways of melodies leading from one part of the song to another. The blend of styles is breathtaking. Not since Metallica has such a synergy of music resonated within the soul.

Opeth may not be commercially playable, or mainstream, and don't get the same media exposure, but true metal heads recognize quality when they hear it. Opeth's songs last as long as they should, whether three minutes to the more usual ten or more minutes. How many groups give you such satisfaction in that, without the song feeling padded out? There are no throwaway songs, just music which is lovingly crafted. Such artistry in their craft, goes beyond the set metal format, putting Opeth in the same league as The Beatles, Pink Floyd, and Radiohead who were/are masters in that field.

As a recent fan to Opeth, introduced last year by a good friend, and owning only two of their nine studio albums, there was blissful revelation at discovering new metal music once thought denied to my ears. The scope of Opeth's music is fully realized and gratefully appreciated, and more cs will be forthcoming. Watershed, the latest album is now a personal top ten album. Watershed may have a mellow sound, but it is not the sign of an ageing, mellowing metal group, but soothing metal music for the discerning listener from a band confident and mature in themselves and their music.

Opeth explore music like no other metal band. Music transcends set boundaries and would appeal to all serious listeners and connoisseurs of music. Metal bands play emotional music, but Opeth takes that emotion and lifts it from doom-laden gloom into an epiphany of joyous sound. Behold Opeth, and their works of sublime nature.

01/Jun/2010

Arts & Humanities
Does today's business professional still find value in the use of a paper notebook?

The Professional's Paper Notebook

A paper notebook still has so many uses that it will never be totally abandoned to the machines and technology of the modern office. Amongst all the laptops, BlackBerries, iPhones, and emails, there is still room for the professional to pull out his or her handy paper notebook and put it to good use.

A paper notepad can be a useful office companion. It can be the first option in writing ideas down and organizing thoughts for the morning meeting. Modern offices can be fast and furious and taking notes will be essential. Instead of tapping into a hand-held device or bringing in sheets of A4 paper, a discreet notepad would add a more efficient air to you, showing your preparedness and keenness for the job ahead. It is a versatile tool in your office locker, which can be quickly edited with words, diagrams, and doodles to prepare your own meeting, report or evaluation.

The professional has a tight schedule to keep and no matter how many large calendars and annual diaries you have on and around your desk, a paper notebook could serve as an ersatz diary. Organizing your daily agenda is the key to getting through the day and the notebook would be a great survival aid. Whether each page is a day or not, the portability and easy access would be a great asset to have to hand in those moments. Quick reminders on important dates, highlights and low lights of the day, venting your emotions in words, and a list of things to do can all be quietly added to the notepad, while on the go, or when a flash of inspiration catches you at an inopportune time.

As well as a diary, the notepad could be a mini-journal, a book-keeping aid, address/contact details book for clients, or a little black book for after-hours meetings. Written information can be personalized with coded references and individualized into a system no electronic gadget could replicate. The notebook would be your personal possession in an office where you sign and account for everything else. Savour the freedom and independence of having your own personal pocket office.

A notebook can be an anonymous medium in collecting, sorting, referencing, and reporting data. In some office environments, things don't always run smoothly and you may need a written back-up or evidence, which you would rather not put into an email. Also, in some jobs, such as security, a notebook can be used as evidence for the police and in court. Hand-written accounts from any professional could aid in a complaints procedure. A professional should always have a notepad to hand to keep a record of any problems, faults, or issue with their work or equipment that cannot be reported or dealt with straight away.

Low tech can be great at times and when the power goes out or the computer crashes, the humble paper notepad will be there with some notes to help you out, especially in a stressed-out PowerPoint conference. Less valuable than hand-held devices and less likely to be stolen, unless you've got the safe codes in it, the notepad will also cost you less. And when finished, the notepad can be stored away for future reference or recycled.

So, a paper notepad is a valuable low-key, must-have for a professional for whatever purpose they use it for. The versatility of the notebook can have many advantages over its electronic counterpart and bring a degree of simplicity and control to a professional office worker's life. Isn't it time you had one?

Environment

02/Nov/2006

Questions and Comments Concerning Global Warming

2020 vision
Research style.
The below research formed part of an article. It put into form questions I had at the time, which would then feature in many articles and even a letter to then Mayor of London, Boris Johnson, January 2009. My articles and essays often started as bullet points and streams of thought before being arranged into something like a readable form of words as seen in the 12/Jan/2008 article below.

I am concerned about the narrow programmer parameters designed for global warming and the seeming absence of reports about the consequences on other energy sources and items listed below.

<u>Natural Cycles</u>
Isostatic bounce-back and effects on earthquakes, volcanoes and sea rise.
Lack of hydrogen test and effect on atmosphere. Water vapour tests, fuel cell development and commercial REMs.
Global cooling (always follows warming) –Atlantic conveyor system.
El Niño/Southern Oscillation (ENSO) effects.
Hurricane seasons and strengths.
Increased droughts and floods.
Volcanoes and cooling cycles.
Methane (land, sea and biomass).
Medieval Warm Period and Little Ice Age investigations.
Solar inclinations –natural warming.
Gaia hypothesis –healthy cool and warm pump cycles.
Forest and jungle loss.
Changing CO_2 levels not only factor.

<u>Green Technology</u>
Solar power –new powerful cells.
Bio-fuels - agricultural land and further land use.
Wind farms – change in wind patterns inevitable due to warming – contingency options.

Wave farms - change in currents inevitable due to warming – contingency options.

Sustainable cities, brown field sites, pedestrianisation, flood-plain housing.

Existing Technology

Oil companies re-tooling for new technologies.

Nuclear technology -security and safety issues vs. need for stable enduring energy.

Human Factors

Media hype

Political short-term thinking.

New world economic models.

Global dimming and pollution.

Technical infrastructure to change during variable changes.

Disaster plans –natural and human epidemics.

Migration issues during land loss, economic and political breakdown.

Human adaptability – for better and worse.

Climate change will not end with lower CO_2 levels. What are the post-catastrophe plans? Climate change is twin to man evolving and growing, as enigmatic in temperament. Each affects the other in a symbiotic relationship. Both self-regulate, but we are now out of phase. A whole new system or lifestyle is needed as the present 'western/capitalist' system cannot be sustained.

Climate change can trigger a technological boom. Man has always used a technological fix to beat climate change, as we will, but to what degree will it work this time?

12/Jan/2008

Sciences, Ecology & Environment
Thoughts on Global Warming

Global Warming Issues

2020 vision
As I prepare this book, apart from more electric vehicles on the road there has been a development by Airbus of a new zero-emission hydrogen-powered aircraft, which may be in service in the next decade. It will remain to be seen the effects of placing more water vapour, the greatest greenhouse gas, into the air.

I am not an environmentalist or a sceptic, a doom-monger or a pessimist, but in reading, researching and watching global warming issues, I still have problems in understanding why some of the subjects I write about below are not discussed more frequently and openly and their implications for fighting global warming. Some of my information may be out of date despite trying to read the latest articles, but I have tried to be as accurate as possible in as little space as I can.

The Hydrogen Economy and water vapour
Many and varied theories, proposals and solutions have been put forth to fight global warming, but to me, none of them seem to have been thought through to their conclusions. The much vaunted hydrogen economy is being set up, the first in Iceland and the next being touted for California. But I have not seen or heard of public discussions about the effects of water vapour in the atmosphere from hydrogen exhaust emissions. Water vapour is the most powerful greenhouse gas, hence our atmosphere and clouds, which protect and nurture us. Apart from fog hazards in cooler seasons, there has been little study, or publicly released studies about the final destination of the water vapour and the potential damaging effects that could make global warming worse. Depending on where water vapour ends up in the atmosphere it could have a detrimental effect on cloud formation and storms (El Niño /Southern Oscillation (ENSO) and Northern Oscillations effects) and could even act to trap more heat and cause more global warming.

Of course, this is not confirmed, but neither are any scientists certain of possible feedback complications. Environmentalists and scientists seem quiet on this subject. I do not think that there is a conspiracy here in any of these issues, just a short-sighted view to fight global warming, when a long-term strategy is needed from start to finish.

Oil companies

As an aside to the hydrogen economy, most of the public do not realise that the hydrogen produced for the new energy revolution will come from hydro-carbons, natural gas and oil products. It is far too costly at the moment to produce hydrogen from water. So, oil companies are holding both ends of the candle and burning the fossil fuel end first, before starting serious work on the other end. We cannot blame oil companies for wanting to hold onto their prime profit cow, but in the end, there has to be some corporate responsibility for their actions. No doubt there will be a transition phase from fossil fuels to hydrogen, but again, there are no time-tables or public relations briefings about this. No one is taking the lead and making sure that the public fully understands the dual role of oil companies. Oil companies could be the saviours of the future! But will we let them?

Nuclear Power

Nuclear energy is a viable energy alternative. France supplies more than 70% of its electricity through nuclear power, and Britain is poised to employ French energy company EDF to build new reactors. But although France has a good safety record and is thinking about building fourth-generation reactors, why is there no talk of the newest generation of pebble bed reactors, which due to the laws of physics could not catastrophically overload like existing plants, could not have its uranium used for weapons production, would be smaller and safer, and have a better waste storage solution. Though it has its drawbacks and is a new technology, outside of Germany, South Africa, and China which have used this kind of reactor, there is no talk of this reactor in wider circles. Even with normal nuclear waste, James Lovelock, creator of the Gaia hypothesis claimed that he would take a chunk of nuclear waste, put it in an underground unit in his backyard and use the radiation emitted to produce heat and power for his home for years. Properly contained, reclaimed energy from nuclear waste could solve some energy problems in local areas. Is pebble bed technology too new and untried or are people just too scared to talk about nuclear energy in any form at the expense of lower carbon emissions and more energy?

Renewable
Renewable energy is not the end all and be all. Alone it cannot combat global warming. Wind and tidal power are limited to their locations and could be affected if wind or sea currents change due to changes in storm patterns and intensity. There is no redundancy in the offing if the 'energy farms' fail for lack of power input. Incentives for solar power are rising slowly, despite huge gains in solar panel technology. Germany is ahead in Europe in both wind and solar power generation because of government incentives to the companies and the public. Solar powered technology alone could ease global warming, yet it lags behind other renewable. No one seems willing to invest, yet, in the potential bonanza readily available from setting up solar farms in sub-Sahara Africa, India or the Middle East.

Most people would say that this is because of less than savoury political climates or lack of infrastructure, but one huge solar farm, possibly supported by an international organization, could provide energy for continents leading to more investment, better social, economic and political environments. Trust funds for the host nation, from land rent and power generation profits, would lead to less social and economic disparities and strife. This is a simplistic view, but people seem to be thinking nationally rather than internationally and nations with the most naturally powerful resource are not having their voices heard when they speak or are not speaking up. The sun's power could actually go to waste!

Food miles and air miles
Air and sea travel, fair trade, and food distribution issues are becoming ridiculous. As Bjorn Lomborg stated in a TV debate, those calling for fair trade also protest about food miles, but you have to have long-distance transport in order to conduct fair trade. Sometimes food coming from New Zealand to Britain is greener and more sustainable than food grown and transported within Britain. There has to be some leeway. There are efforts under way to produce new aircraft fuels and biofuels. Aircraft and airport growth will not subside over the coming decades. Synthetic fuels are being tested by J. Craig Venter and other companies, and new aircraft frames and engines are also being

developed. But is the same for ships? Some ships are reportedly more fuel polluting than other forms of travel, yet few tests or reports have made the media's attention. The oceans provide life with vital oxygen, and though we know that ocean chemistry is changing, ship fuel pollution seems to be missing from the equation.

Policies and education

Overall, I am concerned about the narrow parameters designed for global warming action by governments and policy makers, and the seemingly absence of reports about the consequences of failure, what the contingency options are, and plans for adaptation in case these above scenarios do not work out? I know we have to do something, but nothing we do is guaranteed to work. Media hype and political short-term thinking have acted to confuse and inure people to the more serious issues when they arise. A whole new world economic model, technical infrastructures, and lifestyles are needed as the present system cannot be sustained. Inevitable natural disasters and epidemics will occur, but there seems to be no global voice on the prospect of any post-catastrophe planning.

Global warming will not end with lower CO^2 levels; it is twinned with man, evolving and growing, and as enigmatic in temperament. Each affects the other in a symbiotic relationship. Both self-regulate, but now we are out of phase. There is no real effective global education system to disseminate information about global warming. Governments are fighting the symptoms, but not addressing the main causes: us and our attitudes toward global issues. Climate change to people means more storms, hotter summers and colder winters, but they are forgetting or are ignorant of the small print in the big issues above: Things might not work out. Energy is the key, a selection of sustainable energies will do; but for better or for worse, we have to be ready to adapt to any outcome.

12/Jan/2008

Creative Writing, Humor
Humor: Global Warming

The Great Global Warming Paradox

2020 vision

When I first re-read this without the channel and sub-channel headings, I couldn't remember whether I had actually read this somewhere and reported on it. Then I discovered I had actually written the article in response to a New Scientist job advertisement under the title "Fermi's Global Warming Paradox - Oh, UFO, UFO, wherefore art thou, UFO?" Needless to say no job interview was forthcoming. But who knows, the way the world is going, my theory could be a valid one.

Oh, UFO, UFO, wherefore art thou, UFO? It seems that global warming has claimed yet another scalp. Ever wondered what happened to those once numerous UFO sightings. Well, if some scientists are right, then global warming may have saved us from extraterrestrial invasions.

A cosmologist and his meteorologist colleague were at dinner when they began discussing the Fermi Paradox (basically if the universe is so full of planets with aliens, then why aren't they here). It was a heady debate, but the cosmologist never forgot that conversation and a theory formed in the back of his mind. Finding time to crunch numbers with his friend, the two began linking UFO sightings to our world's climate plight and now according to their work, it seems that as the Earth's temperature has risen, so the sightings of UFOs have dropped dramatically.

'It's not a coincidental correlation,' the cosmologist states. 'The fact of the matter is that as CO_2 has risen, the number of UFO sightings has dropped. But we don't know why.' The data seems to back him up. As CO_2 levels have risen since 1940 levels, the numbers of subsequent UFO sightings have dropped from tens of thousands to a few tens this century.

However, a psychologist sees a different reality, theorizing a memetic reason for this change. 'We've gone from the Cold War and early science fiction scares to modern warfare, GM crops and a science fiction-savvy audience. Of course UFO sightings have dropped. It has absolutely nothing to do with climate change.'

'It sounds a lot of old nonsense,' agreed a xeno-astrobiologist. But added, 'Not all aliens would like warm planets; this heating effect could be our greatest planetary defense shield.'

Apart from environmentalist fears that this will fuel a business-as-usual mode, conspiracy theorists also contend that the real reason why the U.S. has been dragging its heels over curbing greenhouse emissions is because from studying 'cold war era' UFOs, they discovered that greenhouse gases killed off aliens, so the warmer our planet the better. Ironically, the U.S. is risking the wrath of the entire world to save the planet from greenhouse gas-phobic aliens.

The cosmologist laughs when told this. 'Whoda thunk it. This could be the biggest discovery of all time!' He is now preparing to present his theories to the IPCC. It seems that with global warming, space really is the final frontier.

13/Jan/2008

Politics, News & Issues - Energy Issues

2008 Outlook for the Energy Industry

2020 vision
This was a winning entry in a contest by a third-party partner and published exclusively on their platform for which I was compensated.

It will be a mixed bag for the energy industry in the coming year, but mostly positive. The hydrogen economy will acquire huge investments, despite concerns about the effects of water vapour in the atmosphere from hydrogen exhaust emissions on clouds, climate patterns and storm intensities. There will be more research by scientists and environmentalists to ascertain possible feedback complications.

As an aside to the hydrogen economy, oil companies will take more strides in developing cleaner hydro-carbon products while taking more corporate responsibility for their actions. No doubt there will be a transition phase from fossil fuels to hydrogen, but they may have to be pushed into revealing time-tables for this. No one company is taking the lead, yet, but their dual role in creating a new energy economy should be acknowledged and encouraged.

Nuclear energy is a viable energy alternative. France supplies more than seventy percent of its electricity through nuclear power, and Britain is poised to employ French energy company EDF to build new reactors. But while France has a good safety record and is thinking about building fourth-generation reactors, there should be talks about the newest generation of pebble-bed reactors. These relatively new nuclear generators are much safer than existing plants, could not have its uranium used for weapons production, would be smaller and safer, and have a better waste storage solution. Germany and South Africa have trialled them, but China has the only working plant.

Renewable energy will continue to rise, with wind and tidal energy leading the way. But solar energy production will steadily catch up with huge gains in solar technology (e.g. solar panels, towers, and troughs) and efficiency (40%+). Germany is a leader in Europe in solar power generation because of government incentives to the companies and the public, so could be a model for other countries to follow. Solar powered technology alone could ease global warming, yet lags behind other renewable in investments into large solar farms, though the south west U.S., sub-Saharan Africa, India or the Middle East could be potential bonanza areas for solar power production.

Fuels will be a big issue for 2008. Air and sea travel, fair trade, and food distribution issues will be constantly debated. Ships are reportedly more fuel polluting than other forms of travel, yet few reports have made the media's attention. More awareness of this issue will lead to better monitoring of ship pollution. In the air industry, concerted efforts are also under way to produce new aircraft frames, engines and fuels, since aircraft and airport growth will not subside over the coming decades. Biofuels will have a mixed year. Developed countries, like the U.S. might incur higher food prices as crops and/or fields normally used for us and livestock consumption are converted into fuel producing areas. Conversely, in underdeveloped countries, environmental damage will increase as sales in biofuels are increased to export to developed countries. Public outcry to ecological damage and prudent legislation will serve to moderate the rate at which biofuels are produced. This may allow synthetic fuels being tested by scientists like J. Craig Venter and other companies to make important breakthroughs and ease ecological collapses.

The media will continue playing a crucial role in disseminating reports about energy without hype and bias. But their main task will be in the summer when all eyes will be on China for the Olympics. The world will get a rare insight into China and how they are handling their energy industry. No doubt China will show off its green credentials, but prying media eyes will report on all things climate related and the effects on the Chinese population and athletes. But if China is shown to be making some strides in tackling their problems then there will be relief all round.

Overall, policy makers will endorse new economic models, technical infrastructures, greener lifestyles and more education about energy transitions as the present system cannot be sustained. A healthy range of sustainable energies are the key to the future and 2008 will be a year in which these forms of beneficial energy will be in the public's conscience.

15/Jan/2008

Politics, News & Issues - Climate Change
Climate Change and Global Warming:
What should we do about it

Consumer Issues on Climate Change

Climate change is creeping into all parts of life. Apart from environmental and energy concerns, climate change has been linked to obesity, terrorism, economics, marketing, sports, TV shows we watch, and many more issues. But is there an element of overkill in the use of climate change as an all-encompassing Pandora's Box that once opened cannot be closed until a technological hope comes along. How are consumers going to cope with the changing world when government and companies are ambivalent about their commitments to consumer needs?

Consumers want quality, whether in food, cars, sofas, or clothes. They care about value and about savings. They are not interested in saving the Earth en masse, because there is not enough incentive to do so. Energy companies have not assured their costumers that the quality of service will increase and that going green will save them money. Going green is not cheap, people realise, and a companies' transition from greed to green is far from mapped out with no proper plans for energy revitalisation. With no time-table or destination, going green could go off the rails completely.

The marketing of green products is giving companies the opportunity to flaunt their green-tinged credentials, but their practices could leave much to be desired. Consumers are concerned that companies are lining their pockets and taking advantage of the higher costs of supposed green products. Global warming is a big money spinner to some companies and consumers are wary of being stung. Companies have spent decades spreading globalization and global brands and consumers have brought into it. Suddenly, they are being asked to change their ways and buy newly-branded green products for more money and unsubstantiated quality.

There is a sense that there is a deep well of hypocrisy with companies and their prices even prior to any transitional energy changes. Companies are diversifying their ranges and cornering both ends of the pre- and post energy-transition markets (e.g. Monsanto, Shell, and Toyota, etc.) and there is a fear that some companies will profit unnecessarily by passing on costs from new technological breakthroughs onto the public. While green cannot always be cheap, compromises will have to be reached on any pricing of new technology (hydrogen, biofuels, solar, and carbon capture) or re-organized markets (gas, coal, oil, and nuclear). Without sustained energy with reasonable prices, the world could face future energy crises.

One area of overlapping company/public/government concern is low-energy Compact Fluorescent Lighting bulbs (CFL). In *World changing* (2006), it was reported that Philips, a leading European electronics company, marketed their low energy/long lasting CfLs in the U.S. as the Earth Light, without much success. In reassessing the light's performance in market research, Philips decided to change the light's name to the Marathon bulb, and it was a success, because consumers cared more about longevity over cost, the environment, fixture adaptations and quality (Manpower 2006: 390-391). Yet, recently CfLs were found to have dangerously high levels of mercury in them, so the product was green, but toxic. Consumers will not go for such a trade-off, especially when the product could cost your health. Lastly, despite this setback, the Mayor of London, Ken Livingstone, announced plans to establish a lightbulb amnesty where people could exchange their old incandescent bulbs for new energy-efficient CfLs. Aside from toxicity issues, which can be remedied, consumers seem spoiled for choice between green business marketing and political stunts. Consumers can go for green marketing or support politicians by voluntarily going green. The rise of green consumerism and green volunteerism demonstrates the best of both worlds.

If every aspect of our lives is being affected by climate change then that change should be reflected in work life, too. There should be new jobs in climate-related industries and new positions within existing companies to assess, research and find solutions to climate change issues within the work place, such as new energy-saving appliances and materials, natural disaster plans, medical emergencies, and diversification of business to deal with climate change, etc. But is this happening or are companies waiting for government initiatives to lead the way? Consumers should have the right to know if the company they work for or shop in are complying with the laws and regulations concerning climate change, especially if they are a client of a company selling green products or claiming to be green. Green-wash is now applied to companies that spin green tales to the public, so trust and transparency will be a future currency that companies will have to use in order to gain the consumer's appreciation.

Consumers will have to change aspects of their lifestyles if they want to build and live on flood plains, in fire-prone areas, under-serviced areas or in the countryside where freak weather can bring disaster to those communities. Now consumers are learning to be more proactive in community defense, rather than reactive or even counteractive. There also has to be better government policies and assurances in their attitudes toward environmental protection that transcends party politics and changes of government.

Media reporting on global warming has to be more accurate and less sensationalist. By trying to tie every, extra-normal weather event into a case for global warming with no other evidence to go on, it only serves to turn consumers off or bias their attitude toward climate change issues. Also, reports seem to be written for businessmen and politicians with the media having to nit-pick their way through weighty tomes about climate change technicalities, statistics, and business analysis, and then translate them for the public on the news. Why not just cut the business-speak and politic-speak and write reports for the public in plain language to lessen confusion and increase perceptiveness of the issues. This is not about dumbing-down or patronizing the public, but about discussing with and not talking at people about how they want their local, national or international world to be run. Politicians have fallen out of the habit of listening, but for the hard times ahead, they will have to listen if they want cooperation.

In the end, consumers do not want to be constantly and punitively legislated into going green if the cost of doing so will be non-effective, complicated or unsustainable to them and their families. Climate change is altering our personal way of life, affecting globalisation, and heralding energy transitions. But it will not pay consumers more wages, so if fighting climate change is going to cost the Earth, consumers will continue on with business-as-usual and exacerbate the problem.

25/Feb/2008

Politics, News & Issues – Energy Issues
The Future of bio-fuel and airplanes

Assessing the Future of Aircraft Biofuels

2020 vision

I think the article has a better effect in the environment section. Since 2008, commercial jet use of biofuels (or biojet) have been approved with second generation sustainable biofuels available from 2011, which do not compete with food supplies. But even with these breakthroughs there's hardly any media coverage on it, which would mute misplaced phobias over global warming exacerbated by flights. But in a Covid-19 world this is all a moot point, for now.

On February 24, 2008, Virgin Atlantic made the first commercial airliner flight from Heathrow to Amsterdam's Schiphol airport with one of its Boeing 747 engines running on biofuel. It marked a new potential era in the greening of the flight industry. After pledging billions to promote and produce biofuels, Sir Richard Branson has started to deliver on his promise.

The biofuel was a mixture of Brazilian coconuts and babassu oil, and though not perfect it is the first real venture into this field of aircraft fuels. Branson is known for his high-flying stunts, but this could be an advantage in this case, as people know his Virgin brand and that he is involved in many practical business opportunities. This flight test was conducted in partnership with Boeing, General Electric and Imperium Renewables. This should be the start of real and positive moves into this field and the basis of corporate and green cooperation.

But already there was dissent from environmentalists who called the flight 'a publicity stunt' and 'a gimmick'. I was very dismayed by their negative comments to this flight. For years, they have been advocating renewable and for airline companies to change, yet when Virgin Atlantic has started on this path, they were set upon as if they had exploded a carbon dioxide bomb. There is no satisfying Greenpeace – who stormed up onto a plane and draped a banner onto the tail to protest against

Heathrow expansion - and other environmental groups. Apart from local groups and communities who actively oppose Heathrow flight expansion, green lobbyists are still on the fringe in the minds of the general public, and this is a critical reason why green issues are not taken seriously and why big corporations will 'win' in the end. They will change; greens will not. Environmentalists are protesters and not participants in the real changes happening within the environment. They are not active enough in positive business and politics except in peripheral policies. And this biofuel flight proves that.

These environmentalists have to get with the programme, as it were, to not just criticise all the time and to at least acknowledge an accomplishment, whether it works or not in the long run. They have to encourage companies to change and not just beat them on the head. Biofuels (and technology) are not the complete answer, they have problems with sustainability, price and performance, but this is only the beginning. Environmentalists should acknowledge this or at the very least put forward their own proposals, build and test their own engines.

Heathrow's expansion in runways, flights and terminals will continue. The aircraft industry will not shrink, aircraft technology cannot be reversed and expansion means economic growth, jobs and competition. Again, if expansion continues, then there will have to be changes in airline operations and aircraft/fuel technology. There have been calls to make Heathrow more focused on international flights and less domestic, investing more in trains for internal travel. Airlines know they have to change, climate change is a big issue and so is energy transition. Aircraft frames, engines and fuels will change. Synthetic fuels, algae-based and other potential fuels are now being developed and could fill the gap if these biofuels are not considered proficient enough. Flights will not decrease and attempts to do so will fail, especially if environmental groups offer nothing in its place except doom and gloom warnings.

This historic flight may be a dead end, but at least someone is trying to find solutions. I find that most greens are the problem and for all their protests, marches, complaints and negativity, they will not achieve anything if they do not try to work with airlines and find some common ground and compromise. If greens really want change, then they will have to change, get with the times and offer substantial and sustainable alternatives, not something for nothing. Give aircraft biofuels a chance.

22/Apr/2008

Politics, News & Issues – Climate Change
Global warming: What's the real truth?

The Privatisation of Climate Change

Climate Change cannot be solved. Climate Change is not the end of the world. Climate Change can have more benefits than disadvantages. Climate Change is a man-made phenomenon that has made man the phenomenal being he is today.

It seems that lately Climate Change is the measure of all things. Reports of climate change crop up from everything weather related, to food prices, politics and economics, education, the Olympics, business, etc. It is now a cast iron paradigm written in stone and it is heresy to question or criticism any aspect of it not related to CO2 limitations. This is a dangerous precedent for science, for science works on the principle of creating new and different interpretations of data and theories, which can be tested, independently recreated, peer reviewed and changed accordingly. But with climate change, there is no courtesy for such debate. Some people, not even in the Intergovernmental Panel on Climate Change (IPCC), have decided that the debate is over and only their solution is practicable. The climate change debate is out of the hands of the scientists.

For some reason, various environmentalists, activists and other green organisations disregard any technological fixes for climate change and resist such technologies as nuclear, carbon sequestration, biofuels, ocean or cloud seeding or a myriad of other cheaper ways to combat climate change. They prefer Kyoto with its almost $200 billion price tag, the most expensive, yet least useful way to help humans. Even the IPCC acknowledges that by the end of the 21st century Kyoto will delay any warming by a few years. So why are these people hell-bent on spending this exorbitant amount of money on an ineffectual policy? Because climate change policy is not in the green-fingered hands of the environmentalists, so Kyoto is their loudest voice.

In Bjorn Lomborg's 'Cool It' (2007), he lists major ways in which humanity could help itself mitigate climate change for a price many times cheaper than Kyoto. Yes, there is the proposed energy transition to come, but climate change will mean millions of less cold deaths compared to heat deaths; more water (more precipitation and better water policies); painting buildings in lighter colors and planting more trees in urban areas would automatically decrease city temperatures; focusing on malaria (and other diseases) will lessen death tolls even with climate change, and implementing better flood plain management policies would mean less flooding. There are many more worthy examples to work from and they are more workable and laudable than Kyoto.

There is also an important message about data usage. Most data on storms, temperatures, glaciers, polar bears and penguins' deaths, have been misleading or ignored. The Medieval Warm period (never a bad word said about that!) and the Little Ice Age have had more of an effect upon modern times than reported, but the data is often misconstrued or details unreported by those wanting to present a picture 'consistent' with the supposed consensus.

For instance, hurricane strengths have not increased over the last century. There was more damage (measured in today's terms) during the early 1900s than today; then there was a lull in strong hurricane activity between the 60s and 80s, until it picked up again. Some scientists only measure from the 1970s, with uncorrected data, so of course it looks like strength has increased, but it ignores natural cycles within storm systems. The same is seen with glaciers melting; many of which were melting before any effects from 20th century climate change and were retreating from their absolute maximums gained during the Little Ice Age, rather than being permanent glaciers on their way out. Depending on populations and territory, more polar bears are killed through hunting rather than by climate change, and most penguin populations are increasing. In both cases, scientists have taken isolated incidences and presented them without context to the wider populations of polar bears and penguins. This selective data-splicing is disingenuous, especially when it gets re-reported and becomes fact. So why all this doom and gloom, eagerly spread by scientists? Who does this benefit?

Well, the media does play up to this, reporting worse case scenarios and Hollywood blockbusters have also shown extreme havoc caused by climate change, but their agendas are to sell news, or to sell tickets; the worse, the bigger, the better. Politicians have also joined the green bandwagon, begging for Kyoto to be implemented, knowing that they cannot deliver on a promise that will damage their own economies if not perceptively planned and enacted. But the media and politicians are not to blame. They have no control over the climate change agenda; they surrendered and are in the hands of the ultimate climate change stewards.

There is money to be made in climate change and the private industry is reaping the rewards. It is in their best interests to trade in carbon taxes, create new technologies, invest in R&D, and promote alternative energy –whether it works or not. But they are engaged in free-rider mode, where in this case collective good intentions and/or actions attract free-riding industries that benefit from subsidies and plaudits, but do nothing constructive in return. Climate change has been privatised. It is a company business with oil companies cornering fossil fuels and hydrogen markets, Food companies championing their natural fertilizers and GM crops, and news outlets calling for change yet still advertising cheap flights and SUV. It is business as usual, hypocritical and disguised, yet advocated by environmentalists, politicians and even the public alike who all either depend upon these companies for their livelihoods, who do not realist there has been a shift towards privatisation or who can do nothing to counter this. Climate change is the new economy, stupid!

But carbon taxes and trading will not work, nor benefit anyone, least of all the poorest nations in the long run. There are cheaper, better and smarter ways to help the world, which would ease the effects of climate change. Our current path to solve climate change will not help any of the problems we have now. With smoking, drugs and alcohol banned, taxed, controlled or outlawed, a replacement money-spinning industry has arrived in the newly formed, privatised and taxable climate change arena. But why would corporations work faithfully together over carbon trading when they do not over their own affairs or against other businesses or to help poorer nations?

It is because climate change has been 'sexed up' like WMDs, terrorism, pandemics and meteor strikes. Each went through hyper-alert stages, but climate change seems to have become a virtual dogma. As long as companies are seen to subscribe to the New Green Order then they can act with impunity. There are no sceptic companies. Sceptics are *persona non grata*, despite the fact that many so-called sceptics do believe in climate change, but not in the way in which it is presented. Any scientific cause so strongly believed in, with no hint of compromise or tolerant debates on alternate ways of remedying the problem, cannot be wholly based upon science. Kyoto might not be worth the stone it is carved in. So, why is there an insistence that the Kyoto ends justify the means? Because logic has given way to fear —fear of losing our current comfortable way of life. But, I predict that soon, a plateau will be reached and 'green fatigue' will set in when it is realized that nothing realistic is being done or that anything drastic needs to be done.

Solving climate change is supposed to help the world, but lowering CO_2 will not have that effect. We will still have warming, with more poorer people dying from disease, hunger and thirst. Climate change does not cause this, but exacerbates the problem. In alleviating these ills for a cost millions of time less than Kyoto, we would be helping these people now and they would be able to survive any ill effects of climate change. They will be richer, healthier, more educated, and able to handle climate change more effectively than now. So why are we denying them that chance?

Climate Change is not one problem. Climate Change has many solutions. Climate Change will help man change. Climate Change is out of our hands, but only if we do nothing. Privatised climate change is not the answer. If we really want to help, then we need to wrest climate change back into the public domain, where we can create, witness and savour the policies, results and benefits of our own handiwork.

05/July/2008

Nuclear and radioactive waste disposal

The Waste of Nuclear Waste

2020 vision

I was so intrigued by the words of James Lovelock that I had to write him, via the EFN (Environmentalists for Nuclear Energy). The EFN are a not-for-profit organisation created in 1996. Initially based in France, they have spread worldwide with over 16,000 members and supporters in 65 countries. I had responses from Bruno Comby, President of the EFN, one of which is presented at the end of this article. I had further correspondence with the EFN in regards to a TV show I was developing while on a work placement at Windfall Films, as featured in my second volume: *Imaginings of an Infovore.*

Waste not, want not. It is a familiar phrase, but can it pertain to everything? Recently in England, the government asked councils around the country to consider applying for underground facilities to bury nuclear waste, with strong financial investments and other incentives offered (Jowit 2008). It made me think about Environmentalist James Lovelock and his statement in the Independent Newspaper (and his book *The Revenge of Gaia* -2006): 'I would be happy to have the nuclear authorities build a concrete pit on my land and put some high-level nuclear waste in it. It gives off heat that could be used for hot water and central heating. It would be entirely safe and a waste not to use it' [1]. So if this was possible, why should we bury nuclear waste without considering alternate uses for it?

Recycling and re-use:

We are learning or encouraged to recycle all our waste. It is then remade into something similar, a part of something else or could be used as fuel to provide energy. So why not do the same with nuclear waste? A suitable containment and heat-to-electrical transfer system (perhaps a piezoelectric structure) could heat water or even power a house, neighborhood or industrial building. If nuclear waste could be made into a reusable fuel, then all the better.

Of course people would object to having a nuclear fuel source fearing some sort of containment leak, explosion, fatal disease or fuel theft, but the amount of nuclear waste needed would be very small, as it is the heat (from decay) that is needed, not the bulk material and it would need not be disturbed as it could continue for several years without replacement. There would be safeguards and monitoring systems to ensure that all health and safety aspects are in place and that any accidents would be negligible. Theft and proliferation would be minimal as the amount of material and its distribution would be non-concentrated, so harder to obtain. Nuclear waste could be the ultimate decentralized energy system for the 21st century.

Nuclear waste vs. Carbon Dioxide:
Setting aside the issues in building the reactors in the first place, re-using nuclear waste could have many more advantages than the Carbon Dioxide tax system that has been set up. Instead of having concentrated areas of nuclear waste that could be potentially dangerous, space consuming and expensive, a series of small dispersed sites could provide power to numerous industry and residential areas. The killer application would be as a power source for a carbon sequestration plant, so that two waste product industries are more beneficial than one.

As Lovelock also pointed out, nuclear waste as a waste product will not (or even potentially) have the capability to harm the human race or the planet, but our CO2 waste does. In not even attempting to put nuclear waste re-use to some good, then climate change will get worse and our solutions less imaginative and effective. While Lovelock is a member of the Environmentalists for Nuclear Energy, he is not a sell-out to the nuclear lobby or a climate change sceptic. His radical ideas about Gaia revolutionised the way we see humans interacting with a living self-regulating world and just as CO2 is a natural part of that, so is nuclear energy. It adds heat to our planet and is a natural background component within the earth. The environment can cope with mass doses of radiation and relatively quickly bounces back to normal with plants and wildlife reacting quicker. Humans perceive nuclear products as wholly untenable until they have to use its life-saving medical applications.

Of course the biggest coup of using nuclear waste would be in not having to build so many actual reactors. While the existing reactors and a handful of new ones could provide power on an industrial scale, localised waste energy could alleviate the need for large structural and costly sites, since the British Geological Survey in their latest research suggested that forty to sixty per cent of Britain was suitable to store reactor waste (Jowit 2008). So there would be the possibility of having regional energy units instead of static dumps wasting their heat. Storage facilities, like the proposed Yucca Mountain Repository in Nevada, U.S., a deep repository for used nuclear reactor fuel and other radioactive waste[2] could be converted into an energy depot, again alleviating fears of stored waste sitting there doing nothing. Nuclear waste would help mankind by doing what it does best: decay. Using waste fuel would also cut the need for 'nuclear miles' –foreign transportation of nuclear waste to storage facilities, reprocessing depots or unauthorised dumps. Nuclear waste would also lessen our dependency on oil, coal and other sources of polluting energy.

The green agenda and the privatisation of climate change (by corporations) have combined to vilify or stall nuclear power for fear of some unrealised accident or because it would hamper the oil industry, but they do not recognise, consider or appreciate that if CO_2 has such a potent affect on man and life if not controlled, then why not approach the nuclear industry for cost-benefit solutions, like waste re-use.

Other incentives:
Likewise, if people say that there is no incentive to build huge solar farms in the Sahara or other desert areas, or huge off-shore wind farms, then saving the human race must not be incentive enough for them. Carbon dioxide is not the only problem and not the only solution. As long as CO_2 remains the main model for fighting Climate Change, then it will be business as usual; a booming business; buying, taxing and trading in dirty air. In our consumer society, one man's waste is anther's boon. Corporations will make tons of money from trading in tons of carbon, which will do little to reduce carbon levels. Our nuclear waste is also up for sale, sent to other countries to process or dump. But sooner or later, an entrepreneurial company or country will realist that nuclear waste is a worthwhile commodity as a new energy source. With worldwide stocks of nuclear waste growing, this new nuclear business could be classed as a renewable (lasting decades, centuries or millennia), with competitive prices and multiple uses, which would cut down on carbon uses. The dreams of yesteryear of a nuclear age could come true.

So let's go nuclear and burn the candle from both ends. Carbon dioxide has no dual use, it is just a dangerous waste product, which so far we can't even store or bury like nuclear waste on a large scale. Nuclear fuel is useful at the beginning of its life and now could be just as important at the end of its reactor life. So let's not waste the nuclear waste. If there is a way to extract more energy from it in a way that mitigates climate change and several more reactors, then far be it for even the non-nuclear minded to object. Our future could be bright –it could be nuclear.

Sources:
Websites accessed as of 16.06.08
[1] The Independent, Monday, 14 August 2006.
HTTP://nonindependent/news/people/James-lovelock-you-ask-the-questions 411765.HTML. (link no longer active)

[2] HTTP://Wikipedia/wiki/Yucca_Mountain
(link active as of September 2020)

Juliette Jowit, environment editor, The Observer, Sunday June 8 2008.
HTTP://guardianship/environment/2008/jun/08/thermonuclear?
Gus=rs&feed=society.
(link active as of September 2020).

My letter to the EFN and James Lovelock below.

To EFN,

I had written a letter for James Lovelock (below), but do not have his email to send it to. I had written an article about nuclear waste for Helium (attached) and wanted to know his views. In your opinion and with the capacity to share such knowledge, would it be possible to forward on this article to James Lovelock and/or is it of a quality to be published by yourselves.

At the moment with my regular job and volunteer job with Helium, I cannot participate as a local correspondent, but I would like to contribute in some way and I hope this article is a start.

Thank you for your time and I look forward to hearing from you soon.

Regards,

Ray Burke

Dear Mr. Lovelock,

My name is Ray Burke, a former archeology student from University College London. Though my background is in Archeology, I write short articles on many subjects, including science and environmental issues. I had read your book The Revenge of Gaia, which I found quite enjoyable and informative, and was interested in a comment you made about nuclear waste, which you also reiterated in a 2006 interview in the Independent Newspaper:

'I would be happy to have the nuclear authorities build a concrete pit on my land and put some high-level nuclear waste in it. It gives off heat that could be used for hot water and central heating. It would be entirely safe and a waste not to use it'.

I was intrigued by this concept, but had heard nothing about it since. Recently, as you probably read or saw in the news, the government asked councils around the country to consider applying for underground facilities to bury nuclear waste, with strong financial investments and other incentives offered. It put me in mind of your above statement and as I write for an online forum, Helium, I wrote an article [attached] arguing for the alternate use of nuclear waste as a new energy source. As a concept, I would be interested to know if you had contact with the government in exploring this possibility.

Though I have no background in such technology and maybe my article is naïve, but I was wondering, if such an operation is feasible, how such a development or company could be set up to research and initiate a programmer to develop a Renewable project that would provide more energy from waste which is already carbon free.

I look forward to hearing your views and advice on the subject. Thank you for your time.

Yours truly,

Ray Burke

EFN response 07.07.08

Dear Ray,

I would myself gladly welcome a cubic meter or so of highly radioactive waste below my ecological home. The idea is good and quite appealing as long as you don't go into the economics. In today's context it just isn't feasible. Locally (for my own budget) the operation would be OK if you consider the waste as free (but it isn't just the handling of nuclear waste today is very expensive).

If you look at the very high cost of simply transporting and storing the waste (with today's very strict regulations which imply very high costs for anything nuclear), it's cheaper to heat a home with gas sold by Putin. Another thing is that the amount of energy remaining in the vitrified waste is only a very small fraction of the energy initially contained in the fuel (if you reprocess the used fuel as is done in France). It's rather cheap to extract (as we do) most of the energy over a short period of time.

Although I haven't done (yet) any precise calculations, it will be much more expensive (because of a multiplication of numerous small installations yielding only a small amount of energy each) to extract the smaller amounts left over longer periods of time. Usually the investment cost increases in part proportional to the number of installations, and the maintenance costs are proportional to time. Energy density (in time and space) is a potential risk, but economically, it is decisive. The low energy density in the waste (compared to the very high energy density in the reactor in operation) makes it safe, but also much more expensive per energy unit extracted. Because the temperature is low (often less than 100°C) the energy from the waste would in any case be used only for heat requirements, not for electricity fabrication.

Saying we would accept nuclear waste on our land (I would be glad to do so!) is certainly a good way of explaining that we are not afraid of nuclear waste and that the fear of it is largely overdone, but not very realistic for energy production (in any case it would remain quite marginal).

Yours sincerely, with kindest regards.

Bruno Comby
President of EFN

11/Aug/2008

Anticipating a life without oil

Is There an End to Oil?

There is a big misconception about the Oil Age: that it will someday end. Well, it will never truly end. For some reason, people anticipate that oil will eventually run out or will be phased out to introduce new energy technologies and reduce carbon dioxide, but oil will be with us for a very long time to come. Why? Well, as one of my favourite sayings goes: 'The Stone Age did not end for lack of stones.' And the same is true for the Oil Age. As one technology replaces another, the older technology is still in use and even today we use stone, bronze and iron for other needs, whether in different forms or functions. And oil will still be needed.

While oil usage may be vastly reduced there are some areas in the world that will continue to use oil for its basic functions (e.g. travel, cooking, manufacturing, etc.), where new technologies will be inaccessible (due to costs, geographical or geopolitical considerations), or are unwanted or unnecessary (no need to change or oil is in low usage). Oil is not just used for transport, but also for plastics, cosmetics, rubberised products, fertilisers, etc. Our world would be completely void of many of the household products and luxuries we own and consume if oil were not a component of their manufacture. Further, oil and gas will still play a major part in the production of its successor technology: the so-called Hydrogen Economy.

New Energy:
It is cheaper and easier to attain hydrogen from natural gas and even if the more expensive water-separation treatment is used, the generators used would still be fossil-fueled. Hydrogen is not as efficient as oil for energy nor can it replace the oil ingredient in other products. So as long as we need hydrogen for the new economy, we will still need the oil companies (now self-styled energy companies) to pump oil and gas to produce hydrogen. For the oil companies -sorry energy companies- to invest in wind, solar, biofuel, and tidal power, they will need the money from oil sales to start up these ventures. At the moment the alternative energies will never return the profits that oil can, so these companies will

continue to milk the cash cow, but at the same time start paying more than lip service to developing alternative sources of energy.

Oil Wars and Finance:
People also anticipate that when the oil runs out, so will major causes of conflict, especially U.S. aggression. But the U.S. was a major 'aggressor' in the Americas before oil was discovered and widely exploited, under cover of the isolationist Monroe Doctrine. Other countries have fought over other resources and if one energy source can be a source of conflict, so can any other; the same was so with the Stone, Bronze and Iron Ages' resources.

Oil is a large part of the global financial market, the real source of conflict, as were/are gold, diamonds, land, water, food, women, etc. Oil is just a means to an end and cannot be replaced easily with any scarcity leading to instability and possible conflict. So with any end to oil will begin a new age of resource conflict. Paradoxically, oil-based products will need to be replaced, there is still less focus on this than say products tested on animals. If there is such a moral imperative to reduce oil/fossil fuel consumption, then surely people would be protesting as vociferously to get rid of oil-based products as they do with animal-tested products. Until such issues are addressed oil will still be used in many everyday products.

Peak Oil:
There are a myriad questions as to if oil has reached its peak and will run out, if companies are over- or under-estimating oil field capacities or reserves and new drilling technologies. Recently, there were questions about the origins of oil, citing the biotic theory. For years experts had contended that oil was only produced from fossilized carbon sources. But why should there be only one formation method? Other hydrocarbon deposits may have naturally formed when the Earth did, the hydrocarbons eventually seeping up to the surface. Akin to volcanic hotspots, pockets of hydrocarbons may have formed, but are located in areas too deep to drill, thus are too unproductive or may consist of the potent greenhouse hydrocarbon methane? If such an oil source were found, would it lead to renewed production, thus pushing back Peak Oil time?

Reserve oil would become a crucial resource. As the new energy sources arrived oil would effectively be stored as a reserve or back-up energy source for some. What else could it become? You could not pour it back into the ground since empty oil fields will either be pumped with sea water to flush out oil or filled with carbon dioxide. So oil would be stored up all over the world maybe to be used in times of emergencies or even in a limited continuous capacity.

The worst case scenario is the premature end to oil without a transition phase or a viable option for alternative energy, oil ingredient replacement, and manufacturing tool as 'cost effective' as oil. If oil has peaked, then all we have is a limited time frame of oil use, reserves, a few pockets of shakes and tar sands, and possibly reclaimable/recyclable oil products. If the Age of Oil does end before its time, then civilisation will be in a catastrophic state even worse than global warming itself. In other words, if there were not a (s)lick of oil left tomorrow, global warming would still occur and be worse by the end of the century, but we would have no alternative energy source or comparable technology to combat it without the input from oil. So give the oil companies time to sort out our collective mess as nascent energy companies.

Climate Change:
Some people anticipate the end of oil as the answer to saving the world, but seeing as the carbon tax is a business as usual model and will continue to make corporations money at our expense, then oil will still be a commodity, maybe even a black market one in post-peak times. In other words, oil usage could be outlawed tomorrow, but the carbon tax will continue for decades with little effect on climate change. So don't be fooled by talk of the end of oil even with hydrogen, wind, solar, bio fuel, tidal, and nuclear power on standby. Oil will still be instrumental in their production and infrastructure. The Oil Age may end in the history books, but its presence will still be felt in the future just as we still use products from the Stone, Bronze and Iron Ages.

Don't get me wrong, oil and other fossil fuel usage are bad for the environment, and Climate Change will figure in the end of oil use, but oil will never run out as completely as some people would love it to. While President Bush stated that we are addicted to oil, and others say we need to wean ourselves off oil, I say we need a prescription for oil. Oil keeps our world prices down and keeps the world economy stable.

Until other proven energy products come online, we need to prescribe our oil usage and not keep on overdosing.

Without the oil industry to research, develop and finance the next energy age and mitigate its own environmentally destabilising actions, then humankind will feel any climate change shifts even more keenly. Oil is our 'frenemy' – our friend in need and our worst enemy. But just as we need to keep our friends close, we also need to keep our oily enemy closer, as oil does all our dirty work for us, but will herald in a new age of energy.

01/Dec/2008

Issues surrounding genetically enhanced foods

The GM Debate

Recently I watched an episode of the science programmer *Horizon: Jimmy's GM Food Fight*, where TV celebrity/rural farmer Jimmy Doherty travelled the world in order to assess the state of GM foods. Jimmy's farm in Suffolk has free range, traditional and rare breeds and he sees himself as working with nature. But he knows that in 50 years time, we will have to double food production in order to survive. As a realist, Jimmy knew that would not be possible through conventional means, and wanted to investigate if GM was safe and what the consequences of biotechnology could be.

Argentina and Soya Beans:
First Doherty went to Argentina where for twelve years over half of its arable land (about the size of Britain) has been turned over to the farming revolution that has come from the GM soya bean. It has been bred to resist weed killer and thus needs less herbicide. But the cost is environmental as huge swathes of forest are cut down to provide more soya bean farms. Soya beans provide vegetable protein and oil for animal feed, without which the industry would collapse. The huge factories provide jobs and an economy for Argentina. As Doherty found out, GM is far from the periphery, it's a global commodity. Ten percent of the world crops are GM. As Doherty realized, GM cannot be brushed aside and it's best to know the facts.

Britain and Europe GM fights:
The attitude of GM in the Americas is in stark contrast to those in Europe. Britain is virtually GM free. To test people attitudes, Doherty cooked some sausages either in GM or non-GM vegetable oil and asked people in a market in Norwich, which they would eat. Overwhelmingly the people asked picked the GM-free vegetable oil cooked sausages with explanations ranging from GM messes with nature, it's 'Frankenfood', and just having a general prejudice against GM. But when Doherty explained that GM biotechnology could potentially feed more people and be better for the environment using fewer pesticides, a handful of

people changed their minds and ate the GM cooked sausages. A little information went a long way and once informed of even basic facts, people began to fear GM less.

The propaganda wars are heating up with one side advocating that GM is safe, nutritious and affordable; against those arguing it's unnecessary and dangerous. Europe remains virtually GM-free due to large-scale protests in the '90s where experimental GM crops were ripped out of the ground, due to fears of contamination of normal crops. This anti-GM feeling was recently demonstrated in Bavaria, Germany when experimental GM rapeseed crops were ripped up and destroyed. All these sabotage efforts have all but deterred pro-GM policies in Europe.

Lord Peter Melchett the Policy Director of the Soil Association thinks GM technology is uncertain and risky, which reduces wildlife, has unknown affects on soils, could lead to human health risks, and normal crop contamination. He thinks that climate change is a bigger problem. But hasn't he missed the point that GM crops could help mitigate climate change problems? GM crops could be bred to absorb more CO_2 like air scrubbers or produce better biofuel options. Melchett seemed agenda driven with no compromise on offer. As Doherty reckoned, how can we truly know all the effects and consequences unless we do the experiments. I think sooner or later we will need GM technology for food, animals and the environment, and the sooner we test under suitable conditions the better.

Genetic modification processes:
Doherty then pointed out that man has been genetically altering our food for thousands of years. To demonstrate this he produced wild carrots and cabbage from the white cliffs of Dover. Broccoli, cauliflower, and brussell sprouts are all bred from wild cabbage and they would not survive outside of farms. Our grains and even pets, such as dogs and cats, have been genetically bred over the centuries. Doherty wondered if GM was just an extension of this process or a step too far. He visited the John Innes Centre to find out about GM procedures. Plants are modified by taking a gene from another organism, usually another plant, and inserting it into another plant to produce an advantageous trait. It is a natural bacterium, the Ti Plasmid agrobacterium, which transfers its own DNA from one plant to another giving it the title of 'Nature's own genetic engineer'. So why shouldn't

we use something that already happens in nature? GM crops would be drought and disease resistant, more nutritious, have anti-cancer properties and more anti-oxidants. But the crops tested here may never come to fruition even with appropriate and regulatory testing as the European Union (EU) has only allowed one GM crop food, maize, in twelve years.

American GMOs:
America has been using GMOs (Genetically modified organisms) for ten years. Either the farmers, companies, or public know what's good for them or they're a vast live experiment in progress. The FDA has no standard or long-term tests, no ongoing surveys and studies, though over fifty scientific reviews have seen no adverse effects, albeit it with a few allergic reactions in animals. How long do we wait for any adverse effects to show? Another ten, twenty, thirty years? It is ironic that so many Europeans are opposed to GM, yet when they visit the US, almost anything they eat will certainly have some component of GM in it, whether it's the meat from GM fed animals or products, GM grown plants, or other ingredients placed in fast food and grocery foods, that aren't routinely labelled.

The Amish in Pennsylvania, the devout religious society that eschews modern technology, also uses GM as it is practicable and profitable to them. To them it is another tool, like pesticide control, which rids them of the corn borer caterpillar. The Bt (*Bacillus thuringiensis*) GM corn has high yields and if the Amish thought GM would harm their soil then they wouldn't use it, as their farms are handed down through the generations. Over fifty-five million hectares of arable land is used for GM crops, which accounts for the eighty percent of GM soya, cotton and corn in the US. So far, no discernible impacts on the environment have manifested themselves through gene contamination or health problems (allergies or cancers) for the 300 million Americans. And for all the quantity of GM eaten in the US, surely that would be the first place to show such affects. But are Americans healthier for GM foods? What benefits have GM foods conferred upon Americans even through the obesity crisis? Shouldn't that be the measure of success rather than what goes wrong?

Uganda and bananas:
GM foods and products don't have to be ubiquitous or a catch-all cure and can help with sustainability. As expressed in the episode, some developed nations do not need GM, but across the world GM products would be needed to fight diseases, adverse climate change and malnourishment. It could be the only way for some communities to be sustainable and self-sufficient. In Uganda, one of the wealthiest African nations where over eighty percent of people are involved in agriculture and food production (compared to only one percent in Britain) productivity is falling. Bananas are their biggest crop and the East African Highland banana is a victim of the disease Black Sigatoka. Bananas are seedless and sterile and can't crossbreed, so if this banana died out, there would be no more. It is hoped that GM solutions from the National Agricultural Biotechnology Centre can produce strains of bananas with a fungal resistant gene from rice, to resist the disease and increase banana production by sixty percent, as fungicides are too expensive for the subsistence farmers.

Trials are ongoing, but it could take ten years for the first GM bananas to become available, depending on governmental policies, which see GM as negative due to EU influences. Even when severe drought and famine struck Southern Africa in 2002, many of the nations refused America's GM seeds, the Zambian President even saying they were 'toxic'. With an attitude like that, millions will starve. Europe has more options than GM, but Africa has less and GM could be their most significant choice of survival.

Advantages and ignorance:
I think GM crops can have another role other than providing food. We know that trying to use crops for both food and fuel won't work. There's not enough land and resources to accomplish this, but GM crops could be used on land that is considered uneconomic, contaminated, marginal or unusable in any either way for food crops. The second generation of biofuels is also considering using parts of the plant that are not edible for us, and again, GM crops could help facilitate more yields. The rather exasperating thought about GM food is that people will rather smoke or drink themselves to death, but not eat GM food. It seems ridiculous that this should be the case when there are scares about mobile phone radiation, microwave ovens, and electricity pylons. So why is it that

people are so ignorant of GM food and dismiss it out of hand while indulging in killer passions and using technology that has ambiguous long term effects? Is GM the killer cure? Will GM turn out to be like cigarettes, where only after years will any adverse effects become known?

Doherty had to tow the line, balancing between his small farmer instincts and his positive views on GM and being seen as a sell-out and convert, which could be detrimental to his own business. He could see the benefits, but he wanted to know the risks, wanted the experiments and testing, as it should be. We should not squander what could be a great boon to humanity, so let's do it right.

02/Jan/2009

Sciences, Ecology & Environment
Should we emphasise adaptation to climate change or mitigation of CO2 emissions?

Climate Change: Adapt or Die

I am a sceptic; not of Climate Change, but of the methods being presented and the way it is handled. Carbon is not king, it is but a pawn in the machinations of politics and industry as they commercialism and privatise Climate Change just as any other commodity. Data from computer models is not certain enough and interpretations about future warming and damage can be very misleading with the media reporting the worst results.

We have to really start adapting our strategies toward Climate Change away from politics and industry or nothing will be done, due to the short-term interests of government and profiteering commercial interests. We vote for change and nothing happens, we consume out of loyalty and get nothing in return. It's time we re-negotiated our asymmetrical pact with these over-arching institutions and established micro-community projects.

Micro-community projects would involve independent areas or the community getting together and deciding what energy needs they desire and how to accomplish this. There are growing numbers of people going off-grid and producing their own power, sourcing their own water and managing their own waste. However, this self-sufficiency and 'free' energy will surely not go unnoticed and could one day be subject to some kind of off-grid taxing. Authorities would soon find themselves out of work if people weren't subject to them, but some kind of post-deregulation of the energy industry will be needed to free the consumer from prohibitive bills and unreliable energy sources. The energy industry, even a green one, are there to make a profit and as long as Climate Change has been privatised and commercialised, there will be no forthcoming New Energy Age for the foreseeable future, so people will have to motivate and demonstrate their commitment in wanting change with or without the government's help or permission.

All our eggs are in one basket in dealing with carbon alone in trading and taxes and not thinking about some kind of adaptation to climate change. The tipping point has probably already arrived as the Earth will continue to warm no matter what we do now. If we do not have a multi-pronged approach, our eggs will literally be scrambled. We are being given no choice, no alternatives, just ultimatums which are not being heeded. This is the time for unilateral action, an international agreement will not be reached with national interests and distrust blocking the way.

Adapting is not about giving in to sceptics or to climate changes. We have to be realistic. We have not learned from the past and seen how many ancient Empires have fallen because of environmental disasters, some caused by human hands. Why can we never learn from past events? Our modern civilizations have never learned from the past whether it is about over-logging/bush clearing/forest fires, flood plain building/coastal erosion/reef destruction allowing more hurricane damage, pollution, over-mining, etc. Issues such as methane and water vapour, which are far worse than carbon dioxide, have barely been mentioned and the hydrogen economy will produce tons of extra water vapour. You name it, we have not learned, so relying on some new technology or tax to save us will not happen in time.

This is not just about energy and resource efficiency, but also about societal changes and the way our society is structured to deal with energy. The public needs a free reign in energy decisions. Environmentalists, protesters and the media have a lot to answer for in over-playing climate change as the ultimate disaster. It turns people off. It is far more appreciable if you do not bang people over the heads with constant dire messages, otherwise people will choose not to hear and care. Climate Change issues have to be re-booted as New Energy Age issues, to highlight green progress in technology and a more efficient society. Instead of setting targets for some far off Climate Change event, implementing a New Energy Age including solar, wind, tidal, hydrothermal programmed with cheaper, smarter recycling and manufacturing projects will naturally bring about a cleaner environment. Climate Change, like other issues in resources, health, protection, food, education, and production, is in the hands of the rich. Like life-saving drugs that rich corporations won't let poorer nations copy, Climate Change will become a fight between the rich and the poor, the haves and the have-nots, unless we adapt to a more sustainable mindset, energy base, and society.

Climate Change is unavoidable and will continue nonetheless even with lower carbon levels. Carbon will always be in the system. It just seems Mother Nature is winning out over Human Nature, but our second nature to defer to the powers-that-be even when they procrastinate has to stop. It is not just about physically adapting to Climate Change, but also adapting our projects, politics, economics, education, and society. Nothing so far has convinced me that we will come out of this unscathed. There are no contingency plans for failure. Our leaders will fail us, whether Kyoto and its successors get ratified or not, because too much time and money has been wasted trying to satisfy industries at the expense of ordinary people. There is no future thinking on the failure of the Carbon economy, based as it is on an capitalist economy that has just gone bust worldwide. How can politicians not see that?

By 2050, we can expect another 2 billion souls on this world. Where are they in the plans for future climate change? Climate Change models do not account for people, only land and they are only as predictable as the data put in and cannot foresee the future with certainty. Working off models will give a false sense of security and when they go wrong will give sceptics a chance to trash the models leading to more uncertainty. There is a moral imperative here that politicians are failing to address; they have put their faith in industry and technology; a business as usual model, which will be unanswerable to their countries and people around them. Yes, economies have to grow, businesses have to be successful, and people have to work, but each of them can adapt in whatever way to Climate Change, or more people will die in vain.

We need to adapt and get away from twentieth century models of linking Climate Change to economics, politics and industry. It's about people. The Earth, its land and seas will survive, but it is the life on this world that is in danger. And the way we are still arguing over carbon trading and treaties and cost benefits and data models, we might as well be talking ourselves into extinction.

25/Jan/2009

How to combat global warming?
Solutions to combating climate change in London, UK

Innovative Green Projects For London

2020 vision

My letter to then Mayor of London, Boris Johnson, upon which this article is based, is at the end of this article. I would like to thank the Mayor of London office for allowing their response to be included in my book. As a side note, I had once applied for the post of Speechwriter for the Lord Mayor of London, in June 2010. Why? I wanted to contribute my skills and words to the city and hopefully make a difference where it counted. Noble, of course.

There are many ways to combat global warming, but in a city like London not all conventional or taxing methods will work or be popular. Mostly, the congestion charge for cars and Carbon Trading will not suffice as they still encourage business-as-usual models of transport and industry. So a more robust system for encouraging businesses to adopt greener measures should be implemented with emphasis on the issues below. Some methods are already in use, others in trial schemes, and others are rapidly being developed. In combination, these greener methods will yield a positive, visible, cost-effective, and direct effect on the climate of London and other cities.

Waste Heat Capture:
This is already being piloted by The London Development Agency. Their plans will harness waste heat from the Barking Power Station and heat homes and help save carbon emissions. The excess heat will produce electricity needed to supply heat and hot water. Almost 100,000 tonnes of CO_2 a year in the Thames Gateway region could be saved, enough for 150,000 homes.

But there are also other ways waste heat can be recycled, such as with Piezoelectric, where some materials like crystals and certain ceramics, can generate electricity in response to applied pressure. All commercial buildings have generator vents that spread their exhaust either at street level or from the roof. Piezoelectric systems could capture waste heat to be used to power internal company systems, not to mention reduce the ambient temperature surrounding buildings that create city hotspots. Saving waste heat in the city this way could also save on generator infrastructure and performance, bring down costs of heating, air conditioning, lighting, and other power-hungry devices. Any surplus heat could be stored or generated electricity sold back to the grid.

Solar Energy:
Solar panels could be placed on roofs of city buildings, either sun-tracking models or static ones. Also, the top or top two floors of taller buildings could have solar panelling taking the place of every other window. The costs would be met by both the companies and the government on a sliding scale depending on the profits of the company. This 'solarisation' of businesses would be retrofit-able, with financial and energy savings being reinvested and any surplus energy sold back to the grid.

Buildings and companies have their own carbon footprints, not just in energy expenditure, but also from its staff, clients, their expenditures, and outgoing and incoming deliveries. In effect, companies will solarise under new legislation to earn economic or other incentives. This 'congestion' charge on buildings would not be a tax, rather a way for companies to re-invest in themselves for the future. The bigger the company the more they would be expected to pay to upgrade to a greener resource. They employ more people, hire more cars/taxis, receive more deliveries, book more flights, etc. By solarising their company, erecting small wind turbines, or utilizing waste heat, the company would earn a government-approved Green Certificate of Achievement. This system would be better than the current CO_2 trading system, which is really a business-as-usual scheme. The building congestion charge would bring down the costs of renewable to competitive prices and would be more cost-effective over time and make a real change to the climate rather than costly carbon trading, which would not take carbon out of the system. The congestion charge could be rolled out on a timetable according to the size and resources of the company.

White buildings:
There is a plethora of glass, concrete, and bare brick buildings around. And they are grand designs for London. However, there is scope for some buildings to be painted white raising their albedo level to reflect solar radiation, thus keeping buildings and the city cool, thus avoiding hotspots and heat islands. Dark buildings absorb heat during the day making the building hotter and release heat during the night which artificially warms the surrounding streets and city. White buildings (or lighter coloured surfaces) and other white-painted structures (maybe even some roads and pavements) would avoid this problem without the need for extra cooling facilities. Smart materials would keep these white buildings clean.

Roof areas could also hold small urban gardens, planted with fresh vegetables for food and/or grass to absorb heat and CO_2, and cool the building interior. More trees could also be planted around buildings to enhance the cooling effect from lighter coloured walls and roofs. This low-tech and practical approach would cost significantly less than other techniques and be much more appreciable to the public.

Park systems:
There are many parks in London's environs. There are also many unused Brownfield sites in London, waiting for builders to construct premium buildings that in this financial era may lay empty or partially filled. Such sites could be used to build a Central Park-type landscape for London, or a series of parks united in a way to provide London with greenery and water.

The benefits of this would be apparent as to cool and clean the air, add more scenic greenery to the city, and provide shelter and relaxation to city workers, residents, and tourists. But the biggest advantage would be to use the parks as urban rainwater catchments. Either with an existing system or a new apparatus, rainwater would be caught and/or channelled to the park which will have reservoirs protected against chances of rapid evaporation or seepage losses. The water could be used for drier summers as cooling aids and for extra water supplies in other emergencies.

Air scrubbing:
This may sound too futuristic, but the latest research in scrubbing CO_2 from the air, is already being carried out as reported by the New Scientist (Cleaning the Air, 10th January, 2009, Vol 201, No 2690, p34-37). There are several different designs using different techniques of capturing CO_2 from the atmosphere, with some units about the size of a shipping container. Whether Heathrow Airport expanded or not, having such so-called artificial trees around the airport would greatly reduce CO_2 emissions. Not to mention the fact that future aircraft will have cleaner blends of fuel (with bio-additives or synthetic fuel) and quieter engines.

Placed on top of buildings or by roadsides, air scrubbers would be a visible and an assured sign that London is serious about restricting CO_2 levels. Air scrubbers could be used in conjunction with the congestion charges. Air scrubbers are technically feasible and with technology growing exponentially, they could be available for London to volunteer for trials, which could be a showcase for the 2012 Olympics.

These innovative measures are either in use or on the cusp of availability. The great benefit is that they can be retrofitted or applied and so our existing architectural infrastructure can be a part of the climate change solution and not the problem.

Mr. Boris Johnson
Mayor of London
Greater London Authority
City Hall
The Queen's Walk
More London
London SE1 2AA

25.01.09

Dear Mayor Johnson,

REF: Innovative green projects for London

I have no doubt that your office has looked into methods of combating global warming and its effects on London, but not all conventional or taxing methods will work or be popular. Mostly, the congestion charge for cars and Carbon Trading will not suffice as they still encourage business-as-usual models of transport and industry.

A more robust system for encouraging businesses to adopt greener measures should be implemented with emphasis on the issues below. Some methods are already in use, others in trial schemes, and others are rapidly being developed. In combination, these greener methods will yield a positive, visible, cost-effective, and direct effect on the climate of London.

Waste Heat Capture:
This is already being piloted by The London Development Agency. Their plans will harness waste heat from the Barking Power Station and heat homes and help save carbon emissions. The excess heat will produce electricity needed to supply heat and hot water. Almost 100,000 tonnes of CO_2 a year in the Thames Gateway region could be saved, enough for 150,000 homes.

But there are also other ways waste heat can be recycled, such as with Piezoelectric, where some materials like

crystals and certain ceramics, can generate electricity in response to applied pressure. All commercial buildings have generator vents that spread their exhaust either at street level or from the roof. Piezoelectric systems could capture waste heat to be used to power internal company systems, not to mention reduce the ambient temperature surrounding buildings that create city hotspots. Saving waste heat in the city this way could also save on generator infrastructure and performance, bring down costs of heating, air conditioning, lighting, and other power-hungry devices. Any surplus heat could be stored or generated electricity sold back to the grid.

Solar Energy:
Solar panels could be placed on roofs of city buildings, either sun-tracking models or static ones. Also, the top or top two floors of taller buildings could have solar paneling taking the place of every other window. The costs would be met by both the companies and the government on a sliding scale depending on the profits of the company. This 'solarisation' of businesses would be retrofitable, with financial and energy savings being reinvested and any surplus energy sold back to the grid.

Buildings and companies have their own carbon footprints, not just in energy expenditure, but also from its staff, clients, their expenditures, and outgoing and incoming deliveries. In effect, companies will solarise under new legislation to earn economic or other incentives. This 'congestion' charge on buildings would not be a tax, rather a way for companies to re-invest in themselves for the future. The bigger the company the more they would be expected to pay to upgrade to a greener resource. They employ more people, hire more cars/taxis, receive more deliveries, book more flights, etc. By solarising their company, erecting small wind turbines, or utilizing waste heat, the company would earn a government-approved Green Certificate of Achievement. This system would be better than the current CO_2 trading system, which is really a business-as-usual scheme. The building congestion charge would bring down the costs of renewable to competitive prices and would be more cost-effective over time and make a real change to the climate rather than costly carbon trading, which would not take carbon out of the system. The congestion charge could be rolled out on a timetable according to the size and resources of the company.

White buildings:
There is a plethora of glass, concrete, and bare brick buildings around. And they are grand designs for London. However, there is scope for some buildings to be painted white raising their albedo level to reflect solar radiation, thus keeping buildings and the city cool, thus avoiding hotspots and heat islands. Dark buildings absorb heat during the day making the building hotter and release heat during the night which artificially warms the surrounding streets and city. White buildings (or lighter colored surfaces) and other white-painted structures (maybe even some roads and pavements) would avoid this problem without the need for extra cooling facilities. Smart materials would keep these white buildings clean.

Roof areas could also hold small urban gardens, planted with fresh vegetables for food and/or grass to absorb heat and CO_2, and cool the building interior. More trees could also be planted around buildings to enhance the cooling effect from lighter colored walls and roofs. This low-tech and practical approach would cost significantly less than other techniques and be much more appreciable to the public.

Park systems:
There are many parks in London's environs. There are also many unused Brownfield sites in London, waiting for builders to construct premium buildings that in this financial era may lay empty or partially filled. Such sites could be used to build a Central Park-type landscape for London, or a series of parks united in a way to provide London with greenery and water.

The benefits of this would be apparent as to cool and clean the air, add more scenic greenery to the city, and provide shelter and relaxation to city workers, residents, and tourists. But the biggest advantage would be to use the parks as urban rainwater catchments. Either with an existing system or a new apparatus, rainwater would be caught and/or channeled to the park which will have reservoirs protected against chances of rapid evaporation or seepage losses. The water could be used for drier summers as cooling aids and for extra water supplies in other emergencies.

Air scrubbing:
This may sound futuristic, but may I refer you to the latest research in scrubbing CO_2 from the air, as reported by Robert Kunming & Wallace Kronecker (featured in New Scientist, Cleaning the Air, 10th January, 2009, Vol 201, No 2690, p34-37). There are several different designs using different techniques of capturing CO_2 from the atmosphere, with some units about the size of a shipping container. Whether Heathrow expanded or not, having such so-called artificial trees around the airport would greatly reduce CO_2 emissions. Not to mention the fact that future aircraft will have cleaner blends of fuel (with bio-additives or synthetic fuel) and quieter engines.

Placed on top of buildings or by roadsides, air scrubbers would be a visible and an assured sign that London is serious about restricting CO_2 levels. Air scrubbers could be used in conjunction with the congestion charges. Air scrubbers are technically feasible and with technology growing exponentially, they could be available for London to volunteer for trials, which could be a showcase for the 2012 Olympics.

Conclusion:

These innovative measures are either in use or on the cusp of availability. The great benefit is that they can be retrofitted or applied and so our existing architectural infrastructure can be a part of the climate change solution and not the problem.

Thank you,

Yours sincerely,

Raymond Burke

The Mayor of London office response to my letter:

Date: Tue, 24 Feb 2009

Dear Mr Burke

Thank you for your email to the Mayor, highlighting proposals for green projects in London. Your email has been passed to the Energy team to respond on the Mayor's behalf. Your letter contained some very interesting ideas, some of which are reflected in the Mayor's existing work in London. Here are some further details:

Waste Heat Capture

You have highlighted the potential for recycling of waste heat. Indeed, the London Energy Partnership's (LEP) Carbon Scenarios report demonstrates that a Combined Heat and Power (CHP) led approach is the most cost-effective mechanism for delivering carbon dioxide reductions in London. The Mayor's policies in the London Plan are based around significantly increasing the use of energy efficiency solutions, producing energy through cleaner more efficient decentralized generation (such as CHP), and to generate onsite energy through the use of renewable technologies. You may be interested in The London Community Heating Development Study (May 2005) which provides indications of heat densities, and the main opportunities for community heating.

Solar Energy
The Mayor believes that renewable energy (including solar, where appropriate) will help reduce London's CO_2 emissions. The Energy Hierarchy set out in the London Plan is used to assess applications for planning permission for buildings of a certain size in London (Policy 4A.1 www.london.gov.uk/thelondonplan/docs/londonplan08.pdf) [link no longer active]

Using less energy, in particular by adopting sustainable design and construction measures (Policy 4A.3) supplying energy efficiently, in particular by prioritizing decentralized energy generation (Policy 4A.6) and using renewable energy (Policy 4A.7).

In addition, the Mayor is working with existing buildings to reduce their carbon footprints. As such, the Mayor supports the following programmes: The Better Buildings Partnership works with commercial landlords to improve the energy efficiency of their buildings - http://www.londonclimatechange.co.uk/greenorganisations/index. php?option=com_content&view=article&id=181&Itemid=202 [link no longer active]

The Green 500 – http://www.green500.co.uk/ [link active as of September 2020]. All Green500 members will be awarded certification that recognizes the carbon saved through the implementation of activities described in their Green500 action plan, together with existing carbon saving practice. There are 5 levels of Green500 Awards: Bronze, Silver, Gold, Platinum, Diamond.

National programmes require all public buildings to show Display Energy Certificates

www.communities.gov.uk/planningandbuilding/theenvironment/e nergyperformance/certificates/displayenergycertificates/ [page archived, but the link is still active as of September 2020].

Information for other businesses is available at: http://www.londonclimatechange.co.uk/greenorganisations/ [though the page was archived in 2008, the link is still active as of September 2020]. The London Development Agency (LDA) has created this website to help London-based SMEs, large organisations and commercial landlords to save money by reducing the energy consumption of London's business.

The Mayor is also working with many world cities to try and encourage them to improve their energy efficiency, and to share best practice. www.c40cities.org/ [link still active as of September 2020]

Park systems
The Mayor believes parks and open spaces are key to the capital's quality of life, and has committed to invest £6 million in improving the quality and safety of London's parks. Many open spaces are not well used because they are run down. The Mayor

has set up a scheme which will improve ten parks across London, and the aim for the winning parks will be to make each one cleaner, safer, greener and nicer places to visit, with actual work on the chosen parks taking place over the following two years.

http://www.london.gov.uk/parksvote/ [link no longer active].

Adaptation
You mention other approaches such as white roofs and green roofs. The Mayor of London, with Design for London published Living Roofs and Walls, which supports a green roof policy in the London Plan. The Mayor of London is also working with external partners to investigate the benefits of cool roofs for London. These ideas are reflected in the draft London Climate Change Adaptation Strategy, which starts the process of planning how London must adapt to all climate change impacts, a first for a world city. The public consultation for the document will be launched in Spring 2009.

http://www.london.gov.uk/mayor/publications/2008/08/climate-change-adapt-strat.jsp [link no longer active].

Thank you again for writing to the Mayor.

Kind regards

28/Jan/2010

Proposals to stop global warming

Get Rid of Global Warming

The best way for getting rid of Global Warming is to change the terminologies and to restructure the economic models for combating climate problems. Global Warming is a misnomer to people as it implies everywhere will get warm and there'll be no winters or storms, hence the heckling of scientists during the latest snow storm to hit the UK. Global Warming will bring harsher winters to some areas and adversely affect the Gulf Stream which keeps North West Europe as warm as it is. This disruption will cause colder climates during winter. But until this is understood by the public, the term Global Warming should be changed.

Climate Change is also too general a term as climate changes every day. Both the terms Climate Change and Global Warming are not adequate to describe what is happening and the effects they will have. That is why the terms should be changed, maybe to Crisis Climate, and the focus of action should be on adaptation to Crisis Climate.

Further, green energy technology should be advanced whether there was Crisis Climate or not. It should be a natural development toward resource management, which is the major problem driving excess CO_2 production. Recycling should be emphasised as should technology (not just green, but also 'blue-sky thinking' –CO_2 scrubbers, carbon capture, and nuclear power heat recycling, etc), along with wind, wave and solar power.

The changes to the climate and rise of CO_2 should be down-played and people educated on how to preserve their resources and reduce pollution rather than bombard them with scientific analyses people don't understand or care about. Leave the graphs, equations, and charts at home, and bring out the fireside chats. Taxing will not be a help except to fill the coffers of bankrupt governments. There are more efficient and cheaper ways to reduce carbon without taxation, but it will require changes to our over-excessive "Western" lifestyles. Agriculture and vehicles make-up the bulk of CO_2 emissions, followed by ships and the internet/computer industry, which are rising faster than air travel emissions. Finding new ways to grow and transport food, supplies, and people should be top of the agenda without corporate greenwash clogging up the system. Our economy will have to blend in with nature's needs, which will reduce pollution and waste, and help humans withstand Crisis Climate.

Adapt, adapt, adapt. Our ancestors couldn't see what was coming and tried to out-live and out-engineer environmental changes, but they died out as their civilisations collapsed. Our politicians, corporations and media are very poor leaders when change is needed. Crisis Climate can only be coped with through grass roots and education. Small scale changes in communities rather than ineffective and inadequate changes from government and business will be the vital key. Or we can live as we are and let Crisis Climate happen and millions will die unnecessarily. This could even out the human race between the haves and the have-nots, as Crisis Climate has no favourites or takes sides. It's our choice as to who lives and who dies.

While we have the technology to change the climate, it should be used in conjunction with nature and not against it. Crisis Climate tells us just that, that we face a crisis with our climate whether it is warming, cooling, becoming stormier, or causing other effects (i.e. sea level rises, desertification, mass extinctions, etc.). Crisis Climate is a neutral term; direct, not misleading, and easier to stomach for the remaining sceptics who could join in to clean the planet regardless of its cause. So, no more Global Warming. Say goodbye to Climate Change. We can handle Crisis Climate.

13/May/2009

Science & Technology
Computers impact on climate change and how to educe it

The Two-percent Solutions: Internet vs Airlines

2020 vision

With the rise of the computer industry for work and play, especially gaming, virtual meetings, cloud systems, and AI development, I still believe the carbon footprint from this will outweigh the airline industry's footprint, even more so now with the Coronavirus pandemic decreasing the demand for flights while virtual activities vastly increase. But even with the development of biofuels and of Airbus' zero-emission hydrogen-powered plane which will further lower aircraft greenhouse emissions, will anyone call for the growing computer industry's carbon footprint to be curtailed to save the world? Uh-uh.

In May, 2009, *The New Scientist* published an article about the internet and its effects on the environment, stating that the internet and its infrastructure as a whole leave a carbon footprint on par with the aviation industry, about two percent. This fact seems to be a well-hidden one or at least under-reported, and evidence that green lobbies, the media, and the general public are either oblivious to this or are biased against other carbon polluters. Even the shipping industry's carbon footprint estimates (most of which aren't even accounted for in European CO2 estimates) are around 4.5 percent. So why is the aviation industry singled out above all other low-percentage polluters? The whiff of hypocrisy surrounding certain climate change issues rears its head once more.

Bad Internet?

So why isn't the internet targeted by people for its growing carbon footprint? With all its applications and services it will provide in the future, especially in helping to combat climate change, the internet will grow exponentially over the years with it's carbon footprint becoming far bigger than shipping and aviation combined. Governments are trying to reduce businesses' carbon footprints by making people work from home and telecommute or teleconference, which would mean more computers, IT infrastructure and more of an internet footprint. Because the internet is seen as a dormant utility, not much thought is given to its polluting nature in hardware/software production and human applications. This is not to say that the internet should be shut down, far from it, it cannot be; it's woven into the fabric of our society. But people should realise that there are things in life that have far more damaging effects to the environment than aircraft and they should be addressed before they resort to trying to end an industry that could clean up its act (just as well as with cars, industry, and agriculture) and yet provides a service many people could not live or work without.

Bad Aircraft?

Is the internet more essential than flying? For all the efforts of the protesters and environmentalists complaining against the airline industry, they are using the internet to plan or research protests, a tool that basically uses the same amount of CO_2 as does their dreaded flying nemesis. The internet doesn't fly low, make noise, or smell of fuel, but people are discriminating between carbon footprints they like and dislike. One must be as bad or as good as the other. Airports and aircraft give people a severe case of 'Nimbyism'. Yes, they understandably want to protect their lives and homes from expanding airports and increased flights, but would they feel the same if told about the internet's looming carbon shadow. Aircraft industry protests are just an excuse; a green screen used by protesters who would not be able to fight against airport expansions with planning objections and petitions alone. The green agenda gives them more power, but it also obscures real issues of climate change, diverts interests elsewhere, and protects other economic agendas. The counter-argument goes that airlines bring in business and tourists on cheap flights; airports are economic necessities, and here to stay. However, while aircraft are highly visible compared to the internet, in relation to its carbon footprint, the attacks against airlines are all out of proportion.

Good Internet?

The New Scientist article listed green internet ideas about green data centres, more efficient computer cooling systems, superior computers, and improved power sources, but will it be enough to absorb the internet's increasing usage? It's Obama's fault. How can computers and the internet be the bad guys, when even President Obama used the internet, extensively, for his campaigning? He is the first Internet President. How would a carbon-sequestered internet have affected his campaign? How much CO2 did the Blackberry-mad Obama internet-drive add to the U.S.'s emissions? Was it worth it, especially when future elections, keen to emulate Obama's success, and more importantly, reality TV shows will increase internet usage? As the internet becomes the new voting booth, surely we will be choosing to elect ourselves into extinction.

Good aircraft?
Airlines know they have to change, climate change is a big issue and so is energy transition. Aircraft frames, engines, and fuels will change; they always have in response to consumer demand. Synthetic fuels, bio-fuels, algae-based and other potential fuels are now being developed and could fill the gap after fossil fuels. Flights will not decrease and attempts to do so will fail. The fact that airlines have been targeted instead shows a prejudice towards targeting visual and perceived 'anti-social' habits of people who want to fly away on holidays or business. Some commentators might say that getting rid of the two-percent carbon footprints will help fight climate change, but even if that is so, then something else will take its place to compensate. We are probably already past the tipping point, so getting rid of the two-percents won't make much difference. Human nature will always want something that will cost the earth to manufacture, use, and dispose of.

There are probably many hidden two-percent carbon footprints in the world that we think of as ubiquitous, yet harmless. The internet's emerging carbon footprint is proof that we are not serious about fighting climate change or else we would have had some legislation in slowing the growth of the internet. The internet gets no mention in the media, as it drives society, the news we receive, and maintains social cohesion. The shipping industry hardly gets a mention as it is perceived of as greener than flying and it brings us food and luxury goods. When will consumer groups start campaigning for shipping and the internet to be curtailed? Who will be brave enough to equate the internet with the excesses of the airline industry? When that day publicly comes, then we will know that people are serious about fighting climate change no matter what it costs. Is the internet too high a price to pay for our foible nature? Time will tell.

Sources:
Brooks, M. 2009. Internet Wonders. New Scientist. May 2. Vol 202, No. 2706, pg 34.

http://www.guardian.co.uk/environment/2008/feb/13/climatechange.pollution
(link for shipping CO2 levels still active as of Sept 2020)

25/Jun/2009

What are eco-friendly burials?

My Body After Death - Just Don't Bury Me

Who wants to be buried in this day and age? It's boring, unnecessary, and so final. There are more exciting and useful things that can be done after death other than being buried in a hard-wood box for eternity. Besides, not all burials are eco-friendly, so whether you want to be buried or not, there are other options available.

Organic burial:
If you want to be buried, go organic. It seems to be the new pagan (or at least a conscientious materialist) craze to be buried in a biodegradable box, wicker-type basket or shroud. All wrapped up in material that will blend with the sub-surface environment, your body will naturally decompose and quite possibly down the decades add nutrients to soil and trees. You'd enjoy new life for a few hundred years more as a tree, a perfect way to help fight climate change and be the ultimate green warrior. A forested community of the deceased could provide a real eco reason to go organic. But you'll still be taking up valuable land space and with population growth and global warming starting to lead to land encroachment, your plot and status as a tree may not be tenable. Burials, organic or not, may not be the choice forward.

Cremation:
So, if burials take up too much space, the next best option is cremation. Less of the Viking funeral pyre, a cremation gives you options on space, price, and added useful functions for the resultant ashes. There are also emission issues, but crematoriums are certainly not top of the global warming emissions list, yet. You could be scattered to the four winds, dumped in the ocean or a river, shot into space (a personal favourite), stored in a mosaic-like wall, or placed on the mantle piece until the cat knocks it over. It's an option, maybe boring, but less space-consuming and a dusty reminder to the family. But how long will the ashes remain in the family before they all die out and the urn is tipped out and sold at a local car boot sale? How much are your ashes worth?

The best ashes option is to be a diamond. Imagine your life, dull and boring, poor and unexciting, but then presto —your body is processed and pressed into a diamond. Now you can become a part of someone's life for generations. No one will throw out a diamond or abuse your new sparkling life. A human-born diamond would be more ethical than a blood diamond and good for the national economy as natural indigenous resources (i.e. you) would be the source of the diamond. Your value to the country would be immense.

Promession:
One of the newer methods of burial is 'Promession' developed by a Swedish soil scientist and former organic farmer. The body is cryogenically frozen just after death, then vibrated by sound until it is reduced it to powder. After more processing, involving moisture removal, a dry, nutrient-rich material is left over, good enough for fertilization uses. Again, the green option arises and your body enriches the land like never before.

Frozen and resuscitation:
Unlike Promession, the frozen body is not disassembled, but cryogenically frozen and then preserved in some laboratory. The residents of the icy abodes hope that one day they will be resuscitated and their diseased bodies cured by some future science. While sounding far-fetched, it has its advantages in that you get to hopefully live another day, intact and healthy. But if it doesn't work, you will have to die again in a future laboratory. Is this false hope? Who can guarantee the safe revival of a frozen corpse? If you die in such a state, can your body be used for other functions as described above? Frozen for science and for posterity may appeal to some, but the outcome could present unforeseen side-effects and dangers.

Excarnation:
The fate of the ancients in Zoroastrian societies and some New World tribes; you die, get stuck on a ceremonial platform, and then the vultures and other wild scavengers deflesh you, leaving the bones. The bones would then be placed in an ossuary and buried, maybe under the ancestral home. The good old days are no longer here, but while such practices may not be urban fare, they might still exist in rural settings in countries, such as India, where it is still legal. For a unique after-death

experience, full of ancient ritual and spiritualism, excarnation would be an extreme expression of going back to nature. Excarnation may no longer be the 21st century option, but it would be a green way to die by letting nature take its course.

Donation to science:
At various places around America are so-called CSI farms where bodies donated to science are buried to decay at varying rates. While the idea and intent is admirable, how much satisfaction would you get knowing that you'll be lying in a bin or a shallow grave or hacked to pieces, and eaten by maggots to assist forensic investigators in assessing length of death, season of death, location of death, etc. It may not be a pleasant or appreciated way to spend death, but some people might like this altruistic concept, more so than just a normal organ donation. How much would your services be worth? Would you consider this cause to be worthy to donate your body to? In retrospect, mummified and bog bodies have been invaluable to science. The fight against disease has also benefited from donated bodies, so maybe donating your body to science may be worth it after all. If you can pick and choose what your body is used for, then so be it. Might as well make the most of it.

There are other choices then the standard burial practices. Just as death rituals have changed over the millennia, so they will continue to change. And as population, cultural, climate, and economic issues come to the fore, burial options will be available, with a difference.

23/Jul/2010

Science & Technology - Environment
New ideas and methods to replace carbon footprint units

The Green Scale

2020 vision
The Green Scale is a concept I created. Maybe there's already something like it out there, but if not, I lay claim to publishing it first.

What is a carbon footprint? What does it relate to? Who can say how much 30 tonnes of CO_2 feels like or looks like much less describe your own carbon footprint in simple terms, except to be vaguely high or low. Most people cannot relate to the carbon footprint or measure it without an online calculator. And experts who try to define and relate the carbon footprint to Climate Change make it unnecessarily complicated. Carbon Footprint units are not needed. We need a new scale, a simpler Green Scale to make things more accessible to people so they can better understand how much CO_2 is being/has been used.

Carbon Footprint defined:
A carbon footprint is a measure of the impact our activities (mostly fossil fuel use) have on the environment. It measures all the greenhouse gases mankind produces in units of tonnes (or kg) of carbon dioxide. There are two types of carbon footprint: direct emission of CO_2 (e.g. fossil fuels, energy consumption, and transportation, etc) and indirect emissions (e.g. emissions from the total lifecycle of the product).

But how is this calculated? Will every household have a user-friendly carbon footprint booklet? Even after begrudgingly logging in to a carbon footprint site and calculating your footprint, then what? No one else has bothered so you're left in your own carbon footprint bubble. Also, and more importantly, the value of the amount of tonnes CO_2 produced is meaningless without some context as to if that value is good or bad. So, again, you have a number, but no meaningful reference. There is no international, one-size-fits-all carbon footprint calculator.

The disadvantage of the carbon footprint unit is in having to comprehend the context of the calculating and relating it to everyday life. All you can do is calculate your CO2 lifestyle, but not individual, everyday events and product use.

The Green Scale defined:
The Green Scale would solve this with an international and industry-standard scale in line with many other global scales. We have the Richter Scale (where numbers 1 up to a nominal number denote the severity of an earthquake), the Mohs Scale (1 to 10 on the hardness of objects), different scales for temperature (Celsius, Fahrenheit, and Kelvin, etc), and the Saffir-Simpson Hurricane Wind Scale, to name a few. And by another analogy there is even a countdown to the end of the world in the Doomsday Clock and its minutes to midnight. Everyone understands these. They are internationally known. So why not establish a new scale that emphasises the greenness or lack thereof regarding personal lifestyle, companies, cities, countries, regions, technology, etc.

It's simple: Zero (0) would be the lowest point being carbon neutral. The upper point (for man-made emissions) would be 10 with decimal points in between. Factors would include carbon-producing gas/oil/electric/coal use, private and public transport, flights, food and drink industry, clothing, manufacturing, housing/building structures, recreation and leisure, financial issues, etc and how CO2 it is being tackled. The Green Scale could also be adapted to non-man-made emissions, like natural events such as volcanoes whose carbon emissions are hundreds of times what humans produce. Here, the Green Scale would continue past the upper (man-made emissions limit) of 10, showing the comparison between natural and man-made emissions.

Visually, the Green Scale would look like a simplified thermometer, but the 'mercury' would be coloured green up to the highest measured point of CO2. The lighter the green, the closer to zero carbon. Such a scale could be placed on vehicles, white goods, aircraft, throughout companies, and anywhere where carbon is produced as an industry-standard symbol denoting its environmentally-friendliness.

On maps, a number within a green symbol would denote the carbon emission level. The world would be split into a Greenscape and every country, region, city and parts thereof would have a number on the

Green Scale as ascertained from existing and new investigations. So for instance, New York might have a rating of 6.0 on the Green Scale while Paris has 5.3 and so on for each city. After each city and area is factored in, the country would get an overall rating, thus the US may have a rating of 7.5 while China has 7.6, Iceland with 4.1, and so on.

The Green Scale would already be 'preloaded' with the indirect CO_2 emissions (e.g. manufacturing process, product packaging, transport, recyclability, etc). So a car might have a value on the Green Scale of 2.0 with a preloaded value of 0.8 for its pre-use value and 1.2 for its usage, expected fuel use, mileage, and post-life use. Essentially, the Green Scale will account for CO_2 cradle-to-grave and cradle-to-cradle usage in man-made products. The car, or any other product, would have a sticker or badge with the Green Scale value assigned to it. All these Green Scale values would have been pre-agreed by an international body with published data and resulting Green Scale values. Every company would be required to have a Green Scale value for their products, like a quality mark.

Monitoring-wise, the Green Scale would have to use recorded data from the now-defunct carbon footprint scheme and be translated/equated into Green Scale units. Open-air Green Scales could be straight-forward CO_2 monitors placed in streets, open areas and the aforementioned features above producing a value for the regional Green Scale. They would be easily accessible and readable without unnecessary online calculations. Of course the Green Scale initiative will cost money and time to establish, but the Green Scale will be a truly global and innovative way to live a low carbon lifestyle and to tackle Climate Change.

The Green Scale would give people a quantitative and qualitative view on Climate Change, with a simple number they would be able to see, understand, measure, and change for their own benefit. The lower the number the better until carbon neutrality was achieved. The Green Scale would be a simple, user-friendly strategy and a sure-fire visual way to engage and educate people in understanding the effects of carbon dioxide emissions and climate change.

27/Aug/2008

Environment
Facts about Antarctica

Antarctican Facts

2020 vision
I am a big Antarctica enthusiast and the two articles below formed part of my research for my book on Antarctica, hopefully to be published one day.

After centuries of speculation and exploration, Antarctica was finally discovered on January 27, 1820, by Estonian Admiral Thaddeus Von Bellingshausen, commanding a Russian voyage. Since then it has captivated explorers, scientists, and the public's imaginations. Though what do people really know about Antarctica? Here are a few facts.

Geography:
Antarctica is the fifth largest continent, with an area of fourteen million square kilometres, compared with Europe's ten million square kilometres and the USA's nine million square kilometres. Containing a tenth of the Earth's total landmass, Antarctica is twice as big as Australia, but if it were to lose its ice, East Antarctica would be Australia-sized, while West Antarctica, comprised of the Peninsula and Marie Byrd Land, would be a series of islands. Ninety-eight percent of Antarctica is covered with ice; the remaining ice-free two percent (including the famed Dry Valleys) would be about the size of New Zealand. Most of the exposed rock is in the Trans-Antarctic Mountains or along sparse and narrow slivers of coast. Antarctica is surrounded by the fierce, wind-lashed, Southern Ocean, which extends from the 40th south parallel to the Antarctic Circle at 66°S. South America is the closest continent at 1100km away while Australia and South Africa are 2500km and 4000km away, respectively. Antarctica is one lonely place.

East Antarctica is formed from old continental crust, heavily folded and metamorphosed. It rises steeply from the coast to the central plateau at over 4000m. The East Antarctic ice sheet was fully formed by at least fourteen million years ago and though there were fluctuations in temperature, the ice sheet has remained intact with no compete de-icing.

The 1200km-long West Antarctica from the Peninsula to the Trans-Antarctic Mountains constitutes 6.8 percent of Antarctica with an average elevation of 2000m. Marie Byrd Land averages 600m to 1000m, with mountains peaking over 2000m, while the Peninsula, is part of an ancient Antarctic-Andean structure that ends near the Ellsworth Mountains. The Ellsworth Mountains at the base of the Peninsula are part of a separate structure to the Trans-Antarctic Mountain system and has some limited bare ground as does the Peninsula, the bare ground existing due to the disappearing ice-cap. The West Antarctic ice sheet was fully formed by at least five million years ago. There is no suggestion of any period where there was a complete ice sheet disappearance.

Climatic processes:
The strong winds around Antarctica circulate in a westerly direction, due to the southern latitude's low temperature and pressure compared to the equator's high temperature and pressure, which combined with the rotation of the Earth, provides the wind system. The temperatures of East Antarctica can reach -89°C, the strong katabatic (downward flowing) winds affecting the Antarctic plateau. But the katabatic winds are lessened on the Peninsula when these winds interact with eastbound cyclonic winds bringing warm, moist air, and precipitation from the sea. These cyclonic storms frequent the Peninsula, as they are further north and in the path of the circumpolar winds.

Ocean circulation close to the continent is from the east, but in the Furious Fifties and Roaring Forties they shift to come in from the west, creating the Antarctic Divergence, where the two currents sweep away from another, which can actually be seen as a physical boundary in the water. Carrying ten percent of the world's oceans, connecting the Atlantic, Pacific and Indian oceans, the circumpolar current's rate is four times that of the Gulf Stream. The storminess of the Southern Ocean is due to a bottleneck effect created by Tierra del Fuego and the Antarctic where the Atlantic, Pacific and Southern Oceans combine. Two thousand miles of ocean are suddenly compressed into a much shallower, 600-mile wide area, with winds forced southward via the Andes mountain range. The prevailing weather system then moves from west to east. In fact, Cape Horn earned the name *wallapak wellek,* meaning 'evil point' from the Yamana Indians on Tierra del Fuego due to its storminess.

Climatic regions and Temperatures:
Four general climatic regions have been identified, including the interior Antarctic plateau (East Antarctica plateau), the Antarctic slope, the Antarctic Coast and Maritime Antarctic (west Antarctic Peninsula, its islands, and the South Sandwich and South Shetland Islands). The Southern and Eastern parts of the Peninsula are completely ice-bound being 4° to 6°C colder and having stronger winds similar to the East Antarctic coast.

The Peninsula receives more sunlight and daylight hours, and sea temperatures are higher even in winter. And because it is mountainous, it disrupts warm, moist air from the northwest garnering the Peninsula the highest precipitation rate for all of Antarctica with more than 1000mm per annum on the Peninsula west coast. The winds cause snowdrifts, sleet, and even rain with temperatures sometimes rising above freezing in the summer. On the Peninsula and adjacent islands in the winter, temperatures can range from -15°C to +5°C, while in the summer rise to 0°C to 10°C. The sub-Antarctic in summer and winter can be warmer by another 5°C and mean annual temperatures on coastal Antarctica can be -10°C

Zoological and Botanical:
Vertical ocean circulation from the Antarctic Bottom, consisting of water up-welling and sinking brings warmer water to the ocean top, which helps to cool the air and also produce nutrients for surface-dwelling organisms. This is important in Antarctica for the food chain in the Southern Ocean is rich with algae blooming after the winter, bringing in phytoplankton and zooplankton which nourishes krill, fish, seal and whales. Penguins, sea birds and small insects make for some of the land animals.

Invertebrates include collembola, mites, rotifers, protozoa, tardigrades, nematodes and others in Antarctica, with 25 mites species and 7 collembola species in Maritime Antarctica, the largest of which is only 5mm. These invertebrates in turn, forage on bacteria, fungi or algae. In modern times, reindeer, cats, and rats have been introduced to the Sub-Antarctic islands, but have had a rather negative effect on native species.

Botanically, there is not much. Antarctica has the coldest and driest climate in the world due to locked-up water, resulting in very low humidity and precipitation, causing the soil-forming process (weathering, etc) to be reduced. Moisture plays an important role over temperature so in order to survive plants may choose anti-dehydration traits over cold resistance, with plant growth reflecting areas of moisture rather than warmth. As Antarctica was covered by ice by the Pleistocene era, any later re-colonisation by plant life had either to take place from existing plant expansion on limited unfrozen land or were imported from the surrounding continents by birds, wind or ocean currents.

Cryptogams make up one group of plants with 350 to 400 species of lichens, 360 species of algae, 9 Genera of liverworts, 28 macro fungi, 75 species of fungi, and 85 mosses most of which grow in the continental or maritime zones, some in both. But there are only two flowering plants on the Peninsula, the Antarctic hair grass and Antarctic Pearlwort or the carnation in the maritime zone. Compared to the fifty species of vascular plants on South Georgia Island this is still paltry when compared to the eighty thousand vascular plant species in the Amazon. Of course the higher north one goes, the diversity of faunal and floral species increases, as does the productivity of the soil. So at 65°S, where temperatures range from 0°C midsummer to around -15°C in the winter there can be a carpeting effect of lichens and mosses in more sheltered areas.

Antarctica is a fascinating place to contemplate and is on many an adventurous tourist's list of pilgrimage, but tourism, climate change, and possible future industrial processes (mining) could spoil our last pristine continent.

Sources:
Argod, R. 2004. *Out of Antarctica: Reflections on the Origin of Peoples.* London: Richmond Editions.

Campbell, I.B. & Claridge, G.G.C. 1987. *Antarctica: Soils, Weathering Processes and Environment.* Amsterdam: Elsevier.

Crossley, L. 2000. *Explore Antarctica.* Cambridge: Cambridge University Press.

Flem-Ath, R & Flem-Ath, R. 1995. *When The Sky Fell: In Search of Atlantis.* London: BCA.

Hansom, J.D. & Gordon, J.E. 1998. Antarctic Environments and Resources –A Geographical Perspective. New York: Addison Wesley Longman, Ltd.

McLeod, L. (ed.) 2002. *Savage Planet: Cape Horn.* Manchester: Granada, 16-17.

Press, F. and Siever, R. 1986. *Earth.* New York: W.H. Freeman and Company, 292.

Pyne. S.J. 2003. *The Ice.* London: Weidenfeld & Nicolson.

Rubin, J. 2000. *Lonely Planet: Antarctica.* London: Lonely Planet Publications Pty Ltd.

27/Aug/2008

Environment
Facts about Antarctic Islands

Antarctic Islands

Before Antarctica had been discovered, there was avid speculation as to what lay at the end of the southern world. Many an explorer, whaler, and adventurer sought their destinies and fortunes in the quest for the Southern Continent. Finally, after centuries, the Southern Ocean gave up its secrets and many islands were discovered dotted around Antarctica. The discoveries and histories of four of the biggest Sub-Antarctic islands are presented below.

The South Shetland Islands:
Only 1000km from Tierra del Fuego are the South Shetland Islands. There are four main groups in this 540km-long island chain, with one hundred and fifty or so islets approximately located 63-degrees south 54-degrees west. They are eighty percent glaciated and cover an area of 3688 sq km, the highest point Mt. Foster (2105m) on Smith Island. These islands, the closest of the big island-groups of the Peninsula, were discovered by William Smith in 1819 who was blown off-course in the Drake Passage.

Elephant Island is at the northeast end of the South Shetland chain. Chinstrap penguins reside here and 2000 year-old moss with 3m deep peat also appear. Landings are precarious due to craggy and rocky shores.

King George Island has less than ten percent of its 1295 sq km area free of ice. Large moss beds are present and it is home to gentoo and Adelie penguins. Upon it are stations and/or personnel from Argentina, Brazil, Chile, China, South Korea, Poland, Russia, Uruguay, Ecuador, Germany, Peru and the U.S., making the largest of the South Shetlands the unofficial capital of Antarctica.

Greenwich Island, a little south west of King George, is the site of Yankee Harbour, a protected almost circular, one-kilometre harbour on its southwest side. It was an anchorage point for 18th and 19th century sealers.

Livingston Island is the next largest island in the chain. It is also the Site of Special Interest No. 6 (according to the Antarctic Treaty) having the "greatest concentration of 19th century historical sites in Antarctica".

Deception Island is a 12km wide broken-ring of a collapsed volcano cone, making it one of the 'safest natural harbours in the world - despite periodic eruptions.' The entrance is through a 230m wide and windy break in the 580m tall wall in which lies a potentially hull-piercing rock just below the surface. Underground volcanic vents remind one that the volcano is dormant, not extinct and had recently erupted in 1969 and again in 1991/2.

The South Orkney Islands:
Located around 47 degrees West and 60 degrees south, this group has four major islands; Coronation, the largest; Signy, Powell and Laurie Islands and includes the remote Inaccessible Islands. Eighty-five percent glaciated and ranging over 622 sq km, the islands suffer cold westerly winds, with less than two hours sun on an overcast day. Discovered in 1821 by sealers; gentoo, Adelie and chinstrap penguins also roost here.

Signy Island, even though a small 6.5km by 5km island, is an important research base for biological studies, especially plant life such as the *Colobanthus* quintensis which can be abundant, grow around 25cm meters wide and make compacted cushions in sheltered low-altitude regions. Signy Island also has many small lakes located in well-vegetated, mossy areas, that are home to blue-green algae, microbes and bacteria, crustaceans, worms, and nematodes, which get enriched by salt spray and seal faeces. Due to the remoteness and recent deglaciation, none of the Antarctic lakes have mollusks or fish.

South Georgia Island:
Discovered in 1675 by a merchant blown further south and off course while rounding Cape Horn, this island is 170km by 40km covering 3755 sq km. At 38 degrees west and 54 degrees south with smaller surrounding islands, it is rugged, heavily glaciated (more on its south side than the north due to its aspect) and mountainous, the Allardyce Range forming the backbone of the island, Mt. Paget at 2934m, the

highest point. Mean average temperatures on South Georgia are two degrees Celsius, with seasonal variations of seven degrees, some summers being 15 to 20 degrees Celsius. This leaves a growing season of a hundred to hundred and thirty five growing days in the Maritime north, while the coastal continent receives around sixty days of growth. Eighteen thousand years ago, temperatures in the south east Atlantic were four degrees lower than today causing an ice cap to form on South Georgia.

While South Georgia is fifty-eight percent glaciated with a periglacial or tundra-like environment, eighty-five percent of the coasts are ice-free, comprised of hard rock cliffs. South Georgia also has twenty-six vascular plants, of which sixty-four percent of the flowering plants share an affinity with South America/Tierra del Fuego, this characteristic likely due to the 'prevailing westerly winds' which bring in nesting birds, air and ocean currents.

The northeast coast is fjorded, though harbour areas (used by early whaling stations) are protected from the westerlies by the mountains. The island is cold, cloudy and windy with hardly any seasonal change. South Georgia also has some of the best and largest of sand and gravel beaches in the Polar Region, due to past glacial action. Ferns grow on the island, which is inhabited by elephant seals, seabirds, Antarctic fur seals, and macaroni and king penguins.

The South Sandwich Islands:
Almost covered in ice, this eleven-island group running in a rough north-south arc was discovered by Captain James Cook in 1775. The islands cover 310 sq km ranging approximately from 59 degrees south to 26 degrees west. There are three small, contained island groups, with three larger, individual islands strung out along the way. However, due to their position near active converging tectonic plates, the islands are volcanic with both basalt and andesite eruptions occurring in this island group.

All the islands, Montagu being the largest, were formed by volcanoes a "relatively short time ago" and some still show volcanic activity as observed in 1908 and by scientists in 1956 when "three jets of glowing material shot 300m into the air" for forty-eight hours. Thirty-five kilometres off the northwest of the chain is also a submarine volcano.

The volcano on Bellingshausen Island in the Southern Thule group of the South Sandwich Islands causes snowmelt and fumaroles, which helps facilitate sporadic but rich vegetation growth. Though more northerly than the South Shetlands and the South Orkney Islands, the South Sandwich Islands are colder due to seawater coming from the Weddell Sea. Claimed by both Britain and Argentina, the islands also have the largest penguin colony in the world.

The four big Sub-Antarctic island groups are wonders in themselves, still holding on to some secrets, while providing springboards for human habitation and scientific experiences in other cases. They are unique worlds and long may they continue to be.

Sources:

Campbell, I.B. & Claridge, G.G.C. 1987. *Antarctica: Soils, Weathering Processes and Environment.* Amsterdam: Elsevier.

Crossley, L. 2000. *Explore Antarctica.* Cambridge: Cambridge University Press.

Flem-Ath, R & Flem-Ath, R. 1995. *When The Sky Fell: In Search of Atlantis.* London: BCA.

Hansom, J.D. & Gordon, J.E. 1998. Antarctic Environments and Resources –A Geographical Perspective. New York: Addison Wesley Longman, Ltd.

Nunn, P.D. 1994. *Oceanic Islands.* Oxford: Blackwell.

Press, F. and Siever, R. 1986. *Earth.* New York: W.H. Freeman and Company.

Rubin, J. 2000. *Lonely Planet: Antarctica.* London: Lonely Planet Publications Pty Ltd.

12/Dec/2009

Will the Copenhagen climate change summit be a success?

Burning Issues for the Copenhagen Summit

Why save the Polar Bears? Why are they the poster child for Global Warming? While climate scientists, environmentalists, and animal lovers fret over the loss of such wildlife, they forget that natural or not, Climate Change will affect evolution and we should be preparing for that instead of trying to preserve an old order on the brink of extinction. There are more important issues to deal with at the Copenhagen Summit.

Animals will have to adapt more so than humans. South-travelling Polar Bears have already been breeding with Grizzly Bears to create hybrid 'Grolar bears'. Likewise around the world, hardy animals will cross breed or adapt as they enter new habitats when theirs disappears. Most animals will evolve and species converge/diverge when Earth's climate changes again, as always. The Inuit will turn to hunt other animals. Former Polar Bear prey will thrive and provide more food, new predators will arrive, new niches will open and evolution will march on. This also goes for Pandas. What benefit are they outside of a zoo? All of us will have to adapt to new food sources (genetically modified or natural) and eating habits to survive.

Scientists aligned to the Global Warming consensus state that we are heading for the sixth great Global Extinction. Let it happen. Humans spend far too much time, resources, and money on saving animals that will become extinct anyway. We are trying to divert evolution and save species that Mother Nature wants rid of. Of course, some of the extinctions are being caused by man through hunting, habitat destruction, domestication, or other means. Man may even become extinct himself due to severe climate change, but that is evolution. Earth will survive global warming, it always has. We will only make things worse by working against nature.

Believe it or not, there are not too many people in the world. The world could take double the amount of people. The current population of the world could all live within the state of Texas, each within the size of a modest house (albeit in high rises). The fact that humans like to live in coastal and popular areas highlights the fact that there are many areas in the world where man does not live today that they could live in if Global Warming changed environmental habitats. The real issue is resource management. There are too many humans using too many resources too fast. Humans squander so many natural resources that could be recycled, better developed, regenerated, diverted, or even left alone. The western world enjoys a lifestyle way beyond the level of Third World countries, but as those poorer nations become richer, they will desire a 'Western' lifestyle, which would be unsustainable. So-called cradle-to-cradle technology (recycled and reusable) and strictly-managed natural resources will enable population growth and still have enough resources.

In the current climate, Copenhagen will be a deadlocked, hung-jury affair. There are no legally binding deals to be made despite interviewed commentators and those summit attendees talking up success. Rich countries involved will act to preserve their way of life while poorer nations will strive to make richer nations pay, even as they aspire to climb up the rich ladder themselves. Nothing will change. The world should plan for Plan B: adaptation. Yes, more people will die, nations and economies rise or fall, but such epic events have been happening for thousands of years. Preservation of an old order cannot save us. New thinking in politics and economics is needed, but there is nothing innovative on the horizon. The little renewable energy there is, is not enough on current political and economic platforms.

The Copenhagen summit is about leadership issues, or lack thereof. While the case for Global Warming may have been proven by science, what has not been proven is the global political consensus on what to do. Politicians are not ready to make changes unpopular with their constituents. They may bully taxes out of us, make the economic and moral cases, but they are afraid to lose elections. If politicians made the tough choices on green issues through combined cross-party action then voters would have no choice but to be green. Nothing will be done about Global Warming, because our political-economic-social system is too well-entrenched to change.

The reason why so many people are sceptical of Climate Change is the evangelical hysteria that some scientists and activists spout on global warming, which puts people off. There should be less scaremongering and more action. Instead of wasting time and CO2 at Copenhagen about what to do, just do it. But our leaders can't, due to our global system, which won't allow nations to act unilaterally, because it will damage other nations' economies. International collaboration will not work unless the system is changed. And so that's where we stand: on the brink of the Tipping Point. There are many high-tech and off-the-shelf technologies that could be emplaced today to mitigate Climate Change, but it is not in the interests of governments and companies who will not benefit politically or financially from them. As long as they hold the key to unlocking Climate Change, the world will burn.

However, contrary to popular opinion, the US government is not the climatic enemy, neither is Europe nor BRIC (Brazil, Russia, India, China). We are: the ordinary people of the world. We, who have demanded our luxuries and voted in our unsustainable way of life, hold the smoking gun of Global Warming. Climate Change is about individual choice and lifestyle. Copenhagen should be our summit, not the governments of the world who will not act. The last Polar Bear is relying on you, and your friend, and your friend's friend to save it; not your leader. We voted the Polar Bear out of existence. Next, it's our turn.

History

01/Jan/2008

Arts & Humanity - History(other)
Commentary: Changing the Course of History

You Can't Change the Course of History

2020 vision
I do hate that phrase: 'changed the course of history'. Who's to say history wasn't supposed to be changed for better or worse? Nothing is set in stone. The sub-channel title was one I created to vent my displeasure.

In Brian Fagan's *The Long Summer: How Climate Changed Civilisation* (2004), he made a statement referring to El Ninos: 'Some of these rapid shifts were brief: others lasted centuries and changed history.' (p.130). Now something about that sentence niggled me and I realised that he had made a statement, that though commonly used by people, especially among historians and archaeologists cannot happen: 'changed history'? Surely not! History or its course cannot be changed.

This may seem an innocuous phrase and a pedantic response as such, but history flows in a linear manner and cannot be subject to change, because you cannot change the past. If Fagan meant that history was changed from the point of view of present-day academics in regards to changing their theories, notions and books about history accordingly to new data, then that is acceptable. But thinking one knows how history would have run had an event occurred or not occurred, thus supposedly changing history is something else entirely.

The Ice Ages, Thermopylae, the Aztec conquest, the Battle of Hastings, and the Fall of Constantinople happened as they were meant to happen. Even if they did not happen, we would not know about it as being different and thinking somehow that history had been changed. History is a living thing as the idea of history resides in the mind of man, who organises events from the past into chronological order to create history. History has happened, it is the past any moment before now. The future will happen moments from now, but there is not a future history: a hypothetical time and place from where one can sit back, see the future, and change events accordingly to suit it. We cannot know how one of these 'alternate' histories would have turned out.

Even now climate change is again affecting our world. However, it is not changing the course of history. Our civilisation is reacting to climate change as it happens in our present. We will not know the affects of our actions until later in this century, but we would not have changed history as we would have been living through the course of those actions, which have no retroactive effects. Our children and children's children will not be living in a future where the course of history was changed due to climate change, whether our actions were effective or not. All they would know is that past events happened, because people made them happen during their past lifetimes and not that people were somehow steering the course of future history. In other words, one cannot know the future in order to change the past, thus changing history.

When William the Conqueror defeated King Harold, there was no course of history to be changed, because it was happening in their present, all things being relative. They were living the event, oblivious to any future histories. For the people of England in 1066, when Harold died in battle, history did not change, the change was in their leaders, country and perception of a new worldview, but life went on. When William won the war, he opened up a new chapter in the history of England, but that is not changing the course of history. History can be made, have momentous moments, be rewritten, and evolve as laid out by man, but not changed.

So why does this phrase keep coming up, that something this or something that changed the course of history? People know that history is a one-time run event, but it seems this phrase is an unconscious throwaway line to increase the significance of an event, that is already significant. It is a symbolic phrase and not literal. Things can affect people and events making history, but not change the process or fabric of history. A counter-temporal storm would be quite amazing, but on this occasion, this past *El Nino* event, discovered through archaeological evidence, changed our interpretation of history, adding to a vast tome of data. History cannot be changed. I wish it could be, though perceptions, theories, and interpretations of history can be changed and often are. And that's a whole different story.

11/Jan/2008

Arts & Humanities - History Mysteries
Whatever Happened to New Age Archaeology?

Is New Age Archaeology Dead?

2020 vision

Another title I added to the channel. I like to indulge in New Age Archaeology books from time to time. They challenge the orthodoxy of the gate keepers of archaeology and anthropology. Some are well reasoned, but unprovable, while others were just outright cash cows. However they often raised good questions and piqued my infovore nature. There were a glut of them during the nineties and noughties, then the interest seemed to bottom out, especially when their theories were publicly challenged by the media and academics. But I can safely say the hardy New Agers are back and raising more questions of the distant past.

Once upon a time in the land of archaeology, there arose would-be usurpers of archaeological thought and theory. They were the New Agers, men of uncertain origins, untrained in the arts of archaeology, but reputedly armed with the rekindled knowledge of the ancients, new theories and the unvarnished proof of their claims.

They were behemoths like Graham Hancock, Andrew Collins, Robert Bauval, Robert Temple, Adrian Gilbert, Maurice Cotterell, Christopher Knight, Robert Lomas, Zecharia Sitchin, Richard Leigh, Michael Baigent, and Henry Lincoln, and many more. They wrote the seminal books of the 90's or awakened people's imaginations to the new insights into archaeology, or so it seemed.

As a student about to begin my archaeology degree, I readily devoured these books wondering if I would be able to investigate any of these new ideas. But sadly, as my course wore on, it gradually dawned on me and my other friends who were also bedazzled by the lights of new age archaeology, that all was not right. Where were the scientific data, the methodical approach to data gathering and the certain proof? There were accusations of information massaging, misleading translations, random site selection and even plagiarism. Then there was the glut in the late 90's, when book after book rapidly followed each other or was a republished edition from earlier pseudo-science forays, or information was regurgitated ad infinitum from book to book or from the same author. The bottom seemed to have fallen out of this market. But had it? Where are the New Agers now?

There are still conferences for New Age archaeology and still some book sales, but with nothing like the hype that preceded previous sales. So, what went wrong? Archaeology was, and still is, regarded as a stuffy profession with dyed-in-the-wool ideas and methods. When the non-archaeologically educated librarians, engineers and authors came along and had a go, it seemed like a breath of fresh ideas sweeping aside the bureaucracy of the old guard. No more would archaeological secrets be for just the academics.

Of course, this had been done before with people like Edgar Cayce in the 30's and Erich Von Daniken in the 70's, but this seemed like the new coming and beginning, starting with the sensational *Fingerprints of the Gods* (1995) by Graham Hancock. It was almost a dream, with all the secrets of an unknown, ancient and technological civilisation laid bare. This book was followed up by other non-archaeologists, would-be adventurers who scoured the world in search of this lost civilisation and found traces of them in every culture with a creation myth and a lost past due to wicked colonialism responsible for the destruction of ancient texts, and thus the truth, etc. The Pyramids of Giza were mirrors of Orion's belt; the Sphinx was really an ancient lion figure with the mythical Hall of Records beneath its paws, and Mesopotamia had been visited by aliens or a race of snake-eyed creatures as depicted on ceramics. Oh -and Atlantis was buried beneath the ice on Antarctica. Ooh, yes, there were pyramids on Mars and a moonbase around Saturn, according to exoarchaeologists. There was no end to the sensationalist claims.

Even before studying as an archaeologist, I had read a lot of these books with caution. There were some very interesting ideas: In Cotterell's *The Mayan Prophecies* (1995) he surmised that the amount of energy from the sun could affect a mother's fertility and a baby's development and personality, which seemed plausible. But then the theory of his so-called 'sun-sign astrology' developed into a super-code to reveal secrets of ancient civilisations and how the world regularly faced catastrophe from the sun. Then there was *The Orion Mystery* (1994) by Bauval. Were the ancient Egyptians building heaven on Earth? Well, actually no, they were not. The Pyramids may have superficially looked like they were lined up with Orion's belt stars, but the angles were wrong, the Pyramids were upside down in relation to the stars and their location was due more to landscape and geology than to the stars. There were also claims from other authors of helicopters depicted in ancient hieroglyphics and from Hancock, an ancient fortress buried under the sea off a Japanese Island (*Heaven's Mirror*, 1998). It all seemed a bit too much for many people, especially when there was no confirmed scientific proof, so the books and accompanying TV shows and special documentaries faded away.

Now, I am not so rigid minded that some of the more rational claims might be true. I do believe that the Chinese treasure ships sailed around the world in 1421, but circumstances then and now have conspired to leave that evidence in the past. I do believe that there were ancient trade routes across the Atlantic to the Americas, but we have no concrete evidence, because the European traders wanted an advantage over competition and so kept no records or maps. Either way, those two examples do not undermine the legitimacy of the peoples living in the Americas or belittle the achievements of later explorers. I do believe that ancient man was more sophisticated than we think or know, not because of alien intervention, but because of evolutionary spurts, like an ancient internet, where ideas seem to spread very fast from the Ice Age to the Stone, Bronze and Iron Age with agriculture, writing and city-building. There would be no need for an ancient care-taker civilisation, aliens or any other mysteries.

But has New-Age archaeology disappeared or died? Has a new era appeared under Dan Brown and his pseudo-history fit for the big screen? Has the Harry Potter generation taken over not caring for history and archaeology old or new, but just magic and fantasy? With the Olympics in the summer, will China be inundated with old and new theorists searching for the 'lost' Chinese pyramids supposedly covered with pine trees to hide their true nature? Will more expeditions to South America, the Caribbean, Mediterranean, and Antarctica be undertaken in the search for Atlantis?

It seemed that good old archaeology had survived the latest onslaught intact. But like Creationism and Intelligent Design in religion, New Age archaeology could mutate into another faux-archaeology and strike once more at the gates of mainstream archaeology. So archaeology has had to adapt and create courses and structures to be able to address new age archaeology within its more organised remit. Now archaeology can tentatively embrace new and radical theories without fear. New Age archaeology might not be dead; but long live archaeology.

22/Jan/2008

Sciences - Anthropology

Is Indiana Jones Bad for Archaeology?

2020 vision
A title from a debate in our first year as BSc archaeology students at the Institute of Archaeology. My debate was on the 'Yes' side. And as Helium was based in the US, archaeology is under the anthropology banner, whereas in the UK, it is under Arts & Humanities.

'Archaeology is the search for facts...forget about lost cities and exotic travel...' so said Indiana Jones in the film *Indiana Jones and the Last Crusade* (1989). Yet the last part of that sentence typifies Indiana Jones and the facts get left by the wayside. His is the life of adventure, where skulduggery, quests and secret societies haunt the world. Yes, these may only be films, but what impression does it give about archaeology, when any self-respected and professional archaeologist is always compared to a fictional adventurer, rather than being appreciated for their real work.

It all started early for Indiana Jones, enjoying adventures that school boys and adults could only dream about. Later, his most famous adventures involved quests for supernatural objects, the Ark of the Covenant and the Holy Grail. 'You can't afford to take mythology at face value,' he says, but off he goes gallivanting around the world; adventure over archaeology. His every adventure has a conspiracy, whether it's Nazis or evil temple worshippers, and there are secret societies such as the Brotherhood of the Cruciform Sword who are sworn to protect the secret of the Holy Grail. Even for an Inter-War period film, there is also a lack of proper procedures and often destruction of viable property is used to reach artefacts. Who can forget that scene in the church in Venice when Indiana Jones discovers that the tomb of Sir Richard lies beneath the 'X' marked on the floor and proceeds to hammer a hole into it, in what is a scene of comic relief. This was an irresponsible action and prejudices people to the way archaeologists behave.

Indiana Jones is driven by a passion to find things. Many of his colleagues and rivals have obsessions and personal ambitions leading to deceit and double-crosses. Even his own father, a historian, is obsessed with finding the Holy Grail and bizarrely states 'The search for the Grail is not archaeology, but a race against evil.'; more supernatural clap-trap and definitely not the words of a devoted professional. The life of Indiana Jones is more adventure than work. Nothing is learned, nor nothing gained through or about archaeology. Through the films, archaeologists are trivialised as treasure hunters, so archaeology is also trivialised. Archaeologists are seen as glory seekers with maps to lost lands, as greedy grave robbers intent on outwitting the 'savage natives', and enduring all sorts of creepy-crawlies and booby-traps to find their treasure. Belief in archaeological truth and evidence is stretched as the implausibility of the story lines slights the profession, which in turn causes people to become wary of archaeological claims.

The films have also stirred controversy, alienating audiences in Asia in the film *Indiana Jones and the Temple of Doom*, which they saw as depicting Asians as untrustworthy, child-enslavers and sacrificers. It also gives credible Biblical Archaeology a bashing in *Raiders of the Lost Ark*, again making archaeologists seem either ultra pious or completely sceptical of heavenly powers. In both cases it could serve to confuse the public with myth and innuendo interwoven into history. Indiana Jones is such a cult figure with his trademark fedora and rugged character that such things are overlooked in favour of action and box office dollars.

A real-life Indiana Jones had been unearthed. He was the late explorer Gene Savoy. He discovered a lost civilisation deep in the Amazon jungle. Now, the mythical Cloud People have emerged from history, but Savoy was marginalised as more coverage was given to scientists who examined the mummified bodies discovered at the site. The archaeological community was more interested in the scientists' research than in Savoy's exploits and he continued to be ignored. There was and is no place for an Indiana Jones in the real world.

Is it a coincidence that because of the Indiana Jones films, there has been a rise in maverick adventurers claiming to have found the secrets of ancient civilisations? These non-archaeologists roam the world, professing great knowledge, and write popular new-age books. It seems that the films broke the mould, allowing discussion and literature to appear about the Ark and the Grail outside of the biblical stories and the Arthur legends. Before the Indiana Jones films, Hollywood archaeologists dealt with untold treasures and haunted tombs, but the arrival of Indiana Jones has added the esoteric factor and now everyone has joined in. This has caused controversy between new age writers and professional archaeologists. Do the faux Indiana Jones' know more than the dedicated archaeologists? I think not, they only offer creative stories, but no archaeological proofs.

The Indiana Jones factor has made adventurism in archaeology desirable, but upon closer inspection, many of the public and would-be archaeologists are disillusioned by the actual reality of archaeology, which is academically based and hard physical work. And that is when they see that Indiana Jones has failed them; his life the stuff of Hollywood myth. And that is why Indiana Jones is bad for archaeology.

29/Jan/2008

Sciences - Anthropology

The Olmec Civilization

2020 vision
Culled from my essay in uni on the same subject. I love the mystery behind the Olmecs and their enigmatic culture.

Who are the Olmecs? As an archaeology student, I was always fascinated by this Mesoamerican culture. They are thought to be the founders of Mesoamerican urban tradition, but the Olmecs themselves are still very much a mystery, their origin and development a continuous source of debate. How did this enigmatic culture become the progenitors of Mesoamerican urban traditions?

History Overview:
Olmec territory is located in the modern Mexican states of Veracruz and Tabasco. Their origins are obscure, rising as they did within gulf coast jungles, though they may have originated from the Tuxtla mountain region (Davies 1982: 55). Even now there may be undiscovered proto-Olmec sites waiting to be unearthed.

In the so-called Formative Period, around 5000 BC, agriculture developed and spread among the farming communities in the lowlands, until a transition point around 1500 BC, the traditional beginnings of Olmec society at San Lorenzo. Mesoamerican societies lacked beasts of burden and wheeled transport, so man-power did all the work. Also, there were no large domestic food animals so dogs and turkeys functioned as the main foodstuff along with fish, river wildlife, wild plants and an early form of maize (Davies 1982: 16; Killion 1996: 380; Allan 1997: 8-9).

Culture:
As well as their real name ('Olmec' was an Aztec term for 'rubber people' and another tribe) and ethnic identity, the Olmec's language is also unknown, though Michael Coe argues for a Mayan-related tongue (Schobinger 1994: 105). This seems plausible considering that the Maya

adopted so much of Olmec culture and perhaps even further expanded upon the Olmec writing system. While no evidence of Olmec writing exists, there are around 108 symbols on works of art that may be classed as glyphs. Nevertheless, the Olmecs did bequeath to Mesoamerica the bar and dot numerical system, astronomy, reverence to the cardinal directions, ceremonial centres with pyramids and plazas, cave rituals, bloodletting and sacrifices (Allan 1997: 11). All the successive cultures developed a form of writing, though it is also thought to have been introduced by the Zapotecs who possess an undeciphered script, which may have some connection with the Olmec (Allan 1997: 12). The development of the calendar from the Olmec source was taken up more successfully by the Aztecs and Maya. Both had a 365-day yearly cycle and a 260-day seasonal cycle, the Mayan including a 52 year cycle -the Calendar Round- which enabled them to keep track of long periods of time (Allan 1997: 116).

Sites:
Olmec Sites include San Lorenzo considered to be the oldest Olmec site, situated overlooking the Coatzacoalcos River. Now considered a triple site, it comprises of itself, Tenochtitlan-San Lorenzo, and Potrero Nuevo (Davies 1982: 34). Also found were rubber balls, early evidence for the ball game that would spread throughout Mesoamerica (Diehl 1996: 622).

La Venta from the Classic Period is the best known of Olmec sites and home to the oldest pyramid in the Americas (Killion 1996: 379). This 30m tall, truncated cone of compacted mud is the topic of much debate since it is not known if the pyramid was built to be fluted along its flanks, as if to imitate a volcano, or if erosion had taken its toll. Up to 18, 000 people may have been present at La Venta.

Tres Zapotes about 170km west of La Venta, close to the Tuxtla Mountains, possesses around fifty mounds in regular patterns (Grove 1984: 15). Here, aspects of sophisticated knowledge that would later be adopted by the Maya are evident. The important Stela 'C' shows the bar and dot numerical system in use, while other evidence points to the advent of the Olmec calendar Stela 'C' having the earliest date carved on it at 31 BC. Both these systems were further developed by the Maya (Schobinger 1994: 113).

Other sites include Laguna de los Cerros south-east of Tres Zapotes, and Laguna de los Cerros (Grove 1984: 14). Chalcatzingo, a jade trader with La Venta could be an Olmec colony or later society. It also had ceremonial buildings with platforms, pyramid mounds, high status residences and freestanding sculptures, like 'a highland ceremonial centre with an Olmec overlay' (Krupp 1997: 43 & 113).

Religion and Art

A 'priestly elite of unknown origin' was in charge of a core population of about 2500 that built the monumental works (Schobinger 1994: 109). The religion at San Lorenzo seems to be a cult of the were-jaguar depicted in numerous works of art and carved into statuettes as jaguar-baby figurines (Schobinger 1994: 112). Olmec art was more realistic and not geometric or abstract. Also, Olmec murals, especially those at Oxtotitlan and Juxtlahuaca are as great as rock paintings from paleolithic Europe. Olmec ceramics are of a varied nature; quite naturalistic with zoomorphic themes (Schobinger 1994: 87).

The most famous artifacts of the Olmec are the colossal heads. In all, 17 monumental heads have been found, ranging in size from 1.6m to 3m (Allan 1997: 10). The basalt rock to make the heads were dragged from the Tuxtla mountains 80km northwest and transported by river, though a trial on the BBC2 show 'Ancient Voices' proved somewhat unsuccessful in the latter manoeuvre, even finding the carving of the heads a difficult process. Davies believes that they were made within a limited lifespan, evidenced by their similarity, but that they weren't for public display, since some of the heads had been buried in a ritual way, rather than at a spur of the moment (Davies 1982: 48). The heads are unique to the Olmecs, begging the question, why weren't they copied elsewhere?

Were the Olmec warriors or traders? While the Olmec bequeathed human sacrifice, bloodletting and other rituals, did they have wars? At the later site of Teotihuacan, there were no defences and no attempt to hide their wealth, unlike the Olmecs (Schobinger 1994: 88). Michael Coe views the Olmec as empire builders, ruling by conquest, though trade was important to them (Davies 1982: 58). Arguments against a warrior-empire include the question of population. San Lorenzo may only have had a core population of about 1000-2000, so was that enough to control a whole region? If the Olmec had been conquerors, then why are there not all types of Olmec art and monuments at all these 'conquered' sites instead of bits and pieces? This suggests a selective borrowing and trading, an unforced action, not just of material, but also of ideology (Davies 1982: 59-60).

Decline:
Not much is known about the end of San Lorenzo except around 900 BC, the site was partially destroyed and abandoned. At La Venta around the 5th century BC, a decline led to the typical phase of destruction, before being abandoned. But the Olmecs continued further west at Tres Zapotes, which declined a few centuries later (Allan 1997: 12-13).

So who are the Olmec?
Olmec achievements might not reflect their advancement, but just their different ideology from the other cultures of the same advancement, seen in the varying styles of art and monuments. The archaeological evidence does not prove that their art work was any earlier than any of the other Gulf Coast cultures. We would have to look at the other contemporary regional cultures and their 'diverse evolutionary trajectories' (Grove 1996: 445). So the Olmecs might not be the only mother culture of Mesoamerica after all.

The Mesoamerican urban tradition seems to encompass a borrowing of iconography, a way of associating oneself with a more venerable society in order to establish supremacy, using elements such as writing, religion and sacrifices, cosmology and astronomy, terracing and monument building in varied forms. It seems to me that the Olmec were cultural founders on the 'fast-track', leaping ahead of their contemporaries. Whoever the Olmec were, I would call them a 'catalyst culture', their dynamism becoming the inspiration for the Zapotec, Mixtec, Maya, Toltec and Aztec and a whole new world.

References
Allan, T. et al. 1997. Gods Of Sun And Sacrifice: *Aztec And Maya Myth*. Amsterdam: Time-Life Books, BV.

Davies, N. 1982. *The Ancient Kingdoms Of Mexico*. London: Allen Lane.

Diehl, R.A. 1996. San Lorenzo. In: Fagan, B.M. (ed.) *The Oxford Companion To Archaeology*. Oxford and New York: Oxford University Press, 622.

Grove, D.C. 1984. *Chalcatzingo -Excavations On The Olmec Frontier*. London: Thames and Hudson.

Grove, D.C. 1996. Formative Period In Mesoamerica. In: Fagan, B.M. (ed.) *The Oxford Companion To Archaeology*. Oxford and New York: Oxford University Press, 441-445.

Killion, T.W. 1996. La Venta. In: Fagan, B.M. (ed.) *The Oxford Companion To Archaeology*. Oxford and New York: Oxford University Press, 379-380.

Krupp, E.C. 1997. *Skywatchers, Shamans And Kings*. New York: John Wiley and Sons Ltd.

Schobinger, J. 1994. "'The First Americans'". Grand Rapids: Eerdmans.

01/Feb/2008

Society & Lifestyle – North American Culture
The First People of America

Kennewick Man

There are many debates about the chronology of colonisation within the Americas and which culture was first. But it is well known that a few sites and human remains seem to run contrary to the perceived data. From Alaska to Chile, there are indications that the Americas were probably visited and colonised in multiple waves over time, but not all of them were successful. Evidence of such an attempt was Kennewick Man.

The remains of a man dubbed 'Kennewick Man' were found near Kennewick, Washington State around the confluence of the Columbia and Snake Rivers in July 1996. Tests conducted by anthropologist Dr. James Chatters indicated that the skull did not resemble that of a Native American and was found to be 9000 years old. DNA tests were to be carried out to determine Kennewick Man's origins.

But Native Americans, under the Native American Graves Protection and Repatriation Act, called for the body to be returned to a five-tribe alliance to be buried as an ancestor. Archaeologists protested, demanding the right to conduct research on the remains. Also, an obscure traditional European religious group called the Asatru Folk Assembly claimed Kennewick Man, citing the non-Indian features made Kennewick Man a European and thus one of their ancestors. To complicate matters, the land upon which Kennewick Man was found, was federal land under the jurisdiction of the Army Corps of Engineers who later re-covered the discovery site, supposedly to conserve the river bank.

Native Americans argue that they have always been in the Americas (despite archaeological evidence citing a 15,000BP entry date), that Kennewick Man is their ancestor and that humans and animals do change over time. To the Native Americans, this issue is about European domination and an attempt to re-write history favouring a European primacy in the Americas. Currently, the remains of Kennewick Man are in a vault. And though a judge deemed that limited tests were allowed in 2005, legalities continue to prolong this political, scientific and cultural Pandora's Box.

In my opinion, Kennewick Man in no way undermines Native Americans' claims to their status. There are older remains and sites than Kennewick Man from Bluefish Cave, Yukon, Canada; Meadowcroft, Pennsylvania; Pedra Furada, Brazil and Monte Verde in Chile attesting to Native American primacy. All Kennewick Man could prove is the diversity of other and later migrations indicating routes, trade and inter-cultural relationships. The fact also remains that Kennewick Man was exposed naturally and not by archaeologists infringing Native American religious beliefs.

Native Americans are extremely conscious of their political clout, growing American government guilt over past actions, empowering the Indians who can have casinos on their land and some of who can hunt whales as a traditional right (illegal in most countries). Native Americans see any attempt by archaeologists to probe their remote past as an attempt to undermine their culture and religious beliefs, though the opposite is true. Kennewick Man could enhance and advance Native American history adding to the richness of American history.

Source:

Radford, T. 1998. *Equinox: Homicide in Kennewick.*

08/Feb/2008

Arts & Humanities - History (Other)
Shortcomings of Discussing the Past Solely on the Evidence of Texts

2020 vision
Another of my uni essays turned into an article.

When it comes to uncovering the past, one means of doing so is through ancient texts. However, there are inherent problems in relying solely on texts. It has always been said that the conqueror writes history, but what if two warring nations write differing outcomes for the same event, as in the case between Pharaoh Ramesses II's Egypt and the Hittites after the battle of Kadesh, c.1285 BC. Both nations recorded themselves as the victor. Who was right? Propaganda has played a part in writing almost from its beginnings. One could say that writing in itself is a form of propaganda, indicating to others the superiority of their civilisation.

Rewriting the past has become associated with many past societies. Many temples and monuments have been found ascribed to someone else, when in fact the original name had been chiselled off, or destroyed when that person fell out of favour or died. Reading these texts alone would introduce a bias, the reader not having the complete information to hand. Looking beyond the texts at other artefacts would help to find the truth.

Many real life figures have been immortalised in text, but the line between myth and reality has become blurred enough that archaeologists and historians have had trouble in verifying their existence. Two cases in point are Gilgamesh and King Arthur. Many people take 'The Epic of Gilgamesh' to be just a tale, but was Gilgamesh a real King of Uruk? In the Sumerian King-List, a Gilgamesh was named as the fifth king after the flood (Sandars 1972), who was a great builder of cities and temples and an avid adventurer. Beyond 'The Epic of Gilgamesh', the actual text, not much was known. Archaeologists have now been able to piece together more information and have discovered that a Gilgamesh, or an archetype, may have lived during the first half of the third millennium BC. Records state that he lived an extremely long life, though there is other conflicting information. Texts can aid and hinder. It is like looking back at the past through a telescope with a warped lens. Only by fine tuning efforts and techniques can the true picture be fully resolved.

One of the greatest searches through texts to unravel myth from reality has come from the King Arthur legends. From Nennius's 'Historia Brittonum' (c. AD 800) to Geoffrey of Monmouth's 'Historia Regum Britanniae' (c. 1130s) and the romanticised versions by De Troyes and Malory, there is still a feeling of awe that commands respect for the man that has become the basis for the mythological King Arthur. Reading the myriad of texts alone would greatly reduce and probably bias any grounds for real evidence, since there have been many versions and additions printed over the years. Early chroniclers, in trying to establish King Arthur as a real king have tied him to different regions, each country, whether England, Germany, France or Spain preferring different parts of the legend to suit their purposes (Littleton and Malcor 1996). This only serves to muddy the waters even more. Yet, there has been a concerted search to find the historical Arthur. There are many candidates for the historical Arthur, the strongest being Riothamus of the mid-fifth century AD, but again, records from that time are scarce and all we have are the stories commemorating his heroic campaigns.

A whole range of New Age books have dedicated themselves to the notion that long lost civilizations, aliens and other mysteries abound on Earth. Their evidence: ancient texts written by ancient people allegedly describing spaceships, aliens, hybrid creatures and extraterrestrial technology. These books sensationalise past texts and invite such speculation as to totally distort their true meaning. But when these highly subjective writings become popular books, they become even more ingrained into people's minds, the myth overcoming reality. Another famous case are Mayan prophesies relating to the end of the world in 2012. In fact, their texts forecast many more such cycles and this one is simply the end of a world cycle and not the world itself.

Geographical places in texts can become the objects of desperate searches. Some are successful, but others remain hidden to haunt the scholars. Three examples include biblical archaeology, Troy, and Atlantis. Biblical texts had been the basis for world chronology. All mankind was descended from Adam and his offspring and thus Bishop Ussher was able to propose from the counting back through genealogies, that the Earth was created in 4004 BC. This stood for decades until Darwin swept all of that aside with his evolutionary brush. But there are still people who firmly believe in the Bible. Sites in Israel, Jordan or old Mesopotamia are found, and matches to the Bible are immediately sought. Where there is no correlation, it is the archaeological evidence that is at fault and not the text. But obsessions can lead to glory or disaster.

Heinrich Schliemann was a believer in Homer's 'Iliad', and ventured out, book in hand, to find the lost city of Troy. He had many critics and went against archaeological conventions, but he adamantly believed in the texts, not as poetry, but as history. Later, on matching up the site of Hissarlik with what the book said, Schliemann began digging and digging. He went through layer after layer until he finally came upon what he thought to be the original Troy. He is now the celebrated discoverer of the ancient city, but in his ruthlessness in destroying the upper levels, he is also branded 'the second destroyer of Troy' (Stefoff 1997).

Atlantis has become an enduring myth since the times of the ancient Greeks, when Plato wrote his 'Timaeus' and 'Critias' in which he tells of the story of Atlantis. The tale has been dismissed by some as an analogy for Athens and a warning against the greed and corruption of society that can cause its self-destruction. Nonetheless it has inspired many to search for this missing place as if it was real, some sites such as the Aegean island of Thera, Izmir in Turkey (ancient Tantalis) and even Antarctica have been considered. Again, this is all text-based exploration, figuring out the precise meanings and details of Plato's story. It has been latched onto with gusto by sensationalist writers and has churned up much consternation among more seriously minded historians who believe that if the story is true, its origins are much closer to Greece than beyond the Atlantic.

Can art be a text? The Yolngu Aborigines of Australia have oral traditions, but they also represent their history through sacred paintings which mediates between the ancestral past and the present (Morphy 1989). The paintings can either be iconographic in nature or abstract in form, yet they tell a story. But if these paintings were represented in textual form, there would still be problems, for some of the stories would be incomplete or misleading. This is because the story may be continued on in a dance, a song or in a ceremony. Yolngu paintings can be highly metaphorical, with an encoded message within the explicit message that can be interpreted different ways by the artist and reader (Morphy 1989). In doing this they preserve a knowledge that only that society can read entirely. An outsider would only see the top layer of the message without knowing the deeper intent. There are many texts around the world which offer this kind of complexity (i.e. Mayan and Egyptian hieroglyphs). Those and other texts deserve special attention before they can be fully understood and appreciated.

As seen, texts are not always truthful. They can be biased, misleading, misinterpreted or misrepresented. They can also turn the basis of reality into myth and vice versa. In the absence of artefactual evidence, texts will need careful consideration and examination if the past is to be fully realised.

References

Littleton, S.C. and Malcor, L.A. 1996. 'Myth and Mankind- Heroes of The Dawn: Celtic Myth". Amsterdam: Time-Life Books.

Morphy, H. 1989. On Representing Ancestral Beings. In: Morphy, H (ed) 'Animals Into Art'. Unwin-Hyman, Chapter 5.

Sandars, N.K. (trans.), 1972. 'The Epic Of Gilgamesh'. London: Penguin.

Stefoff, R. 1997. Troy: Myths And Treasures. In: 'Finding The Lost Cities'. London: British Museum Press, 92-105.

10/Feb/2008

Arts & Humanities - Ancient History
The Inca Civilization

Factors in the Conquistadors Victory over the Inca

2020 vision
A title I introduced from one of my uni essays. It still fascinates me how the Spanish conquered the Inca and at the same time horrifies me at the loss of the Incan culture and history the Spanish destroyed.

It was a moment that defined history when Pizarro arrived on the coast of Peru in 1532. The Spanish Conquistadors, vastly outnumbered, won an astounding victory. But even with advanced weapons and horses, how could this have happened? The numerically superior Inca with their strategic fortresses and home advantage in rough, mountainous terrain should have been victorious. How did it all go wrong?

Pizarro had 62 horsemen and 106 infantrymen. With shining armour, weapons such as cannons and arquebuses (a matchlock weapon), iron axes (iron not known in the Americas), trumpeters and horses, the Conquistadors had the upper hand in technological hardware. Shock factors also included the colour of the Spaniards' white skin and that of their black slaves (Bernand 1988: 19 & 132). The arquebus, when fired, sounded like thunder which the Inca revered, and was demonstrated many a time to the Indians to scare them and to show off its ability to kill at distance (Innes 1969: 218).

'For, after God, we owed the victory to the horses'. The importance of the horse has never been underestimated in the conquest of Peru. They were considered more important than slaves as indicated by the horses' higher place on inventory lists (Cunningham-Graham 1949: 11 & 23). Along with steel armour and helmets, the Conquistador horsemen also wore the jack, a quilted, leather covered (sometimes iron-plated) coat (Quick 1973: 243), which provided light, flexible protection. Horses were also a psychological factor. The Inca thought that the Spanish were too weak to walk up the mountains so they rode horses. They did not expect an attack from such weakened men. But the Inca delay in attacking the Spanish while in the mountains allowed the Spanish to acclimatize to the precipitous conditions. The horses also had small bells attached to them to create more noise, panic and fear when they charged (Gheerbrant 1961: 329 & 342).

On landing at Peru, Pizarro was able to secure the services of Indian informants, spies and auxiliaries for his force. He was informed of the Inca civil war and that the Inca Emperor, Atahualpa, the victor was camped only 350 miles away in Cajamarca, 12 days march away, up 9000 feet (Innes 1969: 232). The Inca, at their height, ruled over 8 million people, in a heterogeneous Empire, where people resented the harsh rule of the Inca (Bernand 1988: 21-2). These peoples welcomed the Spanish to free them from Atahualpa's rule (Rostworowski de Diez Canseco 1999: 91 & 96).

The Inca army probably had more than 200, 000 men armed with bow and arrows, clubs, spears and slings, protected by padded shirts, or strong tunics of cotton (Bernand 1988: 19 & 130), no match for the arquebuses. Some of the elite carried the flint or obsidian-bladed 'macana', a 2-handed, hardwood sword, along with a long-handled battle-axe, a halberd like weapon with a sharp point on one end and a sharp blade on the other (Gheerbrant 1961: 186-7). This army could operate for months and range over hundreds of miles, though there were only a few elite, full-time, professional soldiers among the vast, unskilled commoner army (Kicza 1996: 345). The Inca had a support system consisting of roads, storehouses, and a chain of formidable fortresses and garrisons along the Andes with lightly loaded men and llama with provisions. By the time of the Conquest, the Inca had coordinated logistics, stores and supplies to protect themselves (D'Altroy 1992), but none of their weapons, sheer numbers or territorial advantages prevented the massacre to come.

It has often been stated that the Inca Viracocha (the 8th Emperor) foresaw the coming of the Spaniards, but did not reveal this to the public for fear of causing panic. The Viracochas, as the later Spanish would be called, would be recognised by their beards (un-growable by the Indians) and by their long robes (Gheerbrant 1961: 132 & 147). But when Huayna Capac (the 12th Emperor) lay on his death-bed, he revealed the coming of the Spaniards, the return of the Viracochas

(Gheerbrant 1961: 147), which is why Atahualpa ordered his men not to fight nor offend the Spanish. But the people did not fight against the Spanish so that the conquistadors could defeat the illegitimate heir and tyrant, Atahualpa (Gheerbrant 1961: 132 & 342). But as this story is related by the Inca Garcilaso de la Vega, a half breed of noble descent, it is tainted by his Roman Catholic beliefs and his justification for the Spanish Conquest.

Huayna Capac had created the new city of Quito (in modern Ecuador), and ruled with his favourite son, the illegitimate Atahualpa while giving Huascar, the rightful heir, Cuzco, which Huascar was hated. When small pox, from Mexico, took Huayna Capac's life in 1527, a civil war ensued, in which Huascar was defeated and held captive in Cuzco (Jenkins 1997: 387). After defeating his half-brother, Atahualpa retired to Cajamarca, when he heard of the Conquistadors' approach (Jenkins 1997: 387). Atahualpa only regarded the Spanish as raiders and wanted to capture them (Kicza 1996: 346). Delaying his victory march onto the Imperial capital of Cuzco, Atahualpa ignored warnings from spies, wanting to see the Conquistadors. In contrasting signals, he sent warnings and veiled threats of his own to the advancing invaders in the form of gutted, straw-filled ducks hinting at the fate of the Spaniards and also clay models of his fortresses. But he also sent gifts of camelids, guides and food (Rostworowski de Diez Canseco 1999: 126-7).

At that time, as Pizarro and his men made their way to meet with Atahualpa in his stronghold in Cajamarca, strong defensible mountain passes were left open, allowing easy access with little fear of a lethal ambush. No resistance or challenge was mounted (Bernand 1988: 138-9). At the Conquistadors' arrival, emissaries from both sides agreed a meeting the next day in central Cajamarca. Here, Pizarro strategically placed men and horses on three sides of the village square within various buildings with one group in the open with a cannon (Rostworowski de Diez Canseco 1999: 129).

There is much confusion over what started the massacre at Cajamarca, whether Atahualpa rejected and threw down the bible offered to him by the Spanish priest or whether the priest panicked and gave a predetermined signal to attack. Atahualpa had an army of 30, 000, the majority of which he kept outside the city, his accompanying guard only armed with small battle-axes (Jenkins 1997: 288). After the bible

Incident, Pizarro advanced and captured Atahualpa, his men killing around 6000 Incas out of the 30, 000 (Kicza 1996: 346) with over 3000 Inca captured alive compared to the conquistadors slight wound to a horse (Bernand 1988: 132-3). While imprisoned, Atahualpa somehow ordered Huascar's assassination in Cuzco. Kept alive for ransom and to control the population, Atahualpa was finally executed in 1533 after converting to Christianity; garrotted rather than burned at the stake, an un-Incan death (Innes 1969: 300). Pizarro then marched on Cuzco.

After sacking Cuzco, Pizarro installed his own Emperor, Manco Inca (another of Huayna Capac's sons). Pizarro's forces then defeated the other Inca armies, put down Manco Inca's 1535 rebellion and by 1537 all resistance was quashed (Gheerbrant, 1961). Pizarro lost only 20 men from the beginning of the Conquest (Kicza 1996: 346).

The Inca Empire had been around a hundred years old, but not consolidated enough to withstand an attack from a small zealous Conquistador force. Inca underestimation of the Conquistadors, delay in attacking, confusion and complacency were more debilitating than their technological inferiority. There is no doubt that Conquistador technological superiority was dominant with advantages in both physical and psychological factors, and their timely arrival during the civil war also aided in their quest. Pizarro's victory is a lesson in history that still stands for these times.

References:
Bernand, C. 1988. The Incas -Empire of Blood And Gold. London: Thames and Hudson.

Cunningham-Graham, R.B.1949. The Horses of the Conquest. Norman, Oklahoma: Oklahoma University Press.

D'Altroy, T.N. 1992. Provincial Power in The Inka Empire. Washington: Smithsonian Institution Press.

Gheerbrant, A.1961. The Incas -The Royal Commentaries Of The Inca Garcilaso de la Vega. New York: The Orion Press.

Innes, H. 1969. The Conquistadors. London: Collins.

Jenkins, D. 1997. Peru -The Rough Guide. London: Penguin Books, 288 & 387.

Kicza, J.E. 1996. Pizarro and the Conquest of the Incas. In: Fagan, B.M. (ed) The Oxford Companion To Archaeology. Oxford: Oxford University Press, 345-6.

Quick, J.1973. Dictionary of Weapons and Military Terms. New York: McGraw-Hill, Inc.

Rostworowski de Diez Canseco, M. 1999. History of the Inca Realm. Cambridge: Cambridge University Press.

RAYMOND R. A. BURKE

17/Feb/2008

Arts & Humanities - Ancient History

Factors in the Fall of the Roman Empire

2020 vision
An essay from my Roman Archaeology course for one of my favourite lecturers, Mark Hassall, Emeritus Reader in the Archaeology of the Roman Provinces, Institute of Archaeology, UCL.

The world has seen the rise and fall of many empires. They have peppered the continents, some lasting for a thousand years, others for a few centuries or less, but they have undeniably influenced other spheres of life beyond their own homelands. But no matter how benign or powerful they have been, they have eventually declined and collapsed. The Roman Empire was one of the most famous empires from history. Its Imperial grandeur, innovations, glorious armies, inspired architecture and sheer longevity spawned many imitators and admirers, and will do so for generations to come. So how did the Roman Empire succumb to this inglorious outcome?

There are a few factors involved with the rise and fall of empires. These factors would include charismatic leaders and effective governance, internal/external order/disorder relationships, the role of the army, location, and the function of chaos within and upon an empire.

Rome is said to have been founded in 753 BC on the famous seven hills surrounding the Tiber River. In the early sixth century BC, Rome, tired of Etruscan rule, deposed the kings and set up their own republic ruled by two consuls and a senate. Italy then warred against their enemies, the Celts and Greeks for complete control, ultimately concluding with victory in the epic Punic Wars against the powerful Carthaginian Empire in 206 BC. Rome was now in the ascendancy. But it was not just the territorial power that made Rome an empire. All throughout its territories there was a maintained order which arose from a centralised administration, a strong monetary and trading economy, a transport infrastructure with networks of roads connecting forts and cities, monumental buildings, and famously, a strong military.

However, military power alone could not have carried Rome upon its back for so long. As demonstrated by Roman legions, effective leadership can be more valuable against superior or overwhelming forces. And Rome had that leadership in Caesar. Could a mediocre commander have taken Gaul? Would his men have followed him across the Rubicon? If that commander had been anyone less than Julius Caesar would they have made him dictator? The answer is no. Caesar set the standard for leadership, such was his charismatic presence and leadership qualities. In later defeating his greatest rivals, Pompey and Antony in 31 BC, Rome gained Egypt as well.

Situated on the Mediterranean, the core of the Roman Empire straddled the best temperate zones of Europe, Asia Minor and North Africa and was therefore not subjected to undue meteorological effects. Rome was mostly a land empire, the only obstacles being natural features and there was no threat from natural destruction. So, Rome also endured due to favourable geographic and meteorological conditions. This strategic locale would have attracted traders and barbarians, alike.

One negative factor was the internal/external order/disorder ratio. The more stable the government and its surroundings, the more contented the people, the better the state. Rome grew up fighting for its own identity and sovereignty, expanding as its needs grew, spreading her own laws and administration which eventually led to the Pax Romana. Augustus saw to it that power was seen to be in the hands of the people and not the military. And as any empire is dependent on the economy to expand; so trade and prosperity grew in order. But while one's own territory had to be stable, the enemies had to be held at bay. Rome defended its frontiers with impressive feats of engineering, whether Hadrian's wall to keep out the Picts, or the huge walls and ditches along the Germanic and African borders. But Rome was able to quell most rebellions by allowing some degree of autonomy and by incorporating non-Roman citizens into Roman society, which would essentially ensure a measure of safety. This worked for internal security, but on the other side of the frontier walls, Rome faced battles on two fronts, the Germanic in the west and the Persians in the east. Though future leaders were able to stave off destruction, the slide downhill had begun.

By the time of Diocletian in the early fourth century AD, the empire was becoming too unwieldy for one man to rule. Knowing this, Diocletian, divided the empire up between himself and a joint ruler, which gradually led to an east-west division of the empire. He also hoped that a smoother transition between rulers and their deputies could be established, thereby eliminating battles for succession or external intrusion. But in the fifth century more Germanic armies poured upon helpless Rome, its power virtually diminished.

Internal/external order/disorder can come in many forms, having varying causes and effects which can be readily seen. Chaos factors can be applied to such aspects as population and disease. In looking at population and the degrees to which fertility (and the birth-death ratio) affected the population, a society's survivability could be assessed as being stable, chaotic or on the verge of extinction. Applying this to the Roman Empire, the number and diversity of peoples would have assured a continuing society. However, the estimated population in fourth century AD Rome was about 1.5 million and the crowded conditions, poor city planning and the lack of hygienic would have severely strained the social system. Population growth was outstripping the supply of resources, whether food, building materials or land. If the population spiralled out of control, there could be social and economic disorder. Also, populations going from one land into another introduced new diseases and plagues, such as the plague in the mid third century AD, due to poor public health. Luckily, Rome was spared the indignity of falling through disease.

Rome's fall was due to the human factor, complacency, of the Emperor and his administration. A series of self-indulgent and ineffectual Emperors (e.g. such as Caligula and Nero) led to a failure of insight and foresight causing the gradual breakdown of all the elements that controlled the empire's rise. This brought about political, social and economic unrest exacerbated by continued invasions. The sheer size of the empire, its protection and control would have presented logistical problems (e.g. food, military and building, etc) that could not have been met and sustained under such pressures. The rot started from the top. Without a strong and effectual leader, the army would not have been able to perform its duties properly. Quelling revolts would have been more difficult. In Rome itself, the fire of 64 AD, made worse by haphazard building and the persecution of the Christians under Nero endangered the social order. And later, while internal order was breaking down, external disorder saw the Visogoths (410 AD) and the Ostrogoths (493 AD), invade Rome.

All the factors that caused Rome's rise in the first place turned against them. There were no charismatic individuals to instigate wide sweeping changes to relieve the situation. Thus a chaotic rise in the population and a decline in the economy would have seen internal order break down, inviting external disorder to take over. And all of this was in the territorially strategic western half of the Empire, whereas in the east, reforms had seen to their own survival, until 1453. But while these outside forces hastened Rome's fall they maintained a piece of the Pax Romana, which survived in parts throughout the generations and has helped shape much of the modern world. So there is still a part of the Roman Empire in all of us.

References:
Forte, M. and Siliotti, A. (eds.) 1997. Virtual Archaeology. London: Thames and Hudson.

Gleick, J. 1997. Chaos. London: Minerva.

Parker, G. (ed.) 1997. The Times Atlas of World History. London: Times Books.

Radice, B. (ed.) 1972. Herodotus: The Histories. London: Penguin Books.

Renfrew, C. and Bahn, P. 1996. Archaeology: Theories, Methods and Practice. London: Thames and Hudson, pg. 167.

19/Feb/2008

Sciences – Anthropology
Russia's Lake Baikal: An anthropological overview

The Archaeology of Lake Baikal

2020 vision
This essay is from my Geoarchaeology course; another fascinating area of study, as is the enigmatic Lake Baikal.

Lake Baikal located in Siberia, is about 636 km long, 80 km wide and at 1,620 meters, nearly a mile deep, is the world's deepest lake. Compared to the other great lakes of the world, Lake Baikal contributes approximately 20 percent of the world's surface fresh water. Lake Baikal may seem remote, but in the past it was inhabited by peoples that archaeological and geological teams are beginning to investigate.

The Baikal Archaeological Project
Since the early 1990s, this Russian-Canadian project, has been examining a seventh millennium BC gap in Lake Baikal history at the site of Bugul'deika. The Kitoi (late Mesolithic, early Neolithic 9000-7000BP) and the Serovo-Glazkovo (late Neolithic-bronze age 6000-2500BP) were two major groups in the area, but their origins are not fully understood. They are known to be bio-culturally the same, but discontinuous as the later Serovo-Glazkovo were culturally-structured, demographically different and more resource intensive than the Kitoi.

The goal of the project is to discern these differences through excavation and mortuary studies. The team also hopes to map spatial/chronological patterns, environment and biological contexts, mortuary and world-views and connections between Siberia and North America. These would be understood through paleo-genetic and osteological (bone) studies, radiocarbon dating, climate modelling and micro-regional studies. Landscape simulation through satellite data, digital analysis and field data would compliment geographic information systems (GIS) studies that will analyse climate and landscape models, and the function of the site through topography, landscape use, lithic and faunal assemblages.

The aim of the project is not wholly geoarchaeological in nature, concentrating more on a cultural/behavioural model. But the wealth of their data from remote sensing, via landscape simulation, could be integrated to give a fuller view of the site. Knowing a fuller geoarchaeological history of the area could serve as an interdisciplinary factor in determining settlement patterns, population movements and resource concentrations. No data from this site has yet been published (as of this writing), though it is available to order privately, which is a disadvantage. An over-arcing history of the Lake Baikal region is in the offering with the integration of the first three sections.

Geoarchaeological studies
New techniques have arisen over the years that lay bare the underlying foundations of past sites, reconstruct landscapes and environments and assess areas of resources and their exploitation. The use of remote sensing and satellite data from geophysical prospecting around Lake Baikal, Siberia, has helped to reveal new features.

Remote Sensing denotes information gathering on objects by non-contact, distance measurement. This includes pattern recognition, spectral and spatial analysis. Different types of data gathering methods include geophysical, geochemical, core drilling and aerial/satellite pictures.

The aim of the German company GFZ Potsdam with their EU CONTINENTal [sic] project, was to gain a continuous high-resolution paleoclimatic record of Lake Baikal through 150,000 years. The data was compiled from satellite use analysing geochemical and sediment data, where possible. At other times algae, phytoplankton and other detrial (contamination) inputs were used, using optical water sampling devices and a GER 1500 field spectrometer. Once the information was mapped, the different data was colour-coded to visually show the different areas and contexts of the lake. While the satellite was tasked for a specific task, I was not sure if it could be programmed to resolve other features germane to the geoarchaeology of Lake Baikal sites, like former lake edges and thus former settlement patterns. In this way, valuable evidence charting past lake resources could give Lake Baikal archaeologists a valuable insight into the lake's settlement history.

While the aim of GFZ Potsdam was water-based, the aim for the Centre for Remote Imaging, Sensing and Processing (CRISP) was to map the land cover around Lake Baikal, via satellite analysis (LANDSAT/TM and LANDSAT-7/ETM) of the phenological (climate/biological) aspects of plants. This is to measure the effects of global warming, land degradation, water supplies and anthropologic damage. This geophysical project is under the umbrella of geophysical prospecting, which details the 'location, extent and characteristics of modified terrain.' Surface geophysics can be used in conjunction with magnetic analysis and geochemical prospecting to ascertain man-made contexts. Geophysical prospecting measures contrasts between 'physical properties of target features and their surroundings'.

The study area was the Selenga basin, southern Lake Baikal. It is a three-river system, prone to tree cutting and forest fires in the dry windy season. The technique used by CRISP, the Linear Mixing Model (LMM), bases it data on mixing the spectral (plant class) proportion data with the temporal (annual fluctuation of plant class) to produce improved classification and reliability. This is a new technique and needs to be tested to ensure accuracy and data biases. It would be interesting to note if the resolution of the satellite could detect crop patterning, that, whether cultural or natural in formation, could predict a past settlement location? Would certain crop types (selected through spectral analysis) located upon old, buried cultural structures indicate a settlement or natural area? Past anthropic activities, such as herding, agriculture, forest tending and landscaping may also have altered the landscape. Have these or any modern developments precluded such methods of detection?

Both the GFZ Potsdam and CRISP satellite data have pertinent applications within geoarchaeology. The 'eye in the sky' can often bring out features not seen from the ground, such as wide-scale land and lake changes, settlement formation patterns and resource fluctuations and at a faster and non-destructive rate than human endeavour. Such projects with on-line results should be easily accessible to geoarchaeologists to plan and guide their work. The range of geophysical and remote sensing suites can reach beyond their set tasks retrieving the deep past and deep depths, bringing them to the here and now to be analysed alongside current geoarchaeological and archaeological data, and also to predict future changes.

Both GFZ Potsdam and CRISP data would greatly benefit the Archaeological project saving unnecessary work or duplication of work (unless that is an aim) and saving time and money (an archaeologist's dream). Knowing how the region formed and developed gives clues into why man settled the region and importantly what happened in the so-called temporal hiatus period, when the Kitoi gave way to the Serovo-Glazkovo. The macro-scale of Lake Baikal's environs can then be studied through geophysical and remote sensing techniques (e.g. satellites) focusing down through smaller regional sites (e.g. Selenga Basin), down to specific archaeological sites (e.g. Bugul'deika), and further onto human scales (e.g. Kitoi & Serovo-Glazkovo cultures) and finally down to micro-scales in the lake itself (e.g. algae & phytoplankton). A complete joined-up policy in geophysical and remote sensing techniques could re-revolutionise geoarchaeological studies.

Global Warming and Siberian Archaeology
Geoarchaeological surveys have indicated that global warming is accelerating the arctic thaw, but in Siberia a new threat is emerging as vast stores of methane, twenty times worst than carbon dioxide, start releasing from their permafrost peat bogs. This could have a serious impact on arctic archaeology, as lakes expand and vegetation disappears. Remote sensing and land cover mapping could indicate global warming hotspots in the Siberian arctic.

The Lake Baikal project makes no mention on the origin of Bugul'deika's (and other sites') discovery, whether it was an existing surface site, eroded or thawed out of the land by changing conditions or found through remote sensing. Will global warming help or harm the future of such arctic sites? Thawing could bring more floods, bogs, soil erosion, site exposure and/or destruction, pollution and more human encroachment. How can archaeology be protected from such instances? Remote sensing and geophysical techniques could give an early heads-up and record sites and their changing environments until geoarchaeologists arrived with preventative measures to save or at least record archaeological sites themselves. Will global warming be good or bad for arctic archaeology? Time will tell.

References:

Rapp Jr. G. & Hill, C.L. 1998. Geoarchaeology. Yale University Press: London.

Kunzig, R. 2005: The Year In Science: Siberian Thaw Releases Methane And Accelerates Global Warming. Discover. January 2006 (27) 1, 34.

http://baikal.arts.ualberta.ca/ (link not active)

http://www.crisp.nus.edu.sg/~acrs2001/pdf/159SHIMA.pdf (link still active September 2020)

http://www.gfz-potsdam.de/html/search/index-en.html (link no longer active)

16/Mar/2008

Ancient cities worthy of visiting

My Top Five Ancient City Tours

2020 vision
This was probably in the travel section originally. And it was popular enough to be bought twice by two different third-party publishers, once in September 2008 and again in February 2009. My choices haven't changed over the years and I have been fortunate enough to visit Tiwanaku on holiday in 2000, after a dig at the Moche site Huaca del Sol and the Huaca de la Luna, near Trujillo, Peru.

If I could go back to any ancient city in the past, where would I go? Outside of the usual destinations of Rome, Athens and Egypt, there are a vast amount of other early civilisations that offered their own unique structural and cultural perspectives on cities. The fact that many of the cities were in ruins by the time Europeans re-discovered them underscores their importance to world history in their creativeness and longevity, but also highlights biased Western views of its own supposed superiority in city-building.

My choices, out of potential thousands, are skewed as a student of Archaeology. These cities fascinated me and one especially where if Europeans had come a century earlier could have had a momentous impact on the way the world is now. The descriptions are just brief thumbnails with suggested further reading at the end.

ÇATALHÖYÜK
My first city would be Catalhoyuk, Turkey. It was founded around 9,500 years ago on the Konya Plain in central Turkey. Discovered by James Mellaart in 1958, work/excavations continue to this day with an international team. What I love about this city of cities is the sheer denseness of the dwellings without roads or an outer wall, so movement was probably via rooftops. It was one big mass of settlement, rebuilt upon itself time after time. It is renowned for its cattle cults and murals of bulls, pottery and figurines of the celebrated Mother Goddess as well

as a huge mural of a nearby volcano, which supplied obsidian for tools and weapons. The first proto-city must have been a glorious site to behold and it inspired or at least co-evolved with other early urban centres.

TEOTIHUACAN

Teotihuacán, in the north-eastern part of the Valley of Mexico was founded around AD100 and abandoned around AD750. When the Aztecs came centuries later, they named it 'The City of the Gods'. The site is dominated by the Pyramid of the Sun and Pyramid of the Moon, and various palaces, all connected by the ominous sounding Avenue of the Dead. The overall sense is of a large religious centre, though there is archaeological evidence that the unknown culture traded as far as Guatemala 1000km away and may have been a war-like culture too, depending on interpretations of images of war gods. Though later Mesoamerican civilisations built monumental urban centres, Teotihuacán built the first and most iconic city of all. It is the sheer scale and layout of the city that impresses and the audacity of the makers to envision such a magnificent city that has stood the test of time.

TIWANAKU

Tiwanaku, Bolivia is the next stop on my ancient world tour. Located in the Bolivian altiplano by Lake Titicaca, at an altitude of 3,850m, Tiwanaku emerged from the coalescing of previous civilisations in the area around AD 350 until its decline around AD1200. Tiwanaku is famous for its urban centre buildings of the semi-subterranean Temple, the Kalasasaya with the Ponce Monolith and the famous Gateway of the Sun, and the Akapana pyramid. Tiwanaku is also famous for its raised field system, which helped crops grow and survive in the harsh weather of the altiplano. In fact, they are being revived and reintroduced to the local communities in order to substantially increase crop yields. Tiwanaku has been one of my pilgrimage points which I had the pleasure of visiting in 2001. The eerie setting in the high plains, the remoteness and the romantic air of Lake Titicaca in the near distance lends certain sacredness to the area, considering Tiwanaku's strong domination in the region for so long. And with the raised field technology, Tiwanaku is a living reminder that there is still much to learn from our ancient elders.

CAHOKIA

In south-western Illinois, there exists a city of mounds called Cahokia. Founded around 1000AD, by the Mississippian culture, their expanse and monumental building is not well-known outside of America, since most of their structures were destroyed by later Americans for urbanisation projects. Also, much of Cahokia had been abandoned around 1400AD, possibly due to environmental stresses. And to think, it was built without beasts of burden or the wheel or metallurgy. At 100 feet high, the 4-tiered pyramid Monks Mound was the tallest building in America until 1867. What draws me to Cahokia is the uniqueness of the site within North America and the sense of what-could-have-been if the Mississippians and other Native Americans had continued in their monumental building. But alas, as with other civilisations in North, Central and South America there seems to have some form of systemic collapses, possibly due to the vagaries of the American environment.

DJENNE

Djenne (Jenne) in Mali, West Africa is now famous for its mud brick Great Mosque, the original built in 12th century. In the past Djenne was an independent City State, founded around AD400 sitting between a string of successive West African Empires: Ghana (8-12th centuries), Mali (12-15th centuries) and Songhay after 1500s, the latter two founded by Islamic traders. With economies based upon gold, ivory, pepper, salt and cast metallurgy, European merchants and explorers had long sought the riches of the interior African Empires, but when they finally arrived the heyday of the Empires were long over. Instead of finding equals and being lavished with gold, the Europeans found decay and exploited the existing slave trade. Djenne to me represents the grandeur of West Africa and the tip of the archaeological iceberg in a region where so many ancient cities lay buried beneath sand and grassland.

Further Reading:

Michael Balter. 2005. The Goddess and the Bull.

Sally A. Kitt Chappell. 2002. Cahokia: Mirror of the Cosmos.

Michael Coe. 1994. Mexico: From the Olmecs to the Aztecs.

Felipe Fernandez-Armesto. 2000. Civilizations.

Felipe Fernandez-Armesto. 2006. Pathfinders.

Alan Kolata. 1993. The Tiwanaku: Portrait of an Andean Civilization.

21/Apr/2008

Arts & Humanities -History Mysteries

The Validity of the Piri Re'is Map

2020 vision
Even though Albert Einstein endorsed the theory of the shifting crust, it is still hard to believe. Is the Earth's crust really like a moving orange peel across the surface? Time will tell. It could explain a few environmental mysteries. I loved the History Mysteries section. So many good articles were in that sub-channel.

The Piri Re'is map, a *portolan* from 1513, famously and supposedly shows an ice-free Antarctica. This map, discovered in 1929 Constantinople was signed by Turkish Admiral Piri Re'is. Professor Charles Hapgood from Keene State College, New Hampshire who propelled the Piri Re'is map to stardom in his books *Earth's shifting Crust* (1958) and *Maps of the Ancient Sea Kings* (originally published in 1966), used the map to support his theories for Atlantis. In regarding the map's discovery, Hapgood notes that Turkish nationalism was sweeping the country at the time and that such a discovery like the Piri Re'is map would have been auspicious.

This, alone, raises questions about the map's authenticity. But why would such a map with such accuracy and at such a time have been faked? Antarctica was not discovered until 1821, its coastline not fully mapped until the 1950s, yet this map was discovered in 1929. Turkey only ratified the Antarctic Treaty in 1995, has no claim to any part of Antarctica or a part in its discovery. Nevertheless, after studies by American cartographers and naval personnel at the U.S. Navy Hydrographic Office in 1956, it was concluded that the 'southernmost part of the map represented bays and islands of the Antarctic coast and Queen Maud Land'. So with authenticity of the map's representations sufficiently established, I believe the Piri Re'is map to be real cartographic evidence for a voyage to Antarctica. But when? And by who?

The Piri Re'is map is not the only 16th century map purported to show Antarctica. The Oronteus Finaeus map of 1531, called '*Terra Australis*

Re, center immensa, sed nondii plena cognita' ('Regions of the Southern Land, an immense center, but not fully known to this day') also apparently shows an accurate depiction of Antarctica, though scale problems probably arose due to copying errors or compiling original maps with differing scales.

The famous Mercator (Gerhard Kremer) drew Antarctica in both his 1538 and 1569 Atlases. He may have been working from Finaeus' map or earlier source maps. But did he include Antarctica because of certain knowledge or to balance off his maps? German cartographer Johannes Schöner in 1520 depicted 'Brasilia *Inferior*' a separate piece of land in the south Atlantic and different to '*Papagalli Terra*' (Land of the parrots) as Brasil was then known. Lastly, Athanasius Kircher's 1665 *Mundus Subterraneus* shows a remarkable depiction of Antarctica. Even with latitudinal or scale and copy errors, Kircher's work carried on a long tradition of depicting a large southerly island continent, accurately and where none had yet been discovered. And though writers like the Flem-Aths, Hapgood and Hancock are Atlantis hunters, the discovery of possible early maps of Antarctica does not presuppose the existence of Atlantis in Antarctica, only that there are maps of Antarctica before its discovery.

Another controversial map, not related to Antarctica but nonetheless part of the validity of the Piri Re'is map story, is the famous Vinland map. As discussed below, the map was originally dated to between 1420 and 1440 (a curious spread of years to be dated to, as will be seen later.) The Vinland map vindicated the Norse claims of discovering North America. Recently it has been denounced as a fake, but I think that the researchers missed several points, also discussed later.

But the maps don't stop there. Other maps dating from just after the Columbus voyages show parts of the world that could not have been mapped so soon, including the Waldseemüller map of 1507 depicting Central America and the Jean Rotz map of 1542 bearing Australia over 200 years before Cook discovered it. Gavin Menzies, author and historian explains that the letters and logs of European explorers, including Columbus, clearly state that they had maps. Menzies states: 'What nobody has explained is why the European explorers had maps.' So who drew the maps?

Retired Royal Navy submarine Commanding Officer, Gavin Menzies, has written a remarkable book *1421 – The Year China Discovered The World* (2002) in which he theorises that the Chinese sailed, discovered and mapped much of the unknown world in 1421, seventy years before Columbus discovered the Americas. In their huge 480 foot-long ships accompanied by an armada of hundreds of merchant junks and other warships, the Chinese voyages around the world including Africa, North and South America, Australia and Antarctica, lasted two years. The Chinese fleet was very accomplished, far more than any European navy, and as Menzies contends throughout the book was far more adept at reckoning longitude and latitude. In fact, it was how Australia and Antarctica were discovered three centuries before Cook even sailed to the south Atlantic.

Menzies recounts the voyage of one Admiral Hong Bao who was tasked with sailing to the South Pole in order to fix the positions of southerly stars for aid in navigation maps and charts. Hong Bao may have sailed as far as Graham Land on the Antarctic Peninsula in 1422, which is depicted as largely ice free in the Piri Re'is map. Hong Bao may have also discovered and sailed through Cape Virgines and the Magellan Strait, and if he is the ultimate source of the Piri Re'is map, Hong Bao may have sailed down west coast of Tierra del Fuego. Menzies also estimates that after the trip down Tierra del Fuego, a voyage of fourteen days depending on wind and current speeds, Hong Bao would have come across the South Shetland Islands.

These voyages could help explain the mysterious origins of the Piri Re'is, Vinland and other early European maps accurately depicting lands unknown to the cartographers of the time. The Piri Re'is map notes that its charts were reduced to one scale (presumably from many maps). Menzies corrected the longitudinal errors whereupon the features of the Antarctic Region became all too recognizable.

Regarding the Vinland map, I do not believe that it is a fake as such. The Chinese (for the Norse did not make maps) could have made the original charts, which were then copied through the ages and traded or won from Chinese hands. The parchment and ink could be faked on copied maps, a still highly contested point, but the original drawing from which it was made is still genuine. It does not undermine the validity of the original map. Also, another curious point is that when it was taken to the British Museum in 1965, the Vinland map was dated to between 1420 and 1440, within the timeframe of the voyages of the Chinese fleet. The dating is significant, because at the time Western archaeologists had no inkling about the Chinese fleet, so the dating could reflect a non-biased and verifiable trueness of Chinese voyages around the world seventy years before Columbus.

Menzies' vast appendices lists supporting evidence, which unlike New Age tomes, are quite convincing and well researched. And he is not the first to write about this, only the most recent and popularised of non-Chinese authored books on this subject. Though there are critics aplenty, the subject is worth further investigation.

I see no need to explain accurate maps of pre-1821 Antarctica as the work of Egyptians, aliens, or lost races. Admiral Hong Bao, in 1422, could have beaten the first Europeans by four centuries. The Europeans subsequent ascendancy in history usurped China's historical feat after their fall into inward-isolation after most of the records have been destroyed by the new Imperial administration. But the Piri Re'is map may yet vindicate their place in history.

Sources:
Argod, R. 2004. *Out of Antarctica*. London: Richard Editions.

Crossley, L. 2000. *Explore Antarctica*. Cambridge: Cambridge University Press.

Flem-Ath, R. & Flem-Ath, R. 1995. *When the Sky Fell: In Search of Atlantis*. London: BCA.

Hapgood. C. 1996. *Maps of the Ancient Sea Kings*. Kempton, Illinois: Adventures Unlimited Press.

Highfield, R. 2002. Vinland map debunked as 1920s fake. *The Daily Telegraph*; July 31.

Menzies, G. 2002. 1421 – The Year China Discovered The World. London: Bantam Press.

21/Apr/2008

Arts & Humanities – History Mysteries
Evidence for the origins of the Garden of Eden

The Garden of Eden

2020 vision
This is a shorter counterpart to the article in the Religion section. I do believe there is resistance to such research and conclusions as it doesn't accord with perceived facts and Eden is now thought of as a mythical location or allegorical exercise.

The story of the Garden of Eden is entrenched in everyone's minds as the Biblical setting for the first man and woman, Adam and Eve, and their eventual and forceful exit from paradise. Yet, this enduring story has its roots in reality and its origins are being unravelled everyday by archaeologists and historians. It is an epic story that could also uncover the origins of the ancestral Europeans.

As written in the Bible, there were four rivers emanating from Eden: the Gihon, winding through Cush; the Pishon flowing through gold-rich Havilah; the Hiddekel (the Tigris) flowing east of Ashur and the Perath (the Euphrates).

David Rohl, an archaeologist has been investigating the origins of the Garden of Eden and along with data and the work of the late Reginald Arthur Walker has identified the other two rivers, the area of the Garden of Eden and the origins of Sumerian legends.

The Perath/Euphrates rises near Lake Van, runs 2720km through Mesopotamia and into the Persian Gulf. The Hiddekel/Tigris rises in the Zagros Mountains and flows west and south of Lakes Van and Urmia until it reaches the Persian Gulf, 2033km away. The land of Shinar through which the rivers flowed is Sumer in southern Iraq, so the rivers had to have flowed from the north southward. The two other rivers had to be in this region and once found, their origins were so obvious.

The Gihon was identified by Walker as the modern day river Araxes, rising north of Lakes Van and Urmia into the Caspian Sea. The Gihon became the Araxes or the Jichon-Aras during the 8th Century Islamic invasion of the Caucasus region. The old name was even waning during Victorian times. Yet it was entirely forgotten. The land of Cush through which it flows could be the ancient land of Cossaea near the Caspian Sea and may be the origins of the Kassites culture from the mountain region who invaded and ruled Mesopotamia c.1700-1160BC. In Iran, there is a 4000m high ridge, known as the Kusheh Dagh, the Mountain of Kush. The land of Cush is now in Azerbaijan.

The Pishon was even more obvious to Walker. The river today is the Uizhun and flows east of Lake Urmia into the Caspian Sea. Also known as the Kezel Uzun (long gold) or the Uzun (dark red/gold), Hebrew texts has translated the 'U' into a 'P', thus the river had retained its rightful name all along, with Pishon becoming the Biblical name. Havilah, in the Anguran region of Iran, through which the Uizhun flows, has always been rich in gold with mines dating back to at least 3rd-7th Century AD.

These then were the four rivers and have their origins in the ancient land of Armenia. They were identified through etymological, topological and historical sources, and the very word 'Eden' is also indicative of the Lake Urmia area.

The Mesopotamian word 'Edin' (Sumerian) or 'Edinu' (Akkadian) means 'open plain' or 'uncultivated land'. In Hebrew 'Adhan' means 'to be delighted', 'place of delight'. The Greek 'Paradeisos' our paradise meant 'parkland' and Persian 'Pairidaeza' meant 'enclosed parkland'. Hebrew 'Gan' equalled 'garden' and 'ganan' meant 'hedged in' or 'protect', 'walled garden' or 'enclosed park'. There was also a river that ran through Eden. This has been identified as the Adji Chay River, which has an older name: 'Meidan' -Persian for 'enclosed court' or 'walled garden'. Thus Sumerian, Persian, Greek and Hebrew lexicons had similar meanings for a specific area: The Garden of Eden.

Eden itself is to the east of Lake Urmia and sits in a valley fenced or walled in on its northern, eastern and southern sides. The Adji Chay flows west into Lake Urmia. The set up corresponds to the Biblical description. In ancient times, the region was warmer, more fertile with fruit trees, and extensively wooded. This mountainous area, near Tabriz, Iran, contains secluded valleys and would have sheltered any community.

And so there is the Garden of Eden, shunned for whatever reason and relocated to Mesopotamia. Why is Iraq more expedient as the supposed home of Eden? Is there a modern political/religious/cultural bias to thinking of Eden as existing in a modern third world or non-Christian country? Do people assume that because Sumer was the first great Mesopotamian civilisation that Eden had to be located there? But the Sumerians had to come from somewhere.

The story of the Garden of Eden and the Old Testament is the very story of their migration dressed up in religious overtones after the fact. The Story of Adam and Eve marks the transition from a hunter gatherer society into an agricultural/technological society. These Neolithic inhabitants, possibly our Indo-European ancestors, moved out of their paradise, possibly due to adverse weather conditions of which there were a few major reversals between 12000 and 5000BC and migrated south. But they retained the memory of their origins, probably through oral myths, then cuneiform, and then written down.

The Ubaid culture, the ancestors of the Sumerians, and the probable original inhabitants of Eden had spread their pottery all over the region, even to the Black Sea and it is their cultural signature found in this region, which may have been the origin of the Great Flood, as the Black Sea was flooded from the Mediterranean via the Bosporous. There are still sunken tells to explore, but the Ubaids would have carried with them the story of the flood to Sumer.

There are also new and intriguing finds of cites in northern Syria, that preceded the great cites of Sumer. It is more evidence of a north to south migration and that Eden was located near Lake Urmia. So, the Garden of Eden, may have cradled one of mankind's ancestral lineages after all. It has endured in myth, but we should investigate and celebrate its reality.

Sources:
Rohl, D. 1998. *Legend – The Genesis of Civilsation*. London: Century.

Ryan, B. & Pitman, W. 1999. *Noah's Flood*. Simon & Schuster.

20/Jun/2008

The History of the Calendar

What Year Are We Really In?

When are we? Nominally, we are in the Christian year of 2008, but we are also in the Islamic year 1386, Chinese year 4608 (or 4706, 4705, or 4645, depending on the reign of Huang Di, inventor of the calendar), Egyptian year 5108 (if the Narmer/Menes dates are accurate) and a few more. But whose calendar is more 'valid', more accurate or even needed? Our calendar systems are subjective and disjointed and the world might be better off with one system only and one that pre-dated the rest. If only our Ice Age ancestors had establish a singular or unified calendar for us, beyond lunar and solar cycles. Below are some calendar histories and mysteries.

Christian:
How can the Christian era start at year zero, even after knowing the fact that Jesus was born between 4 and 6BC (as Herod the Great died in 4BC and the Star of Bethlehem may have been any number of extraordinary celestial features that occurred during that time). Since the modern Gregorian calendar started in AD1582, there have been numerous tweaks and many indigenous time systems have been lost. But these chronological curios would have led to a temporal Tower of Babel with solar, lunar, Venusian, stellar, riverine, and countless other seasonal and calendar systems causing confusion over which calendar was more worthy. The Gregorian calendar brought relative order.

Hebrew:
The Hebrew calendar goes back to 3761BC, the supposed date for the beginning of the world in the Old Testament. That makes it the year 5769. Of course this clashes with Christian calendars (and history). How was this date established, by Talmud scribings of genealogies or from ancient scholarly calendars passed down through generations? If it is from a set date and legitimate source rather than a textual context, then why not follow the Hebrew calendar, especially since Christianity has its roots in Judaism?

Chinese and Egyptian:
China and Egypt have unbroken timelines going back thousands of years, but rely on reign dates that are not totally consistent or confirmed. With the Chinese calendar invented around 2600BC and the Egyptian state united around 3100BC, they could easily have spread around the world, but isolation in the case of the Chinese, and the Greeks and Romans in Egypt's case put paid to that and the Julian calendar would go on to rule Europe.

The Gregorian supremacy:
Succeeding the Julian calendar was the Gregorian calendar, created by Pope Gregory XIII. Without it, the world may have been a different place; for instance, a Druidic calendar from the British Isles may have been in vogue now, with Stonehenge the spiritual heart of England with Kings and Queens crowned, married and buried under the Sarsens and Bluestones instead of St. Paul's or Westminster Abbey.

It is this quirk of calendar systems which vividly reveals the myth of the supposed separation between church and state. Modern secular business, politics and life is ruled by a timeframe set by a religious event. Religious calendars hold sway over secular life. Secularism runs on the timestamp of religion. Our weekdays are named for (Norse/pagan) religious deities and symbols. The first half of our year (January to June) are also named for pagan Gods, two for Roman leaders (July and August) and the rest are numerically based. So our year is ruled by a hodgepodge of pagan-named days, willingly accepted by Christian and other religious orders.

Even the concepts of BC (Before Christ) and AD (Anno Domini –'In the Year of Our Lord') are religious markers in the secular working world. The more neutral BCE (Before Common Era) or BP (Before Present -1950) are becoming increasingly popular as people react to the political correctness of using Christian religious terms for time periods not related to it.

We cannot keep resetting our calendar systems and hopefully the Gregorian calendar is the last major reset. This may be a feature of our times, but it takes away what sense of history there was; we lose our prehistoric perspective and think that only the present and future matter. Knowing your cultural history stretches further back into the past and actually having a calendar to reflect that gives a culture a continuity; a sense of identity and deep heritage. As Muslims celebrate their beginnings from AD622, America might as well celebrate their origin as 232 AI (after Independence from 1776), Canada as 141 AI, and Australia 220 SD (Since Discovery). But on the flip side, the indigenous of these colonised worlds needed no calendar to tell them that they had a deep history or what year it was. All one needed to know was that the past shaped the present shaped the future.

The Maya:

The Maya had a trio of sophisticated calendars, which counted out months, years and vaster stretches of time in Great Cycles. As deciphered, the last of their Great Cycles began on 13th August, 3114BC and will end on December 23rd, AD2012. Their Great Cycles are said to end in great cataclysms, but it is not the world that ends, as usually interpreted by New Age writers and doomsdayers, but an age, a new dawn or new millennium. But was 3114BC just an arbitrary date? What happened in the previous cycles? Since the Maya were accomplished astronomers, something celestial must have occurred such as a conjunction of planets or stars, a nova or comet, which then perhaps became a initialising date, a beginning of a new age. If that date is their year zero then we would be in the year 5122 and celebrating some celestial event. The year 2012 could be our next great starting point.

French Revolution calendar:

After the Revolution, the leaders of the Republican Era established a new calendar from 1792 that tried to be as a natural a calendar as could be. The Years, which began at the autumn equinox, were written Roman numerals and were divided into twelve months of 3 ten-day weeks. Hours, minutes and seconds of the day were decimalised into ten hours, each with 100 minutes made of 100 seconds. The months had names based on nature like Brumaire (fog), Germinal (germination), and Messidor (harvest) etc. The Republican Calendar was ended by Napoleon in 1806, after problems with leap years, changes by the Church and partial abandonment of decimal clocks. The twelve year experiment was over and with it any chance of succeeding the Gregorian calendar. If it had continued and been adopted around the world we would now be in 29 Prairial An CCXVI (17th June 216). While the calendar was complicated and unwieldy it has been the only serious attempt to reinvent the calendar in recent times.

Galactic time:
The moon is close enough for Earth time, but Mars is a different story. Its orbit is 669 days and has an extra 39 minutes to its day. Its calendar would be quite dissimilar to Earth's due to its more elliptical orbit and seasons will be uneven. Hopefully they'll get it right on Mars and stick to one system without any fractious cultures settling for different calendars. But as man travels further from Earth new systems will have to be developed in order to cope with different timeframes and stellar references.

So should we continue on with our disparate calendars or even create a neutral one that the whole world could use, from a past date that we can certify as an absolute date (scientifically calibrated)? A man-made artefact, whether a document, site, or burial, would only cause cultural divisions, so a timed and known geological event (volcano, magnetic shift, meteor crash or supernova), might be neutrally accepted. Only time will tell, so keep checking your calendar for changes.

29/Apr/2009

Arts & Humanities
Evidence of Chinese Oceanic Voyages in 1421

Did the Chinese Discover the World in 1421?

2020 vision

Propaganda, fact, or half-truth? The origin of Sinbad? The real discoverers of America half a century before Columbus? You decide...

Retired Royal Navy submarine Commanding Officer, Gavin Menzies, wrote a remarkable book called: *1421 – The Year China Discovered the World* (2002) in which he theorised that the Chinese sailed, discovered, and mapped much of the unknown world in 1421, seventy years before Columbus discovered the Americas. In their huge 480 foot-long ships accompanied by an armada of hundreds of merchant junks and other warships, the Chinese voyages around the world, including Africa, North and South America, Australia and Antarctica, lasted two years. The Chinese fleet was very accomplished, far more than any European navy, and as Menzies contended throughout the book were far more adept at reckoning longitude and latitude. In fact, it was how Australia and Antarctica were discovered three centuries before Cook even sailed to the south Atlantic.

Among others, Menzies recounted the voyage of one Admiral Hong Bao who was tasked with sailing to the South Pole in order to fix the positions of southerly stars for aid in navigation maps and charts. Hong Bao may have sailed as far as Graham Land on the Antarctic Peninsula in 1422 (Menzies 2002: 141-2). In apparent support of Menzies' theory are the Falkland Islands, which may hold two important clues to possible Chinese voyages. There are two supposed on-going investigations, one searching the ground on Mount Adams for possible Chinese carved stones which may have been used to sight Canopus for navigation purposes (Menzies 2002: 128-9) and secondly investigations into the warrah, a thought-to-be indigenous, but now extinct fox or wolf-like animal whose origins are disputed. While DNA tests are carried out to resolve its ancestry, there are also tests being sought to argue for the warrah being descended from Chinese dogs left behind by Hong Bao's sailors (Whipple 2003: 80-1; Menzies 2002: 135). This research may take some time, considering that much doubt has been cast upon the whole theory by academics.

Hong Bao may have also discovered and sailed through Cape Virgines and the Magellan Strait, and down the west coast of Tierra del Fuego (Menzies 2002: 136-7). Menzies also estimates that after the trip down Tierra del Fuego, a voyage of fourteen days depending on wind and current speeds would have led him to the South Shetland Islands, which he would have charted (Menzies 2002: 144-5). Admiral Hong Bao, while charting the position of the South Pole in 1422, could have beaten the first Europeans by four centuries. Who knows, the Chinese may already be searching for their historical treasures from their existing base Chang Cheng station on King George Island. But where is the evidence for the Chinese voyages of 1421? Surely, someone, somewhere, would have recounted stories of strange ships and men.

These voyages could help explain the mysterious origins of the Piri Re'is, Vinland and other early European maps accurately depicting lands unknown to the cartographers of the time. The infamous Piri Re'is map (a portolan from 1513, supposedly showing an ice-free Antarctica) notes that its charts were reduced to one scale (presumably from many maps). Menzies corrected the longitudinal errors whereupon the features of the Antarctic Region became more recognisable (Menzies 2002: 144 & 147). Regarding the Vinland map, this does not have to be a fake as such as many experts reckon. The Chinese (for the Norse did not make maps) could have made the original charts, which were then copied through the ages and traded or won from Chinese hands. The parchment and ink could be faked on copied maps, a still highly contested point, but the original drawing from which it was made is still genuine. It does not undermine the accuracy of the original map. Another curious point is that when it was taken to the British Museum in 1965, the Vinland map was dated to between 1420 and 1440, within the timeframe of the voyages of the Chinese fleet (Highfield 2002; Menzies 2002: 304-5). The dating is significant, because at the time Western archaeologists had no inkling about the Chinese fleet, so the dating could reflect a non-biased and verifiable trueness of Chinese voyages around the world seventy years before Columbus.

Not only maps, but also physical evidence, like human remains, shipwrecks and artefacts, could be still waiting to be discovered. Proof could come in the form of nine supposed sunken Chinese junks from 1421 in the Caribbean. Menzies is waiting for the right opportunity to investigate. Some people, like Gregory Baughen, the First Secretary at the New Zealand High Commission, are happy about such searches: "We're all ears," he says. "Chinese artefacts have been found around the coast for some time" (Grice 2002). However, it is unlikely that any country will allow such marine expeditions in the near future, either to protect their own history or because they do not believe Menzies.

Is there recourse to talk about pre-Columbian (1492) or pre-Sinoan (1421) America? As Gavin Menzies reveals, the Chinese had allegedly discovered the Americas long before the Europeans. Chinese carvings at American Indian sites from 3000 years ago (Rennie 1999), classic Chinese stories like *Shan Hai King* almost 5000 years old, American crops like maize and peanuts found in China also 5000 years ago (Sieveking 1999), and Olmec figurines bearing Chinese-like portraits (Benson & de la Fuente 1996: 174 & 227) hint at a historical relationship with the Americas that goes back much further than thought. But the subsequent ascendancy of Europeans in history usurped China's historical feat after their fall into inward-isolation. And since most of the 1421 Chinese records were apparently destroyed by the new Emperor's administration, we may never know.

Menzies' vast appendices list supporting evidence, which unlike New Age tomes seems quite convincing and well researched. His historical adventure is seemingly plausible and though there are critics aplenty, the subject seems worthy of further investigation, if only because rejection of Menzies' theory stems more from prejudice against the Chinese, more than because of lack of evidence. And Menzies is not the first to write about this, only the most recent and popular of non-Chinese authored books on this subject. But does Menzies' work threaten orthodox history? Western academics have given a cool reception to this idea. It may not threaten history and archaeological paradigms, but it could lead to more spurious works gaining favour over real history. The voyages of the Chinese in 1421 may or may not be old Chinese wives' tales, with recent investigations and criticisms coming to the fore on the internet, especially with Menzies' new book: 1434: The Year a Chinese Fleet Sailed to Italy and Ignited the

Renaissance due out. Whatever credibility Menzies may have had vanished with this particular re-writing of history. History is usually written by the victor, but here, Menzies has won nothing for the shameful treatment of history.

Sources:

Benson, E.P. & de la Fuente, B. (eds.). 1996. *Olmec Art of Ancient Mexico.* Washington: National Gallery of Art; catalogue n°s 25 & 67.

Grice, E. 2002. Explorer from China who 'beat Columbus to America'. The Daily Telegraph; March 4.

Highfield, R. 2002. *Vinland map debunked as 1920s fake.* The Daily Telegraph; July 31.

Maynard, R. 1999. *Ship may put Portuguese 250 years ahead of Cook.* The Times; August 31.

Menzies, G. 2002. *1421 – The Year China Discovered the World.* London: Bantam Press.

Rennie, D. 1999. *China and US linked by ancient writing.* Daily Telegraph; August 25.

Sieveking, P. 1999. *Ancient Chinese king 'led trip to America'.* The Sunday Telegraph; December 12.

Whipple, D. 2003. Histories: Alas, Poor Warrah. *NewScientist.* 20/27 December 2003 - 3 January 2004: 80-1.

08/Jun/2009

Arts & Humanities – History
Archaeology Today

Basics of Archaeology

2020 vision
Your guide to becoming an archaeologist. You're welcome...

Archaeology is the study of Man's past through his physical and artefactual remains. Archaeology is one of those subjects that fascinate people. Why, they think, would someone spend their days and lives, usually in a field, digging for past civilisations' rubbish? Well, for one, because they love it –the thrill of discovering, learning about past lives and societies, and maybe having the chance to travel or to be in the outdoors. As with many jobs, archaeology has its politics, camaraderie, hard graft, analysis, interpretation, and then lots of beer in the end. Being an archaeologist is not just a job, it's a way of life.

We have only discovered a fraction of a percent of what came before us. Archaeology is not just about pyramids, what the Romans did, or Greek statues, it is a global endeavour with every corner of the world involved with its diverse and hidden gems waiting to be uncovered. Entering archaeology does not necessarily mean a past studying history or archaeology, on the contrary, many institutions would rather have a student from a different background in order to bring different perspectives to archaeology. Such courses are open to all no matter age, ethnic background, gender, or experience. All that matters is the determination to learn and work as an archaeologist. Here, below, is a general outline of an archaeology student's journey.

First Year:
In Britain, Archaeology is a subject all of its own, while in the U.S. it comes under the auspices of Anthropology. While it is treated and taught differently, the outcome is the same. A typical course for a Bachelor of Arts (BA) or science (BSc) in Britain begins in the first year with a general introduction to archaeology. Subjects could include an

introduction to anthropology, classical studies, Egyptology, Roman studies, and learning field methods and techniques. Along with essays and exams, the first year is replete with field trips to learn stratigraphy, excavation, field walking, and experimental archaeology.

Second Year:
The second year becomes more specialised and students can branch out in subjects that interest them. Core courses could include archaeological theory, current issues in archaeology, surveying, geoarchaeology, ceramics, osteology, archaeozoology, research and presentation skills, public archaeology, and heritage studies. More field work is also required and can range as far a field as Thailand or Peru.

Third Year:
This is when the student concentrates on his/her dissertation or a field work presentation. There will also be a few courses in the first terms. In some cases during the three years, students can take courses outside of archaeology, especially languages, to enable them to work in different countries.

Graduates:
For students wishing to continue on in their archaeological education, a Master's degree (MSc/MA) course offers a wide range of options. Students can focus on subjects like forensics, museums, conservation, the environment, materials, cultural heritage, field studies, management, maritime archaeology, and public archaeology. Some have essays, field or laboratory work, with dissertations as final assessments. Depending upon the student's situation and the institution, some courses may be available part time over a two year period instead of one. This enables a student to work, whether in an archaeological capacity or not, to fund their education. A student may undertake a graduate degree for love of the subject, to place themselves above the many undergraduate job seekers, or as a stepping stone to the PhD.

Post-Graduates:
There are two main types of post-graduates going for research degrees. The MPhil (Master of Philosophy) is initially a two-year course of original work that can then lead to a full PhD, normally a three-year course. Both have major theses to complete, with the PhD also having

an oral assessment. On successful completion of the PhD, students can then go on to a job in their field, continue with post-Doctorate research or enter into academia.

Excavations:

Archaeology would not be complete without excavating, which comes in a few varieties. Many digs are rescue digs, where time is at a premium, because a construction company, for example, has come across something of archaeological importance that could be destroyed due to construction work. British companies must adhere to guidelines such as PPG 16 (Planning Policy Guidance 16), which basically states that consideration must be given to the archaeological potential of a site. So in theory, no archaeological site could disappear unknowingly under the bulldozer. Once initial investigations are made, usually via non-destructive methods (e.g. geophysics) then the dig may commence. As the construction company is paying, time is of the essence and an effort is made to excavate and record all that is excavated before construction needs to continue.

The other type of excavation is research excavation where time and resources are available to fully excavate a site. Doing this work are private companies or dig units attached to museums or universities. Private companies and museums usually have a core group of staff with a multitude of contract workers or students. University units would be under a member of staff or a funded field unit. Teaching digs are usually run by universities and are becoming popular all over the world, because students have to pay to be on the dig, so they add much needed funds to university archaeological institutions. Heritage companies also employ people to maintain existing sites.

While excavating can be fun, it is hard physical work, usually on your knees for hours on end or transporting buckets or wheelbarrows of spoil around. Digging will continue throughout most weather conditions, so be prepared, plus facilities may be scarce depending on the location. Besides excavating, there is also field walking to find surface artefacts, plotting, processing and cleaning excavated finds, surveying, and artefact drawing.

Projects:
Archaeology is not just field work. There is also laboratory and library research to be done usually in post-excavation phase. Samples could be studies under microscope or made into smaller pellets for scanning electron microscopes (SEM) or X-ray analyses, geoarchaeological analyses, or other computer and scientific processes. Lastly, once all the fieldwork, analyses, and interpretation is done with, the write-up will begin, either as a dissertation, thesis or for general publication.

Archaeology will always be a factor in our growing society as the old life is ploughed under the new. We need to make sense of the past to help us understand our present and future. Archaeology is also changing with the times in using computers, new theoretical models, new techniques, employing dynamic people, and becoming an international institution to further our knowledge about the complex subject that is man. So, whether an archaeological professional, amateur/volunteer, student, or just an interested observer, archaeology is ever-present around you. Go explore and discover the hidden world beneath your feet.

17/Sept/2009

Scientific Evidence of a Worldwide Flood

Ancient Impacts, Mega Tsunamis and Creation Myths

2020 vision

I became fascinated by these unearthly structures after reading about them in The New York Times newspaper, while researching for my book on Antarctica. Our world is a wonder of hidden geological secrets telling us how she was formed and reformed and how that affected ancient humans and civilisations. All the clues are there, we just have to learn how to see and read them.

Recently, evidence for an asteroid or comet impact, 4,800 years ago, in the Indian Ocean was found in Madagascar. Huge "chevrons", wedge-shaped sediment deposits, usually containing deep ocean microfossils fused with asteroid metals and pointing toward the ocean were found by the Holocene Impact Working Group, a collection of researchers, scientists and specialists in geology, geophysics, geomorphology, tsunamis, tree rings, soil science, archaeology and mythology from America, France, Australia, Russia, and Ireland. The cause of these chevrons was a mega-tsunami 183m (600ft) tall, thirteen times bigger than the Indonesian tsunami in 2004.

The Fenambosy Chevron, one of four, near the tip of Madagascar is six-hundred feet high and three miles from the ocean. When the Working Group looked for the cause of the chevron, they found the Burckle crater, 18 miles in diameter, 12,500 feet below the Indian Ocean surface and 900 miles south-east of Madagascar. It is estimated to be 4,500 to 5,000 years old.

Though with no concrete evidence for this, to me, this is suspiciously close to the dates when the first major civilizations of the world began their rise circa 3000BC. Climate change has often been cited as a factor in emerging civilisations, but the cause of the climate change has not been known. Were asteroids and comets providing a catalyst for change? Do world wide flood myths have a common basis in fact describing mega-tsunamis? How much force would be needed to create these chevrons and what are their capabilities?

Chevrons have already been found as far a field as Australia, Africa, Europe –including Scotland and the North Sea, North Korea, Vietnam, the Caribbean, and in the Hudson River, New York. So, they are not unknown events. Dallas Abbott, of the Lamont-Doherty Earth Observatory, New York discovered oceanic craters from the chevrons that point ocean-ward, including the Burckle crater. With Ted Bryant, a geomorphologist at the University of Wollongong, New South Wales, Australia, who found two north-pointing chevrons four miles inland in Carpentaria, north central Australia, Abbott was able to later find two 1,200 year old craters, which matched the age of the chevrons. Without trying to postulate a catch-all cause for climate change, extinctions, migrations and myths; asteroid and comet collisions could be one of the most important factors in the formation of human life and civilisation.

David Morrison from NASA Ames Research Centre, an expert on asteroids and comets supports the Holocene Impact Working Group's research and expects more from deep ocean impact and crater studies. Estimates from the Working Group see evidence of cosmic collisions, on the order of 10-megatons, at a rate of one every 1,000 years. Bruce Masse, an environmental archaeologist at the Los Alamos National Laboratory, New Mexico has dated the Burckle crater comet to the morning of May 10th, 2807BC. He had analysed 175 flood myths from around the world and related them to natural events, like eclipses and volcanoes. Fourteen myths specifically mentioned a full solar eclipse (one occurred in May 2807BC), half told of "torrential downpours", and a third experienced tsunamis and other "hurricane force winds and darkness during the storm". Masse sees these phenomena as related to mega-tsunamis.

So from two disparate corners of science possibly comes a common consensus for asteroid and comet collisions, causing untold damage in the past, igniting myths and possibly forcing a rewrite of history. But we will probably never know the whole truth, until it happens to us.

Source:
Blakeslee, S. 2006. Ancient Crash, Epic Wave. *The New York Times*. Tuesday November 14.

18/Sept/2009

Arts & Humanities – History
The Sican Civilisation

Brief History of the Sican

2020 vision

My MSc dissertation was written on the Sican culture and I had the pleasure of visiting Sican sites in 2000 while on a dig in Peru. During my MSc in 2004-06, I had contacted Izumi Shimada, Professor of Anthropology at Southern Illinois University, Carbondale (SIUC) and one of the foremost experts on the Sican for his assitance. He gave me some advice and then requested that I send him a copy of my thesis once it was finished.

However, I did not as my desk top had given up the ghost during my work and I finished my dissertation on my new laptop. My research (history text, physical specimen preparations write up, and SEM results) was split all over the place between floppy disks not compatible with my laptop and on a memory stick. The only complete copy was the printed copy and I never recreated it as a whole again. I've always felt a bit guilty for not sending Professor Shimada a copy. I could have contributed in some small way to the published study of the Sican.

The Sican culture inhabited the Lambayeque region of North Coastal Peru from c. AD750 to 1400, between the time of the preceding Moche and the succeeding Chimu. Whether the Sican were bio-culturally similar to the Moche and Chimu is not known. The Sican area of control at the height of their power extended four hundred kilometres down the coast. At first, the Sican were not thought to be a distinct culture and were known as the Classic Lambayeque Style, associated with the Chimu. But through archaeological multidisciplinary studies, the Sican's history has been divided into Early, Middle (Classic) and Late (AD1100-1375) periods, with the Middle period AD900-1100, denoted as a complex state.

Archaeologists mostly focus on the Middle Sican period for its wide-scale use of alloyed metals, especially copper-arsenic alloys, so much so that it was called the "Bronze Age" of northern Peru. Sican means "House of the Moon", which was the name of the surrounding area and implied a reference to silver, but the Bronze Age in the Sican world make possible the cultural developments within Middle Sican with metal artefacts being produced by the Sican unlike any previous cultures.

Sican Sites included:
Batan Grande: the most important of the Sican metallurgical production centres. This large site was located in the La Leche River Valley, 35 kilometres inland and at an altitude of 100masl (meters above sea level). Its position suggested its importance as a "nodal point" between the coast and the Amazon basin. Metals, especially arsenical copper, were smelted at industrial levels in small bowl-shaped furnaces. Batan Grande was the sacred site complete with monumental temples and vast mortuary areas.

Pampa del Tablazo was a further 50km inland and southeast of Batan Grande in the Chancay Valley (altitude 200masl), and was a Late Sican period site, occupied occasionally during Chimu/Inca times. The site sat in a fertile valley with a river one kilometre to the east. The buildings were determined to be 10x10m rectangular enclosures with attendant smaller buildings, which have been interpreted to be metallurgical workshops.

Cantagallo was another Middle Sican site, around 5km to the south of Pampa del Tablazo, where batanes, looted burials, and destroyed platforms have been found. Unfortunately, the site has now been destroyed through modern cultivation after the 1983 *El Nino* event.

Cerro Huaringa is another Late Sican era site, around thirteen kilometres from the centre at Batan Grande also occupied by the later Chimu and Inca. Cerro Huaringa boasted a large, industrial arsenical copper smelting base, the processing of which remained unchanged for six hundred years. This was also the first place where pre-Hispanic metal smelted from ore was found.

Naipes:
The most outstanding feature of the Sican was the naipe. Naipes were unique to the Middle Sican period forming part of a specialised group

of artefacts known as axe-monies. They were made exclusively from copper-arsenic and hammered into thin sheet-metal, I-shapes. The function of the naipe (nominally some form of prestigious exchange system), its manufacture (strength, colour and shape), distribution (socially and geographically) and end-use (bundling and burial), still fascinate archaeologists.

Naipes symbolise the Middle Sican polity with its prodigious use of arsenical bronze. A Sican tomb within Huaca Loro, Batan Grande held various bundles of naipes approaching 20,000 in total (25kg in weight), with a further 250 kilograms of other arsenical copper implements; these out of a total of 1.2 tons of grave goods, over three-quarters being metal goods. Making naipes was an expensive and expansive business.

The Sican may have exported the idea of naipes to Ecuador and Mexico, culminating in their own axe-money industries, where their industries lasted longer. Naipes were not strictly currency, where two naipes equals a bag of oranges, some bread and some change, but a more complex and internal Sican exchange system, whether actual or ritual, but important for almost two centuries. The fact that the naipes' existence was intertwined with the Batan Grande centre indicates that naipes were a form of religious or ritual coping mechanism, whose time came to an end when Batan Grande's fortunes waned.

The manufacturing process of naipes gave the naipe a certain mechanical property, even though it could have been made from gold, silver or a ternary alloy. Naipes were pale pink, or paler in colour rather than a copper-red colour, depending on the percentage of arsenic. A higher percentage of arsenic gave a silver colour, possibly used for ritual or decorative materials, while a high tin-bronze percentage, which the Sican did not use for lack of tin resources, would have yielded a gold colour. Out of the sheer thousands of naipes found and analysed none have been found made from gold, silver, copper or ternary alloys. Naipes were the sole reserve of arsenical copper.

The Sican were a complex society whose full nature has yet to be discerned, but they heralded one of the greatest periods of Andean arsenical-copper metallurgy. Ongoing work is still discovering the secrets this culture once held onto and in time they will join the likes of the Inca, Chimu, and Moche.

Sources:
Bezur, A. 2003. Variability in Sican Copper Alloy Artifacts: Its Relation to Material Flow Patterns During the Middle Sicán Period in Peru, AD900-1100. Unpublished Doctoral thesis: The University of Arizona.

Doonan, R.G. 1991. A Prehispanic Metallurgy Site in the Mid-Chancay Valley, Peru. London: Unpublished MSc Thesis.

Epstein, S.M. 1993. Cultural Choice and Technological Consequences: Constraints of Innovation in the Late Prehistoric Copper Smelting Industry of Cerro Huaringa, Peru. Unpublished Doctoral Thesis: University of Pennsylvania.

Hosler, D. 1994. The Sounds and Colors of Power. Cambridge, Massachusetts: The MIT Press.

Lechtman, H. 1980. The Central Andes: Metallurgy Without Iron. In: TA Wertime and JD Muhly (eds.) The Coming of the Age of Iron. New Haven: Yale University Press, 267-334.

Lechtman, H. 1991. The Production of Copper-arsenic Alloys in the Central Andes: Highland Ores and Coastal Smelters? Journal of Field Archaeology. (18), 43-76.

Merkel, J. & Shimada, I. 1988. Arsenical Copper Smelting At Batan Grande, Peru. Institute for ArchaeoMetallurgical Studies (IAMS), 4-7.

Merkel, J. & Shimada, I. Swann, CP. & Doonan, R. 1992. Investigation of Prehistoric Copper Production at Batan Grande, Peru. In: D. Scott & B. Meyers (eds.) Archaeometry of Pre-Columbian Sites and Artifacts. Los Angles: The Getty Conservation Institute, 199-227.

Merkel, J. & Velarde, M.I. 1998. Naipes (Axe Moneys): A pre-Hispanic Currency in Peru. Archaeology International. Institute of Archaeology, University College London, 57-59.

Shimada, I. 1981. The Batan Grande-La Leche Archaeological Project: The First Two Seasons. Journal of Field Archaeology. (8) 405-446.

Shimada, I. Gordus, A. Griffin JA, Merkel JF. 1999. Sican Alloying, Working and Use of Precious Metals: An Interdisciplinary Perspective. In: SM Young, AM Pollard, P. Budd & RA Ixer (eds.) Metals In Antiquity. BAR International Series 792, 301-309.

Shimada, I. Griffin JA, and Gordus, A. 2000. Technology, Iconography, and Social Significance of Metals: A Multi-Dimensional Analysis of Middle Sican Objects. In: C. McEwan (ed.) Precolumbian Gold: Technology, Style and Iconography. British Museum Press.

Shimada, I. & Griffin, J.A. 2005 (updated from 1994). Precious Metal Objects of the Middle Sican. Scientific American, 80-89.

14/Jan/2010

Arts & Humanities
Writing about history

The Ins and Outs of Ancient History

Ancient History means different things to different people. But when is Ancient History? To some people it means 19th Century events, to others it means the Romans, or the Stone Age, or millions of years ago. In [writing site name's] case, Ancient History covers pre-Medieval/Middle Ages times (mostly along European lines), and includes ancient Rome, Greece, Mesopotamia, Egypt, and even Biblical times. There is already a dedicated Middle Ages History channel and others for Europe, Africa, Asia, and the Middle East, etc., so Ancient History is not an arbitrary catch-all designation for any event in the past, but a more defined period of antiquity. This is a general guideline to the ins and outs of Ancient History.

Anthropology, archaeology, and cavemen:
In regards to Neanderthals, Homo erectus, and other pre-modern humans, these would be more suitable for Physical Anthropology, since identifying such specimens is, well, physical anthropology. This is also pre-history, which is not strictly ancient history, because there is no history to contend with. Arguably, a good guide to the start of history is from Ancient Egyptian and Mesopotamian times with the introduction of writing, urbanism, law, etc.

Archaeology also does not necessarily belong in Ancient History. European and American classification of archaeology and anthropology are different. Within Helium, archaeology is under the auspices of Science – Social Science –Anthropology/Archaeology. And just in case you were wondering, dinosaurs and fossils belong in Palaeontology.

Culture:
Many intended historical articles could in fact be cultural articles and be placed in Society & Lifestyle – Culture channels. If you are describing a culture without delving into its ancient history then such articles belong in Culture and not History, and vice versa, if someone writes about 'The

history of such and such a people' it belongs in History. The trick is in the wording and/or meaning of the title. Post Ancient History titles can go astray and inadvertently end up in Ancient History if the titles are not specific or written well.

Facts and interesting details:
Ancient History should be written about in a factual way without personal speculation, which may be more suited for History Mysteries. However, be imaginative. Spicing up the article with interesting details is always good. It draws the reader in, plus presents the opportunity to learn something new or exciting. Also, 'dry' essay-like articles and lists of facts are not easy reads, especially when trying to convey a lot of information. Long school/college essays should have unnecessary information, digressions, and in-text citations edited out.

Sources:
Good Ancient History writing demands great sources so readers can have a further sense of the material. People can read the same book and come to different conclusions, so don't be shy in inviting debate. Sources show your understanding of the material, depth of knowledge, and may encourage or inspire like-minded readers/writers. It also shows that your ideas are you own and that you can express them in an orderly fashion.

Great articles can inspire and as history becomes just that, remembering what has happened in the ancient past is more important than ever. Your Ancient History article is a window through time, so open up the glorious views on a world gone by, in the best possible way.

11/Jun/2010

Arts & Humanities - Ancient History
General abilities of Homo erectus

The Olorgesailie People

If one wanted to study the general abilities of Homo erectus then a visit to Olorgesailie in Kenya would be a worthy place to start. Around sixty-five kilometres southeast of Nairobi, within the Great Rift Valley, sits a large field of Acheulean tools and butchered animal bones. Discovered in 1919, it wasn't until 1943 that it was excavated by Louis and Mary Leakey. Studies indicated that the site was about 1.2 million years old and fell out of use around 200,000 years ago when the lake it sat beside began to dry up. Fossils of extinct species of hippo, elephant, zebra, giraffe, and baboon and others were found, perhaps butchered using the hand axes. The site had been preserved under fallen volcanic ash (which provided the site dates). Further, while ninety-nine percent of the tools were made from local lavas, quartz and obsidian were also used from two distinct and opposite mountain sites, 16-40 km distant, respectively.

The Acheulean hand axes are associated with animal butchering. The site also seems to have been arranged where 'axes' were made in one area, blunt instruments sharpened in another, animals butchered in other areas, and so on. However, on further study and replication of manufacture the tools were shown to be poor at cutting, chopping, scraping, or tasks such tools would seemed to have been made for. It may be that while the stone tools were inadequate, they were good enough for what they were needed for, at that time and place, for a million years.

However, and intriguingly, the bodies of the tool-makers seemed to be absent. The makers were assumed to be Homo erectus, since no other known hominid contender existed at this time. It wasn't until 2003, after sixty years of excavations, that small skull fragments were found. They were assessed to be that of Homo erectus and dated to between 900,000-970,000 years old. So where did the makers live, eat, sleep, hunt, and die? The skull fragments were found about 1.5 kilometres away from the tool site near the highland area of Mt. Olorgesailie, so perhaps the tool-makers' living areas were away from the lake and in the safety of higher ground, caves, and/or rock shelters.

It has to be repeated that this went on for a million years. A million years. Think about that. Modern humans have been around for less than 200,000 years, yet here was a 'primitive' hominid species making the same-type tools over and over for five times longer than our existence. Can our modern minds even comprehend such a notion of deep time and comprehend our society producing the same bit of technology for a millions years? Our technology barely lasts a decade before the next invention takes hold. So what on Earth were the Olorgesailie up to? How can Homo erectus abilities be studied, here? Below are some ideas to ponder.

Communication:
There is no conclusive evidence that Homo erectus could speak, save for speculation upon other studied Homo erectus' skulls that their brains contained a Broca's area, related to speech. As with such claims, they are hotly contested. However, to maintain and use such a site as Olorgesailie over so long, there must have been some form of communication, especially verbal forms, no matter how unsophisticated, for tool-making and group bonding/hunting purposes.

Homo erectus may have travelled the world, survived tough and varied environments, made tools, and used fire, but they essentially had the brain capacity of a modern infant. Making stone tools could have enthralled them and challenged their spatial awareness and perceptions just as puzzles and building blocks do to today's child. Making stone tools enhanced learning and motor-skill coordination. In any case, the skills existed to create the hand axes and bifacial tools in the first place.

Hunting/Fishing stones:
A lake (now dried up) and a stone tradition purposefully set up by the lake and abandoned when the lake dried up: what is the connection? The main use seems to be to hunt and butcher the animals by the lakeshore. But were the stones also used as fishing utensils to skim the water and bring prey up and to the shore? Were the stones used to scare away predators by throwing them at the beasts or even other hominid competitors? Making tools may have been a rite of passage to bond and

to enter manhood and join the hunt, passed down through countless generations.

Art:
Some of the tools weren't fully functional, but they were pretty to look at. Creating stone tools for creation sake could be seen as the beginnings of aesthetics and art. Were some of the tools a show of aesthetics over function? How valued were the tools? Were they owned or shared? Were they reused or recklessly abandoned? The amount of tools found and the superfluous nature in some of their manufacture (e.g. size, stone type, etc) may make a case for the burgeoning of artistic thought.

Trade:
While the Acheulean stone-tool tradition has been found in Africa and Europe, were these specific stone types also found outside of the Olorgesailie area? Have any 'foreign' artefacts turned up that could have been the result of trade? Did the people come together around the scenic lake to trade commodities (stones, food, knowledge, etc) through the stones they collected and fashion into a type of stone currency? Olorgesailie Acheulean 'intellectual property' may have been passed on to other groups who then spread it beyond Africa.

Other uses:
Were the stone tools used as primitive earth-moving tools, digging in the dirt and marshy land for food or resources? Is there any evidence for Homo erectus-influenced landscaping? While territorial markers may not have been a function, surely coming across so many hand axes and bi-facial tools 900,000 years ago would have marked it out as 'private property' and thus an area of importance by the lake.

All these may be fanciful, biased notions, and based upon modern thinking. Many of these scenarios are much too early in time to have happened or have been thought about by Homo erectus, but maybe there are proto-concepts we cannot now conceive of. The Olorgesailie people and area are determined to hold on to their secrets. Excavations are still on-going and hopefully, one day some answers will be found and new shed light on the life and times of Homo erectus.

Sources:
1. Bryson, Bill. 2003. A Short History of Nearly Everything. Black Swan: London.

2. Olorgesailie – Wikipedia: http://en.wikipedia.org/wiki/Olorgesailie (link active as of September 2020)

3. *Olorgesailie: Life and Times of the Handaxe Makers:*

http://humanorigins.si.edu/research/east-african-research/olorgesailie (link active as of September 2020)

10/Jun/2011

The Digital Age of Archaeology

Internet Archaeology

2020 Vision

Uncompleted article, but I believe with the growth and evolution of the computer industry, we'll need specialists to dig through the dead internet worlds and digital civilisations. Don't believe me? Think when Facebook dies and all our digital lives are trapped; irretrievable, buried in red tape. When the physical person dies, who will discover their digital legacy decades, centuries or millennia later? So keep your cute cat pics coming, memes and gifs circulating, and bury your silly secret trolling passions. The archaeologist of the 31st century will base her thesis of the 21st century on them.

In a May 2011 *New Scientist* magazine article 'Digital legacy: The fate of your online soul' Sumit Paul-Choudhury argued about digital world's heritage, its longevity in storage, and the lost information being found by internet archaeologists. But is there really a need for a new type of archaeologist? Will IT specialists be the vanguard in preserving and recovering the internet archives? Or will archaeologists be required to enter a new niche of archaeology?

Geocities – the 'lost' web hosting site.

MySpace - the 'lost' social media website.

There are now revolutions in the Middle East the impetus of which is not the written word or rallying speech, but a tweet. These 'Twitterlutions' are evolving, but their very nature and origin could be lost in the digital realm if Twitter were to merge or archive or disappear. Archaeologists are used to repeated words through the millennia, but the original texts have disappeared. The tweets and Facebook messages which abound during the Arab Spring revolutions may be collated into a book or reported in newspapers, but the original digital print would be gone.

Take the case of the tweeted word of Sohaib Athar who was first, and accidentally, the person who alerted the world about the mission to kill Osama bin Laden, live. His original tweet would be priceless; like a Roman Senator tweeting about the death of Julius Caesar, a first-hand account archaeologists would love to have. In the centuries to come, such original digital information, which would shed light on historical moments, would be lost.

Imagine the first astronaut on Mars tweeting back to Earth. Would his message be preserved as much as Neil Armstrong's historic and grainy black and white images?

Centuries from now when laptops are discovered and not thought of as just ritualistic objects, the data excavated from them will shed light on our digital lives. But who will be carrying out the excavations – 'dirt' archaeologists or IT personnel? Most probably, it will be a multi-disciplinary effort.

Sources:
http://www.newscientist.com/article/mg21028091.400-digital-legacy-the-fate-of-your-online-soul.html
(link active as of September 2020)

InternetArchaeology.org
http://en.wikipedia.org/wiki/InternetArchaeology.org
http://www.internetarchaeology.org/missionstatement.htm
(link active as of September 2020)

Philosophy

08/Jan/2008

Arts & Humanities – Meaning of Life
Why We Exist

Why Are We Here?

2020 vision

Is this why we exist? We are nothing more than the universe's way to remain balanced. Think deeply on this. On some level it means we are destined to be a space-faring race spreading our 'exergeous' presence in order to help the universe by inexorably extracting and destroying resources. Or we will be failures by only destroying ourselves and this world. We would have failed in our primary responsibility to help the universe attain equilibrium. Too big an idea? Maybe, but it's as good an explanation as any, on par with 'we're accidents of evolution' or 'we're here to serve an unseen omnipotent being'. Welcome to the Philosophy section.

Does humankind a have a purpose? Besides religious answers like because God created us, and philosophical ones like are we really real, I came across an interesting article in the *New Scientist* magazine. It purported to answer the question about why we are here from a scientific point of view.

Reducing it down to its bare points, humans exist as 'exergy' machines 'a universal natural tendency to turn concentrated energy into diffuse waste heat' in accordance to the second law of thermodynamics (Minkel 2002: 30). Humans (in a long line of organisms) are helping the universe attain equilibrium, by our creation and destruction of everyday objects, even our very world.

So are humans 'hard wired' to create and destroy? Do we spread chaos wherever we go and nothing else matters? Exergy (a quantity of useful extracted energy) 'is fundamental to human civilisation too. Our history could be seen as a series of leaps towards better ways of extracting energy: first wood, then coal and oil, and on to nuclear power' (Minkel 2002: 30 & 33). Our raison d'être is to create technology, which structures our world, but tends to destroy the natural world. This 'exergy' principal could view humans as randomly mutating into better organisms suited to do the universe's bidding.

But this brings up further issues, like are we the only beings in the universe doing this? Surely our little planet cannot affect the whole of the universe. There must be others out there busily destroying their civilisations. Maybe this is why there are no visiting aliens; they have destroyed themselves as unwitting pawns in the universe's bid to stay in balance. Other natural wonders of the universe are also doing their bit to bring equilibrium, like supernovas, black holes, voids, dark energy and vacuum energy, etc. They explode, break up, absorb, expand and help smoothen out the universe. This could imply that humans, possible other aliens and other exergy-orientated phenomena may just be evolutionary mistakes that the universe is wiping out in order to be at equilibrium.

On the other hand, another and deeper issue is free will. If we are only around for a few millions years, does it really matter what we do? Maybe the asteroid 65 millions years ago was no coincidence and the dinosaurs were not 'exergetic' enough to get the job done, so the universe decided that mammals might do better, and aren't we just. We could be pre-programmed to provide a service to the universe and free will is an illusion within the bigger picture.

Exergy is an old principle, but in applying it to humans in a new way could open up our eyes about human nature and our role within the wider universe. Do we have the free will to change our ways or will the universe win out? It seems we are here to find out that answer before it all ends!

Minkel, J.R. 2002. The Meaning of Life. *New Scientist*. 176 (2363), 30-33.

10/Jan/2008

Education – Educational Philosophy

What is an Infovore?

2020 vision

As with the article above, the inspiration for this article was from a *New Scientist* magazine piece. I used to collect the magazine with a passion until my period of unemployment. Then the eventual loss of my magazine collection (thrown out) and soon after my comic collection (later sold off) left me with more cupboard space and more change in my pocket. But my infovore tendencies have not been diminished. I then rewrote the article slightly on 31/Jan/2008 for Society & Lifestyle – Lifestyles Testimonies: 'The Infovore Within - Are you an Infovore?' Well, are you? Read on...

I am an infovore. I first came across this term in the *New Scientist* (one of many infovore bibles) (July 22, 2006). The term, coined by neuroscientists, describes an infovore as someone who is hungry for information. New knowledge and understanding of that information activates pleasure areas within our brains like certain drugs and endorphins do. Remembering this feeling drives people to want to learn more. All humans are infovores, but I think that there are a few of us who really crave information about the world around us and actually get a high from it.

How and when did I become an infovore? I do not know, but I do know that my parents instilled within me the love of wanting to learn. We also moved around a bit from England, to Barbados, Canada, America and I was also in the Army. All these different learning systems and exposure to new experiences poured into me and I had to digest it or fall behind and not fit in. My heroes are polymaths like Leonardo da Vinci, Isaac Newton, Richard Feynman, Carl Sagan, and lately Stephen Jay Gould and Felipe Fernandez-Armesto. They were/are thinkers par excellence and viewed the world differently. If had an iota of their ability I could die happy.

I love information, gathering information, discovering and connecting information. I hoard newspaper clippings in scrapbooks for future stories, articles, and sheer pleasure. I watch TV, read books and newspapers not just see what is new in the world, but also what is different; what can I learn from it. Helium writers must be infovores; you are spreading and learning new information. You love writing, you want to know what the world thinks, you have friends who you debate with all the time, and you say things, like a devil's advocate, that you might not believe yourself, just to see the response from your friends and explore new avenues of thought, which fuels new ideas, etc. You are always looking for the new idea; new thoughts.

I read on the trains, the thought of wasting my time listening to music on a journey kills me, when I could be reading another 5 or so pages. I buy three or more books at a time, just to have that information that much closer to me. I would not dream of selling my books, they are the bibliography to my life, and I can remember when and where I was when I read them. Information from them pops up at random moments.

But I seem to be a selective infovore as I am not much for statistics. I could not remember who my favourite football team played last week, let alone who was the highest scorer during the 1980s. There is a limit to infovorism and if you do not want to or cannot learn something, then maybe there is a way to infuse information into people through studying their infovore tendencies. I am a big fan of learning through creativity. My mind wanders, I am always thinking to the point of distraction, but I connect things, put them into context and create a way for myself to learn something new that may have been difficult with 'conventional' rote thinking.

These things may sound excessive or compulsive, I probably am, but as the world is such a small place and you engage with more people, information is a real currency. Some futurist experts like James Martin in *The Meaning of the 21st Century* (2006) have seen the past two centuries as based upon manufacturing and services. This century will be about ideas and information as more and more information is on the internet and businesses dissolve into outsourced and diversified entities. So, to some infovores, all this information is exchangeable, it is liberating and to others it is power. Information alone cannot do much, but connected and shared is a powerful tool. In this century, information may be our saving grace. Let us not waste it.

So are you an infovore? Are you infovorous? Is there an infovorial world out there with more rabid infovorialists sharing an infovorium? I hope so. I am glad to be an infovore and at least I am not a neophilliac. But that is another story.

06/Feb/2008

Arts & Humanities - Meaning of Life
Recognising the big picture when contemplating life

Life: The Big Picture

I am a believer in the Big Picture in that everything is connected; the past, present and the making of the future. From cosmology, religion, chaos and emergence theories, degrees of separation, the environment, globalisation, and individuality, etc., there is a sense that they combine to weave our world, our universe and our visions together.

We are here because we were created. Whether it was by design or not, is neither here nor there because as the universe formed it set into motion the elemental cosmos we now see. And in a supernova's dying moments, the elements that would be needed to create man were dispersed across the cosmos. Those elements are now a part of us and we are literally of the stars. We belong to the same family as the cosmos – we are Homo *Universalis*. Even if some Intelligence made the universe, it still used those elements to create us and the rise of religion within the bounds of the physical laws, so both cosmology and religion can be seen as emergent forces of the universe, regardless of its origin. In other words, because everything in the universe conforms to specific laws of physics, what we see as cosmology and religion are really the same thing, but from different subjective perspectives. Both share the same basic properties within us –the universal elements- so how could they be any different in scope?

Everything is connected; just think of the hypothetical butterfly, its fluttering wings and the resultant hurricane across the world. Chaos theory appears in all shapes and sizes. It affects us through environmental changes, resource availability, conflicts, epidemics, population and societal changes, oil/food/product cycles and prices, government policies, etc. Such changes can be seen in patterns over the years, which over the long term become less random patterns and appear in more or less recurrent cycles. In the Big Picture chaos is surprisingly regular and we live through it every day, oblivious to its background beat. Humans are a part of that chaos and it may be the reason we are here. Chaos is entropy, the universe's tendency to devolve from order to disorder. And as humans create chaos, we are part of the universe's entropic pattern. We are here to help the universe evolve!

Our world is not a bubble. It interacts with the universe at large through solar winds, cosmic rays, countless precipitations of particles and the odd celestial collision. No longer can we just think about ourselves, our city, or our country. There is a whole universe out there and some pioneering people are now beginning to think of how to use it. These visionaries see the future of industry and commerce as it will no longer be totally Earth-bound in the near future. Trickle-back technology will occur within our lifetimes, whether from energy propulsion or production, mining opportunities, building and shelter materials, medical applications, etc. The pace of technology is exponential, not linear like society. Political life-spans are too short-term, the media too unfocused and people too inward looking. We need a vision for the future where space issues are included in political, media and daily life. Space needs to be treated as another country, a resource, an opportunity; an emergent way of human life for the future. We need to return from whence we came.

Gaia cannot sustain us forever, even with new technology, energy and stable populations. We humans have a need to explore and to live in a way that is comfortable and free. At the moment, the Earth is going through changes that affect everyone; problems that Earth will survive, but we might not. There is no grand design for humans to be the end all of civilisation, so Gaia, as a living system could see fit to bring in the next evolutionary model. It has been reported that we are now out of the Holocene and into the Anthropocene. We have created our own human-induced geological era. Gaia is rebelling against this era. We cannot go backward and undo our technology, nor will technology alone save the world. In the big interconnectedness of our world we have to be more proactive instead of reactive against the chaos and emergent feedbacks of Gaia. We need to adapt wisely; not fight harder. While Gaia is our only home, we should play by her rules or she will sweep us under the chaos carpet forever.

Globalisation is the biggest human unit people see, for better or for worse. But the world is hardly any bigger than six degrees of separation. You, the reader, probably know me and the other readers through half a dozen random interacting persons. In a world of over six billion, that is an amazing account of how life is interconnected, though conflict and disharmony throw this into doubt at times. Globalisation is either an inequality machine of politics or a means to level the international playing field. But as an individual, you are your own globalisation entity.

Today, the internet is an unparalleled tool which empowers people around the world, whether though political, social or other means. Instead of Globalisation and degrees of separation, there is now degrees of globalisation. Over time, the über-capitalist society will be replaced as technology, manufacturing and services become less centralised and less commercial (I am no socialist!) and individual and smaller units will inherit the world. This could be because we envisioned a better connected world or because society broke down into chaos and we had to change. Either way, globalisation will evolve. It will have to, because globalisation cannot change who we are, it cannot stem chaos, cannot rule us when we leave Earth, cannot fight Gaia and cannot break the degrees of separation, because in the end globalisation is just a vast collection of individuals.

In this way, individuality is a universal element. The universe is alone, but it is a vast collection of individual elements. Our world is a collection of elements, but is it of anonymous global forces or of individuals who have to be more socially interconnected. For our world to survive, we have to recognise that there is a bigger picture, that we individuals are all connected and that we will someday embrace our place in the universe.

18/Feb/2008

Arts & Humanities – Meaning of Life

My Value to Humanity

2020 vision

This is even more important today. Everyone has value. In this time of the Coronavirus pandemic and heightened racial tensions it's especially easy to lose one's sense of value in a world gone wrong. For some it's even harder to look beyond their insularity to see that differences are positive and a value-added commodity to the social physics of the world. We really are all in this together. Others may deny it and others defy it, but they cannot escape it. All they do is de-value themselves. So, chin up, look out upon the world and see the value in yourself and others.

Everybody adds value to humanity. It is what makes society so fluid and worth living. The big question is how much value is contributed by each person? This includes such factors as interpretations of value, cultural background, education, age, gender, experience, skills, wealth, health, etc. Each of these value factors are then weighed against others by yourself, your family, your society, other cultures and these feedback loops continue, so that your own self-value is constantly changing as you go through life. Actually, depending on the person, your value could continue on after death through ideas and actions established in life. Value is a concept shaped by human perceptions, thus while lauded, value is illusionary, and yet timeless.

My view of my own value to humanity is through the concept of Social Physics. There are a few interpretations of this, but mine is that everything is connected. Because we humans are made from the universal elements, we are part of the universe as a whole and should see humanity as adding value to the universe as it does to us. Humans are like macro-atoms, attracted to each other, forming elemental societies and cohesive structures. In this way, each person is an integral part of society with each individual in their own space-time continuum adding to the energy and mass of society. I add value to humanity by just being alive and part of the global community.

I, as an individual, add as much value to humanity as the proverbial butterfly's wings influence upon hurricanes. That is a lot of energy, which comes down to one's social currency, the gravity of Social Physics and your impact upon others' lives, whether you are a parent, a friend, teacher, a carer, fisherman, priest, policeman, an entrepreneur, celebrity or whatever. We will not always know what effect we have had once we have met another member of humanity; for that is totally within the realms of the chaos effect. So I will also have the possibilities of complex, long-lasting, hidden, delayed or subtle variations of my value to humanity.

For what is it worth, I pay my taxes, which helps the wider community with services and policies even beyond my national borders. I consume products: food, clothing, manufactured goods and other merchandise, which pays the wages of other workers, creates and sustains jobs and keeps the wider economy going. I try to be more responsible for my consumerism practice recycling. My paper, cardboard, tins and plastic are recycled, and I'm thinking about a food compost bin. I am not out to save the world single-handedly, but by doing my part, I help with the saving of resources for the future. Climate change cannot be solved by just big, grandiose capital ventures; it starts with small personal projects. Doing the little things, just like those butterfly wings, adds up and aspects of climate change can be mitigated through fuel and energy saving (I don't drive), recycling, better shopping choices and practices, education in climate change issues and spreading the word. In some small way, in some corner of the world, my consumerism and recycling could be helping others to retain their jobs and resources.

We all know each other. In this globalised world, we all add value to each others' lives through six degrees of separation. Even without the internet, I have met people from all over the world in Europe, Peru, South Africa, West Africa, Canada, America, Australia and China. Having met these people while I was in the Military or at University or from travelling, I have a high chance of knowing a great percentage of the world's population through these friends and acquaintances. I know I am two degrees away from knowing a moon walker. I know a scientist who has worked in Antarctica. My friends and I exchanged and experienced views on everything from politics, religion, sports, life, romance, studying, work, etc. I am now forty years old, but have many friends from teenagers up to septuagenarians. My combined experiences have shaped my personal and world views, some of which I have shared with my friends and some of which I have learned from and adapted from my friends. My value to humanity is magnified by my enduring friendships and their ever-expanding friendships, by listening to and understanding my friends and making sure I help them in their time of need.

While I worked in the security industry I met many fellow workers from South Africa, Nigeria, Ghana, Kenya, Zimbabwe, Nepal, Australia and Poland. When getting to know each other, I would tell them of my history, my studies and my aspirations. If they had no goals beyond working, I would suggest ways for them to engage their time productively while not working or for future studies. With one friend from South Africa, we talked about my studies and my ideas for books, but even though we differed greatly on our views on religion, he still saw me as an inspiration, because he now had ideas for what he would do when going back to South Africa. He had come to England to work for money, but had now learned something about himself and had a better idea of his goals for the future. Some of my other friends have called me an inspiration, because I like to think differently, see the world from a different perspective. I ask deep questions about life and I consider myself an infovore —scooping up knowledge- and adapting it for myself.

My heroes have been the polymaths of old: Da Vinci, Newton, Sagan, Feynman, Gould, etc. This spread of knowledge, or memes (the virus-like ability of ideas to spread and 'infect' people) makes humanity a vast think tank, the first and greatest of the super computers. Ideas and knowledge are powerful and reciprocal systems; their dissemination, sharing and adaptability are ways in which I add value to humanity. We all do.

In the practical sense, I have come up with business ideas, proposals for books, TV programmes, articles and other inventive projects, which I have now brought together on my own website for prospective interested parties. I hold reunions for my friends from university who are now scattered around the world after our degrees finished. I relay news and pictures for my friends on another website I developed especially for this purpose, so my friends from America to Thailand and from Norway to Nigeria can keep in touch and continue to add value to our own little world. I am adding value to humanity in small ways, which then generates a bigger impact as my friends travel around the globe, with memories and experiences we shared together. Through the sharing of knowledge and creating functional projects, I am bettering myself. I am growing as a person, in self-value, and experiencing life in a fashion unique to me.

For the future, I believe that humanity has a great future ahead of it. That is why I am involved with a society that believes passionately in going to Mars. I try to attend conferences, write letters to politicians, write articles about it and tell my friends, to inform them about the realistic issues and up-to-date policies. Going to Mars can be a fully integrated part of society if planned well, which is why I try to make people understand why it is important to go to Mars. It is more than a purely symbolic exploration or a glorified national/international mission. There are issues concerning technology, biology, resources and the survival of the human race. This is just a simplistic overview of Mars missions, but again, my individuality is being added to a greater voice on the future of humanity. Making a difference to the future of humanity would be one of the best ways I could add value to humanity.

So, in many ways I add value to humanity, as much or as little as I can or what society allows me to add. I have added my own worth to the global mass, just by being here, meeting people and sharing ideas, and by thinking about the value of humanity in the future. One day, my value could disappear, but I hope it continues on perhaps with my children or in spirit.

21/Feb/2008

Arts & Humanities – Meaning of Life
Is life worth living?

What Are You Waiting For Before You Die?

2020 vision

Another of my infovore 'bibles' was the TV show *Horizon*. Nowadays, Horizon content seems to have been watered down so the programmes are more about socio-political issues rather than science. I find that a shame if the BBC thinks they are running out of science stories as the horizon is a never-ending destination.

I hope I don't turn into one of those people who gets so old with nothing to do that they are just waiting to die. I have places to go (the travel bug had hit me hard after turning 50, until the pandemic delayed that) and I hope to be writing and being creative until the end.

Is life worth living? I was watching a BBC1 Horizon episode 'Living to 101' about people who live into their 100s. The centenarians were curiously concentrated around Okinawa, Japan; Loma Linda, California, and in Ovodda, Sardinia. Their long-lived tendencies seemed to come down to the obvious good genes and healthy diet, but another factor, especially in Loma Linda was their religion (Seventh Day Adventist), which prescribes a vegetarian diet though research also shows that being part of a religious community also promotes longer living. Juxtaposed to this were some inhabitants of Glasgow, where some life expectancies were in their fifties, quite shocking for a modern country of the west. This was put down to their forefathers' living through hard industrial times in high density tenements. Their immune systems over-compensated against the high rates of child infection, but left them with shorter life spans, it seems. This reminded me of epigenetic theories where the genetics of your grandparents and parents do matter and what affected them could be passed down to their children, contrary to prior belief. So generally, good genes, responsible eating, active communities and past conditions affect life spans.

To all of the people above, life was worth living, for better or for worse. So this got me thinking. What if, with enough of my physical and mental capabilities left, decent amount of money and some family around, I lived until I was101? What would I do? Would I live just for the sake of living? To beat longevity records? Is there anything to live for? Well, I would have a few reasons.

I am forty now, no children, but who knows. With another 61 years to go, I might consider a family, since on average people with partners and children tend to live longer. Once I start to get old, I might need someone to look after me, if I'm not in a care home by then. So to live to 101 would be to see my family grow.

I want to be around for the first Mars mission. I was a year old when we first went to the Moon, but now we're stuck in low Earth orbit. We have the opportunity to launch privately owned spacecraft and we are now looking back to the Moon and beyond. I want to see the first human on Mars, leaving behind a red footprint as he travels off into the red canyons.

I have travelled a fair bit, but there are five places I really want to go; my pilgrimage spots: Machu Picchu, Peru; Tiwanaku, Bolivia; Antarctica, Easter Island and Iceland. I have completed the first two legs and will probably do Iceland. But by the time I reach my century, I want to have completed the lot. I want to expand my horizons, giving me memories well into my century years.

I'm waiting for the bio-tech to be able to allow me to live longer and in better health. Bio-engineering could be an interesting development in the near future and help mitigate the pension time-bomb as people living longer could work longer, but enjoy greater physical and mental anti-ageing affects. I might as well grow old gracefully, and with a few tweaks.

I want to see the shape and condition of the world in the next half-century. Where are we heading? Globalisation, global warming, new technologies and energy transitions, peace in the Middle East, England winning the football world cup, and the remote possibility of encountering extraterrestrial life are all events or systems that could evolve or happen within my long lifetime. I can only imagine what types of technology will be here in sixty years time. I want to be a witness to history.

I like to create things; stories, designs, and projects, and gather knowledge, wisdom and experience. I've done the Army, and university and civilian life. But there is so much out there and so little time to appreciate it all. Crash and burn is not my style, so I want to be around long enough to know that I tried everything I could to have a good life. Living to 101 seems daunting, but the people in the documentary were all happy and active. I would not die happy now. So is life worth living? Give me a few more decades and ask me then.

09/Mar/2008

Relationships & Family - Birthdays

Reflections: Turning 40

2020 vision
More a philosophical reflection, hence pulled it into this group. Another decade on and I'm still holding it together.

I feel fine. Really I do. I don't feel a day over thirty-nine. I don't look forty, I sure don't act like I'm forty and I'm active enough to think that I'm in my sub-prime. Age is a state of mind. Age does catch up to you physically, but mentally and spiritually it can be kept at bay and enhance any physical signs of decay.

When you see documentaries or read articles about centenarians, and what it takes to be 100 years old, they have not been high-flying business people or famous celebrities, but simple folk with simple philosophies and a sense of humour. But most importantly, disregarding diets, physical routines, geography and their family and community support, they have kept active minds. They actively seek out new challenges and give their lives meaning at such a grand old age. As long as the brain is ticking over, the body clock will seek to keep the clogs whirring away.

So, I have no fear at 40. I have an active mind, too much to do, really. I am looking for new career challenges, though if 40 is the new 30, then employers haven't been told this even though they have to follow non-ageism laws. My wealth of experience, knowledge, skills and desire to work long-term for one company seems to be cast aside for the young, dynamic worker who will stay short term before thrusting for a new promotion elsewhere or to start a new family. I am far from my gold watch and have a lot to offer, so watch out you young whipper-snappers.

I am single at 40. No dependants, live by myself and love my own company. I prefer it that way. But I am by no means alone or lonely. I have family who I can turn to and friends, who are mostly ten years or more younger than me; I was a late bloomer in life -a legacy from my

Army and university years. I was not going to celebrate my 40th, I had a party at 39, but it was my friends who threw me a big surprise 40th birthday bash. I was genuinely moved. I had a great time and words could not express my appreciation, surprise, gratitude and dare I say love for them all, for everything they did and the time and effort of their planning. It made my year.

So, 40: another milestone, maybe just over one third of my life done. I'm looking forward to completing the rest of my personal and professional challenges I have set for myself, making new memories and leaving behind any regrets or feelings of guilt over choices I made. I'm setting out to make my 40th year the best so far and for myself to be the best person I can be to myself and to my friends and family. I'm just glad to be 40. Roll on 50!

23/Mar/2008

Arts & Humanities – Meaning of Life
How We Think About Time:
Philosophical and Practical Implications

An Archaeologist's Thoughts on Time

2020 vision
A mixture of philosophy and history, but still a process of conceptual thought. Based on an essay from my BSc archaeological course.

Dealing with concepts of time has played a major role in helping archaeologists explain the contexts of some archaeological finds. The use of different techniques in interpreting time relative to these finds has yielded vast information and enhanced future possibilities of resolving time-related issues in archaeology. The two major components of time are linear and cyclical time, which can be broken down even further, as explored below.

LINEAR TIME
Linear time is an invention of Man to organise and coordinate his surroundings in relation to his life in order to make sense of the inherent disorder (i.e. nature, cosmology, death, etc.) around him. It is highly structuralised (i.e. days, months, years, etc.) and is controlled by man-made devices (i.e. clocks, calendars, deadlines, etc.). For Man, time's arrow points forward in linear time, but for archaeologists, they have to track backward along the line to points where the arrow's line-of-flight is not clear. To aid them, archaeologists can break down linear time into different phases:

Prehistory: Myth and legend

Historical: Dynastic lists, Biblical, calendars, and anthropology.

Scientific: Geological, evolution, modern dating techniques.

Time for the archaeologist stops at the 'time barrier', where myth rules the past of society (Toulmin and Goodfield 1982). History began when legend gave way to prehistory. At one point, Biblical history texts chronicled world history, so much so that Archbishop Ussher used Bible genealogies to propose the date of 4004 BC for the Earth's formation. But it was during the Enlightenment when time was really 'discovered', when artefacts and fossils of extinct animals were found, either separately or together, which did not fit into the Bible's view. Then in 1794, William Smith became 'The father of stratigraphy' after realising that each deepening geological layer was older than its successor, which was further appreciated when fossils were discovered in the lower layers (Toulmin and Goodfield 1982). This paved the way for three works which revolutionised time:

Charles Lyell's 'Principals of Geology' (1830), Charles Darwin's 'Origin of The Species' (1859) and E.B. Tylor's 'Primitive Culture' (1871) all expanded Man's perception of time. Biblical time had severely compressed history, Lyell's work increased time many-fold allowing Darwin's evolution theories to unfold and giving man a prehistory, leading to future anthropology through Tylor's work (McGrane 1989).

Within the geological realm, there are natural events that can happen over long glacial periods or in rapid, violent volcano eruptions. Such changes can be recorded in the stratigraphy of the landscape. That landscape could be of archaeological interest, so when excavated it could be put into a temporal context depending on its stratigraphical position. Complimenting geological studies we have scientific methods of dating, which can reasonably assure the age of a site and any artefacts.

Radiocarbon dating has heavily impacted upon the archaeologists, able to give an accurate date for artefacts. Dates with reference to times BC, AD, BP, BCE as well as bc and ad (lower case understood to be uncalibrated dates) can be recorded (Aitken 1990). This is important in deciding absolute (specific) or relative (assigned to an age) dates. These measurements in time are crucial, thus there are a whole host of more accurate and complex methods that cover longer time-spans.

As mentioned, geological time opened the door for evolution (McGrane 1989). Time was needed for Man to have developed into the being he is today. Evolutionary time, whether in spurts or gradually, gave archaeologists a chance to assess and study the growth of Man through the classification of the Ages of Man into stone, bronze and iron ages; the Stone Age being broken further into Paleo-, Meso- and Neolithic ages. Man's life was sequenced into a linear order.

Geology puts Man within a natural framework, whereas evolution shows Man's growth and adaptability within the framework, and Anthropology brings Man into perspective by studying his society through time (McGrane 1989). Time is an important aspect in the study of past cultures. Instead of looking at those societies in an out-of-time context or perceiving of them as actually being the past, they should be seen and placed within the present temporal context and evaluated as such. With archaeology, an artefact, site or society has to be placed within a temporal context through their remains. The interpretation of these remains, however, can be affected by biases from modern thought, which should be objective. Artefacts from these sites may include texts (i.e. stelae writings, king lists and calendars), from which archaeologists can deal better understand time.

The Egyptians were superb at compiling lists, especially of their rulers. Archaeologists have used these lists to record the different dynastic eras and kingdoms and also to identify excavated bodies. They also invented a sophisticated solar calendar which the Romans adopted in 46 BC (Krupp 1997). Time and its control was a significant aspect in legitimising rulership. This is seen in China, where calendars were used as forward-thinking tools in respect to distributing goods and services in times of need. It authenticated Imperial rule (Krupp 1997).

The Gregorian calendar (invented 1582), though flawed as linear systems are, borders the time line. Within it lays both linear and cyclical elements. Monday December 7th is cyclical, but by adding 2008, it becomes linear. Seeing this interplay may enable archaeologists to see other such patterns.

CYCLICAL TIME

Cyclical time has existed for far longer than linear time. It is the universal clock, the order of nature, from the birth and death of stars down to Earth's climatic patterns. Cyclical time can be independent of or exist within linear time, depending on its use. It is a constant, whereas linear time is an instant within that cycle. And Man cannot control it.

Climatic : Seasonal, agricultural, migration.

Astronomical : monumental sites, great cycles, celestial events.

Ritual/Mystic : renewal, immortality, dreamtime.

Seasonal changes and their information concerning time are a great boon for archaeologists. Agricultural processes can reveal a lot about the time of a society. Time here is measured in linear quantities during a set period, but as it repeats from year to year (i.e. tree rings, varves, crops, etc) the cycle can show various trends through time. Seasonal renewal was important to cultures where birds, fish and animals were seen to go to and fro from their migration lands, providing both nomadic and sedentary peoples with renewed resources (Krupp 1997). To the Egyptians, the Nile's rising was a source of renewal, its waters replenishing the lands from which the crops could be harvested. Failure of this cycle could result in lean periods or famine. Seasonal time is part of the greater climatic time, which in turn is part of global time and so on. This can be seen in deep core samples, where geological changes have resulted in massive climatic changes. These 'deep' time cycles (i.e. glacials, magnetic shifts and extinctions, etc) have affected the linear chronology of Man's evolution. Cyclical time drives linear time, placing Man within a complex temporal context.

Another wide-spread cycle that archaeologists have come across is the astronomical cycle. From Stonehenge to Tiwanaku (Bolivia) there are numerous monumental 'clocks' which foretell the return of celestial events (i.e. moon, sun and star risings for set dates). The nomadic San Bushmen have no calendars and recognise their seasons by the stars, which the San also regard as hunters and nomads (Krupp 1997). The Dogon of West Africa have a calendar system based on the sun and the moon, where the winter solstice begins their new year (Krupp 1997).

Two civilisations with both linear and cyclical systems were the Maya and the Egyptians. The Maya had an everyday linear calendar (The Calendar Round), a cycle based on Venus, and the Long Count calendar for historical dates (Renfrew and Bahn 1996). The Maya calendar systems were part of the all-encompassing Great Cycle which designated the beginning and end of world cycles (Robinson 1995). The Egyptian Sothic cycle was related to mystic renewal. The return of the star, Sirius, heralded a new beginning for life for the dead Pharaoh. He could be seen in the celestial sky, reborn as a star, an immortal being (Krupp 1997). Another view of ritual time comes from the Australian Aborigines. Dreamtime, the past, for them is a plane of reality which exists in the present. It is a peculiar view, but important for archaeologists to conceptualise in order to interpret Aborigine culture.

Both linear and cyclical concepts of time should be examined and interpreted carefully in order to understand the full effect of time upon cultures. Linear time can be measured, structured and sorted into a framework. Cyclical time is a mater of renewal and return. Linear time can be classed as more or less global, but cyclical time can also be 'local' or universal, yet more personal and meaningful. Time, to an archaeologist, is everything and long may it continue.

References:
Aitken, M.J. 1990. Science-Based Dating in Archaeology. London: Longman.

Krupp, E.C. 1997. Skywatchers, Shamans and Kings. New York: John Wiley and Sons, Inc.

McGrane, B. 1989. Beyond Anthropology. New York: Columbia University Press.

Renfrew, C. and Bahn, P. 1996. Archaeology: Theories, Methods and Practice. London: Thames and Hudson.

Robinson, A. 1996. The Story of Writing. London: Thames and Hudson, 126-127.

Toulmin, S. and Goodfield, J. 1982. The Discovery of Time. Chicago: Chicago University Press.

24/Mar/2008

Other - Other
If you could have a one-hour interview with any human being past or present, who would it be?

The One-Hour Interview

First, I would have to resist that old axiom: Never meet your hero. I would then prepare myself to meet the ultimate Vitruvian man: Leonardo da Vinci. He was the circle and the square of art and science; a visionary polymath and Renaissance Man of art, writing, music, invention, engineering, mathematics, sculpting, architecture, anatomy, and more. And I only have an hour!

As one of my heroes and inspirations in my life to better myself as an individual, I would ask Da Vinci about his inspirations. I would delicately ask about how an illegitimate child, surrounded by an average community, embarked upon a journey that would see him celebrated as a genius within his own time. What was his 'world view'? What drove him to be an early infovore, one who seeks knowledge for enjoyment's sake, and turn those ideas into physical reality? And why were his literary ideas hidden within his unique mirror-writing technique?

I would regale him with tales of our times and the scarcity of people possessing both intellectual and practical means. Modern man is over-categorised and restricted to one scope or subject. We have one job and a hobby; one calling and a spot of DIY. There used to be thinkers par excellence who viewed the world differently, but now the Age of the Polymath is ending with even the great inventions of our day being concocted by committee. The individual is subsumed by the community and personal spark is tempered if it threatens to flare out of control. I would ask Leonardo if his time focussed on cults of celebrity, like himself, while normal people were compelled to conform, as our modern world does now.

I would tour Leonardo's workshops, in awe of his artistry and sculptures. I would try to get some practical pointers and learn from a true master the basics of his grand craft. I would walk with him through the city and ask him about his plans for new architectural designs. I would tell him how cities like London, Paris and Washington DC in the New World would be planned as new cities rising from the ashes or their decrepit pasts, only for caution to rein back on innovation and over-ambition. How would Leonardo view our cities of today? What would he make of the skyscrapers and the way our urban spaces have been designed?

We would talk about how some of his inventions were put to the test; where his airplane, parachute, deep sea diving gear, tank and other devices passed the tests of engineering experts today. I would ask why some of his military machines were cleverly constructed so that they would not work properly. Did he build them out of intellectual curiosity and to challenge contemporary notions on weaponry? Or did he see that the balance of power had to be maintained to preserve peace between nations?

More controversially, I would ask Leonardo about his religious beliefs. I would tell him of the more outlandish theories that his paintings have inspired, but would still want to know why some of his painted figures showed peculiar attributes and poses, whether with pointing fingers and/or enigmatic smiles. Was there really a hidden code or message to be seen or have we misinterpreted and over-analysed his works of art?

Leonardo would have been a middle-aged man, aged 40, when Columbus discovered the New World and older at the time Copernicus was becoming a well-known astronomer. Would Leonardo have been the explorer and the astronomer in another age? Think of the world we would live in now. By all accounts Da Vinci was onto the theory of light; he just lacked the instruments. The world of science could be a wholly differently realm now and our world with it. Our dreams of moon travel could have come sooner! What would Leonardo have wanted to accomplish that he had not already conquered? What was left to discover, invent and envision? Which, to him, was his greatest creation? What wonders did Leonardo dream?

Leonardo da Vinci was a man well ahead of his time, trapped in a past that could not contain his ambition and vision. We have his works passed down to us and we have learned a lot since. But we will never see the like of such a man again. Ciao Da Vinci.

28/Apr/2008

Arts & Humanities - Literary Themes & Ideas
Book reviews: Big Ideas, by James Harkin

Big Ideas: by James Harkin (2008)

Ever wondered where some of the latest buzzwords or phrases come from and what they mean? Well James Harkin, a cultural commentator on social trends, has written a new slim-line guide to this world of ideas.

Each word/phrase is defined, its origins traced and examples used to flesh out the concept. Then to make sure we do not take it all too seriously, Harkin then finds a weak point in the idea and provides critical analysis. After all, these are only ideas and ideas are fleetingly imperfect and susceptible to change. Nevertheless, this is a thoroughly enjoyable and informative look at how ideas influence and transform perceptions of the world.

Some of my favourites include the 'experience economy' where contentment through material possessions is replaced by the memorable experience; or the 'Menaissance' the return of the masculine man after the rise of the 'Metrosexual'; or 'Maturialism' – the (usually) baby-boomers living life to the full. 'Infomania' is another one (closely related to my most favourite –Infovore- not mentioned in the book) when raw information is needed in order to fuel an instant need for data. There are many more gems, but I leave you to read the rest.

One might feel that there are a great deal many more words and phrases that could have been added and it should not be too long before the next updated edition is out, for ideas change rapidly and erratically. Harkin may be a cultural commentator on social trends, but so is everyone else to a degree and everyone probably has their own Big Idea and words to describe their world. My words would be the previously mentioned 'Infovore' -someone who gets giddy with the insatiable need for knowledge; and 'Neophiliac' -a lover of the new, especially gadgets; and 'Affluenza' Oliver James' notion of the obsessive, virus-like spread of wannabe celebrity and wealth, that can lead to all kinds of mental distress. Ideas and words for our times.

No doubt as the U.S. political scene, world economic crisis and climate change debates and agendas pan out, there will be new words, ideas and concepts on the tips of our tongues before long. But how long will they last against the standard lexicon and in the minds of society?

Big Ideas is a highly recommended book to sit alongside your dictionary and thesaurus, though it could have been much longer. So don't be a 'slacktavist', go check it out and spread the word.

23/Apr/2008

Sciences – Ecology & Environment
Views on the theories of evolution

The Human Template Theory

2020 vision

For my part, this is more a philosophical view and theory on human evolution than a science. But haven't you noticed this phenomenon? Are we cookie-cutter beings?

Haven't I seen you before in another city, another company, another time? Is evolution playing tricks on our eyes? I think that humans are being manufactured off an evolutionary production line (hints of a hidden designer after all?) where carbon copies of humans are literally churned out every so often? Do you swear you have seen the spitting image of someone or have you even met your own 'twin'? I believe these are all instances of a human template sub-programme within evolution.

There are over 6 billion of us on this world, but even with evolution cooking up new mutations, the recipe for humans is the same, so naturally there are only so many variations that humans can take. A person's looks, traits, dress sense and outlook on life can be virtually duplicated. It is like nature's way of cloning. No matter what your cultural background, parents' looks, your own genes and personalised life, there is someone out there, a slightly distorted mirror image of you, living their own life.

While working and living in London over the years, I have come across this phenomenon frequently, usually in females, probably because out of the millions of combinations in their clothing styles, even girls that look alike should differ just through natural selection of clothing, but they do not. There are certain body types, facial features, hair style and colouring, dress sense, personality types, even down to wearing the same type of glasses that would enable these people to be interchangeable. Why do certain templates of people dress the same and act the same? Is it hardwired, driven by media/advertising or are they 'destined' to be like each other, a part of a whole?

I have never counted how many different templates there are, but they certainly exist beyond national boundaries. How many times have you said 'If that person was black/white/Chinese, etc, he/she would look exactly like...'. Are there some cultures with more templates than others? Would you consider it an advantage or disadvantage? Even some celebrities/actors are touted as looking like another bygone star. There are look-a-likes for hire and political stand-ins/decoys are also known. I have never come across any of my 'twins' before nor heard from anyone who had seen 'me' somewhere else either. How many could there be? Is there a twin or near likeness for everyone? How individual are we really?

Do human templates have an ultimate purpose? When and where were the first 'master template' humans born? Are human templates an epigenetic characteristic that trickles down through generations? Maybe the reason why human templates exist is because since templates are not related to each other, they may have been 'created' to foster familiarity and friendship with different cultures by showing that the unknown outsider is not so different after all. I think that this is a firm sign of the family of man, which shows evolution, human dispersion and eventual convergence at work. I have not seen any human template investigations before, but it would be interesting to note, how many more people have noticed this phenomenon and how wide spread it is. See you later.

07/May/2008

Other - Other
Thinking about the future

Our Last Great Century

2020 vision
Below, I lay claim to inventing the term 'Zenaissance' with a specific meaning. And maybe the tone of the essay is too optimistic in this age, but despite the hatred, terror, indifference, and fear in the world, we still progress, we still face the challenges, by the Grace of Humanity.

This is it! The 21st century will be as great as humans will ever have it! Far from killing ourselves off through war, famine, global warming, nanotechnology, or indifference, and assuming we dodge the killer asteroid and survive other natural global catastrophes, then humans have an open and progressive future ahead.

Why? Being an optimist of informed opinion, this will be the single most challenging century ahead where we will leave behind certain 20th Century paradigms and flaws and set a new agenda. We are ever more aware of our nature and the surrounding environment, including the universe. We are ready to face our Earthly demons and also reach out once more beyond our veil to the moon and then Mars —our first step in humanity's cosmic journey and proof that we deserve to persist as a species. We would lack no ambition, fear no challenge and seek the impossible. This may seem simplistic with all that's going on around us now, but no life, no strand of society will ever be perfect. There will always be conflict, inequality and distress, but we will learn to handle these better, because there will be more freedom through integration and progress between nations and a smoother world system.

While Globalisation is still seen as an attempt to suck nations into a system that does not benefit them, some nations have made the system work for them. But the system is changing with huge consequences. We have the potential to solve a great many problems this century and most will be. Nations will cooperate more to their benefit. People will live wealthier and healthier lives. The energy transition will not only transform global economic and business paradigms, but also political worldviews. Politics will enter a new two-tier model: International and local. With national politics becoming too centralist, their power will wane and local authorities will have more relevance. Internationally, world organisations will direct global affairs, sometimes infringing upon national concerns, but less threatening to individual inalienable rights.

Professor Niall Ferguson, a prominent historian, has categorised the 20th Century as 'History's Age of Hatred'. It marked an undercurrent of tensions caused by the clash of civilisations and manifested in the War on Terror. However, I do not believe another World War will erupt, either between the U.S. and China; or in the Middle East where problems will continue piecemeal, until the elder statesmen die off and younger progressive types take over and finally decide that enough is enough and negotiate compromises enabling a lukewarm Pax Levanta. The so-called 'Age of Terror' will be subdued. Masquerading under the banners of Islam, terror and Anti-Americanism, it is the last gasp effort to resist globalisation. But globalisation is not just one of economics, but also of culture and genetics. Terrorism will not be defeated by military, political or economic means alone, but through bio-cultural changes. The clash of civilisations, our era of alien indifference, will end through genetic alliances, diversified thought processes, and virtual communication and migration.

Progress; why are we addicted to faster and more advanced technology? From personal gadgets, work appliances, to specialised industries (e.g. super colliders, nanotech, quantum computers, space travel, and energy transitions); technology seems to be outstripping human ability to keep up. There is only so much information the human mind can take, only so fast that information can go, and only so long that our information-obsessed way of life will last. So will we merge with technology, become subservient to the robot whip or learn how to moderate our rate of progress? Progress is not the path to perfection, it is only a process. Present-day systems of progress will not last indefinitely.

Sir Martin Rees, Professor of Cosmology and Astrophysics, and Astronomer Royal, wrote about 'Our Final Century'. He had concerns regarding the creation of higher technologies as mentioned above and other possible disasters that if not treated with caution by scientists could potentially destroy the human race. But such progress, speeding at an increasing pace, will be a double-edge sword, with more problems solved because of it. Whether we enter a fully integrated hydrogen economy; build quantum computers, fusion generators, solar panelled buildings, and allow bio-nanotechnology to rewire our bodies, or not, is up to us. There will come a time when we will decide how much we want progress to rule our lives and what benefits it will bring. If this be our final century, then let it not be our greatest in vain.

It was said by Francis Fukuyama, Professor of International Political Economy, that history was over following the fall of Soviet Communism, but of course that has not happened. Classic history doctrines still pervade, but the 20th Century will increasingly be seen as the end of Old Earth history with the 21st Century as herald to a new phase and foundation of humanity. The 21st Century will be the new Renaissance with technology painting and sculpting new sweeping works across the cosmic canvas. Futurologist Ray Kurzweil sees a singularity forming; the merging of genetics, robotics, artificial intelligence and nanotechnology within the human. But I see something greater and more profound and that is a culmination of all that has come before into a coalescent society, where humanity finally realises that their big ideas (the 'zenaissance'), technology maturation and evolutionary path are on a par as never before. It is when we realise that we are satisfied and mature enough in ourselves as a global people, that we become consciously responsible in our stewardship of Earth.

It sounds whimsically simple and clichéd, but Man is driven by old systems derived hundreds of years ago. It is the classic pyramid of society with the elite at the top and the broadening base of lesser peoples below. That time will come to an end and the pyramid will be inverted as the individual gains freedom from past hierarchical strictures. When? People, especially at the top of the pyramid, do not or cannot change. It is a generational bind that will loosen after the baby-boomer generation becomes extinct and late-20th /early 21st Century minds and paradigms take over.

Progress will create a new reality, but not perfection or a Utopia; there will be dark sides to every invention and progressive transformation. As progress evolves, so must chaos; there is turbulence in every wake of creation and progress will churn up the dark waters of 'misinvention' and other false avenues of creation and ideology. But that is the challenge, to preserve and balance order, while progressing. The 21st Century will be the single most important century to achieve this. Our pursuit of progress must be daring, yet tempered; deliberate, but resilient. Our last great century is upon us. Anything less and it just could be our last.

31/May/2008

The Zenaissance

2020 vision

Unfinished article (not sure why that is so) in which I invented a term which encapsulates a new blossoming of human enlightenment and endeavour through technology; though different to Ray Kurweil's Singularity.

Whereas the Singularity is an event, a stage of humanity, the Zenaissance will be an Age, a movement, encompassing the Singularity and other such accomplishments within the next 50 years. It will be when our grandest ideas and creativity are cultivated and realised. It will be the Age when we solve climate change, have unlimited clean energy, defeat our greatest diseases, and live longer. We will be space-faring. Maybe a little too optimistic for some, and not everything will be solved, but technology is accelerating at such a pace that our ideas will lead us into a new world of opportunity and advancement.

The next 50 years will be the new Renaissance, with new technology creating sweeping vistas across the cosmic canvas. I believe that the ideas of Futurologist Ray Kurzweil will come to fruition in the form of the singularity; the merging of genetics, robotics, artificial intelligence and nanotechnology within us humans.

A profound impact from this resultant formation of a coalescent culture will be humanity finally realising that its big ideas and technology maturation are on a par as never before, initiating a resurgent way of thinking and being: the Zenaissance, an implantable and resilient network enabling a human to *be* the internet.

Communications and data management would be irrevocably changed in the global arena as people foster direct interfacial links with technology and each other. Administered by the masses, Zenaissance creativity and pursuit of progress in the 21st Century will lack no ambition, fear no challenge and seek the impossible.

24/Jun/2008

Insights into the brain's sense of perception

The Mind's Eyes and Ears

Can you hear it? Listen; listen very carefully. Say inwardly to yourself: 'That's amazing!' Did you hear it? Your own voice -inside your head. How can you hear that? What is the audiological mechanism and process that allows you to generate a sound inside your head? Do it again. Isn't that amazing?

Now you see it. You are visualising; getting a sneak peak at something in your mind's eye. How can you see that? Was it a person, pet, building or sunset? What is that image imprinting upon that allows you to see something ghostly within your mind?

These moments, those daydreams, the fantasies and dreams, those flashbacks and nightmares; the unreal stuff that goes on inside your head could be the only thing that separates us from so-called 'lower' animals. We share some intelligence, language, culture, tool making abilities and emotions, but the ability to project ourselves inward may be unique to us.

Is this our consciousness or even our soul, the things that cannot be measured or found or fathomed because they are not part of the physical body? They are the result of the entanglement of neurons and proteins, fats and muscle, nature and nurture. Are these voices and images the only things left of us after death floating around in the ether, astray until caught by another on a spiritual plane, seen as a fleeting ghost or heard as laughter on a summer's breeze?

Think of your voice. Where is that sound from? Does it sound like you - or braver, funnier, or sexier? Is it left or right brain oriented? Does it speak another language? Does it tell you to do bad things? Does the voice hurt; is it loud; do you listen to it? Is it the Id, the Ego or the Super Ego, pulling up memories or creating fresh tales? When you talk to yourself (yes you do!) who wins? Does it drive you crazy, especially with that song repeating over and over? Have you ever tried to find the voice deep inside you? Has it ever disappeared? Do you hear multiple voices? Is it really there or a figment of your imagination? Think about it.

Their face is so familiar – almost in sharp relief, but blurred and never exact for more than a fleeting moment. Yet you saw it, somewhere inside your head, plain as day. Where is it playing; on which mental screen? Is it before your eyes or just beyond your vision? How long can you make it last for?... Whoops that hurts –too much concentration. Think of yourself. As with the internal sound system does the image really look like you? Better looking, confident, or smiling? Is the image left or right brain oriented? Is it the Id, the Ego or the Super Ego, pulling up memories or creating fresh images? How vivid is the image –colour or monochrome? Do you imitate the actions in these images? When your inner voice speaks do the words flash before you? Have you ever tried to find the image deep inside you? Is the image in a square box like a TV or diffuse and blurry? Can you see the answer?

What is the voice; what is that image; where are they from? Are they evolutionary advances that provide a coping mechanism, a protective system, a society weaver or anti-sensory deprivation device; a link to the inner self with action rewind and replay? We have something inside us so astounding. The voices and images from another reality, the future or the past, our wishes, messages from beyond, our real self, our other self, the person you want to be. The mind's eyes and ears are us; everything we want to be and more. It grounds us, sends us soaring and unleashes the ultimate you. So watch and listen; don't become trapped within yourself, let the inner voice and vision free.

04/Jul/2008

Society & Lifestyle
What would you do with a million pounds?

What Would I do With Millions of Pounds?

So, I've won millions of pounds or earned it through selling a cracking idea or business; what would I do with my new-found wealth? Needless to say, I've now made myself, parents and siblings comfortable for life. I have distinguished between my needs and wants, and drawn up my budgets and plans for future use of the money. I would not advertise the fact that I was now more affluent to avoid making rash decisions under undue duress from various individuals and organisations. My monetary policies and priorities would be my personal decision alone.

I would invest some money. I am a big believer in space exploration, robotic and manned, and with funding falling for sciences in Britain and with budgetary cuts in space agencies I would lend a private hand. Space exploration in the future would be a private-public adventure and I would want to be at the forefront of new challenges and missions in space. I might even buy a ticket to be onboard a private suborbital flight. Seeing Earth from space would be absolutely priceless.

I would also invest in green technology, especially solar power and strive to set up large solar farms. Any company I set up to achieve this would be publicly owned and operated in such a way that any profit would be returned to the community and not to disinterested share-holders. I would also consider the flip side; the oil companies, the aircraft giants and bio-tech research. Should I invest with them to make money to be used for the greater good? Would the ends justify the means? Should I swim with the sharks in order to save the fish? Could I resist the temptation to fully immerse myself in the money market and forget about my goals? Maybe with the right incentive, I could, but would my money be tainted or my conscience clear? I would have to tread this ethical mine-field carefully.

I would also set up funds. I've been a down and out student, long-term unemployed, and have had to battle with various agencies who think you have unlimited friends, relatives or other means of bail-outs and paying off debts. The bureaucracy is ridiculous and these agencies only care about the bottom line: raking in their money -from you. I would trial my funding organisation on my friends first, by paying off their student loans, for free. Why? Because I could. And because there are people in this world who have worked damned hard to earn their degrees and/or to get a job, but now have a millstone around their neck in the form of crippling debts that decrease their chances for saving money and getting a job they like, but which forces them to get an undesirable job just to pay off debts. I would see how that funding system worked, and then roll out the funding opportunities for others on a case by case basis.

The idea of giving away money does seem strange, but if I'm set for life, invested in what I want to do and am interested in, then I see no reason to save that extra few millions for a rainy day. I can't take it with me; much of it will be invested or donated, so why not put it to good use. Money can't buy happiness, but it can make a difference, plus giving money away would keep my feet on the ground and someone else's dreams alive. If I have children, only some of it will be endowed to a trust and eligible at their maturity.

My parents and my own experiences have taught me the value of money. I know what I can live on and what I need. I've seen the money trap at work (the more you work, the more you spend, the more you have to earn) and have taken steps to strengthen my immunity to it. The millions of pounds I have would enable me to live a little, learn a lot and experience even more. I would work more part-time and volunteer more, write my books, and travel to expand my horizons. Yes, millions would be great, but greater still would be the pleasure in sharing that experience. As priceless as it would be travelling to outer space, the opportunity gifted to me in millions of pounds would enable me to strive to enrich my inner space.

19/Jul/2008

Reflections: Creativity
Brilliant in Solitude

2020 vision

Companion piece to 'The Genius That Is You' 06/Sept/2009 in this section below.

I am brilliant, if I say so myself. But so is everyone else in their own way. There are those intellectuals, actors, celebrities, sportsmen, businessmen, *et al*, who are successful by dint of serendipity, inheritance, intelligence or hard work, but the majority of us are never recognised, remembered through the ages, or acknowledged for our inputs during life.

But do you want to be publicly unveiled as the next big thing or do you, like me, prefer to hide your light under a bushel and plod on developing your own ideas, keeping them to yourself. Granted friends and family might know of your creativeness in thought, word and deed, and you might enjoy some local notoriety, but you like hugging the shadows in the background.

Does the prospect of 15 minutes of fame appeal to you or scare you? Would you rather be admired from afar or enjoy fame in anonymity? Do you want your life changed because of your own hard work ethic? I've been thinking about this for a very long time. For over 20 years, I've been writing stories (along with artwork), first for proposed comic books (which got rejected by publishers) which I later turned into a proposed series of sci-fi novels (again with sample chapters being rejected). Part of me doesn't mind, because the stories then stay mine, to work on and perfect, re-write and re-create. But I have also created, written, and submitted other book ideas, TV programmes (which received some positive feedback, but ultimately rejected), I write songs (which I can sing) and poems, 'designed' aircraft, started photographic projects, and built two websites to facilitate all my works and projects.

Yet my work is not publicly for show, mostly to do with protecting my intellectual property, but also because I like keeping myself and work to myself. It's nice when friends and family encourage your work (which you'd expect them too), but maybe ultimately I am afraid of rejection. After all, these projects are my inner self-expression on display, so does that mean if my ideas are rejected, that I am as a person, too? If my ideas are for me alone, do they remain successful, untainted creations in my eyes? As with many people, I am bursting with creativity and looking for outlets for my ideas. Maybe I have not found the right channels through which to distribute my ideas. I could self-publish or go freelance or hawk my wares on online share sites. Or maybe it is not yet my time, my ideas not yet at that developed stage to fully appreciate and profit from. I am the rough diamond waiting to be discovered.

I am self-critical, a perfectionist (subjectively), and can take constructive criticism and rejection, but if all my work is totally rejected, where does that leave me? Does it really matter what others think? Is it best to be brilliant in solitude or rejected in public? Whatever destiny holds for me I will know that I have tried my best, used my natural and honed abilities to think freely and creatively to make myself as brilliant as I am, as will you.

10/Oct/2008

Why Myths Endure

The Weaponisation of Myth

2020 vision

Right now, myths circulating around the Coronavirus pandemic are rife; from it origins, its existence, 5G propagation, anti-vaxxers, population control with nanobot vaccines, population control especially of BAMEs, fake cures, mask-phobics, the rise of the 'covidiots', and more. Rumours, myths, fake news, whatever, in this case comes from the mismanagement of the response to the outbreak by politicians. Or is that a myth? Come to think of it, myths are like viruses creating harmful outcomes and can be even deadlier than the actual virus. Whatever you believe of the above, take a deeper look. Explore the myth source, its route to the public, who spreads it and who benefits from it. And if you can dismiss it and go on with your life then do so. It will be interesting to see which of the myths above survive into the future.

'When memory dies a people die.'
'But what if we make up false memories?'
'That's worse, that's murder.' [1]

What are myths, but the false memories of mankind? But do myths desensitise us against reality or do they keep alive a half-remembered reality? How have the myths of the past affected us, how are they being generated today, and how will they influence our descendants? We can see this in four areas: Counterknowledge, finance, religion and climate change, before seeing how future myths could destroy us.

Counterknowledge:

I was reading a book called 'Counterknowledge' by Damian Thompson in which he argued against the spread of pseudoscience and pseudo-history being presented as fact[2]. Just recently, the myth that the Large Hadron Collider would create world-engulfing black holes caused a girl in India to commit suicide[3]. The 2012 myth is also a case in point mixing in the Mayan's end of their Great Cycle in that year with the predicted lining up of our solar system's planets; a coincidence that consumes a great deal of people's time in imagining the end of the world in some gravimetric cataclysm. But so it was with the previous Millennium Bug scare and tales of rampant nanotechnology grey goo. The Moon Landing, Princess Di, and 9/11 conspiracies and myths, though debunked by insiders and common sense, have continued to grow and become part of the fabric of history.

Such myths, if left unchecked, could undermine and destabilise whole communities and industries. Never happen? Then just look at the current financial crisis and the loss in belief in the myth of money.

The myth of money:
The value of money is based upon the mutual trust and belief that a piece of paper or metal has an intrinsic worth, so everyone believes that $1 equals whatever the powers-that-be says it does. The current global financial crisis reflects this with perceived values of companies, stocks and currencies plummeting, because the trust or faith in the monetary system collapsed. Myth can perpetuate belief; myth can destroy value. The myth of money construct was broken, because irregularities, bad practices, and management policies caused the breakdown in the myth that money was a constant valued and flowing commodity. Money can't just disappear from the system; its liquidity should ensure that it stays somewhere in the system, but the value of money can depreciate through sheer loss of confidence. The myth is so strong that when you hear the 'experts' speak, their pessimism seeps out and they have 'talked' themselves into a recession; they believed the myth that money has such overwhelming value and shared meaning, but if others do not share that belief then there will always be problems. Such wobbles will stay in the system for some time.

The myth of money is well known; whether it is the root of all evil or that it will never make us happy, but the myth will eventually bounce back because the myth of money is better to believe in than having no system at all; better the myth than anarchy; capitalism over egalitarianism. So you just don't need money to make money, you need the myth to believe that money has worth. Listen to the language of the 'experts' in the coming months and as it becomes more positive, so the myth of money will be reinforced and economies stabilise.

Religion:

Events from the bible have surely passed into myth, no matter how real they were in the past. It is the nature of oral and written traditions through the generations to change, be embellished, and accepted as fact. Just as events from a few decades ago have been spun into near 'mythicdom' with a myriad of theories and strands (e.g. Kennedy's Camelot and assassination, the moon landings, British Monarchy intrigues), the further back we go to Robin Hood, King Arthur, Jesus, Troy, Jericho, and the Garden of Eden, the less we know as fact, even through archaeological, historical and other scientific endeavours.

Intelligent Design (ID) has become the new myth to spin its way from religion in that it purports to be a science, yet uses none of the basics of science to prove itself. It's a 'theory' based on faith and in the myth of the Blind Watchmaker. The myth of (the one true) religion reveals itself in the fact that there are hundreds of religions with different interpretations of the same omnipotent being, yet there is no way to test to see which religious 'hypothesis' is correct (unless all but one religion dies out due to war, out-breeding, conversion, etc). So the myth becomes pseudo-fact and/or faith, which strangles reality into second place, even when proved otherwise (e.g. the Shroud of Turin, the Flood, and Noah's Ark on Mt. Ararat, etc).

The belief in the hereafter is also a powerful concept; people die for it. You won't see many scientists today on the parapets willing to sacrifice themselves for a scientific principle. But all the same, such faith and religious concepts are a suspension of reality; a 'mythality'. To believe in a life beyond reality is a myth. However, just as religion is myth writ large, science is just as mythologically inclined. It can take nature away from man so that man neglects and destroys the environment around him in its pursuit of technology and progress. Scientific myth can obscure one's conscience, create its own dogma, and turn as inward as religion.

Climate Change:

The latest myth to haunt man is climate change. To some, the myth is whether it is actually happening, while to others it is how it can be resolved. In the larger picture, the fight against climate change perpetuates the myth that mankind is the pinnacle of evolution and cannot be destroyed, because of some divine right or fluke that led to our emergence. In the smaller picture, the preferred solution is based on (carbon) taxes and the perpetuation of the industries that caused the problems in the first place. Denial of climate change provokes counter accusations against the sceptic myths, both sides unwilling to bend their myths or meet halfway. The great myth of the 21st century is upon us; it's the classic grassroots campaign that turned into a global phenomenon, bordering on religious fanaticism, with the high priests of the IPCC pontificating to us, the congregation, on how to lead greener pious lives.

So is climate change the myth to forever enrich a green industry and scare us into submission? What if the techno-economic fix fails (due to exorbitant costs or general antipathy), but mankind survives (because there was nothing wrong in the first place or we just adapt to the changes)? The green industry wins either way. And we might never know how much time, energy and money was wasted in combating the green myth. The world would go on, but wouldn't such myths destroy humanity a little bit at a time? As people say: the bigger the lie; the more believable it is. Can the whole world really be duped into believing a myth just because we were told the world might end? Haven't we heard this before? Can we afford not to believe it? That is the power of myth.

The future:
So, to the future; what will myth bring to mankind? With all the myths and pseudo-histories going around now that people absolutely believe in, suppose in fifty years time when we are more technologically connected that a myth so strong sweeps through the human interlinked system, like a virus, and wipes us out? Such a 'weaponised' myth could be more potent than any epidemic or war, as belief is often stronger than fact. So we must beware the virus myth; the spread of unbelievable truths that threaten to destroy us. In a hundred years time, will people hear myths about the Unabomber and think that while he was crazy and violent (if that is not written out of history), he was correct in his thinking that man was moving toward a technological abyss and away from an organic relationship with the environment. Will our future delinquents see him as an 'eco-warrior' and flawed hero to be emulated? Our times are ripe with myths and our descendants will have a hard time picking out the truth from the myth.

The reality of myth:

While some myths are positive; reinforcing certain cultural tenets, all too often they will perpetuate a falsehood and a suspension from reality, whether in religion, economics, science, politics, and culture. 'What?' you say. 'That's the basis of civilisation?' Ah yes, myths are the very stuff of civilisation. Myth underpins everything we believe in, extrapolates from life's experience (e.g. entertainment, education, fashion, etc), colours our views (e.g. racism, stereotypes), brings war (The Nazi Aryan myth), creates belief systems (e.g. Judeo-Christian-Muslim, scientology, etc), and even reaches beyond death (e.g. heaven, hell and reincarnation). Myth lets man and civilisation cheat death, by believing in life after death or by perpetuating the ever-increasing mythologised memory of them.

Myth, unchecked, is the harbinger of death, a weapon of utter mass destruction. If we were told non-mythic news about the world, our lives would be irrevocably changed. Myths keep man in check. But with myth so intertwined in our lives, how can we survive its pervasiveness and destructive qualities? Well, first off, we can't (or is that a myth?). All we can do is limit our exposure to our modern myth-centred Babel and begin to think for ourselves. As a telly addict, an avid reader, and an infovore (a seeker and lover of knowledge for knowledge sake) that is hard to do. But I think; I think about things that may not seem connected, but are (as I'm into the myth of social physics), and I root those things in reality by asking questions; being the devil's advocate, and then writing it down for the whole world to see and question, to criticise or praise, to ignore or disseminate –the myth of the myth. Myth is an equal opportunity creator of order and chaos, so where you choose to place yourself on the myth-believing scale will influence its affect.

If truth is beauty; which is in the eye of the beholder, anything in that subjective realm is open is myth. Any truth, therefore, is susceptible to myth. Is ignorance bliss? Should we believe in the myths that order our world? Do myths make us happy or oblivious to the real world? Myths may be necessary to make humanity appear progressive and alive, while actually protecting us from the scary reality of reality? Our lives are myths within myths and the entangled web myths weave leave us trapped in a nether world of pseudo-realities. So, live the myth; but be aware. It is the danger inside us that we must keep in check, lest it destroy us all in a fit of epic proportions.

References:

1. Sivanandan, A.1997. *When Memory dies*. Arcadia: London, p.235.

2. Thompson, D. 2008. Counterknowledge. Atlantic Books: London.

3. http://news.bbc.co.uk/1/hi/world/south_asia/7609631.stm (link still active as of September 2020)

19/Jan/2009

Essays: Meaning of life

Carpet Marks

What is life about, really? Recently, as I entered my bedroom I noticed, more than before, a well-worn spot over in the corner by a cabinet. And for some reason the thought occurred to me that if I dropped dead what would people make of the trails in my carpet? What would those marks say about my life – my favourite spots in the living room, the best path to the bathroom, the frequency I used the stairs.

Would people deduce that the bare spot in my bedroom carpet was where I stood to sort the contents of the cabinet? Would others say it was where I stood to look out the window? Would others pronounce that I performed some kind of ritualistic ceremony there, hence the less dense patch? As it happens, the last reason would be correct. The bare spot is my alternate working out location –my habitual ritual. It's where I exercise when the downstairs neighbour is in, so I do not make too much noise. That spot represents one facet of my life. It's an important spot to me, but that meaning would be lost to everyone else. My carpet marks would count for nothing after I am gone. They would just be anonymous traces, just a regular feature in the fabric of life.

So what do I have to leave the world as my legacy? I have no children. I am not rich or famous. I've built no grand memorials or written or painted a masterpiece. I am but the sum of my mind, body, and soul. My path through life is marked by fleeting friendships, academic and career records, and internet traces, but I find that my carpet marks must also say a lot about my life and other paths I take. If the carpet marks could be examined in minutiae you would see my 'sidedness' (the preference to sitting down on the left or right hand side on a chair), my favourite side of the bed, the lack of footmarks where I avoided creaky floorboards, the central thoroughfares in the living room or to the bathroom. My private life revealed down to its threads.

So, what is life about really? Carpet marks can represent anything. Where are the carpet marks of your life? What would they say about your life?

Are your paths straight forward or have you had to take a detour to get to where you wanted? If you want to be rich and famous, you will still leave carpet marks in your luxury homes (or scuff marks on hardwood floors). Just make them count for something. If I was gone tomorrow, I would be proud of my carpet marks. They represent me, my life, and my paths. All I can do is to live well in this world and know that I left the best carpet marks that I could.

05/Feb/2009

Arts & Humanities
Essays: Why I write

Food for Thought

This is an ode to the UK show called 'MasterChef'. But I'm not a foodie. I am not really into creating food for pleasure, just survival. I probably couldn't name half the ingredients the wannabe chefs use. And my palate would not be sophisticated enough to savour the culinary delights on offer. Yet, I like watching this particular reality cooking show, something I would never have been caught dead doing a few weeks ago. So what is MasterChef's secret in attracting an unappreciative diner like me? Well, quite simply it reminds me of why I love writing.

First, the hosts John Torode and Gregg Wallace are gentleman chefs; none of the swearing, putdowns, and humiliating of eager chefs. They are honest in their assessments and criticisms, encouraging –not preachy, and who can forget John's cheesy grin when the winner is announced or Gregg giggling after tasting a contestant's dish that absolutely tickled his taste buds. It's an emotional show with real passion for cooking. Second, the contestant chefs themselves are a cut above the wannabe celebrities from other shows. They are here to cook. They want to master their skills, open restaurants, and change their lives. They are not hobbyists, but fervent professionals. Lastly, they show so much creativity in just the way they create their dishes, from the raw ingredients, pouring love into their creations, and producing basic gastronomic works of art.

I'm attracted to that creativity, not the food, for that will never be me. That is what draws me to MasterChef; the creativity, the passion, the energy, and the emotion. What they do to food, I want to do for words. I want to create food for thought. I want to gather the raw ingredients for articles and create a smorgasbord of words that leap off the page and fill the mind with alphabetic flavours. The 'foodsmiths' reminded me that everyone has talent in all facets of life, and mine is to be a wordsmith.

I want to cook literary masterpieces, serve them up to the public, and watch them enjoy the banquet. I want to create three-course articles featuring a well-flavoured intro, textured body, and digestible conclusion. Preparation is a key ingredient with the write utensils, a spread of poetry, a dash of alliteration, and no poison words, to whet the appetite of those who want a juicy read. There are so many recipes to writing, so many platter combinations to consider for the discerning connoisseur. There is no need to over-cook and burn the ears of others –Oh the smell of it. The only scent should be of crisp paper wafting as one turns the pages for the next course of deliciously laid-out morsels. I want people to have cheesy grins and giggle at the sugar rush of words that invade their minds. I want the emotion to show as I stir in added spice and sprinkle seasoning of aromatic prose upon the unsuspecting consumers. Then I want to finish up with a portion of pleasurable dessert that leaves the after-taste of thoughtful repose upon the reader. Writing is my comfort food, but luckily writing has no diet plan –it's all you can write for free.

So while MasterChef has not galvanised my taste buds, it has reinvigorated my obsessive hunger for creating and writing savoury feasts. I want to be a master 'wordchef', open my own 'wordrestaurant', and change my life. No other show, cooking or otherwise, has inspired me to be the best and create a cuisine of articles to feed the masses. Thank you, MasterChef: food for thought, indeed.

26/Feb/2009

The relationship between one's attitude and fate

What is Fate?

What is fate? No dictionary meaning can convey its deep meaning to the people who suffer under the weight of uncertain circumstance. Things happen for no reason, at random, and without warning. Fate knows no boundaries; it has no rules.

Young lives:
A Big Brother (UK) contestant, a boy eaten by crocodile in Australia, a youth knifed outside a train station in London: The fickle finger of fate strikes every second of the day affecting celebrities, the innocent, and ordinary people. Why? Is fate just a consequence of evolution, where Natural Selection is the arbitrary harbinger of eventual destruction and death? Jade Goody, 27, was a Big Brother contestant who was vilified and branded as ignorant and racist for her attitude. But all that changed when she was diagnosed with cancer a couple years ago; a minor celebrity now living her life in the public. If Jade Goody had not been famous, we would not know of her suffering and imminent death, one out of millions afflicted with cancer. Did she get cancer because of her new lifestyle of fame? Would fate have treated her differently if she had never stepped into the Big Brother house? Fate has turned Jade Goody into a cause celebre.

Across the world in Australia, a five year old boy was eaten by a crocodile. His parents worked in a Crocodile-spotting business for eco-tourists for the protected beasts. But their young son fell prey to one. Is this some punishment upon the parents for their choice of work? What reason can there be for this tragedy? What events led to this fateful encounter? Could it have been avoided or is there only one path in life that had the boy escaped, another accident would have befallen him? For the religious –where is God's plan in this? Why does God supposedly work in mysterious ways? Does everything really happen for a reason? What kind of reason is there for a child to die at the hands of a wild beast, except to cause unending grief for family and friends? Fate is a cruel master.

In east London, a 17-year old teenager was stabbed to death outside a train station in a suspected case of gang rivalry. The incident is by no means isolated, nor a special case to Britain. Throughout the world people are killed for a multitude of reasons. Can no one expect to live their lives free from threat of harm or death? Killing seems to be random; an act of complete irrationality, whether accidental or deliberate. We cannot wrap ourselves in cotton wool or flee the world, or live in absolute seclusion. There seems to be no Right to Life any more either through natural means or from man-made terror. There is no defence against being in the wrong place at the wrong time. Life is a lottery now; sometimes you'll live 'til 100, other times life will be interrupted and punctuated, with no warning, no reason, and no sympathy. What could these three young people have ultimately achieved? What will the world miss? Do we even care? There are six billion plus people in the world; fate has a plan for us all.

Unforeseen circumstances:
You don't even have to get out of bed to be hit by fate. In Buffalo, NY, an iced-up commuter plane crashed into a house killing all 49 on board and one on the ground. The solitary death on the ground seems tragic even amongst those on the plane. It's an unusual death, but fate has its ways. Were decisions made by that person to stay in or to go out later? What were the chances of a plane crashing into the house against, say, a meteorite hitting or being struck by lightning? Did the people on the plane buy tickets in the last moment or were they long-held plans? How many flights had they each taken before in safety? What were the chances of a crash in those bad weather conditions versus mechanical failure in good conditions? Contrast that flight against the celebrated 'Hudson River' plane crash, which certainly skimmed across Fate's face. Would another pilot have saved the day so spectacularly? Will this be the crew's and passengers' only brush with death? Was it the pilot's destiny to be the hero (destiny seemingly the positive side to fate)? Flying, as one always hears, is still the safest mode of travel, but with fate as life's pilot, what chance do we have of landing safely? Fate is revenge for living.

Lost potential:
From aborted children, to the disabled and sick, have unused and potential fates been altered? Are various disabilities there to be overcome for success in life? Is this the purpose of fate? How can we go through life like this? Life throws a curveball and you have to deal with

it. There have been great figures from history and today who have been struck by debilitating illness (e.g. President Franklin Roosevelt, Prof. Stephen Hawking, and Muhammad Ali), but there are untold millions suffering in silence and obscurity; their fate decided by class, race, wealth, age, nationality, etc. Fate is an equal opportunity wrecker of lives. If the 'normal' cannot escape fate, then what chance for the less fortunate? Fate is the ultimate tester of life, it's how you deal with it that reveals the human in essence. What about those that don't get to live? What about aborted fate? There must be a world of unborn souls, living in existential limbo. Are they forever doomed by fate or do they achieve their destinies in another spiritual life? What fate conspired to see them never born: the hard decisions, the guilty secrets, or the unwanted reminder? We will never know what fate had in store for them. Fate hates. Fate is inevitable. We cannot fight fate; it is the stuff of universal life.

Future Fate?

Can we cheat fate? Can we create a computer program to predict fate? Scientists think that underlying the unpredictability of quantum mechanics might be a layer of predictability. What does this say about free will? Is there only one outcome to life no matter the path taken? If we found the controls to fate, what would we do? Would we use it as a weapon against others? Would we create an accident-free world or use it for personal gain or to bring peace to the world? The 'fate machine' would make a time machine redundant as we could control events without travelling through time. We could weave our own futures, free from happenstance and error. But would that be any life to live? Where would the unpredictable fun be in that, the challenge, the love of life, if fate were banished? As much as we hate fate, its control over us and the misery it inflicts, fate can bring people together —to live in hope that a better destiny is upon us, before we succumb to fate's vengeful grasp.

06/Sept/2009

How to think like a genius

The Genius That is You

2020 vision
Companion piece to 'Brilliant in Solitude' 19/Jul/2008 in this section above.

Everyone is a genius in their own way, from the first person ever to build a fire or to make the wheel, or to inquisitive babies who learn to build with bricks for the first time. It's that combined spark of unmatched intelligence and imagination, that innate ability to think beyond others, the instinct or intuition to act upon those thoughts, and the capability or authority to be able to persuade others of your genius status. These thoughts may occur in one explosive brainwave or filter through after decades of research and study, but at the core of any genius is an idea. So how does one begin to think like a genius, without being an actual genius (whether by strict IQ definition or perceived as by your peers)? There are several things that could be done to enhance your thought processes to genius level:

Prepare yourself:
Just as with any athlete, the brain also needs to be trained and fed the right kinds of fuel (whether food, knowledge, or meditation, etc.) to be able to function at its peak. A healthy diet of ideas benefits the heart, mind, and soul (as each had its function in the idea process). If you want to think like a genius, you have to think you can think like a genius. Know your mind and its capabilities. Have that self-belief in yourself and your ideas.

How do you think?
There are many philosophies, creative waves, and diverse modes of thinking. Sometimes methodical linear thoughts are not always the best. Chaos can be cool. Channel stress and anger to drive your thoughts and focus your mind. Be counter-intuitive, think outside the box, or be the Devil's advocate. Think in imaginary circles or from dreams. Reality is

not the only thought plane. Be that different person; think, feel, and act differently to thinking patterns and ideas. Push those ideas beyond their limits and use that extreme ideas boundary as your default idea setting. Genius ideas inhabit the outer realm of standard thought. Geniuses are not conservative thinkers.

When to think:
Owls versus Larks; this author is a "nite owl"; the best thoughts and energy to think coming at night. Others think best early in the morning. Use your natural circadian rhythm and figure out when your best thinking time is. There is no real benefit in pushing through half-hearted or poorly thought-out ideas when the brain is still sleeping. Thinking can also come from energetic moments as oxygen cycles around the brain, so think when walking, cycling, or exercising. But always be in the good habit of thinking.

Processing thoughts:
There are three different kinds of people in the world; those who react, those who are pro-active, and those who are counter-active. Genius involves being pro-active. Be an "infovore": a seeker of knowledge just for the sake and love of knowledge. Soak up knowledge and use it creatively; be versatile, and always have an answer, even if it is not the one you were seeking. Be authoritative in disseminating your thoughts (not arrogant or a show-off), but let others know the grand measure of your mind. Remember, ideas are the heart of genius, and to sell ideas, you have to make ideas. Once the idea comes to fruition, you have to have a coherent vision for its presentation to others. And this is the stumbling block for many would-be geniuses.

Putting it all together:
As mentioned, everyone is a genius at some point in their lives, but either the thinker didn't realise it, or others did not realise it, or the thinker could not make the connection to the greater world to reveal their genius. Genius is having the right idea at the right time and in the right place. There is no point in having a genius idea whose time has not come or the application/idea has passed its sell-by date. Genius is the ability to connect all their ideas into that one capsule of demand (need for the idea), supply (ability to sell the idea), marketability (ability to promote/package idea), and profit (whether monetary or otherwise). Genius is capital.

The capital of genius:
Thinking like a genius is a commodity, but not always in the modern sense of financial markets. Genius capital can be academic, spiritual, medical, political, cultural, etc, as genius spans the human gamut of civilisation. Yet despite all the Mensa members and IQ tests, school over-achievers and high earners, there are only a few geniuses who are lauded above all others as true geniuses. This is because they surpassed all the above points. They had that innate spark, the creativity, and that genius capital of mind-and-space-bending ability to convince and shock their contemporary worlds with their genius ideas. Their time had come and they took it.

Genius is a combination of many attributes. It may be an accumulation of test results, but many of the past geniuses even from pre-history never took such tests. Genius transcends man-made tests; genius creates its own tests and resolves them, and in doing so re-creates or re-imagines the world around us. Now that's genius.

08/Jan/2010

The benefits of kinetic thinking

Kinetic Thinking

2020 vision

I still love a good think while walking or jogging. It just frees up my mind and de-stresses me. While thinking of the title for this book, kinetic thinking came to mind, as did carpet marks, big pictures, and brilliance, but Infovore was a natural fit. But maybe I can coin the above term as an original invention by myself.

While some people may be advised to sleep on an idea, others, like myself, are the opposite. We get the best ideas whilst on the move, whether walking, working out, moving to music or even just standing about. I call it kinetic thinking.

A good walk is always a great motivator of thinking. The clatter of music from iPods would be an annoying inconvenience, compromise concentration, and ruin your attention and inspiration to what is around you. Not only is walking good physical exercise, but it is also conducive for a good mental workout and an aid in relieving stress, which unlocks dreaded 'thinker's block'. The pace of walking seems to stimulate the vividness of the ideas, too. And jogging positively provides an endorphin rush, which inspires and pushes good ideas to the forefront. Kinetic thinking is a constant stream of conscious thought activated through motion.

The same is true when working out or dancing. Not only do better visual ideas come with frantic motion, but I also write somewhat more rhythmically to the music; the flow of music, usually riff-driven songs, also bringing out the emotion of the idea and creating more energy. The repetitiveness of physical work outs or dancing can also help the brain remember and reinforce ideas through association with that particular physical action. There are stories I have written where a soundtrack in my mind replays every time I read the story. Other stories are linked through kinetic motion; their compositions flooding back much easier, when needed.

Even while standing, the intellectual juices are still flowing. This may be connected to the fact that you burn more calories while standing than sitting and a good brainstorming session would add to the calorie count. You're trying to maintain balance, run motor functions, stay alert to your surroundings (if standing while at work), expend nervous energy, or you are just a fidgety person. There is an energy to standing and thinking; a sharpness of thought when contemplating alone and on the hoof.

Ideas may come while dreaming, day dreaming, or sitting, but they are usually augmented after some kinetic motion as the stray thoughts sifts through the awakened brain. The thought process seems easier to form, more flowing, and unencumbered when there is physical activity. If writing by hand after clear kinetic thoughts occur, the writing struggles to keep up with the idea and the result is a messy page of scribbles. Kinetic thinking can be chaotic, random in timing, and not easy to connect together. You may be on the move when an idea beckons, but there is nothing structured to write on and memorising even half of it is a job well done. Unlike a note pad by the bedside table when an idea strikes, kinetic thinking entails a great deal of memorisation until the notepad, computer, or ink-on-hand notations take shape. Kinetic thinking is a state of mind, an active and manic mind, constantly striving to create, develop, and share the best idea possible.

Kinetic thinking is a proactive process rather than a reactive one. A fit mind needs a fit body and vice versa. Kinetic thinking is the workout the mind needs. There are many so-called 'brain games', which involves a counter-active, sedentary activity while 'training the brain'. But these games won't work for everyone; not people who think best on the move. So, why not get up and naturally train the brain to think while in motion? Use your brain differently and be inspired by kinetic thinking.

01/Aug/2010

Philosophical views on humanity's sense of global awareness

Mary Shelley's Antennae of the Race

2020 vision
I love reading books with little nutmegs which inspire me to think and write something about it, like the geek and science fanboy I am.

In the book 'Seeing Further – The story of science and the Royal Society', a contributing author, Maggie Gee, references a quote (c. 1826) from Mary Shelley about man being 'the antennae of the race.' It is a strange quote, but what does this mean? How can man be the antennae of his own race? This has such a deep meaning and consequence for our well-being and survival that it is well worth exploring as we acknowledge our antennae's existence.

What are antennae?
Antennae are the sensory organs of Arthropods (insects, arachnids, and crustaceans) though they have differing and sometimes ambiguous functions for different species. Antennae can be used to sense touch, air motion, heat, vibration/sound, smell and taste. So in what sense can man have antennae? How are they used? Man's antennae evolved as they grew from hunters to explorers, farmers, and urbanites. They built social networks as their antennae became attuned to accept and trust others, to read the way of the world's machinations, and to be content in themselves. Man's antennae are no less remarkable than an arthropod's.

Shelley's antenna:
In Shelley's pre-industrial world antennae would have referred to the animal instincts of Man's primitive brain constantly feeling for new wonders and territory to explore and exploit. Western explorers and men of science were creeping around the world discovering, experimenting, documenting, and dominating. Their perceived superior human nature entitled them to swarm over and conquer all before them. These antennae twitched with a thirst for knowledge and power and sought out all such sources for their wealthy royal nests.

Shelley's 1826 antennae were feeble and underdeveloped. Man could hardly have been attuned to his neighbour let alone his own race. The race of man's antennae were skewed toward the west at this time. Any feeling or sensitivity to another culture was detuned from the antenna and only certain cultural, financial, military, and political channels worthy of listening to were picked up. Even then it was realised that humans were flawed and dislocated from nature and themselves. And throughout the centuries nothing much has changed.

Our 21st century antennae:
Far from Shelley's 1826 antennae, our 21st century instinctual antennae are even worse off than our ancestors'. We are engaged in the wholesale destruction of true antennae -the arthropods and other indicator species- which help regulate our world. Long before climate change, man's technological antennae were destroying ourselves without being attuned to each other and the world. We have insensitive and wilted senses. We create and gather crossed signals, transmit the wrong codes in the raw and in imperfect nonsense. No wonder our confused antennae are quivering in conflict between instinct and technology.

In the future, our antennae will become more desensitised to the race of man in the face of and wake of human-caused and natural disasters. Long before we meet our Andorian cousins in space and share our antennaed-affinity, we humans may be long gone. We have no feeling for our race. Our antennae cannot survive in our dumbed-down world. We don't want to admit we are automatons while we attempt to create machines with their own antennae —our surrogate antennae. We have lost touch with the world; our antennae poisoned by the ills we have inflicted upon ourselves.

Man's antennae are now so internalised they only engender a self-absorbed life even when out in the wide world. Beyond our antennae's senses is a blurred sense of reality. We can no longer perceive the danger we are causing to the world, let alone know how to react to it. There's no case for fixing the world as it is not the world that needs fixing, but man's antennae and his ability to sense his environment clearly. As we know from our technological endeavours, antennae are very hard to fix and retune. Man will stumble on as best he can through the fuzzy static landscape forever hoping that his antennae are probing in the right direction. If we cannot develop new antennae and become more externally aware then we will squander that genetic inheritance to the detriment of our race and our world.

Source:
Gee, M. 2010. The End is at hand. In: 'Seeing Further - The story of science and the Royal Society' (Bill Bryson, ed.). London: HarperPress, p. 404-423

25/Oct/2010

Reflections: What future myths will the 21st century leave?

Myths From the 21st Century

2020 vision

With rampant fake news, conspiracies theories, a rapidly digitalising world, and pandemic-driven craziness, god help future archaeologists and anthropologists in interpreting our complex world...

After watching the highly-stylised, fantasy-adventure film '300' which re-imagined the historically-real brave Spartans' stand at Thermopylae against the Persian horde in 480BC, there was a moment of reflection. This tale of an important historical event is two thousand, five hundred years old, one of many incredible events that have been mythologised down the ages. We keep plundering our ancient history for tales of heroics and morality, recycling the themes and characters to suit our generation. But what myths will our time leave to the future? In the year 4510 what tales from the atomic age will survive?

Climate change:

How many cities will be lost to climate change sea level rises and become the new Atlantises? Future archaeologists could be diving off forgotten coastlands and digging for mythological sand-covered cities in the new deserts. Indeed, will climate change turn out to be a myth after all and just a blip on a longer trend of environmental change? Will Climate change and other disasters, man-made or natural, lead to a new Dark Age where technology has been disrupted and man is once again the holder of all knowledge? A new dawn of myths from the technological age could ensue.

Epic battles:

The Gulf Wars will be even more heroically dramatised, as is the case with the Greek/Persian Wars. President Bush, Saddam Hussein, and Osama Bin Laden may become the chief protagonists in 9/11 in a new world Clash of the Titans epic. Surely, the twin towers being on fire and collapsing and the conspiracies surrounding it will survive in some form, oral/written/visual and take on a symbolism all its own. Akin to the Tower of Babel, the Twin Towers may take on the mantle of Man's battle over morality, justice, and the clash of civilisations.

261

The new seven wonders:
What in the next two thousand years will be our biggest lost monuments or ultimate architectural survivors for posterity to ponder over – a collapsed super bridge or caved-in tunnel? Perhaps a buried city lost to the ravages of ocean, sand, or ice? If New Orleans had been abandoned after Hurricane Katrina, would it have been swallowed by the waters and forgotten in time? How many villages will be lost and forgotten under hydroelectric dam projects to power the new megalopolises? We inherited the Great Pyramid, the last of the original wonders, but which of ours will archaeologists of the future find under 'X' marks the spot?

Heroic champions:
Just as the ancient worlders had their mythical champions, could any of our own sportsmen, celebrities, or explorers be immortalised in myth? Will any rival Hercules (Muhammad Ali?), or Hermes (Usain Bolt?), Athena (Oprah?), Aphrodite (Princess Diana?), Apollo (Elvis?), Icarus (Yuri Gagarin?), The House of Troy (The Kennedy family?), or Helen of Troy (Marilyn Monroe?). The adventures of King Arthur and Robin Hood may have been based upon real people, but even our fictional creations, like Sherlock Holmes and James Bond, could become de facto histories of the forgotten past. Our descendants could still be telling tales of our champions and heroines for centuries to come.

Space myths:
As man moves back out into space to the Moon and Mars, will new myths take form such as a revitalised interest in the supposed pyramids and the Face on Mars? What myths from the original moon landings will remain? By then, people should believe that Man did indeed land on the moon once they see Neil Armstrong's footprint on their tours from lunar hotels. But will Little Green (or Grey) men in UFOs still inhabit the imagination or will a new stripe of alien materialise?

Religious and Techno myths:
Will there still be a God or will the supernatural finally be stripped of its veil? The mythical Gods of old were abandoned when the Judeo-Christian-Islamic tradition arose and thus another will appear to supplant the mythical religion of the Atomic Age. Perhaps even an alien one.

Cold fusion may have been as mythical as a perpetual motion machine, but technological progress could still create the myths which will always pervade the world as science becomes more magic-like and for profit. Two thousand years from now, instead of vampires, werewolves, and Frankenstein; grey goo, human clones, and Frankenstein foods could be the new menaces hiding in the shadows?

Internet myths:
Will Microsoft be a footnote in history or continue as the OS of the universe –the hidden force behind The Matrix? Perhaps the internet's capacity to debunk myths will kill off the modern mythological age. Most of the old myths were oral tales told for generations and then written down in epic tomes. Our new internet age ruins the mystique for modern myths as there's no time for stories to resonate with the public, before the next big story comes along. Is our history now too-well documented that it cannot be allowed to slip into myth? Even modern urban myths are being investigated and exposed as such. Everything is under digital scrutiny that the extraordinary becomes mundane and we will never be an innocent civilisation again with anonymous tales of derring-do being our only form of historical news. Our epic Age of Myth could be over.

Whether in a post-apocalyptic or climate-changed world or a stable mature world or a star-faring race, will tales of people and events from the 21st century still be told by the humanity of the future? Would we still need myths? Myths are powerful agents of civilisation. They inform us in a novel way about events from the past. Myths are incredibly resilient and inspiring, but at some point the Spartans will have to give way to the new myths of the 21st century.

21/Nov/2010

Philosophy
Chaos theory and sociology

Chaos: The Law of Unintended Attraction

2020 vision
I frighten myself sometimes. Keep looking up at the skies. It could happen!

There you are sitting at your desk. It's peaceful and you have a little time to read or catch up on your to-do list. Then all of a sudden there's someone in front of you with several deliveries, the phone rings at the same time, and another person comes over with an emergency only you can handle; all this and you suddenly have the urge to go to the loo. That's chaos. It only lasts ten minutes or so and then it is quiet again for a couple of hours before another chaotic quarter-hour arises. How and why does this happen?

People like to talk about the Law of Attraction: like attracts like. This incorporates Cosmic Ordering and positive thinking. Basically, you make the world around you. But now think about the opposite Law of Unintended Attraction and the chaos that brings. You are at work or home, relaxing or doing your own work and a series of unrelated events converge at one time and one point centred around you. You have not caused it or wanted it, but you have unwittingly become a convergence point, an attractor, for several key moments in space and time.

Think about it. At the desk where you work, you may be by yourself or one of many in an office in an inconsequential job and/or building. A courier has journeyed across town from his depot at the mercy of any traffic before he reaches you. A staff member or guest in the building has chosen to call about a pressing issue and after several transfers of varying lengths of time; the call comes through to you as the courier arrives. Your manager decides (s)he needs your immediate attention now. Oh, and you've drunk too much coffee and need to visit the restroom, just as all the other events come together. What are the chances of all those seemingly random factors coming together at one random moment in your day?

In reality, there is no such thing as randomness. Even randomness has a pattern, no matter how long it takes to repeat. The events around you are not random, but a pattern that would be hard to discern in the few hours or days you are at work. It could take a lifetime or more of meticulous recording to make sense of the chaos that surrounds you. Every factor would have to be accounted for like weather, traffic, demographics, geography, biochemistry, online ordering habits, delivery schedules, mealtimes, among other things, but most importantly –that most ephemeral thing- human capriciousness.

Humans bring about their own Law of Unintended Attraction. It is not a wished-for experience and can be made worse by negative thinking. When unrelated events start to gravitate toward you, they can accumulate and increase the pressure upon you. You have two choices: explode under the extreme pressure or go with the flow. The first option is undesirable. It may be best to focus on each new concurrent influx of work in a positive manner until they become separate micro-events floating around you. This will dissipate any pressure, enabling you to handle each event in your own time.

In other words: don't stress. The Law of Unintended Attraction does not last long, unless you are very unlucky or you are unknowingly making yourself the focus of such unwanted attention. Most macro-chaotic systems (e.g. climate, population, disease, traffic, etc,) crash spectacularly when their parameters reach breaking point. But what happens to you at your desk or in life is a clash of micro-chaotic systems centred just on you. These are eddy currents of the macro-chaotic system; blips in the ordered world. We are all walking talking chaos systems and we take our chaos around with us everywhere. We butt up against other chaotic systems and with six billion such systems in the world, surviving in a vast natural chaotic system, there are bound to be moments in the continuum where your own personal chaos system is affected. And it is out of your control.

So, think about this. You are sitting at your desk. The morning rush is over and you have a few quiet minutes to yourself. Three hundred million years ago, a piece of rock began a slow journey through the cosmos and after several million gravitational nudges to its orbit slows down and lines up on an insignificant, small, blue planet. Your urge to visit the restroom arises after your morning coffee; just as your phone rings. You wonder whether to answer it or to tend to your urge. After a breathtaking plummet through the atmosphere at thousands of degrees and surviving as a blazing fragment of itself, the meteor crashes through the building and onto your desk. Were you there or not? Did that space rock have your name written on it three hundred million years ago? In all that time, all that space, the Law of Unintended Attraction will bring together the most unlikely sets of chaos systems.

The Law of Unintended Attraction is blind, affecting anything and everything as it slips through the depths of space and time, unimpeded. It weaves chaos systems together, from all walks of life, from near and far; some stay entangled and others drift apart. The chaos of life is not beautiful to behold, but it has a complex attractiveness, all the same. The Law of Unintended Attraction will drive you crazy as you ponder its reality and machinations, but you will not leave this life without being in its thrall.

Politics

22/Dec/2007

Politics, News & Issues
Politics, News & Issues (Other)

21ST Century Visions

2020 vision

Who would be on this list now? Certainly Elon Musk. Jeff Bezos? Barack Obama? Greta Thunberg? Sir David Attenborough? Lewis Hamilton? Who are the dark horses? And to think, as seen below, Facebook had just exploded onto the scene. But is social media really a leader for a more positive and enlightened future?

Who are the people or organisations that are already leading the way in this youthful century? They are not just politicians, entrepreneurs, scientists and beneficial organisations, these people are setting new agendas for a future in an enlightened world. How did they come to envision a different world? These new ideas and radical concepts are driving through these new 21st century visions. Who is at the heart of new century thinking?

Here is my list, but it is by no means exhaustive (and in no particular order):

Politics

AL GORE: The global face of Climate Change consciousness. An award-winning catalyst, focal point and own force of nature. Whether just the figurehead for climate change awareness or a perennial dark horse in American politics, Al Gore's voice will be heard by billions that it is a time for change.

SIR RICHARD BRANSON: Business tycoon, adventurer, co-initiator of The Elders with singer Peter Gabriel, and creator of Virgin Galactic. Mentioned below, both The Elders and Virgin Galactic could herald bold new eras for politics and space travel, revitalising ailing institutions and driving forth industries for the future. Branson differs from other businessmen in his energy and willingness to step forward and embrace new opportunities other businessmen and politicians would shy away from.

THE ELDERS: The formation of this new independent political force went almost unnoticed in 2007, yet they could be the prelude to a new world political movement. Elected from elder statesmen from around the world, headed by Nelson Mandela, The Elders are an impartial group that could mediate and troubleshoot in certain global situations. But could this undermine the various UN councils? And if successful in the long run, could they replace the unwieldy UN and become the legitimate and dominant global political force themselves? Current members include: Desmond Tutu, Jimmy Carter, Muhammad Yunus, Graca Machel, Ela Bhatt, Lakhdar Brahimi, Li Zhaoxing, Kofi Annan, Mary Robinson, Gro Brundtland, Fernando H. Cardoso, with an empty chair for Aung San Suu Kyi.

Biology

J. CRAIG VENTER: Biologist and genomics pioneer on the threshold of creating synthetic organisms that create among other products synthetic fuels. Venter is likened to the next Bill Gates, with his Microsoft-like grip on a future industry based on synthetic forms of life. But his ambition and controversial biological projects could ultimately create new industries for new energy creation, storage and waste disposal as well as new medical advances.

RAY KURZWEIL: Futurist who envisions the synthesis of human and machine to create the Singularity by mid-century. Is technology becoming so advanced that we may one day have to merge with it to escape extinction? What does it mean to be human? Is it just flesh and blood or are we more than the sum of our parts? Kurzweil has been asking these questions for decades, but within the next half-century, we may see the emergence of a new kind of human. Images of the Borg aside, the next few decades could see if we are in the century of genetics, as Venter sees it, or of the cyborg.

Space

BURT RUTAN: Aircraft designer behind Spaceship One, the first privately owned spacecraft to enter space, financed by Microsoft's Paul Allen. Spaceship Two, its successor, will be sponsored by Sir Richard Branson and be part of the Virgin Galactic fleet. Other private space rocketeers include Armadillo's vertical take-off/vertical landing vehicle, XCOR's EZ-Rocket, Elon Musk's SpaceX, Starchaser and the Canadian Arrow. These new rocketeers are on the threshold of a new revolution in space.

ROBERT ZUBRIN: President of the Mars Society, a group that advocates missions to and colonisation of Mars. With their popular world-wide conferences, political lobbying and Mars research stations, the Mars Society is gaining the ear of NASA with a far more sustainable way of reaching the red planet.

PETER DIAMANDIS: the founder and CEO of the X Prize Foundation, created the multi-million dollar award for the first team to achieve a set goal, chosen by the X Prize Foundation, which has the potential to benefit humanity through competitive and entrepreneurial spirits. The X Prize's first success was the $10 million Ansari X Prize. On October 4, 2004, the Mojave Aerospace Ventures team, led by Burt Rutan, won the Ansari X PRIZE with Spaceship One. New X Prizes include revolutions in the medicine, energy, automotive, education, environmental, and social arenas.

SPACE TOURISTS: the 'thrillionaire' pioneers. On April 28, 2001, Dennis Tito became the first fee-paying space tourist when he visited the International Space Station (ISS) for seven days. He was followed in 2002 by South African computer millionaire Mark Shuttleworth. The third was Gregory Olsen in 2005, a trained scientist. On September 18, 2006, Anousheh Ansari, an Iranian America, became the fourth space tourist or spaceflight participant. On April 7, 2007, Charles Simonyi, an American billionaire of Hungarian descent, joined their ranks.

All four members of this group are contributing in their own way to privatising space and driving down the costs for the likes of you and me for future spaceflight. The commercialisation of space would free up government funding for more earthly pursuits, while the private sector got on with the business of exploring and opening new frontiers.

Environment

BJORN LOMBORG: a latter-day James Lovelock? Once of a green persuasion, Lomborg is now part of a questioning and sceptical movement into the agendas of certain green organisations and the task required to combat climate change. This is not about dissent in the face of climate change, but about the way in which the message comes across and Lomborg, though controversial, has alternative and legitimate ways of dealing with climate change.

11) **THE GLOBAL CROP DIVERSITY TRUST**: Cary Fowler, executive director of the Trust and the Norwegian Government set up the Arctic seed vault on the Svalbard Islands. The seed bank was built to safeguard crop diversity in the event of a global catastrophe. This is a far-reaching event in the face of climate change, though is another 'hidden' news item in the media glare of celebrity.

Social

12) **FACEBOOK**: Love it or loathe it, is this the future of online networking or a flash in the pan before another social revolution? I listed Facebook rather than its 2004 creator Mark Zuckerberg due to ongoing court case regarding Facebook's origins. It may not be the biggest or most popular networking site, but its explosion in members has mesmerised the public and alarmed media minds to the power of social interactivity and business, especially with its controversial advertising plans. Facebook could be this century's successor to Google, Amazon, PayPal, Ebay, and other e-companies.

These then are the individuals and groups with the vision and drive to create century spanning visions, images and technologies. They have succeeded in firmly implanting their brands and brains into this century. This is a very westernised list, besides a few group members. Who else from around the world would be global leaders in their fields for the 21st century?

18/Jan/2008

Politics, News & Issues – [Third party sponsor name]
Can the US Military be effective in nonmilitary efforts to revive a war-battered community?

U.S. Military Effectiveness in Non-Military Operations

Note - The title was endorsed in part by a third party organisation on Crisis Reporting.

Can the US military be effective in non-military efforts to revive a war-battered community? Yes, it can. The U.S. military has been, is and will be always at the front in such situations because it is in the military's interest to revive war-battered communities to such a degree that security of the community is enhanced, private and humanitarian agencies can then move in to work and the military can leave. We have seen this from past conflicts, but the nature of conflicts since the Cold War has changed and so has the military response, both in military and non-military terms.

As a former member of the British Army, I have experienced such non-military operations and I am sure that parallels can be drawn to the U.S. military. One such military unit that performs non-military operations are the Engineers. They are first in; last out, and can build permanent or temporary structures like shelters, runways, roads, schools, and hygienic spaces, etc. Other Logistic units can bring in transport, tents, food, clothing and other supplies for refugees, locals and other war-affected communities, etc. This can be achieved on the ground, through air drops or by sea.

All around the world, from recent and current war zones like the Balkans, Afghanistan, Iraq, Central America and Ethiopia, and also in Indonesia (after the tsunami) and Pakistan (after the Earthquake) among others, the U.S. military has provided non-military services to support these areas in a crisis. Some of the affected communities could be in areas of military or cultural sensitivity that could degrade into local hostilities, so a military presence would be needed.

The military could provide medical facilities, first aid, humanitarian aid and supplies to war ravaged areas. They would be the only effective organisation capable of delivering such supplies and services in dangerous areas. Hearts and Minds campaigns during less turbulent times could include recreational time, setting up playing fields or games with locals and economic possibilities by buying or trading in local shops. Such activities could act to lessen stress and encourage mutual trust.

In post-war scenarios, the military could be the only security around and may have to fill in for police, fire and other emergency services and provide training for local security and protection of the local populace. Communication networks could also be provided to coordinate aid efforts. For any media/news reporters present either embedded or independent, they could broadcast news from secure locations and gain a better perspective of conditions on the ground in order for local, national and international communities to know what is occurring.

All the above operations would be possible and effective, because most jobs in the military are militarised civilian jobs. But the robustness and magnitude of the military would give them the initial advantage over civilian agencies in starting the process of revitalisation. But importantly, the planning of such operations has to be there first and not emerge as an ad-hoc operation or as mission creep. There has to be a proper implementation of resources pre-, mid- and post-war, so that any post-war operation is well-defined and well-equipped. The only problems would be politicisation of the aims, policies and direction of the efforts and also over extension of personnel.

The biggest reason why the U.S. military has to be effective is because America is the only nation that can respond globally in such a way and with the eyes of the world upon them; the pressure to perform is tremendous. When things go wrong, people question that effectiveness and forget all the good that the U.S. military has done. It is all the more appreciated, when the U.S. does assist when your own country needs help. So while the US military can be effective in non-military efforts to revive war-battered communities, the will to do so, the planning behind it and the wherewithal to see it fully through have to be absolutely resolute.

20/Jan/2008

Politics, News & Issues - Constitutional & Contract Law
The State of Britain Today

Great Britain's Place in the Modern World

2020 vision

Despite Brexit, political malaise, racial flare-ups, and now Covid-19, I still believe Great Britain has a bright future to look forward to. Why? Because of her people. Too many may believe in the self-fulfilling doom and gloom prophecies of the above issues, but many more will always strive to be better, to do better, to adapt, and learn. There is always pessimism about any current government in charge and the feeling of helplessness and the country going down the drain while the rich get richer and the poor poorer. And yes, things will probably get worse before getting better. It's inevitable.

Brexit is disruptive; it's a precedent-setting agenda, but necessary. And to be clear, these were my thoughts before Brexit was even an idea. In theory, this is the way I see it, as a naïve non-political expert. One should have the right to say 'no'; to be able to leave an organisation or contract like a marriage, work place, or a sports team. The UK said 'no' to the EU. There should then have been no issues with leaving. Britain was the head of an Empire once, with subjects and countries leaving or granted independence (some violently). Now the UK is part of a wannabe European Empire to rival the US, Russia, and China. But it's not needed, at least not in that present form. Outside of the EU's core of France, Germany and Belgium the surrounding countries are just feeders to another large-scale bureaucracy. It's fine to have inter-nation cooperation, but the EU isn't the answer. Europe isn't a nation to be ruled over as one. And the fact the EU bitterly resisted the UK leaving shows they valued our freedom of choice less than their own survival. Hardly democratic.

And that's the point - if the UK (or another country) can't be allowed to leave without rancour then the EU's remit is suspect. I think it's dangerous to say — 'why should we want to leave?' Without the right to exercise that choice then the EU is a dictatorship dressed up as a democratic union with no members able to leave (the same kind of supposed dictatorship people fear the UK is sliding into). Don't get me wrong. Not everything about the EU is bad; just like the Roman or British Empires, but you have to be attuned to member states and their wants and needs. The UK wants out and fighting against the UK leaving is a testament that the EU needs us more than we need them. It will be a while before the dust settles, but this leaves Britain with a choice in its future, for better or for worse. We have set the precedent. In theory and practice, one can leave EU membership.

In practice, however, the leave process has been chaotic, mostly because this action was not critically foreseen, treated seriously, and not addressed in detail within the treaty contract. The EU stacked the leaving process in its favour and the UK fell into its trap. The UK had no plan either. Both sides have acted with intransigence on leave details. Both want the upper hand, the moral superiority, and most importantly money in their pocket. The EU has always been more about trade and financial security for member states than anything else, sometimes to the detriment of other member or foreign states, companies and individuals. But when other countries leave there will be our precedent and hopefully the EU will behave better in their negotiations. Whether the UK rejoins the EU in the future or not remains to be seen. But while leaving to prove a point may seem churlish, it is an important touchstone in world history. Other nations (including Scotland) strive for their own independence or seek a catalyst for change. They will look back at the UK as an example.

However, Brexit has been coming for years. So-called experts have told people what to expect, mostly negative information about the affect to the economy and people have swallowed it. To them, Brexit is a cliff with no return. What these experts should have done was to inform and teach the government, companies, and individuals how to be agile, flexible, and resilient in the face of the Brexit cliff. As the saying goes 'if you're given lemons, make lemonade'. Brexit is a world-changing lemon, but no one seems to be willing or able to make or taste the lemonade. And that's to their detriment. Doing nothing is a defeatist attitude which goes against the natural Brit fighting spirit. Take advantage of the opportunities Brexit can afford. Others are telling you there aren't any. Are you just going to sit back and believe that or will you use your own intuition and talents to overcome another challenge?

The culture of Britain spreads across the world giving us a special relationship with many other nations. The UK has always has a unique and stand-offish relationship with the world, setting precedents, and being the outsider. And yet this is what draws admirers to our cause and land, despite their differences. While not forgetting the past, Britain has to forge a new future, re-invent itself. And in these uncertain times this will be the best test of our ability to not just survive, but to thrive.

And now to the article...

I believe that Britain is still a major player in world affairs today. There is much hand-wringing at such suggestions and uneasiness at expressing the pride we ought to in our country. Britain has been at the cross-roads of history for centuries and that will not end soon, acting today as a bridge between America, Eurasia and Africa. Britain has controversially dominated the pages of history, but there is no doubting that those past relationships have kept a majority of the world in touch with the departed nanny.

Britain's place in the world continues to be important, due mostly to the 'Anglosphere', those parts of the world that share the English language and culture, like America, Canada and Australia. The Anglosphere is old and new Britain with political, financial, military and social sway in their respective regions. The English language is spoken in almost all parts of the world and no matter which accent it is spoken in it is equated with England (and its former colony America), through the British Empire which spread the language through America, Africa, Asia and beyond.

Because of her past Empire and present Commonwealth, Britain has been host to thousands of immigrants from former colonies, but now sees migrants from non-Empire/Commonwealth countries in Eastern Europe and further afield in Russia and China. There are migrants from all kinds of cultural, economic and religious backgrounds, and out of all the countries in the world, Britain has a relatively stable multi-cultural society that is still one of the most tolerant places to live. This is not ignoring racial issues; there are darker sides to Britain, as in many countries, but that darker side is brighter than the brightest sides of some of the countries that immigrants have come from. Britain is one country that can boast such a diverse blend of peoples that work, live, and socialise together without undue disharmony.

Britain's place in Europe is also unique. As an island nation, Britain still has its isolationist approach to Europe. We are not part of Europe in the sense that we want total integration of policies and other aspects of life, while surrendering our own identity and sovereignty. Britain could retain its independence of European unions and act as a trans-Atlantic or even trans-Pacific bridge. Britain has done this for centuries and its ability to do that so far is a credit to Britain's standing in the world.

Britain also has a distinct role in Africa. Its past there has been hugely influential, for better or worse, but it is not as irrelevant as people think. The reason why President Mugabe of Zimbabwe attacks Britain is because Britain still matters there. It is a back-handed compliment each time Mugabe refers to Britain as if it is the worthy enemy to defeat. It is that respect of Britain's past that he seeks to exorcise, but every time he mentions Britain, it only reflects his feelings of Britain's importance.

Migrants come to Britain for many reasons, better jobs and services, better governing (compared to their own), more freedom, and a new way of life. This only enhances Britain because immigrants add to the economy and cultural life of Britain, and in return our culture is then exported around the world. Immigrants come to Britain and want to stay for many reasons; they are familiar with Britain through various mediums, they love the romance, the myth and the discovery of their own piece of Britain. They believe in a British system and way of life, which is and always has been transforming from one British way of life to another, and the 21st century way of British life will continue that exciting trend.

This is also true for Britain's relationship with America. Many would instantly dismiss any talk of 'special relationships' especially considering current world events. But many people have missed the subtle, but important aspects of the Trans-Atlantic relationship. Tony Blair has always been lampooned as the 'poodle', but when the poodle yapped, Bush listened. Whether it was about Iraq, climate change, economics, African affairs and other issues; Bush listened. Blair was the only foreign premier who could bend Bush's ear and talk to him candidly. 'Yo, Blair!' cut through the political niceties that politicians have to fake while speaking politick, but Bush, not known for his political sense knew his friends. So Blair (and Britain) was not on a leash, he was shoulder to shoulder, and Americans were appreciative of that even if their cousins across the pond were not. While Britain is associated with America as the lesser partner, it is still a partnership that matters in the world, with Britain's moderating effects upon American international affairs.

Sometimes history is thicker than blood. It is why allies, spoilt dictators or other political factions would rather converse with Britain. Because of America's isolationist policies and western hemispheric interactions, America does not understand the history of many countries it is involved in now. However, Britain's past Empire and historical traditions gives it some insight through shared values and history, which both parties could exploit to mutual benefit. Because Britain strides the divide between America and Europe there is a sense that Britain can work around the world as an alternative intermediary.

Britain is a bridge to the East. Within India and Pakistan there are many who still remember and respect British traditions and have maintained British institutions and services. India's economy is attracting British industries and services, while Indian students, businessmen, scientists, sportsmen and families travel to Britain to learn and to explore the roots of the old Empire. Even in the Middle East, Israel, Iran, Iraq and Jordan owe their modern existences to British influence/interference. Britain still has resonance in these areas, now eclipsed by America, but older citizens of these countries remember Britain's involvement all too well. It is these long memories that have kept Britain's place in foreign affairs actively sought after; a political currency that cannot be earned lightly.

This is also true for China. The ties between the two nations are strengthening and the more that happens, no matter what system of government China will have in the future, the effects of sustained British contact will serve to ameliorate internal and international tensions with the Anglosphere. Britain's engagement with China does not condone its ill-treatment toward its citizens; it is a subtle way to confront the Chinese government and keep its actions behind the Great Fire Wall in the public eye.

Even without a nuclear deterrent and place on the U.N. security council, Britain still punches above her weight compared to France, which does not have a global standing outside of its own former colonies and the 'Francosphere'; China, which though an emerging world power does not exercise international missions excepting economic ones and would veto any attempt to counter that; and Russia, which has lost its global political and military voice and is similar to China in its outlook. Britain still spans the globe on diplomatic, humanitarian and military missions as a broker of peace and security. In this Britain shoulders responsibilities that other 'power' nations shirk.

But it is at home where Britain wallows in self-doubt and political correctness. The globalisation effect, cynicism of Big Brother politics and antipathy to the encroaching outside world, has reached these shores. There is a counter-colonialism effect occurring and some people cannot handle that. After years of toil and sacrifice, Britain is now encountering the people of the world that she had once colonised. It is a cultural front that will take time to settle, needing strong leadership and a government that understands the nature of what is transpiring. Some people might not agree with these assessments; Britain is not perfect, but underneath resentments for the Iraq war, the reputation of Britain is still alive and well. And Britons need not fear that. Once Britain is at peace with itself, then its place in the world will be enhanced.

Britain has exported its people, culture, language, industry, energy, films, sports, fashion, monarchy, military, laws, politics, education, and passion across the world, for better or for worse. People come from all over the world to experience British culture, the buzz of the new and the traditions of the old; a country steeped in glory and adventure, a rejuvenated Britannia leading to a brilliant future. It is what makes Britain great, a world beater, and a unique cross-roads for generations to come.

28/Jan/2008

Politics, News & Issues – War & Peace
Will there ever be a chance for world peace?

Man and Peace

Is peace an aberrant phenomenon? I have always thought that man cannot live by peace alone, that peace is the coldest of wars waiting to flare up. But is this true? What are the causes and aims of conflict? Can it be controlled? Whether for territorial or resource gains, alliances, psychological or reproductive power, conflict seems to have been with man from time immemorial. Man's relationship with conflict can be traced in three main areas: evolution and genetics, environmental stresses, and cultural factors. Can we piece together a record of man's violent rejection of peace in the past?

Evolution and Genetics
Ever since man began walking million years ago, he has had to contend with conflict. Bipedalism allowed for better scavenging for food and resources, but in competition with other people and predators. Bipedalism also enabled the hands to become more dexterous. And what did man make? Tools and weapons for survival. This ability put man in a niche above other animals and into one where he could begin to wage war upon other men.

One of the most controversial debates concerns the fate of the Neanderthals. The disappearance of the Neanderthals circa 35,000 BC has prompted some archaeologists to claim that archaic man wiped out the Neanderthals in some widespread campaign leaving man as the predominant humanoid species. But is this so? Or, as others claim, did man and Neanderthals interbreed? In 1997 a study of Neanderthal DNA found that modern human DNA was different enough from Neanderthal DNA for humans not to have been descended from Neanderthals or to have interbred (Irwin 1997). So is ancient man's role in genocide proven or will geneticists yet tease out the mixed blood within us all?

281

Can there be a genetic cause to man's violent heritage? Will genes for violence or potential for aggressiveness be found? Testosterone and cortisol are vital ingredients in the realm of conflict related to aggression and stress, respectively. Ridley in his 1999 work *'Genome'* states that cortisol and testosterone suppress the immune system even as they are at work (as in a conflict), thus seemingly 'kicking you when you are down'. But females will choose males who can defend themselves or fight for mates and, despite their suppressed immune system, remain disease-free in order to father healthy children (Ridley 1999: 149, 158-9). So it would have been advantageous to man not to be without aggressive tendencies and ensure better mating prospects. Man is no stranger to the survival of the fittest, and evolution, long ago, precluded peace as an advantage.

Environmental Stresses

Can chaos theory explain conflict? Studies in population growth reveal that society will break down when subjected to stresses at a certain stage before coming back into balance. 'Everything tends toward disorder' (Gleick 1997: 308). This second law of thermodynamics can apply to any society. Entropy (chaos) flirts everywhere. What look like random societal patterns are in themselves part of larger cycles including factors such as climate change, animal cycles, epidemic cycles, etc, (Gleick 1997: 79). Can downturns in the environment cause conflict? Carneiro's 1970 theory called environmental circumscription could certainly be seen as chaos within society. Conflict is inevitable within a society's environment when disruption occurs. A population within its own restricted area will eventually require more land for its growing population and resources. If they move to another area they will eventually encounter another group, who in their own circumscribed territory would resist any encroachment upon their own resources, bringing them into conflict with one another. Webster, in his reconsideration of Carneiro's work, states that 'Warfare is seen as an adaptive ecological choice under conditions of population growth and resource limitation' (Webster 1975: 464).

In other words, conflict can also organise society. Throughout history, war has been shown to be a great factor in advancing technology on a scale faster than peacetime advances. Greater technological advantage over an enemy meant survival. Carneiro's model saw population growth within a circumscribed area leading to warfare which resulted in greater social hierarchy, a military, and administrative and tax systems under centralised control. So conflict decreased internal stresses within a society ensuring survival against external stresses (Webster 1975: 467 & 469). The environment's ever-changing nature constantly makes man adapt, making lasting peace inherently impossible. Conflict rules the world within man himself and the outside world. It is nature.

Cultural Factors

Myth and art can also play their part in revealing man's aberration to peace. The Lascaux cave paintings, France, date to around 30,000 years ago. In some of the paintings, men are seen with spear-like objects. These weapons were no doubt for hunting, but they could have been used for conflict. This is true for Aborigine art in Australia where there are depictions of conflict as old as 10, 000 years in Arnham Land, Australia. These show scenes of fighting in hunter-gatherer times. Later phases of conflict-art appear around 6000 years ago, and in the early twentieth century when Aborigines came into contact with Europeans. Exact interpretations are unknown since Aborigine art can be both literal and abstract (Tacon & Chippindale 1994: 211 & 217), but it is plain to see that conflict, whether real or imagined is depicted.

Since the dawn of time, man has told tales about the creation of their world. Gods are envisioned as warring amongst themselves, resulting in general mayhem for man. That the gods themselves are not above such base emotions and conflicts must mean that man had just projected his own culture's perceptions and customs upon the gods. Though these gods can be beneficent, it is conflict that drives the pantheons whether Greek, Roman, Egyptian, Aztec or Maya. Look at the fall of the angel Lucifer after his failed rebellion against Heaven in a religion that awaits Armageddon. If peace is not an aberrant phenomenon to man, then it is to the gods of man. Ancient man experienced the inherent violence within nature and attributed these processes to the actions of violent gods. Thus the gods themselves valued conflict over peace which was immortalised by man in his myths. Worldwide, myth and art, whether based on fact or fiction indicates that man's aberration to peace extends into the world of gods and dreamtime.

The Olympics are considered the games of peace, par excellence, but their origins from the ancient Greeks are based upon elements of war, like javelin throwing, wrestling and boxing, fencing, archery, rowing, etc.

The rubber ball game of the Maya and the American Indian's early form of lacrosse were also violent sports, often resulting in deaths. Even the modern professional wrestlers harkens back to gladiatorial contests. Modern sports have absorbed conflict into their structure to become celebrated entertainment. Lately, films and computer games have come under more scrutiny for their levels of violence; a case of conflict reflecting society?

Religion, though a supposed peaceful outlet for man, is also full of conflict within itself and against others, whether defending one's faith or spreading it. If such a concept based on peace can inspire such acts of violence, then what hope and reason for non-violence is there for the non-religious?

Peace nowadays is subjected upon people. After wars and recent conflicts, peace is being imposed upon the warring factions by external forces 'for their own good'. Even now, the U.N. an organisation for world peace is whispering thoughts of a U.N. fighting force. Is peace aberrant to man? Yes. Man is genetically and environmentally adapted for conflict. Man is still an animal, despite his supposed 'higher' evolutionary state. We are still territorially bound, fighting over boundaries and the resources and families within. If ever there was a need to power a perpetual motion machine, then man's infinite search for lasting peace would be the ideal driving force.

References:
Gleick, J. 1997. *Chaos*. London: Minerva.

Irwin, A.1997. Neanderthal DNA Found in Fossil. *The Daily Telegraph*. July 11.

Ridley, M. 1999.*Genome*. London: Fourth Estate, 147-160.

Tacon, P. & Chippindale, C. 1994. Australia's Ancient Warriors: Changing Depictions of Fighting in the Rock Art of Arnhem Land, N.T. *Cambridge Archaeological Journal*. (4):2, 211-28.

Webster, D. 1975. Warfare and the Evolution of the State: A Reconsideration. *American Antiquity*. (40):4, 464-470.

10/Feb/2008

Politics, News & Issues, International Politics
Discrimination against the indigenous peoples of the world

Indigenous and Stateless Peoples Around the World

2020 vision
An essay-turned-article from a BSc course in archaeology. At least in the US, there have been three recent victories for Native Americans: 1) The controversial Dakota Access oil pipeline in Dakota has been stopped pending a review of the environmental surveys. 2) Half of Oklahoma was officially recognised as Native American tribal land, following a court decision. 3) The Washington Redskins American Football franchise have agreed to remove the Redskins name and mascot to a more politically-correct name.

Discrimination against indigenous people includes their statelessness. The stateless society in modernity is a complex issue fraught with endless debates over the composition, function and stability of such a system. Indigenous and stateless peoples like Native Americans, The Kurds, Palestinians, San, The Saami, Inuit, and the Aborigines are now advocating or have implemented plans for their own states.

In defining a stateless society it would be best to define what it is not, namely a state. The Collins Concise Dictionary (2001) defines state as: 6) A sovereign political power or community. 7) the territory occupied by such a community. 8) the sphere of power in such a community: 'affairs of state'. (p.1471). Stateless is then described as: 1) without nationality: stateless persons. 2) without a state or states (p.1471). A state may have law and order, but that does not mean that a stateless society is anarchistic.

In defining indigenism, the Final Statement of the Consultation on Indigenous Peoples' Knowledge and Intellectual Property Rights in Suva, April 1995 stated that 'We assert the right to define who we are. We do not approve of any other definition.' (Ucko & Sillar: 2000). This is vague, but sufficient enough to give the indigenous leeway to protect themselves from discrimination and 'indigenocide' as they have been assimilated, invaded and colonised, physically and psychologically, over the centuries.

In America, the Bureau of Indian Affairs manages the administration of land held in trust by the U.S. for Native Americans. These tribes once lived off the land, but their ways came to an end in the wars against the U.S. government. They were fragmented and placed on reservations, their cultures threatening to disappear. Now, they are rebuilding their culture and asserting their rights. They are stateless societies, though fully immersed within another state. 'State' cannot just be about the physical trappings and definitions, there must be some intangibles. In a wider sense state also must be about notions of 'home'.

The Kurds are stateless. Their heartland lies within several states, including Iran, Iraq (Kurdistan), Syria and Turkey. These oppressed, semi-nomadic, mountain people are fighting for an independent and autonomous state, a home. Such a place, to them, a sovereign state, territorially defensible from where they could exert their own political, economic and cultural influence would be ideal. Kurds may live in within other states and have local power, but they are not a state. They are without a real national identity, in their eyes.

Ever since the formation of Israel in 1947, the Palestinians have been left without a formal state. At war with the Israelis, their terrorist/defensive acts limited their claims to statehood. But with the emergence of a semblance of political order, some legitimisation of that authority, with new road maps to peace, Palestinian claims may yet reach maturity. Palestine is what I would term a 'mid-state', lying between statelessness and state, an evolutionary rung on the state step-ladder. A mid-state is one in flux achieving each of the criteria of state before becoming a state. But now, it is recognition by other sovereign states that makes a state. With globalisation, sovereignty seems to be no longer a right, but a privilege, thus making the formation of a state a discriminating process.

On April 1, 1999, the Inuit homeland of Nunavut ('our land' in the Inuit language) was created. The size of Western Europe in the east Northern Territory, the Inuit will promote Inuit language and culture (Phillips 1999: 137). But while this may herald a new beginning, many see

Nunavut as Canada's welfare state. One fifth are government employed, 30% on welfare, 22% unemployed, with incomes averaging 50% lower than the rest of Canada, though the Nunavut Implementation Commission hopes to put things right (Broughton 1999). The Arctic peoples are progressively asserting their rights in order to gain independent authority over their own land, culture and heritage 'a privilege taken for granted by most of the millions of people to the south' (Phillips 1999: 137). And though Nunavut is 'Aboriginal self-government' it is 'self-government within the Canadian Federal system' (Daes 1993: 5). The time for true indigenous homelands with policies of self-determination may be some time off.

Since 1956, the Scandinavian Nordic Saami Council have been fighting for their rights. In Greenland, the Kalaallit Inuit and their 'tukaq' theatre use folklore and traditional culture to explore contemporary issues to educate and inspire other indigenous groups. Greenland also hosted the last Inuit Circumpolar Conference in 1998 (Phillips 1999: 135-6). There are about 600,000 circumpolar peoples today in the north, encompassing the Scandinavian Saami, the Kalaallit of Greenland, the various Canadian Inuit tribes, the Even, Evenk and Ket of Siberia and various others (Allan 1999: 11). Whether nomads, herders, hunters or whalers, they have shown a determination to follow their cousins, the Inuit, in asserting their right to autonomy.

The Kalahari tribesmen, the San, have regained some of their ancestral hunting grounds in the Kalahari Gemsbok National Park taken from them by Europeans and Bantus and then by the South African apartheid government. Now the Khomani San have returned. Thirty thousand year old San rock art in the area proved their 'indigeneity' and South Africa is 'recognising its first people and their right to land.' (La Guardia 1999). The San are regaining parts of their homeland, but what about the future of other indigenous peoples, like the Tanzanian Hadzabe and the Sudanese Nuer?

In Australia, the Aborigines have been able to make some breakthroughs in their rights. The 'terra nullius', a colonialist act which claimed that Australia had no previous ownership was reversed in 1992, giving prior ownership back to the Aborigines (Allan 1999: 19 & 134). This was part of a worldwide reversal of the international legal doctrine repealed in the Western Sahara, Canada and the United States in 1975 (Daes 1993:

6). In New Zealand, the Young Maori Party acts for the rights of its people (Allan 1999a: 136). The Ainu of Japan are expressing more concern for their rights, after having been forced northward to Hokkaido over the last few centuries and then assimilated into Japanese culture. Only a few pure-blood Ainu now exist (Allan 2000: 11).

So, what future indigenism? While the United Nations agrees to the indigenous peoples' right to self-determination, the Sub-commission on Prevention of Discrimination and Protection of Minorities states that 'there is no legal definition of 'people'. Nor is there a generally accepted sociological or political definition of 'a people'. There are also no international laws providing rules and principles concerning the term 'indigenous peoples' (Daes 1993: 1 & 5). To that end, Daes would like to see the indigenous having a more 'formal and direct' say about their own concerns, proposing that the indigenous be represented on the United Nations Economic and Social Council to address indigenous issues (Daes 1993, 6). This should ensure non-discriminatory rights.

Indigenous peoples may be discriminated against and restricted to the hinterlands, but in some cases they are beginning to gain control and power over their destiny. Though I hope that while they may control their own destiny as indigenous peoples, they do not have to sacrifice, destroy or reinvent what made them so. Statelessness has somewhat preserved them. The 21st century could see indigenous self-definition and statehood save our past and their future.

References:
Allan, T. 1999. *Journeys Through Dreamtime: Oceanian Myth*. Amsterdam: Time Life Books, 6-21, 134-7.

Allan, T. 1999. The Peoples of the Far North. In: Allan, T. (ed.) *Spirits of the Snow: Arctic Myth*. Amsterdam: Time Life Books, 6-23.

Allan, T. 2000. *Realm of the Rising Sun: Japanese Myth*. Amsterdam: Time Life Books, 6-27.

Broughton, P.D. 1999. *Inuit look to a new homeland to solve old problems*. Daily Telegraph, Tues, February 23.

Daes, E-I. 1993. *Explanatory Note Concerning the Draft Declaration of the Rights of Indigenous Peoples*. At:
www.unhchr.ch/html/menu2/10/c/ind/ind_main.htm
(see E/CN.4/Sub.2/1993/26/Add.1)
Link still active as of September 2020.

La Guardia, A. 1999. *The Lost world of the Kalahari is restored*. Daily Telegraph, Saturday, March 20.

Phillips, C. 1999. The Legacy of Arctic Myth. In: Allan, T. (ed.) *Spirits of the Snow: Arctic Myth*. Amsterdam: Time Life Books, 134-7.

Ucko, P. & Sillar, B. 2000. *Indigenous Archaeology*. unpublished precis.

15/Feb/2008

Politics, News & Issues – Death Penalty
The case against the death penalty

Human Rights and the Death Penalty

I used to support the death penalty. But lately the issues surrounding it have become blurred and I feel that it no longer is an effective deterrent or the best way to deal with murderers. Don't get me wrong, I am no liberal, very far from it, but I do not believe in an eye for an eye or that the death penalty serves a justifiable purpose. Four issues have brought this to the fore.

1. In Britain, even though murder has statistically decreased in numbers over the past decade, almost every week there is a high profile murder reported by the media. Just recently, after three youths were convicted of the murder of a man, his widow said that she wished the death penalty was reinstated in Britain and that she would pull the lever on the electric chair herself. We all grieve with her and her loss, but to me, killing these three would be the easy way out for everyone. Getting rid of them will not bring back the deceased, nor ease any memories of their act. The real tragedy is that these three youths will be out of jail in their thirties, even though they were supposedly jailed for life to be able to have the rest of their lives to live after brutally murdering this father of three. Life should mean life. No parole, enduring hard labour and rotting from the inside thinking about their crime and the life they took. State executions make martyrs of those who do not deserve such recognition. Their lives should be taken away, but by incarceration in perpetuity.

2. The former Conservative MP, Michael Portillo, in an episode of 'Horizon – How to Kill a Human Being' (January 2008) investigated the most humane ways to kill a human. He was unsure of the idea of state-sanctioned murder and the suffering of the executed, whether from problems in lethal injection, electric chair, hanging, or gas chamber. Personally, I see no problems with this, since the executed probably dies in less pain than the person(s) they murdered. In the end, Portillo discovered that by inducing hypoxia, a lack of oxygen to the brain, a person would basically doze of euphorically to death. This technique has

been used to kill lab animals, but could it work with humans? Would we care if the executed felt pain even after the suffering they had inflicted? A humane death penalty makes no difference to the outcome. Treating a murderer with more humanity than his criminal act only tries to render the death penalty more palatable so as to ease our consciences. But death is death.

3. The death penalty has been an ineffective deterrent worldwide. Every country, with or without a death penalty, suffers murders. The US, Saudi Arabia, Iran and China are probably the most notable countries that execute prisoners, but still they have high crime rates and countless prisoners. Then there are grey areas such as who gets executed – all murderers, someone who killed accidentally when drunk or ill, a cop killer, or a shopkeeper murderer? Should degrees of murder really be taken into account? In the US, prisoners can appeal for decades against their convictions and executions, and there have been miscarriages of justice. Executing the wrong person is not unknown and can even serve political expedience. Such ineffectiveness costs the taxpayer money, but is it more cost-effective than paying for life imprisonment? Should that really matter? If the death penalty were a private business, its incompetence in services would have caused bankruptcy long ago. As it is, the death penalty is now morally bankrupt, yet still manages to remain commercially solvent.

4. Lastly, can murderers be fixed? As the evolutionary biologist Richard Dawkins states in The Edge Annual Question (2006) 'What is Your Dangerous Idea?': 'Retribution as a moral principle is incompatible with a scientific view of human behaviour. As scientists, we believe that human brains, though they may not work in the same way as man-made computers, are as surely governed by the laws of physics. When a computer malfunctions, we do not punish it. We track down the problem and fix it, usually by replacing a damaged component, either in hardware or software' (Dawkins 2006). So why can't murderers be fixed? This is not about mind control, creating automatons, or medicating criminals into submissiveness. This is about fixing a part of the human body that has gone wrong, like applying antibiotics for a faulty immune system or a cast for a broken bone. According to leading futurist Ray Kurzweil, in his book 'The Singularity is Near' (2005), within 40 years the brain will be scanned, modelled and reversed engineered enough for us to perform procedures to repair functions and prevent defects.

People get queasy and doubtful about such notions, but the technology is coming. In the future we may have maximum security hospitals for those whose murdering tendencies are not the result of predetermination or a flash of anger, but a neurological disorder, which does not discount the two previous reasons. Mental illness, chemical imbalances and faulty 'wiring' can be fixed. This could allow those rehabilitated and 'cured' to re-enter society, just like a cancer patient in remission or a person with a pacemaker, etc.

So do we really need the death penalty? When life should mean life, when methods are 'inhumane', when it is not an effective deterrent and when there is the possibility of real rehabilitation rather than retribution, the death penalty should be phased out. One real way to address this is to have better crime prevention policies, education and not just tougher laws, penalties and sentences, but smarter ones. Murder is a crime that even the death penalty does not deter any more. And there is one big reason for the ineffectiveness of criminal sentencing: Human Rights law.

Human Rights laws now give criminals more rights even though they have transgressed those laws. A citizen cannot defend themselves in public or in their own residence from criminals for fear of the criminal pressing charges for physical assault. While some prisons may be tough, the inmates still enjoy most of the 'freedoms' practised by the general public. Human Rights laws waters down the justice system, giving the victim no protection or justice. People feel that the death penalty is the only way left to find resolution and closure when the justice system lets them down. The death penalty then is really a symptom, a sign of a failed justice system.

So again, do we really need the death penalty? For me, a once staunch supporter of it, I have to say, no. It has out-lived its usefulness, its function and raison d'être. I say no, not because of accusations of state-sponsored murder is wrong, or because it is inhumane, but because even upon threat of death, murderers still stalk our streets. Criminals are not afraid of the law; they cheat the system and wrong our society. If our society and our elected governments cannot change the system, then we will have more pressing problems down the line with more serious transgressions and burgeoning prison populations. Without any re-assessing of death penalty issues or proposing radical solutions as above, then the rusty old machine of the death penalty will continue on to our society's detriment.

01/Mar/2008

Politics, News & Issues – People in the News
Should Prince Harry Have Been Sent to Afghanistan?

Should Prince Harry Have Served in Afghanistan?

Since the news has broken that Prince Harry, third in line to the British Throne and a Second Lieutenant with the Household Cavalry, had been serving in Afghanistan there has been much debate. The fact is he is a soldier, an officer and part of a unit. There would have been no point in training him for his position if he was going to be kept out of harm's way, while his men were sent into the danger zone.

Prince Harry is setting an example and fulfilling the wishes he has had since a young boy of being in the army. Various members of the Royal Household are or once were serving members of the Armed Forces and the Queen is the Head of the Armed Forces. It is the duty of the Royal Family in being representatives of several Armed Forces Regiments that they should serve in whatever capacity they can, just as Prince Andrew did in the Falklands War in 1982. In this, the twenty-first century, Prince Harry is proud to serve Britain and wanted to serve in the only way he could as an officer, on the front-line. And by all accounts he has been doing a great job. This is not about being gung-ho or staging publicity stunts. If it was then Prince Harry would have just paid a flying visit to the troops in a flag waving exercise, giving speeches, driving a tank and firing a symbolic shoot towards the Taliban before returning home, as many politicians and celebrities have done. But this was about doing the duty the Prince voluntarily enlisted to do and with the full knowledge of the dangers involved. Putting a Royal Family member's life on the line is not a publicity stunt.

The danger to himself was enormous as to any other British and coalition soldier in Afghanistan. But, once German, Australian and American sources had broken the story about his already ten-week old mission, he might still have been safe. But in pinpointing his location, his position became a bit more precarious and now he has been ordered home. Part of me hopes that this is a bluff and that he can complete the remaining four weeks of his tour of duty. It is not like the Taliban have the extra luxury, time or resources to identify and engage the Prince in combat. There are now fears he may be a more likely target for terrorists in Britain, but again, as a member of the Monarchy and the Armed Forces, he was already in the danger zone anyway.

Morally, the war in Afghanistan is different to Iraq, where Prince Harry's deployment was aborted last year due to media leaks, because most people see this as a justified war to end the Taliban regime. There is a moral compulsion to be there rather than in Iraq. Prince Harry is not fighting a crusade, but against the Taliban who aided in 9/11 and also suppressed the Afghans. Prince Harry is just one soldier carrying out NATO's mission to fight for the survival of the Afghan State and their democracy.

Our nation should be proud of Prince Harry, not because he is any more special than other troops, but because he could have chosen not to go. He has shown real courage, leadership and maturity that will stand him in good stead for his future army career and as a leader of the country. Prince Harry also gains the respect from his fellow soldiers who he can now empathise with. Prince Harry's deployment in Afghanistan has not been a hollow exercise in spin or PR. He has boosted morale, become a prince of substance and shown the nation that duty should not be shirked or taken for granted. Well done Prince Harry.

05/Apr/2008

Politics, News & Issues – People in the news

Reflections on the Death of Charlton Heston

2020 vision
Maybe this should be in the entertainment section for the great actor Heston was, or even religion for the amount of biblical characters he portrayed. But he was also a big part of the political scene on pro-gun issues.

April 5th, 2008: One of my favourite actors of all time has passed away, but even the ravages of time will not succeed in erasing our memories of the presence and character of Charlton Heston, a legend in his own time.

Charlton Heston was a man of conviction. Every character he played in Biblical epics, Classic dramas, Westerns and Science Fiction were men of faith, determination and resolve. I could list the films which have affected my life, like *Ben Hur*, which makes me shed a tear at the end for his mother and sister; *El Cid* –which has one of the most unforgettable endings ever; *The Big Country*, one of my favourite westerns with that throat-choking moment of loyalty in following the Major; *Planet of the Apes* and that immortal line; to the little-touted *The Warlord* with a hair-raising castle siege. The list could go on, but Heston set the archetype as the heroic man for all seasons A-Lister across many film genres.

Outside of films, Heston showed more conviction as a supporter and later leader on gun control as the President of the National Rifle Association. It is one thing for an actor to play a man of conviction, but to live by it in one's personal life is courageous and shows a rare quality of humanness for an actor. Not many actors of our generation fly their colours up the flag pole, at least not without a publicity machine, but Heston transcended the generations, growing up in a time of segregation to march with Martin Luther King to fighting for the freedoms enshrined in the Constitution. His association with the NRA has not endeared him to many Americans or with my native Britons, but he was not deterred or afraid to add his voice to the causes he believed in.

In this day of celebrity marriages that last a brief trilogy, Charlton Heston was married for 64 years to Lydia. Again, even at the age of 84, Heston revealed a personal conviction that at its heart must have set the agenda for the rest of his life. For his marriage and career to have survived for so long through the turbulence of six decades calls for inner fortitude, adaptability and understanding, all the qualities Heston brought to his films.

There is no modern day Charlton Heston in Hollywood; he broke the mould. No more epics for a man of a thousand beards, booming voice and sheer physical presence. The lights of Hollywood are dimmed by his absence, a great man of great conviction, and a hero forever in my memories. Thank you for so much, Charlton Heston.

Charlton Heston Filmography
http://www.imdb.com/name/nm0000032/
(link still active as of September 2020)

30/May/2008

Politics, News & Issues - Economics
Would a 'flat world' economic policy be a fairer way?

Flat World Economics

2020 vision

I remember a fellow site writer complaining about the article title and asking what 'fairer' meant – fairer for whom? I don't know, not for me to figure out! And of course this isn't about a flat Earth!

Part of me does ask why drag the top earners down when we should be raising the economic bottom? There are many rich people who have attained their wealth earnestly and created their businesses from nothing. They deserve their prosperity, their top salaries. Some give away more money than most people earn in a lifetime. Why drag them down? Yes, there are those less well off who work hard, but they don't earn a great deal or some don't work to their full potential to earn promotion or high earnings. There are companies who hoard their assets to boost their status when that could be shared out to employees. There are those companies and individuals who evade taxes. But even without those factors it is a fact that the rich/poor divide is growing. What can be done about this? Change the system? Invest in people? Reinvent the business model?

A more recent economic system I heard about during 2016 was Social Capitalism (lots of different definitions, but essentially using capital for social good rather than amassing fortunes – however, it is often mistaken for socialism, which it is not). It may have been one answer to heave the UK away from disparities between social orders. But that was squandered right at the beginning of then Prime Minister Theresa May's tenure in one of her first speeches. We have an opportunity with Brexit to find our own economic balance, re-invent our economy, breaking free of entrenched European or US systems, and forge a lucrative, and perhaps a more moral, path forward. But will we take it?

Why can't the world be flat? Does our society have to depend on materialistic gains to be deemed worthy of praise and acceptance? First of all, let me say that my background is in archaeology, not economics, so forgive my naivety and simplistic arguments, but I read a lot and have discussed these views with others. Recently, I had been reading about Milton Friedman and the Chicago School movement regarding economics, in 'The Shock Doctrine' by Naomi Klein. Previously, I had been reading about the rise of the virus-like 'Affluenza' in the English-speaking world, as eloquently captured by Oliver James, 2007. There does seem to be a correlation between rampant capitalism and wellness deterioration.

Friedman's use of unfettered capitalism (deregulation, privatisation, and cutbacks), the shock to the system (renamed as 'Disaster Capitalism' by social commentators) has created the disparate world we live in today, rather than the economically-balanced world that Friedman nominally envisioned. His problem was/is that he could not implement his version of the free-market economy from scratch, because global society was already entrenched in an old (Keynesian) system of government-led policies. The free-market economy would not work within that system, so Friedman found his opportunities elsewhere (mostly South America), say after a coup or a natural disaster, enabling that country's government or leaders to wipe the slate clean and re-format on a free-market remit.

But such a system did not work as intended, because the markets were still controlled by governments (and military) and individuals (the elite) who took advantage of that system to enforce their policies and become richer at the expense of the general population. There can be no free-market system until that flaw, the naked pursuit of power and profits, is fixed. But at the heart of that flaw is the human being. And humans aren't getting any better at being less greedy.

There is a disease spreading amongst humans called affluenza. It is that rapacious inner need for money, or fame, or power, at the cost of one's health and happiness. It is a virus spawned and spoon-fed at birth through childcare policies, instilled within us through the education system and perpetuated within us through employment systems. Affluenza destroys our needs over our wants. Oliver James has many 'vaccines' for affluenza, but that would mean a radical over-haul of our deep-seated politico-economic systems, a shock to the system, as it were, just like a pure free-market economy.

But could a flat version of the pure free-market economy work and be a cure for affluenza? Financial profit does not have to be the end-all and be-all. I once had a discussion with a friend about my future desire to set up a flat company, where the top earner did not make an exorbitant amount more than the bottom earner. It would be fairer, I said, and people would be happier in a company where profits were ploughed back into the employees and the community. With stars in my eyes and my head in the clouds, my friend said then my company would die, as there would be no incentive to work, no drive for promotion, no ambition, and no company. I did not have an answer then, but I do now: Let them go!

I realised that was the whole point of a flat economy. If people want to work for pure profit at the expense of others, then let them go. A flat company would weed out those not focused on their work, but on profits. Their materialistic outlook on life, their ambitious drive for promotion and bonuses, possibly beyond their means, would expose their insecurities, unhappiness and mental distress. Sure not everyone is affected by such financial gains and rewards are needed for work, but a flatter economy across the board would mediate affluenza. And with all companies on the same level playing field, profits would not be the influencer for customers.

Flatness does not mean flat rates of pay, or no advancement, or no profits at all; it just means that the biggest earners or the company would not be sitting on unassailable amounts of profits, that corporate responsibility and meritocracy would be at the forefront of company needs, and that a company's work ethic and reputation would be their biggest selling point. A person would work for a flat company, because they like the job, there would be promotion, a fair share of the profits and knowledge that their colleagues were also there for intrinsic reasons rather than materialistic gain. A sense of accomplishment, success and challenge, would be the rewards in such a system. As more companies encompassed this, the need for obscene profits would dissipate as they vied for wellness profit instead.

This may seem like communism or socialism, but so what? Or rather, if those systems had worked like they were supposed to then we may have seen a pure meritocracy. Properly run, the free-market system of Friedman and socialism had essentially the same outcome: individual freedom. But whether through the private sector or the public sector, in both cases, human nature interfered again, and they brought coups, wars, torture and death. The elite feared their loss of power and wealth in a world that worshipped these things. Free-market capitalism would make them stronger, affluenza would make them ill, a flat economy would make them weaker, but within a relatively stable world. In a flat world, instead of using their materialism for status, the elite would have to use themselves as a commodity to draw any further attention or wealth.

Flat companies would free up profits for social funds, reinvigorating and regenerating their employees and communities. Such private funding would take the lead from government taxation. Such central governance processes would also lead to a flatter government with less regulation. Such flat governments and companies would lead to the rise of wealthier and healthier individuals, unencumbered by materialism and political control. Of course, a flat world policy would bring conflict as elites fought against it, thus marking flatness as a subjective economic policy with a (subjective) authoritarian leadership having to impose flatness around the world. Is flatness itself then totally fair and just?

Obviously, not just one system will work and total flatness is not the only answer, but our mindset on such matters has to change. What is this obsessive need for profit? Who are you measuring yourself against when we can only look to ourselves for happiness? Why be measured by your house, car, money or fame, than just for yourself? If those are what you are measured for, then look inside yourself as a person who has none of these. If you find yourself lacking then the emptiness inside is affluenza.

I myself have recently 'downshifted' to another job. It took me eight months of unemployment to find my balance between needs and wants, happiness and stress. I know what I want out of life and I am happier for it; but I look around and see so much unhappiness in people supposedly living the good life, due to the indoctrination policies of our society. The real shock to the system will be when people realise that there is another way and that they can change or demand change. The 21st Century could see a new rising breed of believers in a flat world.

31/May/2008

Politics, News & Issues

Identifying the Illuminati

There have been reams of paper written about the shadowy group of masters who have allegedly ruled the world through the ages, but they are often dismissed as a myth. However, an Illuminati do exist, they have ruled the world for the past 50 years and spanned the globe with their epoch-making policies. Their individual names might not be known, but they are well-known in the upper echelons of governments and corporations alike. They are not kings, generals or presidents (though they make and break them); but a select group of economists, known as the Chicago Boys.

You may not have heard of the Chicago Boys, but their hand has had its prints (along with the CIA) on every single 1970s/1980s South American coup, on South Africa's ripped up Freedom Charter, Poland's broken Solidarity movement, Russia's rise of the Oligarchs, direct influence on Tiananmen Square, even Post-Katherine New Orleans, and more. I thought that I knew world history and the reasons behind some of the last century's momentous events, but upon reading Naomi Klein's 'The Shock Doctrine' (2008), I was literally shocked at the involvement of the University of Chicago's Economics Department, the philosophy of its one-time 'Zen' master, the late Milton Friedman and the policies that wrecked and shocked one country after another and which still continues today in Iraq and Afghanistan. The Chicago Boys are alumni of that Economics Department, their successors and students (whether American or foreign), and other economists who follow their tenets.

Milton Friedman, the architect of the Chicago Boys, was an unabashed capitalist. He believed in total free-market systems and was opposed to New Deal (Keynesian) systems, or half-way capitalist/socialist systems or third world developmental economies. He even thought the U.S. economic system was still too strict and wanted freer controls. He instilled in his students that same fervour, the so-called Chicago Boys, who in the coming years would find themselves at the centre of coups, wars and massacres; sitting on the Boards of the IMF, World Bank and corporations; and getting away scot-free, while lurking in the shadows for the next opportunity. Friedman himself even won the Nobel Prize for Economics in 1976, which nominally absolved him of his part in Chile's 1973 coup.

The Chicago Boys are the progenitors of what has been dubbed 'Disaster Capitalism'. Once they precipitated coups so that the foreign government could instigate their economic reforms (privatisation, deregulation, and cut-backs), when the country was still in shock, but coups were not the only disasters as hurricanes, tsunamis and terrorist attacks also alerted the Chicago Boys to new avenues of potential wealth at the expense individuality and democracy.

The tragedy is that Friedman and possibly some, but not all, of his colleagues and mentors actually believed that their free-market economies would work, but they had to be pure, free of human influence and allowed to balance themselves out. But this never happened. In order for Friedman's version of free markets to work, said government had to be authoritarian and impose it, much to the detriment of that country. But the link between his (and said government's) reforms and the violence, torture and deaths were never directly linked to him, especially not by the media or the human rights groups. It was assumed that people were fighting against the loss of democracy, while the governments were fighting against left-wing insurgents. The Chicago Boys economics, which was laid out prior to the coup were never mentioned, as if economics was divorced from political and military actions, when in fact it drove them.

The outside world assumed that the economy was the victim of the fighting, but it was in truth the underlying cause as people revolted against the selling off of their country. It is why the Chicago Boys have survived ever since and why they are still so integral to the world affairs today. They operate in the daylight, out in the open, but people don't notice, don't care or accept it, because we have been indoctrinated under the mantra of capitalism. And as long as the capitalist/corporate structure exists, the Chicago Boys will exercise their will over the rights of others.

There is no conspiracy theory to this. The Chicago Boys exist; their exploits are a matter of record in documents, letters, truth commissions, senate hearings and manifestos, and mostly in the lecture halls of universities; they are alive and well and living it large in the 21ˢᵗ Century. Their philosophy has many other names, such as Reaganomics and Thatcherism; the Oligarchs of Russia and the Princelings of China are acolytes, and it gave rise to Neo-conservatism. There is no doubt that they have transformed the economic fortunes of many a nation throughout the 70s and 80s, but the Chicago Boys' economic footprint is heavy, especially felt in under-developed countries and at the cost of thousands of lives and livelihoods. They and their client countries' elite have creamed the profits from privatisation and deregulation, and while said country may recover (hailed as an economic miracle), the rich are richer and the poor poorer. The Chicago Boys create puppet elites.

Now that the Chicago Boys have the reins of the IMF and the World Bank, whenever you hear of a disaster around the world, listen and read carefully reports about economic aid from those institutions, or about reform bills, redevelopment and the rise of left-wing insurgents. These are hallmarks of Chicago Boy intervention. They have policies ready for any occasion and the shock of a disaster, to them, necessitates the need for an economic shock in order to wipe the slate clean and bring in new reforms.

No continent has remained untouched by them and even Russia and China have invited the Chicago Boys to help them out. Friedman even persuaded the Chinese Government to tough it out over the students protests of 1989, which led directly to the Tiananmen Square massacre, but again, the link to Friedman was ignored, because the media depicted the riots as a fight against communist rule, when in fact it was the Chinese government who wanted capitalism under communist rule against the people's desire for slower reform. The Chicago Boys won out and many Chinese lost their lives, for the sake of instant profits, seen now in new dams, Grand Prix racing and the Olympics. (It is one reason I think why China and America will not go to war with each other –it would be economically unthinkable!).

To test my Chicago Boy/Illuminati theory, here are three predictions for the coming year:

1. Zimbabwe:
When Morgan Tsvangirai is elected, listen for news reports about aid from World Bank and IMF and about economic reform that involves

privatisation of former state run industries. Zimbabwe may have no oil (the usual reason for non-intervention by America and Britain), but it does have gold and diamond mines, fertile land and is in a strategic position to act as a bulwark against further Chinese resource gains in Africa. When Tsvangirai takes power look for riots to start, which will be blamed on pro-Mugabe forces, but which will really be a wider range of people, who are now even poorer because of the new economic regime. It would not surprise me if the Chicago Boys deliberately held back (if they were not already advising Mugabe) to precipitate this crisis so as to get ready to shock the people of Zimbabwe into a new economy.

2. The world economic crisis:

The credit crunch and housing crisis has hit across the world, especially in America and Britain. Here, in Britain, Prime Minister Brown is being battered in the polls, with the Tories now commanding a double-digit lead over Brown's Labour. But Brown is not dead yet, and I have a feeling that there is bad medicine on the way in new economic reforms, whether through stealth or other taxes. But any shock tactics will not be met with too many protests, because 1. we will be told it is for the country's benefit and 2. the law has already been changed by former presi...(sorry) Prime Minister Blair during the last shock of terror attacks, so dissent in Britain is already covered with police cordons.

3. If Barack Obama is elected president:

Clinton and McCain are not the ones to worry about. We know their policies and that nothing will substantially change. But beware Obama. Look at his background: He lived in Indonesia (as a child), 2 years after the coup set up by the CIA and the Berkeley Mafia (University of California at Berkeley economists, the precursor and ideological opposite to the Chicago Boys). He went to Harvard 1988, where one Jeffrey Sachs a Chicago Boyesque economist made his name in Bolivia and Poland with his 'shock' tactics. Obama is Senator for Illinois, the home of the Chicago Boys and he also attended the Law School, in 1993. Of course these are coincidences in life, but such incidences do rub off on you. There is no way he would not know about University of Chicago's influential economics department or the history of the Indonesian coup. He is a child of the ideological battle between the Chicago Boys and the 'free world'. Which way will he swing? To me, Obama won't change the world; it will be business as usual with a new face.

The Chicago Boys transcend governments and countries. They may not be the classic archetypal Illuminati, but they are the closest thing the modern world has to an all-pervading shadowy law unto themselves. Their policies are the fabric of life, they have woven a web of capitalism and power, controlling the world economy; privatising, deregulating, and cutting services, so much so that people do not realise they are part of a global shock programme; we cannot see the wood, for the trees. They are all around us; just look past the headlines. And that is the Chicago Boys; the real Illuminati.

26/June/2008

Politics, news and Issues - Other
Satire: President George Bush

Will the Real George W. Bush Stand Up?

After seeing such films as 'Vantage Point' and 'Dave', and hearing that Stalin and Saddam Hussein had doubles, I began to wonder if George W. Bush had a double and then, which one was the real one: the lucid, straight-talking CEO of the nation or the seemingly simple, malapropism-prone 'gaffester'? Who was the Commander-in-Chief we saw on TV comforting the nation after 9/11 with fine speeches? Who was the prime target of Michael Moore's documentary 'Fahrenheit 9/11' providing fodder for all those who suspected the President was a bit mentally lightweight?

We know Bush wasn't the brightest of students, but his charisma has been lauded. He might not have been the best of businessmen, but his choices of oil and baseball couldn't be closer to America's heart. He might not have been the best of governors, but he was well-equipped to run for the White House. And we know he wasn't the best of sons, but hey, Bush Sr. has three more sons, so Bush Jr. was going to be a mediocre president at best.

But there are two sides to him, that witty rancher from Texas who has few eloquent moments and who can front the media with no answers, and the tough talking politico who takes the flak without flinching? Does the Bush double have to act more like the real Bush or vice versa? Whose poll numbers are down? Which Bush has the most biographies about him, which one flies to Iraq, and which one can't wait to leave office? Who's cleverer, or greyer, funnier or taller? The real Bush may be a Texan rancher, but who is the avid jogger and cyclist? Is Bush double really a stunt double; falling off bikes, choking on pretzels or carving turkeys in Iraq for comic relief?

Was the double groomed for this moment from Bush's governorship? When did it begin? How much did he resemble Bush beforehand in looks and speech? Is there a school of 'Presidential Look-alikes that he had to go to learn mannerisms and speech? Does the double do things that the real Bush can or cannot do; something that may give the double away or bolster the real Bush's image? How much does such a job pay? Where does he live in his 'off time'? What are the perks of the job? Can he ever retire or is there a 'Prisoner' type village awaiting him for former spies, Presidents and dictators?

What are the double's duties and how much 'air time' does he get on TV? Has he made major addresses and fooled other heads of state face to face? When Bush was told in an Oval Office briefing that five Brazilian soldiers had died from a bomb and the visibly shocked Bush asked how many was a Brazilian —who was that? Who wanted Osama 'dead or alive'? Who stood shoulder to shoulder with Blair? How far is the double willing to go to protect his country? If the double died while on duty —what would happen to the real Bush? Would the government have to come clean or would Bush make a miraculous recovery? Why be a double for Bush in the first place? Or did it not begin this way, the double life slowly deteriorating into a lame duck double. Has the double life been worth it?

We will never know if the President has a double. No such claims, other than films, have ever been made public, even after generations. Either it is the closest kept secret, even more so than Area 51, or maybe there is no Bush double; the funniest and scariest thought being that they are one and the same.

11/Sept/2008

Politics, News & Issues – US elections 2008
Who would make a better President?

Welcome to the McCain Presidency

2020 vision

I really did think McCain/Palin would win. Stranger things have happened since. But I believe the 2008 recession and the decisions McCain made around that time (to suspend the campaign, etc) hindered his chances. And then there was Sarah Palin, the gift that kept on giving...

This is what I see from across the pond and as someone who has lived in New York, studied American history in high school, and experienced many US elections. While a lot of my British friends do not understand American politics or have a knee-jerk reaction to like Obama for his novelty, I think I have more of an insight (compared to them) on America, its politicians, and people. First off, I would liken myself as a Republican, analogous to the British Conservatives, so my views could be considered biased, maybe even naïve and simplistic, but there are many other reasons as to why I think McCain is going to win, and dare I say win big.

John McCain

Maverick, radical, outsider, a non-neocon, and hero: that is John McCain to the Republican Party and to the electorate who follow politics. McCain is no Bush III. He's a more liberal Republican. There is daylight between what the Bush Administration has done and what McCain will do whether with climate change, energy, gun laws, and taxes. McCain understands politics and as the next Commander-in-Chief, he has demonstrated an understanding of military tactics. The 'Surge' in Iraq was attributed to his efforts, which led to fewer troop deaths and a semblance of some peace. McCain makes the hard choices, unpopular as they may be.

In picking Sarah Palin as his running mate, McCain has stuck to his maverick style of politicking. I actually think that he was inspired by Britain (where he has visited often), where all the main parties 'skipped' a generation and went for younger leaders who in turn selected a new generation of men and women, thereby breaking up the old boys club. The Conservatives and Labour have also taken up positions commonly associated with the other, which attracts undecided voters. As a non-traditional Republican, McCain is somewhat centralist, a winning formula for undecided Americans. In his choice of VP, McCain has shown a forward thinking agenda and in one fell swoop he has highlighted the next generation of the Republicans.

Sarah Palin
What a breath of fresh air. A lot of commentators on both sides of the Atlantic see this as a cynical move by McCain. So what? Any Governor or Senator, once eligible is capable of being plucked for the big jobs. The way I see it, any State Governor of the US is almost equal to many Prime Ministers around the world, such is the complexity and wealth of those States. Palin is a typical, can-do woman, wife and mother and with her undoubted ambition has achieved a much vaunted position on a State level, which can now be transferred onto the national stage.

Palin ticks all the boxes; married to a half-Native American Inuit, with five children, one of whom has Downs Syndrome and her eldest son is bound for Iraq. She's already fought corruption within her own party and against corporations in Alaska and her stints as Mayor and Governor have been accompanied by approval ratings of over 80 percent. It also seems that the 'October Surprise' came early, not only with her nomination, but with the revelation of her unwed teen daughter's pregnancy and allegations of affairs. The mud is out, though no doubt the Democrats are busy ski-dooing all over Alaska for more dirty snow. While in Britain, a politician's religion is a private thing, Palin's (as are most candidates') religion is out and proud, which will garner more approval there as McCain himself has not enamoured himself with the Christian Right.

Does Palin have what it takes to be in the top job if anything happened to McCain? Will she turn out to be a Quayle? We'll have to see, but her barnstorming speech and record so far have signalled her determination not to be underestimated and she seems a formidable politician in the making.

Barack Obama

While some states like California, some newspapers like the New York Times (among others), and millions of individuals are liberals, the US as a whole is not. It's a corporate state run on conservative values with big government and welfare agendas a far second. Although Senator Obama will seek to maintain a diverse business economy, his speech at the Democratic National Convention underlined a more liberal outlook, which could panic some corporations and damage their bottom lines, American jobs and the economy as a whole.

Obama has three problems as I see it: First, as a black man myself; colour is an issue, despite what people say, with prejudice still percolating within the melting pot. He is the first black candidate. That matters. That is news. And his wife, Michelle and the Reverend Wright will have to take responsibility for their outdated remarks about Race and America. It will be a factor come election day, but it is a minor problem compared to the others. Second, I believe that his liberalism will deter many voters, as discussed above. His policies will alienate true blue believers and I also believe that Hilary Clinton took many votes away from him so that many disaffected Democratic voters will either stay away or cross to the Republicans who offer a more balanced candidacy. Third, his youth and inexperience shouldn't really be a hindrance, but it is showing in his inability to get any depth across in his policies. There is a Cult of Personality forming which will overshadow any policies he has. The fact that he is a Black, inexperienced politician and his inability to land policy punches has tied his hands and led to him make a cautious decision by bringing in Biden.

With his celebrity status, great orations, campaign coffers brimming, and the whole world willing him on, Obama has really missed a trick in picking a safe pair of second hands in Biden. Obama could have 'done a McCain', shown a more radical and flexible approach to the future, but instead Obama is thinking only about this election. By choosing Biden, Obama has shown his weakness by admitting his foreign and defence policies are not up to scratch, but he may neglect other aspects of policy, which may frustrate many voters. He should be way out in front on points, but the Convention bounce did not come and 'Change' might not be enough without substance.

Joe Biden

What to say about him? The main thing the British Media remember about him is the incident where he had plagiarised a speech by a British politician (Neil Kinnock) in 1988, though the fact that it was during a failed Presidential bid is not usually mentioned. My dad also laughed at the fact that Americans would elect a man called Joe as their President. Obama can gloat all he wants about how much he opposed the Iraq War, but his running mate Biden voted for the Iraq War and is a strong Hawk, already having influenced US entry into the 1990s Balkans Conflict. This could conflict with Obama's message come tough times ahead.

As mentioned above, Biden is part of the old guard of liberal Democrats and a safe pair of hands. But how ambitious will he be as the number two? Will he be Gore or Cheney; chomping at the bit to lead or the power behind the throne? Biden may be Obama's biggest liability either out-shining the young would-be president on policy or reminding voters of why he twice failed in his own bid for President.

British Media

The media here has succumbed to Obamamania. It is treated as some reality game where everyone says: 'I hope Obama wins' without any further qualification. There is an obvious bias toward him in the newspapers and TV news as if he can cure our ills as well. I've watched our newscasters constantly praise the Obama campaign while downplaying McCain; setbacks are disasters for McCain, but for Obama —one more obstacle to overcome.

I truly think that the Media here do not understand American politics and are taken in by the glitz and pizzazz of the Conventions and the personalities of the candidates rather than focusing on the policies. The media also does not understand the American people and think that after eight years of Bush and the Iraq War, they will automatically vote Democratic. But the American electorate are more worried about their jobs and homes at the moment and who can deliver on their promises. America will not take a huge liberal swing if it is not in their interest to do so. In these tight times they'll be looking for experience and outward and forward thinking to guide them with the flexibility of compromise. With the combination of experience, youth, liberal conservatism, Christian Right fortitude and regular American appeal McCain and Palin fit the bill.

Bearing in mind that this superficial view is from early September and that the TV debates have not happened yet, I won't change my opinion. McCain and Palin will win by a large margin. Watch this space.

03/Oct/2008

Politics, News & Issues - US elections 2008
Lipstick politics and Sarah Palin

Sarah, lipstick, and the Witches

Oh God! (oops, maybe I shouldn't say that!) Odin's eye! What the Zeus is going on with Sarah Palin? There is so much to discuss here, but I will try to encapsulate it in a couple of pages. So, Sarah Palin, the be-lipsticked pit-bull, Creationist Governor of Alaska, and the Republican Vice-Presidential candidate was allegedly caught on camera receiving a blessing from a witch hunting Pastor to protect her from all forms of witchcraft, as reported in the British Press from a YouTube clip. I'm going to go with the 'So What!' club on this one. It makes so much sense. Apart from the fact that I believe McCain and Palin will win, this story will probably add to the rich tapestry of her already eventful life, so what's a few witches' skeletons in the closet going to do?

Mrs. Palin's religiosity is well known, but to some of us who are less than total believers, it makes sense that if a person from one made up religion would want to protect themselves from another made up religion, then why not? It would be like a couple of players in a virtual reality game attacking each other over the Ethernet: It doesn't really matter because none of it is real! I won't even suggest that because her husband is part Inuit that maybe some of his ancestor's tall tales from their pre-Christian days got the better of her and she decided to act and forestall any Polar Bear spirits derailing her campaigns. But as a true believer, Palin has decided to take out an insurance policy against ungodly spiritual acts. You have to admire her devotion.

But how will this translate in the real world of politics? How damaging would it be? Would we find many Democrats ski-dooing around the State for more dirty snow on her or heavens forbid even converting to Wicca in any attempt to scare her and to learn new spells to vanquish her and the maverick political sorcerer that is McCain? Also, it was ONLY witchcraft being singled out here, if it had been a blessing to protect against Jews or Muslims or Chinese people, or even if she had been a male candidate, then the political stakes might have been a bit higher. Was this a religious hate crime? There have been sources claiming that there are veiled references equating witches with Jews, but no high profile Government official has come out and demanded an official apology from Palin. The biggest indication in the Palin factor will be the witch vote and the proportion that McCain and Palin receive. The 'witches for lipstick' campaign' should be one section focussed upon in post-election analysis on CNN. Let us see that slice of the electorate pie!

Don't forget Wicca, witchcraft, and paganism are fast-rising religions in the US. Palin would find this very distressing and have to take action, which could actually constitute Palin's first foreign policy initiative as she tours the world visiting Wicca councils, Pagan circles, Shaman and Witchdoctor seminars in order to fight the fight against them and try to re-convert them as Born Again Christians. No doubt such a bold move will draw criticism as much as Obama's pledge to talk to Iran. After all, if the witches won't give up their spells and mysterious ways, what action should be taken against them? Will all hell and spell break lose? Will Palin, an avid hunter and already in command of Alaska's military, be in command of the Homeland Security Witch Finder General Corps? How much of the Pentagon's budget would be taken up by anti-spell bombs and stealth planes to combat the broom brigades? Would there be a Palin Act declaring all forms of witchcraft illegal (again) or could this serve to highlight the plight of the minority witches and bring out the Free-Witches banners from Hollywood? Palin's blessing could turn out to be a curse, strengthening the base of witchcraft.

In a bizarre twist, two of Palin's daughters are the namesakes of famed TV witches. Willow and Piper from 'Buffy the Vampire Slayer' and 'Charmed', respectively, are celebrated good witches, though Willow did have a bad spell (no pun intended!). Maybe this blessing was actually a pre-emptive strike by a superstitious Palin to be immune from her two younger daughters if they grew up to emulate their TV doppelgangers and be artistes of the Craft! Has the Harry Potter generation spooked Palin? Is the whole Harry Potter filmography seen as an insider's biographical documentary on the rise of witchcraft? Would such films be banned? Would witchcraft be driven back underground like American socialism? Be that as it may, the witch community could be a vital swing vote and actually favour Palin just because of her choice of daughters' names.

Lastly, in watching the YouTube segment, there is a lot of 'in the name of Jesus', but without a full transcript and any confirmation from Palin, the Pastor, or the congregation present then, his exact words and meaning could be taken out of context. I could be a dubbed put-up job by a Democrat or even a witch to raise their profile before the election and trigger the next global crisis. But crucially, what if the blessing was genuine and it worked? Suppose Palin is now fully protected from all forms of witchcraft. Would this be the beginning of 'Voodoo Politics'? Maybe Palin can now see the world as it really is, un-blurred by the hypnotic spells cast by financial institutions, the rabid environmental lobby and the industrial-military complex.

Palin is the novice among the group, but is un-jaded by the years of political spin and indoctrination. She has fresh eyes, a new mind set and the spirit of America inside her. The blessing against Witchcraft could be an analogy, a modern parable if you like, of what is needed in the world today; to turn away from the perceived unknowns of evil, greed and conflict. In fact, on inauguration day, on the Capitol steps I want to see the blessing added as a measure of added protection. So, despite what people think about Palin and her lipstick, she might have actually done us all a favour!

13/Oct/2008

Politics, news & Issues – economics
Could a single global currency work?

Do we need a single global currency?

2020 vision

I do hate the idea of putting all our eggs in one basket whether it be Empire building (What's wrong with the nation-state?), language, or money. It's why I'm glad the UK has stuck with Pounds Sterling. As we've seen with evolution, stagnant one-trick ponies die out without new stimuli to create growth, competition, or offspring. Brexit is an outcome of this, too. Keep our differences, keep our choice, keep our freedom.

I think it was Margaret Thatcher who said we already have a single global currency –it's called the US dollar. That was in relation to the impending Euro. Not that the dollar is performing at its best at the moment, but it does get around, albeit it in tandem with other local currencies. And there's the rub; a single global currency sounds good and may make sense, but after investigating both sides of the issue, I don't think it will work for several reasons.

The Pros:

A single global currency would get rid of exchange rates and a myriad of other languishing currencies, thereby making financial trading easier and less perilous in less secure times. There'd be no more news reports of dollars to sterling; yen to euros; or roubles to rupees. This would also get rid of a whole industry of money changers and dealers, possibly leading to a more streamlined and manageable banking system. That could be a good thing. Would that have made this financial crisis better to deal with, with no foreign exchange rates and foreign money devaluations to live through? A single global currency couldn't be devalued against another country's making any funding more accessible.

Many countries around the world have updated their currencies with a few minor disruptions (e.g. Britain's shillings to sterling, Continental Europe's conversion to Euros), so adopting a single global currency maybe one continent at a time may help ease any disruptions.

Having a single currency would benefit financial security as black markets of alternative currencies would cease. Since everyone would own and know what a legitimate bill/coin looked like, it would be far easier to spot a fake. Better re-use and recycling of bills and coins would also be a benefit of a single currency. The costs in savings from not having to set up language translations of various currencies in shops, travel agents, banks, and on signs, would also be an advantage. Advertising, marketing and promotion could be targeted more effectively for one currency rather than several. A single currency would save money in bureaucracy.

Having a single currency would make it easier to have a cashless system. Paying by a credit system, chip and pin card, mobile phone, etc would be easier when spending or sending money around the world with no exchange commission or charges applied.

In an age of globalisation, a single global currency would add to the already growing arena of the global village. Weaker nations would feel akin to larger nations, sharing in the same currency of wealth, while confident in the knowledge that their smaller economies wouldn't be swamped with foreign investment currencies. A single currency would bring the world together, perhaps acting as a precursor to joined-up world governance; one currency, one voice, one world.

Or is that the case?

The Cons:
As was seen in the run up to the introduction to the Euro, the monopoly-like money of the European continent, countries hated the fact that they were giving up centuries-old currencies. People believed that they were giving up their independence, identity, and sovereignty to the European Union, whose parliament is made up of faceless bureaucrats, to most Europeans. The fate of one's own economic policy would lie away from their native countries. Luckily Britain has so far declined to join and has survived well without it, proving that a joined-up currency policy is not needed to prosper.

Not all nations are equal in their economies. Continent-wide single currencies may the precursor to a single global currency, but the third world countries and other weaker nations would have to come up to a certain economic standard, before a strong global currency overwhelmed their system. Even throughout Europe, the Euro is worth different values between the more prosperous west than in the east. Products and labour have differing values; prices will change in accordance to more local conditions, so there would still be some kind of discrepancies and 'exchange' rates from country to country. How could this be controlled?

How would institutions like the IMF and World Bank fare in this currency transition? A new global financial institution would have to be created, along with more bureaucracy and administration. The location of any central currency administration may be disputed so not to imply that a powerful nation controlled all of the world's money. Surely some of the multinationals would lose several divisions and others become defunct? Far from being streamlined, the banking system would be gutted, leaving thousands unemployed with lost revenue and taxes from foreign exchanges.

A single global currency would instigate globalisation, trade imbalances, and elimination of competition. It is also classic putting your eggs in one basket; a financial no-no. There would be no fall back just in case. Globalisation through a global currency would seem very Big Brother like. No world government plan has succeeded (League of Nations, -even the UN is a mess), a world language has failed (Esperanto); in fact there is no world spanning system that has succeeded or does not have some sort of tandem or back up system. A global currency would be a footnote with the League of Nations and Esperanto.

Lesser problems would include negotiations over what symbols to put on the currency and what denominations to have, what to call it, and who would have authority over printing and minting. Symbols on the bills and coins, would probably be neutral to avoid any accusations of bias over ownership and sovereignty. Even the currency's name would have to be neutral to avoid the same issues.

The myth of money and alternative currencies:
The myth of money lies in the fact that we give some intrinsic worth to bits of paper and metal. Anything could be used as money, but currencies are perceived at being at that value because a central power tells us what it is worth. Not all cultures believe in hard currency and its

power, thus unequal dominance would reign with larger countries and multinationals controlling weaker economies. Some countries, either because of ideological, religious, or cultural beliefs would not want to share a currency with another nation or their enemy or submit to what in effect could turn out to be neo-economic-colonialism. Because of the nature of free market economies and more socialist states, a single currency would end up in the hands of the marketers.

Alternatives to money would not also work. The Gold Standard is not the same as a single currency as the general population at large doesn't use gold. It was the preserve of the government and elite. Diamonds, like any other mineral/element, would necessarily lead to environmental degradation as miners sought evermore declining resources in sensitive areas. Plus with the general population walking around with pockets and pouches full of gold or diamond bits and dust, crime rates would soar, destabilising the market. A cashless system could also rival bills and coins, negating the need for a single currency.

Some people say that in the past, the Romans and other conquering empires established single 'global' currencies, but really there were other local currencies and trading systems in effect, as seem in archaeological investigations. There has never been a true global currency and there never will be. No other single global system has worked. Mankind is and always will be an individualistic-inclined, protectionist being and the temptation to impose any single global system upon him will be doomed to fail, as two World Wars have found. A single global currency would lead to a world of less choice, less character, and less freedom.

26/Oct/2008

Politics - US elections 2008
US elections 2008: The impact of race on the choice for Obama

Why I wouldn't vote for Obama:

First of all, I'm British, so I couldn't vote for him, but I really hope that Barack Obama does not become president just because he is black or despite of his 'blackness'. He should be judged as the man first and what he stands for. As a black man myself, I've always hated the fact that my blackness has either opened doors or caused others to speak on my behalf because of my colour. Case in point was my time in the British Army. I wanted to be taken at my own merit and prove things to myself, but when I failed one course and was back-squadded others tried to play the race card and get me back, as I later found out. I was not happy with that. I failed because I was not good enough, not because I was black [2020 vision – my white partner on the same failed exercise was also back-squadded, but there was no out-cry for him]. And so it is with Obama. If he wins it should be because he was the best candidate not because his blackness will somehow absolve America of slavery issues or show the world that America cares. If he loses then he lost not due to his colour, but because people doubted his message and social policies.

Obama's background is not that of the typical African American. His father was from Kenya and his mother from Kansas so he does not have that slavery issue hanging over him. That is attractive to white Americans who do not want to be constantly hearing about the sins of their fathers. However, to African Americans, Obama has the chance to lay to rest the stigma of slavery, even though Obama's ancestry is not their history (though Obama's wife and former pastor certainly do carry chips on their shoulders about it). Though race has not been an overt part of the campaign it is a factor and it has to be addressed so there are no festering undercurrents of racial hostility should Obama win.

To me, Obama is an empty shell of a politician. His orations are mesmerising, but preachy and mechanical, like the lecturer he was. He may be intelligent and eloquent, but you need more than that to be president, you need policies, not platitudes. Obama will not change America in the sense that the whole world is looking for in regards to foreign policy and economics. No matter the political affiliation, the US has been in some form of conflict every three years or so, since WWII. Not all have been senseless or unavoidable and in choosing Joe Biden as his running mate, a seasoned foreign policy champion, who voted for the Iraq war and backed Clinton into the Balkans, Obama is hedging his bets. Obama has never been tested under fire as a politician and has been a politician long on conviction; but short on action. Obama will have to become a hard-boiled President or he will crack under pressure.

Obama is the new face of young black ambitious talent as recognisable as Lewis Hamilton, Theo Walcott and Usain Bolt. He is fast becoming a cult of personality with more authored books than national policies; he is still only a first term senator. Even the increasingly mocked Sarah Palin has more executive and legislative experience than Obama, yet people feel she is not even up to Vice Presidential duties. America does not want a black president, just a president who can do the job. If Obama is seen as not helping the black communities, he could become a lame duck president in their eyes, just as David Dinkins was as New York's first black mayor from the early 90s, then came Rudy Giuliani, and the rest is history. If Obama does not deliver what blacks expect, what white America wants, and what the rest of the world needs then his legacy for future black presidential candidates could be lost.

Obama has come at the crux of a new age; a new age of economics (supposedly to arrive after the global financial crisis), a new age of energy (to meet the challenge of climate change), and a new age of politics (a softer, gentler US foreign policy). But that is similar to the Carter Presidency, who Obama's presidency could well emulate. But as an American friend told me, Carter actually believed in what he said, but his plans though real were a little bit too ambitious for the time. Obama, of course, will actually be the second black president, after Bill Clinton. Clinton was another cult of personality, much beloved by African Americans, who did not achieve much in two terms and whose wife could have been the first woman President if not for her marmite nature. People love Obama, because he promises a new vision after the Bush age, but the Bush era has cast a long shadow over the world militarily, economically, environmentally, and politically that Obama will find hard to dispel.

Over here in Britain, people are looking for our own Obama, but Britain is a long way from that with no viable black parliamentary offerings for the top job for some time to come. It is a class thing more than a race thing since Britain has a more-or-less better integrated society where blacks, whites and Asians can socialise and inter-marry more freely than most other nations. But there is seemingly a stained-glass ceiling for blacks in the boardrooms, public institutions, politics, etc. Will Change in America lead to change here? Or will it just lead to Obama envy and disillusionment?

If Obama fails to lift the African American community (or if they don't use his inspiration and help themselves) or if he is seen as pandering to them by the white community then Obama will find himself in a difficult position. His performance or lack thereof could also affect later black presidential candidates' chances if people remember Obama and any failures. The trust will not be there for future black candidates. The future of American politics could not only be about the blue Republicans or the red Democrats, but also about black and white America, which could cause further schisms. Obama has a mighty task on his hands and for a novice, I do not think that he has the political nous and experience to handle such pressures. So will America's future be black, bleak or bleached of past racial divides? I think Obama's time has come too soon and will lead to a more unsettled America; change indeed!

06/Nov/2008

Politics, News & Issues - US elections 2008
Why Obama won the election

Obama: The Zeitgeist of America

The Second Coming is upon us: America has elected the first President of the World. On my way to work in London, I could even hear fireworks, or was that just for the Diwali Festival or Bonfire Night? I am also waiting for the Concert for Obama to be announced. There are many reasons why Barack Obama won the election, not all obvious, and as a black Briton who was more inclined towards McCain, it was a bit frustrating to see the superficiality of the Obama movement grow into some worldwide cathartic Event. But that is why Obama won, he is the man of the moment (a little too soon perhaps) at a period when the world is at a crux in time in many ways. So why did Obama win?

First off are the obvious issues: following Bush, the worst rated President and the economic crisis which wrong-footed McCain. But most of all, it was because Obama had his whole party behind him, while McCain fractured his. Those were the evident reasons, but there is so much more to it.

The new eras:
As I have written before, Barack Obama has come at a time of change in energy concerns, economics and politics. He has not instigated the changes, nor will signing up to any feel-good global policies work any more than before. The world is full of subliminal messages and coincidences, and Climate Change issues and the matter of new energy sources has been weighing on people's minds. With oil associated with the Republicans, environmental issues drifted into the Democrat domain and the new Energy Age would naturally get kick-started with a new energised regime in place. Obama would stand for green and not just black issues.

Old Capitalism is dead, or so it has been announced. Some new banking system and monitoring process will have to be established during and after the recession. Of course this was caused by Republican failures to control the free market and reign in unworkable practices. But Obama's redistribution of finances and tax cuts will herald in a new Social Capitalism, more socially beneficial and just. Obama is a kinder tax man for the new money age.

Obamapoliticks will involve adopting a centralist role, if the Democrats will allow him, having also just won more seats in Congress and the Senate. He will speak to enemies, shake their hands, look them in the eyes, and get to know what makes them tick. But what happens when the talking stops? No matter who is in the White House, there will always be someone taking advantage, showing off their power, and ruffling feathers. Well, Obama will need the hawks, as well as the doves. On average, the U.S. has been involved in a conflict every six years since WWII, except during the Carter years, a notable weaker period for America. Even if Obama ceases all Iraq operations, there will still be Afghanistan and any other threat after that. Some conflicts will be unavoidable and Obama will have to walk the walk after the talk.

The new political era will spread across the world to Obama's ancestral homes of England, Kenya, and Indonesia; places where he and/or his family lived and grew up. But the touchstone of his honeymoon period will have to be a visit to South Africa; for Obama is also the new Nelson Mandela, a new 'African' son to take up the mantle. You can see the photo op now, surrounded by dancing Zulu girls, with Archbishop Tutu beaming and praying away to the soothing sounds of Ladysmith Black Mambazo. But here is also a chance for real change in Africa; Obama has the chance to truly reach out and save lives in Africa by educating the remaining superstitious and sceptical Africans about AIDS and other diseases they believe were created by white men to destroy them or that there are natural cures for them. Africans will see the example set by Obama and be inspired to choose their own Obamas for the future. A new era could be dawning for Africa.

The new eras continue with celebrity, the media, and sports.

Charisma:
I hate this word. It is without qualification a very false image to attribute to someone. Bush, Blair, and Clinton have charisma, even Hitler did. Charisma is only the surface reflection, like an iceberg hiding the rest of the flaws below. There is a danger of a Cult of Personality forming around Obama, where hype and his celebrity status overshadow

character and policy weaknesses, as with Clinton. Add charisma to the new era of Celebrity and reality TV and you can see why Obama was more popular than McCain in the youth and Hollywood vote. His orations (to me) were quite monotonous; it was his strong, rapturous voice and not the words which carried the real message. Just imagine Bush or McCain saying those exact same words and you get the point. Obama talked himself into the White House. But what will happen when the shock of the new wears off and Obama faces real scrutiny?

Media:
While Hollywood has been full of black actors and entertainers, with Denzel Washington and Hallie Berry winning recent Oscars, the small-screen media has also played a huge, if unwitting, role in Obama's win. Besides Obama dominating sound bites and news spots, at least in Britain, two highly-rated TV shows have portrayed a Democratic President. The 'West Wing' featured Martin Sheen and '24' featured a black American President played by Dennis Haysbert, who in at least one internet poll came top of best TV American Presidents. While not entirely endorsing Democrats or Obama, it would have set the scene in people's minds; a vision of a black Democrat President, thereby nullifying and pre-empting the race issue. There would be no mystery as to what a black President would do while in the Oval Office. So, while not an overt media ploy, such portrayals would have predisposed people to think: Why not Obama?

Sports:
A new era of sports was already underway with Tiger Woods and the Williams sisters winning everything in sight. But the new generation has pushed black athletes and coaches into a global limelight. Almost two years ago, the first two black American head coaches met in the Super Bowl - Tony Dungy for the Indianapolis Colts and Lovie Smith of the Chicago Bears. Black coaches have been slowly filtering into the NFL top spots, showing younger sportsmen that their careers won't end just as athletes and sports pundits. Add Lewis Hamilton into the mix, the youngest and first black Formula 1 Champion and people now see that new challenges and options are opening up to young black sportsmen.

It is plain to see that the rise of the black American was coming, but this rise was not reflected in the political arena which was lagging far behind. Into this new age of energy, economics, politics, celebrity, media and sports, stepped Obama. Whereas many others filled those slots before, Obama became a one-man gap-filler breathlessly and effortlessly donning the responsibility of the entire world upon his shoulders. Even his side-kick Biden disappeared in the glare of victory. Obama now has to switch from campaigner to practitioner and practice what he preached or he'll find that his coming will only lead to the wilderness. When once Obama followed in the wake of others, he is now on the crest of a tidal wave of power and responsibility, inspiring the next crop of black achievers.

As not to appear bitter and a sore loser, I will congratulate Obama. But I can only hope that once his picture is up in the White House, it is not on a separate wall to the others. Few men have stood on such a precipice of goodwill and admiration; greater men have not lived to tell the tale of such success. But whatever the consequences ahead and whatever it means to people, Obama has began the Era of Change.

24/Nov/2008

Politics, News & Issues
How can modern sea pirates be defeated?

Gunboat Diplomacy

Blow them out the water; give no quarter; show no mercy; take no prisoners: we need to deal with the pirates of the high seas. I believe an international armada should steam into pirate territory, sink all their attack ships and hijacked ships, and turn the areas into huge ships' graveyards to warn other pirates of the folly of taking ships. Hit the pirates where it hurts the most and show what we are willing to sacrifice to get rid of them.

No doubt other people think we should negotiate and understand their grievances, because they have human rights. Pirates are not terrorists per se, though some may share their ideas; they are criminals, whether Somalis, Chinese, or foreign mercenaries in the pay of onshore warlords, corrupt government officials, or other criminal organisations. Terrorists usually have political agendas and target such specific institutions for their cause, but these pirates are economic criminals, making money for their own gain. Whether they operate in territorial waters or international waters, pirates should not be allowed to keep on carrying out their attacks. Yes, some Somali pirates have been captured recently and handed over to Kenyan authorities, but it is no deterrent to other pirates. As long as they are safe out at sea or protected by some government or organisation, then piracy will be a constant problem.

The taking of the Sirius Star, the largest oil tanker taken by Somali pirates to be ransomed off for millions should be the wake-up call that dire action is needed. These Somali pirates have their stronghold at the port of Eyl, surely a tempting target for air and sea attacks by the international community. The Gulf of Aden and the adjoining Indian Ocean have become some of the most dangerous seas to sail through, even with patrols from various navies to help. Though few of the hijacked crews have been killed and many crewmen still sign up, this is still no reason to think that the pirates aren't ruthless thugs. They are affecting the lives and economies of global citizens and societies.

If such an international armada did attack pirate strongholds to deprive pirates of ports, ships and booty, the companies with hijacked ships should have insurance claims honoured and pirates made to pay reparations from all their ill-gotten ransoms, once all the crews are safe. In such situations, I do not think that any cost is too high to rid ourselves of these modern day brigands. I would ignore environmentalists on eco issues of contaminations and oil spills and have all the ships scuttled. If we the free world can't have the ships returned other than by ransom, than neither will the pirates. Some sunken ships could provide reef-like barriers for fish or storm breaks and become protected areas under international law, thus shrinking the areas that pirates (and other ships) could operate within.

Recently, an Indian warship destroyed a pirate ship, but there are still calls to have more patrols protecting commercial ships further out from Somali waters. Maersk, a Dutch merchant shipping company, is considering re-routing some of its fleet to avoid areas at a greater cost to itself, which could be passed on to consumers. With the global credit crunch, how soon will it be before piracy directly affects prices closer to home, whether with higher costs of products or taxes to help our navies combat piracy?

But are there other options to protect ships from pirates? Labelling pirates as terrorists and using anti-terrorism laws against them only affects their status upon capture. Maybe targeting the host nations of the pirates with threats of sanctions, payments of compensation to victims, and other serious consequences, will flush out the pirate sponsors and embolden these nations to give up the pirates. Will armed marshals or guards introduced on ships, like the airline industry be effective? How much firepower and force should a commercial ship have to possess just to be able to sail the seas safely? Is it better to deal with the symptoms or the cause? International talks about devising new approaches to piracy are on-going, but in this upcoming age of soft and consensual US foreign policy, the pirates will test the resolve of the nations and UN. The strong-arm approach will have to be used in tandem with any negotiations, where the law can then be applied, if that really makes a difference.

So who will blink first and end up walking the plank? For our sake and the lives of the merchant crews before they even set sail, bring back the gunboat, then we'll talk.

27/Dec/2008

Politics, News & Issues
Political theory: The needs of the individuals vs. the state

Political Lefts, Rights, and Wrongs

2020 vision
Below, I stated I don't vote, but since then I've participated in General Elections and the Brexit vote.

Sometimes I wonder what my own politics stand for. I used to be quite sure of my political leanings to the right, but lately, I have come to reconsider a lot of my convictions. Don't get me wrong, I will never be a limp, left-wing, liberal, do-gooder, but I feel that politics is no longer just about left, right or centre policies, but about common sense and decency.

In a rundown of issues I used to be sure of, some things have changed: I don't believe that the death penalty works as a deterrent; it seems to be an arbitrary punishment, when other methods could be used. I still believe that war can be justified even as a means to a political end, but that there are actually effective and just ways to wage war to achieve a lasting conclusion. I still believe in the private sector over pure governmental programmes that gives people less choice and freedom, but that a flatter economy and more public-private ventures are needed to create an equalised wealthy society. Politics now is either/or, for or against, black or white; the common ground is missing.

My charity begins at home and I direct my funds to organisations of personal interest and let my taxes take care of the rest, since I cannot control where they go. Having read the Unabomber's manifesto (only out of interest not devotion), I could see his point in Surrogate Activity, where one activity, say charity work, is actually an 'artificial' goal to achieve for the sake of accomplishment. But I also see surrogate activity in politics as a systemising activity.

If there is a hidden agenda in charity and foreign aid then it is to build up the Third World with foreign aid and charity and turn them into consumers for First World industries; to get them into the system where they can be controlled and taxed; to make them more like us - Westernised. That, to me, is the point of modern democracy; whether right or left politics, the only difference is how to achieve this. Politics is really a surrogate activity that will never achieve an ultimate goal, so why should I really follow any particular ideology? Why do I consider myself to be on the right?

What are left and right politics in the larger political scene? Why is there a political Newton's 3rd law where 'for every action there is an equal and opposite reaction', where political forces line up against each other and react in the opposite direction to the political force in power, even when they know they are wrong? Watching MPs in England engaging in 'yah-boo' politics is almost a farce where hardly anything is agreed upon, even within political parties. Is there a biological imperative with the right or left side of the brain ruling over the other creating a left or right politicising person? Is politics hard-wired into us, until a political epiphany hits us? Mine came after reading Naomi Klein's 'The Shock Doctrine.' Until then, I viewed the world in a certain way, and still do to an extent, but there are many destructive things done in our name, for freedom, and our way of life, that will be constant negative features of our history, because we rely on the yin yang of international politics.

Globalisation, the right-sided policy and Socialism, the left-sided agenda are really the same thing, but from different directions. They both seek dominance and can throw up a multitude of despots and dictators to fight against each other's doctrine. Take Hugo Chavez of Venezuela. He resists and taunts the U.S. in order to protect his country from perceived or real unfair economic practices and to strengthen his own power base, but in order to do this he has become a dictator and practically bully vast swathes of his own population. His democracy is demonstrably crazy as it offers no better alternative than globalisation. On the other hand, Globalisation has widened the wealth gap, made financial systems more susceptible to systemic collapse, and caused more stress and unhappiness within the Anglosphere (those parts of the world that share the English language and culture) so why are we pursuing unsustainable and destructive courses of action that are spreading across the world? Where are the politics of the common ground, the neutral laws, and the objective path?

Maybe Micro-politics and not macro-politics will be the way forward, where politics are decided from the ground up and funding provided by special micro-organisations without the need for a vast, central over-arching government with its own self-interests. Governments lose touch with the people too often and too much, but the situation is never resolved with a new leader who often implements the same programmes or changes for the worse. Some might say that people do not know best and we need to be governed, yes, but let the macro-government stand off and let people power reign. Will some kind of Third Way be the norm? If so, it will have to be stronger than it is now, with the private sector providing more for its own workers instead of out-sourcing. Profits should be for people and not for piling up for the Fortune 500.

In what may seem abhorrent to others, I do not vote. I know people have fought and given their lives so that others may be free and decide upon their own political fate and I should know better having been part of the Armed Forces. But I find that the people up for election are not inspiring enough and are all part of the same elite no matter their political philosophy. It is not about apathy or giving up on the system, I actually feel more empowered for not voting as I am not giving in to any political indoctrination. Change of any colour is not enough when the same people are in control. Coalitions rarely work and political objectives are too orthodox and short-term. Real change has to come from the population and their attitudes as to what they really want instead of being told what they want. But what I want is not on the political menu and that is a dissolvable political party; micro-interventionists who only convene at times of emergency; why do we need standing political institutions?

As I write, President Mahmoud Ahmedinejad of Iran has just given the alternative Christmas message on Channel 4 drawing widespread criticism from around the world. But here I see hypocrisy laid bare, since President-elect Obama had said that he would talk to Ahmedinejad (and other pariah leaders) to change American foreign policy and bring about peace, which is one reason why he was elected. So why should not Ahmedinejad offer a fig-leaf with a Christmas message? Shouldn't we forget the past and start a new future, if he really means it? Many other terrorist organisations and states have renounced their past deeds and turned over a new leaf. Iran is constantly challenged and denigrated for its ambitions so they bite back in belligerence. A few years ago, I would have been spoiling for a war with Iran, but in this case, there is no cause for one if some progress is made in peace. If Ahmedinejad offers conciliation for past words and deeds, then let him, without grudges and resentment, just as with the IRA, various Truth and Reconciliation tribunals, and Libya. There is room for talk, but just in case also have a big stick ready. There sometimes has to be a 'live and let live' attitude, but politics gets in the way. Politics creates divisions to exploit and one cannot trust the 'truth' of one's own politics to be entirely sure of reality.

A case in point: I often get into trouble for saying I think George W. Bush is okay. Even when I explain I mean as a person, rather than as the President, they sometimes still don't understand, unable to separate man from duty. I explain that Bush is not a bad person; that good people sometimes make mistakes or make the wrong decisions that they do not recognise, cannot correct or learn from. It happens – we're human. That is why I would not vote for someone else. Maybe I'm a conscientious objector to voting. The only person that can take care of me is me. I am responsible for my own actions in the larger scheme of things. I can change my own actions rather than that of the State, no matter who is in power. I vote for me. I am my own state; my own reality.

You can only be true to yourself, follow your own morals, and think for yourself. My politics have changed over the years, but are still governed by a right leaning compass; whatever that means -it is just a label, a portfolio of personal experiences, upbringing, self-invention, and ideas. And I am learning more about me everyday. If the above seems rambling and contradictory, therein lays the crux of my problem: I cannot be apolitical, but as my ideology drifts, where does that leave me in a world still ruled and contested by right and left? I will have to make my own way, my own choices, and be contented that my own politics do stand for something. That's all I need.

22/Feb/2009

Politics, News, & Issues
Political theory: Relevant or passé

World Orders

2020 vision

When I was a night concierge, I would bring in all sorts of books to read to pass the time during the quiet night shifts, usually sci-fi novels, but also history, science, and political books. One of the residents cottoned on to the fact I liked 'high brow' fare and so passed on a couple of Noam Chomsky books for me to read. Though not my normal stripe of politics, I gave the books a read and the more impressionable subjects gave me ideas for essays of my own.

Recently, while reading Chomsky's views on 'The Origins of the "Special Relationship"' between the U.S. and Israel, it was noted that 'the Israeli press speaks of "The Fifth World —Israel, South Africa, and Taiwan —a new alliance of technologically advanced states..." That didn't exactly develop, but where did this 'Fifth World' title come from? The Fifth World seemed democratic if somewhat highly militarised. Political theories were and still are all the rage, since defining oneself against others is still part of our human nature. But such theories encompassing World Orders are only brief labels over a period of time and their relevance soon becomes passé, once a new order is established.

Terms such as First World, Third World, Old Europe, the New World, the G8 (expanded from the G7), and BRIC (Brazil, Russia, Indian, China), are familiar to us, but what happened to the Second and Fourth Worlds? How could anything be lower than the Third World? Are economics the only way to categorise the world? Has the New World Order since the Cold War changed the world for the better when the global economy suppresses smaller nations? Any such system has no got us closer to international equality.

So what of the fallen World Orders? The Second World was used to denote the Soviet Communist states (Regan's 'Evil Empire'), China, and Cuba. Since the fall of the U.S.S.R., most of the European Second

World countries are now deemed as part of the First World (either in the European Union/NATO, G8, or waiting to join), while Asian countries are now relegated to Third World status. Other Third World countries are also designated as non-aligned or neutral and under the current banner of Developing Countries.

The Fourth World represents the stateless peoples such as the Kurds, Palestinians, Native Americans, Sami, various Asian and African indigenous tribes, etc. They are relics of the past living as nomads, herders, or hunter gatherers. The Fourth World is not used much outside of academic circles, maybe due to politically correct attitudes (with terms such as Stateless Peoples, Aboriginals, or Indigenous used) or publicising of the term. But there has been some action in trying to 'raise' the lot of the Fourth Worlders. In 1999, the Inuit homeland of Nunavut was created within Canadian territory. Since 1956, the Scandinavian Nordic Saami Council have been fighting for their rights and Greenland hosting the last Inuit Circumpolar Conference in 1998. The Kalahari tribesmen, the San, have regained some of their ancestral hunting grounds in the Kalahari Gemsbok National Park. In Australia, the Aborigines have been able to make some breakthroughs in their rights with the 'terra nullius', a colonialist act which claimed that Australia had no previous ownership was reversed in 1992. The few Ainu of Japan are asserting their rights. The United Nations Economic and Social Council is now seriously addressing indigenous issues. But does living in the so-called Fourth World just leave us in some misguided belief that there is a notional ladder of state progress that has to be followed? These peoples should be judged on their own merit and not as part of a larger structure.

There was a 1970s alternative World Order theory proffered by China's Mao. In his theory, the Superpowers of America and the Soviet Union were alone in the first world. Their allies (the rich Europe, Japan, Australia, Canada, and the Soviet satellite states) were in the Second World. China and other non-aligned states were in the Third World. But this notion was never taken as a mainstream theory and it eventually fell out of favour.

In recent times, the J-Curve –the index of stability and openness- has come to express a World Order. On a graph, Openness is measured on the x-axis and the y-axis measures Stability. So while some dictatorial states can be stable, they are not open, thus sit higher up on the 'j' than other states. States can move up and down the curve and along the x-axis. So, apart from just economics, nations can find themselves anywhere along the curve according to their internal and external factors. Many nations could thus escape Third or Second World fates if they could also avoid other nations exploiting their lower status.

When, if ever, will we be a global First-World planet? Will Climate Change, war, Neo-Colonialism, and resource issues further separate the World Order? Since the Cold War there has been the 'Axis of Evil' and the War against Terror; will other nations band together and create another arbitrary World Order as nations react to perceived or real World Orders? Should we still be promoting and living in these World Orders? Globalisation is destabilising equality, keeping nations in their place, but as it is controlled by the First World, under the nascent American Empire (Pax Americana), this current World Order could persist for some time. But as the Fifth World never materialised, maybe our current World Orders will also change over time to meet a future need for global cooperation. Hopefully this change will be a smooth transition and not precipitated by a global crisis or an unpredictable event, or the Next World Order could be our last. Then it would not matter if our political theories were relevant or passé.

Sources:
Chomsky, N. 2008. The Origins of the "Special Relationship". In The Essential Chomsky. A. Arnove (ed.). The New Press: London, 216.

http://en.wikipedia.org/wiki/BRIC
http://en.wikipedia.org/wiki/Second_World
http://en.wikipedia.org/wiki/Fourth_World
http://en.wikipedia.org/wiki/Three_Worlds_Theory
http://news.bbc.co.uk/1/hi/programmes/newsnight/5411212.stm
All links active as of September 2020.

23/Feb/2009

Politics, News & Issues
War in Gaza

The Plight of Gaza

Why has there been so much outpouring of grief for the Palestinians of Gaza? In this latest bout of tit for tat attacks, Hamas – the military wing of the elected Palestinian political party finally (re)provoked Israel into another attack by unleashing rockets into Israeli cities. As usual, the Israelis responded with its typical unrestrained nature, determined once and for all to put an end to the rocket strikes.

But who is really to blame for all the Palestinian civilian deaths? Hamas' actions of firing sporadic rockets into Israel were a deliberate provocation. Almost forgotten in the media reporting was the fact that Hamas initially attacked Israeli citizens and not Israeli military bases. Hamas was resorting to terrorist tactics. Also, in basing themselves among the general population of Palestinians, Hamas was also adopting guerrilla tactics for cover, for popular support, and maybe even to coerce cooperation from its own people. Israel, for its part, played the bad guy, uncaringly targeting areas in an effort to kill the Hamas leadership and military support structure. At least that was reported in the news, but once Israel banned all access to reporters, then all bets were off as to what was really happening. However, as the Palestinian civilian death toll rose, so the sympathy seemed to swell for the Palestinians.

But that support was not felt everywhere, especially in the Middle East, where people know what the Israeli/Palestinian fight is all about. Westerners forget that the Palestine/Israel conflict is now in the larger context of the U.S.-Iran proxy war. The other Middle East nations aren't publicly complaining too much or aiding the Palestinians because they understand the proxy war and are keeping a wary eye on Iran. Iran supplies Hamas and Hezbollah with the means (politically, economically, and militarily) to fight. While the other Middle East nations might not favour Israel, they fear Iran more and they would rather have Hezbollah and Hamas' wings clipped, as they are the current destabilising factions of the region, at the behest of Iran. It is a wait-and-see, tug of war, cat and mouse game, to see who will gain the upper ground.

This is one reason why the U.S. is heavily involved in Iraq and Afghanistan. The War on Terror neatly encapsulates America's plans to isolate Iran, encircle it by also trying to build U.S. bases in the former Soviet south central Asian states. If Oil was the primary motive to be in Iraq, it was not to keep it for itself, but to keep it out of Iranian hands. (As a counter to the oil motive, the U.S. has been involved in many wars in countries without oil or other resources. For example in Zimbabwe, there is no oil, but neither is there a threat from Islamic terrorists, the Russians, or the Chinese, so the U.S. will not act significantly there. It is not in their 'national interest' to do so unless another 'power' is involved; besides they can act indirectly in Africa through intermediaries such as Israel).

Ever since the U.S. lost its installed Shah in Iran and Saddam proved unreliable and surplus to requirements after the Iran-Iraq War (1980-1988), Iran's dominance was surely going to cross the America's radar sooner or later. Also, it was Iran through Hezbollah that chastened America (and France) from Lebanon in the 1980s. Now Iran is again testing the America's resolve in Iraq and Palestine. The U.S. in response has left Israel to take matters into their firm hand, though on the long outstretched leash of America. Iran's arming of Hamas is not only harming Israelis, but also killing their own people. Hamas has to bear the responsibility that they are martyring their own people for their own cause.

But recently, as revealed in the TV programme 'Iran and the West' Iran and America had at least two real chances since 9/11 for peace as their interests combined in the common enemy in the Taliban and al-Qaeda, but for whatever reason, the respective top authorities in Washington and Tehran both spurned chances, with Iran ending up in The Axis of Evil. Iran is now recalcitrant, reflected in their shadowy presence in Palestinian affairs. Gaza is paying the price for mistrust and decisions made far away.

Biased reporting and appeals for aid to Gaza with hardly any mention of Israeli casualties is somewhat galling. If Hamas militants live and work among the general population, then there will be 'collateral damage' whether wilful or accidental. When the brouhaha with the BBC refusing to air the Gaza Appeal occurred, some wondered why they did it. Surely it was not because they felt that there should have been a corresponding appeal for the Israelis that had died, or do Palestinian lives mean more than Israelis' just because Palestinians died in greater numbers? Rather than some concern for objectiveness, it may have been due to behind the scene factors and politics. The media should not take sides, their impartiality is crucial in times such as these. In the end, the mini scandal garnered more donations for the Palestinians. The cynic may wonder who really got the financial aid and supplies, the people or their culpable leaders.

The next time this happens, and it will, watch the news for what is said and not said. Which countries around the Middle East get involved? Who remains silent? The Palestinians are really just cannon fodder in the proxy war. Iran does not care about Palestine, so the Palestinians are victims of circumstance caught up in the buffer zone between East and West. They the victims of their own leaders, though Israel gets the blame (not that they are totally innocent). The larger picture has to be seen and understood in order to understand who is really pulling the strings. The Israelis are enthusiastic pawns in the international chess game. If there's any sympathy for the Palestinians it should be because whether they know it or not, they are paying the price as sacrificial lambs to the slaughter. No one country as such is to blame; it's an ideological stalemate burdened upon the East and West and someone had to bear the brunt between the Immovable Object of the Middle Eastern nations and the Irresistible Force of America. The plight of Gaza will continue until something breaks or someone shifts bringing all out war or all out peace, but Gaza will have no choice in which it is.

18/Mar/2009

Politics, News & Issues
Should there be a special tax on junk foods?

Junk Food Taxing

In this increasingly health conscious age, there has been intense debate about the effects of junk foods. One such issue revolves around taxing junk food to try and phase them out of our diets. But there is no need for a special tax on junk food, nor an extra tax, or any other kind of tax. Several factors are involved including questions over stealth taxing, what to tax and how, who it hurts or benefits, and how society should deal with junk foods.

Stealth taxes:
Junk foods and other foods should have their prices altered wholesale so that healthier foods cost less than junk food. At least that way the good companies would get the profits from their healthy produce and others would be penalised from pumping out the junk. If there was any tax, that would go to the government for their own use, no matter the stipulations placed upon the tax to be used to tackle obesity and healthy causes. We here in Britain have heard it all before with other tax initiatives obstinately to help in certain causes, but they just end up as stealth taxes - extra revenue-boosting schemes for the government that get channelled away from public works. A junk food tax would just be another stealth tax; a waste of time and effort.

Chocolate Tax?
This debate about junk food taxing was raised recently in the UK when Dr. David Walker, a food scientist and nutritionist, argued that chocolate should be taxed in order to reduce obesity levels and type 2 diabetes occurrences. He reckoned that chocolate had slipped through the net, escaping being maligned as an unhealthy habit as bad as fast foods, alcohol, and cigarettes. In the end, this comfort food could be damaging to your health. But should it be taxed? No, rather chocolate prices should be regulated so that the price goes up and those nations that grow the cacao bean are paid their fair share, rather than our own governments squandering any chocolate taxes. Taxing Chocolate would be a preposterous idea and it would be better to re-market such confections away from children or to have more restraint over its consumption.

Natural Law:

Junk food could alter human evolution. Most societies are becoming more obese due to high calorific intakes and low exercise regimes. The physical human is getting bigger, but living longer, and costing health services much more to maintain our unhealthy lifestyles. There is a solution here and that is to refuse or reduce medical services to those who make themselves ill though the over-abundance of junk food (or cigarettes and alcohol). But that isn't the politically correct option. But it could be under a literal reading of the Survival of the Fittest paradigm. If people cannot look after their genes, which will corrupt future generations, then they should be left to die off naturally, leaving the fittest behind. Simplistic, flawed maybe, but such actions could bear fruit (no pun intended) and create a more health-conscious society. Otherwise if obesity becomes the norm, for whatever reason, it could be seen as an advantage and positively selected for in future genetic mutations. Special taxes would not discourage junk food eating, thus Mother Nature would still win out, with humanity possibly evolving into a naturally obese species.

To balance the equation, for those who do not believe in natural selection, then as their body is a temple, they shouldn't ruin it through unhealthy practices, like eating unnecessary junk food. While Jesus may have befriended tax collectors, he was against unnecessary or excessive taxes, which junk food taxes would be as they would not benefit people affected by junk food illnesses. Society should be a self-regulating system with reasonable constraints and better incentives and if a bad diet means dying early, then so be it. If self-preservation and respect for others is not incentive enough to live healthily, then special taxes will not help deter junk food eating either.

Poor and Hungry:

Special junk food taxes would deprive poorer people of food since cheap junk food is a main food source. But if poorer people subsisted on poor food then they would not be around long enough to enjoy any benefits (no pun intended) from eating healthy food. If they cannot afford to pay for junk food which may be taxed, then they might as well buy healthier food at lower prices. There is no excuse for keeping poorer people on unhealthy food, but again, taxing them is not the answer. A nanny state trying to deprive people of junk food through higher taxes won't work. It has not worked for cigarettes or alcohol. Even now, the

UK government is debating whether to raise prices on beer, rather than solely relying on taxes. Taxes will only harm someone buying junk food, which is the point, but the poor will be deprived twice over, by having extra money taken from them and then not having that money invested back into their health services. There are other options to taxing, which will not make the poor, poorer and hungry.

The Future:
Imagine the future of taxes. We would end up with scenarios from the Sylvester Stallone film Demolition Man (1993), where every bad thing, including human bodily contact, was either taxed or banned. On the surface everything seemed perfect, but in reality there was a thriving black market underground in all things bad. We might not be going down this extreme route, but over-taxing will just lead to an equal and opposite reaction and a rise in black market activities. The laissez faire attitude towards foods should be tightened with food prices being regulated to fit the crime: Good food –low prices; bad foods –high prices. Simple. The only thing that should be taxed is our attitude towards changing our eating habits and that should be achieved through education, rather than monetary punishment.

Last, is a plea that will no doubt fall upon deaf ears. The food industry has to take a look at itself and the service it provides. Yes, their remit is to make lots of food for lots of money, but they have a responsibility in what they produce. Sooner or later, more legislation will force them to provide healthier foods at cheaper prices, negating the need for special junk food taxes. The best policies against junk food diets are education, physical exercise, and regulation of the food industry. This can be done without hurting people in the pocket.

24/Mar/2009

Politics, News & Issues
Humor: Politics

Noam Chomsky: American Spy – An Alternative Life

After reading a few of Noam Chomsky's books and also the Anti-Chomsky Reader, I have come to a startling revelation: That Noam Chomsky, the hated doyen of Anti-America is in fact the greatest American spy that ever lived*. I jest, you think! But no, think about it; Chomsky's Anti-American/Jewish/Capitalist rants and rallies provide perfect cover for his operations in counter-secret agency. America's secret champion travels the world under the guise of the Oppressed's Messiah in order to glean information and uncover nefarious plots against Chomsky's beloved government. Here below are the alleged true pieces of Chomsky's life construed from various factions, under no torturous means whatsoever (I think).

Early Life:
My investigations through secret U.S. documents and unnamed sources have revealed that from a young age, Chomsky was schooled in a C.I.A. college for gifted youngsters, trained to denounce America and gain favour among the communists and terrorists of the world. Under a pseudonym he later graduated top of his class from West Point as a Lieutenant and has worked as a spy ever since. His cover as a linguist allowed him to supposedly study world language, but in reality he was working to create, decipher, and destroy secret codes. His lack of continuation training in linguistics courses can be seen in his somewhat recent erratic theories on language. Chomsky's apparent deficiency in political nous is deliberate, since it is really his expertise. This throws Chomsky's detractors off the scent with ease; such is his commitment to his undercover role.

Early Career:
Parts of this section are selected moments from Chomsky's secret bio from unnamed sources at various U.S. Institutions. Lieutenant Chomsky's first major job in the 1970s was Vietnam. With Senator 'Communist witch-hunt' McCarthy down and out, Chomsky was ordered to take his place as the new national hate figure and establish his

credentials by befriending and drawing out the Leftist, Socialist, Anarcho-Communists from American Society, through decrying American actions in Vietnam. Chomsky bonded with these 'unsavoury elements' (as he allegedly called them) and garnered their support while gathering lists for his governmental cohorts. Even to this day the most rabid of his followers are on government files. Many people now believe Chomsky's manufactured assertions that America is the world's greatest terrorist (it pains him to do so), but his clandestine work has brought down many a terrorist cell. Due to his selfless work, Chomsky was promoted to Captain.

Mid Career:
During the 1980s, with his great friend and fellow Communicator, Ronald Reagan, Captain Chomsky formulated the 'Chomsky Doctrine' which was to manufacture the myth that the wars in Central America were all America's fault. In this way, Chomsky could pander to dictators, gain their trust, and steal their secrets; which would lead to America bringing freedom to the region. Chomsky really had to bear the pressure of criticism and hatred, but he persevered for the good of his country. At the same time, Chomsky had to malign his own heritage and attack Israelis and Jews. The fact that he was not assassinated for his views is testament to the fact that those in high circles knew of his exalted position in the spy hierarchy and he was protected. Due to Chomsky's work in pushing the Soviets over the edge, making them believe that Communism could work by stockpiling more nuclear weapons and then bankrupting them, Chomsky was promoted to Major and given an office with a window at C.I.A. HQ, which he cannot take at the moment (obviously). With the Cold War over, Chomsky was due to retire, with a gold watch and a slew of medals in hand, but he was offered one last mission, which he eagerly undertook.

Late Career:
Major Chomsky's new objective was to root out Osama bin Laden and his terrorist horde. To do this, Chomsky had to ratchet up his anti-American rhetoric and blame the U.S. for all the ills in the word since Columbus. Word had it that from his cave in the mountains OBL (as bin Laden is known in higher circles) declined Chomsky's invitation to a world anarchy party to be thrown in his honour –though this is just a rumour of a rumour. Chomsky himself still treks in the wilds of the Afghan/Pakistan border looking for his foe, but to no avail. It is

understood that OBL believes Chomsky should convert to Islam before he will meet with him to prove himself. It is not known at this point whether Chomsky is under going such training. In recognition of Chomsky's work, President Bush II almost named Guantanamo, 'Camp Chomsky', but after being reminded that Chomsky was a 'secret' agent, Bush decided not to.

Movie Career:
From sources unnamed, though close to the White House, it was often known that Chomsky went bowling with Condi Rice, where they formulated U.S. policy (in fact the Domino Theory was originally called the Bowling Pin Theory). At one bowling session was ex-British Labour MP, George Galloway, Chomsky's English equivalent. Galloway's mission was to indefatigably set up his old friend Saddam Hussein for a fall, though it took two wars to succeed. For his part, Galloway was secretly knighted, though of course this could never be revealed publicly. But Galloway also revealed that he was the model for James Bond, a fact acknowledged by sources from MI6 (far from me to name names).

But even more astonishing is the fact that Jason Bourne, Robert Ludlum's literary hero was inspired by Chomsky himself. The cast iron proof is the casting of dour, humourless, boring Matt Damon in the role, who captured Chomsky's affected personality to a tee. Bourne's amnesia mirrors Chomsky's initial training and suppression of his true 'Americaness'. Bourne's fight against the system accords with Chomsky's fight to end tyranny. Of course the action was updated and spruced up to protect Chomsky's identity, but his intellectual jousts were just as brutal. If these facts were known, then the Bourne trilogy would have earned several Oscars instead of Lord of the Rings (a factual predication of the fall of the Soviet Empire)**. So Chomsky has been honoured with a big screen biopic, which coincided with his promotion to General.

For over forty years, General Noam Chomsky has been America's most selfless servant. He is a brave man bearing the slings and arrows from a general public that will never know what he has done for them. As I write these words for an anonymous agent, I salute the General for his dedication to the American cause. God bless you, Chomsky.

Footnotes:
* see text above. It is all true, if it isn't a lie, which it could be.

** More to be revealed in my future book: Chomsky 2012: The Mayan Capitalist Conspiracy – How the Mayans predicted America would rule and destroy the world in 2012.

26/Mar/2009

Politics, News & Issues
Will the current global financial crisis cause wars?

The Credit Crunch War

2020 vision
It seems to me that during such lean years and now with the pandemic, with every nation practically in each others pockets, there isn't the time, energy or money for war. At least not an overt declaration. However, as we know certain clandestine operations are afoot with the Russians involved in UK and the US election interference. Why wage open war when you can influence from the dark fringes? (note - link still available as of September 2020)

So, we've come to this? Dominique Strauss-Khan, head of the International Monetary Fund stated that the economic crisis is so bad that it 'could lead to war', if not sorted out soon. War? Things may be tough all over, millions facing poverty, job losses, and emigration, but this just sounds too alarmist. The IMF may be just issuing some form of verbal insurance policy to protect itself if things really go wrong and they failed to predict it or is just throwing out ideas, but this seems too far-fetched and irresponsible.

Rich v Poor:
First off, who besides the rich nations has the money and clout to wage war in this economic downturn? Is Strauss-Khan thinking of the pre-WWII Depression and how history could repeat itself? Certainly the First World nations won't fight each other so would they fight the poor nations? Well, this is already happening, with wars for resources, energy and land, so that cannot be blamed on the credit crunch. The credit crunch may make things worse, but these wars may have happened anyway. Will poor countries fight poor countries? Well, this is already happening too and if they can fight a war, then where have they got the money from to fight it? Why waste money on a war for no gain? The only countries that would gain are the rich ones, but what is there to gain from a poor country? They are poor for a reason (no resources, work force, or exports). Anything stolen in a credit crunch war would probably be worthless anyway.

Would the credit crunch cause a civil war with the haves and have-nots fighting for resources? Again, this already happens and the credit crunch could not shoulder the blame alone in causing tension that may have already existed. Any of the warring factions could just use the credit crunch as an excuse, when in reality there were other underlying problems. In the end, a Credit Crunch War would not be worth it.

E-Wars:

Strauss-Khan did not expand on his views of future wars, so maybe there are other explanations for his outburst. If the war is not a hot one, then will it be economic? Will the war be cyber-based with bankers, bloggers, and hackers on the front line? As most of the money precipitating the credit crunch was virtual, even more of it could disappear into the void. This 'e-Credit Crunch War' could actually be quite devastating, leading to a hot war and causing a total economic collapse. Denial of service and virus attacks could be just as crippling to a nation as hundreds of cruise missiles, affecting millions of people than a hot war thousands of miles away. The fears of Strauss-Khan are echoed by the Pentagon, whose cyber-warfare assessments however came on the back of climate change issues and terrorism. If Strauss-Khan meant this kind of war then surely he would have directed banks and other institutions to toughen up their online security as the Pentagon had already foreseen. Cyber wars are also already happening, but it is yet to be seen if the credit crunch will affect hacking intensity and frequency.

Bank wars:

In a perverse way, the IMF could be direct sponsors of any credit crunch war having loaned many countries funds that could subsequently be used to acquire arms to fight wars. So any war would be part-funded by the very banks and institutions that are themselves in financial trouble. The Banking Wars would be even worse than before the crisis. Before, the banks were friendly and lending to each other, bending lax regulations, and profiteering. Now they are jittery, afraid to lend, yet still wanting to be bailed out. The banks are already in a war for survival, so they could be more conservative in their future investments. Lack of investment, loans, and other support could push other countries over the brink, leading to conflicts, not just against people, but also against the banks themselves, even to the IMF's doorstep.

There are many ways to define war, with its many targets and objectives, but how did Strauss-Khan see the any credit crunch war ending? Does he privately concede that the IMF is partially culpable for any impending war through its funding programmes? Who will rescue those at war if the financial system collapsed? The credit crunch war could not only cause a revolution in society, but also a revolution in economics. War could lead to a level economic playing field. Maybe the IMF should welcome this and help pick up the pieces after any war and function as it was suppose to do when it was first established.

Wars of liberty:
Will liberty and democracy be threatened by the credit crunch as Strauss-Khan proposed? Well, the world won't become Socialists because of this. Terrorism Laws in many countries have already restricted some activities with their application to credit crunch problems already causing rifts between the UK and Iceland. But Strauss-Khan's assertions are a dangerous route to go down, for as mentioned, it would give anyone an excuse to act out in violence and then blame the financial crisis. Riots, strikes, and anti-social behaviour may arise from financial frustration, but both governments and local communities should be working to forestall such outcomes. Argentina's economy went into meltdown in the late 1990s (with the IMF not entirely blameless), yet they survived as have many countries. This may be the biggest crisis yet, but there is no reason to suppose that we will not survive, despite IMF interventions, and stay democratic

If Strauss-Khan is playing the provocateur or devil's advocate then he is doing a good job of stoking up fear, resentment, and the war drums. This could give an excuse to anyone looking for whatever gain from the credit crunch, making Strauss-Khan's dire warning a self-fulfilling prophecy. While the IMF has a duty to foresee future problems, they should also provide solutions or at least elaborate on the problems instead of just floating out doomsday scenarios with no basis in fact. Dominique Strauss-Khan should take responsibility for his words and work to avoid such a drastic outcome. If there were to be a credit crunch war, it would not be the sole trigger, sharing top billing with climate change aggravation, terrorism, resource shortages, and energy concerns; any one of which is already exploited for whatever reason. Let us hope that the IMF will be part of a creative solution and not stirring up the problem.

29/Mar/2009

Why Join The Military?

2020 vision

This was probably in Politics & News – Occupations. It was written 12 years after I had left the army. And almost another 12 years on since the article, I still look back in pride at my time in the army, the people I met and am still friends with (and the ones lost along the way), the places I visited, and the work I did on helicopters all while serving my country. It wasn't always easy, but I would do it all again.

Of course, in my particular role while I was enlisted, I wasn't in a front-line war theatre; close, in the Former Republic of Yugoslavia, but not the same. I had joined just before the Gulf War and left by the Iraq War, so my experiences are different. And I salute those who have sacrificed themselves protecting us.

In this uncertain day and age for conflicts and emerging disasters, why would young men and women want to voluntarily join the military? Is it just about national pride, for Queen and country, or is it about a life experience on a different level? There are many reasons to join, as I discovered myself. I liked helicopters, and was fortunate to work on helicopters in the British Army. It changed my life for the better and now I use my experiences to enhance my life and career prospects.

In my younger days, I lived in New York, so the TV ads proclaiming: 'Be all you can be' and 'We do more before 9am than most people do in a day!' were quite un-missable. Even while at High School, Armed Forces representatives would visit my on recruitment drives and drum up patriotism. Some of my friends answered the call after graduation. I returned home to England in 1990 and followed in my dad's footsteps into the British Army, who had served in the 1960s. My parents were supportive of my choice. So, besides my love of helicopters, why did I do it?

I did it for the adventure, the challenge, to find myself, to grow up and become a man. I wanted to learn a trade and travel, through which I became more confident and organised. There wasn't a conscious decision to follow my dad into the army like a family tradition; it was just something I wanted to do. I found my youthful anger and stress channelled into doing something I loved. Not all was rosy, however, such as the technical training, firing ranges, drill practice, and field exercises, but I did enjoy the social life and camaraderie from a bunch of zany characters. Luckily, I have kept in touch with old friends, some of who have started families and are a few years away from completing 22 years of service, a real achievement.

Also, the experience was different for me, being slightly older than the other recruits, at 22 years old, and also in being black. During my time in, there were about five or six other black people in my various units, much less than the influx of women who started joining around the early nineties. While there was initial ribbing for my age, there were a few slight racist issues, which mostly and overtly occurred in Germany and Croatia, though I didn't let them affect me. However, while I found that my colour wasn't a barrier to progress and that ability counted for a lot, a more important criterion seemed to be if your face fitted, which mine apparently did. The saying went 'Play the game', -keep your head down and do the work, which I did. There were other technicians with better abilities than me, but for whatever reason some didn't fit in or who were teased for something or another. I found the army to be like any other institution, made up from a British society which divides normal from the abnormal. I found that by just being myself, making friends, and getting on with life in the army made me more acceptable than others who could not fit in, black or white.

To dispel a few misconceptions, not all the jobs in the army require you to fight or kill someone. You may be a soldier first (with weapons training) and your skilled job second, but they are not all front-line positions. Not all soldiers are aggressive, in your face or misogynistic, I certainly wasn't and am still not, so don't expect to change into a yob. Depending on the job and posting, you won't be isolated and out of touch from friends and family (though it may be difficult to communicate the things you've been through). And the army is actually a great place to save money, stay fit, and hone new non-military skills. The army is what you make of it; the opportunities to travel during overseas postings are great and the chance to study is encouraged. While the army has invested time and money in you to obey orders, there is still scope to be an individual, to grow, and to offer the army a multifaceted soldier ready for promotion and to set an example to those that follow.

So after all of this, why did I leave the military after six and a half years if I wanted to join so much in the first place? Well, I got bored, bored of the same job day in day out, as one could get in any other job. I needed a new challenge, to stretch my mental abilities, which in fact the army had inspired. After all the travelling to some exciting historic and cultural places on postings or leave (Germany, Canada, Croatia, Belize, Peru, and Hawaii), I wanted to continue that and study archaeology. Being in the army helped me into university and into work. The army also helped build my confidence and keep me organised and self-disciplined.

My years in the army will never be forgotten and I do highly recommend it. If I ever had children I would certainly entertain the idea of them joining the military. Even in this dangerous time, the military can offer a life training experience found nowhere else in the world. There is that sense of duty, but that call has to come from within, to be dedicated, positive, and willing to learn. So, be all you can be, and more in the military.

13/Jun/2009

Strike action serves no purpose anymore

Tube Strike: London

June 2009, and once again, London was held hostage by the selfish actions of the RMT (the national Rail, Maritime and Transport workers) union who forced through a strike action by all, but one, of London Underground's unions. It has become an annual rite for this organisation to commit to strike action under the banner of higher salaries, better conditions, and health and safety matters for its 80, 000 members.

The RMT may have the best interests of its members at heart, but this sustained assault of strikes is not gaining sympathy from the public who have to suffer from 24 or 48 hour strikes and travel misery. Yes, that is the point of strikes, but in yesteryear, strikers used to have the support of the public and they went on strike for valid reasons. Nowadays, for a tube driver, who is on £40,000 per year on a 36-hour shift with 43 days holiday and free travel on the tube, to want more money, particularly in these times is absolutely unfounded. For a supervisor on £35,000 (plus) a year to turn around and blame the fat cat bosses of rail companies is a disingenuous diversion tactic; the bosses aren't on strike and have nothing to do with the cause of the strike. For the RMT to change their reasons for the strike, flipping between pay conditions, redundancy and job security issues, solidarity for a sacked worker, safety matters, and difficulties with the London Mayor, Boris Johnson, is also shameful.

The RMT leader of the strike, Bob Crow, even boasted that he was glad the strike had caused disruption. There was no contrition or understanding for the plight of the public, no forthcoming apology; nothing except the threat that another strike could loom in the following weeks. This last strike cost London an estimated £100 million pounds -"a roaring success" said Crow. He wanted maximum disruption and London to shut down. For someone in charge of such a transport union, his comments should spark calls for his own resignation. His attitude will not garner sympathy for their cause and will invoke future hostility.

Despite this latest strike, London did not come to a complete halt. One union, Aslef, did not back the strike and only two of the eleven underground lines were completely halted. Hundreds of extra buses were brought in (though were still overcrowded), more people biked to work, walked, took ferries and boats, or worked from home. Driving a car was the worst option, clogging up the roads. Londoners do understand strike action, but it is the manner of the strike which gets under people's skin.

As mentioned, this is a frequent occurrence, sometimes with multiple threats of strikes in a year. While people are at opposite sides to the debate over strike action, a fundamental issue has to be with the cause, effect, and process of the strike action. Quite often there are undercover media investigative-reporting on underground workers, which often uncover bad practices from the workers and sub-contractors. When the RMT strikes for health and safety matters, then they should take this issue up with the companies, internally, and clean their house first before harping on publicly about such issues. When arguing over sacked worker issues, in most cases the worker had been found to contravene health and safety regulations and was fairly sacked, but the union steps in and protests. If these were legitimate protests, then the RMT should publish all such details on the web, or in newspapers, instead of arguing publicly with government officials and other rail companies and unions. The public does not have the salient facts, thus the public's non-understanding of the RMT's strike demands undermines the union's credibility.

However, the biggest issue is with pay. Underground workers get paid handsomely for the job they do, especially compared to other transport workers. Yes, they endure stress from verbal and physical abuse, running over people on tracks, and confined work spaces, but many other jobs have the same or higher stress levels, yet do not go on strike. Bus drivers share the same issues, but do not strike, and while postmen, rubbish collectors, cleaners, hospital workers, teachers, lorry drivers, firemen, and other workers may strike for the same reasons as underground workers, it is not a yearly event or even a threat of one. Only tube workers consistently strike, with each one diminishing their reputation. The police are banned from striking, but recently had a walkout (2008), the closest to a strike for ninety years. Tube workers get paid more than double an average soldier's wage, yet soldiers do not strike. The hypocrisy of the RMT is breathtaking. There are many more jobs out there which do not have the benefits and luxuries that tube workers have, yet they do not strike. While they may provide an essential service, they are not immutable. And some form of action should be taken against the RMT.

No matter the allegiance of people to one strain of thought on strikes, the fact is that strike action is a breakdown of communication. Other organisations have settled their disputes without strikes. The fact that the RMT cannot suggests a flaw in their organisation and communications policy. It is trying to justify its existence and membership fees. Their fall back/re-set condition is to strike and an organisation with such a mindset is not fit for purpose. It shows a general lack of understanding in the principles of public transport, is against the spirit of worker union issues, and is showing contempt of the general public. The RMT is out of step with modern world politics.

Actions against the RMT or for any strike action could range from fines for striking, limited bans (yearly or phased), contract changes or losses, or other suitable punishments. Some people might say that that will lead to more disruptions and costs passed on to the public, but at the same time, some form of action has to be taken to limit the power and frequency of strikes. In the case of the RMT, there are hidden political agendas (as implied by media reports), so stronger action could see the government step in to control the transport network in a larger public-private partnership. At least the public would then have some say in how their underground network runs. The best course of action may be just to fire the vast majority of the London Underground network and go the route of the DLR (Docklands Light Railway) by having the system automated. Machines won't strike (yet) and the public is used to a faceless technology running many everyday systems.

Will the RMT get its act together and show some sign of civility to the public and their workers? It can only be hoped so. Any more strike action and the RMT could find itself facing counter-strike action by the public who will refuse to take it any longer and take their grievances to court or to the RMT offices. Enough is enough.

20/Jun/2009

The case of legalizing drugs

The Legalisation of Drugs

All drugs currently illegal should be legalised. The war on drugs cannot be won due to human nature and our socio-politico-economic polices. There is no need to quote statistics to justify or denounce this issue, since statistics can be manipulated, misquoted, misinterpreted, de-contextualised, and classified/re-classified, *ad nauseam*, etc. Society changes the use of statistics and the status of drugs changes throughout time to suit those societies.

Society:
To ban anything goes against human nature. It's the proverbial forbidden fruit. Put something out of reach and someone will always strive for it. Making drugs illegal has not stopped the use of drugs. The idea that it is illegal actually draws some people, mostly the young and disaffected, to use them. They get a thrill from drug use (including cigarettes and alcohol) or may be forced to use them whether unwillingly under peer pressure or to escape everyday life conflicts. What stops people from using even legal drugs is their own common sense and moral aptitude. People would use these same judgements if all drugs were legalised.

Putting it another way, crime is illegal, yet even the threat of the death penalty does not deter criminal activity in even the harshest of states. In fact, states with the harshest penalties have higher rates of criminal activity, often involving drugs. In these current times with society at a low ebb, drugs will alleviate people's worries or illegally increase their wealth. Society is pressurised and all kinds of temptations will drive people to drugs. So what can be done to relieve this malaise?

Legalising drugs would go some way to addressing this system. As with crime, it is effective law enforcement, understanding the underlying causes, and people's own respect for the law that prevents crime. As with any legal and/or prescription drug, effective drug regulation is strictly controlled. Yes, there are abuses of the system, but far less damage would be caused to society. Legalising drugs in a social context would eliminate the desire to do drugs as an anti-social statement or to drop out of society. The tendency to demonise children as drug-using delinquents would decrease, and drugs would be seen as no more good or evil as cigarettes and alcohol. For those who would want to use them, drugs would be sold and administered by professionals in controlled doses. Education and counselling would be offered and children taught about the dangers of unmanaged drug use. While drugs would be legal, they would still be dangerous, so they would be kept behind counters, though the stigma of using them would be taken away. Controlled drug use would lead to less and harmful drugs as dangerous additives would be eliminated or diminished. Children would grow up in a world where drugs would be de-mystified, the 'coolness' stripped away, and people responsible for their use. This policy will not create a perpetually drug-induced society under Big Brother control, but one more in control of and aware of drugs.

Politics:
We already use harmful legalised drugs, far worse than some illegal drugs, in the form of cigarettes and alcohol, two of the biggest killers of mankind. But political and business decisions were made long ago to legalise them, as their stock crops could be controlled and taxed. And that is the crux of the whole debate and the root of hypocrisy when dealing with legalisation of drugs. Poppy seeds, coca leaves, cannabis (hemp), etc are drugs that cannot be effectively controlled by western governments, but tobacco and certain grains (e.g. barley, hops, wheat, etc) to make beer (and to a certain extent tea and coffee) can be controlled, so they are deemed legal. The fears that western governments are actually secretly controlling illicit growth, movements, and sales of illegal drugs to finance and conduct wars would also disappear. There would be no point in "Do as I say policies; not as I do" double-standard practices or pandering to drug companies. Legalised drugs would create a level economic and political playing field.

The countries and organisations that grow and profit from illegal crops are also stigmatised and marginalised. Such countries like Columbia, Afghanistan, Morocco, The Philippines, and Thailand then become targets for war, civil unrest, famine, and poverty. Illegal drugs have not made any country prosper, except for their crime lords and corrupt politicians. Depravity and violence often set in. Contrast this to Holland which has a more liberalised attitude towards drugs. Again, it is not a perfect system, but Holland is not a degrading crime den. Drugs are used responsibly in a social setting, safe and non-threatening. Following such enlightened political decisions could foster a world-wide template in the legalisation of drugs. Either that, or cigarettes and alcohol are made just as illegal, but the reasons why they are not are economic.

Economy:
Imagine those drug-rich countries from above as rich countries in the G20, boosted by the sales of legalised drugs. Countries would have licensed farms to grow drugs, turning illegal drugs into legal cash crops to help their economies boom. The farmers would be providing drugs for medicinal and other legal purposes. Those afflicted with chronic pain would be able to use coca leaves or cannabis without the threat of being arrested. In the case of coca leaves, the base ingredient for cocaine, it was once used in coca cola, but now alternative extracts or synthetic drugs are used, like caffeine. Instead of just being tied to the Andean highlands, coca leaves could be enjoyed again in its pure form as a tea ingredient and a pain/fatigue reliever. Hemp also has industrial uses as fuel, construction material, and food. Such dual purposes from illegal drugs would make them more palatable as legal commodities.

The world spends more time and money in fighting drug wars, pursuing, prosecuting and detaining drug offenders than it would in regulating drugs. Low-dosage and controlled drug use would effectively cut down on users involved in crime, in disease, psychological problems, infections, and other situations, saving the tax payer millions. Medical, police, social and other services would be freed financially and physically from having to deal with illegal drug problems. In all of this, there would be a debate about how drugs would be legalised and in what dosages, though drugs would be rendered less addictive and potent (possibly through genetic means). Some variations on drugs would have to be 'phased out' (like skunk, crack, and LSD), but that dilemma would be resolved once trial tests of legalised drugs took place.

There is a dearth of political action and wanton lack of responsibility in dealing with the drug legalisation problems or even raising the debate. There is the fear that legalising drugs would lead to a more drug-fuelled society. But regulated in the right way (and yes, there are many debates as to what is the right way) legalised drugs would cut crime dramatically. Black markets, street dealers, drug smuggling, and money-laundering, etc would be under-mined, with money going straight to governments or legal institutions and not into criminal hands. Just as oil money and taxes are petering out due to global warming scares, legalised drug money could take up the slack, just as cigarettes and alcohol taxes and sales have been doing for decades. For its past sins, legalised drug money might as well be put to good use in national and community projects.

Legalising drugs could end centuries of social, political, and economics quagmires. The benefits of such a move would undoubtedly outweigh all present negative effects drugs have. Legalising drugs would be a case of "Better the devil you know", where drugs would be in the open and able to be controlled and legislated for more effectively. Coming from a non-user of drugs, the case to legalise drugs is the best option available and the least that could be done is to start the debate. Drugs will never go away so let's put them to the best possible legal use.

25/Jul/2009

The role of horses in policing

When the Police Don't Need Police Cars: Mounted Police

Sometimes on the streets of London, there is the not unusual sight of seeing mounted police patrolling the streets, though people still stop and stare. You may wonder what is the use of mounted police in modern society, when they have cars, bikes, motorbikes, helicopters, boats, inline skates, and even Segway transporters? Is the horse just an anachronistic show of force for an intimidating effect? Do the public see mounted police as modern knights in flak jackets or fanciful cowboys? The history and use of mounted police in London is an often forgotten and unappreciated duty.

The first horse patrols were in London in the 1760s. John Fielding, who was the Bow Street Magistrate, and founder of the Bow Street Runners (a prototype police force) organised government funding for the horse patrols to secure main roads. Though this was discontinued around 1764, it proved a success. Patrols began again in 1805, again from Bow Street, employing the services of ex-cavalrymen with proper uniforms and weapons (pistol, sword, and truncheon). In 1829, the Horse Patrol was formally incorporated into London's police force, by the Police Act of 1829.

What kind of training is involved for the mounted police? Nowadays, police horses are a "three-quarter bred" Heavy Hunter, "(three parts Thoroughbred and a quarter of a heavier breed)". They and their riders are trained in Thames Ditton in Surrey. The horses are trained to handle noise such as gunfire and crowds, cope with fire and smoke, and withstand long hours on urban roads –horses fitted with special shoes and even head armour in some cases. But is a horse more cost-effective compared to the other modes of transport? How many police and civilian staff does it take to raise, train, and maintain a police horse? In the same way as the car industry can benefit from supplying police cars; farms, food suppliers, traditional crafts and equipment, and staff benefit from the continued police horse service.

Most people in London associate mounted police with football game crowd control, Trooping the Colour, or from the notorious horse charges during the London Poll Tax riots in 1990. So why keep them around? What kinds of incidences do they report to –surely not domestic cases or bank robberies (excepting McCloud)? Where do you park your horse outside of the stables? And what, if any, are the detrimental effects to horses facing modern criminals armed with guns and cars? Horses can provide 'high ground' protection, crowd control, cover long and hard distances and terrain that transport vehicles cannot go, like the small, tight alleys of Central London, and also horses are also quieter. In east London, Bow police station has a mounted police section, routinely providing patrols for West Ham football games, the Olympic site, and other local areas. The horses are thus exercised and kept active with these patrols.

Are police horse injuries and fatalities from modern crime recorded? Thus far, this author has never heard or read a news report about injuries or fatalities to police horses compared to frequent stories of random or deliberate injuries and abuses to 'normal' horses on farms or race horses. Whether this is due to the nature of the report or non-interest from the media is not known.

Some counties are now bringing back the mounted police service in order to control rowdy crowds, provide high visibility, and increase cost-effectiveness. Of course, with children and horse-lovers, seeing mounted police may open up another avenue of communication and respect for police.

There is still a fascination with mounted police, whether in their day-to-day operations or in their ceremonial roles for the state. They are not cowboys, but this old-fashion service still provides a very modern role.

Sources:
http://en.wikipedia.org/wiki/Mounted_police (link active as of September 2020)

http://www.met.police.uk/mountedbranch/index.htm (link no longer active)

http://britishaffairs.suite101.com/article.cfm/mounted_police_and_cro wd_control#ixzz0JfK2pSJD&D (link no longer active)

09/Dec/2009

Politics, News & Issues
Analyzing the war on Iraq: Justified or not

Iraq War Issues

Is the war in Iraq Justified? Who cares! The question if this, or any other war, is legal or justified is a nonsensical aspect of 21st century political correctness. No war can be or should be judged on a legal aspect, because war in itself is a gross break down of legality. Legalities are suspended. Any war can be justified; you just have to find the right reasons for it. While individual actions can be judged, the war itself cannot be. The belated War Inquiries in the UK are a case of sour grapes by the blame culture and Political Correct Brigade trying to absolve their own guilt and appease a current public not used to drawn-out wars. So who cares if the war is legal or not, it is being fought now, the troops should be supported, and any retroactive witch-hunt will not stop it. Lastly, history will show that the war was about security; security of energy, politics, economics, and territory.

Energy:
The war, as many people believe, was not just about oil. Oil is just the slick surface gloss, which detracts from the real reasons of the war, which even the media does not fully address. While oil is a major concern, it is not the main reason for the war. Petrodollars and the oil companies have not saved the US from the recession. The Middle East provides oil for the entire world, so if any country threatened that resource then the US would act to mitigate that threat as it does in any region. Any person who doubts this action should consider the world economic order and personal finances should any nation hold the world to ransom through oil and the consequences if they went unchallenged. While the US wants to reduce its dependence on oil, it still has to defend the world's access to oil. It's a common goal the world should share, for the time being and while oil resources are replete. In any case, the Iraqi Oil Laws have not been signed so the US, UK, Japan, China and other EU nations itching for oil have not seen the oil revenues pour in. Securing world oil resources would have been a justifiable reason for war.

Politics:

Blair and Bush are being made scapegoats for their unpopularity and the dragging on of the war. If the war had been decisive and finished early when Bush made his infamous 'Mission Accomplished' speech then things would have been different and any legal qualms quashed. Resolution 1441 (concerning WMDs) was a unanimous vote in the UN in 2002, but the contentious passage of 'serious consequences' should Iraq breach the resolution split the UN. The term 'serious consequences' concerned many nations who saw it as an 'automatic trigger' to war, with no further resolutions or safeguards. That they could see this serves to show that the resolution was acceptable nonetheless, but that the wording was weak. Resolution 1441 was legal in its formation. Its intent was well known. The interpretation was ambiguous.

The war was justified in that one statement, but the other nations sought to void it. The fact that 1441 was not strong enough is the collective fault of all the nations that rallied to strengthen it after the fact. The fact that the UK and US could obfuscate and circumvent the Resolution, and launch an attack speaks volumes to the weakness of the Resolution and the UN. Despite Kofi Annan's assertions that the war was illegal, he did nothing beforehand to avert it. To make matters muddier, the UN is involved in the Iraq War, in a humanitarian capacity, but which partially legitimises the US and UK's involvement. Hindsight is perfect, but even though no WMDs were found and despite sexed-up dossiers, the contradictory Intelligence and International Atomic Energy Agency (IAEA) reports along with the blustering of Saddam Hussein about his arsenal made it essential that the WMD threat be taken seriously, no matter how tenuous the case.

Economics:

The War in Iraq was not just about oil; it was also about the UK being at the heart of Europe (from its periphery) and about the US gaining 'independence' from China. While the UK is still a viable force in international politics, there is still an Imperial tint in their foreign policy. It's a hard habit to give up after ruling half the world. While Blair firmly believed what he believed about Iraq, there was still an eye cast toward proving himself to the US and enhancing himself within Europe. Bringing the UK to the European table with a swift Iraq victory would have been a boost to UK industry and trade. While America is the 'Land of the Free', it has the yoke of financial burden hanging over it. The US wants independence from China in that China virtually pays American social security cheques through investments and bonds (which is one reason there won't be a war between China and the US. They are so deep in each others' pockets; it wouldn't be financially worth it). A successful war for the US would have bolstered its international clout enabling the US able to gently bully others into line and to command more favourable terms in global financial markets. The justifiable plan was to 'liberate' Iraq economically and democratically, but it has not materialised, yet.

Territory:
The main reason for the war was Iran and boxing them in between allies in Russia, Saudi Arabia, Israel, Afghanistan, Central Asia, and Pakistan. But the former ally, Saddam, needed to go as he could not be trusted anymore. Just as the recent conflicts between Israel and Syria/Palestine has been a proxy war between the US and Iran, so has the Iraq War. Iran's ambitions on political, religious, oil, and nuclear control over Iraq and their neighbours ran counter to US policy. The far-forward-thinking strategy on Iran is the concerted effort to marginalise Iran until it gives up its nuclear ambition or is forced to fight. There are rumours that there are such groups in the US who desire such an outcome and that war with Iran should have been the real target. Accordingly, Iraq is a pretext for future US objectives against Iran. Iraq is a lynchpin in this future plan and its stability in any conflict with Iran would be highly sought.

Morality:
Is the war morally justified? Is any war moral? Again, morals in general are not the issue. Did Bush and Blair know there were no weapon of mass destruction, yet attacked anyway? Was Bush's, or rather certain Neo-Con elements in his government, thirst for revenge against Saddam the overriding force? Was the Iraq War a case of personal ego overshadowing common sense? The public jury has said 'yes'. The UK Inquiries are still continuing, but the verdict seems certain to be non-conclusive with no legal ramifications or punishment come the outcome. Why? Because any future US or UK leader faced with a future war with a very justifiable reason may baulk at the wrong moment, causing further damage and death, scared that he may be placed on trial for the consequences of his actions. And no one wants that responsibility of restricting a leader's capability to defend their country.

The public can push and push for some resolution to the Iraq War case, but it will be a long time before anything is settled. Bush and Blair are right in that history will be their judge and they'll be long gone by the time the events of the Iraq War are over.

27/Jan/2010

Politics, News & Issues
Reflections: Why the Iraq war is justified

Reflections on the Iraq War

Is the war in Iraq Justified? Yes, it is. While many mistakes have been made, the war was justified in many ways, including oil security, economic stability and defeating terrorism. The Chilcot Inquiry in the UK has been set up to reflect upon the UK's involvement in Iraq, including the decisions and actions taken, and to identify the lessons that can be learned. Already there are discussions on the legality of the war, but the main way in which the war was justified was Resolution 1441.

Resolution 1441 regarding Iraq's WMDs was a unanimous vote in the UN in 2002. However, the contentious passage of 'serious consequences' should Iraq breach the resolution split the UN. The term 'serious consequences' concerned a great many nations who saw it as an 'automatic trigger' to war, with no further resolutions or safeguards to prevent a pre-emptive attack. That they could see this serves to show that the resolution was acceptable in its initial state nonetheless, but that the wording was weak. Resolution 1441 was legal in its formation. Its intent was well known. The interpretation was ambiguous. The war was justified in that one statement, but the other nations sought to void it once the situation became more serious.

The fact that 1441 was not strong enough is the collective fault of all the nations that rallied to strengthen it after the fact. If they did not want war then they could have strengthened the wording or sought further legal action. The fact that the UK and US could circumvent the Resolution, and launch an attack speaks volumes to the weakness of the Resolution and the UN. And despite Kofi Annan's assertions that the war was illegal, he did nothing beforehand to avert it. He was powerless to stop a legal Resolution. To make matters muddier, the UN is involved in the Iraq War, in a humanitarian capacity, but which partially legitimises the US and UK's involvement. This is why UN targets are attacked in Iraq. Their involvement has endorsed US/UK action despite their 'illegal war' accusations.

Hindsight is perfect. Even though no WMDs were found and despite sexed-up dossiers, the contradictory Intelligence reports and the International Atomic Energy Agency's (IAEA) dithering, along with the blustering of Saddam Hussein about his arsenal made it essential that the WMD threat be taken seriously, no matter how tenuous the case. Imagine if Iraq had a fraction of the weapons imagined and nothing was done about it.

There was no absolute law concerning having to secure a second resolution. It was only the interpretation of the law that muddied the waters. And it was mostly argued for after the event. Participants in the Chilcot Inquiry are all back-tracking and claiming they were against an illegal war, yet most did nothing beforehand. Some resigned their positions in government, but there was no concerted legal effort at shouting out their views, which is deeply hypocritical as they do so now. There seems to be a backlash at the way the war was/is being handled and against an unpopular Prime Minister who supported an even more unpopular US president, rather than at the legality of the war. They are seeking to turn misgivings on the war into issues of legality, which is not right. There is no excuse for all those people suddenly now finding their tongues and consciences. If there is anyone to blame then these turncoats are as guilty as anyone who they seek to blame for the war due to their own inaction and silence. Shame on them.

However, while the war was justified, not everything has gone according to plan. There was no post-war or post-Saddam planning for peace. There was no Nation-building strategy afterward. The terrorist threat has increased and many innocent people have died, because of bad tactics and strategies. The War may be justified, but peace as of yet, is not. Peace has to be earned. And that will not happen until the political will is there on both sides to plan for Iraq's future.

25/Apr/2010

Politics, News & Issues
What to expect from the 2010 UK General Election

The 2010 UK General Election

2020 vision

My political predictions are seldom correct. It was a Hung Parliament and since then there have been two more general elections with the Conservatives staying in power. Labour seem down and out and the Liberal Democrats are clawing their way back up. Unfortunately, nothing will change in the foreseeable future; Brexit, break-away parties, nor the Covid-19 pandemic will change the politics of the land. For now we are stuck with two main irreconcilable parties and a few smaller parties nipping at their heels looking for scraps. Maybe if the Scots vote for independence that will shake things up a bit. But that's another article, which I never got to write.

Hung Parliament. That is what everyone is predicting and expecting for the 2010 UK General Election. But will it happen? What does that even mean? This General Election is one of the most important voting decisions for a very long time, but what will the outcome mean for Britain and the world? While there are many issues to discuss, like all political dalliances there are few clear black and white, right or wrong answers. So, here are a few points and comments to shed light on these matters.

There are three main parties vying for control of the British government: the incumbent Labour Party led by Prime Minister Gordon Brown; the opposition Conservative Party led by David Cameron; and the surging Liberal Democrats led by Nick Clegg. Until recently, Britain was predominantly a two-party state, but after the first-ever, nationally-televised Leader Debates, Nick Clegg brought his lowly party to the table of power. Now the scrap is on for Labour and the Conservatives to refocus and recoup their campaigns and power bases.

For thirteen long years, Labour held power after the Tories' (Conservative) own lengthy eighteen years of Thatcherism and its successor politics. Many Britons still remember Margaret Thatcher's reign and not with fond memories. The current Tories still have not recovered from her shadow, which led to Tony Blair's emphatic rise to power, only for him to squander Labour's popularity, mostly due to the Iraq War. Both parties are seen as tainted, old, arrogant edifices of cronyism and school-tie rule. The new party on the block, the Lib Dems, with their Blair-like leader, seems to have stepped into the void as the old parties feud. This has created a situation where the voting public may not to vote for any party majority, thereby causing a Hung Parliament.

Currently, the House of Common seats stand at: Labour - 349 seats, Conservatives - 210, and Liberal Democrats - 62. Other parties make up the total 650 seats with 29 of their own. The winning elected party would need 326 seats for a slim majority. If this majority does not happen, it will lead to a Hung Parliament. There are many variations that can happen in a Hung Parliament.

First, the Tories may win, but not with enough seats for a majority and may have to seek a Lib Dem alliance to overpower Labour's still probable superior seat number. Labour may not win outright, but could still hold sway with its number of seats in the House of Commons over the other two parties. Labour could even finish third and still have enough seats for Gordon Brown to remain Prime Minister. This would be untenable for many Britons as Brown was never publicly elected upon taking over from Tony Blair and to 'lose' his first election, but still remain in Number 10, would surely trigger another election. Lastly, the Lib Dems could remain riding high in the polls and cause an upset landslide, sneaking in between Labour and the Tories, but such an upswing for a third party has never happen before. Nevertheless, the Liberal Democrats could hold the balance of power and the other two parties may have to cosy up to Nick Clegg. However, there are already very public indications that Labour and the Lib Dems would never have such a pact. Interestingly, although the Conservatives and Lib Dems are opposed on many issues, many news pundits and insider commentators feel this would be a more preferable alliance. These are but a few of the scenarios for a Hung parliament.

While many Britons think a Hung Parliament would be a good thing, forcing the politicians to work together, it would not be good for Britain as a whole. The UK's last coalition government was in 1974, which didn't last long. Britain has always traditionally voted for strong governments through the Plurality voting method. There is much talk about power sharing in many European states such as Italy, Ireland, Germany, and further afield in Israel. But as seen on the news, politics in both Israel and Italy is far from smooth with very frequent elections and government changes. Germany has a Proportional Representation voting system, which frequently leads to minority governments. But one wonders if Germans have good reason to be suspicious of strong government as it led to WWII. Their co-operative political system suits their country as it ensures internal stability and a less threatening stance to its neighbours.

Britain is not a country tolerant of frequent elections and politics have been fairly stable for decades, even in this current recession. People can't vote for a Hung Parliament, it is just a situation that is reached upon election results. Personally, there's a feeling there will not be a hung parliament. Voters are being galvanised more than ever and turn-out should be better than average. My personal opinion also sees the Conservatives and Lib Dems sucking seats away from Labour enough to give the Tories a slim majority, the Lib Dems in second, and Labour coming a surprise third.

Why this outcome? Many people want a change; a change from Labour. For years, voters looked to the new fashionable Tories with some trepidation. A vote for the Lib Dems was usually seen as a wasted vote, because an upstart third party would never accede to power. But things have changed. The Conservative's huge and often double-figure lead in the polls has evaporated with the Lib Dems benefiting the most, but their accumulation of seats will not be enough to overcome gains Tories will make from Labour and undecided voters. Though a few see Nick Clegg rising a la Obama, the Liberal Democrats will still be seen as untried outsiders this time around. Labour could come third in the vote, but still be the Opposition Party with its many seats.

The main issues being discussed are the Economy (for obvious reasons), Defence/foreign policy, Environmental issues, Crime, Europe, Immigration Education, and the NHS (National Health Service). There is no consensus on any of the issues, though there is much rhetoric that each party wants to do the best for everyone on each issue. Also, many

Britons do not like the American-style debates, feeling they promote style over substance, which is why Clegg is deemed the winner in the debates. There is certainly passion and conviction politics at play, but the UK election campaign is a short one: five weeks, compared to almost a year in the US. The leaders needed to find new ways to connect with the public after the expense scandals, banking crisis, and other issues; hence debates and internet campaigns. At least the debates have got people talking about politics again and many more people, especially younger constituents, have been galvanised to sign up to vote.

Britain needs a decisive government even with a slight majority. An election where Labour finish third, but still remained in power with enough seats would de-legitimise British politics. British voters seriously need to think beyond themselves and a wishful want for a Hung Parliament with its false notions of party cooperation, but with a real threat of continued recession for Britain. The other smaller parties, including UKIP (UK Independence Party), the Green Party, SNP (the Scottish National Party), Plaid Cymru (Welsh National Party), DUP (Democratic Unionist Party), Sinn Fein, and even the BNP (British National Party) are hoping for some form of power-sharing government to drive their own party agendas and claims. They sense a weakened government will be in their best interests. If that cynical view is not incentive enough to vote for an outright government then nothing will be, for such thoughts would have repercussions world-wide.

A Hung Parliament would weaken Britain's role in the world. The credibility of the government would be lessened in dealing with Europe, China, and America in areas such as trade and the economy, foreign policy and defence, climate change, and sheer political status. Britain is always seen as a strong, combative government punching above its weight in world affairs. Britain is at the cross-roads of Europe and America, able to bridge gaps between two unsure allies. Better Britain's government continue to stand on the bridge as a majority government rather than to hang from it as a disjointed Parliament.

So, while Britons do want a change, they must see the wider picture and vote for a majority government that will deliver consensual governance in these troubled times. And barring any last gaffes or slips in the polls, and contrary to popular belief, it looks like it will be the Conservatives with a slim majority.

Religion &
Spirituality

25/Dec/2007

Religion & Spirituality - Religion & Spirituality (Other)

Science versus Religion

2020 vision

Sometimes it doesn't feel like it is science versus religion as there is a rise in both anti or pseudo sciences and religions. There used to be cross-fire, but now it seems they are both being attacked from factions within each other. Belief is withering and it is as if both have hit a wall in furthering their missions. There's nothing new under the sun (or son) and people looking for guidance have nowhere to turn except to the new altar of theories and worship – social media. For worse (not better) it is filling the gap vacated by the two pillars of society and bit by bit tearing them down with its own created, re-defined, and regurgitated versions of reality by the new self-informed scientists and Gods of the internet – we the people. Nothing is sacred. Nothing is true. The internet is all. And science and religion are facing a losing battle to remain relevant in the world let alone continuing to be pitched against each other.

Personally, I have a healthy scepticism for religion, not of spirituality per se, but in the man-made, organised religions which have arisen since the time hunter-gatherers became civilisation builders and created the post-ice-age, catastrophe religions in the Eurasian region. Since then, expansion, indoctrination, and control has dominated most of history with modern-day theocracies and personality cults surfing the undercurrents of the socio-political realm. I'm more on the Humanist scale; atheist, scientific-minded trying to grasp the reality of the world. But even here are zealots, unwilling to look beyond their cognitive bias, falling into the well of hubris, and worshipping technology as a panacea for the world's ills. But I still have more faith in science than in religion.

While I attack religion for its flaws and practices, hopefully below are questions and critical thoughts to expand the debate.

I am not especially religious, but if God did exist then he would be seen as a scientist. It does make sense in that if God created the universe, then he created and used all chemistry a nd physics, etc., needed to kick start the universe in a big bang. Even human scientists when creating precursors to life needed a big spark to set things off (as in Urey and Miller's experiments in the 1950's). God set the parameters for the constants and made the universe elegant. If the universe was some kind of experiment, then God would have used a scientific method to create and run it. Crucially, God has let us in on some of the secrets of science by allowing mankind to use science to measure the universe, the world and ourselves. It is how we can measure cosmological, geological and archaeological time by using the very products (atoms, elements, isotopes, etc) that the ultimate scientist created himself. Even the Pope has an astronomer so as to be closer to God through the stars.

There is no dichotomy between science and religion because they are one and the same. The universe itself is not just a physical scientific thing; it resonates with morality and faith in that the galaxies, stars and planets behave in a rational way. They also are born, live, spread life and die; there is a respect for their environment and for us a world that shares its wealth. It is not science nor religion that is the problem, but man's propensity to name and separate things. Such words cannot describe the universe; it cannot be devolved of either science or religion. The universe has its own commandments, its constants of nature, physical laws that are obeyed, which constitutes a deep belief in the infinite and everlasting. That is the religion of the universe, which is an organised system of forces, which controls our destiny. Every single galaxy, star, planet and particle has an effect on us through whichever force manifests itself. Indeed, we are made of the same universal stuff having elements within us that can only come from stars. We are truly one with the universe. How could we not see the universe as a religious entity in itself?

As for the supposed ultimate scientist, could God be a Boltzmann Brain? Religious minded think of God as some kind of disembodied force watching over us. Cosmologists have theorised that in our ever-expanding universe (due to vacuum energy), it may be possible that during the universe's lifetime a conscious being, a Boltzmann Brain, could spontaneously appear, if only for a microsecond. It is not actually a brain, but a representation of something that could consciously observe the universe. But could one have appeared at the beginning of the universe, its spontaneous presence growing and precipitating all that we see now? Is it still observing? Wherever and whatever God is, he has surely given mankind pause to think about it and the universe. Should we have to worship God, just because he created us or just show obedience like any child would its creator/parent? It seems mankind is in its rebellious teenage years, questioning the authority of the creator. What will happen when mankind matures and succeeds their creator?

So the universe, God, science and religion are intertwined like space-time. Even if God did not exist there would be religion, as seen in prehistoric worship of abstract symbols, the sun and moon, idols and inanimate objects. And if there was a God, all around us would still behave according to the laws of physics. Religion is not just for use as a moral compass, nor science for just an objective view of life. Science is the fabric of space, while religion is the mass (excuse the pun) that dents space, causing a congregation of force, gravity, to bring harmony and order to the universe, keeping it together, for now —as it is expanding forever. Whether man or God-made, science and religion created and shaped each other, they have nurtured mankind, inspired new heights, caused untold grief, and brought hope to us all. Whatever you believe, life without an inkling of understanding of both, is only half a life. And if God is both and we are creations in his image, then so must we be the children of both science and religion.

02/Jan/2008

Religion & Spirituality – Thoughts on God
The Debate over Creation and Evolution

Evolution and Religion

It strikes me as strange that some religious groups attack science on its record concerning evolution, but totally ignore the evolution of their own religion. Even today, religion is evolving to fit into the modern world, whether through ordaining women and homosexual priests, arising pagan groups, creations such as Intelligent Design, and cross-cultural pollination. These issues could split church groups leading to new branches of religious sects. Just as humans branched off due to evolution, so too can religion, their divergent paths flowing backward in time to common origins.

There is commonality in the origin of Eurasian religions. Christianity, Islam, Buddhism, Hinduism and Judaism have such intertwined relationships with each other and Zoroastrianism and Egyptian religions that one can say that these religions are related to each other through evolution of cultural beliefs. Take the repeated transformations and branching off from Gnosticism, Mithraism, Roman Catholicism, Coptics, Presbyterianism, Lutheranism, Protestantism, and Mormonism, etc. Likewise with Islam which is split into Sunni, Shiite, Sufi, Druze and Wahhabism sects, etc. Judaism has its different sects between the Ashkenazi and the Sephardi including Reform, Conservative and Orthodox, with the mystic Kabbala sect having a possible, yet vague, relationship to the Essenes who wrote the Dead Sea Scrolls. In China, Confucianism preceded Taoism, which blended with Buddhism to provide the basis for Falun Gong. These are only a few of the hundreds of religions with their own specific traits that have mutated from parent religions. And like man, religions have evolved due to the environment around them, whether from man-made situations (like Henry VIII's break with the Pope) or through natural events (Sun God worship from Egypt and Mithraism in the Middle East), which gave rise to Christianity.

Survival of the fittest
Islam evolved from the Old Testament and local traditions. Mohammad had to fight off various other would-be Muslim sects for his religion to

prevail. In effect, he caused the extinction of competing Muslim religions, until events after his death. It is survival of the fittest for religions too. This is entirely the case for the conquering Europeans in the new world, where disease ravaged and decimated the American Indian populations. As the colonists moved across both North and South America, they spread more than their religion and evolutionary tracts of religion either involved extinction where the natives resisted and were killed, mutation where the natives tolerated and blended their religion with the European religion, and survival where they were wholly converted. Where populations survived and grew, so did religion, sometimes to branch off again into a new religion.

Consider the ways in which Jesus is worshipped and the divergent evolutionary courses this has caused in religion. The Mandeans in Iraq see John the Baptist as being central to their faith while Jesus is seen as almost evil, akin to a traitor as in traditional Judaism. While Christianity sees Jesus as human and divine, Islam views him as a man and a prophet. The Copts, Christian descendants of the original Egyptians, practice monophysitism viewing Jesus as wholly divine. Just these few examples are enough to divide religions and create new religious pathways.

The Four 'I's
The four 'I's are: internalisation, immigration, invention and interpretation. Religion is not dying out as feared, but is being internalised by many individuals who pray or express religious feelings in private, reflecting a secular society. This may also be a reaction against the rise of fundamentalism in some major religions. People also feel that they do not have to necessarily worship in church as God is always with them. However, the slight rise in church going in England has been due to the influx of immigrants from African nations and Eastern Europe. This will also increase the rate of religious evolution as these immigrants adjust their ceremonies and beliefs to their adopted countries. Immigration in the past has proved to be a major factor in the history of some countries as in the case of the Moors and the Puritans.

The invention of religions and other religious rites has been going on for centuries. Scientology is growing with numbers each year, though is based on extraterrestrial intervention. Pagan groups are being (re)invented with Gardnerian, Druidry, Wicca attracting members from different religions. Intelligent Design (ID), which grew from Creationism, could be an evolutionary dead end. Already it is causing another divergence within the church in regards to their interpretation of the world around them. ID will out-evolve itself and be replaced. Just as wooden sticks were replaced by stone and then metal tools, ID as a tool to define science within religion will not work, as science and religion are not self-contained entities. They over-lap and co-evolve, strengthening and validating each other. Interpretation is man's most potent effect upon religion. Translation errors, misunderstandings and selective 'breeding' of scriptures occur as with Hebrew to Greek to Latin, etc and the Council of Nicaea verdicts on selecting Gospels to the bible while leaving out many others, which have been coming to light in modern times. While not out of malice, this decision led to a defined and stream-lined Christian church, while trimming off excess religious baggage. But this also deprived the so-called heretics and Gnostics of their scriptures. Such actions lead to religions that may be isolated, persecuted, killed off, and forgotten until their fossils are discovered in hidden texts like the Dead Sea scrolls.

Scientific religion

Can religious evolution be studied scientifically? Yes it can, in many ways. One could lay out the traces of religion like a family tree, stretching back for millennia and crossing entire continents to their roots. The reasons for their branching off could be studied statistically. For example, religions are not just about their religious texts, but also about the cultures that adhere to them. The so-called God gene and who is susceptible to believing in God or the divine can lead to a psychological study of religion, as can the theory of memes and the way ideas spread like a virus. With immigrants, there are also geopolitical studies in religion and the statistics behind them, language being such a facet, whether Aramaic, Latin, Chinese or Polish, etc. Coming to another country and worshipping in unfamiliar surroundings, with local customs and another language also introduces another evolutionary factor into the frame. Biologically, the Lemba tribe from Africa were recently confirmed as being a Jewish off-shoot through genetic analysis. This is a real evolutionary change in religion through immigration and cultural divergence, while keeping the Jewish faith. These examples are few, but are only the tip of the iceberg.

In the end, the reason why religion evolves is because man evolves and takes his culture, including religion, with him on his journey through life.

If religion did not evolve, it would not be around today in such numbers, continuing to affect the lives of billions. Every believer is a religion unto themselves and for better or for worse it is in your hands, your heads and your hearts; evolution at its best.

09/Jan/2008

Religion & Spirituality - Thoughts on God
Thoughts on the Nature of God

What is the Nature of God?

What is the nature of God? What stuff is God made of? Is God a corporeal being somewhere out there, a spirit within the universe –if not the universe itself, or something else entirely? Did God create man or man create God? These are issues that have intrigued man since the beginning of organised religion. Here are a few explorations into this theme.

Is God corporeal, a real and living being, whether an extraterrestrial, from the future, or an other-dimensional being? Is God outside the universal bounds watching over his dominions? Is God a singular or a multiple entity? To create a whole new universe would take a lot of work even for a scientist the likes of God would have to be. As scientists do on Earth, would God have collaborated with 'team members' to do this or was he/she a maverick working alone to achieve a new creation?

Is God a supernatural entity? Whatever the nature of God, he/she is not beyond the realms of science even as a supernatural being. Supernaturalism may include powers and abilities that may seem like magic or miracles to us, but magic is just a higher form of science that we cannot yet understand or use. Magic/supernatural ability still affects the physical world and uses the universal elements/forces to create something within our universe. If a supernatural being can supersede our universal physics then they would not be of this universe for they would have to obey the laws of physics. This would make God extra-universal and able to access our universe with other technology.

Could God be a Boltzmann Brain? Religious minded think of God as some kind of disembodied force watching over us, while cosmologists have theorised that in our ever-expanding universe (due to vacuum energy), it may be possible that during the universe's lifetime a conscious being, a Boltzmann Brain, could spontaneously appear, if only for a microsecond. It is not actually a brain, but a representation of something that could consciously observe the universe. But could one have appeared at the beginning of the universe? This entity may have created our world and us, but how long could such a being survive and why would it want to be worshipped?

Is God an atheist? Can God worship another God? Who would he/she pray to? Should we worship God with no present evidence (like new prophets, visiting angels and new miracles) that he/she is still around? If God is atheist, are atheist people made in God's image? Even if an atheist does not believe in God, is there something they believe in 'out there' that would qualify as some sort of 'supreme being', deity or is there nothing to believe in except the will of man? Is God just an idea, a hard-wired tendency to believe in God because of our genes and memes, the virus-like way ideas spread and are believed. Are we God? Is God a feeling within us that over millennia has been anthropomorphised into an external being? Does thinking about God make you a better person than someone who does not believe? I am not especially religious, but this debate does not undermine the foundations of religion. If anything, such a debate may bring others closer to God just by reflecting upon this issue.

Is God male or female? Does such a term apply to God who could be an androgynous being, both and neither gender, though he/she supposedly created humans in his own image? For humanity, females were Earth mothers/Mother Earth –Gaia, Goddesses of the land, Venuses of Earthly beauty and daughters of the moon. Males were the power of the sky, Dyeus the Sanskrit Sky Father from which Zeus/Jupiter and Thor came. So, if God is male, female or other, how does this reflect upon our creation and the way we view God? Would it matter if God was black, white, brown, yellow, or other?

Of course, before organised religion, people all over the world worshipped their own gods or had their own beliefs: idols, animism, druidism, shamanism, and other pagan religions. Why and how after millions of years of human evolution did God suddenly appear? Even from at least 60-40 thousand years ago, man had the cognitive abilities to create art, sophisticated tools and artifacts, and think about burials and their place in the environment, so why did not organised religion and God appear then? What was God doing before this? It would have been simpler for God to appear then, unite the people under one religion before man spread out too far and wide. It seems that in the middle-east, the confluence of peoples created the atmosphere for religion and God in times of crises and uncertainty. This leads to the conclusion that man created God to address this, rather than God creating us. And now, with our rich appetite for war, terror, global warming, and other international crises, why has God not returned?

On the other hand, all the holy texts assert God's omnipresence and creation of the universe and everything in it, but for billions of years waited for the 'right' time to reveal himself and then disappeared after his 'son's' death. As for Jesus, how was he the son of God? Did he share God's genes and DNA? Was he just a representative of God's word, or truly part of God, a clone maybe? This leads back to God's corporealness and how he could have a physical son and not be physically corporeal himself. It would involve some form of high science to achieve this feat of procreation. Did God do this himself, did he have a wife to bear a son and why was there no further off-spring even after Jesus taught us about sacrifice and love?

What is God's job? Besides creating the universe and all in its domain, what else does God do? Is he a scientist, mathematician, economist, diplomat, etc., who sits around on a throne attended to by angels? Is he out creating more universes, pressing the 'flesh' with other Gods in an ultimate council or universal government? Is God one of many Gods, especially assigned to us, while his/her colleagues attend to other extraterrestrial worlds? He cannot just be waiting for our worshipful praise, so maybe he is out maintaining order to the universe.

Is God relevant for the world today? Two thousand years ago, religion was at a cross-roads having being born from Zoroastrianism, Hinduism, Egyptian and Judaism and leading to Islam and other modern religious sects and schisms. Today, religion is at another cross-road re-ordering itself and dogmas for the new century. Is science the new religion? Hardly, but faith alone is not enough? God does not love, redeem or create alone, nor science discover, prove or create in a vacuum either. Whether you believe in God, science, both or neither; God plays an important part in people's lives and like many other aspects of people's lives is a lifestyle choice, which adds to the variety of life on this world and maybe the next.

20/Jun/2008

Religion & Spirituality - Other
Exploring the effect life on other planets
would have on religion

Aliens and Gods

The Vatican, it seems, is ready to boldly go where no Pope has gone before. Recently, two of the Vatican's top Astronomers have stepped out from behind the telescope and into the public pulpit to speak about their cosmological beliefs. While Vatican Astronomer Brother Guy Consolmagno is to speak at the 11th Annual International Mars Society Convention discussing what impact (if any) space exploration will have on religion; the Pope's chief astronomer Father Gabriel Funes announced in the official Vatican newspaper that life on Mars cannot be ruled out and that intelligent beings created by God could exist in outer space. Such announcements and debates could have astonishing implications for the future. Here are a few scenarios:

Human proselytising of aliens:
Our world is already a jumbled world of religions. When we explore space, our beliefs will go with us and upon meeting any intelligent extraterrestrials, cultural exchanges will take place and religion will no doubt be one of the issues discussed.

1. Aliens have own Gods:
Our intelligent aliens have their own religions. Would we humans be so arrogant, bold, and stupid enough to try and convert our cosmic friends to our religion, whichever they may feel akin too or would we leave them to their beliefs? If our alien brothers were so inclined to accept religious indoctrination, then which Earthly religion would be best? There is no way that any of the major religions would agree on letting an entire alien race adopt one religion. If the said extraterrestrial civilisation did engage in multiple religious practices, then surely they have already or would repeat the mistakes of man by trying to expand their religious beliefs leading to strife on their own world. We would have to live and let live.

2. Aliens have no Gods:

Our galactic neighbours have no Gods or religion. Will they see us as a backward species still worshipping non-existent beings? Could they be a species that had no concept or desire for spirituality? Would we see these poor non-religious aliens as inferior? Would we humans have the moral right to teach and convert them, even though our alien brothers had passed that primitive religious phase and had moved on to a more mature belief or scientific calling. Who are we to try and pass on our morals and inhibit other species from their own path, spiritual or not. What would happen if our beliefs were rejected? Would human fundamentalists have no further contact with these aliens? Would the aliens be denigrated for their non-beliefs? We should refrain from forcibly spreading our religion on other worlds.

3. Aliens have same God:

We arrive at planet Zog to find aliens awaiting us with open arms with greetings from a God that is not too dissimilar from Earthly beliefs. Would we humans feel less unique and superior to find another world graced by a God we thought was solely ours? Would this increase human belief in God or threaten the Church's authority? Would common beliefs between hundreds of religions on Earth and Zog be enough to unite our civilisations in peace or would familiarity breed contempt? We may have to adapt and evolution evolve in order to encompass a larger cosmic congregation.

Alien proselytising of Earth:

1. Aliens have own Gods:

The aliens have landed. They come in peace. Out steps the Extraterrestrial Pope of planet Zog. He's here to convert us. How would Earth respond to an alien conversion programme? We would not countenance such alien high-handedness and would fight back. Or would we? Our newly arrived alien neighbours may be so advanced that we may feel obliged to convert even if the aliens may believe in something else; the universe as a God-being, another spiritual plane; or even themselves as Gods. Even if the alien religion was highly spiritual, noble and non-violent, would we humans accept an entirely new religious paradigm? Would an alien presence increase humanity's religious beliefs? Could this cause a Cosmic Holy War? We will finally find out what religion really means to the billions of believers.

2. Aliens have no Gods:

On the other hand (since aliens might have more than two), they may have no religious beliefs whatsoever and work to cleanse us humans of our confused, unoriginal, unscientific and archaic religions. To join the cosmic club, would humanity have to ditch the idea of God, spelling the end of Earth religions? How would this 'de-religionising' take place; by peace or by force? Could we resist such a process? What if it was successful and the Earth became a non-religious world? Are humans meant to be non-spiritual or will we find that our newfound freedom from religion produces a more mature phase in humanity? We may find that there is an adequate replacement for religion after all.

3. Aliens have same God:

Lastly, what if there is a God and he did create all the aliens in the universe, each civilisation having a different creation story, but the essential tenets were there? Would we welcome our intergalactic cousins with open arms or still view their beliefs with suspicion as we do to our closer neighbours on Earth? How many different versions of God's Word could there be and how would they fit into the larger scheme of life? Would our alien friends try to 'correct' our religion to the one true God, sparking a holy diplomatic incident or war? Or would religion really bring about a final world peace? Peoples' dreams and belief in God come true, but at a price: We are not God's only children. We are not special. Now what?

Hopefully, while the Vatican Astronomers are looking through their telescopes, they have been thinking through these scenarios and they'll be able to see what's coming. While scientists will be thinking about alien technology and the boon or damage it will do to us, the same could be said for religion. Be careful what you wish for. Maybe in some far distant corner of the galaxy, an alien priest is thinking the same thing and suggesting to his superiors to stay away from the little blue planet of quixotic believers.

09/Jul/2008

Religion & Spirituality

The Discovery of the Garden of Eden

2020 vision

Longer version to the piece in the History section; one of my longest articles. This was published in an online magazine *'Gods & Empires'* issue 1, by Patrick C. Chouinard. He also published the New Archaeology Review for which I was briefly assistant editor for a few articles in 2008, after seeing an advertisement on the Helium platform.

There were originally pictures with this article, but removed for publication of this book. For further information on sites in the area, I had written to two professors who had conducted investigations in the Lake Urmia region. Looking back now, while they had taken pictures in the area, they were probably not the right people to write to. I didn't get a response, but my letter to them is at the end. I still think the so-called Garden of Eden was real, but that its origins are more earthly and pedestrian. It was a place where people lived and practised agriculture until something made them leave (War? Environmental change? Exploration? Societal change? The Shining Ones?) and descend the mountains.

Some commentators have now associated Gobekli Tepe (the oldest temple in the world and not far from where agriculture was invented) in Turkey with Eden. Maybe, but this may be too far east. But wherever the Edenites came from, they remembered the journey in tales passed down through generations which was then incorporated into the bible, where the tale was later mythologised and the rest is history or rather, religion...

The story of the Garden of Eden is entrenched in everyone's mind as the Biblical setting for the first man and woman, Adam and Eve, and their fateful exit from paradise. Yet, this enduring story has its roots in reality and its origins are being pieced together through multidisciplinary studies and methods. It is an epic story that could also trace Eden to the ancestral Europeans and map the dispersion of civilisation to Mesopotamia.

Eden's Biblical Origins.

As described in the Bible, Genesis 2:8 to 2:14[1], a river flowed through Eden, from where four other rivers emanated. They were called: the Gihon, winding through Cush; the Pishon flowing through gold-rich Havilah; the Hiddekel (the Tigris) flowing east of Asshur, and the Perath (the Euphrates).

Over the centuries historians, academics and theologians had theorised and searched for the fabled Garden using the rivers as a starting point, without success. But in the late 1980s, University College London archaeologist David Rohl had been conducting his own investigations into the origins of the Garden of Eden. His data led him to the 1987 work *The Garden of Eden* by the late Reginald Arthur Walker, who had allegedly identified the other two rivers, the area of the Garden of Eden, and the origins of Sumerian legends.

As established, the Euphrates (Perath) rises in the Zagros Mountains near Lake Van, runs 2720km through Mesopotamia and into the Persian Gulf. The Tigris (Hiddekel) also rises in the Zagros range and flows west and south of Lakes Van and Urmia until it reaches the Persian Gulf, 2033km away. The land of Shinar through which the rivers flowed is Sumer in southern Iraq (Rohl 1998: 47 & 52). So any other river associated with the Biblical events would have originated in this northerly region to concur with the Biblical account. And once found, their origins were so obvious.

In his research, Walker had identified the Gihon as the modern day river Araxes, rising north of Lakes Van and Urmia and flowing east into the Caspian Sea. The Gihon became the Araxes or the Jichon-Aras during the 8th Century Islamic invasion of the Caucasus region. The old name was just waning during Victorian times and then somehow forgotten. The land of Cush through which the Gihon flowed could be the ancient land of Cossaea near the Caspian Sea. It could also be from where the Kassites, the mountain people, who invaded and ruled Mesopotamia c.1700-1160BC, originally hailed from. This land of Cush is now in Azerbaijan and across the border in Iran, there is a 4000m high ridge, known as the Kusheh Dagh, the Mountain of Kush. (Rohl 1998: 51-53 & 55-57).

The river Pishon was even more evident to Walker. The river today is called the Uizhun and flows east of Lake Urmia into the Caspian Sea. Also known as the Kezel Uzun (long gold) or the Uzun (dark red/gold), Hebrew texts had transposed the 'U' into a 'P', thus the river had retained its rightful name all along, with Pishon becoming the Biblical name. Havilah, in the Anguran region of Iran, through which the Uizhun flows, has always been rich in gold with documented mines dating back to at least 3rd to 7th Century AD (Rohl 1998: 53-54).

These then were the four rivers of Eden and have their origins in the ancient land of Armenia. They were identified through etymological, topological and historical sources. The very word 'Eden' is also indicative of the Lake Urmia area. The Mesopotamian word 'Edin' (Sumerian) or 'Edinu' (Akkadian) means 'open plain' or 'uncultivated land'. In Hebrew 'Adhan' means 'to be delighted', or 'place of delight'. Even the Greek word 'Paradeisos' [paradise] meant 'parkland' and the Persian word 'Pairidaeza' meant 'enclosed parkland'. Hebrew 'Gan' equalled 'garden' and 'ganan' meant 'hedged in' or 'protect', 'walled garden' or 'enclosed park'(Rohl 1998: 49-50). All these words described the areas and the rivers around the Garden of Eden.

Of the river that 'flowed from Eden to water the garden', Walker identified it as the modern Adji Chay River, which has an older name: 'Meidan' -Persian for 'enclosed court' or 'walled garden' (Rohl 1998: 59-60). The Meidan, as the possible original ancient name for the river running through the garden, seems to be the origin of the area's name: [M]eidan. Thus Sumerian, Persian, Greek and Hebrew lexicons had similar meanings for a specific area: The Garden of Eden. It thus becomes interesting that all the modern English translations of Eden just mean 'pleasurable place' or 'place of desire'. We have forgotten or ignored the ancient literal meaning, thus denying ourselves the clues as to the origins of Eden; a real, enclosed, sheltered, and well-watered land in which man prospered before being expelled from paradise.

Eden itself is to the east of Lake Urmia and sits in a valley 'fenced' or walled off on its northern, eastern and southern sides. The Adji Chay flows west into Lake Urmia. The physical setting corresponds to the Biblical description with amazing accuracy. In ancient times, the region was warmer, more fertile with fruit trees, and extensively wooded. This mountainous area, near Tabriz, Iran, contains secluded valleys (Rohl

1998: 59) and would have sheltered any developing community, as such similar environmental systems had around the world.

Criticisms in Discovering Eden.

Here then are our ancients forbearers telling us specifically where they came from, with names and all, and yet that evidence is ignored, because: 1) The Garden of Eden was found by non-religious means by men of science. 2) The vanity of the religious minded is offended that the Garden of Eden could be found at all and so easily. 3) The Garden of Eden was found in a place not 'sacred' or 'cultured' enough to have been a paradise. 4) Lastly, no one, not the countries harbouring areas of Eden, Church authorities, popular press or academic community has reported, endorsed or publicised the proposed discovery of Eden. Opponents scoff at the mere mention that Eden has been discovered.

And so the Garden of Eden, shunned for whatever reason was relocated to and obstinately remains in Mesopotamia. Why is Iraq more expedient as the supposed home of Eden? Is there a modern political/religious/cultural bias against Eden existing in an unknown third world country? Do people assume that because Sumer was the first great Mesopotamian civilisation that Eden had to be located near there, even though the Sumerians did not originate in Mesopotamia and had to come from somewhere else.

The story of the Garden of Eden in the Old Testament is the very story of the Sumerian ancestors' migration from paradise, dressed up in religious overtones long after the fact. The time of Adam and Eve marks the transition from a hunter gatherer society into an agricultural/technological society. These Neolithic inhabitants moved out of their paradise, quite possibly due to adverse weather conditions after the last Ice Age of which there were at least two major reversals, such as the Younger Dryas 9,600 to 10,800 BC and Mini Ice Age/Event c.6200 BC (Mithen 2003: 12-13). They migrated south, probably following the very rivers that become enshrined within the Bible. But they retained the memory of their origins, almost certainly through oral myths, then in cuneiform, and then written down and translated through the ages. So who were the people of Eden?

Eden and the ancient Europeans.

Is there a genetic trace to and from Eden? Can we back track and relate this to the so called Seven Daughters of Eve? Proposed by Bryan Sykes, Professor of Human Genetics at the University of Oxford, in his 2001 book of the same name, Sykes used mitochondrial genetics (mtDNA) to trace the origins of modern Europeans, identifying seven different haplogroups (or specific genetic characteristics within populations). He gave these haplogroups 'clan mother' names according to their geographic location. Our interest lies in Haplogroup X, represented by Xenia. After diverging from Haplogroup N, Xenia originated 20,000 to 30,000 years ago in the Georgia/Caucasus Region, north of the Zagros Mountains[2]. Could Xenia and her kin be the progenitors of the Edenites? Meanwhile, to the south, between Turkey and the Euphrates, Haplogroup J (Jasmine) had originally mutated around 45,000 years ago in the Caucasus region. Around 10,000 years ago this group began their journey toward the Neolithic Revolution in Anatolia [2]. Further more, the situation is more complicated due to local variations and interbreeding so Xenia and Jasmine could have had further splinter groups and daughters of their own that migrated and mutated.

Whether the people of Eden can be traced to Xenia, a mixture of Xenia and Jasmine, or to their Haplogroup relatives would also link archaeo-genetics and the Bible together bringing the Genesis epic to life. It would also raise the fascinating possibility that certain people around the world with the same specific Haplotype may be rightly and directly descended from the Edenites, a prestigious birthright! But all this is a matter of speculation and timing. We would need to know which clan mother descendant group lived in Eden, when and for how long.

Biblical identification of Edenites.

Biblical evidence could also tell us the origins and nature of Adam and his clan. In Genesis 2:15, Adam was placed in Eden by God 'to work it and take care of it'. In Genesis 4:2 it is stated that '...Abel kept flocks, and Cain worked the soil[1]. Thus Adam and his sons are already farmers and herdsmen. This places them in a certain timeframe and at a certain location, the Lake Urmia region c. 10,000BC (if not slightly before) to c.3000BC, just prior to the Bronze Age. As examined below, the archaeological data from this time and region is scarce and under represented, but it is very important to the story of Eden for in Genesis

4:3 to 4:8, Abel and Cain present their produce of firstborn meat portions and fruits of the soil, respectively, to the Lord. The Lord favours Abel's offering of meat, rejecting Cain's fruit, which causes Cain to kill Abel in jealousy[1].

This has some varied and startling implications. First, this violent episode seems to be an allegorical reflection of ancient climate change. The Lord in not favouring Cain's fruits could mean that there was a downturn in crop production, while Abel's mobile and versatile herd could graze and not be affected by such agricultural losses. Second, the herds of animals would provide more protein from milk and meat and materials from hides, furs, horns, and sinew, etc. Animals were multipurpose resources, thus more valuable in a time of uncertainty, so the Lord 'favoured' them. Lastly, the Bible is pointedly telling us that such scarcities in crops, probably caused by climate change, and no doubt exacerbated by grazing flocks caused conflict. In a once plentiful land, where sedentary lifestyles had emerged, climate change threatened first the agricultural lands and eventually a growing population, enough to cause stresses, conflict and migration; an expulsion from Eden. Land utilisation, crop depletion and water wars are nothing new. So what kind of climate change event would reveal more clues as to why and when Eden was abandoned?

Evidence from the Great Flood.
One clue to the abandonment of Eden comes from the shores of the Black Sea. When Oceanographer Dr. Bill Ryan and geophysicist Dr. Walter Pitman, both from Columbia University, investigated a huge, ancient flood event in the Black Sea, they also discovered that higher plateau areas were hit by an extended period of coolness and dryness, a mini Ice Age, c. 6200 to 5800 BC. Even sites such as Catalhoyuk, the 7th millennium BC urban centre in central Anatolia, were abandoned around this time. As people left their previous habitation areas they found a more hospitable climate in the lower Black Sea basin or further south. But around 5600 to 5500 BC, another disaster occurred as the then fresh-water Black Sea was catastrophically inundated by the salt waters of the Mediterranean via the Bosporous, which until then had a portal that acted as a natural dam (Ryan & Pitman 1999: 15-17).

After 5500 BC, a seemingly new culture arrived, identified by their distinctive face pots. Called the Ubaids, these ancestors of the Sumerians had spread their pots all over the region, including the Black Sea. And it is their cultural signature found in this region, at the time of the Black Sea flood. The Ubaids may have produced the first stories of the Biblical Great Flood. To see if there was a link to the flood event and the Biblical story (usually placed at 2300 BC), Ryan and Pitman had studies undertaken of the seabed. With the help of sonar profilers, possible Tell-like structures emerged from the murky depths, 55 meters down, and possibly datable to the time of the flood, which could give a more compelling picture of what really happened during that time (Ryan & Pitman 1999: 18 & 21-22). But, no doubt, the surviving Ubaids would have carried the memories of the flood to Sumer, where they were perpetuated via the Mesopotamian Ziusudra and Utnapishtim legends, which were then spread to later cultures, becoming part of the Biblical fabric through Noah.

When the Israelites were later taken captive in Babylon, they were exposed to and receptive to the myths, legends and religions of the time. They fused their religion with the prevalent Babylonian ones and incorporated them into their own new religious canon, which would later become the Christian Bible. They thus unwittingly kept the names of the ancient rivers, regions and events, even though they had never been there themselves or written the original stories. Their Hebrew translations into Greek, Latin and then English kept the original place names, clearly corroborating ancient Sumerian stories that the original Garden of Eden was in the Iranian/Armenian highlands and not in Mesopotamia.

The Black Sea event, the Mini Ice Age, resource scarcity, and possible localised (yet undiscovered) climate fluctuations caused a time of conflict (enough to turn brother against brother) and migration (away from ancestral lands). As more data is detected and collected through archaeological analysis, the closer we will get to understanding the reality of the Garden of Eden.

The Archaeology of Eden.
Are there any archaeological remains in Eden? Two documented sites excavated in the Lake Urmia area are the Early Bronze Age I site of Yanik Tepe, east of Lake Urmia (in Azerbaijan) and Haftavân Tepe (c.2600 BCE), one of three large settlement mounds in the Urmia basin[3], both excavated in the 1960s and 1970s, respectively, by Charles

Allan Burney from the University of Manchester (Amiran 1965)[3]. A major feature of this period is the Khirbet Kerak Ware, or Red-Black ceramics, found in various locations from Anatolia and the Levant, which originated from the 'Araxes Valleys of Transcaucasia (modern Georgia, Armenia and Azerbaijan) or the Kura-Arax culture, where it is referred to as Karaz or Pulur Ware' from the Early Bronze III 2700-2300 BCE (Amiran 1965)[4].

In a clear archaeological progression, pottery was 'invented in the mountains of Western Iran during the seventh millennium BC', the suspected area being around Kermanshah (now Luristan) and the archaeological site of Tepe Sarab, 6300 to 6000 BC (Rohl 1998: 136 & 138), and later spread by the Ubaids. Evidently, the lights weren't all turned off after the 'expulsion' from Eden and whatever the reason was that Eden was abandoned, it did not remain a lasting deterrent. Indeed, new technological advances were occurring, perhaps as a coping mechanism to the changed climate or from an influx of new people and/or ideas. Haftavân Tepe, Yanik Tepe and other contemporary sites could represent either a partial continuation or re-population of the Lake Urmia/Eden region, which given time, could have become a fledgling city state in the Zagros Mountains.

However, the information from Yanik Tepe and Haftavân Tepe is almost fifty years old and any current Urmia basin excavation data is limited. If this was any other Biblical site or area archaeologists, the media, and pilgrims would be descending in rabid anticipation and rapture. Even the hint of such a discovery would pique their interest, but not Eden, even after tantalising new evidence is revealed. It is still too controversial and unnecessarily treated like New Age sensationalism without discussion or investigation. What do archaeologists have to do; produce the engraved headstone and bones of Adam at the head of Lake Urmia?

To make matters worse, some archaeologists are notoriously deficient in publishing in a prompt fashion, preferring or compelled to continue excavating for funds and/or prestige, so information is slow in dissemination. From the standpoint of the Lake Urmia/Eden area, archaeological sites are surely under-represented in discovery, excavation, recording, and publishing. In its own right, the Lake Urmia area should be investigated, better documented, and publicised more so due to its importance in regards to pottery, animal husbandry, agriculture and metallurgy. But Eden is seemingly considered either off limits or undiscoverable. Such a school of thought could soon be coming to an end.

Rohl has unquestionably (re)opened the window into informed debate about Eden. Instead of ridicule, there should be interest; instead of disbelief, there should be evidence review; and instead of rejection, there should be more excavations, the only practical measure that would prove or disprove the case for or against the reality of Eden. Because the idea of Eden is taken literally as the first place of Man (ignoring evidence from East Africa), some religious scholars and people think that archaeologically, Eden would be the last place found; or deny that Eden was a living site with a full community. Eden was a paradise, which though destroyed by God should somehow still be in a (modern) paradisaical setting, but is now in a third-world state. There is an undeniable whiff of prejudice in the face of mounting evidence that Eden was located in the Zagros Mountains, until some event caused a migration from north to south and possibly provided the catalyst for the great civilisation revolutions.

From Eden to Mesopotamia.
Further supporting the role of Edenites in founding the future civilisations in Mesopotamia, are the intriguing finds of early cities in north eastern Syria. The sites of Tell Brak and Tell Hamoukar so far predate the great 'first' cities of Sumer, which grew from their settlement origins in the 8th millennium BC to fully-fledged cities by 3500 BC. Located 600km North West of Uruk, Tell Hamoukar was a city by 3700 BC, with influences from Uruk appearing around 3200 BC. Tell Brak, situated on a major trade route from the Tigris, may be even older with origins going back into 5th millennium BC. It was once known as the ancient city of Nagar, a later capital of the Akkaddian Empire in 2000 BC.

Such evidence has spurred archaeologists into wanting to investigate Sumer once again to find older sites. Tell el-Oueili, near Uruk, once investigated in the 1980s may have roots in 6th millennium BC and the search is on for more sites (Lawton 2004: 32-35). While the north to south migration to Mesopotamia is well known, the origins of the Sumerians are not clearly defined. The 'Out of Eden' hypothesis: the forced abandonment of Zagros mountain valley sites because of changing climate conditions; would fit the time, location and motive for the long and eventual migration into Mesopotamia and the beginnings of urbanisation. The Garden of Eden has now been placed in a physical context, but over time it has built up an enduring metaphysical construct. It is now time to investigate and celebrate its reality, which is now emerging from the myth.

Nevertheless between the Garden of Eden, Yanik Tepe, Tells Brak and Hamoukar, and Uruk, there are gaps in our knowledge. How much more biological and cultural affinity, whether burials (e.g. customs), artefacts (e.g. pottery), and resources (e.g. trade) is there that could be traced from the original mountain homeland of Eden? From the time of Eden to Tells Brak and Hamoukar, where were the people of Eden? Where will we find the interim settlements as they migrated from their protective valleys and finally into the land between the rivers? Is the Black Sea area one such brief refuge? Besides pottery, what other artefacts could used to trace the Edenites migration? It seems to me that major archaeological, anthropological and genetic investigations will be needed in order to solve this dilemma. Whether created by God or not, the people of Eden were real people that can be traced archaeologically, and we owe it to them and ourselves to trace the origins of the people who established several major pillars of our modern global society.

Conclusion.

If only modern religious scholars' minds were open enough to perceive the apparent truth in Eden's discovery. If only the Iranian and Azeri governments were open enough to explore these ideas and areas. Are there more Western fears that a fiercely open Muslim country holds the key site of Christendom? Would this undermine the legitimacy of the Garden of Eden? Imagine the peaceful ramifications between the religions surrounding the Lake Urmia/Eden area in that they were venerated for their sacredness and that pilgrimages were allowed to take place. But we know it will not happen. Or is that the point? To some, the Garden of Eden, once a paradise and scene of Man's greatest expulsion, was forbidden to us; not just then, but forever. In reality, the Garden of Eden is still lost to us and will never be rediscovered, at least not in a physical sense.

Sources:

Websites accessed as of 16.06.08 (and links active as of September 2020).

[1] http://www.biblegateway.com/
[2] http://en.wikipedia.org/wiki/The_Seven_Daughters_of_Eve
[3] http://www.cais-soas.com/CAIS/Archaeology/Pre-History/haftavan_tepe.htm
[4] http://www.archaeowiki.org/Khirbet_Kerak_Ware
Amiran, R. 1965. Yanik Tepe, Shengavit, and the Khirbet Kerak Ware. *Anatolian Studies*. (Vol. 15), 165-167: British Institute at Ankara.
Lawton, G. 2004. Urban Legends. *NewScientist*. (Vol. 183. No. 2465). September 18, 32-35.
Mithen, S. 2003. After The Ice. London: Weidenfeld and Nicolson.
Rohl, D. 1998. *Legend – The Genesis of Civilisation*. London: Century.
Ryan, B. & Pitman, W. 1999. *Noah's Flood*. Simon & Schuster.

Letter to Professors Sheila Blair and Jonathan Bloom 04/07/2008. 1st Link active as of September 2020.

Dear Ms. Blair and Mr. Bloom,

REF: Haftavan General View IMG09724 (Source ID –Box 66B, Slide 0399)

from:

http://archnet.org/library/images/one-image.jsp?image_id=115765

My name is Ray Burke, and I'm a former archaeology student from University College London. I had been in contact with ArchNet and they supplied me with your contact details. I am writing an article for http://www.ancientarcheology.net/ regarding the on-going re-interpretations for the location of the Garden of Eden in the Lake Urmia Region.

I wanted to include archaeological data about later Bronze Age sites in the area. I would like your permission to re-publish the image above, to illustrate: 1) What the area is/was like; 2) That the proposed area around the Garden of Eden was re-occupied after the 'Expulsion' or abandonment of Eden; 3) That archaeological sites exist in the area, which are under represented in excavation and publication; and 4) that more investigations and excavations should be carried out, if only to better document such an important area in regards to pottery, animal husbandry, agriculture and metallurgy.

I am not using Haftavan Tepe or any other Bronze Age site to represent Eden, but to put Eden into a wider archaeological context. Also, to your knowledge, has there been further work there since 1984?

Thank you for your time and I look forward to hearing from you soon.

Regards,

Ray Burke

20/Jul/2008

Can Intelligent Design be considered a science?

The Flaws of ID

2020 vision
With some channel headers missing from my records, I have elected to place this in the Religion & Spirituality channel rather than Sciences.

Thank you ID. Once again, a pseudoscience has shown itself up to be a lame duck because of its innate flaws. Intelligent Design is the idea that life is too complicated to have arisen without the intervention of an intelligent and/or supernatural agent. Intelligent Design was supposed to be a rival to the scientific theory of evolution, but ID has such obvious design flaws that it is a wonder they weren't identified ages ago and ID put to bed with Creationism.

The fact is that scientists think too linearly and challenge things in logical, orderly ways, following a forward procedure. But with ID, they threw this out the window and tried to pick apart ID at its roots, with arguments targeted at its religious base. But if scientists or anyone else followed through and worked out the 'logical' conclusions of ID, then ID would fizzle out, due to the illogical ideas ID would have to study.

Unseen, unnamed creator:
First, to circumvent the argument that ID is a fundamentally religious doctrine (which it is) in order to undermine scientists' attacks and gain secular approval, the word God, specifically a Judeo-Christian God, is left out. God is the implied intelligent and supernatural designer, but without Her explicit mention, interpretation of ID is thus wide open to other religious and non-religious ideas. Thus shouldn't ID proponents be asking us to believe that any other God or being, like Allah, Re-Atum, Gaia, or Izanagi, etc, could have created life? There could be any number of beings that we don't even worship, intelligent robots, and even aliens that could have created us. Extraterrestrials are favoured by many as progenitors of humankind, and any ID taught course would have to include these other ideas or be accused of bias and not teaching the whole story (as they accuse evolutionists). After all, ID is being taught

under the 'academic freedom' banner, so without a specific creator-entity mentioned, all potential non-evolution ideas would have to be considered, including a balanced debate over alien creators, seeding and intervention.

Supernatural what?:
Second, without defining what supernatural means within ID, it opens itself up to the idea of the creation of humans through Boltzmann Brains (spontaneously appearing sentient beings), or mythical Gods and Goddesses, and even magic (magic being just a higher form of science). We thus have the possibility that a pagan witch or sorcerer created the cosmos and life with magic, with attendant Druids, fairies and unicorns. Thus the universe is magic, held together by spells and incantations. Supernatural encompasses a myriad of terms and thus ID should teach all of these aspects too, so that people can make up their mind over which Wicca, wizard, demon or spirit (holy or not) created life. Is God, or any other creator, really a supernatural being, or just someone with the magic of science at their disposal? How can 'supernaturalness' be measured to prove such a being's existence and intelligence?

This is beyond the realm of science, but the boast that ID can understand such things without resorting to theology is just hollow. ID also misses another trick: There is 96% of the universe that is not made of normal matter (e.g. so-called dark matter and dark energy). Who's to say that these mysterious forces, fields or particles are not proponents of an intelligent or supernatural force, so far undetectable by science? If ID claims to be a science, it should be using existing scientific frameworks to define and investigate these scientific curiosities, but its rejection of certain scientific principles exposes its religious foundations.

Creating the Creator:
Third, whichever mythical or sentient being (whether alien, Brain, witch or robot) created us, then how did they arise? Did they evolve or were they created by another race of beings, aliens, Brains, pixies or other artificial intelligences? There could be as many facets of ID as there are string theories. If science is black and white, then ID is the rest of the spectrum, but it has decided to only concentrate on, say, green, rather than the rest of the colours. Science defines things; ID does not. If ID will not study all of the permutations of its own doctrine, then it cannot be viewed as anything other than a vehicle for religious encroachment

into scientific and secular life. ID is too diffuse in nature, undefined and inclusive of anything else, except science. If that is ID's agenda, then so be it, but I don't think it was supposed to be. These flaws in ID have opened it up to all comers of a pseudoscientific or non-religious colour in appropriating it, which could lead to more court cases with other versions of ID suing each other for not teaching their side of ID. Paradoxically, this could serve to dilute ID's religious backbone, but also eliminate any credibility it had in claiming to be a science.

Random or directed life:
Lastly, evolution is not the explanation for the origins of the universe and life, only the process of life. Evolution explains (even in theory) aspects of why, how, when and where life evolved; ID has no purpose other than to state that evolution is not the prime designer during life, without further discourse into the whats, whens, wheres or whys. Again, that is not science. ID is a one-trick pony, not even offering its own analytical methods in detecting this intelligent designer. Even given that the universe could have been created by an intelligent being, then why does the life that arose have to be directed, as ID claims, and not an undirected process like natural selection. The designer may have wanted blind experiments to test Her own theories, to see how life evolved in random ways, without direction. ID cannot even admit to this, a blindsided, non-scientific view to say the least.

Evolution may not be perfect, but as a theory, it is nowhere near as flawed as ID. ID has no scientific basis, no measurable qualities, no original meaningful data, and no function other than to say that an intelligent/supernatural designer exists; thus ID has no future as a relevant doctrine. It is a religious masquerade designed to outwit scientists and court case actions, and cross the religious/secular divide. ID has one last flaw: the inability to see that it is also a product of natural selection, evolving from past creation ideas, and that it will die a death when all its ideas become extinct.

27/Aug/2008

Religion & Spirituality
Christian evangelists: Helpful or hurtful

Get Off My Doorstep: The Problem With Proselytising

2020 vision

Now there seems to be a switch in strategy with those of the religious persuasion standing passively outside tube and train stations beside stands with pamphlets and with copies in their hands. Some have even approached me while I'm out jogging in the park. The advertising arm of the church better be getting their cut -in souls- from their roving sales people.

One nice, peaceful Saturday morning my doorbell rang, jolting me away from my pastime of watching TV. I rushed downstairs to see who it was: the postman with a package? The gas or electric man to read the meter? Or a member of some organisation doing a meaningless and time-consuming survey? No. These things I can handle, but when I opened the door, I saw two happy, smiley, clean-shaven men, suited and booted, and ready to give me some spiel. Having worked very briefly in the sales business, I saw it coming, looked at their hands and there it was – The Watchtower. They were a couple of Jehovah Witnesses. I looked at the men and said 'Sorry guys, not interested, gotta go!' before one of them could mount a comeback. I closed the door and went back to having an uninterrupted Saturday.

Why do some Christian denominations still go door to door or from country to country trying to enlist people? I thought the Crusades were over! I thought I'd be safe in my own house away from that; but no. It is one thing to canvas and recruit in neighbourhoods, but mine is predominantly Muslim, Hindu, Jewish, and probably dye-in-the wool C of E, so their conversion rate can't be great. I also have no sympathy for Christian aid workers who get caught and punished in Muslim countries for trying to convert the un/non-convertible or who inadvertently stir up trouble for the Christian minority groups already leading a precarious life there. Those countries are not set up for religious freedom even within their own factions, so why be tempted by the devil into interfering with other countries' religion?

Islam is creeping up in numbers in Britain, but not through active door to door selling. People might not like that, but at least it's in their own mosques and classes. No Koran wielding huckster will ever come to my door extolling the benefits of Islam. People go to them for instruction. It would be interesting to see their conversion rate and compare it to the Jehovah Witnesses door-stepping techniques. What do they hope to gain? A friendly chat? An invite for tea and biscuits? An actual convert whose soul they can save? Or a slammed door in their face as my downstairs neighbour offers? England may still consider itself a 'Christian Country', but religion is a private matter for a secular country, and religion should be kept off the doorsteps of the nation.

Should we now 'preach' science, evolution and Darwinism in the same way, door to door, with a book of Richard Dawkins under one arm and a microscope in the other? Is this a last ditch attempt by some religions to get congregation and subscription numbers up by adopting the techniques of sales and marketing? If so, it is almost crass in operation and will probably have the reverse effect of turning people away from the Word. In fact, door to door selling of any kind should be discouraged, if not banned, as most have become unscrupulous toward the unsuspecting and vulnerable elderly and other naïve consumers. But for now, let's just start with ending the religious doorstep industry.

25/Sept/2008

Religion & Spirituality
Problems with religion and hypocrisy

I Won't Go To Heaven – So What?

I had a debate in my head one day, as I often do. I was at work and had been reading a big, thick book, when a colleague came up and asked if I was reading the Bible. I recoiled in horror and said no, 'I'm a scientist; it's a book about evolution'. He then retorted –'The Bible is Revelation'. While I had been reading a book about evolution, my remark had been flippant, but his had been serious. I left him to his thoughts.

But in my own mind, I thought about his world and those of others who believe that religion is the only thing that matters. And this bothered me. It bothered me because most people do not know the history of their own religion and only know the Bible in its now modern form, which leads to hypocrisy. They don't know that Christianity is a blend of Judaism, Zoroastrianism, Egyptian Mystery/Resurrection cults, Gnosticism, and more. You can see this shift in religious thought when the future 'heretical' Jews came back from exile or imprisonment in Babylon and Egypt and brought back these novel ideas with them and mixed them with other local religious traditions. So why should this mongrel blend of religion be any more special than other religions, including paganism? Here's how such debates start leading to other ideas:

As often debated, the Bible is full of mistranslations and copy errors from its original form. The Old Testament stories (Eden, The Flood, etc) are originally Sumerian and transplanted to Israel in later migrating generations. None of the Biblical stories are contemporary and are written-down versions of much earlier oral traditions which changed with political and social moods, and further translated and mistranslated with omissions and 'corrections' to suit particular conditions. The Lost Gospels of the New Testament are one such omission. They did not conform to the 'appropriate' Gospels of Matthew, Mark, Luke and John; even though some of these lost Gospels are older (closer to the time of Jesus) with some written by the very people that were probably of Jesus' socio-cultural group. The accepted Gospels, chosen by a European council, centuries later each contain varying accounts of the accepted story of Christ. They reflect changing times over the course of a century during which the Jews and Romans became the later enemy and ally of Christianity, respectively. The Bible is essentially an epic story of a peoples' migration from one part of the world to another dressed up in terms they used to explain their world and navigate their way.

There are also other contradictions and historical inaccuracies. Take the birth of Jesus. First of all he couldn't have been born in the year zero, or around our Christmas date. That is the 'fault' of Pope Gregory in inventing the modern calendar. Jesus was born a few years 'before' his time, due to the fact that King Herod died in 4BC, so Jesus had to have been born a year or two before that, so our calendar is somewhat out of kilter. Add the fact that most Christian festival days just overrode pagan ceremonial days, then it becomes apparent how contrived Christian history and celebrations are.

There have been many documentaries by serious theologians (to distinguish from the conspiracy theorists and Dan Brown Brigade), which shed light on the early church run by Jesus' family. His biological brothers James, Joses, Simon, and Judas/Jude, some of which were disciples carried on in their own 'Christian' family-run church for almost a century, yet this particular religion was allowed to die out. The Christianity of today bears little resemblance to the original Christianity. It has evolved. Religion is as man-made as science; hence I would ask my friend: Why he believes in the Church of England when it was 'invented' by King Henry VIII in the 1500s so that he could divorce his then wife? Henry protested against the rule of the Pope, hence the PROTESTant church. Why should anyone have faith in that religion, than say over Calvinism, Lutheranism or any other contemporary religious revolt of that time? Some people do not know the evolution of their own religion and how the Church had moulded and perpetuated a hol(y)istic image presentable to the masses. But all companies do that, and the Church is just another business selling the notion of God, with the effect of keeping its congregations ignorant to certain facts about its own religion, which is an unpalatable act perpetrated upon the believers of this world.

Going back to my flippant scientist remark, I know that science does not have all the answers and that it can be as indoctrinating as religion, but religious people have to understand that if there is a God and he made everything, then he made the natural/scientific world, too. Science is a part of God's nature, so for those who turn their back upon science, they are also turning their backs, or even denying, the work of God. Just as priests disseminate the word of God, scientists discover the science of God. Not all teachings of science and religion are good. Fundamentalists and Ultra zealots can be as bad as some Applied Sciences, but the danger in a narrow view of the world from only a religious perspective deprives one of the whole nature of God, including science. One has to know both sides of the equation to argue their point.

Some people then might say that science has brought evil into the world, despite its good intentions, while others counter that most of the biggest wars are fought because of religion. I tend to agree with the latter, though detractors will always cite Hitler and Stalin, forgetting that they, and even the modern 'atheist' Chinese state, targeted religious groups. So whether or not religion started a war, it has always been at the heart of war. Religion is more divisive than science, despite its so-claimed peaceful cloak of sheep's clothing. Intelligent Design is the wolf of religion, claiming to be something that it is not: science. This is another evolution of religion, a false one, just as The Theory of Everything will not know the mind of God. Religion and science are mutually exclusive, differing aspects of any God.

So, to get to the crux of this debate: A religious person will probably tell me that I won't go to heaven because of my beliefs, but there are good people in this world of different or no religion. There are many supposed Christians in this world who do very bad things. What will happen to them when they die? Is there a heaven or hell for them? Why not? Does it really matter? Are there sections in heaven for believers and non-believers? There has to be some afterlife for everyone, doesn't there? What about the reincarnated? Will they ever die or pass through heaven? With so many Gods (Christian, Jew, Muslim, Hindu, etc) how can any one religion be more legitimate than any other, especially when most of the major religions are split because of human frailties? Why would I want to go to Heaven? Some people, Christians and non-Christians, are living a life of hell on Earth, as I write. What does heaven mean; a life of luxury, non-drudgery, and celestial beauties in a mist-filled city of light? Of course, people will say that heaven is unexplainable, inexpressible, and undeniable, but I don't care. Whether there's a flash of light, black nothingness, a new life, or my soul dissolves into a disembodied soup of wandering atoms, I don't care. I've had my life and I've loved it, so far. What more could I want, a piece of heaven? Naah!

29/Nov/2008

Religion & Spirituality
Conception of Heaven

I'm in Heaven – Now what?

I've died and now stand at the Pearly Gates. I'm checked in, my bags are taken by the patron saint of porters, and I find myself in a blank white room awaiting my heaven orientation lecture and document package. Some bikini clad angels-to-be run past me, but my thoughts must be pure, lest I'm evicted. And then I realise something: I'm bored. What in Heaven's name will I do in Heaven, forever?

What is Heaven?
I guess Heaven is a paradisaical after-life on another plane of existence. It's where the good, just, and believers in God go for their reward during life. A Heaven may have been conceived and used by the Judeo-Christian-Muslim trinity, but other adherents could no doubt join if they have been just enough. Presumably, Heaven only opened for business around the time of Christ, so no Neanderthals or Homo erectus are likely to be found there; it's exclusively for us modern types and not back-dateable. It's a stress-free zone where the light always shines and people are happy, eternally so.

Who goes to Heaven?
Some people are already happy on Earth in life. If Heaven is what people make it, then how much happier can they be in death? Some people, Christians and non-Christians, are living a life of hell on Earth. Will the good non-believers in such lives be compensated in Heaven? There are many Christians in this world who do very bad things. What will happen to them when they die? Is it Heaven or hell for them? Does it really matter? Are there sections in Heaven for believers and non-believers? Are there multiple Heavens? There has to be some afterlife for everyone, doesn't there? With so many Gods (Christian, Jew, Muslim, Hindu, etc) how can any one religion be more legitimate than any other, especially when most of the major religions are split because of human frailties? Why would I want to go to Heaven? Life is so enjoyable.

What happens there?

Er, not sure, there hasn't been a complete description of Heaven in the Bible. People imagine you spend all your time being happy. But doing what? Do you live the life you would have had, like a virtual reality game? Do you get to spend time watching over family and friends? Can you use cosmic Facebook to find family and friends you lost over the years or will they be the ones to welcome you? Would you live in some idyllic house or something similar to when you were alive? Can you train to be an angel? Do you spend it in total contemplation and prayer? How free is Heaven to explore? Is there anything scenic to see beyond blinding white lights? Will you seek knowledge of the universe and travel the cosmos? Is there TV to watch and what would be on? Would you see Jesus or Mary or commune with the Holy Spirit? Once there, why is it not possible to pass back to Earth and tell people of the heavenly experience in a manner that is emphatically clear beyond séances, ghosts and visions? Why would God not allow such endorsements from beyond the grave? Is that the true test of faith in Heaven – to believe is to be there?

What is the future of Heaven?

Will we be assigned to guide someone like Guardian Angels? Can we do that in the past, present and future? Are there Guardian Angels for everyone, believers or not, different faiths and beliefs? Will we be trained to fight come Revelation, the Apocalypse of Armageddon and the following Rapture? Will we dead in Heaven live again? How many people will that leave on Earth and then what? Will life then start all over; from what stage – pre-historic, pre-industrial, the present or the future? Will it start from the Big Bang and everything is reincarnated? What will Jesus do the second time around if everyone is already converted to Christianity? Christ will only rule for a 1000 years after his victory, then what? Who's next? Will life and/or history come to an end with Heaven on Earth? Will that be the end of Homo Sapiens –God's experiment over? Is Heaven the ultimate Ark, saving those from the apocalyptic storms to come? Can Heaven end?

Can Heaven really be that good?

The so-called martyrs (Terrorists) claim that they will have a myriad of virgins if they accomplished their mission? So what? Once they're no longer virgins do they get more or are they stuck there with no one to talk to? Would you have a job in heaven? Tending gardens, looking after children, or preening angel wings? Would you get paid? How would God pay you for work; with happiness, love or a promotion? What kind of satisfaction would you get from working in heaven? Everything would be the same, day in, day out, like Groundhog Day. There would be no challenges, nothing to achieve. Can you really be happy forever and ever? At least in Hell there is motivation to keep working; be punished or tortured. The saying goes: Better to rule in Hell than to serve in Heaven -words of a cynic or of someone experienced in the downsides of paradise? What does eternal life mean to the dead? Will the soul live on forever?

Those were only a few of the questions that one can ask. Whether you believe or not, the role and state of Heaven in people's lives is constantly changing and the only way to know for sure is to go there; a one way trip down the tunnel of lights. Of course, people will say that Heaven is unexplainable, inexpressible, and undeniable. Whether there's a flash of light, black nothingness, a new life, or my soul dissolves into a disembodied soup of wandering atoms, would I really want to be in Heaven? I will have to wait and see, for life is heaven enough for me.

29/Nov/2008

Religion & Spirituality
Contemplating the existence of God

God the Scientist

2020 vision

Think about it. If God created the universe, using all the tools of physics, biology, and chemistry, then he is a scientist – at least in our understanding of the word scientist. And yet, God insisted on being worshipped. Are all scientists so egotistical? Maybe in God's realm science and religion are the same. We humans created the dichotomy in ignorance, not knowing what science was thousands of years ago. But either way, whether God exists or not as the creator, science created the universe.

For years now I have been telling people that if there was a God, then he and science can be reconciled, but either I did not explain it well enough or people just did not accept it. To believers and non-believers, God and science are two mutually exclusive realms. But they are not; they are one and the same. Note that I have not said religion and science; that is a different issue that will also be addressed. This is not intended to shake anyone's faith either way, but just to give an underlying understanding on how God and science are interlinked. By the time you come to the end of this article you may well have a whole new view on God, religion and science. The least it will do is to get you thinking.

God's science qualifications:

So first off, the premise is that if there is a God, he/she/it is a being not too dissimilar to us in nature, but is omnipotent, rather than just being some disembodied cosmic force. This God sits somewhere in the universe he made, overlooking us and any other of his other universal creations. And that is the first point. No matter what God is and how he made it, he used matter and energy; atoms, molecules, and photons, etc, to create galaxies, stars, planets, the conditions for life, and us. That is understanding the depths of cosmic composition: chemistry. That is the physical manipulation of basic energy and matter: physics. That is building and terraforming worlds: geology. That is creating and sustaining life: biology. Even if science is just a label we use and some people believe that God's power is above science, he has still used those physical elements, not belief or prayer, to create everything. Science, even by any other name, is still science. So God is a qualified scientist.

Evolution:
What about evolution and genetics? Surely, random processes have created all the myriad species on Earth and the (supposed) pinnacle of all animals: humans? Let's suppose that God is directing evolution. Almost every week in magazines like the New Scientist, I read articles about new genetic discoveries, about random mutations, and the way genes are transmitted over time. There is DNA, RNA, Messenger RNA, Introns, Exons, proteins, viruses, Junk DNA, Amino Acids, etc. So, sort it out and build me a human from scratch. What, too hard? The combinations of just those few components of a human are astronomical. We would need a quantum computer and countless years to build anything that complex from scratch, yet God apparently did it; the ultimate biologist. He would have to know how to spark life from organic compounds, anticipate all the evolutionary traits and combinations, programme all the mutations, cause decay, and yet enable us to reproduce imperfect copies of ourselves. Why would he do that?

Yet, Godless evolution would explain that; the randomness and complexity are there as a trace of our 'accidental' selection and arrival through catastrophes and adaptation. Humans were designed, by natural evolution that has had millions of years to practice and learn from its mistakes, yet still create us imperfect humans. If God designed us, he designed us to evolve, flaws and all, and he is no longer actively directing it a la Intelligent Design. Paradoxically, ID tacitly admits that a supernatural being created everything, thus that God uses/d science, but at the same time ID entirely divorces God from science. In trying to disprove 'natural' evolution, ID ignores the fact that God has to be an evolutionist in the highest scientific sense. God believes in evolution.

Nature:
It would have been better if man had stuck to worshipping the sun, moon and other cosmic bodies/phenomena. At least they were worshipping in the natural science realm and God would have been the God of nature. Natural science would then have been the original 'religion' and God would have been truly super natural. This is not to say

411

that science should be worshipped in itself; cold logic might not be the most enlightened way to live. Some people argue that science teaches worldly matters, but that religion teaches morals. However, with reason comes morality and law. There are people of all persuasions and beliefs, religious and scientific, both and neither, who have different moral compasses. Such reasoned beliefs have been around longer than religion otherwise there would have been no collective societies or civilisations prior to the first organised cults (e.g. Catalhoyuk, Turkey, c.7,500 BC) and religions, which funnily enough never mentioned The God, but which used primitive science to urbanise and survive.

Religion:
So where does religion fit in? Religion is a man-made response to the natural world. It's ironic that as man first worshipped the scientific world through the sun and moon, etc, the more man moved away from equating God with science. So why has this been so? Well quite simply, as with pagan celebrations and sites, religion, especially Christianity has co-opted God for itself and transplanted science with faith and belief; two tenets that take away certainty from people and use it to control the masses through superstition. Some Pagans in a way worship natural science at solstices and our calendars are based upon scientific principles such as the sun and moon's movements, and atomic clocks. Science rules our lives. God is both supernatural and super natural and he gave us the intelligence to investigate the scientific and natural world around us, which religion seeks to demonise.

And that is the ultimate secret of religion. It has obscured the fact that God was originally (and still is) a God of Science. The intangible and abstract notions of faith, the after-life and the supernatural has now immersed itself so deeply into human consciousness that it has become a meme (coined by the arch-anti-religionist Richard Dawkins); the 'DNA' of human transmitted thoughts, ideas, and culture. That in itself is interesting for if memes are a component of the human psyche, a function of the brain, created through biology, and thus by God; then God is behind the rise of faith (but not organised religion an invention of man). So faith and reason arose from our combination of genes and thoughts, but it is faith that has been utterly corrupted by religion in its selfish and supposed sole ownership of God. There is no harm in thinking of God, if he exists, as a God of science, but that faith should be subordinate to science. It's how God created the world in the first place; but man has sullied the scientific message with a subversive movement called religion.

So there you have it: God is science. There is no reason to suppose that God did create us, but for the believers here is a one explanation of how God and science can co-exist. God the Scientist can be worshipped; it's the natural thing to do. So if someone says they've had a calling to do God's work, don't be surprised if they become a scientist.

25/Dec/2008

Religion & Spirituality
Arguing the existence of the devil

Hell on Earth

After watching the BBC TV series 'Apparitions'[1] it made me think that if the Devil did exist, then what is his ultimate goal? There are references in the TV show that the Devil is trying to create his own Messiah of a son, born of a virgin, followed by an army of unborn souls. I thought that was an interesting premise, seeing as we always depict the Devil as just tempting people. But recently, his plots against God, as also shown in the film 'Constantine' have become more sophisticated, though he still usually loses in the end.

The idea that the Devil would try to imitate God's 'procreational' deed by delivering a son upon the Earth, pre-empting the Second Coming, would be the most audacious and cynical plot from Satan. But what kind of world would it be? Who would worship Satan and why? At total random I saw an ad for a TV documentary about The Devil's Bible (The Codex Gigas or the biggest book in the world)[2], allegedly created by a 13th century monk who sold his soul to the Devil and had a large picture of the Devil incorporated into the book. But then I wondered, beyond the Satanist cults, is there a true Bible of Satan where everything in the otherwise well-known Bible is mirrored in the Devil's bible, but from his point of view; everything from his fall, through the Crucifixion, to Revelations. What would this mirror universe look like? How would it read? Is there a parallel world where the Devil is the 'star' of the Bible?

As I delved further, I found an interesting reference to Satanism[3]. It is not what people think it is. It is not the worship of the Judeo-Christian devil or Satan, or related to Devil worship; as God, the Devil, Heaven and Hell do not exist to the real Satanist. In a very basic sense, Satanism is a religious form of Humanism, but the former 'worships' man as a God in himself and the carnal life that each leads. Satan is just a symbol of that sinful nature, just as a cross is a symbol to Christianity and fire to Zoroastrianism. The Church of Satan, founded by Anton LaVey (1966), was the first organisation to identify itself as such and the Satanic Bible lays out rules, meanings, and teachings in what it means to be a Satanist.

Inevitably, as with any religion, it has split into a few factions, some more obscure, but there is still misunderstanding from traditional religions as to the purpose of Satanism. Traditional or Theistic Satanism does view the Devil as a being worthy of worship. So, even Satanists are caught between atheists, agnostics, Judeo-Christians, and Muslims in their conflicting beliefs between man and God - truly the work of Satan.

There are also societies that are often accused of worshipping Satan. The Yezidi are a Kurdish religious group from around Mosul, northern Iraq. Their religion is often said to be that of Devil worship because their chief Angel, the Peacock Angel (Melek Taus) is also known as 'Shaytan', the same name the Koran has for Satan. Melek Taus did not respect Adam, as he was an Angel and Adam merely made from dust, which led to Melek Taus' fall, a parallel to Satan. However, the Yezidis do not believe Melek Taus, still their archangel, to be evil; that comes from within humans themselves. There just seems an agenda by Muslims to demonise this minority religious group with the Satanism tag, which often sticks, without further research.

History is littered with other satanic groups and evil organisations, but the truth often lies in the words of their accusing enemies. Occult writers such as Nostradamus have been seized upon as predicting the rise of various Antichrists: Napoleon, Hitler, Saddam Hussein, and Bin Laden are such names that have been proffered over the centuries, but none have risen to the heights of the original fallen angel; can any human really? Devil worshipping killers, satanic sacrifices, and demonic exorcisms are figments of religious minds or the works of a sensationalist film industry. It seems to me that evil comes from within man who then justifies and excuses his actions on behalf of some evil metaphysical being.

It is strange that we know or imagine more about Hell than we do about Heaven. The Devil is always depicted as a horned being or demon; a suave, sinister man; or possessing another being; whereas God is usually remembered as George Burns or Morgan Freeman. Hell is always depicted, rather brilliantly in 'Constantine' or in Dante's 'Divine Comedy' as Circles of Hell in the Inferno and Purgatory. Hell is there to frighten us away from a sinful life, but why is Heaven a sketchy image? Why is Heaven unknowable, beyond white lights and eternal happiness?

The more we know about the Devil, evil and Hell, the better we can recognise them and fight them. Maybe a life in Heaven will show that we humans cannot live without sin to drive us. Lucifer was only cast from Heaven and not destroyed; thus sin lives as the devil inside us all.

So, perhaps the Devil does not need to manifest himself through his son on Earth. His demonic armies can stand down. Maybe Satanism has the answers – for each man is already sin incarnate and better the devil you know.

1. Apparitions TV show:
http://www.locatetv.com/tv/apparitions/5911071
(link not available)

2. The Devil's Bible: http://en.wikipedia.org/wiki/Codex_Gigas
(link available as of September 2020)

3 The Satanic Bible:
http://www.dpjs.co.uk/modern.html
(link available as of September 2020)

06/Jan/2009

Religion & Spirituality
What is your understanding of God?

God's Assets

2020 vision
A later companion piece to The universe's assets essay in Science section 30/11/08.

Occasionally, I ponder the very stuff of God's divine nature and wonder about his existence. Now in this time of global financial crisis, I wondered how such a crisis would affect God. The universe is God's greatest asset, so how rich is God? Since he created the universe, does he have sole ownership, or is his universal property divided among lesser Gods, angels, mystical forces and probably the Devil and demons (someone has to own hell). Is heaven the penthouse of the universe and hell the basement? Let us consider God's assets.

How much does the universe cost? Has anyone ever costed the universe; all the galaxies, stars, clusters and planets? We humans put values on the universal elements (like carbon, iron, gold, etc), but does God put such values on the cosmic stuff he has made? Where is the costliest place in the universe? Is it in a dense stellar cluster, the centre of the universe, or is there a universal equivalent to the French Riviera? Are black holes universal stock collapses and the rest of the galaxy whips around to create stars to pay off the cosmic debt? Are dark matter and dark energy shadowy investors in the material world, supplying cosmic funds in terms of gravity? The universe must have some kind of value even to a God, whether financial or spiritual, and the interest from its expansion must be astronomical.

Is God an entrepreneur? Is the universe a business venture? Did God have to buy up the matter and energy to create the universe or was he a speculator just gathering what was freely floating around and creating a patented network called the universe? Does he own the cosmic software, keeping a tight grip on the laws of the universe or is he a philanthropist ceding certain laws and property to other masters of the universe, like a wiki? The universal company is definitely in the black, but as it operates in a vacuum, God will have to watch out that the bubble doesn't burst one day.

Along with the matter of the universe, which can be totalled up into material assets, what about the intangibles, the priceless life-giving energy of the cosmic green machine, like the solar winds, nuclear fusion, lunar tidal power, comet water, and star light; what price they in the larger scheme? If humans are not the only life form to inhabit this cosmic real estate, then how much value do we add to the system? Are we living rent-free? Is the universe a *des res* because of our presence or a squatter's den for humanity? Are humans a tax on the system? The universe is worth more than the sum of its parts, just as a human soul is more than flesh and blood. The energy quotient and the efficiency rating of the universe could go a long way in raising the value of the universe. The verdict is still out on human worth.

Will God ever go bankrupt as the universe nears the end of its life as a hypersphere of hot gas? Or will he repackage it and sell it as a newly refurbished, unfurnished accommodation to another God or alien willing to take on any further remodelling and redesign work? The universe could loose its value and be repossessed by whatever force of nature God may have been in debt to. The boom and bust of the universal industry could then begin again with a big bang heralding a new universal era.

Of course, God might not need money or finance, but would count his assets in spiritual ways, amassing a fortune from the laws of nature and the growth value of the Gross Universal Product. The universe produces unlimited energy, perpetual and profitable power; the universe manufactures goods in the form of galaxies, stars, planets and life forms; and the universe in all likelihood trades with other universes, through other quantum dimensional banking systems via gravity leaks, neutrinos, or other exotic means. A spiritual banking system may be better than a material one, but would depend on the strength of faith and belief which could also suffer in confidence. If God places no value on anything, if there is no universal value system, then is the universe (including humanity) a worthless waste of time, energy and space? No, for just by the act of creating the universe God must have placed some value in that one deed. But are we the beneficiaries of that act, the future evaluators or mere inconsequential observers?

So is the universe in good financial shape? Is God looking after the pennies? What could happen to cause a universal financial collapse, leaving God needing financial assistance? Well, first of all, God's assets are unlimited, whether material, energy or spiritual. The universe is of such vastness and of a divested nature that no financial calamity should be able to bring the whole system down like a supernova. Black holes, pulsars, gravity quakes, solar storms, time and space instabilities would just be local blips and if worse came to worse, any collapsed solar system or galaxy would get an injection of fresh capital and be rebuilt over a few billion years, a wink of an eye in the larger scheme of things.

But ultimately, if things went wrong, who is there to bail out God? Is this where religious minded people come in? Is belief in God and faith, his fallback and emergency refinance package? Is religion propping up the financial base of the universe? God has many strings to his bow, a trans-universal company pumping out cosmic products and abundant energy, but his greatest asset could be an insignificant expenditure on a tiny blue world who are present to witness his wealth and enjoy in the proceeds. So while we suffer through the global financial crisis, just remember that no matter the value of the universe, God or no God, treasure the assets that you already possess.

15/Jan/2009

Religion & Spirituality
Questioning the reality of God

Dinner with God

So, I'm at the top table with God, a few archangels, angels and fellow newly deceased, (incredible, as I am basically a non-believer) and I ask the question: "God, are you really real?"

The various heavenly dinner table conversations go quiet and I hear an angel mutter, "Hear we go, again. Not another one."

God, or the bright light at the head of the table, answered: "I am as real as you want me to be. I exist everywhere and am all things to all people."

I ask: "So, who are you and why should people worship you?"

And he answered (not by voice of course, but the warmth of the light conveys the answer): "I am but myself: the way and the light. I am Jehovah, Yahweh, Allah and a whole host of Gods. You worship me for I created you, as it should be."

"But how are you all things at once?" I ask.

"Think of quantum theory. I am the universal superposition, like a photon making all choices on its path at the same time. I am the one to all; there is no conflicting or contrary belief, as I am everything and everywhere at once. I love and I smite; I am the lamb, I am vengeance. Everything at the same time."

I kind of understood, but I had to ask for myself, as a non-believer if we had to believe in him: "How relevant are you then? Not everyone will worship you."

"Haha," God laughed. "I am as relevant as I need to be. Whosoever needs and wants me can worship me in their own fashion. I will never be alone without believers. I will always exist, and as long as people believe in existence, here I am."

"I believe, therefore I exist. Is that it?" I asked.

"Something like that. But you do not believe in me, yet here you are talking to me."

"I'm dreaming," I said. "This is an existential journey I am taking in order to deny you; but to deny you, I have to confront you."

"Oh," said God, somewhat disappointed.

I asked: "Where are you from? Were you born? Are you from our universe? Are you an alien?"

God seemed cautious here. "I've been around, done this, done that, you know. I'm not an extraterrestrial nor am I really corporeal. I walk many planes of existence, many times, and a few dimensions. I am of the body, mind, and spirit. I have always been and ever will be." He looked a bit smug or at least the light seemed to dance.

"Not an entirely satisfactory answer." I said, "Which is why I and many others don't believe in you. There are no straightforward answers forthcoming."

"Why should I reveal everything to you? Why should I have to answer your questions? There are men who seek to be Gods in their own right; those false idols and prophets whether scientists, so-called priests, or politicians who also do not have all the answers, yet you follow them blindly."

"Ah," I replied. "I guess we're just sheep." I changed the subject: "Why did you cast out Lucifer? Can't you reconcile with him as you want us humans to do on Earth? Why should everyone in the afterlife follow you blindly?"

"It is Lucifer who prolongs his own exile. His pride is unbridled and he will not accept any conditions. He really would rather rule in Hell than serve in Heaven. And as the creator, I should be followed, not just blindly, but with open hearts and minds."

"Serve in Heaven? Why don't people or angels have free will in Heaven?"

God smiled. "They do, but free will is governed by me of course. Free will is but quantum fluctuations of the mind and I created it all, so I get to say how it works and who it works for."

"You sound like a scientist."

"I am. I created everything that you would call biology, physics and chemistry. I created you to evolve. I am the Scientist God!"

Some of the dinner guests were shocked by this. They thought science and God could not be reconciled. Now they knew better. I continued. "So do you think people use you as an excuse for all their actions? Do you deny people their true inheritance of thought, word, and deed?"

He looked at me, or at least the searing light beamed brighter in my direction. "Am I making you ask me these questions?"

"I don't know. Are you? The illusion of free will is still but a prison. Why keep us locked up, God? Why not let us see our jailer? Show yourself!" I trembled in fear as the light flared, and then all was warmth again.

"To see me is to see yourself. Remember, I am God to everyone, a reflection of their beliefs. If everyone on Earth saw me at the same time, they would see and describe different things; their own interpretations, their dreams, fears and prayers. I am but the light and not as you are."

"Good answer, God. But that is the problem. One day, as scientists near discovering the Theory of Everything –knowing the mind of God, religionists will want to know the mysteries of God; who you are, why you created us to worship you, what is your ultimate role for us, and when your son will return." I looked around for Jesus, but he wasn't at the table. "You are secretive to the point of paranoia. You portray yourself as an all-mysterious force without proof of existence and that scares a lot of people. Some affirmation should be forthcoming in this life, rather than the next. Why can't you just show yourself?"

"Are you a psychologist, now?"

"No. But I think that if we knew everything about you, then your power would be gone. You need us humans more than we need you!"

But God was dismissive: "As God I have nothing to prove. You either believe in me or you don't. That really is your choice. And that's all I have to say. But just for you, I will tell you this secret to prove my existence..."

Just then a cherub flew by and offered me dessert; angel cake, of course. But the distraction broke my concentration. And I woke up from my dream. I swore I heard fading laughter.

Did God mean for that to happen or did I not want to know the truth? I couldn't decide, so I went back to sleep and dreamed of lunch with Satan.

04/Feb/2009

Religion & Spirituality
God and time

Happy Birthday God

In the Satanic Bible it states that 'the highest of all holidays in the Satanic religion is the date of one's own birth' rather than some stolen pagan celebration or of someone nobody ever knew like a famous celebrity or politician. This is highly commendable as each person is a God unto themselves. The same should be true of God when he has a birthday.

But if God did exist, when would his birthday be? It is not Christmas, which is not even his supposed son's birthday, since Jesus was allegedly born around Easter time (and before year 0). Some might say that maybe everyday is God's birthday, but that is only if man is a God unto himself, then yes, everyday would be a god's birthday. Is every Sunday God's birthday, or a Saturday, or a Friday? Is the Sabbath just a day of rest for him? What does God do during the week that he needs one day to rest, presumably to listen and catch up (omnibus style) on our prayers. God's birthday won't be on Walpurgisnacht (May Day) or All Hallows' Eve (Halloween). Maybe God follows a totally different calendar, a universal one not known to man. In this case God's time would run differently to ours and he may only be mere decades old to a billennia (hence his making of everything in seven days rather than millions of years). Maybe the spin of the universe sets God's clock, thus his birthday would be immeasurable to us.

Having a birthday implies one was born. So when was God born -when and where? Where did God grow up? His life is a mystery —the ultimate holy ghost in the universal machine. How old is God, 13.8 odd billion years old (or more depending what's behind the cosmic horizon)? Does he regenerate like a Time Lord? Has God been reincarnated? I assume God has gone through the tweenager years and past his quarter-life crisis, but maybe not as far as a mid-life crisis. Is God so old that he doesn't bother celebrating his birthday —too many candles? Is God just a title like Pharaoh, Caesar, or King, thus a hereditary job with one God following another? Does each God have a personal name like Jehovah,

Yahweh and Allah, who are just Gods from different dynasties or a family of Gods? Whether God invented man or Man invented god, surely there must be a date from which we can pin on the calendar the day God was born.

Would God have a big birthday party (not a big bang)? What kind of cake would God eat, besides angel cake! Do the angels make him presents? What gift would you give a God who has everything, including a universe of his own? Like Queen Elizabeth II on her official birthday, would God present an honours list to those deserving in heaven or like the Thai King Bhumibol Adulyadej would he grant amnesty to certain sinners? Do those in Hell escape punishment while God celebrates? Would Satan send a grudging congratulatory card? Does God even believe in birthdays? Or believe in anything? Does he pray to his own Gods from a universe before or beyond? In supposedly creating man in his own image and inventing the birth process, God must have had knowledge of this procedure as it would have happened to him and his only begotten son. So he must celebrate each birth on Earth as he would his own, even with a modest bit of wine and bread. Cheers!

Should we humans pick an arbitrary date to celebrate God's birthday, like President's Day, Valentines, or Father's Day? When would be the best day for God? Christmas is already taken, but as the calendar is man-made would choosing such a date suffice. Would the Pope know more about this? Has the Vatican looked into declaring an official day of God to wish him Happy Returns? If God had a star sign (since if religion exists then so does magical astrology), which of the countless constellations in the universe would he come under? Was God born an Aries or a Pisces, Leo or is God really just a Cancer? Was God born in the year of the Goat, the Dragon, or the Rat? In any event, the world's religions could probably never agree which date to commemorate, so God's birthday will probably never be celebrated and that would mean one less bank holiday for us.

God only knows when his own birthday is and how he would celebrate, but whenever it is and if God does exist, then Happy Birthday God.

19/Apr/2009

Religion & Spirituality
What's wrong with religion?

Church Hurts

The divisions today between religions seems ever wider than before as each attacks the other for being the cause of all the ills of the world. But the real problem is not with religion *per se*, but with the churches, which concentrates religion, spreads division, and deprives people of free religious thoughts, words, and deeds. It is the church which hurts the cause of religion on many levels and religion may never recover from it.

There is no one true religion. However, because of the church's insistence on keeping denominational traditions, each one believes they have some kind of superiority over the other. This alone can fuel conflict and without even bringing up war, local communities can be divided over religion and the churches that lead them. Religion used to be its own master, but churches have subverted religion for its own purposes and it is not always for divine intentions. Man's whim can make up any religion and enforce it through church rules. The church has taken over and crushed the spirit of religion.

The Bible does not discriminate against or even legislate for who can preach, yet man, in the guise of Popes, cardinals, bishops and other senior figures try to tell the layman who can and cannot preach and all this is from a personal view point. It is a human decision, not on authority from the bible. These people are out of touch. Lately, there has been a growth of non-denominational churches, some of which have grown into independent 'mega-churches'. Anyone from any denomination can come and be with like-minded people. There are no hard sermons, just places for people to go and express their religiosity, rather than being targeted with fire and brimstone. But the majority of churches are still tied to the monolithic, traditional cultures of the Middle Ages and for some reason cling to this mode of existence even in the face of changes in modern society. Churches cannot keep up in a modern world and are not fit for purpose any more.

Churches have an agenda to indoctrinate people from Sunday school onwards. They spread propaganda, like businesses using marketing and advertising. Churches today are still some of the biggest landowners and operate as business rather than places of worship. Collections are for investment rather than fixing the leaky roof. In some places, separation of church and state hardly exists or is masked by lobbyists. Money may not be the root of all evil, but it could plant the seeds of corruption in the minds of priests and their churches. Many a scandal in churches has arisen from money, sex, and power. While churches preach that science has made society immoral, there are many church leaders and goers leading quite immoral lives. Society is not moral because of religion; people have lived morally for millennia without having religion and churches. Churches are not always the moral centres they claim to be and have strayed far from the religions they claim to represent.

With so many denominations of every religion, all with churches and/or meeting places, the church takes away the right for people to worship their religion the way they want to. Religion is a deeply personal thing. Religion could probably be tolerated more by the non-religious if not for the churches that continually try to erode personal freedoms and dictate to their flocks. Churches are trying to order national and international policies in regards to teaching evolution, AIDS prevention, abortion and sexual advice/orientation, women's rights, and even war. There is a hypocrisy that emanates from church authorities, which causes religion to polarise society. Church authorities have no place in the political process and such forays into politics are blatant attempts to hold onto some former power. Religion in itself is free of any political doctrines, yet the church drags in its religion, tainting religion in the view of many. Hiding behind the banner of religion, churches harbour politicos, sexists, bigots, and ignorance within their doctrines.

Religion may be hard-wired in the human brain, but the cult of the church is not. Once again, a man-made institution has tainted what was once a 'pure' concept and could be a perfectly acceptable and personal practice. Religion has become more internalised, so there is no need to visit a special place on a special day to worship. Churches should accept this and either change their ways or go out of business. Getting rid of churches may go some way to ridding the world of sectarian conflict, promoting more tolerance, rehabilitating religion to its original teachings, and making religion appealing to more people. Ditch the hurt; get rid of church.

15/May/2009

Religion & Spirituality
If God is so powerful, why does evil exist?

Is God Evil?

This is an interesting concept. At first, the question seems to ask if the traditional God of Western thought is actually an evil entity and how and why this manifests itself. But there are also deeper questions that must make one think about the wider implications of this concept. Three issues that stand out are: If there is a God, is he evil? If there isn't a God, then why did man create a God who can be evil? And, what is evil?

There is a God:
First of all, we cannot know if God is evil, because he is the only God we have. There is no comparison with another God to know if our God is any more evil or benevolent than another God. How do we not know that in another world or universe, a God is supposed to walk among his people, speak to and teach his children, and be more open and visible? Our God hides away in the dark recesses of space or within the religious mind, behind religious veils, doctrines, and prayers. We only know about God from what has been 'told' to ancient witnesses and written down in the Bible, by men. The word of God may be heretical to another God, but we only have one side of the story.

But who is God? Is he Jehovah, Yahweh, Allah, or another? If these names are for the same God, then none of them are exactly peaceable. They effect war and make us wage war without end. Religious arguments condemning man to a life of sin from the legends of Adam and Eve in the Garden of Eden do not tell the whole story. If we are indeed in the image of our God, then our war-like nature would stem from a war-like God. To be fair, God has a dual nature in that he is both vengeance and love, good and evil, and we humans could be no less so than our creator's vision. Then again, what is evil? It's a human term for things that are natural to the universe, but immoral to us thinking beings. It would be fascinating if an 'evil' gene were found, especially if it was related to the recently discovered 'God' gene. Would God splice into us an evil gene if it was not already part of his holy body or experience? In any case, any evil in us stems from a God who has the capacity to create and commit evil as well.

There's no God:
If God does not exist, then who is benefiting from spreading the word that God exists and evil is man's fault. In modern times, not one war or act of evil has been stopped by invoking religion. The lightness and darkness of our created God is reflected in the tales of Ahura Mazda and Ahriman, the deities of Zoroastrianism, the oldest monotheistic religion in the world. In fact, God is a culmination of the legends from Persia, Egypt, Greece, and Rome. Their Gods were capable of great heroics or evil, it was just part of their supernatural nature, continued by God and Satan, the fallen angel. In the Satanic religion, Man is a God unto himself, and if evil is committed, he must be prepared to face the consequences. Is that what evil is for? Evil must be expressed, for it is natural, but it comes with dire consequences. The concept of evil was not created by God, but by men who now try to absolve their sins through a deity that does not exist, but which helps such men to rule us. If that is not evil, then what is? Man uses God to commit evil. God is a manufactured concept that takes away man's right and capacity for self-determination. In such a way, God is evil.

We do not know the supernatural state of God in our cosmological and evolved world. Our mythical God is as impenetrable as dark matter and dark energy. The universe is a dark place, because it was created within a vacuum of darkness. Would a more understanding deity have produced a more hospitable environment for us to travel within? It seems a cosmic joke that the ever expanding universe only has one life-bearing world with people who yearn to know it secrets, yet cannot physically journey beyond its own moon. God could be keeping us in a gilded cage of a universe for all we know, so the joke is on us and God is laughing away. Maybe God just has an evil sense of humour. Our scientists think that quantum string theory may reveal a multiverse. Each one could conceivably have its own God. Who knows, the creation of our universe and of man may have been an evil act, by an evil renegade God, who wanted people to worship him, which in itself could be an evil act. Again, we have no other experience of prior or other Gods to let us know what a God is supposed to do. Just because we humans are still here, does not mean that our God is not evil and ready to cause our extinction as has happened many times in the past. Our universe could be one big experiment of an evil mad scientist God; tinkering and testing, and distorting our sense of good and evil. And if God was evil, there would be nothing we could do about it anyway. So, in an Anthropocentric universe, we are here not to witness the universe in its life-bearing phase, but to observe the evil act of God.

So, is God evil? Yes and no. God, whether he exists or not, has gone through many incarnations and is very much a product of the prevailing times, so our views on him do change. But the underlying factor is in relativism: we have no one to compare to God. All we have are his supposed reflections, and if we take a good hard look at ourselves in that cosmic mirror, in spite of all the evil that occurs, we are still here, for better evil or for worse evil, forever and ever. Amen.

13/Jun/2009

Religion & Spirituality
Is Heaven a real place or a state of being?

God in Heaven or Heaven in God?

The great scientist and experimenter JBS Haldane once said that maybe "heaven was in God..." rather than God being in heaven. The context was the beginning of the Space Race when Russia had sent up Laika (the dog) into space and thus held an early lead in the race. Haldane wondered if because Americans believed God was in heaven and space was God's domain that American space agencies would have difficulty in dealing with God's preserve. They would not be as eager and as atheistically bold in exploring space as the Russians. After all astronomy, cosmology, and physics contribute (even if unconsciously) to proving or disproving God's existence.

But what if heaven was just a state of being? If God is a state of being, a sentient force permeating the universe or just a human-formed metaphysical construct, then heaven can be in God. How would this affect our view of God, the universe, life and death?

Our concept of heaven could be absolutely wrong, as we have no experience of other worlds, lives, or heavens (or Gods for that matter). Life here could be as good as it gets. Other worlds or the 'real world' could actually be hell. Our cosmological wanderings and wonderings may never find God. Heaven may not be a physical place, but just a state of human or even God's mind. If you believe in God, then you believe in heaven, so heaven can be in God.

In string theory, there is a possibility that there are up eleven dimensions. Suppose one of those hidden dimensions was heaven, curled up so tiny that it could not be seen. When we die and dissolve into atoms, space in heaven would be no problem. Or heaven could be so large as to be on a different or higher plane of existence, well outside of our perception. Heaven may be the string that holds everything together, a quantum property in the theory of everything. So far no heaven has emerged. Heaven remains in the Schrodinger-like state of being or not being.

In the bible, there is talk of ascending to heaven at one's death. But suppose this life we are in is already heaven? 'Real life' could be another plane, from our dreams, or beyond the universal horizon. Our lives and memories could be an echo from a past life where heaven is what you make it, thus life is recreated from past experiences —hence the continuation of good and evil. So what happens when people die? Maybe they are rejections from this kingdom of heaven and so go back to 'real life'. Near death experiences may just that, but in reality those 'saved' have actually died in the real world and are now in heaven. But if our world is heaven or if no religious heaven exists, heaven may just be a hole six feet under. As a state of being, the lure of heaven may also be an accomplice to self-destruction. Is heaven so rewarding that it is worth dying for? If heaven is a state of being in the here and now then death would not matter. But as one heaven dies, many more are born.

So, what is heaven? In a sense heaven is a state of being, for if God did create us all then we all have a piece of heaven within us, whether the spark of life or a soul. Likewise, we are Gods unto ourselves so we each have our own self-made heavens (and hells) inside us. In time, we shall all seek out our inner heaven and whichever God resides there.

08/Dec/2009

Religion & Spirituality
Does our spirit or soul survive after death

Death and Soul

A 14-year old girl died recently. An accidental drug overdose took her life. Stories such as this appear in the newspapers all the time. People die from senseless murders, accidents, their own hand, and of course when their time has come. But is there a soul and what happens to it upon death? And why do we need to be comforted that there is something after death? Delving into such issues is among the deeper questions on what it means to be human.

We humans dwell on death, a condition we can do nothing about, yet we are dead longer than we are alive. If that is all there is, if death is the end all and be all, and if there is no soul and no way back then humanity is in a sad state indeed. Our lives are too short and meaningless without an afterlife to balance out our existence. Wasted death just seems so unnatural that there must be something on the other side. If the soul is the residue of human energy then it should persist in the ether somewhere beyond our perceptions. There may be a universe of the dead where all dead souls can live either as ethereal beings or in some facsimile to their former lives on Earth. Life may be a series of existences with life on Earth a mere short term, physical state among many non-corporeal forms.

I want to know where I go after death. I deserve that much after putting so much into life, don't I? Are there different types of afterlives depending on how you led your life? Surely an innocent's life on Earth should have another chance in the afterlife, a better chance at life? What purpose does a short life serve? Is there redemption in death? For every wasted life and death is there some solace on the other side that their death will not go unredeemed? Karma may have a big part to play in life and death; as you lived, so shall you die. Your destiny in death may shadow your life. This would be enough to make me live a better life, make the most of what I have, and prepare for the day I finally leave this mortal coil. Another life awaits me, but different in nature. And when that dead life ends, another is waiting, and so on. I live for eternity through death.

Death is stranger than fiction. Real people die in unimaginable circumstances, their deaths not solved or the perpetrator unpunished. It's a reminder that death is uncertain, unpredictable, and not confined to celluloid entertainment. TV/movie deaths are seen as cheap entertainment, but my life is not so cheap as to have such a dramatic ending. Death is serious; an ending to some or a new beginning to others. Is there a choice in which you choose or are you just 'born' to the other world, oblivious to your former life? Being reincarnated may apply to both the beginning and end of life, where the destination of the soul is determined by any amount of unknown factors. But are we in control of our souls, so we may go and be what we want to be after death? Death may trigger a re-set button on the soul, beginning a new life.

What is death like? Lying cold, dead in the ground for eternity is a wasteful shame. But where does the soul go, if not to some form of heaven or hell? If the soul is a separate entity to our body then where does it come from and why do we have one? This is in no way a religious question, for if religion is considered then anything is possible and our souls are controlled by some non-existent being to live forever in some distant, sunny, wonderland. The soul is a problem for science, beyond supernatural superstitions, and a fundamental point of life. If the soul exists then it can be investigated by science as the soul's nature would be an emergent property of the human body. Humans are made up of atoms; matter which cannot be destroyed, only transformed. Death then would be a transformative process. If the soul is just an emergent property of the electrical activity of the brain, the air from our lungs, and warm blood from our heart then the soul may be conserved, like energy, and not destroyed. But a soul is not a form of energy that can re-animate a body once it has ceased. The soul is not a battery. The soul must be a residual and evolved effect of humanity. The soul is inextricably bound to us.

If, however, souls are transcendent why cannot we see the 'other side' by travelling through our souls to these places and then returning? Are the tunnels of light and the feeling of warmth of a world beyond an actual view of the afterlife or just tricks of our brain as we experience out-of-body experiences? Are our souls locked inside us while we live, only to be released upon death? Why should this be so? What is the mechanism whereby the soul is released? Science has not found the seat of the soul, yet there is something fundamentally different in us that sets us apart from the 'lower' animals. As evolved animals, we humans have acquired something unique that allows us to contemplate life beyond death and visualise such an afterlife. Our souls are messengers of hope beyond our world.

The mystery of the soul is unfathomable. How, why, and where it exists may never be known, but death is a part of life, which still fills us with fear. For the 14-year old girl who died so tragically, let us hope that her soul is free and living the life she was meant to.

21/Dec/2009

Religion & Spirituality
What is heaven like?

House of God

Where does God live? Heaven, you say? But what and where is heaven? Even as a metaphysical place, what form would heaven take? And within the realm of heaven, where is the house of God, his personal abode? Heaven is never physically described in the Bible in concrete concepts, beyond a place of salvation, peace, and love. But if one is fated to end up there, wouldn't it be nice to envision heaven? Visualising the state of heaven could bring some closer to God while accepting their demise.

Where is heaven? Even if not a physical world within our reality, is it a planet in a higher dimension or is heaven just a cosmic plane of reality mirroring our universe, expanding forever? Is heaven controlled by other physical forces? The planet of heaven would probably be a world like ours, but more benign in climate and geology. Heaven could well be Earth's twin, invisible to our consciousness by the merest of dimensional walls. Maybe heaven guides the forces and has done so ever since the Big Bang (since God is a scientist who created all the physical aspects of the cosmos). If heaven is the seat of control of the universe, is that where God works or does he also live there –like a live-in caretaker? Heaven may not be adequately described or totally comprehended in life, but then again, life may not be what we think it is.

One theory from physics claims that our universe is a holographic projection resulting from energy particles interacting off two higher dimensional surfaces, like a credit card hologram. But if we are holograms, is heaven also a holographic projection? Would heaven still be a valid concept? Would people still be willing to go to a place that could be a holographic projection dreamed up by a holographic projection? Has physics ruined the foundation of heaven? Would it matter if life and death were just mere differences in the state of the holographic projection? Maybe heaven is real and we are not, hence humans were made in God's (holographic) image. Is the House of God nothing more than holographic smoke and mirrors? So, as heaven is the light, and light creates holograms, then maybe God really was being literal when he said 'Let there be light'. The writers of the Bible may not have understood physics, but they may have transcribed the first scientific act and the secret to our existence.

Somewhere in heaven, real, holographic, or imaginary is the House of God. What kind of house would God have? If it can be assumed that God is not a disembodied spirit, then God would probably have a place of private abode, because we were apparently built in God's image and our lives would reflect the kind of life God may have led in his early existence, thus God could live in some dwelling. Would it be a temple or a humble house, surely not some grand palatial sprawl? Would it be of wood, brick, stone, or even steel and glass – modernising as man has changed through the ages. Would it be open to all, an open house for an audience with God? Would there be a spare room for Jesus, places for angels, and some special guests like Saints, Popes, and Bishops? Would there be a heavenly Garden of Eden out back, all neatly mowed, with orchards and rivers? The House of God would probably be a simple, yet all-encompassing structure; wall-less, yet private; light and airy; contemplatively peaceful, and a home away from home. The House of God would be one of belonging.

Even if God and the inhabitants were disembodied spirits, would they still create an image reflecting our world with houses, roads, shops, and other infrastructures of life, in order to feel more connected to the world of the living? Or would they reside in the open, living under the stars? How can we conceive of disembodied spirits not having any place to live or rest in peace? Everyone has their own concept of heaven, thus the House of God would mean different things to them. The House of God could reside in the consciousness of each person or it could be a place for their soul to reside after death. Heaven could just be a concept for the living and there is nothing after death. The House of God may be an empty shell, never visited in death, but coveted in life. No one has returned from heaven to tell us these things. The House of God could be what we make of it on Earth, how we shape it, and how we want to live for now and the future.

So, in trying to peer through the keyhole into the House of God, we may just find us staring back at ourselves, so either draw the curtains or fling open the windows and live peacefully in your own House of God.

06/Apr/2010

Religion & Spirituality
Creationism vs. evolution: Will the controversy end?

America's Dilemma

America is a real dichotomy between religion and evolution, but not just in the usual way people think. The financial collapse and Obama's reach for medical care for all has brought this issue into sharp relief on several fronts: God, socialism, capitalism, and evolution have confusing roles.

In both the above cases of the financial collapse and medical care (as reported here in Britain), the majority of regular 'Joes' interviewed stated that America is not a socialist state and should let the banks and big businesses fail without bailouts and that everyone should be able to take care of themselves without having to pay for others' healthcare. These are very capitalist opinions. They are also very 'evolutionary' statements, evoking survival of the fittest thoughts. If you're not a good bank; you fail and become extinct, likewise car companies, and any other unsound institution. If you can't take care of yourself and pay your own way in health, then don't rely on the rest of society to bail you out. In those cases, America is a dog-eat-dog world. Natural selection decides who the winners and survivors are.

But hang on, America is also afflicted by an epidemic of religion, especially creationism, the anti-evolution doctrine. How can such a society, so avidly devout, operate under such a open evolutionary capitalist government? The American lifestyle is unabashedly set in evolutionary terms; co-opted to so-called Social Darwinism - one adapts and mutates to suit the times or you become a low-rated species ripe for extinction in the 21st Century Empire. The consumption society is based upon surviving to spread one's genes or financial legacy. How can creationism survive in the evolutionary capitalist atmosphere? That Creationism can survive within evolutionary capitalism must mean that it is also evolving. Is that a major flaw or part of the grand design? Can you believe in both religious non-evolution and the American brand of capitalism that is inherently evolutionary-based?

Where does this leave God? God must be a socialist entity (in nature not politics *per se*); being so benevolent towards all. God would want everyone to have free healthcare, God would want everyone to keep their jobs, and to let thy neighbour cross the U.S. borders without being harassed. If America is such a devout nation then why does it not stick to the socialist tenets of God? Or has God gone all capitalist and is out for Himself as well? Why does America fear Socialist policies, when they know the mistakes their former Socialist enemies made and can adapt them; the so-called Third Way politics? Why don't the Creationists see that they are living the evolutionist life? The Creationists fear their own extinction, so they act accordingly to make sure their legacy survives. They must successfully outlive and outbreed their competitors. Evolution, whether biological or social, is the undercurrent of the American's life, liberty, and the pursuit of happiness, despite the Creationists' best efforts to dictate otherwise.

The God-fearing, top-heavy American government also acts in an evolutionary way as the top predator and protector. To survive, you have to make your own environment safe, which at the moment includes the whole world. Again, the socialist and capitalist nature of America collides as it wants to do the best for everyone (by itself) and profit (for itself), a selfish collectivism. Americans have chosen to turn away from the socialist God and worship the God of evolution and capitalism. Even with Obama at the helm, even with God-fearing leaders, and resources for all, evolution is dictating the life of America. The drive to survive; the need to breed, both personally and professionally, must belie many religious creeds. Some religions would create a 'flat' world, all equal under one God, a socialist utopia, where none wanted for anything. It is a laudable goal, but the fact that America resists it so much (unless it rules it), underlines its evolution-based strategy and market-forecast society. Social Darwinism rules, for better or for worse, which drives biological evolution, which breeds successive leaders to keep the status quo of American supremacy.

So while the world may think that the U.S. is a burgeoning theocracy, ruled by Super-God Republicans and Soft-God Democrats, shored up by adoring creationists; it is not. It is a pure Darwinian State upholding principles the Great Man would have been ambivalent to. Long live the American wolf in religious sheep clothing; the longer this great nation deceives itself about its evolutionary nature, the worse it will be for Americans and the world.

22/Aug/2010

Religion & Spirituality
Can science prove the existence of God?

The God Equation

Einstein once asked: Did God have any choice in his creation? An ultimate question if there was one. But how was God created? Can we assume a conscious decision was made to create God? By whom, how, when, and why? Is God just a conscious part of the universe created by the Big Bang? Or did God cause the Big Bang so he could be created? Is God a Boltzmann Brain, spontaneously spawned at some point and time in the universe, and who created worshippers to intuit his presence? And in a universe or multiverse so infinite and diverse, was there more than one God created; each in an infinite series of Gods? We may never know the answers to these questions, because if there is a God, he has chosen not to reveal his part in his own creation.

So, what would the creation of God depend on? Can an equation for the creation of God be devised? In 1961, the radio astronomer Frank Drake devised the famous equation which bears his name for the estimation of other civilisations in the galaxy: $N = N^* f_p n_e f_l f_i f_c f_L$ with 'f' meaning fraction and the 'fraction of what' as a subscript.

Where: N = number of communicative civilisations

N^* = the number of stars in the Milky Way Galaxy
f_p = fraction of stars with planetary systems
n_e = number of ecologically stable planets per system
f_l = fraction of those suitable planets with life
f_i = fraction of those planets with intelligent life
f_c = fraction of those intelligent-life planets with communication technology
f_L = fraction of lifetime of such a civilisation

In some calculations, N could potentially equal millions of civilisations. It could just as easily equal one: us. Can this equation be adapted to estimate the creation of a God? We could begin with: $E = A i f_b f_s f_l f_c f_L$

Where: E = the existence of God(s)
A = the age of the universe
I = initial conditions of the universe conducive to conceiving God(s)
f_b = fraction of the number of Gods actually born to a universe
f_s = fraction of the number of born Gods who became self-aware they were Gods
f_l = fraction of the number of self-aware Gods who created other life
f_c = fraction of the number of such Gods who communicate with their creations
f_L = fraction of the lifetime of such God(s)

Is there an answer in that equation?

A: the age of the universe is estimated at 13.7 billion years.

I = initial conditions of the universe conducive to conceiving God(s).
If God was born at the beginning, middle or end of the universe would he be a different God, depending on the state of the universe at that time? Would a Big Bang induced God be different to a Big Crunch God? Are there more favourable times to be a God when the universe became suitable to God's needs? If God had a choice in his creation, did he choose the universe to be born in or did the universe form around God? God's creation could be a product of the prevailing universal environment.

f_b = fraction of the number of Gods actually born to a universe.
When or if the Godly baby boom ended, how many Gods would there be? Is there only one God per universe or time period or a Many Gods Worlds interpretation with different Gods per universe? Could one God span all time and universes? God's creation could depend on the frequency and extent of such births. Whether it was by choice or a random event would not be known.

f_s = fraction of the number of born Gods who became self-aware they were Gods.
Would God already know he was born God or would it take time? Why did God not create us sooner than 13.7 billion years down the cosmic road? God may have had to mature as the universe did and wait for the right universal time to get to work.

f_l = fraction of the number of self-aware Gods who created other life.
We do not know the answer to Drake's equation: are we alone in the universe? Further, we do not know if any extraterrestrial civilisations would have been created by a God. If future human space explorers discover extraterrestrial civilisations are created by a God, the better we would know this value.

f_c = fraction of the number of such Gods who communicate with their creations.
If God ever did communicate directly to his creations, he basically stopped 2000 years ago when his only begotten son died (and apparently rose again). The only evidence for God's existence disappeared from the physical realm. We cannot know if this is normal behaviour for a God, having nothing to it compare to.

f_L = fraction of the lifetime of such God(s).
Is God eternal? From the Big Bang to the Big Crunch and beyond either way, how long does a God live? Does God have a choice in his own demise? As a universe dies, so might God. Maybe then he will start playing dice!

E: the existence of God(s) would thus be very hard to discern without the known quantities after the age of the universe. However, many billions of people on Earth believe there is at least one God. But until a new theory is proposed the same could be true for God's non-existence. So the answer to E is (theoretically): zero, one, or more.

Why should an equation be able to discern God's existence? Because we have observed that the universe exists in a law-abiding physical state. There is no reason to presume that God, if he exists, operates outside of those laws. Even if God created the world in six days, all he did was to speed up the process. God cannot be divorced from physics, mathematics, or science being either master or subject to the same laws we are, the universe being immutable. So God should be subject to scientific scrutiny. However, our technology is not sufficiently advanced enough to detect him, yet.

Maybe God exists on a philosophical plane: God thinks, therefore he is! But no matter the nature of God; whether of magical, supernatural, transcendental, or exotic being-ness, there will be an underlying law of physics he must obey. We humans have come so far in our scientific endeavours so it will not surprise many if one day we came face to face with whatever we call or whatever calls itself God.

20/Nov/2010

Religion & Spirituality
What if God only had an only-begotten daughter?

God's Only Begotten Daughter

In many traditions, stories, TV shows and films involving the Devil, he is usually depicted as having a plurality of children, both male and female spawn, who want to rule the world with their hell-daddy. However, God has only ever delivered unto humanity, one child – an only begotten son. Indeed, people are ridiculed when they claim to be a new son of God. The rationale whereby everyone is God's child is invalid here. This is about being the 'Only Begotten' one. But what if God did not have a son? What if Mary had given birth to a daughter instead? Would the world have been different with a 'Messiahress'?

Mother Goddesses:
Why did God bequeath to the world a son? Was this just a reflection of the times? Male heirs were seen as the traditional choice and able to perpetuate the family line? But Jesus would not have been expected to start a family, so again, why a son and not a daughter? Suppose God had decided to send his offspring to earth at an earlier time, before the rise of civilisation, when more egalitarian communities existed. A female saviour could have been born a few thousand years earlier during the reign of the Earth Goddesses with its images of Venus figurines and fertility goddesses.

If God really wanted to send a message and connect with humans who were just out of the throes of worshipping Mother Goddesses, he could have sent his only begotten daughter. But with the advent of agriculture and urbanisation, men usurped the matrilineal world order and took over. The world of man arose and women were relegated to the background in most cases. With Jesus, the son of God on Earth and with his all-male disciples, this sent a powerful message that men were in charge. Women have been catching up ever since.

Bishopesses and Popesses:
There are myths that the ascension of a black Pope would see in the end of the world. Whether this means a black-skinned man or black as in

dark and evil is another matter, but what about a female Pope? It seems never in their wildest dreams did the early proponents of the black Pope myth consider a female Pope's accession; and God-forbid if she were black. Right now, the Anglican Church is tearing itself apart just arguing on the matter of female clergy. Elements of both the Catholic and Protestant Churches are bulwarks against such 'radical' changes even though there is nothing in the bible which explicitly forbids a woman's right to preach or be ordained as a Bishop. If a daughter of God had been born, several female disciples and apostles could have been chosen, leading to today's 'Bishopesses', (anachronistically-named) High Priestesses, or even a female Pope.

Somewhere along the line of the early Christian Church, devoted women were erased from the pages of early Christianity, even though the early church had been more accepting of woman, attested to by female-dedicated shrines in Asia Minor and Europe (i.e. Ephesus and St. Priscilla's Catacombs) and by endorsements and correspondence with the much misquoted, misunderstood, and ambivalent figure of St Paul (with Thecla and Junia, among many others). Mary Magdalene would certainly not have been accused of being a prostitute. If anything, Magdalene probably had a high role in Jesus' ministry, which was seen as unbecoming (by men) and thus were the rumours borne against her. As men had taken firm charge of religion, women were kept in their place and away from the male self-empowering rituals.

Witches:
If a female Messiah had died for our sins, would God's daughter's crucifixion have cancelled out Eve's sins? Women have been blamed for humanity's sins ever since Eve's temptation, so the sacrifice of a female Messiah may have balanced the equation. Because the only begotten daughter of God would have had performed miracles, women with peculiar or claimed powers and abilities may have been less likely to be denounced as witches. Witchcraft was seen as a pagan art in league with the devil. However, with a female Messiah, there would have been no witches, just female prophets, endowed with the spirit of the 'Messiahress', and in touch with their God. Joan of Arc would certainly be a saint among saints and possibly a Pope (not withstanding myths of Pope Joan from the Middle Ages). Maybe men who heard the voices of God would have been persecuted and burned at the stake instead.

The modern Wicca 'church' might not have turned out to be an ostracised section of society, but an organised and accepted font of ancient knowledge handed down mother to daughter through the generations. English Witch-finder General, Matthew Hopkins, may have been a seeker of prophetesses, while Salem, Massachusetts (possibly thriving on the manna of prescribed ergot) may have developed into a Western Vatican, permeated with medicine, philosophy, art, and even science.

Thoroughly modern women:
Because women may have been less persecuted for their womanly ways, for learning, or being left behind in the home, the world of Science and the Arts may have been more open to them. With more women inspired by their messiah there may have been a female Columbus, Da Vinci, Newton, Einstein, and more? Women may have integrated more within a once male-dominated society, rightfully taking up places alongside the giants of history. Only now are such women coming to the fore. There would still be war if women were in charge of the church and were more politically entrenched, but a woman would be more likely to fight and die for her God. There would not still be a fight for women's rights after two thousand years, but would modern society be more egalitarian or would men now be striving for their equal rights, their masculinity threatened by the perceived stronger sex?

With a female Messiah, the rights of females would have been asserted more. The fairer sex would have been seen as God's preferred line: the Messiahress a woman in his image. Families may now be wishing for a first-born daughter or looking after their daughters better. Even in China, a cult of reverence for daughters in a one-child policy nation may have blossomed, stemming from China's early assimilation of Christianity from the mid-millennium AD. In all, the only begotten daughter of God may have brought more benefits to mankind than Jesus. If only God had taken a chance.

23/Jan/2011

Religion & Spirituality
Where is God?

Is God Afraid of Us?

Show yourself, God. Where are you? You may be omnipotent, but the one thing you, (and all Gods) are afraid of are your own creations. In Spy Kids 2: The Island of Lost Dreams (2002), the character Dr. Romero (Steve Buscemi) who genetically creates new animals, fears for his life, thinking his creations want to destroy him for his experiments on them. In a famous line, he mutters: "Do you think God stays in Heaven because He's afraid of what He's created on Earth?" It was a very thoughtful line and maybe gives some insight as to why God does not appear on Earth. He is afraid of us.

Why should he be afraid of us? An all-powerful being is always afraid of being unloved, usurped, surpassed, forgotten, and rejected. So God has to maintain a discreet distance, lest he be mistaken for anything less than the Supreme Being.

God would be afraid of us, because though he created us in his image; we humans are flawed and surely we would ask God why he created us so and why we are not more perfect. If God were on Earth, we would see him reflected in ourselves and slowly grow to dislike him out of familiarity or our human nature to dislike and alienate others. Like some parents who are afraid of their children; they don't want to be disappointments or failures to them, God is afraid of us because no matter his power, he will be seen as a disappointment to many. He would not have answers to everything for everyone. He would have let people down, destroying any faith or trust in him.

With six billion humans on Earth, and counting, not every single person will worship God. In fact, there are many who would openly rebel against God, even if he revealed his presence on Earth. There would never be peace on Earth whether God showed himself or not, as the many hundreds of religious and non-religious factions would always be fighting amongst each other. There is no one true religion, even among God worshippers and the many misinterpretations and man-made iterations of God's word would only serve to further negate God's power. Which religion could God possibly favour after so many millennia of religious dilution?

Once God was revealed, his majesty and power uncovered, God would be rejected as the Supreme Being. No matter if God came down to Earth in the form of an old man with a flowing white beard or as a wispy entity we would be disappointed in God as he could not be all things to all people. We humans demand exclusivity from God and if God favoured one strain of religion or one peoples over others, we would not convert to that other religion and that favoured religion would then feel obliged to attack the other non-believers. That is the status quo now on Earth, so God's presence would not alter anything.

God the scientist would be revealed. How he created the universe and let evolution flow would be scrutinised. He would no longer be seen as purely supernatural and his powers could one day be approached and surpassed by us. We would surely hunt him down wherever he dwelled and encroach upon his person. Once science and God came face to face there would only be one winner: science. For if God created the universe using physics, chemistry, and biology, but still expected us to worship him, that would not make sense. There would be no dichotomy between science and faith; they would be the same, but fall into the scientific realm, because God would be seen as the ultimate scientist.

We humans could then no longer be asked by any religious person or organisation to accept a non-scientific creation of Creation. In that way, God would be diminished as a religious figure. If God wants sovereignty over humans he has to promote that element of faith, the belief in him. He must be unknowable and omnipotent. A God among us would bring too much temptation to interfere in each others affairs. We would not even worship a scientist God, though some people might set up new religions around this theme. Nevertheless, knowing God's science secrets would make him fear us. No matter our peaceful intentions, there would always be a military application and one day God would end up in someone's sights for whatever reason.

We may be God's creations, but whatever we create, we destroy something to make it. Humans have created many religions and destroyed many lives in their wakes. If God physically came to Earth, we would eventually end up destroying him to make him into our own image of what we thought he was. God would lose his identity, his power, and purpose. And that is why God is afraid of us. Where is God? He is lost without us.

Sciences

26/Apr/2006 (original)

Sciences - Sciences (Other)

Thoughts on Mars: Past Goals and Future Exploration

2020 Vision

As a member of the Mars Society, the world's largest space advocacy group dedicated to exploring and settling Mars, I have written several articles on the Red Planet; why we should go, how to get there, what to do once there, and more. The Mars Society was founded by Dr. Robert Zubrin and others in 1998, with chapters worldwide.

I sent off my first International Money Order in April 1999 to become a member. My first European Mars conference was (the 4th one) in Oct 2004 held at the Open University, Milton Keynes and I was delighted to meet Dr. Zubrin. I have several signed books from him. The European Mars Conferences were suppose to rotate amongst the European chapters but the 5th conference (EMC5) stayed in the UK - Swindon, November 2005. For my first and only time (so far) I saw Mars through a telescope. I also met the best guys from the Dutch and Aussie chapters whom after hearing I was leaving before the exclusive conference dinner paid for me to stay for the guest-speaker banquet and I slept on the floor of one of their hotel rooms afterwards. It meant I got to see and hear more of Colin Pillinger on the failed Beagle 2 Mars mission. I was so inspired over the weekend that I thought about volunteering for the European Mars Analogue Research Station (Euro-MARS) for the 2007 crew in Iceland, but that project fizzled out with funding. Oh, plus, I probably didn't have the relevant skills anyway. But I can live in hope for the future. See you on Mars!

As I put the finishing touches to this book, I've just attended the 23rd annual Mars Society teleconference. These are usually held annually in Colorado, US, but of course the pandemic has altered that in-person event, so it was great to attend the 2020 streaming event for free. But, despite a lot of brilliant talks by experts, what struck me and other attendees after the session by Rick Tumlinson of the Spaceflight Revolution (and other space initiative start-ups) is that for all the conferences, academic papers, and advocacy movements over the decades we're still no nearer to a manned mission to Mars. And only one person is actively trying to change that. The fact that Elon Musk joined the conference to discuss his efforts, his reasoning for the missions, and proposed timelines was a great boost to the Mars movement. But there is so much more to do.

There were several versions of this essay, some shorter, some slightly different, but this version is the definitive one. I had also sent this updated article (10/Jan/2008) to the Mars Society which was published in The Mars Quarterly, Vol. 1, issue 4 Fall 2009.

WE are in danger, danger of not realising our dreams. I had attended the 4th European Mars Conference at the Open University in the UK, 2004, and was inspired and impressed by the varied presentations and the visionary goals. Since then, the whole experience and the story of reaching the Martian Grail has been further impressed upon me by two books I had recently read.

The first book, *The Arctic Grail* (1988), by Pierre Berton, chronicled the explorations of the British Navy in the 18th Century, highlighting the intransigence of the Admiralty in its attempts to conquer the Northwest Passage. The nationalistic approach, the non-adoption of native survival customs, the ill-preparedness for the cold, scurvy and overland-travel even after almost a century of documented successes in those areas by seasoned Arctic explorers, was wholly negligent. Some might think that that was a sign of the times, that is true; but NASA is a sign of our times. And things were not looking good.

NASA reminded me of the old Admiralty. Obstinate in its approaches to space travel and not heeding advice and warnings from experienced scientists, technicians and senior astronauts, NASA had rekindled the complacent culture of the Admiralty, both organisations suffering loss of life and folly after folly. Just think of the Challenger and Columbia shuttle disasters, which surely rank with the Franklin Expedition (among other near disasters). With failed robotic Mars expeditions, the cancelled orbital space plane programme, the re-jinked Space Exploration Initiative and the lustreless International Space Station, NASA had failed to recapture the glory days of its moon shots, just as the Arctic expeditions employed idle sailors to glorify the Empire after Napoleon's defeat.

The parallels are striking. I can only hope that in a century's time, people do not look back at our time and wonder with dismay, what went wrong? The second book is Friedrich Nietzsche's *Thus Spake Zarathustra* (2003 translation). In it, the character Zarathustra muses: Mankind still has no goal... if the goal of mankind is still lacking, is not also mankind itself still lacking?'(pg 45). Well, to me the answer must be a resounding 'yes'!

You may be thinking that mankind has goals! Alleviating poverty, eliminating diseases, increasing education, cleaning air, land and sea, and forestalling starvation, etc, are all goals of mankind are they not? Well, no. They are not goals; they are Rights. Everyone has the Right to be free of poverty and disease, to be educated, to have clean food, water and air, etc. Going to Mars is not a Right. It has to be strove for; attained to. Going to Mars continues our long and proud heritage of human exploration. A worthy goal indeed for mankind. But everyone has to believe in the goal.

How can we achieve this? We would need a joined-up Mars programme. In an ideal world, NASA, ESA, the Russians, Japanese, Chinese and other space-orientated nations would establish a joined-up policy from all of the individual national pursuits. We would learn from each other, learn from the past and from our collective mistakes so that one overall Mars programme would be instituted. We would need to create a balance between public, corporate and private initiative, sustained effort, financing, and continued support for decades.

But that is in an ideal world. In reality, each nation is pursuing their own agenda, like the British, (and later) American and Scandinavian efforts to discover the Northwest Passage and the North Pole. Each nation has the same goal, but achieving it with diminishing funds and support will be next to impossible, unless there is a radical shake-up of the space establishment'. The goals of exploration, whether to the ends of the Earth or Mars, mean different things to different people, but in the end, it can only benefit mankind.

Is Mars too far or too expensive? Tell that to Columbus or the Pilgrims or to Neil Armstrong. Why have costly Olympics or other world sporting events or fly around the world on holidays? They, among other entertainment and adventures, may benefit and enrich human life, but are costly pursuits. In all honesty, Mars would not benefit the public for some time, perhaps not for a generation. But who does not save for their children's further education or wedding in a generation's time, with no immediate benefits? Who does not invest in mortgages, pensions, insurance or other financial plans? They are risk investments that mature or bear fruit in a generation's time. Going to Mars is the same; a small investment now will bring future benefits and security for humans. At this moment private corporations, interests and other public/private industries are bringing costs down by investing their own time and money so that the public does not have to bear all the costs. The private industries will profit initially, but that private profit will be the guarantor of future missions and public benefit and involvement in Mars.

Maybe we are learning. It is ironic that the Mars Society, dedicated to the exploration and colonisation of Mars, has its Flashline Mars Arctic Research Station (FMARS) in the high Arctic on Devon Island. What would the Admiralty of old have made of that? Now NASA has announced plans to return to the moon and possibly launch missions to Mars from there. Let us hope that there is a resurgence of the old NASA can-do spirit, that they have learned the lessons from the past and are keen to set a new goal for all mankind.

Is it too dangerous to go to Mars? No, it is not. Some people cite the dangers of cosmic radiation, technical difficulties, bone mass loss, the deep isolation, food issues, etc., but in all honesty, these issues will be solved before we go, whether from all the growing research upon Earth, on the ISS, or on future moon missions. The only danger is not having the political will to do it and more importantly, to continue with the missions and not have a one-off, flag-planting exercise. Both the expense and danger of going to Mars will lessen significantly over the course of a few missions with the 'live off the land' philosophy. The more we discover about Mars from rovers, satellites and human missions, the more we could depend on Martian resources (oxygen, fuel, minerals, water, etc.) to survive. The danger really is in not trying.

I do not believe that we humans lack the courage to go to Mars when the time comes, but we will need to do it soon so that the fear of trying does not prevail and that the survival of our race is more secure. Going to Mars would be the most selfless thing that mankind has done.

10/Dec/2007

The Way to Mars

2020 vision

This is not an original article for the Helium writing website, but I found it nestled in file between the article above and a letter to Lord Sainsbury (at the end of the article) and to David King, then Chief Scientific Advisor to HM Government and Head of the Office of Science and Technology regarding the UK's participation in ESA's Aurora project. This was instigated by the Mars Society UK chapter in order to support the project and was one of my first advocacy letters sent out. I received similar form replies from both David King and Lord Sainsbury reiterating their support for the UK's involvement with ESA and the Aurora Project. Ultimately, this project is no longer active, but it has evolved into another strategy to continue both human and robotic exploration of space.

I'm not sure why the article wasn't finished, but I'm glad some of those mentioned below have made great strides in getting us closer to Mars. The names in the last paragraph were just made up to represent the public.

Show us the way to Mars, ye old heroes of old: Voyagers, explorers, adventurers, all. New astronauts for the new century. Who are these bold and undaunted souls:

Burt Rutan, Chuck Lauer, John Carmack, Jeff Greason...
Those that have succeeded or failed to touch the edge of space. The leaders of a new vision behind Scaled Composites, Rocketplane Ltd, Armadillo Aerospace and Xcor Aerospace. Builders of spaceports.

Peter Diamandis, Paul Allen, Elon Musk, Sir Richard Branson...
A few of the men that will show us the way to Mars with their private businesses tied into the space race. The X-Prize that spurred these men on is the future of competition and should be adopted to reign in the expenses and time-scales of space missions.

The role of Scaled composites and the successful Spaceship one have provided the way for Sir Richard to envision Virgin Galactic, a private company providing personal access to space.

Starchasers, Pioneer Astronautics, Spacefleet Associations, Virgin Galactic, Space X...
Private companies committed to the pursuit of space and Mars exploration.

NASA, ESA, Roskosmos, JAXA, ISRO,...
The Stalwarts of space travel and the new space agencies. Can they re-invent themselves for the new century and new challenges therein and emerge as effective organisations able to commit a man to Mars.

Dennis Tito, Mark Shuttleworth, Gregory Olsen, Mike Melvill...
Space tourists, the first participants and pilots in a new breed of spacemen: the private citizen?

Ted Perkin, Ronald Schuckman, Dave Braun, Holly Fennick...
You, the public. Your support is needed beyond what those mentioned above bring for without the public, your voices of support, funding, enthusiasm, the governments and organisations won't budge or be as effective.

My letter to Lord Sainsbury on the Aurora Programme.

The Science Minister
House of Lords
London
SW1A 0PW

23.11.05

Dear Lord Sainsbury,

I am writing to you in order to add my support to Aurora, the European Space Agency's programme of moon and Mars exploration, and the next 5-year phase in 2006. Britain has a great and heroic history of exploration from pole to pole and on every ocean and continent. The next logical step is to explore new frontiers and emphasise the 'Great' in Great Britain.

Aurora is the UK's chance to step up and take a prominent role in space exploration, the benefits would be enormous economically, politically and culturally. Economically, there are scientific breakthroughs and rewards, but also industrial and manufacturing jobs; politically a strong space programme with Europe would boost our international standing and bring national prestige; and culturally, education would benefit as more students would become inspired, interested and involved in science. As a Black Briton, I would truly love to see Britain diversify through the future and a space programme cuts across all British socio-cultural lines. Media exposure, tourism, jobs and a positive outlook toward the future are all things to look forward to from a robust space programme from Aurora.

Currently, the public is riding the tide of positive publicity from Mars Express, the Spirit and Opportunity rovers, Mar Global Surveyor and even Cassini-Huygens. Britain cannot afford not to be in the forefront of Aurora and the next five-year phase. I urge you to commit to the next five-year phase and secure Great Britain's future into the new century.

Yours sincerely,

Ray Burke

Lord Sainsbury's response 30 November 2005. The DTI has a new identity so I have removed contact details.

Department of
Trade and Industry

V 359
1 Victoria Street
London
SW1H 0ET

Enquiries

Direct line
Local fax
Our ref
Your ref
    Date 30 November 2005

URL
Telex
Minicom

Dear Mr Burke,

Thank you for your letter of 23 November to Lord Sainsbury about the UK's involvement in ESA's Aurora programme. I have been asked to reply.

As you will probably appreciate, Aurora is an optional ESA programme, meaning that countries can choose whether or not to participate and at what level. Aurora is distinct and separate from the mandatory space science programme of ESA to which the UK is a GDP-based contributor. In October last year, the UK made the decision to join the preparatory programme for Aurora which allowed detailed study and technology development work to start and which assisted definition of the future programme. A draft programme proposal from ESA has been prepared and is being considered.

The Particle Physics and Astronomy Research Council (PPARC), which decides on the funding for the UK's participation in Aurora, will very shortly consider the UK's involvement in the programme including its priority in scientific terms and whether it is affordable. The final proposed Aurora programme will then be subject to a decision at the ESA Council meeting in early December which will be attended by Lord Sainsbury.

I hope this is helpful.

Yours sincerely

dti
Department of Trade and Industry

30/Dec/2007

Sciences - Astronomy

The Possibility of Other Intelligent Life Forms in the Universe

Are we alone in the universe? My natural inclination is to say no, because everything in this universe comes in multiples, whether it be galaxy clusters, galaxies, stars and planets. The only singular things found so far in the universe are our habitable world and the universe itself. Now apart from the wastage of unused real estate, the universe has gone through a lot of trouble to create one singular habitable world in all its vastness. Is our world really just some toy wrapped in a ridiculous amount of packaging? If the conditions are right for us in our peripheral position within the galaxy, then surely somewhere out there is another form of life. What would happen if the human race disappeared in such a singular universe? Would another life form arise to take our place to fill the vacuum, as it were? Is this why we are finding so many new worlds and proto star systems, so that the universe is primed in the event of our premature or maybe even timely demise?

We know that nature abhors a vacuum and demonstrates this by filling up our universe with more energy, seemingly from nowhere. If the universe is constantly 'refueling' itself with particles and using energy to create stars, some with planets and ours with life, then life in some form seems to be a key component of our universe. Interstellar space is teeming with organic chemical matter floating through space, not alive – as far as we know- but the very fact that organic matter is present in the vacuum of space speaks volumes for the universe's ability to produce such material. So the universe has all the key elements to produce life: A star's energy (and elements), suitable planet/moons, organic material and sustenance (whether comet water or chemical diets). It may be rare that they all come together, but it is not impossible.

Drake's equation basically boils down to the fact that there at least between one and millions of other civilisations out there. Our galaxy is vast and the universe is unimaginably vast. The chances of us hearing from another civilisation would be very remote. That explains the Fermi Paradox; we will not hear from another civilisation because they are so far away or are living/have lived at different times to us. Also consider

461

Olber's paradox and why space is black and not lit up with all that star light. The universe is expanding and as it does the energy from stars is diluted, thus light cannot illuminate the entire universe. Now if light cannot get everywhere even at the speed of light, then how can us slow-paced civilisations hope to. Taken together Drake's equation is not totally positive nor Fermi's paradox entirely negative. They reinforce each other. Olber's paradox is neutral in that it also reiterates the vastness of space, but unlike the other two factors is a natural occurrence, rather than a man-made inference. So we have three key factors in determining the prospects of other life in the universe, which as with the above paragraph on materials for life, do not rule out the possibility of other life, just that we would be incredibly far away from another civilisation, even with light and radio signals.

I am not an advocate of the anthropic principle, but there may be a relationship between the universe's energy production and humankind. Just as we need oxygen, nitrogen, argon, etc., and the trace elements in our atmosphere to live, the universe could need its essential 'nutrients' to breed galaxies, stars, planet and life; after all, these dimensional particles and forces form the basics of all the elements and us. So we are here because the universe gets the right 'diet' of energy and is at an age to allow life to form. So whether we are alone or not, I do think that we are here at a privileged time of the universe, just as we are on the earth, because we could not be here at any other point in time due to the prevailing conditions. As above, so below; there is symmetry between us and the universe.

Are there extraterrestrials watching us now, benignly or ready to invade, from another planet, time or dimension? Who knows? Whenever or however they come, at least we will be comforted in knowing that we are not alone and that life somewhere will continue.

31/Dec/2007

Sciences - Physics

The Structure of the Universe and Why Humanity is Here

2020 vision

Way back in the Arts & Humanities section on the subject of my favourite books, I wrote about the book - Brave New Universe – followed up by a letter to the authors Paul Halpern and Paul Wesson. This essay -my view of the universe- is the result of my short correspondence Paul Halpern.

As a student of archaeology, this may be a strange place to write an article about cosmology, but archaeologists and cosmologists do the same thing -look into the past- just on different scales. I have always been interested in the structure and mysteries behind our universe. Archaeo-astronomy crosses both boundaries studying the cosmology of ancient civilisations, asking similar questions as cosmologists: how old are artefacts/stars? How did civilisations/galaxies form or societies/black holes collapse? What are our origins? The trowel is our telescope! So just think of the ancient Egyptians, Mali or Inca empires as galaxies and work from there with all your questions.

I wondered if there was a simpler way, a different way, to look at the universe. There is a tendency now to look at Big History and emergence theories and I tend to also view the big picture, because nothing exists without interactions on different levels. I imagine that theories like this have been suggested before and the way I would see the universe is as a series of interacting dimensions along the so-called branes. The universe would have its well-known dimensions and the lesser known ones to make up the suspected eleven dimensions: Length, breadth, depth, time (entropic field), mass (Higgs boson field), gravity (gravitons), strong force, weak force, electromagnetic force, dark matter (solitons/axions/neutralinos) and dark energy.

These eleven dimensions mesh together tightly to form an interweaving fabric that is the universal plane or brane. We know of the first four dimensions (length, breadth, depth, and time). The fifth would be an extra large dimension, which I would assume to be a hyper-field of Higgs bosons which gives everything its mass. Dimensions six to eleven are the tightly curled Kaluza-Klein spaces. Their spaces are so tightly curled that they would become almost fluidic in nature and 'leak' through the other larger dimensions in varying concentrations. On passing through the fifth dimension, they would gain their mass or loop quantum/string qualities before appearing in dimensions one to three. This could suggest a hierarchy among dimensions in that the 'particles' pass from one dimension to another in such an order as to give rise to the universe we see.

This further suggests a preferred direction in time, the fourth dimension (time) seen as an entropic field through which the other forces flow, causing a scalar flow across branes, manifested as cause and effect. There is not so much a time particle, but the way in which the other dimensional particles and forces flow creates mass and space leading to gravity, which in turn creates a preferred direction through the dimensions and our universe. So we are locked in a 'clockwork quantum universe', where even quantum effects are non-random, because they have to traverse the dimensions in a certain order and at a certain intensity for our universe to exist and work. Maybe this explains the superposition aspects of quantum particles as they are coming from over-lapping dimensions and thus appear to be in different states at once, because they exist simultaneously in other dimensions. Apart from our own three large dimensions, we do not have the technology yet to be able to view the other dimensions, thus superposition may be evidence of other-dimensional effects upon the particles.

The intensity of particle flow across the dimensions could explain the weakness of gravity relative to the other forces (strong, weak and electromagnetic) in our universe. While gravitons are yet to be detected, if ever, there may be some sort of filtering mechanism from one of the other branes or dimensions, which affects the graviton's movement. Either the Higgs boson field drags back gravitons, 'stealing' their energy or they are attracted somewhere else, like another universe where gravity is stronger.

Lastly, the issue of origins is also a commonality between archaeologists and cosmologists: Are we alone? Is this the only universe? My natural inclination is to say no, because everything in this universe comes in multiples, whether it be galaxy clusters, galaxies, stars and planets. The only singular things found so far in the universe are our habitable world and the universe itself. Now apart from the wastage of unused real estate, the universe has gone through a lot of trouble to create one singular habitable world in all its vastness. Is our world really just some toy wrapped in a ridiculous amount of packaging? If the conditions are right for us in our peripheral position within the galaxy, then surely somewhere out there is another form of life. What would happen if the human race disappeared in such a singular universe? Would another life form appear to take our place to fill the vacuum, as it were? Is this why we are finding so many new worlds and proto star systems, so that the universe is primed in the event of our premature or maybe even timely demise?

That could make sense, because nature abhors a vacuum and demonstrates this by seemingly filling up our universe with more energy, seemingly from nowhere -another brane or 'leaking' universe? Even that idea could lead to the theory of the ultimate recycling machine. If energy cannot be created or destroyed, just transformed, then our universe could be the recipient of or medium for recycled energy from other universes. This constant flow of energy through the dimensions replenishes each universe, topping it up with the right amount and kind of energy, maybe even to the point where life could begin.

I am not an advocate of the anthropic principle, but there may be a relationship between that energy flow and humankind. Just as we need oxygen, nitrogen, argon, etc., and the trace elements in our atmosphere to live, the universe could need its essential 'nutrients' to breed galaxies, stars, planet and life; after all, these dimensional particles and forces form the basics of all the elements. So we are here because the universe gets the right 'diet' of energy and is at an age to allow life to form. So whether we are alone or not, I do think that we are here at a privileged time of the universe, just as we are on the earth; we could not be here at any other point in time due to the prevailing conditions. As above, so below; there is symmetry between us and the universe, but we just have to know the scale and the right way to look at it.

RAYMOND R. A. BURKE

04/Jan/2008

Sciences - Astronomy
Could there be life on other planets?

The Star Trek Theory of Extraterrestrial Evolution

Have you ever wondered why there were so many humanoid aliens in *Star Trek*? Well, according to *Star Trek* lore, the Preservers, an ancient and long dead super-race seeded the galaxy with humans, which eventually evolved into separate, but similar civilisations throughout the galaxy. While the Preservers were fictional, how true could the notion of other humanoid species populating the universe be?

I had read a long time ago that there could indeed be other humanoid races in our galaxy and that this is mostly due to the physics of our universe. While extraterrestrials can be based on other elements besides carbon like humans, interstellar space is itself seeded with organic hydrocarbons, which could literally form the basis of the backbones of many species on future worlds. Also, the stars themselves pump out many elements up to iron, with supernovas and other exotic stellar phenomena contributing the rest. So any alien species in its formative stage could receive the same basic elemental building blocks that we did and so start out on the same biological path.

Next is the 'Goldilocks' hypothesis. So far, the only planet with life is ours and we have noticed that this is because of our position from the sun: not too close and not too far, but just right. Venus and Mars may have been more Earth-like in the past, but conditions proved that ultimately without any planetary checks and balances (e.g. cooling processes and stable atmosphere, respectively) the doomed worlds could not cope with their solar position. With over 200 extra-solar planets now discovered few of which are in the Goldilocks zone, astronomers are keen to seek that all-important small, stable rocky world. There have been some candidate solar systems with gaps in between the gas giants, but nothing has been observed so far. Hopefully this will change with the next generation of telescopes. Also, the sun would have to be an average star, yellow, maybe orange, and of a stable nature and temperature.

The size of the planet and any moons could also affect evolution. The size of humans has varied over the years, but averages are generally between 4-6 feet (1.2 to 1.8m) Gravity would limit the size of humans, so we would not have 12 foot giants roaming around. Maybe on Mars, man would grow taller and slimmer due to the lighter gravity and on a larger planet would be shorter and squatter, but could still be recognisably humanoid. Humans have an average life span of between 60-70 years and from this we could estimate generational information from the past and project guesstimates for the future, especially if new genetic technology is available to tweak our life spans even further. Our size, age, birth rate, death rate, resource use and other factors would determine our ability to survive and become a technologically advanced race and thereby able to explore other planets and stars. Also, our moon is large and in the perfect position to influence our planet through tides and its affects on human biology. It might also give us some protection from cosmic impacts. It certainly inspired human philosophy, religion and technology.

We humans are tetrapods, sharing a four-limbed existence with thousands of other creatures from land, sea and air. It seems to be the basic template from which more complex life evolved from. And since our world is the only example of this and since this evolutionary path has been copied for millions of years even after extinctions, it seems nature prefers this template as it is a successful formula for life. This includes multiple and independent evolution for eyes and other organs. Our sensory organs, appendages, and big brains are not the end-all of evolution, but another variation on a theme. Stalks, tentacles, tendrils, claws, wings, trunks, beaks, proboscises, fins, gills, flippers, etc, are evolutionary adaptations of tetrapods, but only humans have truly mastered technology over the millennia with our cleverly adapted limbs.

An extraterrestrial being, on another planet such as ours, around a stable star pumping out the same elements, even in an atmosphere different to our own could certainly end up looking humanoid. To build technology you would need to have appendages, whether hands (preferably with opposable digits) or tentacles to build and to manipulate things. You would need a big brain and senses to experience the world. Organs might not be the same, but to communicate you would need some kind of apparatus to do that, which could look similar to our eyes, mouth, nose and ears, whatever their size, location and effectiveness. Beings from ocean worlds may be amphibious in nature, but again, to build a lasting technical civilisation they would need to be beyond the form of frogs, toads and salamanders; likewise with mammals such as whales, dolphins, seals and walruses and any airborne species. A certain amount of dexterity would be needed to manipulate complex technology, so fingers, tentacles, or other fine-shaped appendages would be a necessity. This aspect of evolution could be borne out by theories that a certain dinosaur species, the Troodons, could have evolved into a dinosauroid, so two separate species could have shared one world, depending on evolutionary processes after the 65 million year crash. The odds for this would be astronomical. Could Earth really be this rich in life in a universe so barren?

There are alternatives to humanoids. Extraterrestrials evolving as telepaths or telekinetics able to communicate and move things with their minds, might not need a physical body such as ours. Also, there might be the possibility of energy beings, but they may have evolved from humanoids or could take the form of humanoids if needed. Aliens could be totally or partially machine in nature, maybe built by humanoids, so their form could be totally different depending on their function. Lastly, there could be shape-shifting aliens, so their form could vary, again according to function. These extraterrestrials may seem non-conformist, but could be the dominant form in the universe. Humanoids may be redundant, under-evolved or an evolutionary fluke.

So the physics of our universe could dictate the form of life available. In *Star Trek*, other humanoid races were usually highly distinguished through varying cranial ridges, stalks/antennae or pointy ears. Our 'real' extraterrestrials will be different, but the general humanoid look, size, recognisable features and maybe an outstretched hand to shake would be welcomed.

05/Jan/2008

Sciences, Sciences (Other)
Essays: The Concept of Time

The Definite Existence of Time

This is a 'Yes-Yes' issue. Yes, time does exist and yes, man has also invented the idea of time. Change is time. No matter what we call it, when something changes it takes whatever interval of a moment to do so and we called that time. Absence of change equals no time and without time then nothing would happen. Time is an emergent property of our three dimensions of space, which interact to create another tenuous dimension called time. This dimension is not physical, but exists because space exists and space changes. We know that the universe is expanding and has been expanding for some time otherwise billions of years would not have passed and we would not be here. Atoms have finite lives and half-lives, suns are born and die, planets form, and humans experience changes over a lifetime.

Man has invented his own notion of time. We would have to otherwise there would be no context to life, no expression of the here and now, of yesterday, millions of years ago and tomorrow. Tomorrow is another aspect of time that although is in the future gives people some reassurance that the world around them will continue and that there is something to live or die for. Human adjustment to and invention of time has come with evolution. Even without modern devices, there are natural clocks in the seasons, the sun and the moon, and biological clocks (circadian, diurnal/nocturnal, body, etc). Without any modern devices, humans could still live life knowing that time passes as things change. It will be interesting for biological clocks for long-time spacefarers and those living on Mars in the future where the day is thirty-eight minutes longer than Earth's. Jewish and Muslim astronauts had to consult with their religious leaders on how to pray in space when the sun rises every ninety minutes. Synchronising man-made time to the universal time of our solar orbits (years), lunar and sidereal revolutions (months and days) and ticking of atoms (atomic clock seconds), has given man more of an insight into the workings of the universe.

Is there a direction to time? As stated above, time does not drive events; it is a consequence of change, a cause, a movement that produces an effect. Ageing causes time to go by, but time can be kind to you depending on the speed of the ageing process. Time heals all wounds or time will tell, speaks of the future, a forward direction to time, since we cannot go back in time. The structure of the universe seems to prefer this direction since broken things do not put themselves together again or age backwards. The expansion of the universe outward could be the cause of this preferred time direction. So time might not be a physical feature with particles to discover and analyse, but it has a direction whether the universe has a beginning or not. There are horizons we cannot see beyond at the beginning and the end of the universe, so time is also as infinite as space.

There is no problem with the dual nature of time being a universal and man-made feature. Time does exist, it is a consequence of change, it is a function of the physical reality of space and it has a direction. The only problem with time is that there is not enough of it.

07/Jan/2008

Computers & Technology - Computers & Technology (Other)
The Science of Star Trek

The Inventions of Star Trek

Star Trek is full of the stuff of life: drama, adventure, philosophy, emotion, etc. But the one thing that caught people's imagination was the technology; some practical, some possible and others fanciful. The technologies I have listed below have been debated over for decades and while I have thought about this subject, I have also added information from the TV show 'How William Shatner Changed the World', and books by Lawrence Krauss' 1997 *The physics of Star Trek* and Douglas Mulhall's 2002 '*Our Molecular Future*'. These show how far we have come in technology since the original programme and how 23rd century technology is closer than we think or know.

Computers in Star Trek brought several innovations to our world. Computer disks were used by Mr. Spock in 'The Menagerie' when trying to escape with Capt. Pike. But since disks are going out of fashion now, then maybe they were more like flash drives, big ones, but more sophisticated. There was also voice-recognition, conversational computers (that must have passed the Turing Test) and also on Voyager, a computer that was constructed of bioneural gel packs. Scientists now are working on neural interfaces to produce better thinking computers. Translators are also a part of his revolution. PDA translators are in use in Iraq and Afghanistan by soldiers which speaks to civilians in Arabic. Computers on Star Trek also allowed video conferencing and computer note pads.

Our first real PC was named 'Altair', named after a solar system in Star Trek, according to 'How William Shatner...'. This computer directly influenced Steve Jobs (Apple) and Bill Gates (Microsoft) into creating software. Related to computers are crystal storage devices of varying shapes and sizes used by different cultures in Star Trek. Instead of tapes, disks, CDs/DVDs, memory sticks or drives, we use crystal units ourselves for holograph memory.

Communicators were the mobile phones of the future, limited in scope, but they were the inspirations for some of our mobiles. In fact, Martin Cooper envisaged the mobile phone while at Motorola after watching Star Trek; and the rest was history – from the brick to Razr. With the Next Generation came the comm-badge, which could be a reality as new types of batteries could be printed onto surfaces and made more powerful and flexible. This means that the shape and size of any electronic device would not depend on its battery shape as most current mobiles do. A triangular comm-badge capable with mobile applications could be just around the corner.

Tricorders were the workhorse of the Federation. In 'How William Shatner...' Steve Perlman, a software programmer, admitted that in trying to copy the tricorder's abilities at Apple, he came up with something else: QuickTime, which led to the MP3 and finally the iPod. PDAs of the future may also one day evolve into a more versatile version of the tricorder. As we will see below Perlman is far from finished.

Holographs and holograms are in use now, but holodecks are some way off. In 'How William Shatner...' Perlman, now president of MOVA, was also working on this problem with a new motion capture system. However, as Lawrence Krauss states, holograms, like the EMH, could not exist as a solid object because holograms are just light. So unless there's a way to hardened photons, then no real interaction with holograms could occur.

Transporters may have no part in our world, but scientists have managed to perform teleportation, though on quantum scales using entanglement. However, the original object (photon/particle) is destroyed before being created somewhere else. Not ideal for us. So in the absence of Heisenberg compensators, we may only be able to transport photons, especially for quantum computers. Without transporters we could just listen for aliens as Star Trek inspired astronomers do at SETI.

Anti-gravity experiments in mag-lev trains using superconducting materials have been around for years. Shanghai currently operates such a train, though teams in America, U.K., Japan, France, and elsewhere are trying to find the holy grail of anti-gravity. This would involve strong magnetic fields operating on superconducting materials causing an object to lose weight.

The pre-Star Trek invention of hypo-sprays already exists, while t-ray (terahertz) scanners could be the basis for the medical tricorders. T-rays can penetrate clothing, but are not as strong and damaging as x-rays, and are now being used at airports. They could be the basis for future non-invasive procedures. Dr. John Adler at Stanford created the CyberKnife, a robotic laser that zaps tumours without invasive surgery. His inspiration was watching Star Trek.

Replicators are machines that are in an infancy stage today with 3D printers, or printable technology and digital fabricators. Imagine being sent the raw materials, load it in a machine and it builds whatever you programme it to, according to Douglas Mulhall. This is happening now and working bicycles have also been 'printed up'. Replicators could revolutionise our way of manufacturing our own products and the economy as we know it leaving large manufacturing companies redundant.

Ion engines, which Scotty practically drooled over in 'Spock's Brain' are in use now. Mark Raymond at NASA JPL, a Star Trek fan helped construct the first ion engines for two probes Deep Space 1 and the Dawn mission to Asteroids. They are ten times faster than conventional chemical propulsion.

Warp drive is the bear-bug. Scientists would love to say that it could be here one day, driven by some exotic energy, but as Lawrence Krauss puts it in his book, the amount of anti-matter needed would require a huge 'scoop' to collect anti-matter for storage and use. This has not stopped physicists from working on the principles, however.

Space elevator technology has been muted for decades and features in an episode of ST: Voyager. Competitions are held in US every year to teams, sometimes even making it onto the news. Every year reaches a new milestone with tethers and power beams to lift them.

In phasers, we already have stun guns (tasers) and lasers, microwave and other non-lethal weapons, but not a combined weapon. Well, the US has unveiled a 'non-lethal' laser rifle called the Personnel Halting and Stimulation Response (PHASR) rifle which can dazzle the enemy while causing non-permanent harm. Before use, it will need to comply with UN protocols on blinding laser weapons.

Geordie's visor would be an interesting concept, a portable device that could scan all frequencies of the spectrum, though he could selectively screen out what he wanted, just as we screen out conversations in a busy place. Would this be possible? Bionic eyes, as Geordie later had, would probably be more readily available in the coming decades. Cybernetics are also coming to the fore as implants would allow us to control machines, access the web and talk to each other 'telepathically'. Resistance just might be futile.

Cloaking devices (though in microwave region) have been invented, but plans are afoot to create materials which alter light around them and make them invisible. Other technologies to explore would be bridge controls, turbo lifts, forcefields/deflector shields, tractor beams, sensors and sonic showers.

There is so much technology to explore and make real, but Gene Roddenberry's vision has inspired future scientists, astronauts and entrepreneurs to create the world we live in today.

22/Feb/2008

Sciences – Astronomy

UFOs: A Scientific Point of View

The very term UFO conjures up exotic images of strange lights and shapes of graceful movement and speed in the twilight skies. These flying saucers or hovering cigars that are glimpsed fleetingly between the trees leaving behind tripod landing marks have become ingrained in popular imagination. But how can we tell what they really are? Their erratic, high-speed manoeuvres or exhilarating flying formations belie the fact that they are from human manufacturing plants. Or are they? Can our science begin to explain the case for UFOs, when most 'official' organisations have closed the book on their own investigations into extraterrestrial vehicular activities?

The Unknown:
The spacecraft in this category are theories, myths and imaginary. They are the spaceships of science fiction and fantasies of film, minds and dreamers. Are UFOs from the distant galaxies, from the future or from different dimensions? We do not know why they have come whether as observers, invaders or universal guides. Who are the voyagers, navigators or captains of these ships? How do they survive the cosmic vacuum for so long between interstellar space?

Science has answered one of these questions: where are the aliens? Drake's equation basically figures that there are at least between one and millions of other civilisations out there. Our galaxy is vast and the universe is unimaginably infinite. The chances of us hearing from another civilisation would be very remote. That explains the Fermi Paradox; if the galaxy is so full of planets, then where are the aliens? We will not hear from another civilisation because they are so far away or are living/have lived at different times to us. Also, Olber's paradox asks why space is black and not lit up with all the stars' light. The universe is expanding and as it does the energy from stars is diluted, thus light cannot illuminate the entire universe. Now if light cannot get everywhere even at the speed of light, then how can us slow-paced civilisations hope to. These factors reiterate the vastness of space.

So UFOs are a mystery to science, because they don't exist as we have imagined them, they have not arrived yet or they are something else completely.

The Unknown Unknowns:
This class of UFOs are the unknown unknowns, at least to the public. They are real, but are secret and classified man-made objects, whether crafted from hypothetical extraterrestrial sources or entirely 100% earthly elements. Ever since the Roswell incident in 1947, there have been claims about secret areas, hangars, aircraft and projects. These conspiracies and controversies have been fuelled by Air Force hardware such as the stealth fighter F-117A, stealth bomber B-2, the supposedly secret Aurora spy plane with its alleged distinctive pulse drive, and the latest suite of unmanned aircraft. Also on the 'radar' is the 'Bird of Prey' (so called after Klingon ships from 'Star Trek'. These futuristic looking aircraft have been the result of decades of testing from the original X-Plane projects and reams of computer programming and software, rather than reverse engineering of alien craft.

Mysterious aircraft noises, lights, formations and manoeuvres could be down to the exotic nature of the UFOs' construction and propulsion. New stealth aircraft have faceted features and new composite materials, which render them invisible to radar and peculiar to the human eye. Proposed and experimental propulsion systems could include anti-gravity, nuclear fission or fusion engines, electromagnetic or super-conducting power plants, pulse detonation drives and ramjets, all of which would leave distinctive sounds, trails or other signs/effects behind. They could easily be mistaken for UFOs.

So, man-made science has created the UFOs, but the testing of these military craft and applications have increased sightings, press leaks, misinformation and covered-up accidents, which fuel the UFO debate.

Known Unknowns:
UFOs are all around us, but we know them as jetliners, satellites, and weather balloons reflected from strange angles in unusual, low or bad lighting. They are flares, helicopters, training flights and fog-light sightings. They are hallucinations, hysteria, hoaxes, lies, confusion, and tales from UFO believers. They are the crop circles, sheep killers and missing moments of one's life.

Humans have to make sense of what we feel, see, hear and touch. We see patterns and signs where there are none. Sensory deprivation and certain frequency vibrations can cause sensations of being uplifted and dream-like states can lead to claims of being abducted by aliens. In further and extreme cases, some might claim that they had been subjected to invasive procedures and implanted with mysterious devices. So far, no open or public admission to this alien modus operandi has been reported by the scientific community.

The UFO is a combined product of the imagination and the surrounding environment.

Unknown Knowns:
Lightning never strikes twice, they say, but what about ball lightning? Ball lightning is a rare phenomenon of controversial nature. Its composition is not known, but may be formed from lightning-vapourised silicon, and it has been known to 'float' in the sky after formation as a bright ball of light before disappearing. St. Elmo's fire is another rare occurrence, but is of a different nature than ball lightning, being made from plasma. Meteorites, whether man-made junk or falling stars, can also be mistaken for UFOs, especially if it explodes upon entry just like the suspected meteor in Tunguska, 1908.

Such rare natural events seen in unfamiliar surroundings could tempt people to claim they saw a UFO.

UFOs are non-existent, man-made, natural phenomena. They are secret, yet fly in the open. They are piloted, unmanned, spontaneously appearing figments of the imagination, but real to the touch. Scientific enigmas; Universally Forever Out-there.

27/Feb/2008

Politics, News & Issues – Political Issues

Space vs. Earth: Where to Invest?

2020 vision

My notes state this was the 50th article I wrote. I think it works better in sciences than politics. And look where we are now with commercial space enterprises taking on the established space agencies. The costs are orders cheaper with more directed missions and quicker turnaround flight times. They can do more for less and bring those benefits back to Earth forming a virtuous circle of investment.

There is only one answer to this: there is enough money for both. But, I am a big believer in space exploration, which is starting to get back on track, set new goals and compete against other countries and private investors. It is the new Space Race and we need to invest in it.

Cost:

There is no argument against the cost of space investment whatsoever. The UK contributes only around £125 million pounds to ESA (European Space Agency) annually. By comparison, the UK for 2007/8 will spend £62 billion on education, over £96 billion on the National Health Service, £33 billion on defence and so far the 2012 Olympics will cost over £9 billion. In the US, NASA's budget is $17 billion, in real terms the same as NASA's Apollo budget. This is less than 1% of the US budget. The US spends $480 billion on defence, which is over 20% of the national budget and also spends over 19% on medical services.

One can argue that for what the UK and US space agencies do, their organisations are actually under-funded. As seen above, space investment does not detract from public services investments, the big difference being that space agencies now have to spend more wisely. ESA has to run a tight ship while representing several countries. NASA has opted to retire the expensive space shuttle, continue with satellite/probe missions and plan appropriately for future moon and possible Mars missions. No amount of money thrown at badly run and wasteful public services will help, so cutting or transferring space investment is not the answer.

Exploration:
Bizarrely, exploring space seems cheaper and safer than exploring our oceans, hence the reason we know more about our solar system than our deepest oceanic trenches. Water pressure is a big issue and it is easier to protect a vessel and its occupants from the vacuum of space. The expenses involved and technology to totally explore the oceans have not been sufficiently mastered, though such explorations do occur. Look how long it took robotic submersibles to find and explore the Titanic (Alvin 1985) and to fully record the depth of the Marianas Trench (Kaikō 1995) compared to sending probes to Mars (Viking 1976), Venus (Mariner 1962), and Saturn (Voyagers 1 & 2 1980-81). This practice continues today with missions to Mercury and Pluto.

For those who claim that orbiters and rovers are the only way forward, then consider that for all the fine work that the Spirit and Opportunity rovers have done on Mars in four years, a human could have done it within weeks. Humans have a totally independent nature for exploring, rather than having to be programmed to investigate. Also more is spent on Earth on investment in oil, gas and minerals, which is despoiling the Earth. Taking such industries off Earth would help with climate change and resource depletion concerns.

Human survival is paramount. One day we will have to colonise other worlds, just as past societies explored and colonised other parts of this world. Exploration is part of the human way of life whether physically, spiritually or mentally. Leaving it to robots and other remote means will be detrimental to us. We have to invest in our future, whether on Earth or in space.

Danger:
So-called dangerous aspects of space travel, though while not insignificant, are not unexpected nor insurmountable. People like to highlight US and Russian space disasters, but forget that people die on Earth from car/plane/ship accidents, murder and other instances every single day. Being an astronaut/cosmonaut/taikonaut is an extraordinarily heroic job that they train for. Nobody expects to die in their job and all precautions are taken to see to their safety. NASA had slipped up in this recently, with its high-profile shuttle disasters, but this in no way signifies that space is inherently too dangerous to continue investment. We should not be afraid of danger, only failure.

Technology:
Some governments are no longer the sole funder of space programmes. Private businesses and individuals are much more involved, as with the X-Prize competitions and organisations such as the Mars Society. They are running their own programmes that will ultimately save the tax payer money. Investments on Earth can lead to more space investment and vice versa. Space creates jobs, new industries and technology, spin-off and trickle-back technologies, and more education and involvement in science and space matters. Exploring new worlds and building new habitats in space will help scientists to think outside the box and bring greater benefits to our lives.

The new Space Race started the day SpaceShip One won the X-Prize as the first privately funded spaceship into space (2004). Now with SpaceShip Two on the way for Virgin Galactic, other private space programmes and possible space ports, mostly privately funded with some state financing, investments in space will be less public and more private, leaving more investment for Earth.

So there is enough money for investment in both, though it has to be used smartly, with proper planning and the political will power to see projects through, for the good of all mankind.

06/Mar/2008

Sciences – Sciences (Other)
Are We Alone in the Universe

Where Are the Aliens?

Are we alone in the Universe? At this very moment someone, somewhere around the world is bombarding the galactic airwaves with our radio, TV, microwave, infrared and other communicative signals. We are peering into the distant cosmos with huge telescopic eyes, from within and beyond our atmosphere, and listening with straining radio-telescopic ears for that historic First Contact with beings from another world. So far we have found no other life. But why would aliens want to advertise their presence, contact us, visit us to spy or invade or integrate or probe us, or even acknowledge us? There are several reasons why we are alone and why aliens would not reveal themselves to us.

First, let's imagine that Drake's equation has been right all along and that there are thousands of other technological space-faring civilisations out there. Let's also assume that the Fermi Paradox has been invalidated by aliens that can travel around the universe in other-Einsteinian ways, whether through space, time or other dimensions. These aliens then intercept our space-bound signals or secretly orbit our world. What would they see?

The aliens would surely be distressed at our hostility towards aliens; human or otherwise. We are a destructive and hateful species when we want to be. This would be borne out in almost every single science fiction film, where even good aliens are wiped out either by mistake or because some megalomaniac distrusted those who came in peace. No alien in his/her/it right mind/minds would want to be taken to our leader. Our entertainment would seem like anti-alien propaganda to any alien. It would be a bleak warning to stay away from our world.

Some people suggest that aliens watch us to assess our potential to see whether or not we would be mature enough to join the interstellar community one day. They are waiting to see if we will use our technology to destroy ourselves or propel ourselves to the stars. But they know full well that we would use it to destroy other aliens. Our solar system is quite full of moons. It would not surprise me if some were alien beacons warning the whole inter-galactic village to stay clear of the innocent-looking blue planet that packs a mean punch.

Next, apart from violence, the next big threat would be disease. H.G. Wells started the whole human/alien germ warfare industry and even if an alien doctor told the 'away team' that it was safe, who knows what type of genocide a ten-year old human child with the sniffles would unleash. This world has recently suffered from SARS, Bird Flu, Anthrax scares, Mad Cow Disease, Ebola, HIV/AIDS, and other contagious/spreadable diseases. Having watched humanity spread these malicious bacteria, why would any alien risk its own neck for a quickie visit? We are alone because Aliens don't want to be around us. We scare them.

But here comes the mental bit. What if there really are no aliens? There are two ways to look at this. What if there really is a God? And that God created us and only us. Is that really an Intelligent Design? The universe would be ours to spread out in and inhabit, with no other God-created alien play/pray mates. In that case, God has a lot to answer for. In the other view; what if we evolved alone? What if man is the first of the greatest of the universal civilisations: Homo Universalis? Is that an arrogant assumption? Is Anthropocentricism really that wrong? The universe might only support one life-form at a time? So why not think of ourselves as the first inhabitants? In this case, we humans have a lot to answer for. We are the sole care-takers of the Universe.

So in the end, we are the aliens. We may spread out so far and wide in the future that our descendants are visiting us through space, time and other dimensions. This would be a good thing. Think about it, if you came back from the future, why screw up the past by revealing yourself if your past worked out well? We should be worried if the aliens had come to warn us that we did something wrong that would screw up the future. As the saying goes 'If it ain't broke, don't fix it'. We are both alone and surrounded by the aliens that are us.

So I reckon that the human race is doing okay whether we are alone or not. If there are aliens, then they are not revealing themselves to us or coming to observe, invade, sterilise, test, prod, or anything else for fear of our xenophobic nature. Or we are alone, because it is our destiny to be the only universal civilisation. But just in case: Aliens beware – leave us alone or we'll whack you!

16/Mar/2008

Sciences – Earth Science (Other)

Is Space Travel to the Planet Mars too Dangerous?

2020 vision

You may recognise some of this from the 'Thoughts on Mars' essay, but expanded into a different perspective.

Is it too dangerous to go to Mars? No, it is not. Some people cite the dangers of cosmic radiation, technical difficulties, bone mass loss, the deep isolation, food and water issues, etc., but in all honesty, these issues will be solved or addressable before we go, whether from all the growing research upon Earth, the ISS, or on future moon missions. The only danger is not having the political will to do it and more importantly, to continue with the missions and not have a one-off, flag-planting exercise.

What people have to remember is that astronauts are willing participants in this mission, their chosen job. Just as people smoke, join the army, drive fast cars, become stuntmen, skydive, etc., there is danger in everything we do, so danger is relative. When people say it is too dangerous to go to Mars they are likely thinking of today's technology and not of the many innovations and experiments that are being tested and practiced for the future by NASA, organisations like the Mars Society, Universities and other institutions, especially the new private companies involved in the so-called New Space Race. Just as with any industry, these preparations will lessen the dangers and make space travel safer than it is, as safe as it can be, and as safe as any other occupation with inherent dangers. Space to other people now and to our future generations is and will be just another medium for their work and life.

Going to Mars will not be a one-nation mission either, but an international mission, so any danger will be shared. The danger and expense of going to Mars will lessen significantly over the course of a few missions with the 'live off the land' philosophy being advocated by NASA. The Mars mission will not just be about scientific advances and pure exploration, but about expanding knowledge about ourselves and what we can truly achieve, spreading our genes and gaining new resources and territory across the cosmos so we can survive longer and prosper as a race. The more we discover about Mars from rovers, satellites and human missions, the more we could depend on Martian resources (oxygen, fuel, minerals, water, etc.) to survive. The danger really is in not trying.

I do not believe that we humans will lack the courage to go to Mars when the time comes, but we will need to do it soon so that the fear of trying does not prevail and that the survival of our race is more secure. Going to Mars would be the most selfless thing that mankind has done and if that is dangerous, then it would be worth it.

02/Apr/2008

Computers & Technology – Internet Issues
Satire: The End of the Internet

2008 Speculation: The End of the Internet

I first read this article on April 1st and thought it was an April Fools' joke, but it seems that within six months, the Internet will die. This is the authoritative word from Professor J. Walkin and scientists at the Braham Institute. So how will this happen? Well Professor Walkin describes the internet like a room and as it fills up with furniture there will come a time when there is no more room for more furniture, let alone people. So as more emails, forums, spam and other extraneous ether material fills up the internet, it will crash and die. But it's not true, for several reasons:

1. The internet is not a closed system. Taking the analogy of the internet as a room, this room has doors that can lead off to other rooms, building extensions, or out into the garden, to other streets, neighbourhoods, cities, floodplains, etc. It is ever-expanding and growing. The only thing that would stop it is the technological growth of the computer. This is 'ruled' by Moore's Law which basically states that the power of the computer will roughly double every 18 months or so. Any physical crash of the computer system is decades away until new technology, perhaps quantum or nanotech, takes over. So hardware is not the immediate problem for the internet.

2. Neither is software a problem. Computer programmes seem to have a life of their own and can affect the world with the words and the numbers we write. But these words are just data, organised to and fro between bits into words. Storage of this data can be compressed, moved, filed or deleted. If the Internet was going to die in six months there would have been signs in the software like the signs from Revelations. Doom and gloom would have persisted as war over internet access would have occurred followed a famine of information as a pestilence of viruses and spam hit the internet to cause death. Yet the signs have yet to appear. The internet is still safe.

3. The big reason why I would not believe that the Internet is dying is because of the media. They would hype it up and leap on this story as it would affect their business and the governments around the world. Imagine India, China, the US and Europe without the internet, and those developing nations that are now investing in computer technology. Such a devastating news story would bring out the media vultures so that they could practice their long-honed scaremongering skills. It would be bigger than climate change and the media would insist upon Kyoto-type agreements to safeguard the internet and limit email messaging to 1990 levels. Governments would treat violators and spammers like terrorists, throw them into 'Spamtanemo' prison and throw away the encryption key. Internet pollution would drop drastically, but would it be enough?

So those are the main reasons the internet is not dying. Even if it was, would we, could we, do anything about it? Climate change is a big enough issue and look at the debates, controversies, and procrastination there. As a global tool, the internet is a repository of information and a world unifier, but humanity has lived without the internet for 99.99% of its lifetime. But what would be the consequences if it were to disappear now? What would we do? Would we build a better internet or revert to the snail-mail dark ages? Could we live without the internet in the 21st century? 'The End of the Internet' is a cautionary tale; maybe we should heed the forewarning.

29/Apr/2008

Science – Astronomy
The first humans on Mars

What to do on Mars?

Life on Mars, what would it be like? A lot of science fact and fiction has been written about Mars, regarding the reality, politics, economics and technological feasibility of going to Mars. But let us assume that we have made it there and the first manned Mars mission is taking its first steps upon the red soil. To survive beyond a flag-planting, boot-print, Kodak moment, what must we do to maintain a presence on Mars?

The current mission scenario envisions an unmanned habitat module (hab) and fuel-making plant (an Earth Return Vehicle –ERV) being sent to Mars first, followed many months later by astronauts in another hab. As explained below this allows less weight to be carried in fuel and other resources as they would be produced on Mars. Once on Mars, the astronauts would be there for around 18 months before returning to Earth, when Mars is once again closest to Earth. There will be a lot to do to ensure that those 18 months are productive enough to encourage further missions and eventual colonisation.

Mars will not be just about science and exploration, it will be a way of life. So just like the frontiersmen of old, Martian voyagers would have to learn to live off the land, getting to know the area and what resources are available. How? Part of this would have already been accomplished by the first ERV. The air of Mars is high in carbon dioxide and reacted in chemical plants with liquid hydrogen brought from Earth would yield high amounts of methane for fuel, with oxygen and water by-products. The fuel, air and water would enable ERVs, rovers, habs and other appliances to be powered and re-supplied. This brings down costs and ensures efficient resource use.

More water would be available in areas just below the surface and perhaps in deeper aquifers, ready to be pumped out. Mixing the water with regolith would enable bricks to be made in order to build sheltering structures, probably semi-subterranean in nature, to offer pressurised facilities and also more protection from harsh radiation and temperatures. Martian elements and minerals are as ubiquitous as they are on Earth and so with the right technology could be used to build anything on Mars. Light and flexible materials, including glass, could be used to build greenhouses for food, maybe with hydroponics units. Human ingenuity will sustain Man on Mars.

With manned and robotic rovers, currently being tested and built by universities and other companies for competitions, the future colonists could be more mobile and set up small frontier stations for stop-overs, scientific experiments or bolt-holes from dust storms. The first Martian colonies will not be stationary outposts, but hustling-bustling staging posts. Fuel, food, travel and shelter would be taken care of and be more sustainable as wholly Martian industries with minimal re-supply from Earth.

So what on earth shall we do on Mars once the initial mission has succeeded? With logistical problems anticipated and overcome, colonists would be able to move out and explore and in safer conditions than any explorer before them on Earth. This would be due to the substantial amount of data and maps from rover, telescopic and orbital missions. Mars' surface area is about the same as all of Earth's continents put together and without any oceans obscuring the landscape, precise geological images and maps could be produced for any explorer/prospector to use. This would apply for all latitudes, even the north and south poles, which are ice covered. It would remain to be seen if old territorial patterns arise again or if new models for Martian land management could be established for a fairer land distribution system.

Not only will there be professional and private astronauts and colonisers, but the big driving force would be commercial ventures seeking new avenues in resource mining, virtual-tourism, adventurism and extreme sports, and other businesses, such as law, education and medical jobs. Martian commerce would be vital for its own and Earth's economy in terms of trade and new employment opportunities. These commercial factors may also include any moral obligations in searching for indigenous life before any large scale terraforming projects began. Though this process will take centuries to complete just to allow humans to breathe through a light mask and wear a lightweight spacesuit. Such moral dilemmas may prove distracting, yet entirely welcome if non-terrestrial life is found on Mars. So before bringing a little piece of Earth to Mars, we would have to make sure that no one was at home first.

With further settlements up and running, with commercial industries finding their way, the stage would be set for the next phase: full colonisation. In the last half of this century, pioneers will find their way to Mars to live a hard life, creating a new home for humans. Their children will be the first of a new generation born on a new world, granddaughters and grandsons of Earth, though maybe unable to return, depending on theirs and their children's weaker Martian physiology. The social aspect of Martian newborns may be tremendous as it will define what it means to be human or indeed Martian.

Going to Mars would be a Generational Mission of the 21st Century, guaranteeing a feel-good, can-do factor in accomplishment and pride at the birth of a new human civilisation. Mars will not be a one-trip mission, but a prelude to a whole new way of human life. Mars will not be a dead world for there are resources waiting to be used to sustain us, to help mankind grow and expand. We are ready for Mars. Let's go!

Source:
Zubrin, R. 1996. The Case For Mars. London: Simon & Schuster.

25/May/2008

Great Air shows around the World

Farnborough Air Show and RAF Fairford RIAT

I love aircraft, especially the military variety, and if you want to see them in action, besides in a theatre of war, then head along to one of the many air shows that take place in Britain and around the world. Depending on the host airfield, there are a few types of air shows, some of an international variety, some focusing on WWII airplanes and some with specialised aircraft, like helicopters. My favourite is the Farnborough International Air Show.

The three times that I have been to Farnborough in Hampshire, England, reminds me that it can be a place of varying, peculiar weather contrasts; it is either somewhat hot or rather rainy with all parts in between during the day; never a dull moment. I usually go on a Saturday, but the biennial Farnborough Air Show is now a week-long event with five days allocated to the Trade Show for professionals, industry insiders and budding aerospace students, within a top-notch exhibition space. The Saturday and Sunday are open to the public, featuring static displays, flying performances and the remaining trade vendors in the exhibit halls. I first like to walk around the static displays of the great and the good aircraft, classics and modern alike. In 1990, my first air show, I had more than my fair share of minuscule pictures of aircraft from my 35mm camera, so much so that my pictures for that time have disappeared, though I was inspired to return by the attractions and flying spectacle alone.

At Farnborough 1998, I hadn't gone digital yet, but while there I brought a second-hand 300mm lens which was well worth it. At that time there was a penchant for slide shows so I converted my film into slides (why?). But with a keen eye and a lightbox, I spied that highlights included the Airbus super transporter -The 'fat brained' Beluga; Concorde and the Red Arrows, a rare outing for the de Havilland Vampire, the Bell 609 –the first civilian tilt-rotor aircraft, the Airbus A330, a C-17 Globemaster, a JAS 39 Gripen, 'bowing' Harriers, and the ever-so-graceful MIG 29s and Sukhoi 27s. I also remember the food, typical fairground fare, though the freshly baked, sugared doughnuts were outstanding, especially after queuing for ages for it.

By the 2006 air show I had a compact 500mm lens; great for high altitude shots. This was a rainy weekend and my souvenir programme cover looked like a (water)moth-eaten page. Highlights included regular turnouts as above, the ubiquitous flash of American firepower (F-14, F-15, F-16, F-18, B1 Bomber, the Apache, and Blackhawk helicopters), the Eurofighter Typhoon, the EH-101 Merlin, Chinook, the V-22 Osprey, the rare Catalina 'amphibious flying boat', a F-35 JSF (Joint Strike Fighter) mock-up, a few static UAVs and other lesser lights. The Blue Eagles display team (British Army Lynx and Gazelle) also performed quite spectacular feats performing barrel rolls and loop-the-loops. And as I found out earlier in my army career, such feats required gear box changes at the end, so I appreciated the efforts of the pilots and their training to pull off amazing manoeuvres for our enjoyment.

The Airbus A380, the biggest airliner in the world, was debuted here, effortlessly and almost silently rumbling into the sky, juxtaposed against the heart-rendering power of the Harrier Jump Jet and Tornado, interspersed between various civilian business jets and sports planes hurtling out of control to gasps of wonder. But best of all were the superlative Russian MIG 29 Fulcrum and Sukhoi Su-27 Flanker jets -never a more acrobatic jet set was assembled as witnessed during their cobra manoeuvres and impossible tail slides: absolutely 'aerogenic'. Of course the Spitfires, Hurricanes, Avro Lancasters and the ever-present Red Arrows were there to close out the show. Farnborough is worth the time, effort and money to get there. There is more than a day's worth of entertainment available with added special tours and flights, and tons of fun and thrills for kids of all ages.

RIAT (Royal International Air Tattoo) -RAF Fairford:
In 1997, I went to RAF Fairford, Gloucestershire, and was treated to the first UK visit of the stealth bomber B2 Spirit (at least in public) accompanied by a couple of F-117 Stealth Fighters. Highlights included sights of some old classics such as the F-4 Phantom, F-100 Super Sabre, MIG-15, Saab JA37 Viggen, and B-52 Stratofortress. While the A-10 Thunderbolt, B-1, F-3 Tornado, Sepecat Jaguar, and Hercules represented more modern era, the P-51 Mustang, Spitfire and Lancaster reminded us of the past. Great display teams also arrived in the form of the lively Cadbury Crunchie Flying Circus complete with a brave soul strapped to the top wing of the Boeing Stearman; the Silver Swallows of the Irish Aircorps in their unique V-tailed Fouga Magisters; the Freece

Tricolori (Italian Airforce), outdone by the brilliant Ukrainian Sukhoi SU-27 Flanker aerial display team, with their outstanding feats of glorious, breath-taking, and awesome flying. Lastly, there was Concorde, only a few years before its official 'retirement'; a final salute to a great icon.

While I love jets, the sameness of the displays, both static and air, can leave one wishing for the Cold War inventiveness of aircraft. The UAVs of today (Predators, Global Hawks, Firescouts, and Scan Eagles, etc.) and the future, will not be as exciting as the aerial stunts of man and machine. I'm waiting for the flying displays of the F-22 Raptor, the F-35 JSF, but mostly the Kamov KA-50 Black Shark (aka Werewolf), the coaxial-rotor designed devil of a helicopter, specifically in its menacing black livery with the tell-tale red star on the tail. It's a mean-looking, thick-metalled skinned, snub-nosed, sleek beast from the minds of aerial hell. I hope to see it stalk the sky one day.

Now that I've seen everything I've wanted to see, except for the above, I can enjoy air shows more and wander around the expansive exhibit halls. I usually go alone and have the freedom and time to take in the experience, take pictures or buy souvenirs, but I still usually see at least one or two people I know doing the same. So if you have never experienced the roar of jet engines up close, the sheer brilliance of the pilots and teams involved, and great day out, then I highly recommend an air show. So, what are you waiting for: chocks away!

30/Nov/2008

Reflections: The Universe

The Universe's Assets

2020 vision
This is a counterpart to the 'God's Assets' essay 06/01/09 in the Religion section.

How much does the universe cost? Has anyone ever costed the universe; all the galaxies, stars, clusters and planets? How? Who has the catalogue? We humans put values on the universal elements (like carbon, iron, gold, etc), but how much would it all be worth if it were up for sale? Where is the costliest place in the universe? Is it in a dense stellar cluster, the centre of the universe, or is there a universal equivalent to the French Riviera? Are black holes universal stock collapses and the rest of the galaxy whips around to create stars to pay off the cosmic debt? If matter is only four percent of the universe, then how much more would dark matter and dark energy cost? Are dark matter and dark energy shadowy investors in the material world, supplying cosmic funds in terms of gravity? The universe must have some kind of value and the interest from its expansion must be astronomical.

Along with the material assets, what about the intangible, priceless, life-giving energy of the cosmic green machine, like the solar winds, nuclear fusion, lunar tidal power, comet water, and star light; what price they in the larger scheme? The universe is worth more than the sum of its parts, just as a human soul is more than flesh and blood. If humans are the only life form to inhabit this cosmic real estate, then how much value do we add to the system? Are we living rent-free? Is the universe a *des res* because of our presence or a human squatter's den? Are humans a tax on the system? The energy quotient and the efficiency rating of the universe could go a long way in raising the value of the universe. The verdict is still out on human worth.

Will the universe ever go bankrupt? Can it be repackaged for the next dominant species? If there was a God, would the value of the universe change as a result of a God-made creation rather than a natural cosmic gem? If God placed no value on the universe, then is the universe (including humanity) a worthless waste of time, energy and space? Surely just by the act of creation God must have placed some value in that one deed. But are we the beneficiaries of that act or mere inconsequential observers? How would a universe full of aliens affect the value? Will the super technology of advanced civilisations create more wealth to the system or will space travel and colonisation cause wear and tear and ultimate destruction?

The universe produces unlimited energy, perpetual and profitable power; the universe manufactures goods in the form of galaxies, stars, planets and life forms; and the universe in all likelihood trades with other universes, through other quantum dimensional banking systems via gravity leaks, neutrinos, or other exotic means. How much does a dimension go for? How much is a cosmic string worth? Will ten dimensions be cost effective and will time itself be quantifiable? Is time money?

So, is the universe in good financial shape? The universe is of such vastness and of a divested nature that no financial calamity should be able to bring the whole system down like a supernova. Black holes, pulsars, gravity quakes, solar storms, time and space instabilities would just be local blips and if worse came to worse, any collapsed solar system or galaxy would get an injection of fresh capital and be rebuilt over a few billion years, a wink of an eye in the larger scheme of things. The universe is a valuable asset and it should be treasured for as long as we are here, and beyond.

17/Dec/2008

Sciences

57 Alien Species: Are We Alone in the Universe?

2020 vision

This and the following two articles are variations of each other. They cover slightly different angles of the same topic which has a finely crafted air of authenticity, without any credible evidence. The best of conspiracies? Or an unbelievable secret revealed? The truth is out there!

Are we alone in the universe? My natural inclination is to say no. It would be an incredible waste of unused real estate if the universe had gone through all this trouble to create only one habitable world in all its vastness. If the conditions for life are right for us in our relatively peripheral position within the galaxy, then surely somewhere out there is another form of life.

So it came as no shock, when according to the Disclosure Project, an organisation dedicated to uncovering UFO and alien truths, and Sergeant Clifford Stone, an ex-top-secret government worker, that we Earthlings have 57 alien species as potential inter-stellar neighbours. In 2001 the Disclosure Project publicised Stone's extraterrestrial catalogue. But the conference was hardly convincing. To announce something like this one would need hard evidence, but there was scant mention of all fifty-seven aliens or their origins or purpose of visitation, or any accompanying graphic information. There were no grainy pictures or files or any detailed descriptions which would have been needed for absolute proof. Why couldn't the Disclosure Project offer anything more than a substandard conference? Where are these aliens now? The most momentous news ever was reduced to a Kolchak moment.

The Disclosure Project also dropped another bombshell, alleging that various secret agencies and aerospace contractors had successfully reversed-engineered alien craft that can travel faster than light. Not only that, but these craft have been exhibited at air shows as advanced human-built craft. If the Disclosure Project had an agenda, I would say that it is to deny humans with the element of self-ingenuity. There was also no detailed analysis of the spacecraft's technical workings or any physical/digital data for the public domain. Even Star Trek technical manuals have more believable specifications.

To be fair to Sergeant Stone there could indeed be other humanoid races in our galaxy, due to the physics and chemistry of our universe and its ability to create the seedlings of life. Stone is not afraid to come forward, though he will be doubted and his integrity challenged. But is he brave, a whistle-blower, disgruntled, a patsy, a conman, or just part of a military machine that occasionally spits out people who have seen too much? Sergeant Stone might have done better than present his story through the Disclosure Project, a rather obscure outlet, when he could have been better served choosing a more credible news source. How can any independent scientist or physicist verify Stone's claims without evidence? He should have known this, so far his part Sergeant Stone has failed to convince me.

What did this conference tell us about the state of our national space defences and programmes, our politicians and scientists in on the secret, and the Disclosure Project itself? What is there to be gained? There is no fame from such claims except in UFOlogist and New Age circles; the wider public would not care. Does the Disclosure Project think that they can con people with claims that cannot be substantiated or are they after something bigger? How much publicity did the Disclosure Project get from Sergeant Stone? How many truths have they uncovered in the years since? Seven years later and we are still waiting for answers, waiting for the evidence, waiting for the fifty-seven aliens to be revealed. For their part, the Disclosure Project is just a forum for UFOlogists, alien hunters, and fringe technologists. There is no convincing substance to their project, they have also failed Sergeant Stone and they confirm to the public that they are as much in the dark as we are.

We may, after all, be alone in the universe, but the Disclosure Project and Sergeant Stone must feel even lonelier as they try to convince us otherwise. All that can be said is if the Disclosure Project and Sergeant Stone really believe in what they are saying then it is up to us only to believe them or not. And unfortunately I do not.

01/Jan/2009

Sciences

57 Alien Species: Are We Alone in the Universe?

2020 vision

The preceding and this similar article were probably under different titles, but they are lost now. If the below were ever true, I'd actually be scared for our survival. Humans and Earth are just exploitable resources with hardly any defences. If it's not true then let's make up some nice aliens. And of course, there's always the theory that all the sci-fi TV shows and films are made to make us more receptive to the idea for when the aliens finally do arrive whether in peace or to resist invasion. Note – only the 2nd YouTube link is active as of Sept 2020.

Are we alone in the universe? My natural inclination is to say no as everything in this universe comes in multiples, whether it be galaxies, stars and planets. The only singular thing found so far in the universe is our habitable world. Now apart from the wastage of unused real estate, the universe has gone through a lot of trouble to create our unique habitable world in all its vastness. Is our world really just some toy wrapped in a ridiculous amount of packaging? If the conditions for life are right for us in our relatively peripheral position within the galaxy, then surely somewhere out there is another form of life.

Well, now it seems we Earthlings have 57 potential inter-stellar neighbours out there, thanks to the work of the Disclosure Project and Sergeant Clifford Stone who, in 2001, publicised their extraterrestrial catalogue. But in the brief youtube segment (http://www.youtube.com/watch?v=rpAPxdjXLCQ) there was hardly mention of all these aliens or their origins, or accompanying graphic or stellar charts. You would think that would have been included for absolute proof. But on another link (http://uk.youtube.com/watch?v=xih43EZuXyI&feature=related) this site lists aliens such as The Greys, The Ancient Mantis, The Blues, the Pleiadians, Tau Cetians, Alpha Centurans, The Vogan, a cat-like species from Sirius A, Reptillians, Draconians, Chubacabra, Orange Eben, and various hybrids.

That's only 12 main species and a few hybrids. There are probably more listed on other sites, but if so, then where are the aliens?

Drake's equation basically boils down to the fact that there at least between one and millions of other civilisations out there. Our galaxy is immense and the universe is unimaginably vaster, so the chances of us hearing from another civilisation would be very remote. That explains the Fermi Paradox; we will not hear from another civilisation because they are so far away or are living/have lived at different times to us. So how can no less than 57 alien species have found their way to Earth?

The Disclosure Project Conference has an answer for this as it lets loose another bombshell: various secret agencies/aerospace contractors have successfully reversed-engineered alien craft that can travel faster than light. Not only that, but these craft have been exhibited at air shows. If the Disclosure Project had an agenda, I would say that it is to deny humans with the element of self-ingenuity. There was also no detailed analysis of the spacecraft's technical workings or any physical/digital data for the public domain. Even Star Trek technical manuals have more believable specifications.

To be fair to Sergeant Stone there could indeed be other humanoid races in our galaxy, due to the physics of our universe. Interstellar space is itself seeded with organic hydrocarbons, which could literally form the basis of the backbones of many species. So any alien species in its formative stage could start out on the same biological path and more than likely be humanoid looking in size, recognisable features, and maybe an outstretched hand to welcome us.

But why would aliens want to visit us? They would surely be distressed at our hostility towards aliens. Almost every single science fiction film depicts even good aliens being wiped out either by mistake or because some megalomaniac distrusted those who came in peace. No alien in his/her/it right mind/minds would want to be taken to our leader. Our entertainment would seem like anti-alien propaganda; a bleak warning to stay away from our world. If there are aliens, then they are not revealing themselves to us or coming to observe, invade, sterilise, test, prod, or anything else for fear of our xenophobic nature.

Sergeant Stone might be doing a classic Rumsfeldian shuffle by letting those aliens know that we know the unknown unknowns. He could be a part of a massive military-industrial complex conspiracy to lull us humans into a false sense of security, or preparing us for alien arrivals, or an elaborate cover-up to obfuscate any other truths and secret projects. We all hope, Disclosure Project, that you are speaking from your earthly heart and not from Uranus.

06/Jan/2009

Sciences
Do you believe that aliens have already visited our planet?

Why Aliens Visit the Earth

2020 vision

If you have ever watch the *Ancient Aliens* programme then you'll know that aliens have come to Earth to: create humanity, destroy humanity, make humans dig for gold, fight amongst themselves thus creating our mythologies, create hybrid creatures, build every single ancient pyramid and megalithic structure, give humanity weapons, hand secrets down to humanity, guide humanity, and much more. I do like a good New Age tome every now and again, but it's a wonder we humans have done anything ourselves and survived.

In 2001, a conference held by the Disclosure Project, a group who investigate the truth about alien visits to Earth, revealed that over the years 57 alien species had been identified. But if this was true, why would aliens visit Earth, a primitive, backward planet with an epic history of violence? However, thinking deeper about the reasons for any alien visit could reveal more about us humans.

First, any alien arriving here would be alarmed at our hostility towards aliens of any kind because we can be a destructive and hateful species. All they would need to do is access our sci-fi back-catalogue of DVDs and witness even good aliens being wiped out either accidentally or because some megalomaniac distrusted those who came in peace and became a monster themselves. No alien in his/her/it right mind/minds would willingly want to be taken to our leader. Our entertainment would read like an anti-alien manifesto; a bleak warning to stay away from our little blue world. Yet, apparently, 57 alien species have dropped by, some repeatedly, to take a peek.

Some people suggest that aliens observe us to assess our potential to mature enough and join the interstellar community one day. They are waiting to see if we will destroy ourselves or fulfil our technological destiny and propel ourselves to the stars. The 21st century will be an important crux in human history as the potential grows to destroy ourselves. So aliens could be weighing up the data on our innocent-looking blue planet which could either pack a mean punch or become a productive member of the inter-galactic village. Aliens are not revealing themselves to us while they stealthily abduct us, test, prod, or whatever else for fear of our xenophobic nature. But there must be something else that makes us such a cosmic curiosity? The aliens must see something in us to continue stalking our world; something unique.

Evolution drives the course of our world, but how universal is it? Human life is in the hands of natural selection, but suppose that it is not the case on other worlds. Suppose evolution itself evolves and throws up different types of progressive development in species. Who says that it is imperative for animals to have to compete to survive for better genes? Maybe that is so for Earth, but other worlds may have evolved differently and that is one reason why visiting aliens are so much more advanced. Earth could be an atavistic throwback on an anomalous evolutionary path and that is why aliens are so fascinated with us, like moths to a flame. We humans shouldn't have survived our evolutionary path. We're a live experiment to watch, a cautionary tale to other aliens and worthy of a fieldtrip from alien 'xenothologists'. Earth is evolution gone wrong. But are the aliens here to fix us with impromptu abductions? Invade and rule? Are they just going to stand by and watch nature take its course like some Star Trek Prime Directive mission? We humans may end up being quarantined to this world if we cannot overcome our twisted evolution.

More intriguingly, if aliens have been in contact with various individuals and/or organisations, or if the military have captured them, and scientists have 'examined' them, then what have they learned from any the 57 alien species? It seems that no biological advantage has come from any alien source. We have no modern miracle cures for the major diseases and we are still fiddling around with stem cells and biotechnology. The only supposed advances have been technological, to wage war and advance science to wage war. Does this mean our biology is incompatible with aliens? Has our evolutionary path has made us too different, no matter the fact that so many of the 57 species were humanoid with some able to pass as human. Is this why some abductees have implants in them to monitor their conditions for whatever reason?

In another twist, in the UFO drama, 'Taken' (2002), aliens were creating a special hybrid human in order to recover a part of themselves lost through evolution, but still present in humans. Humans could be the real missing link in universal evolution. We think we're the superior animal, just as the dinosaurs, mammoths and dodos thought. But these aliens could be the big game hunters, a la the Predators breeding Aliens for sport. Now Earth is due for a massive cull for our precious quirky genes, just as we get smart enough to leave our world and spread our evolutionary infection. The Anthropic Principle, that the universe is here and like it is, otherwise we wouldn't be here to observe it, must make a mockery of cosmic order. Our self-obsessed beliefs and arrogance must truly appal aliens as they try to fathom our skewered logic. Our deeply flawed human psyche might offend alien sensibilities as they try to figure out how and why we chaotic beings exist in an otherwise universal splendour.

But there is another dimension to humans in that many believe that a supernatural being created them and the universe. Imagine if that were true. Are aliens visiting us to see how we were made and to investigate 'God' through man? Aliens might not have such a concept, so they are laughing away at us and our belief in the unbelievable? Will the aliens descend and destroy the belief in God and shock us into the bright reality of the galactic order around us. Will we humans ever be the same once the alien neighbourhood replaced God? Will we lose that evolutionary 'zing' that made us so (supposedly) special? Maybe aliens enjoy seeing a reflection of themselves at an earlier stage of innocence.

Should we be scared of these 57 species of aliens and the rest? After all, we supposedly shoot down their craft, capture and dissect them, and scavenge their technology. Do these strange visitors from another planet really travel hundreds of light years just to be our cannon fodder? Are we evolutionarily incapable of living in peace with other species? There are those on Earth, notably the military-industrial complex, who have a lot to protect in power and wealth and might stop at nothing to conceal the truth from us. Others maybe have true altruistic reasons in wanting to protect us from panic and fear. But what do the aliens gain? Why not show themselves, help us, guide us? All I can think of is that we humans are not ready. Our evolutionary path is still unwinding and the possibilities of our destination are too numerous to predict; so our future is uncertain. Humanity is a work in progress, a quantum flux, which will either decohere into nothingness or become positively entangled with the universe at large.

So, to any of the 57 species of aliens reading or sensing this article, give us the chance to evolve into the beings you want us to become and to join you in the cosmic journey of life.

12/Jan/2009

Science & Technology
The price of Progress

How Much Progress Do We Really Need?

What is the aim of progress? Where are we heading? There is no doubt that progress has enriched lives, but it seems there is a global agenda to push progress for progress sake, which can actually degrade lives. With no defined destination and aims, we are haphazardly planning for the short term, repeatedly fixing things short term, and remembering a short term past. There is a distinct lack of vision, a well-thought out worldview on our journey that will inspire the next generation. Our cultural evolution (memes) is outrunning our biological evolution (genes) and we are now paying the price. Our world, bodies, and technology cannot withstand the relentless pace of unfettered progress, which is killing us through cancers, climate change, and chaos.

Our technologies got us into these problems in the first place, now we're expecting those same technologies to get us out and that somehow we'll mature into a more stable global community. But the world is not a box of tricks that can be tweaked. Our engineered solutions will just turn into disillusionment as failure looms. Progress in nature, technology, and man will progressively and negatively end our lives as we know it.

Nature:
Climate change issues and so-called corporate science are now part of a commercialised and privatised industry. Our industries and corporate science which were created to save us from such catastrophes have caused more misery and now we still look to them to save us once more. But their solutions will be short-term, to paper over the cracks, leaving a ticking time bomb for the future. Will technology and science save us from climate change? No, international politics and business will see to it that such treaties will never be fulfilled, not out of some conspiracy, but because of their intrinsic structures. We compete, not cooperate. We hoard, not share. We enrich ourselves, not spread the wealth. Thus no deal without severe compromises will be forthcoming. It's everyone for themselves.

There is no such thing as sustainable growth and living for six billion plus people. Whether the technology is Genetically Modified food and animals, new energy sources, human biotech, or re-engineered environments, the effect will be to destabilise that which we seek to emulate –Mother Nature. We might as well let climate change continue unabated. Let it kill millions, flood cities and islands, create new ecosystems, create a new world; fresh, cropped and less industrialised. To progress we should adapt more than fight, for Mother Nature will fight back harder and our technological fixes will be for nought. For what climate change will do to the poorest of the world, is what we are already inflicting upon them with economic, political, military, and cultural wars. Progress in nature is imperative, or we will die –simple. But the progress has to work with nature, not against it. So far, the effort made does not look promising.

Technology:
Every year our computers get faster. Why, because Moore's Law says it can? Which is in control of which, the law or technology? Why do we have to reach the limit of everything? Surely consumers are not demanding this everlasting process. Once industries have figured out a way to do something better, faster, and stronger, then the genie is out of the bottle and our wishes are theirs to command.

Why is the pace of progress so fast? Who set the bar so high? Technology is crippling our evolution. Our obese and dumb-downed children will suffer immensely as technology takes over their lives and produces a society dependent upon others to do things for them. Who needs to think and act accurately and effectively when machines can do it for you? They are already plugged and tuned into systems that rule their lives. Ideas and knowledge will be the currency of the future, but it will be computer-aided. Creativity will be lost as artificial intelligence creates a logical mist across the world. The human machine will be subsumed by the mechanical machine and nature will lose out as industry spreads across the surface of the Earth draining natural and human resources in the name of progress. Technological progress is a degenerative process, and again, nothing is standing in its way.

Man:
The Singularity: Have you heard of it? It is the synthesis of Genetics, Robotics, Artificial Intelligence, and Nanotechnology (GRAIN) within a

human. By the mid 21st Century, man will become more than man, more than machine: stronger, faster, smarter, forever. But actually, this process will see the evolution of something less than a man. From mechanical implants, bionics, genetic manipulation, cloning, and so on, man will infect himself with artificial products and unnatural processes. The goal of man is to spread forth and multiply, but in the end the outcome is to die. Interfering with this process, even for the stated benefits of mankind will lead to unforeseen circumstances if used indiscriminately.

Are we creatures of the universe at large or small insignificant beings trapped on a single slither of life in the cosmos? We are accelerating our lives enough to leave this world, leaving behind the dispossessed. We are heading for the 'supercosm' where the universe will be filled will technologically-enhanced humans in an increasingly artificial universe. In the 21st Century, we will either reach the stars or become increasing extinct from all our progressive efforts. The only alternative is to exist – as we are; warring, dying and suffering with no objective in sight. Progress for humans has increased living standards over the millennia, but it is still a prejudicial tool used to build artificial environments and people with no purpose in sight.

What price progress?
Progress, without rhyme or reason, is unwarranted. Progress is now an end to the means; the real runaway effect. Progress curses our civilisation to keep on striving and attaining when there is no goal ahead, just more progress once a new target is arbitrarily set. Progress keeps man busy so he can forget his problems, stay out of trouble, and be a good little consumer for the powers-that-be. Of course, not all progress is bad, but in effect progress is the control of the masses. We progress and enslave ourselves to our wants rather than our needs. We need to slow down, take stock, and re-direct our progress to benefit all, all the time. Progress is the real Perpetual Motion machine; it cannot be stopped, we don't know how, and it only goes one way, faster and faster. Sometime, in the not so distant future, progress will cost us dearly. All we can hope is that someone is left around after the inevitable crash to pick up the pieces.

17/Mar/2009

Science & Technology
Pondering the consequences of scientists discovering the secrets of the universe

We Know Everything. Now What?

So, it is Day Zero, the time scientists finally discover all the secrets of the universe. The mind of God has been unravelled, time and space laid bare, and mankind stands on the threshold of infinity. What will it be like? What would we do with all that power and knowledge? Will life be at an end? Will there be nothing left to discover? Will unlocking the universe's secrets be the end of everything? Mankind's quest for everything could lead to having nothing. The main areas which would be profoundly affected would be in science, religion, and humanity.

Science:
Whether in this or the next century, man will surely and decisively render unto themselves the greatest of all prizes –unlocking the mysteries of the cosmos, whether by string theory, quantum loop gravity, or another exotic theory. Man will unite all the forces and energies into one colossal nutshell. The world will celebrate, the planets tremble, and the stars quake at the thought of humans understanding the universe. But then what? Will we do everything at once, quantum style, or bit by bit? Will quantum computers solve all our problems? Who will own this miracle scientific progress –the scientists? The rich countries, or everyone? Will corporations withhold vital pieces of the universal code, ransoming human survival for a few dollars more? Indeed, if scientists discovered the ultimate cosmic key, would they keep and use it in secret, never to be divulged? What other arcane unknowns would they delve into? Who has the right to keep such secrets and power? Maybe it would be in the public's best interest not to know or wars could begin to control such secrets. After all, we have fought over lesser matters.

Could we travel time? Would time be meaningless? Would space have meaning? All the visible and dark matter and dark energy would be entwined into a comprehensible tale of cosmology? Would limitless energy power the world and thrust humanity to the stars and beyond? Or would we simply teleport there by thought? Would we unleash deadly forces beyond our control –an equal and opposite reaction to us opening Pandora's Box? But instead of Hope at the bottom of the box, we would find despair. What if the secrets of the universe held nothing but empty promises? The grandest of secrets and all the questions that were asked just answered by more vexing questions. But surely knowing everything would let us see everything to come? Well, yes, but knowing something does not mean you could do anything about it. The universe could be one great big unending question, even though we have the answers, we might not understand them.

Religion:
So we've peeked behind the curtain and found no God peering back. Will Man be a God unto himself? Or will Man instead worship natural law? Will we enter heaven or descend to hell having tasted all the forbidden fruits? Will scientific claims of killing God cause wars on earth? Will the religious minded accept the scientific doctrine? How could they go on believing in something that had been disproved or would they believe that God is outside of the universe and thus our complete understanding? Religion could evolve into something new, something all encompassing and beyond the belief in a supernatural being. Knowing the secrets of the universe would still mean different things to different people and what they would still believe in.

What would happen if we actually found God? Would this be the day of Ascension or Armageddon? Would everyone be forced to worship God? Will God draw back the veil and laugh as he destroyed the universe in another Big Bang, ready for his next test subjects? We human lab rats took 14 billion years to finish the test –is that good or bad? Okay, really, modern human thinking has been around for almost 50 thousand years, so have we excelled ourselves or are we just Johnny-come-latelys to the cosmic club of total understanding? God's purpose for humanity may be just for us to strive as far as we can, reach the finish line, and then watch as the goal line is pushed further away. The nebulous heavens in deep space could be there for a reason, to shroud the darkest secrets from us and stop us from going blind with ambition as we stare at the stars. There just may be someone out there hiding the Universe's commandments away from us. We shouldn't know what we cannot know.

Humanity:
Life on Earth would be irrevocably changed as the full import of harnessing the power of the universe became apparent. But can knowing everything be enough? Would we be able to put an end to the world's ills: poverty? disease? climate change? war? And even death itself? We humans would live forever. There would be no more death; there would be selective evolution, transgression of body and machine, and the unbounding of the mind. Physical man could cease to exist as he transcended to a higher plane of existence. This omnipotent being would stride the galaxies upon wings of thought. There would be no more secrets, nothing to learn, nothing to teach, nothing to live for. The end of humankind would begin with the decoding of the last revealing universal equation.

But we are nowhere near this tipping point (even with the Large Hadron Collider). However, like climate change, the feedback loops from our endeavours could be devastating. The universe could be polluted by unseen particles or forces and warmed up beyond absolute zero, defrosting space, causing extra solar precipitation in one galaxy, gravity droughts in another, and cause huge galactic storms. Once the secret is out and if it goes wrong, how can we fix the universe? Yes, we have discovered everything, but we do not know what is beyond the discovered horizon. Humanity could destroy itself and the universe in seeking what created them in the first place.

Is this a precautionary tale? Perhaps; each time we have discovered something, even for the benefit of mankind, it has brought its own problems. So, instead of lining up for the ultimate Nobel Prize ceremony, scientists should be thinking ahead —way ahead- to the day someone finds the golden key to the universe's door. Either they shut the door (and forever wonder if Schrodinger's cat is alive or dead) or they have to get a great screen door to filter what is worth processing (and control their Pavlovian urges). Which is it to be? Time will tell.

21/May/2009

Who are Britain's Astronauts
Astronaut biographies

British Astronauts

2020 vision

It was a great pleasure to see and hear astronaut Tim Peake in person at the New Scientist Live event at the ExCel, London 22.09.16. It's not every day you get to see an astronaut, especially one who had just recently been on the International Space Station.

Britain's newest astronaut was announced recently, as Major Timothy Peake, a veteran helicopter test pilot in the British Army. The 37-year-old was chosen for ESA's Astronaut Corps, along with two Italians, a Frenchman, a German, and a Dane. Peake is not the first British astronaut, nor will he be the last, but the media have seemingly celebrated his achievement more so than other British astronauts, probably because he has remained British and with ESA, the European Space Agency. Britain's astronaut list is short, but nonetheless, it is a tradition that is growing

Timothy Peake:

Peake, who has a degree in flight dynamics, is the first British ESA astronaut, as other British-born astronauts are NASA-trained, with some becoming U.S. citizens to secure better Space Shuttle berths and advancement. This is because Britain opted out of the Human Spaceflight, deeming it too expensive. In some quarters, this is seen as an expensive mistake by Britain and short-sighted. While Britain is committed to ESA and robotic space programmes, it could miss vital experience in a manned programme to compete with NASA and the Russians. This point was reiterated by Jean-Jacques Dordain, director-general of ESA, when he stated: "I hope it [the appointment of Timothy Peake] will now encourage the British government to contribute." To the proponents of human spaceflight, this could entice Britain to contribute, but to the cynics, this could just be a political ploy to placate Britain, since it is a major financial contributor to ESA. Either way, this is still a milestone in British spaceflight history. Major Peake, however, is just the latest in a modest line of British astronauts.

Helen Sharman:
The Girl from Mars, as the first Briton in space Helen Sharman was called, worked as a chemist in the Mars Company. In 1989, the Sheffield-born Sharman applied to a radio advertisement calling for a British astronaut, which she eventually won selection for after an intensive testing regime. The prize was Project Juno, a Soviet/British initiative, which offered a private flight to the Mir Space Station via a Russian Soyuz spacecraft. Sharman's week-long spaceflight was in 1991. She did not fly again, and although she was awarded an OBE in 1993 and inducted as an honorary fellow into the Royal Society of Chemistry, her spectacular achievement is somewhat forgotten by the British public. She has written two books, one being her biography, and she currently undertakes broadcasting and lecturing work on space and science.

Michael Foale:
The best-known, British-born astronaut is Michael Foale, although to enhance his prospects, he also holds dual American citizenship. Foale's moment in the sun in the UK media and public spotlight was in 1997, when he was aboard the Russian Space Station Mir. It was hit and damaged by a re-supply ship and Foale had to conduct an EVA to help examine the exterior for damage. Foale is also the first British Astronaut to accomplish an EVA in 1995, and has also worked on the Hubble Space telescope in 1999. From joining NASA in 1987, Foale is not only Britain's most accomplished astronaut, but must also be considered one of NASA's most qualified astronauts as well, due to his long-service and experience.

Piers Sellers:
Not as well-known as Foale, research scientist Dr. Piers Sellers was born in England, joining NASA in 1996, and is now a naturalised American. His first shuttle flight (Atlantis) was in 2002 and his second (Discovery) in 2006, both of which involved significant amounts of EVAs while helping with the construction and maintenance of the International Space Station (ISS).

Nicholas Patrick:
Hardly garnering any publicity in the UK, is Nicolas Patrick. Born in North Yorkshire, Patrick's background is in mechanical engineering. He joined NASA in 1998 and is also a naturalised American citizen. So far, Patrick has completed only one shuttle flight in 2006.

Gregory Johnson:
A USAF Colonel, Johnson was born in Middlesex, but this one-time space voyager is now an American citizen. He was selected for NASA in 1998 and flew on an Endeavour shuttle mission in 2008. Besides his flight experience, Johnson has also been part of the Shuttle Cockpit Avionics upgrade unit, was part of the investigation team into the cause of the 2003 Columbia disaster, and from 2005, was involved in designing and testing of the Crew Exploration Vehicle, which eventually became the Orion spacecraft. Colonel Johnson may not be in the public eye, but he is amassing some serious behind-the-scenes experience that will see NASA possibly return to the moon.

Antecedents:
Interestingly enough, while Helen Sharman was the first British astronaut in space, she was not the first British astronaut. That honour went to John Anthony Llewellyn, a Welshman, who had the "right stuff" in 1967 as a scientist-astronaut. But before he could fly into space, he resigned in 1968 due to personal reasons. Llewellyn currently serves as the Professor Emeritus in the department of Chemical Engineering at the University of South Florida, where he had worked in several positions for decades.

Space tourists:
Whether seen as real astronauts or not, the future seems to be open to space tourists and private ventures with British participants at the forefront.

The first British space tourist was Mark Shuttleworth, in 2002, who holds dual South African and British citizenship. Paying over $20 million to be a 'space participant' on the ISS, the South African businessman spent eight days in space, helped with biological research in AIDS, and held a radio conversation with Nelson Mandela.

The second British-born space tourist was Richard Garriott, a computer games developer. In 2008, the now-American citizen Garriott spent around $30 million on a twelve-day visit the ISS via a Russian Soyuz spacecraft. Though Garriott made history as the first second-generation American in space after his astronaut father Owen Garriott, he sported the Union Jack flag on his uniform. Besides communicating with school children, and testing the Windows on Earth software project, Garriott also participated in the first sci-fi film shot in space called Apogee of Fear.

Private enterprises:
The leader in the market to develop private space planes is Sir Richard Branson's Virgin Galactic. He has teamed up with Burt Rutan, the winner of the X-Prize with his SpaceShipOne, the first privately own spacecraft to voyage into space. SpaceShipTwo is in development by Rutan's Scaled Composites Company and within a few short years could produce many more British astronauts for a nominal fee.

From 1967 to 2009, and beyond, British astronauts have contributed to national, European, American, Russian, and other international space agencies and endeavours, and fired the public's imagination. When the next missions to the Moon and Mars take off, there is no doubting that a Briton will be among the crew.

08/Jan/2010

What are Ultraterrestrials?

The Supernatural Terrestrials

2020 vision
This may be the only reason I might take drugs, to test this theory and seek something beyond our understanding. However, in expressing this thought, am I now biasing the experiment to predetermine what I would experience? The connections between Stone Age rituals, shamanistic depictions and our modern alien beings concepts are an intriguing thought and maybe not so far-fetched.

The concept of Ultraterrestrials is a fascinating one to encounter. There was not such a belief on my part in the supernatural and even less as an advocate on the merits of mind altering drugs. But then came "Supernatural – Meetings of the Ancient Teachers of Mankind". Written by Graham Hancock, he of "Fingerprints of the Gods" fame, "Supernatural" could have been written-off as a throwaway New Age tome, but it is so much more. It is an opening into the world of the Ultraterrestrials.

What connects Stone Age cave paintings and their spirit worlds in Europe, Africa, the Americas and Australia to the Middle Ages' elves, fairies, changelings, and prophetic visions to modern-day shaman, UFOs, and aliens? It is the commonality of the hallucinatory themes as experienced under the effects of certain mind-altering drugs, trance dances, meditation, and other extreme physical exertions. For over 30,000 years, man has been having hallucinations sharing the same basic visual elements no matter the era or culture. The only thing that has changed is what we called these beings encountered in these altered states of consciousness. Surely these are Ultraterrestrials by any other name.

In the Stone Age, the spirits took the shaman on magical trips; their visions may have led to the beginnings of art and religion. The experience included surgical-like procedures with spears/arrows being stuck into the shaman, as painted on European cave walls. Also painted were therianthropes (half men/half beasts), magical animals, and strange, pear-shaped-headed men. This was also repeated in African iconography and the supernatural quality of their trances was reiterated in ethnographical accounts by the San Bushmen. Without a doubt, Shaman from around the world were in contact with beings beyond the realm of normal reality.

In the Middle Ages, the elves, fairies, little people, and women in white also took people (permanently or temporarily) into other realms, seemingly experimented on them, tried to create changeling hybrids, and lured people to them through animals, and dances. The Fairy circle dances seemed to be a mode of portal transportation, but flying vehicles were also seen. Witches in later centuries were reported to be able to see the occult world (possibly due to ergot-infected rye which induced hallucinations) and were condemned to death for this gift/curse. Several famous sightings of the Virgin Mary or angels may have been caused by hallucinations, these venerated sites being previously well-associated with fairies, until the Church supplanted them.

In our modern era, we have millions of tales of alien abductions, invasive procedures, inter-breeding, strange flying vehicles, and loss of time. The aliens have pear-shaped heads, try to communicate knowledge to us, and can also morph into animals. The commonalities between the paintings on pre-historic caves, pictures or engravings of Middle Age magical beings, and images of modern-day aliens seem to point to a common origin for these beings, with a strong sense of supernatural reality.

Ultraterrestrials can be accessed, contacted, seen, and interacted with through an altered state of reality (i.e. when we have hallucinations, whatever their cause), which can seem as real as physical reality. The continued common visual themes throughout time and across cultures attests to the fact that all these spirits/magical beings/aliens are one and the same manifestation, perhaps evolving as we do or just perceived through the eyes of the current times. No one sees elves now; the Middle Ages peasants and Stone Age dwellers did not see aliens, but they are one and the same beings, whatever they call themselves or whatever we call them. They seem to be tied to Earth's supernatural gravity, possibly evolved on Earth, and then transcended to another plane of existence only accessible now through telepathy or hallucination.

The supernatural element cannot be dismissed, yet Western science scoffs at this notion even though scientists toy with such ethereal theories such as 11-dimensional string theory or quantum loop gravity. They search for hidden dimensions, wormholes, and dark energy, yet wholly discount the belief that the supernatural world may exist and may even be what they're looking for. The Ultraterrestrials are always spoken of as trying to impart to us knowledge either through books or telepathy. Science can investigate this through carefully controlled experiments, using trance-induced hallucinations. It would be as worthy as the Large Hadron Collider searching for elusive God particles and Theories of Everything. Ultraterrestrials could be ascended or evolved dark matter. We won't know until we investigate. If scientists had poured as much research and effort into exploring the supernatural world then we could have been in contact with the Ultraterrestrials for decades, learning much about ourselves and the universe.

Hancock, or none of the other experts/shaman, have ever named the beings, only referring to spirits/guides, elves/fairies, and Grays/aliens, etc, but surely these are the Ultraterrestrials, in different guises, on another plane of existence trying to communicate with us. Apart from trying to procreate with us and perform strange physical procedures upon us, they also try to convey that our DNA has a message within it; that we are the carriers of important information related to them. Apparently, within our junk DNA is a unique pattern, documented by biologists, which contains vast amounts of data that so far we cannot read. The codes to unlock the data may just lie in the supernatural world of the Ultraterrestrials.

There is a fear that in trying to contact or study Ultraterrestrials, this could demean religion in some way if it turns out that these entities kick-started religion and have been mistakenly worshipped as deities. There would be fears that science would be able to disprove God and take over all facets of life. So be it. We would then know either way, that there is a proven supernatural world to believe in, which could still make religion stronger rather than redundant. Of course, drug-induced experimentation is illegal under the various anti-drug laws and wars. But is this for our protection by the politico-religious, military-industrial complex or is it to control us; steer us away from our natural right to contact higher beings? The Ultraterrestrials would be less mysterious and thus make our world less superstitious, but also free us from a controlling human hierarchy.

The Ultraterrestrials have been encountered in all-too-real hallucinations, out of body experiences, and altered states of consciousness throughout the world and throughout different millennia. It is time that science acknowledged these phenomena and their presence and probe more deeply into supernatural cosmic territory, revealing the supernatural terrestrials all around us. Until then, it may also be time to contemplate a personal trip to meet them myself.

30/Jan/2010

Is the anthropic principle valid?

We Are The Aliens

Scientists from around the world have gathered at London's Royal Society to debate the merits of contacting alien civilisations, but they should also discuss another pertinent problem: that humankind may be living anomalies in an anomalous universe, whether there is extraterrestrial life out there or not.

We humans are very arrogant about our place in the universe; and quite naturally so, as we are the only known beings in the universe. We assume we are living at a special time in the universe as only we alone can witness its grandness and presume a special relationship with the cosmos. This is known as the Anthropic Principle. Well, we should rethink our Anthropic view of the universe and see ourselves in a very different light.

For years, we have known that the universe is made up of only five percent of ordinary matter; that is the visible universe: galaxies, stars, planets, you and me. The rest of the universe is dark matter (some twenty-three percent) and the even more of it is mysterious dark energy (around seventy-two percent). The question is: is our five-percent of matter the norm or is it to be considered an anomalous and random inclusion within a naturally Dark Universe? We see our five-percent bit of the universe as the normal condition of the universe, because we live in it. But it is not.

There could be dark-matter beings out there in the universe viewing us with disdain and wondering why our five percent speck of matter survives. The majority of the universe could have a Xenocentric view on our existence. All the supposed alien abductions, invasive surgeries, and attempted/alleged hybrid creations could all be in order to determine what we are; to make us better, to cure our baryonic nature. We humans are the aliens, the anomalies of the universe, the dregs of creation in our little bubble of visible matter.

This begs the further question of our existence: Is this a natural state of events where we inhabit an oasis of ordinary space or were we created and live in what is in effect a safari of 'normal' matter designed by the bored indigenous dark matter inhabitants? The Xenocentric universe may be multidimensional, supernatural, or so dark we will never penetrate it with our toy-like instruments. We humans are a minority in a universe of dark matter and energy. The state of the universe is not going to change any time soon so the proportions of matter/energy will stay the same. No matter how far we explored in the universe, we could only ever experience five-percent of it.

So, we are not special; just left-over bits from the Big Bang, whose natural inclination was to create a Dark Universe. Our small visible-light universe makes us an endangered species. How are we to cope with that? Are we making the most of our lives? Are we lucky? Yes, we are lucky to be here, but at the same time we have to accept that we might not have the right to exist and can be culled by the universe at any time. In fact, we exist to help the universe return to a state of chaos. All our building, wars, exploration, even breathing creates more and more chaos or thermodynamic entropy, so we are doing our bit to destroy ourselves naturally. Maybe that's our five-percent universe's function: to create chaos and return the universe to its natural state before the next Big Bang.

So scientists at the Royal Society needn't worry about aliens invading or watching us whether there is finally first contact or not, for our existence may be totally random, innocuous, short-lived, and less than a blip on the Xenocentric radar. Like a certain thought-experiment with a cat, we won't know whether the validity of Anthropic Principle is dead or alive until the box is opened, in this case by extraterrestrial communication. However, the best bet is the universe has chosen the majority dark side as its primary breeding ground and that our Anthropic view of the universe is a presumptuous belief.

06/Apr/2010

Exploring man's fascination with the universe

A Universe by any Other Name

Man may be fascinated by the universe, but the thing that fascinates me is that our universe has no name. If our universe was to have a name, what would it be? We've named everything from the Milky Way (a prosaic name at best), stars –like our sun Sol-, planets, moons, asteroids, comets, and even lumps of cold rock beyond Pluto. Surely we will discover another universe and will have to differentiate between us and them with names, rather than boring catalogue numbers. So what kind of names would the universe have?

The universe is a hypersphere; what the sphere is to a circle, a whole other dimension. Are all other universes like ours? Are they flat or saddle-shaped, curved or round or blob-like? Are they balanced and static, or closed and finite ready to collapse, or open and infinitely expanding forever? Have their inhabitants named their universe or are they wondering like us humans why we are here? Should we humans, since we seem to be the only ones here, name our universe after ourselves: The Anthroverse? If we're arrogant enough to think we are the only life in our universe then we may as well cement that view and name the whole she(big)bang after ourselves.

We should have a name fitting the character of the universe. Our Earth has often been alternatively named Gaia. If the Sol system begat Gaia, and if the Milky Way begat Sol then who begat the Milky Way and its brothers and sisters (whether or not our galaxy is male or female, of course)? Chaos was the mother of Gaia, but such a name would not do for us. Our universe has a strange disproportionate spattering of matter in that only five percent is normal matter and the rest dark matter and dark energy. Since we are made of the normal matter, the universe could be called Matteria, to honour this unique composition of our universe.

Maybe there should be a global contest to name our universe taking it out of the hands of scientists who would plumb for a generic number. With six billion of us on this world someone would come up with a fitting name. An obscure name from a mythological tome might be desirable as it is already in use for planets, stars, and galaxies. But are there nomenclatures for universes? Is cosmos already a name? Is Heaven an apt title? If we are a holographic projection on the edge of a higher plane then are we in the Holoversia? Let the contest begin.

Why does our universe have no name after 13 billion years? Whether a single universe or part of a multiverse, hyperverse, bubble universe, etc, we still need a name. When these other universes are discovered we will not be the centre of them, we won't be the oldest of them, nor the best, nor the brightest. We will need to distinguish ourselves from the others and no number will do. We won't be Universe Prime (as in comic books) or Universe 1, nor 100, nor universe 1 million. Douglas "Hitchhiker's Guide to the Galaxy" Adams may well have named us Universe 42. Is universe in itself a name? Not really it's a designation of a category, like galaxy, star, planet, but they all get to have discrete names. Dispersia (after the Big Bang?), Quintessence? Hubbleverse? Existia?

But would the name of the universe be male or female? This would matter for how could we be taken seriously if we didn't even know that? We would have to split the difference and go with a gender neutral name so as not to cause offence to the universe and fellow humans. Does it matter if the universe has no name? If we meet other beings from our universe would they have named it already? Would they agree with our name and we with theirs? Is the universe a possession that can be named or is worth naming or is it too grand and unique to have a name? We humans are built to name and describe things, it defines us. How can we not name the universe? Quantuma? Newton-Einstein? Chronos? We can go on.

When we are visited by extra-universal beings, we should welcome them: Welcome to Earth, 3rd from Sol, in the Orion Arm of the Milky Way, not far from Andromeda in the universe of ...erm. Exactly - Not a fitting welcome and we would probably be seen as the primitive beings we are for not naming our universe. And we couldn't blame them. So, think of a fitting name for our venerable 13.7 billion year-old universe and let's become more aware and appreciative of our fascinating universe.

16/May/2010

Science & Technology
The mystery surrounding Edwin Hubble's death

The Hubble Mystery

2020 vision
This was probably originally in History Mysteries, but I've put the title I created into Science.

In Bill Bryson's "A Short History of Nearly Everything" there is the curious tale of Edwin Hubble, the 'discoverer' of Galaxies and the fact that they are rapidly receding away from each other. In 1953, Hubble died of a heart attack (or a cerebral thrombosis –a blood clot in the brain, in some sources). His wife, Grace, never held a funeral for him (at least not publicly) nor did she say what had happened to the body. And his body has never been found. Hubble disappeared as fast as his red-shifted nebulae.

So where is Hubble? His wife must have had a reasonable motive for this mysterious move. Are there surviving relatives who could shed light on this mystery of the disappearing cosmologist? Was his body donated to science? Was he cremated? Was his disappearance done to enhance his enigmatic nature? Or did Hubble disdain the frivolities of funerals, wakes, and rituals? Whatever the reason, it has piqued the curiosity of many people.

Is there an air of arrogance lingering after his death; one of Hubble's riddles, as he often made extravagant boasts in life? Imagine you are a famous scientist. You are feted through life, but know that even with your awards and world-changing discoveries you may be forgotten in death. What better way to keep your name alive far beyond death and the mere feats of your scientific endeavours? Will Hubble be the Percy Fawcett of the scientific world – mysteriously lost with tantalising new evidence on his whereabouts emerging every so often? Imagine Hubble's remains being found a hundred or more years from now; what a news story that would be, even in 2110.

Is this only a myth? A search of online sites seems to perpetuate the story of his wife not revealing where and how the body was interred or disposed of. In a couple of websites, there are references to what Grace Hubble did do and why. After Hubble suffered a cerebral thrombosis at home, Grace cremated his body. She held no service or a memorial. Apparently, she then boxed up and buried his ashes, which have never been found. Another source suggests that Hubble wanted no service for himself and that he is either buried in an unmarked grave or was indeed cremated. Whichever is true, the location has remained safe for almost sixty years: some hiding place, Grace!

Did Hubble want no fuss over his death, not wishing for worshippers coming to view his grave as in a pilgrimage to a scientific saint? Did he want a private death; to die and remain in peace with dignity? It is a rare thing for a famous scientist to crave anonymity in death, but maybe Hubble felt he had done enough in life that his death was unimportant and not wanting it to overshadow his achievements? The mysterious disappearance after his death has certainly bolstered the mystery surrounding him? Hubble's grave site location is as uncertain as Hubble's constant.

But for how much longer can Hubble's body go undiscovered? If his remains (cremated or not) are found in an unmarked grave or cemetery, how would we know if they are Hubble's? Did Grace Hubble leave any indication of where he was in a diary, or private notes, a whispered confession to a friend or family member? Is Hubble buried close to home, in a cemetery or crematorium, or by his beloved observatory where he made history? Would forensics be able to determine his identity if a body was found? If his ashes were found, could we be sure it was him? And then what: would Hubble be re-interred, whether in a private ceremony or in a public celebration, and allowed to rest in peace? I'm sure there would be a petition to have his ashes carried into space to join his beloved galaxies.

Is this all too much of a contrived mystery? Would a search of the Los Angeles county death certificate records solve the problem or do we want Hubble's disappearance in death to be some romantic myth? Wouldn't it be great if Hubble's remains were secretly entombed in his eponymous telescope, the ultimate cryogenic coffin and eye on the universe? Wherever Hubble is and in whatever condition, we can only hope that he is not lost forever. Hubble's law defines our universe, but it seems Hubble himself wanted to be a law unto himself in death, resting as enigmatically in the afterlife as he did in life.

Sources:

1. Edwin Hubble: King of the Hill
http://www.vision.org/visionmedia/article.aspx?id=3722

2. Edwin Hubble:
http://en.allexperts.com/e/e/ed/edwin_hubble.htm

Both links are no longer active.

25/May/2010

Science & Technology - Cosmology
Going to Mars

Dying to get to Mars

2020 vision

I had submitted this to the Mars Society for publication, but The Mars Quarterly stopped publication soon after. For info, I had contacted the United Nations Coordination of Outer Space Activities (letter below) to enquire if there is a global policy among space agencies in the event of an astronaut dying in space or on another planet. I didn't get a response. This article is not intended to knock the positiveness of Mars Missions, but to bring to the fore our own fears, to meet and understand them, and to move on. We cannot let the fear of death on a space mission rule the public's (and thus politicians') minds, so let's confront it. Be bold.

There are always arguments as to why some explorations should not be undertaken. One of those reasons is the risk of death. But why should this be so when exploration is a necessary part of human discovery, growth, and survival. Exploration is part of human nature, whether in the physical, psychological, or emotional realm. We humans need to know what is around us, near and far, known and unknown. There are a few intrepid few who have travelled to the ends of the Earth, to the deepest oceans, the highest mountains, and even to the moon. In each and every endeavour, along the way or at their destination travellers, adventurers, voyagers, and explorers have died. They died in their pursuit of adventure, science, faith, dreams and advancing mankind towards a destiny of greatness.

Such things may well happen on the way to Mars. Some astronauts, Mars explorers, and colonists will die, whether from accidents in training on Earth or in space, an accident on the voyage to Mars or on Mars itself, through radiation-induced cancer, spaceship malfunction, inadequate resources, some unknown factor, or just plain bad luck. But it will still be necessary to go to Mars.

We all know about the accidental deaths in Apollo I and the Shuttles Challenger and Columbia disasters under full media-glare. Much less known is the fate of Soyuz I and the fatality of a cosmonaut from parachute failures in 1967. However, the only true deaths in space occurred on June 30th, 1971 when three cosmonauts, Georgi Dobrovolsky, Viktor Patsayev, and Vladislav Volkov in Soyuz 11, were asphyxiated after a faulty valve opened while preparing for re-entry. They were still above the Kármán Line, the 100km marker of outer space. While the bodies were recovered upon landing, what if they had been left in orbit or drifted further into space? What if Apollo astronauts had been stranded on the moon or forced to drift past the moon and into the black yonder? Success cannot be guaranteed every time, but any failures cannot detract from the mission.

While we want to accentuate the positives of a Mars mission, we cannot be squeamish about discussing any possible deaths. It is one reason why much of the public oppose such an epic space voyage; they fear death. But in transferring their own fear of death to the strangers in the sky, the public unnecessarily hamper the political will and responsibility to undertake the journey to the red planet. We need to know what precautions and directives would be given by the various governments and space agencies of the countries involved if an astronaut died. We would also need to gauge and mollify the public's reaction and perception of Mars Missions in the case of such a tragic incident.

Is this a cold-hearted view? Is this scare-mongering or pandering to the sensationalist? No, this is an attempt to rationalise an important and natural point of exploration. How many sailors died from scurvy and other diseases exploring the world —hundreds, thousands? If the old European governments knew then what we know now about scurvy and the deaths it would cause, would they still have sent their navies out? Well, they did anyway. The benefits of exploration out-weighed the deaths of men. It is a callous statement, but such exploration and inevitable disasters led to new territories, resources, and discoveries - scientific or otherwise- some of which helped to cure the diseases that killed so many explorers. There are many more examples of exploration/death occurrences as in yellow fever, small pox, malaria, hostile inhabitants, and extreme climatic conditions, to name but a few. But just because we sit on cosy Earth does not mean that death by exploration is a thing of the past. Those who venture to Mars for the sake of Mankind may inevitably have to face death.

Is it because there is no air to breathe in space, through which astronauts will travel and live upon a tiny, fragile spaceship, and enjoy little resources upon a cold, rusted world, which biases the public's perception about the success and survival of astronauts on Mars? Is it down to costs? Would the public rather have a hundred astronauts travel to Mars for fifty billion dollars rather than four, six or eight astronauts? Does it come down to value for money deaths? Would it matter if their taxes were footing the bill or if it came from private coffers? The public want assurances that astronauts will not die and that if they do, what will happen. Will they be 'buried' in space? Will they be interred on Mars, never to be repatriated to Earth? We will need to deal with death quickly and responsibly, especially if the death is on the probable nine-month voyage out to Mars, when a death is most likely to occur, or during an exploratory mission on Mars during a likely two-year stay.

Are there international conventions on the procedures for the death of an astronaut in space? Do NASA, Roscosmos (Russian Federal Space Agency), ESA, or CNSA (China National Space Administration), the main contenders to send Mars missions; practice missions where a member dies? There seems to be no unified charter on space deaths. It seems such a policy will be ad hoc in the event of a death in space. Groups and Conventions such as the United Nations Coordination of Outer Space Activities, the Committee on the Peaceful Uses of Outer Space (COPUOS), Unispace III, and the International Association for the Advancement of Space Safety, and other groups concentrate on safety standards, space debris management, a non-nuclear space, technological discoveries, environmental benefits, and other such matters. They involve specialists in their fields and national space agencies, but there is no mention of a common agreement in the event of a death in space or another planetary body. In fact, there is no mention of any space law to deal with this issue.

If a Mars Mission went awry would the mission continue? How would the news be broken? The world's population and the media would need to be prepared in the event that astronauts died in space or on Mars. Is this too morbid a thought; because it could be a real situation that the world will have to deal with? There is a psychological price to pay when humans leave the protection of Earth. There is already the physical isolation, the disconnect from reality, and the fragility of the surroundings. What could a death do in such confined quarters? Will the astronauts have psychological training for such an event? They would have to cope so far away and alone.

What ever happen to the "Give me liberty or give me death?" sentiment? Is that spirit dead, so to speak? Exploration of Mars is the liberty from Earth mankind seeks; a new world to discover and live on; freedom for our species doomed to die if it lingers on one world. We should not be afraid of the risks, nor of death, for if it comes we will be prepared. We will mourn, but we shall also understand and acknowledge the reason for it. A few with the Right Stuff are willing to take the risks and potentially sacrifice their lives for the greater good of mankind. Death will not be a failure. Death will not be the end. Mars awaits its new life.

Sat 22/05/2010

To: oosa@unvienna.org

To the Office for Outer Space Affairs,

My name is Ray Burke and I am contacting you for research purposes regarding writing an article about the unfortunate eventuality of astronaut deaths on a mission to Mars or on Mars. I know this is a somewhat morbid subject and such a mission some time off, but as with high costs and political will concerning Mars missions, the death of an astronaut on a Mars mission is another reason why the public would baulk at such a mission. My article would put the case forward as to why, despite such a dreadful scenario occurring, a Mars mission should go ahead.

I am primarily interested as to if there is an international accord between the UN, NASA, ESA, Roscosmos, and the CNSA, and others as to what procedures would be taken if an astronaut died in space (i.e. above the Kaman Line) or on another planetary body, especially on a joint mission. I had looked through documents from groups and conventions such as the International Association for the Advancement of Space Safety, Unispace III, the Committee on the Peaceful Uses of Outer Space (COPUOS), but did not find any mention on aspects of a mission should an astronaut die in space or on another planetary body. Perhaps it was outside of their scope? Does the UN have remit over such international issues and the psychological implications of such a tragedy? Is it a topic mentioned at all in space industry circles? Or is it a situation that can only be dealt with as it arises, hence no overall policy? To quell media and public outbursts, should such a policy be advocated and publicised to put to rest any perceptions of helplessness, conspiracies, or lack of planning, if a death occurred on a Mars mission.

My article will be posted on Helium.com and may be presented for publication on the Mars Society quarterly magazine. The subject is unorthodox, but without pandering to the sensationalists, and in the interest of space exploration, my article would address the fears many do not mention. I would appreciate any information you could supply. For any quotes, specific information or citations, I would gladly write for your permission first.

Thank you for your time and I look forward to hearing from you.

Regards,

Ray Burke

01/Jun/2010

Science & Technology
World first: How scientists have created artificial life

Craig Venter: Man God?

2020 vision

Where is the man of tomorrow, now? The former 2-time *Time Magazine* member of the top 100 influential people in the world may still be CEO of his eponymous institute and winning awards, but the media seems to have forgotten him. I last remember watching his Dimbleby lecture on the BBC in 2007 and thinking we'd have all these wonderful genetic cures and inventions. But perhaps mother nature is still too hard to recreate indefinitely.

A scientific team led by Dr. Craig Venter of the J. Craig Venter Institute in Maryland and California has succeeded in developing the first synthetic living cell. The scientific landmark used cutting-edge technology over fifteen years to construct a bacterium's 'genetic programming' from an off-the-shelf DNA package. This was then transplanted into a yeast cell to promote growth and after several more processes, finally transplanted into a recipient cell which had its own DNA removed. The new cell divided over a billion times under its own programming to become new life.

Venter has been touting the synthetic life form, dubbed "Synthia", as a near-panacea for most of the world's ills, perhaps able to produce medicines, fuels, clean water, new foods, and absorb greenhouse gases. Will this be the start of a new biological revolution? Venter hopes so, but his critics are many, not appeased by the claims that Synthia will cure the world and also because Venter's team received $40 million in funding from drug companies, oil companies, and the US Department of Energy, fuelling suspicions about commercial agendas ruling over humanitarian interests.

Fears that military or rogue elements could create their own synthetic organisms for use a biological weapons, have been countered by Venter with the fact that the Massachusetts Institute of Technology (MIT) and a Washington defence think tank, reported that there was only a small occurrence of this happening.

Dr Helen Wallace from Genewatch UK, which monitors genetic technologies, stated her fears that new organisms released into the environment to clean up pollution would be akin to adding new pollution. She has called for new safety evaluations against misuse and abuse by the military and terrorists. However, it has been noted that the synthetic organism would not be able to survive outside of the environment created for it, thus avoiding Prince Charles' once fabled fears of a global 'grey goo' takeover. Venter has already begun discussions regarding new biological and ethical regulations and accountability to prevent misuse of the technology.

Meanwhile, University of Cambridge geneticist Dr Gos Micklem admitted that cheaper, established methods for genetic engineering already exist and Synthia would not necessarily supersede these techniques. Likewise, others have noted that GM foods were also thought to be the next best thing, but have failed, due to resistance from the public. Cloning has also failed the public test, which has moratoriums on its development in many countries. This new bio-tech could yet fall by the wayside. The public do not like the idea of life being manipulated, even for their own good. Time will tell if the results of Venter's work will overcome that resistance.

So is Venter playing God? No, the synthetic life form was not created from scratch. The DNA had existed before, but it and its host cell had been manipulated, before Synthia could live. But even if Venter had created new life from nothing, it would still be a far cry from creating an animal or a human being. Venter's achievement is on the bottommost rung of being a God. He has a long way to catch up. But whether the experimentation continues, the latest bio-genie is out of the bottle and everyone will be wishing that Synthia is a gift and not a curse.

15/Jun/2010

Why the human race is doomed to extinction

Intelligent Extinction

It struck me, while reading Bill Bryson's "A Short History of Nearly Everything" that we humans are really here by the skin of our teeth. Our ancestors have dodged every single extinction event going for millions of years. They bided their time in holes, up trees, and avoided being eaten, until we became the predominant species. For those who advocate Intelligent Design for our existence, this writer would have to counter with Intelligent Extinction. Someone, something, somewhere in the universe has favoured directed extinction so that we could be here today —and gone tomorrow.

Think about it. There are creatures that once lived who survived tens of millions of years as a species only to be wiped out by meteor impacts, volcanic cataclysms, violent climate change, etc., which favoured the creation and perpetuation of a furry mammal that would one day evolve and dominate the Earth. There were species with more or less the same characteristics as their close neighbours, but where one type died out and the other lived. There are so many inconsistencies in extinctions that one can't help but think that something wanted humans to evolve.

Did the other species fail in some way? Were they not wanted anymore? All the ancient water creatures, plants, all the reptiles, dinosaurs, and past mammals seemed to have served their purpose and produced the right environment for the next species to dominate until we humans arrived. Intelligent Extinction is of course an anthropocentric and scientific view on how humans got here. So, did extinctions happen because we humans were meant to be?

We may be the shortest lived of the major species that have ever lived, but we have demonstrated our superiority in civilisation over longevity. The Earth could wipe us out in an instant and any future extraterrestrial visitors would never know of our presence after a few millennia. In our pursuit to live life to the fullest, we could be causing our own extinction. Indeed, some environmentalists believe that the Sixth Great Extinction is happening now, possibly caused by humans, but happening on a scale that we cannot see clearly. However, what kind of world would we leave behind and what would come next?

Maybe the Earth is looking for the right animal to inhabit it and thus is its own intelligent designer. Then there is no need for an external or supernatural source for life. The Earth is its own source of life and knows what it prefers. When an Earthly or cosmic event shatters the prevailing ecosystem, the Earth helps design a new environment for new species to evolve. Likewise, the new species help the Earth to thrive. Evolution through natural selection is strong enough on its own, but it helps that the Earth is with you and not against you. But if a species reaches the tipping point of destroying enough of the biosphere then Earth will retaliate with an extinction event. This does not denote intelligence on Earth's behalf, just the fact that Earth is a reactionary system and sensitive to changes made by its inhabitants.

Most of this is part of the Gaia Hypothesis laid out by James Lovelock, but Intelligent Extinction would go further and say that Earth, as a natural system, wants to reach a state of equilibrium; whether chaotic or not. And just as the Universe tends toward entropy so does the Earth; thus it will search for the right organism to attain that state. But if that organism does not provide the right requirements or goes too far then Earth will reciprocate and find an organism that will. Hence us humans; we are a chaotic species by nature. Right now in this time, we are right for Earth's needs. But is climate change tipping things too far? We have extended the normal interglacial, balancing a warm Earth with glacial caps, unique in Earth's history. We are using non-replenishing resources and killing off many species which are necessary for land and sea stewarding. We are the intelligent species, yet may be causing our own extinction.

This is the true Intelligent Extinction. Earth hasn't hit back hard, yet. The cosmos has not sent down hurling meteors or solar flares to destroy us. It is we Homo sapiens, the wise man, causing the self-inflicting wounds. We won't be here forever. We are readying the Earth for the next organism to succeed us. It could take a thousand years or millions of years, but it will happen. Intelligent Extinction is inevitable.

25/Jun/2010

Science & Technology - Cosmology
What is the theory of dark fluid

What is Dark Fluid?

There is so much darkness in the universe, no more so than man's knowledge about what is out there and what it is made of. We used to think we knew the Standard Model, but every so often a new theory arises and filters through the scientific consciousness and darkens the cosmic waters again. Enter: Dark Fluid.

First, we had Dark Matter to explain the fact that there aren't enough visible stars or gas in the structure of galaxies to explain their high rate of rotation. This non-visible Dark Matter is so-called, because it is unseen and it does not interact with the light-bearing electromagnetic force. Second, came Dark Energy to explain that the universe was not only expanding, but accelerating in its expansion. This Dark Energy was accounted for by the fact that Type Ia supernovae in distant galaxies were fainter, and thus further away than expected. Lastly, there is Dark Flow, the controversial observation that certain galaxy clusters, indifferent to the prevailing cosmic microwave background radiation, are moving toward one specific universal location. Now we have another dark and mysterious conundrum regarding the universe.

Dark Fluid seeks to explain Dark Matter and Dark Energy as emergent properties of Dark Fluid. Theorised in 2008 by Dr HongSheng Zhao, a British astrophysicist at the University of St Andrew's School of Physics and Astronomy, he proposed that Dark Matter and Dark Energy are not separate physical phenomena with separate origins, but are "specific sub-effects of new extended laws of gravity at very large scales."

Dark Fluid sees the Einsteinian spacetime fabric as a fluid that flows, condenses, or expands just like any other fluid. Around matter, Dark Fluid slows down and thickens, drawing more space around it, intensifying the gravity around it, much as Dark Matter is supposed to do. Also, where there is less matter, as in interstellar space, Dark Fluid expands, stretching away from itself becoming like a repulsive force, which is the same effect as Dark Energy. Dark Fluid could also be the model behind Inflation (after the Big Bang), Quintessence (a negative pressure scalar field), MOND (Modified Newtonian Dynamics) and more.

But what is Dark Fluid made of? Is it the same stuff theorised to comprise Dark Matter? Are neutrinos, neutralinos, or gravitinos the missing matter, clumping and expanding to cause the emergent properties seen as dark matter and dark energy? Is there a prevailing neutralino field or force that is the key to understanding gravity on large scales? Dr Zhao believes efforts to find large dark-matter particles with the Large Hadron Collider at CERN will fail as Dark Fluid would be a low-energy particle, too low and undetectable for the Large Hadron Collider. However, Dark Fluid may point to the absence of dark-matter particles. Dark Fluid may not be particles of energy, but just a modification of the law of gravity.

So if Dark Fluid is a modification of gravity then are gravitons its primary component? If neither gravitons nor neutrinos, or neutralinos are discovered or are not responsible for any of the Dark materials, then could a new particle, a hypothesised graviphoton perhaps (which can be repulsive in force), be responsible? How can a force be attractive and repulsive at the same time? Would Dark Fluid matter change, depending if it manifested as Dark Matter or Dark Energy? Can Dark Fluid be hot, cold or warm like Dark Matter? Just as water can freeze, become liquid, and turn into gas; the same material under different conditions, can Dark Fluid have differing effects and manifestations under different cosmic conditions? If space is basically a super-fluid stretching and contracting according to the matter around it, Dark Fluid could cause varying effects which to the outside observer would seem to be several different manifestations, when in fact it is just the same phenomenon reacting in different ways.

In this writer's speculative opinion, Dark Fluid's properties are similar, yet different to water. Assuming Dark Fluid concentrates around other matter; its relative particle temperature should fractionally increase due to pressure, friction, drag, density, etc, thus it should expand like liquid water or gas. Hence, around large cosmic structures like galaxies there should be less gravitational effects/less density (Dark Matter) but more energy/more velocity (Dark Energy). Galaxies should have flown apart. But the opposite is true. The gravitational force, though weak, must be binding the Dark Fluid as a cohesive unit. This manifests as Dark Matter.

Liquids contract in the cold. Hence, interstellar space should have large masses of cold, clumped Dark Fluid and be less energetic. But the opposite is true. Dark Fluid expands in the 'colder' regions of interstellar space as when water turns to ice. Thus Dark Fluid's density is lower than surrounding space, thus it floats away at an accelerated rate. Gravity, as a weak force, cannot bind the particles together. This manifests as Dark Energy.

So is Dark Fluid the answer? Whatever the properties of Dark Fluid and its relationship to Dark Matter and Dark Energy, there is much to ponder. Many different cosmological models turned out to be part of the same String Theory. Dark Matter and Dark Energy may be strings on the same Dark Fluid bow. Maybe Dark Flow is Dark Fluid heading down the universal drain. At the moment, Dark Fluid is an elegant theory, which answers many questions, is testable through existing models, and makes predictions. How long that lasts is a Dark Mystery.

Sources:

http://en.wikipedia.org/wiki/Dark_fluid
Link still active as of September 2020

http://www.sciencedaily.com/releases/2008/01/080131094056.htm
Link still active as of September 2020

Gilliland, B. 2010. A shot in the dark: Has Jupiter led science astray? Metro, June 18, 2010, p 22-23.

21/Jul/2010

Science & Technology - Cosmology
Philosophical arguments on whether
mankind should go to Mars

Mars: Spiders, Ants, and Bees

Francis Bacon, the 17th century natural philosopher, once said "Knowledge is power" and that knowledge has been used to great effect in powering the civilisation we have today. However, the knowledge to power process has hit a prolonged snag in regards to taking Man's next giant leap onto Mars. And here, Bacon's new philosophy from 1620 sums it up nicely. In his work, *Novum Organum*, Bacon critiques natural philosophy of the bygone era. He describes sterile philosophical academics as spiders endlessly spinning silky and groundless philosophy. Then there are the ants of the automaton ilk; blindly and ceaselessly producing technology for the sake of it. Bacon favoured the bee, which like a real scientist sourced and gathered the best from nature in order to manufacture practical products. But Bacon's pre-Reformation ideas also relate directly to reforming a mission to Mars.

In the pre-space era and early space age, our spiders were ignorant of the realities on Mars and dreamt up fantastic scenarios and adventures. Even with probes and rovers preparing the way for man, spiders still held sway with reasons not to go to Mars; like costs, risks, and unrealised technology. But in our modern era the biggest spiders are evident in the political system. The political science advisors spin endless philosophical yarns on space policy, trapping the unawares in webs of circling logic, rhetoric, and Obamaian platitudes so the public are unable to penetrate the true meaning of the words. These scientific courtiers theorise, lobby, pontificate, and set up lofty commissions. The spiders dragged their sticky heels through the tangled Augustine Commission report making airy and eerie pronouncements on the future of manned space. We do not need these spiders to lead us onto Mars. Spiders are the past; yet crucially and unfortunately, they hold the power, but without the knowledge.

Ants have been around for countless generations inventing, assembling, and engineering the Industrial revolution. But ants became more prevalent after WWII, eager to manufacture the future; usually through nuclear power. With all due respect and without denigrating all their rocket science brilliance and heroic endeavours, NASA became a giant ant colony creating a self-sustaining contracts organisation and producing the space shuttle industry –going nowhere, but soldiering on. The subsequent ISS is the ants' colony in space with 'antonauts' feverishly shuttling back and forth like leaf-cutter ants in Soyuz spacecraft, building and feeding as if programmed. Ants are technology-driven; their destination determined by what technology they can make. The latest ants' inventions are the unmanned probes toiling away on and around Mars. For the technologist ant, their machines will always be evolving as needed, but they will never be as sophisticated, wide-ranging, or as adaptable as humans. Ants have promise, but their potential has to be reformed and directed into one defining mission. Ants have the knowledge, but lack the power to make things happen without the spiders' authority.

We need bees; and lots of them. Bees pollinate; they make the world like honey, they help nature bear fruit and many other things besides. Without bees humanity would crumble; some say within five years. The ultimate bee project was Apollo, which bore fruit for a scant ten years. We lost those bees after Apollo and manned spaceflight shrivelled to low Earth orbit. Bees are experience-seekers and destination-driven, their waggling technology determined by their mission. A Mars mission with international bees might not be as pretty as a butterfly, but even an improbable and ungainly bumblebee will fly. Bees, especially from private corporations, will counter the spiders and the take the best from the ants, producing useful things. They know how to work in the spidery political realm and be rewarded with the necessary funding and public endorsement for their work. For a mission to Mars, bees will have to pollinate the political landscape so that the leaders can taste the golden dream. Bees also get the best from ants by inspiring them into action with clear directives and end goals. To get to Mars, bees will have to tap into the vast ant technological database and manual skills pool. Bees recognise knowledge is power, but they have to navigate through the intricate webs of politics and harness the labour of the ants.

Only by working together with empirical bees in the ascendancy will Mankind ever get to Mars. Spiders need to direct their thoughts on the reality of a Mars mission. Ants need to adapt their mechanistic manner.

Francis Bacon would be astonished today that mankind still has not learned from his natural philosophy from four hundred years ago and put the busy bees in charge. Hopefully, our 21st century bees will become Bacon's latter day reformers on Mars.

20/Oct/2010

Sciences & Technology - Cosmology
The history and future of the universe

The Past and Future Universe

October 2010 – the TV science programme 'Horizon', examined the theories of what came before the Big Bang by several prominent physicists. The notion that anything could come before the Big Bang has been dismissed by many who cannot fathom such a concept or who still abide by a God-made universe. But thinking of a time before the Big Bang is no longer a fringe idea.

According to some theories, the Big Bang may not even have happened at all and our universe may have been preceded by another one. One factor in theorising the non-Big Bang was that of cause and effect. We humans can see the effect of the Big Bang; an expanding universe through which cosmologists can peer back 10^{-34} seconds to after the Big Bang. But what caused its formation 13.7 billion years ago? What came before it? And what would it look like? Horizon queried the theorists.

Nothingness into Something:
Professor Michio Kaku thinks that the nothingness from which the Big Bang arose, needs to be redefined. While there's a state of absolutely nothing (no time, space, energy, etc) there is also the nothingness of the vacuum, which in reality is only the absence of matter. In Kaku's version of the pre-Big Bang universe, a high-energy vacuum existed where the energy temporarily transformed into matter. One of these transformations became self-sustaining causing a chain-reaction, which led to the Big Bang. So rather than absolutely nothing producing the universe; there was just nothing, which became something.

Eternal Inflation:
At Stanford University, Professor Andre Linde thinks the Big Bang idea is flawed. The universe is relatively smooth and ordered materially, not something that could have emerged from the chaos of a Big Bang. He now thinks that not only did Inflation greatly expand the size of the universe just after the Big Bang, hence the universe's smoothness, but that Inflation was the creation event. Further, Linde posits Inflation as

an eternal process with countless other universes, which sit in a 'heavy vacuum' superstructure, inflating from each other, like bubbles in Swiss cheese. Above all, Inflation has seen many of its predictions about the universe emerge, which some of the other theories have not.

The Big Bounce:
It is well known that Classical Newtonian theory and Quantum Mechanics do not mix, but Dr. Param Singh has discovered a possible paradigm-shifting mathematical equation that could explain the Big Bang. Classical theory breaks down when approaching Quantum levels, bringing with it problems with Infinity. But Singh's ingenious mathematical formula using both Classical and Quantum theory equations revealed that the attractive force of the contracting universe became repulsive before a singularity was achieved. In other words, as the universe collapsed, before it could reach zero, the force became repulsive, rebounding to create a new universe. This Big Bounce could be an eternal and cyclical event making new universes each time. [But if Singh's formula is so revolutionary, how come the world at large has not heard of it, á la the great formulae of Newton and Einstein?]

Black Hole babies:
What do you get when you mix Darwin and Einstein? Cosmological Natural Selection. Professor Lee Smolin is convinced that Black Holes are the progenitors of other universes. As with evolution, Smolin sees ancestor universes with black holes living and dying, sucking in matter and energy, and spewing them out into a new universe. Do universes evolve? Perhaps like Stephen J. Gould's Punctuated Equilibrium, nothing happens for a long time and then –Bang! A new species of universe evolves?

Brane game:
Neil Turok, the Director of the Perimeter Institute for Theoretical Physics, believes that the universe sits on a 3D brane (short for membrane), which floats in a higher dimension with at least one other brane. At some point, the branes collide, releasing energy, and a new universe is the result. This is a sharp paradigm shift and an idea still in progress.

The Future Past:
What happens at the end of the universe? Professor Sir Roger Penrose sees the end of our cooled and expanded universe possessing no time or mass, just photons. The photons convert into energy, which at some point explode resembling a Big Bang event. However, this is no point of nothingness, the old remotely-stretched universe becomes the focal point of the new Big Bang, negating the need for an infinitely small singularity point. From our point of view, the explosion would look like a small origin point but in fact, a whole photonic universe would be the source. An elegant theory.

Waves and Strings:
Perhaps the most complex idea belongs to Dr. Laura Mersini-Houghton. Mersini-Houghton realised that the universe could be represented as a wave function and used with String Theory equations. Such an equation explained the whys of the universe's birth and survival in relation to a Big Bang. But even more important is that her theory predicted three (now observable) separate and unexplained cosmological phenomena not seen by the other theories; namely, the existence of Dark Flow, voids in the Cosmic Microwave Background, and discrepancies with the temperature of space. These seemingly point to the effects of neighbouring universes.

How to prove them:
While these theories compete, there are at least two instruments which while seeking confirmation of the Standard Model could prove or disprove some of the theories. The Low Frequency Array (LOFAR) radio telescope, when built, will be able to see backward one billion years after the Big Bang and check for the randomness of material in the universe, verifying or disproving Inflation. Meanwhile, the Laser Interferometer Gravity-wave Observatory (LIGO) in Louisiana searches for gravity waves caused by the Big Bang. But any results could take decades.

The elephant in the room:
However, a main point not addressed among all the counter proposals was that the theories seemed very compatible on complicated levels, as if feeling around the proverbial elephant. The maths and philosophy may be different, but there were more commonalities, which didn't seem to be appreciated and discussed. Each wanted their own theory to win

out. Surely they all remember how String Theory started out as several strands only to be recognised as many pieces of one stringy puzzle.

For instance: Michio Kaku's high-energy vacuum of nothingness resembles Penrose's future photonic state of the universe. The resultant energy burst could manifest as Inflation or the repulsive Big Bounce of Linde and Singh, respectively. The effect is a Mersini-Houghton-type universe, with accurate predictive qualities for the existence of other universes. Whether the beginning and end of the universe is played out on branes is another matter, plus black holes may have a role in restricting or ameliorating such cosmic processes. Perhaps there are shared emergent properties which could be discovered.

While the origins, mathematics, resultant outcomes, and predictions of each theory are different, the over-arching themes seem to point to a complex relationship between all the theories. However, it seems that the stellar personalities involved are the real unknowns. Horizon will no doubt follow up on the theories depicted and hopefully by then the main contenders will resolve any commonalities and come together with one grand and unified theory.

11/Mar/2011

Science & Technology - Cosmology
Alternative theories of the universe

The Gender of the Universe

2020 vision

Of course, as with humans, gender can mean more than just male, female or neuter. The fluidity of gender can slide up and down a scale and I have no doubt that universes, galaxies, stars, and planets, and constituent atoms inhabit that scale in ways humans cannot fathom. Why should living organisms be the only ones to have gender? Quantum and classical particles and their macro structures may have gender in their own way. And if we are made of star matter, then our parental cosmos are our star daddies or mommies.

Does the universe have a gender? Which sex would it be? We humans brand everything male or female or perhaps gender neutral, but what if gender extended right down from the Newtonian universe to the quantum universe? Our cars are 'old girls', airplanes and ships are emblazoned and adorned with female images, trains gendered by their names, and even countries have gendered names being the Motherland or the Fatherland. Our world is the Goddess/'bio-spheric' spirit of Gaia. As we investigate further into the depths of the universe, we may find that our understanding of gender reaches much deeper than we thought.

The universe is awash with gender, ascribed to it by humans with our planets named for male or female Gods; the moon is Luna and the sun – the masculine Sol. Even stars, constellations, and galaxies (when not under sexless NGC numbers) have gender through names like Centaurus, Orion, and Andromeda. Galaxies could be clusters of stars drawn together not just by gravity, but through the attractive force of gender and sex, as material is thrown across the cosmos to fertilise new stars, solar systems, and ultimately, life. And as humans are made from star dust, it may not just be a natural tendency to ascribe gender randomly, but a biological imperative to impart gender to the universe, because we humans have an intrinsic feeling that the universe is a gendered entity. The only thing which precludes us from acknowledging and pursuing this theory is our own scientific and cultural bias and lack of deep cosmological understanding.

Put forth, here, is a new radical theory of the physical universe:

1. The universe has a gender.

2. This gender arises from the fact that all atoms and their constituent parts (from quarks, electrons, protons, neutrons, etc) also have gender.

3. The quantum nature of the particles allows for gender to be ascribed to the universe and that while gender may or may not change, the gender affects the properties and nature of the Newtonian universe.

**

1. The universe has a gender:

Whether the universe is male or female, we may never know. But why should this be so? The universe may have a gender stemming from its emergent constituent parts, which also have a gender, thus conferring upon the universe a distinct gender. As human genders have differing structural and genetic natures, so the sex of the universe could be visualised through the universe being flat or curved, due to its 'genetic' make-up.

Two recent studies discovered distinct characteristics of the universe: its sound and its colour. If the universe was likened to an animal, it could be a large flat, beige whale in a multiverse singing a universal song in order to attract a mate or navigate its way. Procreating could involve two universes (or branes) colliding together to produce a baby universe in a Big Bang. Such speculation may be too far, but you get the picture: the universe may not be a sexless entity.

2. The gender of the universe arises from the fact that all atoms and their constituent parts also have gender:

Baryons and mesons are made up from varying numbers of quarks, the particles of which have a spin (a quantum property which imparts magnetic nature) of a whole or half integer. The spin, charge, or other inherent qualities may representative of differing genders. Quarks, with their flavours (Charm, Strange, Up, Down, Top, and Bottom) could be the gender imparters, akin to the hypothetical graviton which imparts gravity, and the equally hypothetical Higgs which imparts mass upon particles. The amount and combinations of quarks could be the gender initiators.

So while quarks make up electrons, protons, and neutrons, which in turn make up atoms, which in turn make up atoms within all elements; materials such as Oxygen could be male, while Helium could be female, for instance. Some elements already produce 'daughters' within isotopes from radioactive decay, but the make up of elements within genes could be the initial factor when creating a human baby's gender. So emerging from the gender of quarks could be the determined outcome of a human's sexual world.

3. The quantum nature of the particles allows for gender to be ascribed to the universe:

Even within quantum theory, strings may be male or female. Their 'vibrational' natures may be representative of their gender imparting a gender upon all things in the universe. A rival to String Theory is Loop Quantum Gravity, where there are no particles or strings, but finely-weaved gravity fields of loops which 'fold' in varying ways to create the familiar quantum structures. The directions in which the loops fold could also be gender indicators.

But can particles change gender? What could affect universal genders? There are five main candidates: 1. neutrinos, 2. vacuum energy, 3. Higgs field, 4. anti-particles, and 5. Superposition.

1. Neutrinos may be trans-gender as while they are known not to interact with other particles; they do change in nature while in flight through the cosmos due to high-energy collisions. Maybe the gender neutral electron-neutrino changes either into a male or female muon-neutrino or a tau-neutrino, which may affect gender in local regions.

2. The universe is not completely empty, with vacuum energy constantly pumping out new particles, their origin and nature unknown. But if vacuum energy spills out an equal number or disproportionate number

of male and female particles, then that could stabilise or upset the balance of universal gender. Gravity (gravitons) and dark energy may also be opposite genders one attractive, one repulsive, each having a different function due to their gender.

3. The theorised Higgs field may also impart mass upon particles depending upon their gender, thus also compensate to balance gender in the universe. Proportioning gender through mass, or vice versa, could explain the ratio of certain particles to others.

4. Anti-particles (such as the anti-electron or positron) probably do not differ in gender, but anti-matter does not exist in the same quantities as normal matter. For whatever reason, anti-matter did not evolve at the same rate as normal matter though gender issues may not be the cause.

5. In superposition, particles can exist in simultaneous states, maybe as both male and female, until a measurement fixes their gender. Just by exploring the universe, humans may be altering the gender of their cosmic surroundings. We perhaps should not talk of the Anthropic Principle, but also the Gender Principle when discussing why human life exists in the universe. Life may be dependent on the gender of the universe.

Lastly, even if spin, or charge, or matter/anti-matter nature is not a characteristic of atomic gender, this does not preclude the idea of gender. After all, these terms are human constructs and could actually be describing gender characteristics. If particles are gender neutral, then why do they not have gender? This brings up the deeper question about life and inorganic particles. Can inorganic particles have gender? Does gender mean having to be alive? We humans assume that gender means having physical sexual organs. While not being sexual in nature, particles may be asexual or procreate in a transformational manner through fusion or fission, since energy cannot be destroyed or created; only transformed. But if that transformation is gender driven, where more female particles create an electron or a proton, etc, then the state of the universe may be a reflection in the change of gender throughout its existence. The emergent properties of particle gender could be the reason for the structure of the universe.

The whole universe may be alive in ways human cannot measure or fathom. So with alpha male particles, Earth mothers, and daughter isotopes floating around the universe, will there ever come a time when we will know whether the universe is male or female? Who knows, but it is worth finding out.

Links still active as of September 2020

Universe sound:
http://phschool.com/science/science_news/articles/cosmic_melody.html

Universe colour:
http://www.newscientist.com/article/dn2013-the-universe-is-not-turquoise--its-beige.html

04/Jul/2011

Science & Technology - Cosmology
Alternative views on String Theory

Noisy Strings

Scientists often use the analogy of quantum strings as being like instrument strings, under tension and vibrating through dimensions. But they never talk about the quantum strings themselves making a sound. This always seemed peculiar. If strings were isolated from the vacuum would they make a noise and could that noise be detected by us? What would such noises tell us? Strings give rise to photons with which we use to see and also to phonons from which we can use to hear and make sound. It would seem reasonable that if a string was isolated in some ideal environment and through experiment, one would be able to hear the string as it vibrated.

Vibrating strings create our elementary world, whether perceived as a force or as thermal or electromagnetic or gravimetric particles. The emergent sound from quantum strings into classical particles can be picked up by radio-telescopes and analysed for their identification and to give their origin. Hence we have the static-sound of the Cosmic Background Microwave radiation left over from the Big Bang and even the sound of the universe itself.

When particles collide in the cavernous tubes of the Large Hadron Collider would they conceivably clash in a crescendo of noise along with the light and energy they emit? Is there an inherent sound quality that emerges from strings into the classical world? Would strings hum, or crackle, pop, whine, drone, or hiss? Would a string be a pure solitary tone or a combined note assemblage? Would the pitch be high, low, or off our human-held scales? Would the frequency be long or short bursts or something completely random? Could string sounds be super partners of 'normal' classical sounds we humans hear? Perhaps, as with trying to physically detect strings, their sound would be far and away beyond our detection range. Noisy strings could reveal the rhythm of universe, the heartbeat of a dimension; quantum sounds in the cosmic darkness.

So, why is string noise important? Why can't we hear them, if indeed they do squeak? What kind of frequencies would they emit at? And could string noise be formulated and used in equations? If physicists think about such things, here are a few proposed answers.

Why would string noise be important?
Each particle, dimension, universe might have its own vibrational frequency; hence its own sound and identification. Photons are strings that bring forth light and phonons (a quantum of vibrational energy in the acoustic vibrations of a crystal lattice) are strings that herald sound. Strings can be open or closed (the former represented by the weak nuclear, strong nuclear, and electromagnetic forces; the latter making up the proposed graviton). Knowing which sound characterised which string-type particle may preclude scientists from having to see the string, when they could just listen to it.

Why can't we hear strings?
One theory could be related to the Heisenberg Uncertainty Principle in that even if we could see the strings we could not hear them due to the uncertainty of their probability in location or velocity. In trying to listen to the string we would alter the ability to detect it because of the act of interference of the measurement. As with pinpointing the position and momentum of atoms, or its direction of spin, we could do only one with certainty and thus with sound we could only measure certain aspects of it, an echo of it so to speak, if at all.

What kind of frequencies would strings emit at?
Strings may be transmitting sound through higher dimensions. Different strings may emit different sounds. Each higher dimensional and particle may have its own unique sound. We cannot see strings, but suppose we could hear them and use the sound to interpret the type of other universes or particles out there. In an analogy, suppose you were walking past a zoo with a large wall separating you from the menagerie on the other side. You could not see the animals, but on walking past you could hear trumpeting, roaring and tweeting. You would then interpret the sounds as elephants, lions, and birds. Further, you could theorise the type and size of those animals' environments and maybe predict their behaviour. With strings, if they had sound and cosmologists could hear them, perhaps they could interpret the environment around the string and its properties.

How could string noise be formulated?
A whole new quantum mechanical discipline could take shape. Perhaps Quantum Audiodynamics (QAD) would be its designation. As sound can be musical and music 'translated' into mathematical formula, the underlying quantum structure of the universe may be more related to sound than we thought. What would a formula in Quantum Audiodynamics look like? Would such formulae be interconnected to current mathematical formulae? Are there mathematical formulae which describe the noise of strings? Such an emergent set of mathematical formulae could aid in the hunt for a Theory of Everything. Surely sound, as with light, energy, and mass would help fill out the fabric of the universe.

So, are strings noisy? We do not know. But it would be important to think that they are. String Theorists have come a long way by thinking out of the box. And in the cosmic symphony of theories and particles, string sounds could be another element of the Theory of Everything that strikes the right note.

11/Nov/2013

Science & Technology – Cosmology

Mars: What Are We Waiting For?
Who Do We Need Permission From?

2020 vision

It looks like Elon Musk's SpaceX is leading the way to get humans to Mars. They are building spaceship after spaceship and testing them to their limits, something NASA could never do due to budget, engineering, and political constraints. Commercial space companies are just too agile for wieldy governmental agencies who will have to buy space on their competitor's spacecraft. Musk has a vision for Mars; all his current companies are geared to this (SpaceX, Tesla, SolarCity) and within the next decade humans will be on our way to Mars.

How close are we in getting to Mars? Currently, there is not an international collaborative Mars strategy between nations, space agencies, private companies or the media. The Mars Society chapters have been lobbying and hoping for years, but maybe it is time to start new (or explore old) debates, start looking at new ways to publicise manned Mars missions, find new avenues to raise funds, and determine new ways to involve other countries, agencies, and individuals. We are no nearer in getting to Mars. What can we do about it?

Martian politics:

Our politicians are not the leaders of old. They do not have the vision beyond their short office terms to commit to a manned Mars mission within a 10-year time scale, which is feasible. And to our detriment we are only telling them, not showing them what a Mars mission will do. Words will fall upon deaf ears. Words won't get us to Mars, actions will. We cannot rely on the 'can't do' attitude of the politicians. There will be no political Mars solution.

Concurrent to the problem of lackadaisical politicians is the issue of permission to go to Mars. It occurs to me that every time I see Robert Zubrin at a Senate committee hearing lobbying for a Mars Mission he is talking to the wrong people for decisions on Mars missions. These sessions, and others like it, just seem to be a succession of debates, designed to gain various permissions from Congress, NASA, funding committees, etc, at the end of which nothing of significance leading to a Mars mission would be done.

So do we need permission to go to Mars? If so, from who? If not, then what can the combined Mars Societies do to make a manned Mars mission a reality?

New Mars Society goals:
The combined Mars Societies should make it their goal to get things started beyond the volunteer and lobbying stages. We are the ones who want the manned Mars missions, not the politicians. To that end, we should make it our goal to raise, say, $5 million over 5 years to show our ambition and commitment in making a Mars mission happen. Is a 5-year goal ambitious? Very, but what else can we be?

Crowd funding: We should raise money directly for Mars missions and put into a Global Mars Society fund: monies for training, infrastructure (cargo fees, space centre fees, etc), rocket usage fees, and hiring the necessary people with the technological and scientific expertise for the job. More fund raising could involve highly, lucrative sponsored Mars reality-TV/Springwatch type programmes at MDARS and especially at FMARS and any subsequent MARS Arctic 365. The analogue astronauts would be conducting the same outreach activities as Mars astronauts in the near future, so why not practice it now on a global audience to get the public interested and involved.

United Nations Mars:
No nation will take unilateral missions to Mars, not even China, who will take another 10-15 years to gain the experience the other manned-space nations and ESA have. Subsequently, there should be an integrated international Mars mission programme. Perhaps the UN should be brought on board to spearhead the Mars campaign. If they are already, then the UN needs to be more vocal about it. People need to know that this will be an international effort with a purpose and not just a technical exercise. There are many conventions regarding space under the auspices of the UN. The United Nations Office for Outer Space Affairs (UNOOSA) promotes international cooperation in the peaceful uses of outer space and also prepares and distributes reports on space science

and technology, and international space law. One such report discusses the human habitation of Mars[1]. A collaborative Mars programme should be instituted so that all nations have an invested interest in a Mars mission.

International Mars Taxes:
Would individual nations donate towards a Mars mission fund? Could a 'Mars Tax' introduced whereby $1 per person in the world would be annually raised, putting billions into the Mars pot. Those billions could pay for the first years of the Mars mission. Such a tax could be balanced between nations; means-tested to avoid nations paying more or less than needed. The Mars Tax would be an inclusive project enabling nations to invest and participate in the process of building the programme and getting their populations involved. Such tax schemes would enable Mars missions to be more visible and readily accepted by people, for they would have a more direct interest.

The key to Mars:
The most important factor relating to Mars missions is in convincing people we are ready to go to Mars. So how should this be done? By demonstrating we can provide the key for the Mar missions: survivability. Back in 1990, Robert Zubrin and others at Martin Marietta Astronautics built and tested an In-Situ Propellant Production system (ISPP) capable of producing rocket fuel (Methane and Oxygen) from the Martian atmosphere (for the return journey to Earth)[2] as part of a future Mars Sample Return mission. Though the system was criticised by other engineers for not being efficient enough, it was applauded by others as a key component of a Mars mission.

The ISPP system should be the cornerstone of the Mars missions. It should be paraded through the corridors of power to show the can't-do politicians that there is a practical application to the Mars missions. But where is the ISPP now? Have modifications been made to satisfy the critics? Does it actually work? Yes? Then let's build more! And furthermore, just don't keep testing it on Earth. Its place is on Mars! So let's send it to Mars! Feature it in documentaries or on YouTube spots about Mars missions. It might be boring to look at, but showing the mechanical and chemical processes of how man will be able to 'live off the land' and survive on Mars will convince politicians, space agencies, the media and the public of the viability of Mars missions. Telling people how it will work is not good enough. They have to see it working, believe it can work, evaluate and repeat the tests. An ISPP test bed has to go to Mars for people to really understand that a Mars mission is achievable!

There are engineers out there who would gladly give their eye teeth to work on such a project. How long would the ISPP take to build now? How much would it cost now (back in 1990 it was $47,000). There are companies who would also give their all in time, research, resources, and money to help sponsor such projects; companies with a stake or potential stake in future Mars missions like aerospace companies, energy companies, pharmaceutical and agricultural companies, communication, transport, and financial companies, etc would all have an interest and stake in funding a Mars mission to increase their own growth and future success.

Once the ISPP system is proven, we have the basis of the whole Mars mission in place and waiting to go. So, send it and they will come: the politicians, the scientists, space agencies, media, and the public. There will always be critics and 'Earth Firsters', but in the end we would need people to stay behind on Earth anyway.

Mars Businesses:
If space entrepreneurs like Paul Allen, Jeff Bezos, Robert Bigelow, Sir Richard Branson, Elon Musk, Dennis Tito, the X-Prize Foundation, and others want to prove their space worthiness then they should be pooling their resources together to form an organisation (where for profit or not for profit) dedicated to promoting, developing, and launching technologies and systems to go to Mars. Let's get the ISPP on one of Musk's Falcons or other launch system and send it to Mars. There is nothing like a field demonstration to prove a point. The ISPP and rocket delivery system would be the first elements to be built and tested. Focus: that is what we need; an interconnected, integrated Mars mission programme and these space entrepreneurs and others could help provide that impetus to get to Mars.

And so we come back to the politics of Mars. We're falling into the trap of thinking like our predecessors. The government used to run everything. But no longer. Private space industries are a growing force. They have the know-how and can-do attitudes. We don't need to rely on the government as our main partner in Mars. We need to be self-starters and to build our own Mars businesses and Mars missions.

Does this all sound too simplistic, idealistic, or naïve? Perhaps, but we need to start new debates and challenge the status quo. People want to know the 'what', 'why' and 'how' regarding the Mars missions. We are stuck in a rut telling people what we want to do. We need to physically demonstrate how we will survive on Mars. That is vital. Some people will never understand why manned Mars missions are needed. That is not their vision. But we can still trust the rest of the world to believe in a manned Mars mission. So, what are we waiting for? Who do we need permission from?

Links and further information:

UNOOSA -http://www.unoosa.org/pdf/pres/stsc2013/tech-43E.pdf Link active as of September 2020.

Zubrin, R. 1996. *The Case For Mars* – The Plan to Settle The Red Planet and Why We Must.

23/Nov/2013

The Superstring God

2020 vision

Whether we are Exergy machines for the universe, or God-made or God-free, or holograms lost in a nameless gender-fluid universe, humanity has it rough. We are living without a reason for being, without a destination, at the whim of the cosmos. What is out there for us? Or are we to look within? Time, if it exists, will tell. Or maybe not...

In Brian Greene's 'The Hidden Reality' (2011), there was one line which caught my imagination concerning branes and Holographic Universes: '...strings that move, vibrate, and wiggle along the branes themselves...' (pg 263) It is an intriguing line, with provocative images of strings living some sort of life on the edges of reality casting their quantum shadows over the rest of creation, including us humans. In one version of the multiverse, we humans may just be holographic reflections of string interactions from a higher plane of reality's boundary.

Think of Princess Leia in Star Wars when her hologram shoots out of R2D2. The image is a product of lines, etchings and light combining on a 2D surface to form a 3D image. Similarly, strings may also have the ability to produce holographic images. Definitively described by Argentinian string theorist Juan Maldacena in the late 1990s, Maldacena envision that '...branes influence their immediate environment gravitationally'. Maldecena made the connection that the moving strings on the brane and the brane's action upon spacetime are the same natural condition, but from different perspectives. More technically, open strings can move within and through the brane, while closed strings can travel off the brane and through all spacetime. Strings and their interactions produce everything we see in the universe, including us. We are holographic projections, though we live and think because of strings in the 'real' reality.

It is an insight that is truly amazing. It makes you think what really is life. Are strings the true lifeforms in the multiverse and humans just an after-thought through their brane-interactions? There is no suggestion that strings are alive, conscious and sentient, but they could represent the ultimate lifeform of the universe and we humans and everything in the universe are a consequence of their interaction on the edges of branes. This could be the very process and defining argument as to how inorganic becomes organic.

Think of a two-dimensional string you. That is the real you living on the boundary of a brane. But it is a string you. So is the string you alive or just doing what comes naturally by moving in and through branes. If strings were alive somehow then they would be a higher lifeform. If strings are the makers of everything we perceive and experience then they are God. Strings are everywhere —omnipresent: the all-pervading alpha, omega, and beyond of the universe. Strings are all powerful -omnipotent: creating and controlling all the forces of the universe, including gravity. Strings are all-knowing – omniscient: forming the laws and rules of the universe. Strings don't need to be alive to do this, it's something they do. It's their nature; they move, vibrate and wiggle -and behold, there was light! And everything followed in a flash, a very big one.

If there is a God then it is pulling the strings, because God is a string. And strings work in mysterious ways. Or maybe the strings themselves were made, in which case, it is back to square one. The strings may be sentient so while we are looking for God in the biggest of spaces —the universe- God may be in the smallest: God is a superstring who thought big. That's what creators do - think big!

Source:
Greene, B. 2011. The Hidden Reality.

03/Sept/2014

Mars, Media, and the Public

A Proposed Media Strategy for Popularising Mars Missions

2020 vision

This was not an article for Helium, though from my research it was started in 2009. Still incomplete, I may have intended it for the Mars Society UK journal, which then didn't work out. Though I had been accepted as the editor for the journal during our conference at the National Space Center, Leicester, in 2013, I couldn't ultimately fulfil the role due to other work commitments. And soon after the Mars Society UK Chapter had disbanded once again. But fear not, the Mars Society UK was resurrected in 2019 (and a London Chapter established in 2018) so all is not lost.

Recently a Mars University has been set up with academic courses each summer to educate and mentor those with visions of building professional careers geared towards Mars. That should capture the imagination of the young and experienced alike and establish more global Mars-orientated academic centres and businesses. And on that hearty note, this is the end of the Sciences section.

People of Earth, we are going to Mars! It will happen and it will happen within your lifetime. But how will you benefit from it? How will you be involved? What will Mars do for you?

A TV channel dedicated to Mars, whether sponsored/run by Discovery or National Geographic. There are more than enough old archive and current documentaries on Mars to keep the channel going, live feeds and interviews from NASA and other space agencies, experts and reports. It could even include book reviews, films (fiction and non-fiction), and access to FMARS (Flashline Mars Arctic Research Station) on Devon Island, Canada or MDRS (Mars Desert Research Station) in Utah, USA. Mars 365 would make a great reality TV show or even FMARS on TV – Discovery or Nat Geo TV? The channel does not have to be 24/7, but it can also be a PBS type set-up involving donations, whatever it takes to get the public interested.

Why wait for the future when we need to be doing it now. Fact files could be put on YouTube or other online outlets and also connected to radio and online shows. There has to be a total media integration to involve the and interest the public.

The Mars Society can play a big part in this, showing off Chapters around the world so there's an international feel to the channel with different countries producing different shows like their contests for robotic Mars exploration, other scientific developments, televised conferences. There is a vast opportunity here that is being missed.

This will bring Mars to the public without the subject being the niche preserve of 'nerds' and 'space cadets' as is perceived by the public. Mars exploration is about everyone. It is about their future.

Internet
Of course, the internet will be used to communicate with those during a mission to Mars, on Mars, and between Mars and Earth. I think domains like www.site.Mars and name@webmail.Mars should be created/protected by the Mars Societies. ICANN, the Internet Corporation for Assigned Names and Numbers. To apply for a top-level domain requires paying a fee of $185,000. Why now? This will pre-empt others, especially non-Mars related entities, from expropriating the sites and then being extortionate in releasing them.

If we get lapel badges they could be of the Martian flag (red, blue, green) design. Produce little (7.5" x 5.5") Martian flags to wave.

Society & Lifestyle

23/Jan/2008

Society & Lifestyle (Other)
Life isn't Perfect:
How to beat 'the system' and live successfully

We are the System

2020 vision
The show I was watching was 'The Wright Stuff', though I can't recall the celebrity panelist who stated 'it was just the system.'

While watching a TV debate about stress and illness in our society one of the panellists asked why they were on the rise. What caused it? Nothing, was the answer, they were products of the system. But I thought 'We are the system!' You, me, your family and peers, politicians, the media and the lady down the street -everyone from the bottom up has created the system, whether passively or actively endorsing it. And if things go wrong, then a share of the blame is upon us! So what are the systems that most affect our lives? They are social, political, judicial, corporate, technological, and media, among others.

I do not have the answers in this article. What answers there are is for you to decide, but hopefully this will make people think about the world around them and inspire others to make better choices and to find the answers.

Social
People have noticed how modern life causes stress though materialism, capitalism, advertising, progress, life-styling and more. Studies have shown that happier people seem to be less wealthy, because they are not materialistic workaholics, but conversely they have shorter lives, because they live in third-world countries or are less-privileged westerners. Wealthier citizens may have longer lifespans, but work too long, are more depressed, and are generally less happy in their lives. This is more prevalent in English speaking countries, or the 'Anglosphere': Britain, The U.S., Canada, and Australia. There seems to be a cultural schism, which sees certain societies inflicted with life-style diseases and other ailments.

565

So if we are locked into some kind of system where our lifestyles dictates our well-being, then what can we do to alleviate the stresses and fears within ourselves and others. I have been taught that my behaviour affects your behaviour, which affects my actions, which affects your actions. In other words the system begins with you. Our behaviour and actions are what creates laws to manage our behaviour and actions. As individuals who interact with others we could actually stem the course of more punitive laws by curtailing our behaviour within ourselves and towards others. This is not some namby-pamby, new age love-your-neighbour theme, but a way to look at oneself and decide what you want to do and how you want society to be. There are those who feel disadvantage or antagonistic toward society, but that is because they have made it so themselves by 'locking' into a supposed system way of thinking.

Politics
Everything is politics. People complain about the political systems, about crime, the food they eat, health care, public transport, the environment and immigration, etc. They blame the politicians and the system, but again we vote them in, or don't do, which can be just as bad and which I am guilty of. We hope for the best when we vote, but there is an element of cynicism creeping in and a realisation that many of these issues are about us as a society. Prominent politicians have said that there is no such thing as society or that our society is broken. In a way they are right; society has become individualised —each to his own and we do not take care or notice of each other. So the system breaks and the rules and bureaucracy created to fix it does not work because they were created to fix something that does not exist. The only way the system can be fixed is from the bottom up, with parents, family, and local communities setting the agenda. Government has become far too removed and centralised to know how to address the system. Government is trying to rectify this by devolving responsibility and delegating power to the local councils, but Government themselves are still in a centralised mode of behaviour and their behaviour ultimately affects our behaviour and actions. So unless the system changes and becomes an inverted pyramid with us at the top, then nothing will change.

Judicial
The Justice System has let society down many say, with lighter sentences and unfair laws giving criminals rights and more power than the victims.

Human Rights laws have made a travesty of court laws and victims have less protection than they ought to. Criminals are not rehabilitated in prison and re-offend more often than not. It is nonsense that criminals get to shroud themselves in human rights laws after they have breached them in the first place. Criminals are not victims of the system; they made a choice to transgress the system. They are responsible for their own actions and the system is no excuse. So when did the laws change? Who made it happen? We did —when we voted in politicians who then unceremoniously unshackled those laws and surrendered them to faceless bureaucrats and judges. Human Rights laws are now so liberal that they hurt the very people they are supposed to protect. The system is out of balance and we have to find some way to prevent system abuse.

Corporate

Corporate responsibility, transparency and flatter companies should be pushed for as the norm. With globalisation, monetary and policy concerns affecting the world, why are there no transparent global corporations? Why is there such a discrepancy between the top and the bottom workers' wages and a drive for astronomical profits? Don't forget money is a belief system; we have to trust a system where issued bills of paper have value. Some countries and cultures are not so dependent on monetary systems so their idea of wealth and 'wealth-being' is different. As an individual in a company —what is your goal, or path or ambition? Do you have to drive straight toward it or can you go sideways and feel more contented? Is there such a thing as a work/life balance where you can have what you want? The system here is rigid, but you can gain some 'wriggle room' if you really want to. So, downshift, delegate, transfer, quit; join, relocate, assume responsibility, get promoted —whatever it takes for you to shake the system and be the best and happiest you can be.

Technology

Why does the world have to progress faster and faster? We are demanding faster and more complex systems to run our lives. From wired to wireless, we are still entangled in energy and technology. When the 21st Century energy transition comes we had better be ready to transform ourselves, our lives and thus the system to work more in harmony with each other and the world; for like the oceans, humankind is one big connected system. There will be haves and have-nots and any transformation will have to include everyone or the system will remain distorted.

Media

The media, the biggest system manager, reflects the system in print, online, TV and radio form. They advertise, programme and show what we want to see, so we cannot complain about what is seen and heard. There is a perceived notion by the public that that news programmes cannot be fully trusted because of bias and spin by controlling authorities. Many news programmes do not ask the questions we want or bring up subjects that may offend the establishment, so people are sceptical, because they do not see the 'official events' as truly reflecting their worldview. Why do some media outlets show a perceived bias? Who controls the media and what do they gain from their subjective broadcasts? The public want more than a news desk reporter with repeating news. They want to know what else they may not be hearing, they want fresh perspectives, reassurance that their views are aired, and they want news with their questions answered. This system is all pervasive. You can turn off or tune out. Or you can make the news yourselves and become a non-system reporter. Most importantly, think; think for yourself and not system-think.

So how can the system be managed or even beaten? Can you be in the system and change it from within, withdraw from the system or fight it on the fringes? We can change our behaviour and actions to lessen the stress within life; we can be happy and wealthy whether physically, mentally or spiritually. We are the system. We created the problems and hopefully we will have the solutions.

25/Jan/2008

Relationships & Family – Gift Advice

Gift Ideas For A Best Friend

How well do you know your best friend? Over the years you have given and collected many gifts to and from them, but have they meant anything to you? How personalised were they? Were they thoughtful and meaningful gifts or were they just off-the-shelf last minute thoughts? Your best friend deserves a gift worthy of their friendship, so giving thought to that gift is pertinent. My gifts tend to be of the books, arts and crafts variety. Creativity is the key. The gift can be simple, non-extravagant, long lasting and personalised, so think of that person and what they mean to you.

First off, start with a card, preferably hand-made, with a front cover that suits your friend and a blank interior for your own personalised message that emphasises your long friendship and appreciation for them. This can be in the form of a poem or memories of friendship. If you have friends that have moved away, have started a family or have had changes in their life, then you can refer to that in the card to let them know that you empathise with them, that they are special, that they are not forgotten or under-appreciated. Your card will be a keep-sake; your hand-written word your bond of friendship. So, decide how your best friend makes you feel, write a few lines to be proud of and above all, be creative.

Favourite gifts of mine are gifts that involve daily or frequent interaction, so your friend remembers when they received it and from whom. Journals are a preferred choice of mine to give. A sturdy, hardback journal for the busy person, a budding writer, a frequent traveller, or a meticulous jotter, is a perfect gift. Again, the inside flap can contain a personalised message, giving the journal an old-fashioned feel. Blank pages can then be individualised by your friend giving an extra special meaning to that journal. It becomes part of the story of their life.

A book will also add a personal touch, especially if it piques your friend's interest or which means something to them. Books are underrated as presents, but the right book can stay with someone forever. Knowing your friend's interests will help, so make sure it is not a general weighty tome that anyone would read, make sure it is specifically tailor-made for your friend and would sit proudly on their shelf.

Creative gifts can include a model kit, if your friend is interested in airplanes, cars or whatever. It takes patience to build and when proudly displayed will remind your friend of the achievement of completing the task. If you had gone on a trip of a lifetime, then collect a memento and save it for prosperity (e.g. a small bottle of sea water, a special mineral or fossil). Label it, mount it or frame it and present it as a reminder of good times. One-off gifts from foreign places should reflect your friend's character. Scrapbooks and photo-albums can also be fun for keeping mementos and collecting memories from the past and adding those from times to come.

There are many shops with eclectic collections and unique gifts for almost anyone. So find that special shop and throughout the year, earmark those special gifts for your best friends. My best tips are to be creative, personalise your gift and try to keep it simple. Gifts do not have to be generic, extravagant or a fleeting moment of surprise. You appreciate your friend, so show it and give them a gift that truly reflects your feelings for them.

02/Feb/2008

Society & Lifestyle – Personal Morals & Values
Tips to good manners while walking in public

Good Manners: Walking Outdoors

2020 vision

This is still a big personal gripe of mine, especially in our social distancing times. Some people just have no concept of courtesy and would rather ignore you or argue with you on the street. But, I suppose as with the theme of the essay above and below, that is the system we live in. And the system is us.

Why do some people have no manners while walking in public? Even if I am in a rush, I make sure that I walk responsibly and do not hinder another pedestrian's path. Should there be some kind of walking etiquette taught to people so that they can be safer and aware while walking down the street? Here are some tips in the meantime.

There are times when you are walking down a high street, when all of a sudden someone pops out from a shop without looking, oblivious to your presence and you have to swerve out of their way and they still do not notice. They are 'street blind' seeing only what's in front of them. This kind of narrow focus could be dangerous if you are not aware of your immediate surroundings, from thieves, bike riders on pavements, other pedestrians and other hazards.

Being aware is very important as a pedestrian. As above, some people are blind to their surroundings and are not conscious of other people around them. As I am walking, I am looking at everyone and everything. I'm not paranoid or suspicious, but I do want to be more aware of who is around me, especially at night. It's my 'radar', my defence mechanism, always making me aware of my surroundings. My safety is important and if any one else is around, I would let them know that I see them. Don't be aggressive, or stare down people, but keep looking behind you every so often. Walk confidently and at an even pace; be in control of your own walking experience.

Amazingly, there are pedestrians who walk around reading books and listening to iPods, because they would be bored otherwise on their mundane trip to work. But at the same time, they are isolating themselves from other pedestrians, potential dangerous situations where they would need to instantly react, or they could be hit by the inevitable bicycle that runs the red light or rides on the pavement. I make walking more interesting by looking at and thinking about the environment around me, whether an urban setting or a less built up area. Too me, those isolated people are missing life, the hustle and bustle of the street.

When out walking, it's important to be able to anticipate people's movements if they are going to suddenly stop in front of me, start walking erratically or whatever. At bus stops there are always people who stand in the middle of the pavement blocking pedestrian progress, there are those slow walkers, people with unruly umbrellas, litter-bugs and loiterers, groups hogging the pavement, hand-holding couples, parents with baby buggies and tourists gently ambling about with backpacks. It takes patience, planning and concentration to anticipate their possible movements and reactions, and to avoid any accidents, making for a better walking experience for all.

Another way to experience a peaceful walk is by 'signalling', like in a car, but more subtlety when changing direction to make people aware you will be moving across them. It's not a complicated action, just by glancing behind you or using your peripheral vision you would be able to avoid bumping into people or cutting people off. Also by walking on the side of the pavement you need to enter a building instead of weaving about, you would also avoid any mishaps. Signalling can also include making people walk where you want them to. If a person is approaching you on the same 'walking plane', you can do a shuffle to alter the other person's direction or watch the other person's movements and leave them the space to move about themselves (usually through a puddle – just a joke!).

So what to do to those who cut you off or walk carelessly in front of you, especially on stairs? Unfortunately, I may resort to clipping their heels to let them know, but say sorry. Don't trip them, but they either move out the way or at least apologise for their 'supposed' walking transgression. It is not recommended, but necessary some times. Sometimes it is necessary to walk in the road just off the pavement to circumvent busy areas, pedestrian groups or other situations, but you should be careful, watching for buses, cars or bikes. Here again, anticipation of others' movement, or non-movement, is needed. Really, it's all about awareness and anticipation.

Walking is good exercise and relieves stress. It helps with digestion and gets creative juices flowing. Why should we let others spoil our walks? Remember, there are people out there who do not possess the grace, manners and the wherewithal to care about others while on the street. It is time we had some kind of general public campaign on the etiquette of walking along the street. Until then, do your best and happy walking.

09/Feb/2008

Society & Lifestyle - Social Values & Norms
Has British Society lost touch with the meaning of respect?

Pessimism in Britain

Whatever happened to the good old days? Even when things were going badly, there was still a sense of humour in the air, general trust and respect in society and government and the feeling that Britain was a nation to be proud of. But those sentiments seem to be missing and a pall of pessimism has shrouded our nation. Whether it is about crime, immigration, taxes, credit crunches, climate change or whatever, even in our relatively prosperous nation, we are not happy or at peace within ourselves. Is there nothing to be optimistic about in these times? And what are the elements creating this general malaise?

We always hear about unruly youths, yobs, gangs and hoodies, but never about the good kids. When we do emphasise the good kids, people always say –'Yeah, but what about the bad ones?'. We never seem to praise the good teenagers/young adults and this is bound to affect them and turn them into pessimistic adults and parents. They are the future of our country and need more positive role models and systems to work with. Hugging a hoodie might not be the answer, but communication is, through whichever medium –talking, music, sport, etc. Young adults need to know that they are not being neglected, scorned, or forgotten. This creates a base of respect and potential optimists.

Some politicians, rock stars, models, actors and other celebrities set bad examples in their behaviour and get away with it because of their 'star' status. If they were normal people some would be in jail, but because they have 'talent' or power they can flaunt the laws. People then get used to that idea, turn against normal values and support the 'victimised' celebrity. But if you cannot support, appreciate or admire your leaders and role models, then what is there left to aspire to? All you can do is emulate these 'fallen leaders' and become a wayward member of society. Some people reach too far in their ambition and their failure is too much to take. They develop insecurities, accept the unrewarding life given to them and forget about their own unrealised dreams. Self-respect and optimism for the future drains away as society also fails in its dreams, as there are no strong and positive leaders to show the way.

Because Britain is a 'build them up/knock them down' society, we expect mediocrity, whether from our sportsman, politicians and celebrities. We applaud failure if you have tried your hardest; yet play down victory and overt celebrations. Our sportsmen can go from heroes to scapegoat zeroes in days. This is probably because once upon a time sportsmen were once a part of their local communities, but now they are commercialised commodities and removed from their surroundings. People believe that they do not give back and thus do not deserve any more adulation than they need. So when local or national teams lose we take out our frustrations on them. Such feelings are almost alive in themselves and can either lift crowds' emotions or send them into despair. Sports are escapes from the drudgery of life and though a certain team might not be doing well, it does well to support them through thick and thin and savour the good times, while filtering out the bad times. Just like in life.

The media are very much to blame for our pessimistic society. The media is all doom and gloom, it is drama-induced, because people watch that more than warm-hearted 'And Finally' stories about stupid furry animals on skateboards. The media harps on about controversies, deaths and scandals because it makes for better reading/viewing and the public accepts and endorses that. It seems we thrill to the lowest denominator of man, we even identify with it, which is why we celebrate the underdog and cheer for the loveable rogue. Without drama in the world, we would be bored, complaining that 'nothing ever happens'. It is why we are hooked on conflict and violence in our TV shows, sports, news, books, etc. But what is important to remember is how we assimilate all this conflict. We can let it get us down, or we can learn from it and use it to create new challenges.

We Brits are impatient. We are apologetic complainers. We are reserved patriots and strangely pessimistic optimists. We are too self-critical and not appreciative of what we have, preferring to want more even if we do not need it. In a way, I think pessimism and stress drives us, it creates challenges to overcome and makes us feel better. But, pessimism is only good if there's light on the other side. It can promote soul-searching and resolution, but to wallow in self-doubt can be self-destructive. We do not feel happy, whether that is through prolific materialism or a fractured society is an issue that needs to be addressed. Nobody celebrates the best of Britain, least of all our nation leaders, excepting special one-off

TV shows. We should have a 'Ministry of Happiness' which encourages our Green and Pleasant Land to return to respect and optimism. It would not be about happy pills, constant wealth accumulation or subliminal media happy messages, but more about why we are the great nation that we are and why we should be proud of it, despite any shortcomings.

Pessimism is contagious and is not caused by events outside our country, but is an internal affliction. So what are any possible cures? Well, society starts with the individual. This includes you, me, the government, our teachers, doctors and everyone else. So as a society we have to be more respectful, responsible, transparent, communicative and trusting. Society reflects the collective individual so if we do not trust or respect our society, then we have to look within ourselves for the reasons why and the answers. And then do something about it.

12/Feb/2008

Society & Lifestyle - Australia & South Pacific Culture
Australian Aborigines: Trying to understand their plight

Aborigine Art and Ownership

2020 vision

An essay from my Indigenous Archaeology course at uni. Part of the essay concerned didgeridoos. One of the best nights of my life was in a Mongolian yurt in the wild fields of Sussex where the Institute of Archaeology held its annual PrimTech course, an introductory course for first-year students in the arts of primary technologies. In my second year, I was part of the elected Student Archaeology Society (SAS) as the mature student representative, who accompanied the new first-years on this course. On one of the nights some of us gathered in a circle within the yurt and while one of the guys played the didgeridoo, another tuned up his tabla drums from India and started tapping out a rhythmic beat; some alcohol was passed around, cigars smoked (I did not partake in the latter) and the whole concoction produced a heady night, almost trance-inducing. I had given the didgeridoo a go and though I can't remember if I could make a noise, I do remember the circular breathing process between mouth and nose you have to endure to get a constant air current from you to the instrument. But what a night!

Aborigines have gone through many phases of Colonial and modern Australian suffering, but a constant and growing plight is the further destruction of their art culture. Aboriginal art and didgeridoos are icons of the Australian Aborigines, but they are increasingly being used by non-Aboriginal peoples for the international markets, causing outrage and offence to the Aborigines. Aborigine art and artefacts should be protected for their use, ownership and sale.

Aborigines make up only 1.7% of the total Australian population, but contribute 25-50% of the visual arts and more in art sales. But Aboriginal art, like the common dot and circle paintings and bark painting X-ray styles (Maughan 2000: 4-5) are increasingly being imitated by non-Aboriginals. The art represents different meanings to the Aborigines who see their art as expressing their homeland, a 'spiritual landscape', and a sense of loss, whereas non-Aboriginals see Aborigine-inspired art as 'the taming of a wild, hostile place' (Langton 2000: 12).

Art scandals have plagued the Australian art market, but some say that to call it an Aboriginal art scandal, when it is non-Aboriginals imitating Aboriginal art, is to wrongly implicate the genuine Aboriginal artist. It is the media and the anti-Aborigine minority which discredits Aboriginal art, either to gain more news mileage and publicity or to damage the Aborigines' ability to communicate their values to everyday audiences (Johnson 2000: 32). Further, I feel that the replication of Aborigine art can be seen as a continuation of colonialism. To the Aborigines, not only have they lost their lands to non-Aborigines, but those same non-Aborigines are also trying to diminish or subjugate Aborigine history through the appropriation of their art.

It is the expectation that Aboriginal art has to mean something that makes non-Aborigines want to understand something about Aborigines and their culture. But it is Aborigines who sometimes reinforce this notion in order to sell more art. And because of the abstractness of Aborigine art some non-Aborigines feel that the art actually has no meaning and hence can be copied. Yet it is that very abstractness that defines Aboriginal art. Art is an ideological form in flux, reflecting society. It is an indestructible concept, ingrained into a culture who owns the meanings, concepts and interpretations, but its form and implementation can be copied. So how can Aborigines protect their art from being replicated against their will?

Organisations like the Papunya Tula Artists P/L and the Aboriginal Arts Board of the Australia Council, among others, try to protect and encourage Aborigine artists and their work. But importantly, Maughan states that '...it is not the medium that defines 'Aboriginality'; but its cultural origin and the statement made that dictates Aboriginality (Maughan 2000: 5). So whether canvas, paper or textiles are used by non-Aboriginal imitators, no matter how sincere they are in regards to Aboriginal art, they cannot hope to claim or present their work as Aboriginal. They might know the workings of the artistic 'language', but the 'grammar' and 'syntax' would be garbled, the symbolism of the artwork lost in translation. An Australian Authenticity Mark scheme to answer 'who authenticates the authenticators?' is now being established with ongoing work by Johnson addressing 'cultural appropriation and copyright issues' (Johnson 2000: 34-5).

Australian didgeridoos are very popular tourist items, but poachers are now stripping the bush land of the wood in order to make didgeridoos. Now the Western Australia Department of Conservation and Land Management has begun a tagging system whereby licensed woodcutters attach a label to each branch cut which stays on the branch throughout the instrument-making process. Selling or owning a tag-less didgeridoo would be an offence. This would also protect trees from needless damage from poachers who destroy whole trees for one decent branch (Squires 2000).

But Aborigines state that 'didgeridoos should not be cut or made by non-Aboriginal Australians at all, and are offended by the appropriation of the instrument, which is considered sacred' (Squires 2000). Didgeridoos have been around for at least 20,000 years as evidenced in cave art. But Aborigines are seen as an 'alternative culture' which attracts backpackers, especially women who offend Aborigines by handling or playing didgeridoos, the preserve of Aboriginal men. But to the Department of Conservation and Land Management this issue is only a matter of preserving and protecting the 'sustainability' of the tree cutting (Squires 2000).

The didgeridoo has 'become the victim of its own success' (Squires 2000), and like Aboriginal art is entirely an Aboriginal product being targeted by non-Aboriginal Australians in order to promote tourism and trade. I think that the lack of (though rising) Aboriginal socio-political power is detrimental in their cause. Indigenous rights, even under the auspices of the United Nations, have not done enough to protect Aboriginal culture and their artefacts. Trademarks, authenticity schemes and tagging may be trying to address the problems, but it is still the Aborigines themselves who are in danger of losing their culture, let alone ownership over their artefacts.

With the Aborigines, their art and artefacts define them and only them, not Australia as a whole. But with an increasingly global market system seeking new avenues of sales, non-Aboriginals are adopting Aboriginal images and artefacts to sell for their own benefit. This loss of Aboriginal ownership is distressing and can only be seen as cultural theft, eroding

Aboriginal culture. While steps are being taken to protect Aboriginal images, there still seems to be no Aboriginal patent or no definition of what are Aboriginal art and artefacts and who can own and copy it.

Aborigine ownership issues should be more vigorously addressed by UNESCO, with provisions for Indigenous peoples' to hold patents on their art and artefacts with monies from sales going into their communities. Representatives for the Aborigines should be on national arts, trade and tourist councils to protect and inspect the authenticity of artefacts. Aboriginal art and artefacts are world famous. They should be controlled and entrusted to the peoples who have invented, developed and preserved them over the millennia.

References:
Johnson, V. 2000. The Aboriginal Art Scandal Scandals. In: Britton S. (ed.) Artlink. Vol. 20, No.1. South Australia: Artlink Australia, 32-35.

Langton, M. 2000. Homeland: Sacred Visions and the Settler State. In: Britton S. (ed.) Artlink. Vol. 20, No.. South Australia: Artlink Australia, 11-16.

Maughan, J. 2000. From the 21st Century and Through the Telescope. In: Britton S. (ed.) Artlink. Vol. 20, No.1. South Australia: Artlink Australia, 4-5.

Squires, N. 2000. Didgeridoos to be tagged to stop poachers. The Sunday Telegraph. December, 31.

13/Mar/2008

Autos – Autos (Other)

Reasons Why It's Better to be a Non-driver

2020 vision
Twelve years on and I still don't drive. It really doesn't appeal to me. But in these pandemic times, it would beat having to wear a mask on public transport all the time. Still, I can't complain as the 'benefits' below still outweigh my hankering to learn.

At 40, I have never really considered it in my life plan to learn how to drive. It has never really interested me. Besides my dad, I come from a family of late learners, my mom and sister learned to drive well into their fifties and thirties, respectively, and my brother, in his mid twenties only drives on his computer games. Considering that our family has lived in England, Canada, America and Barbados and that I was also in the military only adds to the fact that driving, for me, is not an indispensable tool.

General reasons.
Some of you, like me, might like the look and design of a car, but getting behind the wheel does not give you the buzz, power or independence that others feel. Maybe you felt independent enough with your friends in your local community and did not have to venture far. If you did, you had your own personal chauffeur (mom/dad) to take you. Maybe you felt you were not mature enough in your abilities to drive, due to bad car experiences, or physical/mental inabilities. There are also no responsibilities of people depending on you for rides all the time. Also, if you want to move, you can choose a company that delivers boxes and packing materials, decent vans and drivers for an affordable cost. Whatever the reason, being a non-driver has suited you and you feel better for it and more self-reliant.

Costs.
Another obvious reason is the financial burdens a car brings with it. Initial sales costs, insurance, road taxes, congestion charges, toll booths, service and repair bills, parking permits and fines, refuelling, cleaning,

baby chairs, etc are costs that accumulate over the years and can drain a person's or families' accounts. My job or lifestyle does not depend upon me having a car and I walk and use public transport, which for my part of London is not too bad. As a single person, a whole car for myself would be a waste of resources and money. Driving in any city is becoming more expensive and for me is not worth the cost and effort.

There are other costs, but ones that could benefit a non-driver. You can save money from such a heavy investment and divert it elsewhere more meaningful. If you have a house with a garage and/or driveway, but are not using them, you could rent them out to other drivers or use the garage for storage or convert it into a rentable space.

Health and Safety.
Being a non-driver means I walk a lot more and get more exercise. I get to see and experience my surroundings more. I have a great park five minutes from me, which is a great shortcut away from the roads, so I can avoid car fumes and noise. A non-driver also avoids stress over a stolen or damaged car. Being on the roads nowadays is a question of keeping your wits about you, with road rage, speeders and untrustworthy drivers major issues. People eating, smoking, talking on mobiles, or applying make-up behind the wheel endangers other drivers and pedestrians. Being a non-driver, one escapes becoming a likely car-crash victim. Yes, non-drivers and pedestrians can be victims of a crash too, but accidents between vehicles happen more often and are more likely to be fatal.

Environment and technology.
Recently, global warming had raised the issue of fuel-guzzling vehicles, vehicle overuse and fossil fuels. This, to me, is not the main reason for being a non-driver, since there are and will be better green-manufactured and fuelled cars in the future, no doubt with self-drive capabilities. Even biofuels are controversial, because their production can cause further environmental degradation of forests and other countries' economies if the crops are not grown in a sustainable manner. As a non-driver you dodge the negative aspects of polluting and encouraging fossil fuels use. With technology, some people worry about monitoring systems with LoJack, GPS and other tracking systems able to trace and monitor your journeys. While this technology exists in other personal devices, some people might not like their movements monitored so much.

So there are many reasons why it's better to be a non-driver and to be independent of the hazards, ill benefits and costs of driving, no matter how good a car or its driver is.

24/Mar/2008

Society & Lifestyle – Personal Morals & Values
Modern-day conveniences: Whatever did we do without them?

Living Without A Fridge in Modern Times

2020 vision
Been 15 years now. Get over it!

What? No refrigerator? Yes, I do not have a fridge. No, I do not live at the North Pole. Here's my story. While at my former residence, I defrosted the fridge – with a chisel. Not recommended –Do not try that at home! So of course, gases escaped rendering the fridge useless. I was due to move in a few months and the landlord was going to refurbish anyway, so I just got used to not having a fridge. When I did move, just outside of London, into an unfurnished flat, I didn't bother getting a new one.

First off, I am a single male, so I am a bit of a self-confessed heathen when it comes to cooking gourmet meals. I eat properly, so don't tease me. I just do not need a fridge stocked full of food that would only go to waste. This is not about having a non-environmentally-friendly electrical unit, but about cost and practicality. I have extra room in my kitchen, no maintenance problems and I save money and energy. I can afford the luxury of not having a fridge.

I had previously switched my diet months before the defrosting incident, cutting out most dairy products. I drink Soya milk as a preference and yes there are good tasting ones, and it is not around for long enough to need refrigerating. I don't eat bread, toast or sandwiches; at least not at home. I buy my vegetables fresh and meat when I need it, so don't have frozen peas, carrots or left-over scraps. I don't have frozen ready-meals or useless condiment packages, like congealed mayonnaise. If I need ice cream or frozen dessert I can get it on the day before dinner. I do not drink alcohol at home, so there is no need for beer and wine cold storage or ice for mixers.

I do get eggs, though my kitchen is the coolest room in the house and they can be stored away from the sunlight and heat sources. My fruit prefers the fruit bowl and any other food is comfortable in the cupboard. So, no need for an extra expense that isn't used. It's been more than a year now and to tell the truth I hardly miss it.

In fact this seems to be a trend in my life. I do not drive, so have no car. I have no microwave, no MP3/iPod, washing machine and only recently did I receive a digital camera as a gift. I am not a technophobe or some environmentally conscious hang-wringer. I just find that there are things in life that are not really needed. Conversely, I could not live without my TV and find people weird who do not watch TV or even more frightening, people who do not read a book. So there are many needs we think we want, but many wants we do not need. So may my lack of a fridge not cause concern for my well-being. I hope it inspires others to think about the things they can really live without. It was done in the past; it can be done now. Chill.

30/Mar/2008

Jobs & Careers – Trade & Manufacturing Jobs
Occupations: Ice Road Truckers

The Ice Road Truckers

2020 vision

I believe I had also put this under a title for 'dangerous jobs' though someone did question why teachers and such weren't included. True, any job can be dangerous, but the title implied non-every-day hazardous jobs, and this was certainly one of them.

The concept and execution of the first few seasons was great, but like most shows of this ilk it became a victim of its own success and it seemed to morph into a reality show which seemed more and more staged, bringing in new characters and trucking locations (like India). I had initially been interested in the reasons why such truck treks and equipment were needed in the mines of the far north, how climate change was affecting this, how technology overcame this, and a chance to see a different part of the world.

The Ice Road Truckers are an eclectic group of 18-wheeler drivers who annually trek to the Canadian north in order to deliver high value goods and supplies to mines for high amounts of money. The truckers can earn as much within a two-month season than in a year of their regular jobs. The Ice Road Truckers were popularised in a documentary of the same name in 2007. It focused on regular veteran adventurers Hugh 'the Polar Bear' Rowland, Alex Debogorski, Jay Westgard, and Rick Yemm in his second year, and the rookies TJ Tilcox and Drew Sherwood. Alex calls the winter ice road season: 'The dash for the cash'. It is highly dangerous, but lucrative.

The Ice Roads replaced dog sleds and barges from the days when gold was discovered in the 1850s, followed by discoveries of pitchblende (for radium and uranium), then silver and finally diamonds in 1990s. The temporary frozen highways lead from the Tli Cho base in Yellowknife and cross over 300 miles of frozen lakes, connected by portages (ice covered islands) over which 100,000 tons of material goods are delivered via ten thousand truck loads to diamond mines and other industries in the far Canadian north. It is a non-stop business to the mines of De Beers Snap Lake, BHP Ekati and Diavik, as well as clearing out other old mines of their equipment.

The drivers face constant danger and have to avoid going through the ice, spillages, crashes, breakdowns, isolation, storms, and working relationship problems. Twenty people have died since the inception of the Ice Roads in the early 1940s by John Dennison, an ex-Mountie, and modern technology and know-how has not made the transport any less perilous. Why not airlift supplies or build bridges? Airplanes, such as the C-130, are six times more expensive for delivering loads and cannot carry as much as a truck. The minimum the ice has to be is 16", but at 50" thick, the ice can handle 85 tons and is stronger than a steel bridge. There is talk about future tarmac roads leading from the north down to the mines, but such road works and industrial plans could blight the northern environment and make local climate conditions worse.

Temperatures can plummet to -40°C with blinding snow blizzards and there is only a nominal two month season or 70 days for the ice roads to survive. In 2006, there were only 45 days of ice roads and people wondered if global warming was having an affect. How much longer will the ice roads last and how sustainable will the mines be without a regular flow of equipment in the winter? While the lifetime of the resources and mines are not strictly known, the ice roads will continue to supply the mines and keep the local economy alive.

One wonders why such resources of fuel, money, transport and man-power are utilised in such a spectacular and hazardous fashion. Even if it is vital for local community survival, the diamond mining industry is driven by commercial considerations for public consumption. So if people ask why professionals risk their lives to mine in the frozen north, to drive there, and risk environmental contamination and damage, then look no further than our high streets, businesses, industries and homes. Our economies and lives run on precious goods and as long as our insatiable demand for these products last, then such dangerous jobs like the Ice Road Truckers have will exist and seek to fuel that demand. The dash for the cash is truly on.

16/Apr/2008

Relationships & Family – The Single Life

Being Single and Happy

2020 vision
My 70th article, so my notes say. And the same is more or less true, below... though there was the one who got away. Her loss!

I love being single. I am a 40 year old, happy male who just hasn't found that one woman and I am contented with that until I do. I won't fret or have regrets nor settle for second best.

Maybe my 'condition' stems from my childhood moving around from the age of 11 from England to Canada, where our family moved five times in six years, or in New York, where we moved twice in six years. At school, while I had friends, was on the sport teams and got on well with everyone, I was kind of the outsider, a black Brit that didn't quite fit the Cannuck way of life or the rough and tumble streetwise kids of Brooklyn and Queens. But I was self-sufficient, smart enough and confident to know that friends did not define me as a person. So I did my own thing.

When I joined the British Army, I had several short relationships, but promised myself never to marry while enlisted; it was too much of a risk if posted for even for short terms and even back then trust was an issue for me and I didn't trust many women while in the army. There was heartache and heartbreaking on either side, so maybe I was protecting myself from further pain. After the Army and into university, I worked night shifts, so having no money and being unavailable during sociable hours was not conducive to long relationships. So, relationships in my adult life have been ones of misadventure, missed opportunities and indifference.

I have my own set ways, tastes and preferences. I can be independent and actually enjoy my own company, whether going to films, concerts or travelling by myself where I can learn and partake in a personal experience even in a crowd. I can screen out the world and set my own agenda. I have crafted my own persona. I like to be different, I strive to be different, and singleness gives me the freedom to explore both my inner and external world on my own terms.

Speaking to a friend recently, he was shocked that I was still single and had no children. His tribe in Nigeria would see single-dom as being selfish, as children would never had been born to carry on the family. Luckily my parents are not that pushy —so far. The way I see it, as do some other 'westerners', having too many children is selfish, especially in England if you survive only on benefits. Since I don't drive, pollute as much, father children irresponsibly and neglectfully, I am doing my duty toward the planet. Am I selfish for wanting to live my life before potentially devoting my life as a selfless parent? Who knows! But only I can answer that in time.

Do I want children? I'm not sure. I am not a 'regretful loner' or lonely, but alone; a big difference, but I do not miss anyone and I am surrounded by good friends, who incidentally are coupling up and having babies. I don't feel the clock ticking away imploring me to settle down. Yet after a lifetime of second childhoods in the Army and university, is it time I should settle down? I still have a lot to do, more to learn, places to go, people to see. I'm only just getting started, finding my way, enjoying my life.

There are times when I think I want a girlfriend, but my single-minded brain convinces me otherwise. Why give up the good life? If, perchance the right girl did come along, I'm not sure how I would react. She would have to be both patient and independent and probably have her own flat and peculiarities, since she would be like me: a committed singleton, ready to commit to a mutual, exclusive, singleton pact. So who knows, I may surrender, since no man is an island unto himself. I've held out for so long, but I have another 40-50 years to go at least. So I am content for now and wedded to the single life.

08/May/2008

Hobbies & Games – Scrapbooking & Paper Crafts
The joy of scrapbooking your memories

My Scrapbook Memories

2020 vision

Unfortunately, my scrapbooks have been lost; some during my parents move from their house in 1997 and more recently around 2013 to make room for my then-girlfriend. I should have kept the scrapbooks... better memories.

I used to scrapbook avidly in my youth while living in Canada and the States, cutting out newspaper clippings on sundry topics and taping them neatly into an over-sized, blank-paged artist's sketchbook. Over the years, I found dedicated scrapbooks and even continued my hobby during my stint in the military. This changed when I left and most of my things were placed into storage. I had a few new scrapbooks, but I didn't have the time to organise them and sort out scrapbook space.

I still remember my first scrapbook pieces. One of the Canadian papers, in 1980, had a picture of Ronald Reagan sitting at his desk in the Oval Office, smiling away, eyes closed and reaching for one of his beloved jelly beans which rested perilously close to the nuclear button. As a kid, that made me laugh and I wanted to keep the picture. The next was 'Turkish find predates the Pyramids' about an early urban site in Turkey, which turned out to be Catalhoyuk, built way before the pyramids of Egypt. Another was a programme from a school play I did, an updated version of Snow White and the Seven Dwarfs. Alas, my early scrapbooks disappeared somewhere into the mists of time, maybe lost in storage or lost forever, I do not know.

Over time, my scrapbook empire became more sophisticated. All articles were dated and its newspaper noted. I had dedicated scrapbooks for different topics, some even taking up 3 or 4 volumes. Scrapbook titles included: The Universe (mostly Hubble pictures, articles on stars and planets, etc), Man in Space (Space shuttle missions, robotic missions, etc), Aircraft (I was a bit of a spotter), News and current events (started after Berlin Wall came down), Science & technology, History & archaeology, and Entertainment (comic books, films, sports, music, and personal pieces).

But later, on moving back to England, and not finding the types of glorious scrapbooks I had collected in Canada and the States, I fell behind in updating or buying new books. Instead, I still cut clippings out, but store them in folders by year, then archive them in plastic sleeves. At least I still have a data-base, which I guess is why I do it. Textbooks are not updated fast enough and I found that newspaper articles were a good way of keeping up to date and useful for my course essays when I went to university. I guess I'm also a bit of a hoarder in collecting bits of paper for no real intrinsic purpose. I'm afraid to open some of the older scrapbooks I have, they may just fall apart into dust. At one point I even considered scanning them into my own online scrapbook, but now with online search engines and magazines out there, I found it would be too much work. Besides, the smell and feel of old paper and seeing the old words brings back those nostalgic memories.

I also have a large, artist's portfolio case for the events of 9/11 up until the first 'end' of the Iraq War. That event was so momentous with so much written, re-written and 'sexed up', that in years to come, re-reading the raw news as it came out will certainly be different to the sanitised and politically spun stuff that will be published later.

Scrapbooks are a good reminder of the past; personal, un-rewritable, re-accessible, and a fun hobby for an actively inquiring and creative mind. Start one today and record history for yourself.

03/Jul/2008

Society & Lifestyle – Relationships & Family
Looking for Mr or Miss "Right"

Finding Miss Right

2020 vision

Since writing this I've had two fairly long relationships: one where she thought of me as her soul-mate though I didn't reciprocate and the other whom I'd thought of as the love of my life, but ultimately she didn't feel the same way though we were engaged for what seemed like all of five minutes. Love can hurt, but you have to move on, and more importantly, love yourself whether you stay single or if love finds you again.

Now that I've started my fourth decade, finding Miss Right has started to enter my mind. Do I watch out while shopping, in the laundrette, or in pubs and clubs? Do I internet date, catch her eye while on the tube or bus, or just walking down the street? Should I cast my net far and wide in a sea of strangers or search through my circle of friends and friends of friends? It's tough, but whatever happens I have a general guideline to stick to: the 4 'I's:

Eyes; Intelligence; Independence; and Interests.

The eyes are so important. There at least has to be a light on inside. The eyes should smile and Miss Right should be able to hold your attention just by gaze alone, no matter whether her eyes are startling blue, deepest brown or that rarity of gray. Eyes are my starting point, and convey such information as friendliness, trust, intelligence and inner beauty. With the eye factor comes the smile. It's nice when Miss Right smiles, again another sign of friendliness and trust. It lights up a room and also your life (and you also get to see if her teeth are clean).

Intelligence is another key factor. As an educated person myself, I expect to be able to hold intelligent conversations with Miss Right. Not that she has to be super intelligent or even university educated, but she must have some knowledge of the world about her, whether through reading or travelling or just common sense and reasoning. Having a sense of humour is included here since you need intelligence and wit to tell and appreciate a joke, or to negotiate your way through a difficult time.

Independence is an issue of trust. I'm not one to want to spend 24/7 with Miss Right. Familiarity could breed contempt if you crowd each other, especially if you already work or study together. There should be some element of independent development with your own sets of friends, plans and thoughts and there should be that healthy bout of jealousy, just so that the other partner knows there are boundaries. I am no dog, but have lots of female friends, and would never cheat on Miss Right. And I would have to trust that she acted the same. Trust is a valuable commodity and once it is tainted it is very hard to regain.

Interest covers many subjects and is the glue that holds you together. I find that you have to have a spark, that natural bond and chemistry that cannot be faked. It is more than flirting; it's not lust, nor love, but that inner buzz, that fulfilling sensation you have when the other is around or when you think of them. Some people call it having a soul mate. You have to have things in common and want to keep the interest going well into the relationship, whether through sharing experiences, keeping fit or working the brain. Find ways to keep the zing alive. Interest balances against Independence to create a lasting relationship.

Notice I have not talked about looks. Beauty is in the eye of the beholder, so what I or you like others may not. There are many types of women; shapes and sizes, and I have no set rules on hair style or colour, eye colour, body shapes, or for the most part nationality, though I prefer British girls. I find that as a girl grows older, she likes to migrate closer to where she grew up or out of the city to raise a brood, so if you are not prepared to move, then choose a Miss Right who has set down roots and is already at home. Other personal parameters for my Miss Right would be: not to be taller than me, be a non-smoker, and not overly fat (I like curves) nor too skinny. I still like to work out and find it's good for the mind and soul as well as the body, and I would hope Miss Right would want to stay fit and healthy too. Beauty comes from intrinsic values such as personality, vitality, individuality and creativeness. Miss Right would remain youthful by wanting to enjoy life, wanting to learn and experience what is out there; to live and not just to exist.

Mostly, finding Miss Right means not ending up with second choice and wondering if I made the right choice. At the moment, it is through choice that I am single, mainly for selfish reasons. I have a lot to do that I personally want to achieve before settling down with Miss Right. Secondly, while I know and like a lot of girls, each have some of the 4 'I's, but not all of them and though I favour flawed diamonds, should I compromise and settle for less or hold out for first choice Miss Right? Of course Miss Right could come into my life and totally sweep me off my feet, but I have to be willing to give up on my bachelorhood status, which will not be easy.

Actually, I already know who my Miss Right is. And she knows it, but she has her own issues to work out. Whether we end up together, only the universe knows. Maybe she is only Miss Right for this stage in my life. How many more can there be? All I know is that no one else stands a chance against her, she's everything to me and I will wait until the end of the universe for her or until she makes up her mind, whichever comes sooner. So for now I am alone, and happy, and for some time to come. Or is it time for me to change, to amend my selfish ways, re-set my goals and declare my love for my Miss Right...?

19/Jul/2008

Reflections - Choices

Freedom of Choice

Since when did freedom of choice become a good thing? By 2012, the UK will be switching off its analogue TV signal and everyone will be 'forced' to go digital. It's all in a drive to modernise TV services. But as the five existing terrestrial channels provide adequate TV for me, a self-proclaimed TV addict, then why should I want hundreds of channels that would add next to nothing to my viewing pleasure?

Yes, there are movie, sports and documentary channels that I would probably watch, but their content is already repeated or repackaged for normal TV. I don't miss much and what I can't see, I don't miss, so why the push to give me something I don't need or want? The government says this will benefit everyone's TV experience and be more efficient, but they have not given anyone the choice to remain digital-free, which means losing your TV if you are not with their programme.

I suspect it all has to do with money and corporate influence. I already pay a TV license fee for the BBC channels, but for the extra digital/satellite/cable channels, I would need to pay for their hardware and any subscription fees, not to mention special pay-per-view channels for extra channels, most of which would be redundant to me. And all this without my consent or consultation; digital TV is a *fait accompli*. Extra channels have been foisted upon the nation and the viewers are burdened with more energy consumption and viewing costs.

Choice can be a buzz word, mesmerising you at the supermarket, thinking of all the different brands or flavours or styles of one product even if you have a shopping list with you. Choice is paralysing, it overwhelms the brain with too much information, so we do not think about what is important; and advertisers, politicians and corporations know this. Choice replaces needs with wants. Given the choice, we go for what we want. The once monopoly of needs is gone. Choice is the real product of the modern world; we are conditioned from childhood to be good consumers and accept choice, but not our own choices; but what society thinks you should choose. So we are told there is no need to change our TVs, but a digital image will mean better quality and a desire to purchase a bigger, HDTV or jumbo flatscreen, with attendant applications. The Digital Age will have an inevitable inbuilt requirement for people to upgrade to better viewing facilities, when their old TV was good enough, because in true consumer fashion, you have the choice to.

The multitude of choices is forever expanding, invading our private lives and thoughts. There is a thing as too much choice, too much freedom of choice; it dilutes the individual, seizes the mind and offers no alternative. It's choice or more choice. For those who can resist, I salute you and long may you live under the choice radar. As for me, I will continue to resist the digital/download onslaught and live with my own choices.

12/Aug/2008

Society & Lifestyle – relationships & Family
Being complete as a man without a woman

21st Century Caveman

That's me! Not quite the knuckle-dragging behemoth, but a man of my time, my own personal world, and I'm not about to change. I was not nor will be a New Man, a metrosexual or any other trendy label. I just want to be me.

At 40, I should be settled, married with kids, mortgaged to the hilt, juggling a business career, and having nights out with the lads (when permitted by the missus), but that has not been my path. Maybe I don't want the responsibility of commitment or to conform. I've seen what this 'normal' life does to people and it does not fit me.

I'm no free spirit, I still have to work, but I've never done a normal 9-5 job; whether growing up helping my dad with work, or in the Army, or through university; and I prefer night work. Why am I such a night owl? Do my ideas and writing of articles and stories come more freely with time on my hands after dark? Whatever it is, such unsociable hours in work and life are not always conducive to relationships. Am I selfish, not caring for or listening to anyone else, but myself? I want to find out more about me, by myself. Does it take another to complete someone? Do I dare try and risk losing myself, my independence; my caveman? If I sort myself out, whatever that means, will I be ready to abdicate my caveman throne and relinquish my feelings to someone else? For now, the caveman rules and any woman brave enough to embrace my inner caveman might just be worth it.

I am self-controlled, in check, though positive in outlook, and a perfectionist in my own way. My own universe is a selfish one; no room for anyone else's universe to collide into mine and produce a baby universe as I imagine the real universe does (though I can't speculate on the universe's genitalia!). Do I want to pass on my caveman genes? What is there to look forward to? I don't have the patience or the will to raise a new me, for surely I would want to mould an independent and intelligent mind for the future as a non-conformist who could adapt and hone their talents to anything they wanted to be and do. But I also think of my social gravity and my place within the world. I want to be a facilitator of ideas, sharing my views and thoughts and ways to do things. I want to be different, strive to be different –an infovore; collecting knowledge for knowledge's sake- while remaining steadfastfully me.

My caveman is wary of his inner emotions. I used to be quick to anger in my youth, but as I grew older and wiser, and discovered things I could do, my anger was tempered and re-directed. It fuels my passion for knowledge; so little time, so much to learn. That may not sound too much like a caveman, but cavemen were intelligent beings. I'm intelligent, but my emotional quotient isn't on a par. It's the stiff upper lip mentality and the strong silent type attitude, though I'm no 'roughty toughty'. Real men can cry, even if I tend not to show my emotions. That side of me is personal, too personal to be laid bare. Yes, I've been hurt, but the reserve has always been a part of me; maybe a selfprotective mechanism for having moved around as much as I have during my younger years. The wall is up, and few will get to see what's within the fortress of my soul. That's my core, my reservoir of ideas, my emotional being; the caveman. He lets me get away from the claustrophobic throng of people, to be alone once and awhile.

I like my inner caveman, solitary; always hunting for new ideas, a fighter for his way of life, wary of distractions to his goals. Yet, while the caveman can live on an island, he is alert to new means of staving off isolation. So I don't neglect my friends. I am no island unto myself, so I come out from my cave and reunite with friends so I can keep in touch, listen more, stay grounded, stay sane. Doing the nice things keeps the caveman from doing the bad things, from being too alone. It makes me happy, which makes others happy. This caveman can crack a smile.

Life for me is not some static dance or rehearsal for some next life and it's more than just existing. It is good to have a dream away from the reality of life; whether you follow it is up to you. I know what I want to do and it will take time to get there, not through the finesse of the New Man, but by the caveman bludgeoning his way forth with ideas and knowledge; staying the course of non-conformitism. If it means putting relationships off, then so be it!

I recently found out that I could belong to the SPURMOs (Straight, Proud, Unmarried, Men Over-30. A crap group title to be sure!), or could be part of the Menaissance movement, with perhaps a tinge of being a Regretful Loner; basically an anachronistic and selfish male, though I'm not so chauvinistic to believe that women don't count or cannot feel the same about being happily single. The world is made up of different people who do not conform or who do not want to be tied down or intellectually stifled. There are many cavemen and cavewomen around, some hiding it better than others; they are proud of their lives and intensely protective of them. We choose our own independent paths, away from the strictures (and scriptures) of 'organised civilisation'.

The Age of the Caveman cannot end, no matter what technological advances come; the caveman was meant to survive and even help drive forward civilisation even from within his cave. So, seek your inner cave-dweller, make yourself happy first and see where life will lead you. My caveman is restless and I might have to look to new horizons, roam further afield, and explore life in other worlds before those worlds and my caveman become extinct.

04/Sept/2008

Are pennies worth the same as before

Minding the Pennies

Are pennies worth the same as before? I used to hate pennies with a passion; the copper-coloured coins, the 1p and 2p. I used to throw them away. I don't know when I started to dislike them or what it was about them —maybe they weren't shiny enough or they just cluttered up my wallet or hung around the backs of sofas needlessly and generally never came in handy.

Some might ask: well why didn't I just collect them in a jar or piggy bank and then take them to a bank to be cashed in. Do I look like a five year old? I hated wrapping those measly coins up in those special paper wraps or putting them in designated bags. It was annoying, time consuming, and the payback never amounted to much after all of that effort. Pennies were a waste of time and space.

So each time I came back from shopping or a night out, I would 'sterilise' my wallet, clean it out of unwanted pennies and receipts and literally throw them in the bin. Or in shops I would say to the person behind the till to keep the pennies or put them in the charity boxes. Luckily, no one gave me back pounds and pounds worth of change in coppers. Even shopkeepers thought I was crazy, but as I always said to them: the pennies would never come in handy since I would have just spent them on nothing useful anyway, so it was already wasted money not going to waste, because the pennies had no value, in my view. Not my problem. How could you waste nothing? I would even just discreetly drop them along the street or in a street bin. The streets were literally paved with copper and someone else could find them and use them. I just didn't want them in my wallet, in my house, in my life.

But then things took a turn for the worst and I was out of work for a long while. Money got tight. I had to sell possessions, look for food and household bargains, and most of all I had to save every penny. I even had to retrieve pennies from my bins at home. I was amazed that even a few pennies were the difference between getting one more item of food for a decent meal or for posting an item I had sold. Everything was added up before I went shopping, my tightest ever budgeting period, and I learned if not to love pennies then at least to respect them. Pennies came in handy in my darkest hour of need.

Now I'm back at work and I keep the pennies in my wallet, though I do still try to get rid of them first when paying for something. They're not as beloved as the silver or golden coins, but I now know that the pennies' beauty comes not from any attractiveness, but from their intrinsic value. So there's an uneasy truce with my pennies; they don't bother me and I won't chuck them away so cheaply. I've learned my lesson and look after my pennies. Pennies are worth a lot more than you know.

26/Oct/2008

Jobs & Careers
How to survive shift work

Working Night Shifts

2020 vision

While I'm glad I got out of the night shift racket, I do miss the quiet nights when I could look out over the city at night or read, write, study, and sing a song to myself while on patrol.

For most of my adult life I have worked shifts; usually twelve hour shifts with differing patterns of days and nights, though I stick to nights now. Do I like shift work? I suppose I do; I'm used to it and working opposite times to the majority of workers and having extra days off is also a benefit. But there are many factors involved and if one is not suited to shift work then they could find their personal or professional lives a bit disrupted.

Team work:

Finding the right type of shift work is important no matter where you are. I was in the security industry for nine years working at elite London companies, yet I did not fully enjoy the shift experiences, so I have since kind of 'downshifted' to residential work, which suited what I was looking for. My night shifts are relatively peaceful and less stressful than the city jobs, away from office politics and cliques. My charges are less stressed and the working atmosphere is friendly. Any shift worker needs such a community to feel worthwhile and appreciated, no matter where they work or how much they earn.

The changing face of shift work is another factor. When I first started security, sites usually consisted of a few white British guys, Nigerians and a few South Africans. The British and few Caribbean guys were usually older and of ex-military /police backgrounds, like myself. Then there was a glut of South Africans who burnt the candle at both ends and went home early well before their visas ran out. Now I find there are a lot more Ghurkas around, who do as they are asked and also the Polish, who are more laid-back and amazed me with their ultimate commutes home to Poland on cheap flights for their four days off and then back to work. The increasing demographic is now younger Brits, especially women. Along with security, there were caterers mostly from continental Europe, northern and eastern Africa, and Antipodeans, while cleaners were usually West African or South American. Shift work offers a lot of opportunities in meeting a myriad of people, developing character, and working together, but you also have to be willing to take advantage of the benefits and make the most of their time.

Time and mind management:
I'm a night-owl and do more reading, writing, and (once upon a time) more studying at night. It takes a lot of preparation and some good sleep during the day before shift to stave off any sleeping at work, which ruins your already topsy-turvy sleep cycle. Over the past decade, I have honed my pre-, during, and post-work routines so as to maximise as much time possible doing the things that need to be done. I even break my night down into different activities at work so as not to get bored or complacent and to stay alert.

Boredom can be the biggest soul destroyer in shift working, especially at nights. I've seen too many people waste their time watching videos or playing games when they should be working; or they're sleeping on duty (a bad habit I hate to see in colleagues), because they're lazy or have been out all day. They have nothing to stimulate them, nothing to think about or aspire to and that dismays me. One of my friends was in his mid 60s and one of the sharpest grafters around always learning, while there were guys less than half his age ready to write their lives off and be content with their lot. Shift work was clearly not for the youngsters, but as the security industry grows, such people will inevitably be drafted in. But with the new security industry licenses required, which involves training and examinations, only those dedicated and serious enough should be occupied in certain shift work.

Social and Personal issues:
As a mentor said to me once; 'nobody comes to work to do a bad job'. But it does become clear when people are not suited to their work, especially shift work. I always told younger workers to find something to occupy their time, whether studying or a hobby. Security sucks you in with money, but with no real qualifications required or acquired, it could be a dead end job for some. This leads to problems in relationships or

with a person's social life or professional life if they do not work as a team. There was one man who was clearly either in the wrong job or wrong relationship, when his girlfriend stayed outside his workplace in her car during his night shifts, because she was afraid to be home alone. A positive mentality and strong sense of duty are needed to succeed in shift work.

I prefer the night shifts also, because it's quiet, away from the hustle and bustle, and you see the city in another light. When I worked in the city you saw all the night cleaning and deliveries; those whose work the day city workers thought was probably done by pixies, if they even noticed. The urban foxes came out, bedraggled specimens eking out a life as precarious as the human night shift. The streets were empty and quiet and a quick exterior patrol revealed a city at rest. The views from roofs or top floor windows were also more spectacular whether to St. Paul's Cathedral, Canary Wharf or the London Eye. Most people think they can see the city on street level, but the architecture is really in the air. The hidden balconies and roof gardens, the ornate decorations or stonework and glass atriums revealing spiral staircases will never be seen by normal passers-by and tourists; it is the privileged domain of those who guard the towers of finance.

So at the moment, I am loving my shift work though I think about the next step up in my career. I have barely done proper nine to five work and any aspiration to do so will be hard to adjust to, but am I willing to sacrifice my long nights of blissful solitude for the harsh daylight of normal commuting? Maybe a new shift in life is on the way.

21/Nov/2008

Society & Lifestyle – relationships & Family
Being single and child-free

Am I Selfish For Not Wanting Children?

2020 vision

I think I have mellowed enough to admit that if I met someone now she'd probably be maturer and have children. Though hopefully they wouldn't be too young as I'd want my partner and I to have some quality time and freedom alone.

To be brutally honest, I'm not sure if I want children. I don't have the patience, the paternal or loving instinct. I don't think the door is totally closed, but it would depend on meeting the right woman. The fact is, I like being single and have never seriously envisioned having children. Some might think it's a phase I'll grow out of, but I'm forty years old and quite happy being a bachelor. It's not about having a swinging lifestyle or being a dog, I think by now that if I wanted to be settled, I would have done it long ago and be happily married with kids, but that's not for me.

Some might think me selfish for not wanting to have kids or share a life with someone else, but in this day and age, I'm probably better off alone, taking care of number one. I'm not in a position or frame of mind yet to settle or have kids. I was once in the Army and told myself I would never marry while serving, after seeing some unsavoury goings on with wives/girlfriends while their men were away. Why subject myself to that? After that I was at university, so I was a poor student with a night time job and I would have had little time for a wife and kids, though others managed to muddle their way through. Now I have yet to sort myself out after a few career turns and dreams to satisfy before considering letting someone else into my life.

I think people would rather I be gay than admit I like being alone. Every time I mention I'm single I feel I have to mention I had an ex-girlfriend once or start looking at girls to satisfy others' curiosity over my sexuality. Single people probably get less understanding than gay people from others and even in government social policies. It's like single people are a burden on society and should want to eventually shack up with someone rather than be an anti-social outcast. I say leave me alone and let me get on with my single life –thank you.

I often joke with my friends that if I did have children I would soon cart them off to military school, like the Spartans, and they would learn discipline and survival skills, but also have an education and opportunity unlike other kids and experience the world from a different perspective. Maybe they would be in my image; perfectionists, knowledge seekers, free thinkers, and emotionally in charge, or at least that's how I imagine myself. I did dream about having children; an older girl, followed by twins (one boy/one girl); don't know where it came from, but it was a funny dream to have seeing that when I see children of friends and family, I don't wish I had some of my own. I'm not broody or feel my own biological clock running out. In fact they probably put me off, especially when I see unruly infants on the streets, while shopping or on public transport. Are children really worth it? Don't answer that –I know I was a kid once and people had to put up with me. But I don't have to repeat the everlasting cycle of reproduction. There's plenty more people out there doing that in my stead.

Do I mind not passing on my genes, or my father's and his ancestors? Sometimes, but it still could happen. I had mooted donating reproductive fluid, but my female friends talked me out of it as complications could arise further down the line if Junior came looking for me years later (and found himself carted off to military school) or due to future laws changes a woman I never laid eyes on before could claim child benefit from me, so to avoid these legal mine fields, I will probably avoid donating. If I did, I wonder if my offspring would either be miraculously well-adjusted or come back with an Oedipus complex. Well, if I'm going to do it, it'll be natural, and face to face, so to speak. Would I worry about not having someone to look after me when I'm old?

Well, at the moment I'm too busy to think about that and if I'm lucky I aim to stay fit and healthy for the next two-thirds of my life. Would I worry if a future partner got pregnant? What my reaction would be? Would I have to learn to love our child and not resent my partner for ruining my life? It would be a harsh decision, so for now I'm better off alone. Am I just scared of commitment and responsibility of having a child? After seeing and hearing horror stories from new parents, it does put me off. Also, I wouldn't want to be one of those guys who just went along with what their partner wanted only to find himself being a bad father and partner. It would be totally negligent of me to be in a situation like that.

So there we go. If my parents read this, understand it's not your fault I like being alone. I've cultivated my own lifestyle and so far it does not involve a wife and kids. Looks like the buck stops with me.

22/Nov/2008

Society & Lifestyle
Reflections: Heroes

Where Have Our Heroes Gone?

2020 vision

I still feel this way. Where have the larger than life personalities and daredevils gone? Does Elon Musk fit this mode now? Felix Baumgartner? Usain Bolt has retired. Even Obama has been turned into a black Superman. Have YouTube and reality TV given us 15-minute watered-down wannabes? Of course people will chirp in that there are so many unsung heroes in our everyday life and maybe we should focus on them. You can do that. I think big.

After watching a made-for-TV film about Evel Knievel and the spectacle he created, I wondered where our modern daredevils and heroes were. The Seventies had Mohammed Ali, John Wayne, Elvis, the Jackson 5, and the Osmonds, etc. Even David Copperfield was a later must see attraction. We get stuck with David Blaine, David Hasselhoff, and a whole host of mediocre celebrities.

The Golden Age of Hollywood has gone and been replaced by adequate actors-cum-superstars, but will they ever be mentioned in the same breath as the true Legends? Were the heroes defeated by the politically correct villains or did they bow out like the ancient Gods who knew their time was up? There are many actors with charitable causes, political agendas, and even some with decent films, but there is still that unique mystical quality missing; acting is a job to them rather than the stuff of life.

Was the 20th Century heroes' popularity and success artefacts of simpler times? Would they have survived in this internet age of celebrity-dom? We have niche heroes —those who occupy a particular section of the population's imagination and adoration, whether sportsman or extreme-sportsman, entertainers or politicians. Astronauts with household names are gone and their space tourist counterparts get more airtime. Name the man who just flew across the English Channel in a home-made jet pack (It was Swiss pilot Yves Rossy a.k.a Fusion Man) or the man who plans to jump from a balloon on the edge of space in a special carbon-fibre suit (It is former French Colonel Michel Fournier). These two one-time wonders will fade into history while Charles Lindbergh is still revered. After adventurers Sir Richard Branson and the late Steve Fossett, voyager Burt Rutan, and Sir Ranulph Fiennes, where are our adventurers and explorers going to come from? In this Health and Safety age, it's a wonder that any of our wrapped-in-cotton-wool kids will ever venture out to boldly go where no one has gone before.

Where are our polymaths and celebrity boffins? Carl Sagan and Richard Feynman were great thinkers and 'popularisers' of science. They knew a lot about a lot of things. No one now carries that responsibility. Knowledge is compartmented, more niches within niches, and rather than individual inventors, there are a whole slew of collaborators queuing up for Nobel Prizes that the public doesn't care about anymore, outside of the Peace Prize. Al Gore hardly fits the bill as champion of the Climate Change era; where is he now after his Oscar. Please don't place Obama on the pedestal just yet. He is the train that said 'yes it can' but his staying power has yet to be tested and his legacy won't be known for maybe a generation. He has to prove his worth over time as any hero has to. Political heroes are on the wane, the Cult of Personality has taken over the Courage of Conviction.

Our sportsman create spectacle, but are they worth looking up to in this age of hype and overpay after the world stage was graced by Pele, Maradonna and George Best? Is David Beckham their heir following Zidane and Figo? After Michael Jordan, vintage Iron Mike Tyson and Carl Lewis, who are our new sporting superstars? As much as past sportsmen were stoned or drunk, some of our sportsmen are still revered after being in jail for varying anti-social infractions. Will Lewis Hamilton become the new sports icon after winning the Formula One title? As with science collaborations, the new sports era is about teams; teams tour all over the world, but now for lucrative sponsorship deals rather than to pay homage to their fans. The sporting hero has been lifted by image rights, advertising and media hype, but the charisma and sheer presence had been drained away. There will never be another 'Thrilla in Manilla' or a Snake Canyon rocket-cycle jump.

Will the likes of the Rolling Stones, Led Zeppelin or Pink Floyd come our way again? Are the Beatles and Elvis destined to be reincarnated for the modern age? Has X-Factor and the internet killed off true superstardom, again creating mediocre niches for specialised audiences. Will the Spice Girls and their 'Girl Power' be remembered in generation's time? Madonna is still in vogue, Metallica is still as hard and fast as ever and Radiohead continue to bend music, but new artists seem to be derivative of past classics; everyone has to be placed in a box —this group sounds like (insert group name) or he/she sings/plays like (insert name here), it's no wonder that music has become the dominating element on the internet. Anyone can be a star, but success and longevity is fleeting as they enjoy a 'Warholian' 15 minutes of fame.

Our heroes have all but disappeared, the spectacle is an anti-climax, and mediocrity is the norm. But have the heroes really gone, or have the public just become disinterested in grand finales and individual heroics discovering the flawed human behind the hero's mask? Are we being taught, through politics and the media, that standing out as the hero, the solo icon is not the cool thing to do, even though films says otherwise? Surely it's down to the individual to make that choice themselves; to be man or superman. We all know that there are heroes around us at home, work and play, but the true, global giants of spectacle that inspired generations now only remain in our hearts and minds forever.

23/Nov/2008

Society & Lifestyle
Organ donation registers should move from an opt-in to an opt-out system

Organ Donations: Opting In or Out?

I have never really thought about donating my organs once I was gone. I probably wouldn't have minded either way, but then the subject of Opting Out or Presumed Consent hit the headlines in England and it was rejected by government advisors. The main reasons were it could undermine trust between doctors and patients if patients thought they were mere ready-made-organs-to-go and that better run organ donation campaigns would be a better system. But there must be other reasons why people like myself are still in a quandary over whether to opt in or out, whether for cultural, scientific or religious reasons.

Cultural:
While the Opt Out option is a well-meaning way to get more organs into the system for transplants, it's also a simplistic notion. Yes, there may be more organs available, but matches to recipients, bureaucracy, potential organ surpluses and storage issues, and illegal organ sales could all still be problems under the Opt Out system. People would be lulled into thinking that enough organs are available and opt out, leading to cycles of shortages and Opt In/Out debates again. Such apathy could lead to disruptions in blood and bone marrow donations, as people lose trust in such procedures. Not everyone feels that a person should automatically be a donor upon death. Organ donation should be a gift rather than obligation, so stealth legalisation with little or no choice over options is not the way to go.

Spain has had the Opt Out system for years, but credits donation increases from its high-profile public awareness campaign. While most continental European countries can be a bit more enlightened on social issues, Britain's government has tended to extend state powers into the personal arena, but its poor record on data collection, protection, interpretation, dissemination, and costs has not endeared it to the public. On this basis, most people would reject the Opt Out system, no matter how beneficial, just because of the government's involvement.

Scientific:
Personally, I wouldn't mind being cremated, being sent into space (though at the back of my mind there would be the thought that aliens would find me and reanimate me), or made into diamonds, so I probably would not need my organs. Or I could donate my body to science or to one of those CSI farms where they study the effects of decomposition on bodies over time, where I might need my organs. I might want to be cryogenically frozen for some future purpose where my intactness would be needed. Opting out would give me freedom of choice over what I wanted my body to be used for.

Cloning, stem cell, artificial organs, and other advances could make donations obsolete. The Opt out system could be an unnecessary stop-gap measure until science finds a way to replace organs in an alternative fashion. An Opt Out system could prevent another Alder Hey scandal where baby organs and human tissue had been illegally removed and kept in the Hospital. There would be no need for such secretive operations for research if donations were more freely available, but would there be the choice over how exactly you wanted your donation to be used.

Religious:
Some religious factions could be exempt from any donation option, owing to their beliefs, but as mentioned, trust issues were paramount as patients close to death would be worried about having their plug pulled in order to harvest their organs. There are some people who just want to be buried whole, for no other reason than they want to be –which is their right. God made them; only God can dismember them. Only God can opt them out. Religious people could want their body intact for heaven, feeling an incompleteness of body and soul may make them seem less worthy. Even if their worldly goods are given up upon death, in a way, the religious minded are just as materialistic in attitude when it comes to their bodies.

I think in this day and age of Big Brother, no matter what the government says about opting out, people would wonder how hard it would be to opt out and the pressures not to. Just as stealth taxes have crept up on people, stealth legislation could make donations compulsory as people become apathetic to opting out and it becomes a de facto law. This seems a choice of free will versus government legislation over our own bodies. Is there a fight brewing in the future or will common sense and science make the Opt Out system and even donations a redundant element of the medical world? For now, I think I will opt out.

24/Jan/2009

Banning Smoking – Taxes and Health issues
Arguments for banning smoking

Smokers Beware

2020 vision

Yes, yes, there are other and worse habits out there and I have friends who smoke (and hypocritical of me an ex who smoked) but hey, these were my honest thoughts. This was one of the few articles I posted to Reddit, trying out a new platform, and basically the article was attacked for my bias. Nothing I can do about that.

There is nothing worse than enjoying a lovely walk through a park or down a road when all of a sudden the disgusting smell of cigarette smoke comes wafting your way and follows you like, well, a bad smell. You cannot always see the culprit or hear them, but you certainly can smell them. It takes the absolute pleasure out of breathing fresh air and ruins a peaceful state of mind while trying to have some quality time.

Smoking is an absolute selfish addiction and should be on a par with CO_2 pollution, since you can readily smell and be affected by cigarette pollution. Yet smoking is a legalised drug by governments since they can control tobacco, but not cocaine, poppies, or marijuana plants (This is the same for alcohol, but that's another story). It is why tobacco products are allowed to thrive and will not or cannot be totally banned due to their revenue from taxes. For governments to be implicit in the deaths of millions during peacetime for the sake of raising money for public concerns seems perverse. How many more lives would have been saved had smoking not been legalised and promoted to such mountainous heights (Some might say the same for driving accidents, plane crashes, drinking and drugs, but the effects within societies from smoking and smoking deaths are just not comparable).

As much as I like some of my female friends that smoke, the fact that they do would preclude them from being my girlfriend. The thought of them harming their own health would be hard to take, but also they would be harming mine with a constant pall of smoke that would cling to them and their effects. Killing themselves and me is as bad as physical, mental and verbal abuse. They are deriving pleasure from slow suicide and this personally upsets me. For smokers with children, they are condemning them to a possible life of respiratory illness, addiction, or even rejection/resentment for smoking. If a parent cannot give up for the sake of their children it is as much an abuse as smacking, or verbal and mental abuse. Some cultures are practising genocide of the next generation by not curtailing tobacco.

Smokers claim that their taxes (from cigarette tax) pay for a majority of public health services, but that should not be an excuse to continue smoking. Smokers drain National Health Service resources with their illnesses and complications. But taxes, pricing and legislation are not the only issues, as smoking will not go away with bans, restrictions, and higher prices. Solutions have to be sought to combat smoking and its negative effects. This won't come from reinstating indoor smoking, banning all outdoor smoking, or even a total ban, but by eradicating the social aspects that gives rise to smoking like poverty, stress, peer pressure to smoke, and tobacco advertising. Emphasising negative health issues or even refusing medical services to habitual smokers may have to be used. Other solutions are synthetic cigarettes, nicotine patches, and less addictive substances.

The 'pleasure' of smoking causes irreparable physical damage to the body, even if outwardly the smoker seems fitter than a non-smoker. There are always exceptions to the rule, but smoking kills sooner rather than later. But the irrational need to smoke, even after knowing the dangers from lung disease, cancer, other complications, and negative social aspects also points to psychological issues like denial of the risks involved and the pleasure derived from such a subversive activity.

Like the fossil fuel industry to climate change, like alcohol to binge drinking, and like fast foods to obesity, the tobacco industry will be legislated heavily against with companies restricted in ingredients and advertising, to bring about a healthier life. The tobacco industry (like the oil industry) will always be around in some form, but the idea is to make cigarettes less potent within society and the companies more responsible for their actions. There is no such thing as responsible smoking, which immediately affects others with second-hand smoke. There are a whole host of other vices (drinking, over-eating, over-exercising, drug-taking, etc), but smoking is the most visibly ubiquitous and divisive of them all.

When the indoor smoking ban came along, people cheered; it meant that pubs, clubs, restaurants, and places of business would be clean and clear. But now you have to run the gauntlet of outdoor smokers crowded around doors they should legally be well-away from shivering in the cold and wet and wade through piles of cigarette-butt litter. Apart from providing jobs for street sweepers, there is nothing to gain from pushing smokers outside where a haze of smoke now greets customers and pedestrians, especially when smokers blow smoke into buildings after their final exhale. There is a non-chalant air (no pun intended) to the way a smoker puffs away while walking down the street oblivious to whoever's face he/she blows smoke into. They are as blasé to that as they are to filling their lungs with black tar and eventual death.

As mentioned, smokers participate in the most visible and inherent anti-social habit. It is a way of showing an assumed maturity, toughness, and coolness, especially amongst youngsters. Smokers show a non-conformist attitude in the midst of our politically-correct world and cigarette bans. They can ostracise and be ostracised by others, yet be included into a minority group, with a sense of belonging and powerful lobby. Smoking is a self-identity, a badge of honour among peers, a supposed stress reliever and pleasurable practice. There is no acknowledgement of their intimidating and arrogant actions and no humane defence as to why they should continue smoking, despite their self-righteous and coveted Right to smoke. But in a fast globalising world where minorities are being broken and lost to history, it will not be long before more pressure is placed on tobacco to clean up its act.

The Climate change industry will be a template to work from as it is the new tax industry following on from tobacco, especially since climate change will exacerbate smoking illnesses. Just as fossil fuels are being phased out to ease climate change, so cigarette smoking will be replaced by other safer inhalation devices and substances or eliminated altogether to improve general wellbeing. We all have vices and guilty pleasures, but some are more dangerous than others. If you don't hate yourself or feel shame towards harming yourselves or other people, and about how people feel about you when you smoke, then just do us non-smokers the courtesy of smoking in your own homes, taking an alternative, or just dying off and leaving us non-smokers a cleaner world.

13/Jun/2009

Modern life and the absence of quality time

Being Time Poor

This almost didn't get written. There was no time; just floating ideas and fleeting moments of prose. I used to work 12-hour night shifts where I had tons of time to read and write. It was perfect. But circumstances changed and now I work day shifts, which aren't exactly conducive to all-out assaults on writing. There are quiet times to contemplate and write things down, but overall, my quantity and quality of time to think, to read, and to write has declined.

Even on my days off there is no time to catch up on TV, read, write, get chores done, work out, and meet friends in real time or online. Some people might think these are trivial matters compared with what's happening in the world today, but they are integral to me and in maintaining links to society and to my own state of mind.

So where does my time go? How come I barely have time to think [hold on, work to do......okay, back now]? I admit that I'm a telly addict, but even then, I can multitask with concurrent activities: watch TV while ironing, or writing emails, or working out. Should I sacrifice sleep to get more done? I am a natural night owl, so staying up late isn't a problem, but early mornings can be non-starters. It takes a while for the creative juices to get flowing, thus time is lost. I even set up schedules, minute by minute, hour by hour, but time still slips away. Has Global Warming made time go faster? Is the world and life just happening faster? Am I just filling my time with useless bits of junk to stave off boredom? I'm intelligent and curious and I want to know about what's happening around me, so I read, watch, think, and write about things. But working, sleeping and eating can get in the way of that.

My time is precious to me, I hate wasting time and my time being wasted by others (though I confess that due to my own selfish time-obsession, I am late for others). Time is a commodity I can ill-afford to give away cheaply; it can be more valuable than friendship and money and more pleasurable than sex (though time for that is great). Time to myself is paramount, the better to have my own sense of worth and well-being so as to live and work with others.

So how can I save time from creeping through the hour glass? As mentioned I do schedule, but planning doesn't always work. I scrimp and scrape to save time, but then something unforeseen occurs and steals my hard-earned time. It is those unanticipated moments that are time killers, so it does not matter how much you plan. I have a saying stolen from Star Trek's Scotty: "You cannae break the laws of physics." Each day, I know how long it takes to get ready for work, to shave, to dress, organise things, pack lunch, walk to the train station, etc. Everything is timed. But if one thing takes longer than usual, if time slips out of control, then there's no way to make it up. Shortcuts can be taken, but inevitably the quantity and quality of the time left is depreciated.

I am so time poor. Why can't there be more hours in the day? Mars has thirty eight extra minutes –great, send me there! Is my life such a rush that I can't stop to appreciate time or am I actually more appreciative of time, because you never know how much is left? I have so much to do and so little time to do it –what's a man to do? Modern gadgets don't save that much time or give little value for time. Sometimes the more technology surrounding you the more distracted you are from real-time caring and sharing. All I can do is shuffle time; it cannot be controlled. Time cannot be shackled; only monitored. Time cannot be tamed nor understood. We can only ride time at its own pace. We are at time's mercy.

So please, Sir, may I have some more time? A little bit more to enjoy and be creative in, where time can overlap and help me double up on duties, relaxation, and writing. I'm not greedy for time or desperate, but at least let me break even on time. I'm in the red for time and I cannot borrow more. I am so indebted to time that it's running my life and I can't catch up. Oh, time please spare a few mere moments, a minute or two, an hour, even? I would beg for a day.

I am glad I had the time to write this, to share my plight of time 'devoidness'. All I can do is go with the flow, save time here and there, and to use it purposefully. And hopefully, when I get to the end of my days, I won't look back and say it was all a waste a time.

19/Feb/2010

Customer care in supermarkets

Where's the Customer Service Care in Supermarkets?

Don't you just hate it when you go to the supermarket and things go wrong, like your favourite item is out of stock yet all the crappy alternatives are there, or the checkout person packs things wrongly, or people disregard the etiquette of the store? These are some of the bugbears you have to face at the supermarket. It comes down to customer care and attention to detail, which would be so easy to rectify. So why can't supermarkets get it right?

Packing:
Why can't cashiers pack bags properly? You put the items on the conveyor belt how you want them to be packed (usually by yourself), yet the person will pick up items in random order and plonk them in the bag willy-nilly. You have to physically take them from their hands and placed them in the bag you want in the order you want. They then give you a funny look, but you have to say to them not to put the eggs at the bottom of the bag with the potatoes on top. And who wants a toilet cleanser sitting beside your fruit. It makes sense. And please never, never fold the magazine/newspaper. It's the basic law of packing.

Yes, it may be busy and the checkout person wants to move things along, but not at the expense of quality care. It is up to the store to train in packing skills and we customers can also help. One good tip is to be polite to the checkout staff, sort your own packing, and remember to say "Thank you". Hopefully this will give the cashiers incentive to be more considerate towards your goods.

Out of stock items:
Why do the in-demand things run out and the cheap, rubbishy, unhealthy stuff stay on the shelves? Surely there are rules for pre-provisioning and stocking up on items people actually buy, rather than what shops find cheap to buy and flog. Take healthy cereals and sweetened Soya milk, which go out of stock and the cheap, sugary cereals are in vast abundance and the unpalatable, unsweetened Soya milks which really do taste like the cardboard they're packaged in are also left in greater quantities. What do the store managers actually do?

Who orders these things? If the supermarkets want consumer loyalty then they should show loyalty to their consumers, do better stock checks or consumer surveys and find out what their customers want, and it's not the unhealthy, sugary stuff.

If there is really an item you want or need, it is always good to ask a member of staff or preferably a manager and make your feelings known. Really express the fact that that in this day and age with healthy eating concerns, under-stocking the good stuff is not good enough. Yes, these supermarkets have deals with producers and are raking in millions by the day so one customer might not matter, but that customer is you and you shouldn't have to settle for anything less than the quality you deserve.

Empty checkouts:
We all know supermarkets can't employ an infinite amount of checkout staff. But there comes a time during shopping rush hour when the vast majority of such staff are on breaks. When there are a couple dozen checkouts and only three that are manned with queues backing up in the aisles then it makes sense to call in the reserves until the backlog is taken care of. But no, this is a slow process of a supervisor getting on the store tannoy and urging staff to man the checkouts. There is also the reverse of this when you spot an empty till and you rush over, only to find that the checkout person is clocking off and has put the 'this till is closing sign' out and by the time you rush back to the original checkout the whole world and his dog is in front of you. Lastly, who likes the self-service checkouts? More and more of these are popping up, but no one uses them. Checkouts are being outsourced to machines.

Man management and time management skills are important. The manager should know when rush hours and bottlenecks of customers will occur. If he doesn't have the staff, why not? Can the self-service checkouts be made less awkward and more user-friendly? Patience is not in abundance in such situations and it is down to the manager to have these things under control.

Store etiquette:
There is a way to manoeuvre around a supermarket; the supermarket has usually spent vast sums of money making sure people can find what they are looking for and also the best route around the shop. But there

are people who are directionally-challenged. They meander from aisle to aisle, picking random things as they go around. A simple shopping list really is effective as it helps the shopper disregard any random buys, helps in the navigation of the shop, and also makes packing of the basket or trolley easier, unless the basket is an awkward shape and can't hold more than a bag of potatoes and a box of cereal. People stand in the middle of the aisles, sometimes chatting to a co-shopper; baby buggies are always in the way, especially when little sir or miss is the one pushing it; and most annoyingly of all are the staff who have decided to re-stock during peak times and park their large trolleys in front of the very item you want.

Here's the problem: people are such random creatures that they will never adhere to any one system while shopping. What can be done about it? Plan, plan, plan. Have a list, know where everything is, get in and out as fast as you can, and rise above the maddening crowd of shoppers. Or just shop online, if you can stomach the charges they stick on for deliveries. If something is really bugging you, make it known to staff and hopefully it will be addressed as it is in their interest to provide quality customer care.

Shopping at the supermarket can be very frustrating. You have to be patient, organised and plan your trip to the last second and to the last penny. Customer service at supermarkets is the key to not wasting your valuable time and money. Make your voices heard and help your supermarket be the best it can be.

30/May/2010

What is holding back the paperless office?

The ever-lasting paper office

2020 vision

From what I can see, the paper-littered office is still here. There's paper for office memos and reports, notice-boards, signing in sheets, job forms and certificates, delivery notices, etc. The electronic gadgets and pens to replace paper seem to develop faults or not work with coffee or food-stained fingers or just don't display what we want, when we want. Technology isn't the end all, be all, and sometimes the humble, low-tech paper sheet is the best option.

The electronic and email age will render the office paperless. So was the claim a few decades back. Yet, with all the technical wonders of email, palm pilots, blackberries, iPhones, iPads, etc, the office is still overflowing with paper. What people forget is that even the Stone Age did not end for lack of stones; it ended due to successful, superseding technology, though we still use stone today for many things. Paper has yet to be so succeeded and superseded as to be irrelevant to today's professional. It is vital to them and around the world as much as papyrus was in ancient times. There are many reasons for this, ten of which are listed below. Feel free to print it out.

1. First port of call for idea jotting. Paper is brilliant for jotting down those all-important kernels of knowledge, ideas, and brainstorming thoughts. It's there on bedside tables for those late night flashes of inspiration and ready for thoughts of fancy throughout the day. It's more amenable to making margin notes, drawing diagrams, and organising thoughts on the go. Darwin's sketch of the tree of life on a page of the nascent "On the Origins of Species" is a case in point; it conveyed the essence of his thoughts in one doodle.

2. The look, touch and smell of paper are palpable. Is it the caveman inside us all that likes the touch of paper? Our ancestors walked among the ancient forests; we hunted in them; the trees provided shelter, food, and comfort, and still do. But is paper our subconscious way of

connecting to the lost wooded worlds? Our senses are stimulated by paper. Who hasn't smelled the old-style photocopied pages? Stacked and bound paper is more imposing than stashed disks and memory sticks in drawers. People still love the feel of a book or magazine in their hands, turning the pages, and just owning a piece of organised and printed pulp.

3. An acknowledgement of professionalism. Who isn't impressed when walking into an office and seeing stacks of books, files and reports on shelves? Many a professional has a certificate of achievement, framed and admired, on the desk or hanging in the office. The paper has meaning. It had to be earned. Professionals rate each other and compare businesses on those pieces of paper; it's how businesses and professionals build their reputations. Indeed, many successful companies built their reputations before the digital age. No amount of technological devices and gadgets will make up for professional status. Professionals have to be worth the paper their reputations are printed on.

4. A link in the Information Age. Paper doesn't need booting up; it's constantly on-stream or 'on-ream'. Paper can be a backup to technological databases and, especially in those all-important PowerPoint presentations liable to crash. Despite guarantees of durable data storage, it is not definitively known how long digital data can be stored and retain its data. There are still first-print books in circulation older than the digital age. In rare cases there are readable texts and paper from the last two thousand years that will still be around when digital data starts to degrade. Paper is a failsafe that can be copied time and time again, as the Bible has shown.

5. The personal touch seals relationships. A hand-written note or letter means a lot to a person, whether a personal note or a hand-written cover letter for work. Writing shows a level of confidence, dedication, and meaning, but unfortunately, penmanship is becoming a lost art. Books to some are not centres of learning, but obstacles to avoid. Libraries might as well be museums. But on those rare occasions when the arcane art of writing might be needed (for a flowing personal tribute on a card, or a draft report, or chairing a meeting or when the power fails), the professional with that skill (along with editing nous) may be a valued asset to the company.

6. Paper is ultimately versatile in presentation, mobility and portability. It can come in many forms, sizes, colours, plain or ruled paper and shift between an art form (paper airplanes, origami, boats, hats, etc) to a work base (envelopes, post-it notes, out-to-lunch/do-not-disturb signs, and more). Ten people cannot crowd around an email on a laptop, but paper copies can be distributed round. A laptop or hand-held device may be instantaneous at transmitting information, but until they are paper-thin, foldable e-paper then paper wins in the practicality stakes.

7. Print-version newspapers are still kingmakers and ball-breakers. The Financial Times, the Wall Street Journal, and The Economist, among others are still leaders in their markets. All professionals have some type of industry magazine or newspaper on their desk or central filing area. They are indispensable founts of knowledge. A news story could make or break a company and while the story may be internet-friendly, it's the front-page headlines in the paper which grab the headlines. Paper news cannot be ignored by professionals.

8. While more and more businesses and professionals deal in electronic payments and transactions, paper money is still valuable in professional circles. Money talks, it greases the wheels of industry, and it buys influence and possibly friends. While such paper has value, it is not the root of all evil; that comes from the minds of people who value money above all else. Petty cash is still needed for whip-rounds, lotteries, tea money, and after-work dinner and drinks that can't be claimed on expenses. So, show me the money; the professional's preferred paper of choice.

9. Absolutely 'shreddable', recyclable, and in some ways greener than technological plastic and silicon. Paper is cradle to cradle technology. One man's dodgy dossier can be transformed into another's report on the latest technological breakthrough and then perhaps turned into toilet paper. And it's virtually free compared to technical products.

10. Paper means jobs. If the office went paperless, whole industries (from newspapers, magazines, books, stationary, signage, decorations, and art, etc) would suffer and economies collapse. While environmentalists may laud saving paper, such a move would require a whole new paradigm in business thinking, cost more money in data production and storage industries, and cause excess pollution while

producing alternatives to paper and computer manufacturing. Paper is an important industry covering almost every aspect of life to a professional. It is no paper tiger.

The paperless office may never happen, but when it does it will be because the professional industry is ready for it. Until then when using paper, make sure it is from a sustainable source and that it is recycled so that many others can enjoy the sensation of paper for a long time.

Sport & Recreation

10/Jan/2008

Sports & Recreation - American Sport: A British Perspective

In Defence of American Sports

I am British and have lived in England, Canada, America, and been in the British Army. As someone who has played football, rugby, volleyball, ice hockey, baseball, cricket, American football, basketball, athletics, I believe that I have a very good insight into these sports than an armchair viewer and casual commentator.

Football/soccer is rapidly becoming the fifth sport of America. It probably will not overtake the main sports in America commercially, but it is a big game for schools and universities. Major League Soccer is a much better league now with quality Americans, ex-premiership and British players and managers. With numerous American players in the Premiership, this strengthens their national team, which competes regularly in world cups now. The women's team is better and is one of the world leaders in football, if one watched the exciting women's world cup games on TV recently. The quality can only get better; it is certainly not boring and as with the other major sports is shown, albeit in highlights, on Channel 5.

American Football is one of my favourite sports. There can be boring games as with other sports, but again, it is not boring overall. Brits for some reason just cannot get over the rugby analogies and the padding. Get over it, it's part of their game and it's not meant to be American rugby or a free-flowing game. You cannot hope to understand or appreciate this sport from highlights. Again I have played this game at high school and even now, while watching coverage from Channel 5, I have learned a lot about the game. It is all about strategy, which is way the game stops and starts; you have four chances to go ten yards, running or throwing, if it doesn't work you kick it to the opposition. But in between plays, the team has to set new play agendas, huddle or maybe not, regroup, sort things out and fake the other team out. Every team member on the offence, defence and special teams has their own position to cover while watching the whole field for action. It is a technical game, which is why for a one-hour game it lasts up to three hours, but the frequent ads do not take away from the game. There's no attention span deficit, if there was the game would not last three hours and still be enjoyable. There is hardly anything better than seeing a quarterback throwing to a receiver, both knowing they could be hit and yet still making the play, or a running-back finding the hole to run through for a long run. The excitement comes from watching the strategic game unfold, like a military campaign, capturing land, falling back, advancing, etc.

As for the fans, they love the game. I have never seen other sports fans dress for a game like it's Halloween every single week. The fans are also better behaved. I cannot remember a time over decades when there was a riot at an American football game or any crowd problems. It is more family orientated, with tailgate parties (barbeques and picnics) in the parking lot before each game. Also, in America you have university and college players drafted into the NFL. There is nothing like that in Britain, which taps a schoolboy on the shoulder for greatness with hardly any further education. Sure there may be some NFL dunces, but at least they have some sort of academic background after sports. Britain could learn a thing or two about nurturing young sports stars.

American Football IS played outside of the US, hence the (now) defunct NFL Europe, which hosted and traded American and European players for the NFL, and the newly formed and very popular British Universities American Football League (BUAFL). Look at their website. Even the NFL TV coverage is better with split screen views, overhead shots, better telestration and replay technology. Lastly, if anything, Brits do not have the patience for a dynamic and strategic game. I have even watched back-to-back games on Saturday while living in New York. As for cheerleaders, who can be male or female, it's a job and they are proud to represent their team and get involved. One former cheerleader is now BUAFL Head of Research, Dr. Elesa Argent.

I would watch a baseball game over cricket any day. It's not a jumped-up version of rounders or cricket and the aim is not always to hit the ball as far and hard as you can. There is a strategy to batting and pitching, which is why teams can change batters and pitchers to suit the situation. A batter can try and place the ball where he wants to whether in the infield (bunting), outfield, left, right or centre field in order for his team mate to get another base. This could even involve sacrificing yourself in order to do this. At least gloves weren't mentioned, because it's not that easy to catch with them and then make a play. And pitchers have a vast arsenal of pitches to strike out a batter, too. Baseball is played all over the Americas, Europe, China, in Japan (from the 1920s), and I played it in the Army in England, which has a baseball league, as do other countries around the world. Baseball is an Olympic sport from 1992, with Cuba beating Australia in the 2004 final, so it can't be that boring to others. There is an uncertain myth that the World Series was named after a newspaper *The New York World*, but it is more likely because in 1903 when the modern World Series began, the team who won was the best in the world, because only Americans played it. The name may be an anachronism now, but no one really cares about it, except pernickety Brits.

Basketball and volleyball are also popular world-wide and Olympic sports. Basketball is a fast-paced game, which attracts players to the NBA from Africa and Europe. Athletics in America is not hugely followed outside of high school and college, and because of this, they can concentrate on their sport and become champions without all the media hype, unlike British athletes who wilt from all the stress.

Ice Hockey is one of the most physical sports around. It demands tremendous fitness while skating, keeping your balance while hitting the puck or other players, dodging those same hits and trying to score. There's hardly a still moment in the game and is physically exhausting. Again it is a winter Olympic sport, enjoying success in Europe with Sweden the current champions.

A big difference, as a black man, is the high number of black players, coaches and staff on American teams, in sports which are not considered elitist fare. Only football here offers a suitable comparison. In my opinion, Brits need to come to terms that other nations play sports that may not be to their tastes. America may have TV markets for their sports, but other countries like Canada (lacrosse), Ireland (hurling), India (kabaddi), etc., also have strange sports, which may seem boring to us, but are hugely popular to others. The only thing to do is to research these sports and see how popular they are outside of America and also see rugby and cricket being played across America and Canada. You'd be surprised.

23/Jan/2008

Sports & Recreation – Super Bowl
Who will win 2008 Super Bowl XLII:
New England Patriots vs. New York Giants?

Go Giants

2020 vision

And the Giants did win 17-14, a classic game most memorable for 'that catch' – David Tyree's helmet catch – to keep the Giant's drive going with time running out.

And Spurs also won the Carling Cup, 2-1 against Chelsea – Spur's last trophy to date. 'Twas a good year for me.

Oh, the Giants are so gonna win!! I am so chuffed that they have made the Super Bowl. I am also doubly on cloud nine because across the Atlantic in my hometown London, my football (soccer) team Tottenham Hotspur have made the final of the Carling Cup after beating their fiercest rivals Arsenal after nine years. The Giants and Spurs are so alike in that they have great traditions and great former players, yet they under-achieve, are inconsistent, and come unravelled at the end of the season. But not this year. No one rated the Giants to make it past the wild card game yet they have beaten two great teams in the Cowboys and the Packers. So they are due this honour.

Other teams have under-estimated the resolve of the Giants, a team coming together at the right time. The Patriots are a machine. You know their go to weapons, their strengths and weaknesses, but they play to a system and beat teams on sheer reputation sometimes. The Giants are more organic and can be more adaptable because they have had injuries to contend with and new guys (Wilson, Bradshaw) have stepped into the breech. The defence is becoming stronger and they will give Brady all kinds of trouble. I don't think the Patriots can stop Jacobs, and in Eli Manning we have a quarterback who is still learning, yet coming into his own so much so that the team is drawing around him. His leadership and confidence are shining through. What a dynasty the Mannings will make if Eli wins a year after older brother Peyton did. The dynasty would be better than the political Bush's.

The Giants are the under-dogs. They will be under-estimated, but they did give the Patriots a good run for their money in the last game of the season. They have nothing to lose, nothing; while the Patriots have the perfect season to contend with. They might say that this is just another game, but the pressure will be on. The stain of the scandal upon the Patriots may sway more neutral fans towards the Giants and it would be a fitting end to the season if a team constructed of passion and honest hard work beat a team whose halo had slipped.

But the reason the Giants will win is because of Jeremy Shockey. He might not be there, but I once heard a commentator remarked on Shockey's commitment to the game. When he was in College, he lost a championship game and he was so devastated that he picked up some dirt from the field and ate it. He hated losing, so he wanted to remember the taste of defeat. So his exuberance and commitment comes from that and if that energy transfers to the rest of the team, then the Giants will win hands down. And champagne is better than dirt.

So not only do I hope to make Wembley for one final, I sincerely hope to make a Super Bowl party somewhere in London. GO GIANTS!

28/Jan/2008

A Short Guide to Sheepdog Trials

The Trials of a Sheepdog

I am not into the countryside as such, nor farms, dogs, or sheep, but there is something that compels me to watch sheepdog trials when they come on TV, typically around Christmas time with the programme 'One Man and His Dog'. I just love that interaction between the man/woman/child whistling or calling to the dog(s) to herd the sheep over varied field conditions and through various obstacles. It's great.

You quickly get to know the stories and personalities of the handler and his/her dog(s), a Border Collie breed. The control of the dogs through voice and whistled commands to guide the sheep through obstacles and gates is a fascinating thing to watch, a game of cat and mouse (or rather dog and sheep).

Points are awarded for successful completion of the course in the quickest time with fewest penalties. Components of the trials include:

The Fetch —where the handler, from a fixed position, sends the dog over a distance to collect the sheep. This is important for the dog cannot always see the sheep as it runs out and has to listen to the handler's calls.

The Lift —where the dog, from behind the sheep, then brings the sheep toward the handler, usually through a gate. This takes control, as the sheep can bolt away and miss the gate completely, losing the handler points.

The Away Drive —as the dog brings the sheep around the handler, the dog is instructed to drive the sheep away and through another set of gates, followed by

The Cross Drive —where the dog then drives the sheep horizontally across the field and hopefully through another set of gates. Of course, more points are lost if some sheep go around the gates and not through them.

The Shed is where the sheep are led into a prescribed circle, held, and the dog instructed to separate one or more sheep from the group in a controlled manner. The handler can leave his position in order to direct which sheep are to be separated.

Finally, the dog is required to drive the sheep from the shed and into a pen, with the handler closing the gate behind them. The winner of the trials is the handler/dog team with the most points.

There are several variations to these trials, such as having two dogs, two groups of sheep, or corralling into a vehicle rather than a pen, but those are the usual elements. It never fails to amaze me, the skill needed to accomplish this.

The TV commentators are quite informative and pick up details I would never imagine would really matter, like the wetness of the ground which sheep apparently dislike or the over-eagerness of the dog. The emotions of both the dogs and the sheep really do play an important part and if the sheep are skittish, it takes patient dog to deal with them.

Sheep dog trials are something I would never compete in, but it's something I still like to watch. I look forward to the day it is an Olympic sport. Until then, I'll be here at Christmas ready to watch one man and his dog and assorted sheep.

07/Apr/2008

Politics, News & Issues – International Politics (Other)
2008 Olympics : Should the Olympic torch be greeted by celebration or protest?

Olympic Ideals

We should celebrate the Olympic ideals and the torch, which encapsulate the spirit of brotherly competitiveness throughout the world. The torch is not the symbol of any one country, but an international beacon for sporting excellence. The disruption of the torch relay in London only insults those athletes preparing for the games, in some instances for years. This is their job, their forte, their livelihood, and they are not involved in the political processes of any country.

Britain has always had a healthy history of protesting and demonstrating, and long may that continue. But the levels of vitriol against the torch relay runners were against that spirit of protest. Trying to pull the torch from the hand of TV presenter, Konnie Huq, was an act of aggression and not a part of protesting. A fire extinguisher was also used against the torch. These protesters misrepresent the genuine protesters who act for Tibetan freedom. They undermine the earnestness and validity of anyone who speaks for Tibetan freedom. They turn any sympathy for the Tibetan cause into antipathy.

Chinese flags can be burned in protest or demonstrators could line or block the route or make grandiose speeches, but an assault upon the torch and torchbearer is not conducive to the Tibetan cause. People know about the Chinese actions in Tibet, but freedom campaigners will lose credibility if protesters act like violent hooligans. Their misdirected anger at the torch should instead be turned on the politicians who are indecisive; caught in the middle of condemning such acts and having to maintain diplomatic decorum when their own citizens are running riot.

People like to say that politics and sport do not mix, but that is not strictly true. In England, when foreign businessmen are eyeing football clubs, there is much political hand-wringing as to which and how many foreign owners (and even players) there should be. There is even much political debate over involvement with Zimbabwe's cricket team. The

(Soccer) World Cup is rotated and awarded to nations due in part to political considerations, as are the Olympics. No part of society is untouched by politics, including sport. So Politicians should be out in force, voicing their opinions, one way or another.

Media bias was evident in the reporting of the London torch relay. Only pictures of police intervention and interception of the violent protesters was beamed around the world. The police were right in their actions for they would be facing unknown threats to relay runners. Sure there were other protesters caught up in the police operations, but on one TV talk show phone-in the following morning, one of the spectators present in Trafalgar Square commented on the peaceful nature of both protesters and police, yet those pictures were not shown on TV. Yes, some police may have acted over the top, but by and large demonstrations were peaceful. If the media is going to report on such a controversial issue, then they should show both sides and not fan the flames of the already raging politicised debate, for viewing figures.

The Paris torch relay has also suffered protests and disruptions with the torch allegedly extinguished three times as to evade protesters. But the protesters' actions will not affect the Olympic reality. No one will remember these protests in years to come. They never do. Because whatever the outcome of the Tibet unrest, the games will go on. The Olympics in China will not be cancelled, boycotted, postponed or interrupted. There will be protests, demonstrations, and no doubt a few conflicts, but an international Olympic Committee did pick China, knowing full well the controversies and implications. Celebration of the torch relay is in no way condoning Chinese actions, I could care less about China, but the Olympic Games should transcend such ideologies and politicking.

Protest all you want, but focus on the real issues and the people behind them. The Olympics are not the real issue, but a smoke screen and sleight of hand tactics by political manipulators on both sides to deflect attention away from the real problems -and solutions- within China and Tibet. Think about it. I fully intend to celebrate the torch relay and the Olympics, so will millions more. The torch is a symbol, an important one, and a celebration of hope and glory, in a world of uncertainty. Why extinguish it?

26/Aug/2008

Sports & Recreation - Olympics
Reflections: 2008 summer Olympics in Beijing, China

Thoughts on the Beijing 2008 Olympics

What a fantastic Games! Where to start? Well, to be truthful I'm not a big fan of Opening/Closing Ceremonies so I only watched the highlights, but despite all the reports of 'jiggery fakery' on fireworks, the singing-girl swap incident and other identity swaps, the opening ceremony was an extravaganza to behold and the Olympic Torch embedded in the Bird's Nest Stadium was an inspiring sight.

Stadiums:
Speaking of which: the Stadiums were magnificent. The Bird's Nest has to be recognised as one of the most iconic buildings in the world now. Not many national stadiums are as instantly recognisable worldwide and that is a tribute to Chinese vision and technology. Even the athletes loved the track. The Water Cube was also a sensational swimming arena that swirled in colour from the outside and resounded to cheers on the inside. The Laoshan Velodrome was awesome; having not really watched cycling before I was blown away by the sheer pace the 'speedy boards' seemed to impart to the cyclists. The golden block for basketball was also top class as was the Pagoda-like media centre for the world's press.

Games of Records and Confidence:
This was supposed to be the Games of Chinese 110m hurdler Liu Xiang, but after his hobbling act from physical and mental stress, that honour passed to Usain Bolt, the newly crowned 100m, 200m and 4x100m champion and world record holder. Only non-athletes and casual viewers of athletics were cynical of his wins with whispers of some kind of assisted help, but that would be totally disingenuous to Bolt. As other ex- and current athletes knew Bolt was already a sporting prodigy at age 15. His height and raw power marked him out to greatness and he has successfully married up his strength, long stride, leg speed, and most importantly his confidence into a winning technique. He will be around for some time and who knows if he will return to 400m running! For a country of only 2.8 million and for a team of 51, comprising 39 track athletes, Jamaica is punching above its weight. Both

the Jamaican men's and women's teams grew more confident after each win, while the Americans' confidence seemed to evaporate on the track, saved by the men's 400m relay.

Well done to Michael Phelps who will also be a top name from these Games, although to some he will still be second to Bolt's achievements even though he won a record-setting 8 Golds with 7 world records. Who is the best ever Olympian? Does it come down to performance over one Game, multiple Games (like rower Sir Steve Redgrave) or world records (like Michael Johnson) or racial defiance (like Jesse Owens)? Phelps will be in that elite group, but depending on how you measure Olympic greatness, he will not necessarily be on top.

Drugs:
Usain Bolt's training was his only weapon; no drugs were needed. The Athletes were drug tested to destruction, especially the Jamaican team, like it was an Olympic sport in itself, and it netted a few athletes including heptathlete Bronze medallist Lyudmila Blonska. Phelps was on top of his game with no suggestion (from other athletes) about drugs. I was also pleased for Christine Ohuruogu, the 400m runner winning the gold. A lot of people still misunderstand the reasons for her suspension and reinstatement over 3 missed drug tests, but the British Olympic Association is one of the most stringent organisations around on the issues of drugs (witness Dwain Chambers) and her clearance by them should indicate her complete innocence. The strangest drug incident was the positive tests of 4 horses, though the circumstances are still disputed by the four different teams. Beijing has proved so far to be quite clean.

Politics:
I hope people will look past the politics. Yes, there were protests, violent actions, and repression, but that should be dealt with separately. These are professional athletes who ply their trade at the highest levels and if they objected then they would not have gone; the politicians would not have gone. Rather than use any protest action or boycotts against China, the Games could be used to spotlight the good areas and impress upon China the need to expand on them, while also shining a light on the darker aspects of China. But first and foremost let the Games speak for themselves.

London is doing the same thing as Beijing in relocating residents and businesses from Stratford, many of whom have operated and lived in that area for generations, but now regeneration for the Games is uprooting them. The clearance programme, though not as forceful as Beijing's, was reported on at first, but now hardly merits a mention.

Despite some bad publicity on the 'jiggery judging' (on Taekwondo, boxing and gymnastics), the murder of an American man, a suspected terrorist attack, the scare stories of pollution (in fact, despite a few downpours, the weather and air seemed to agree with the Games), and protests, these have not dented the fact that the Chinese are human after all and were proud to show off their country, history and skills.

Britain and 2012:
This was Britain's best Olympics for 100 years with 19 Golds, 47 medals in total, and 4th in the table overall; the goal UK Athletics had set for 2012. So much more is achievable for the future with 3rd place behind China and the US a distinct possibility.

The British media was pretty well balanced in their reporting. They did reflect on Tibet and other disputes throughout China, but they stuck to the games and celebrated the wins of other athletes from different countries. They were also giddy with excitement over Britain's overall success and now look forward to 2012, though I hope they don't over-hype our prospects as is usual for sporting events.

So what can Britain bring to the Games of 2012? Well, some say we won't live up to Beijing, but we won't have to. China had something to prove at any cost; Britain does not. We do pageantry like no other country, whether for the monarchy, sports finals, music festivals and other national events. Britons celebrate in the streets and the atmosphere will be electric and festive, not like the empty, sterile Beijing streets. The Games of 2012 will be a cosy affair and we will stick the kettle on for the world!

Legacy:
I hope the legacy from these great games will reflect in China's dedication to sport, the environment and over all in politics. China need not be afraid of the world, nor we of China and I think the Olympics have shown that and why it was created in the first place to bring nations together.

26/Aug/2008

Sports & Recreation - Olympics
Sports that should be added to the Olympics

New sports for the Olympics

Having watched the Beijing Olympics and a bewildering array of different categories for sport (e.g. Mountain Biking, trampoline, handball and Canadian canoeing), I wondered what other types of wacky sports could be included.

Rodeo:
In the Equestrian events, I would like to see the Rodeo; with the cowboys riding, roping and branding (read inking) skills. It might be better suited for the Americans, but I'm sure it would spread, though it might be a man-only event for now. Are there female rodeo riders? The 'how long can they stay on the bucking bronco' would be a great World and Olympic record to set.

Bull Fighting:
This might favour Latino nations, but again it is a sport where other nations could catch up. No bulls would be killed, just daubed in paint to indicate 'kill' strikes. Points would be awarded for speed, accuracy and difficulty in approach and evasive skills. Shouts of 'Ole' would echo around the Olympics.

Sheep Herding:
One Man and his Dog has been a feature of the British farmlands, with Christmas specials shown on TV following cancellation of its regular timeslot. You quickly get to know the stories and personalities of the herder and his/her dog(s). The control of the dogs through voice and whistled commands to guide the sheep through obstacles and gates is a fascinating thing to watch, a game of cat and mouse (or rather dog and sheep) and points would be awarded again for successful completion of the course in the quickest time with fewest penalties.

British Bulldog:
I wonder if school kids still play this or if it's 'outlawed' as too dangerous. It's an 'accumulative tag' game with as many players as you

want so would be great for single or mixed categories. You start off with one person as 'it' (the Bulldog) who is faced by how-ever many along a baseline in a set field with boundaries. At a signal the competitors on the baseline have to run to the other side of the field, avoiding being tackled by the Bulldog. Once captured, you are now part of the Bulldog team and so on until there is one remaining, who can take his chances, or not. With Olympic Bulldog, the competitors would be from different countries, who would take turns being 'it' and points awarded for captures, escaped tackles, successful runs, etc.

Air Sports:
The Olympic ideals are higher, faster, stronger; so let's take to the air with Olympic Hot Air Ballooning, parachuting, air surfing, and forget about propeller air racing —let's go for the rocketplane racers soon to start in Oshkosh, Wisconsin. Each event would be a simple showcasing of speed and skills with hot air ballooning having to navigate a set course with speed; parachuting would offer solo and formation skydiving and landing targets; air surfing would be judged on trick skills and slalom racing; and the spectacle of rocketplane racing would bring the Olympics into the 21st Century.

Cultural sports:
Both modern and ancient sports could be included from around the world like Kabaddi from India, Sumo wrestling, Lacrosse, and the ancient Mesoamerican ballgame, though no one would be sacrificed at the end to consecrate the (Olympic) ground, and it would be funny watching the athletes play a ball game using their hips.

War:
Yes, war! On average, since WWII, the US had been engaged in conflict almost every 3 and a bit years, so why not codify war for the Olympics, which was supposed to end conflicts between nations. It would not be to the death as bombs, bullets and bayonets would be replaced by laser tag devices (for the less squeamish). People might assume that the US would win more medals in Olympic Warfare, but it might not always be the Gold. There'd be points and penalties for tactics, logistics, friendly fire, attacks and counterattacks, successful conclusions and peace settlements. But the points would also be spread among the 'host' war nation, the 'visiting' war nation, nation allies, the 'Olympic UN', protesters (who influence political will), mercenaries/terrorist/freedom

fighters, and the peace treaty members. As many nations as possible can take part in Olympic Warfare.

Incorporating War as an Olympic sport, thus nullifying its deadly implications could help to bring about world peace and also wars would only come about every 4 years and last 16 days without bloodshed. How good is that?

25/Sept/2008

Sports & Recreation - Keeping fit despite your age

Keeping Fit and Healthy in Your 40s

2020 vision

While I enjoyed a casual jog, in 2011, I had run an organised local 10K event attended by former Olympian Tessa Sanderson. But while training for another event, I hurt myself and took a while to recover. After that, I only stuck to 5K or less. Then in 2015, I joined Parkrun, the international 5K run initiative. I loved running, but hadn't done so properly in the intervening years with my lower back, knees, groin and hamstrings giving me problems. I ran with knee and hamstring braces and it took me days to recover after a run.

I'm sure it was a combination of things, one being a change of trainers (the heels had worn unevenly causing pain in my knees and hips) and another being the purchase of a cross-trainer in early 2015 to take the strain off my joints. Also, I've been quite glad my hernia repair way back in 1991, while in the Army has behaved itself for the past two decades. So, gradually, I could run without the braces and I recovered a lot quicker between runs. I can now run weekly without that pain. I'm up to 76 Parkruns and was hoping to complete 100 by the end of 2020, but the pandemic put an end to that. But now I am back out running Notparkruns getting ready for when we go again. I'm eating more healthily and in the article below still working out at home, keeping the mind going, staying stress-free, and safe.

There is usually that look of surprise on a person's face when I tell them my age. They wonder how I can look so young and handsome (okay I added the last bit), but all I can say is that it's a combination of genes and my own fitness regime. My parents still look quite young for their ages (in their 60s and 70s) and they are relatively active with the usual age-related niggles. I just hope I'm as healthy as them when I reach my 'senior' years.

But as every aspect of life is a varied permutation of nature and nurture so is staying healthy. My interest in physical fitness started when I moved to Canada from England around age 11. The Phys-ed teacher, Mr. Fox, seemed aged to me, but he was as strong as an ox, able to climb that thick heavy gym rope hand-over-hand. It was the feat of strength all the boys in class aspired to. After that it was the sports teams and I enjoyed several levels of jock-ism throughout high school. This continued when I moved to New York and the high school track team was my highest achievement with my best performances. This was the first phase of my physical fitness journey: the growing up and learning about your body and competition.

The post-high school era was different as I had nothing to do. I wanted to join the military, but was undecided on what to join. I had also discontinued any sports becoming a couch potato and putting on a few pounds. But then I decided to come back home and join the British Army, so I had to get into shape. And here's where the first part of my physical fitness experience helped me. I was able to get back into my own training regime quite quickly and by the time I joined the army, at a relatively 'old' 22, I was fitter than some of the younger recruits. Again, there was more to learn about my own endurance and performance levels, whether in combat fitness or playing for army sports teams, but physical fitness in the army was also about survival. So my second phase of fitness consisted of the strategic and tactical aspects of physicality.

Such lessons took me into my 30s as the army had taken its toll on me. I had over done it. I thought I was bionic and indestructible, but a hernia, broken bones and pulled muscles (all sports injuries) taught me otherwise. I had to slow down and re-adapt my training programme. At this time I entered university as a mature student. I could have blended in with the students in looks regarding age, if not a year or two older, but I wasn't, so I had to keep in shape for any team I joined, the usual parties and drinking sessions. As a matter of fact, drinking was never my strong point and I only started drinking in the army (cider first, then shandies, then snake bites) and it was the army that taught me that spirits are not to my stomach's liking. Even now, I'm a light drinker of beer. And fortunately I never was interested in smoking or drugs. So, throughout university I worked out, keeping myself trim. The whole university experience was a continuation of the first two phases: learning, competing, and survival, but my strategy was now in looking forward to the next decades ahead and staying healthy.

So as I hit my 40s and people asked how I could be so young looking, healthy and handsome (whoops –done that), I always told them about my parents, but then I told them it's by working out and eating right; basically taking care of myself. After all these years, I know my body. I know why something hurts and generally how to take care of it and I'm not afraid to see the doctor. In fact, one visit to the doc, about my over-worked hip, ended in his surprise at how 'bendy' I was in my late 30s. I stretch out before and after workouts. Also, if I am injured and have to reduce or stop working out, my recovery is still better and faster due to muscle memory. I surprise myself sometimes at how quickly I can bounce back from a muscle pull. It always reminds me of another story a former gym teacher told me about an American Football player who severely injured his neck and survived a serious break by dint of all the muscles that held it together. That may have been an old wives' tale, but it still impressed upon his young class that fitness could make injuries less serious, but also aid in the recovery time. I've been fortunate to benefit from this.

There are also other benefits to keeping fit. In addition to changing my diet over the years to its healthiest yet (though I'm a big believer in 'Everything in Moderation'), my stress/anger level is also lowered. Exercise is great for the mind, easing any stresses. Also, I have never suffered with flu in my adult years (flu being the end-of-days affliction that leaves one bed-ridden). I have colds, but I let them run its course and now don't take any medicine, except paracetamol, vitamins, and helpful foods. That could be down to genes, but I'd like to think that my body is a honed anti-flu machine. I also don't drive, so I do a lot of walking often with a heavy bag on my back or in my hands. People also ask me if I go to the gym, but I haven't been to any since the army. I work out exclusively at home, one hour of music, which I dance around to in lieu of running that serves to get the heart going, work up a sweat and save wear and tear on muscles and bones. Then I stretch out from head to toe, before doing alternate sets of different sit ups and press ups. I sometimes use light strap-on weights for the arms. So while my earlier years have banged me up somewhat due to my own over-exuberance in working out, I believe I have finally found the balance of fitness training that will carry me through to my later years.

So far from my youthful aspirations to have big muscles and without the need to avoid the enemy (depending on the neighbourhood I'm walking through), I find I just need to let my muscles know they're there and how useful they are. My fitness journey started early, which I am grateful for. There's no need for the gym and working out can relieve stress and increase creativity, with the incidental benefit of keeping you fit and healthy for a long time.

14/Oct/2008

Sports & Recreation

Home Workouts

2020 vision

Twelve years on and I still work out at home with my own series of warm-up and cool-down stretches, press-ups and sit-ups, with occasional light-weight work-outs. I'm not after big muscles or to get thin, though I do watch my weight and waist. But it's mostly to keep the muscles maintained so I can lift myself off the floor at least. I find I heal faster after an injury, suffer much less with colds, and I've never had the flu as an adult. But I guess no matter what and how much exercise you do, you never know what could hit you out the blue. While I'm not a work-out addict, I certainly couldn't sit around and not do any exercise. It's good for my mind, body, and soul. Essentially, I'm experimenting with my body, hoping I have the right ingredients to stay fit and healthy for my next half century. Each to their own and everything in moderation.

I work out exclusively at home. I found that you do not need to expend time and money at a gym to have a good workout. Working out at home is less stressful, flexible, and you won't get any self-conscious complexes about anyone looking at or judging you. In familiar surroundings and at your own pace, your fitness levels can increase at your own leisure.

I have built up my own home workout regime over the years with exercises cobbled together from school, the Army, university and from TV workouts, but each phase is adaptable, with minimum equipment needed, and a workout can consist of a quick half-hour workout or a two hour session.

Warm up cardio:

First is the cardio dance session, in lieu of running, which can be done in your own living room or bedroom. Essentially, for me, it is around one hour of music, any type, which gets the heart going, works up a sweat, and saves wear and tear on muscles and bones. You can even sing to it, adding to the cardio workout. It is such a stress reliever and fun. It gets you in the mood for the next part.

Stretching out:
The dance session has warmed your muscles up, now it's time to stretch from head to toe. I start with the neck, rotating and articulating the neck, moving on down to arm and shoulder stretches. Hula-hoop movements loosen up the lower back. Next are stretches of the hamstrings, thighs, calves, ankles, and even some butt-clenching; nothing is missed out. Stretching usually takes about twenty minutes.

Main work out:
I sometimes start with light strap-on weights (5lbs) for the arms. With high repetitions, I can work out the biceps and triceps, and work the traps with upright rowing action. After that, I then go back to the floor and start an alternate set of different sit ups and press ups. To protect an old shoulder injury, instead of the extended press up position, I am on my knees, but in the same press up position. This also adds more of an upper body workload.

The first set is essentially normal press ups. You will feel the pressure along the top of your chest. Then for the sit ups, my feet are up on the sofa or bed to do stomach crunches, including cross-body crunches.

The second press up set are cross-thumb press ups and diamond-tip press ups, where your thumb and forefinger tips form a diamond shape. Along with maintaining balance, these mainly work out the upper chest and triceps. The sit ups are essentially the same as the first, but on the floor, feet on the ground.

The third press up set are wide arm press ups, with a slightly wider arm position that the first set of press ups. With the sit ups, it's a straight crunch, but with my thighs vertical of the ground; then leg raises, followed by bicycle kicks, and kick outs. The last press up session is a repeat of the first set. This is followed by a warm down stretch, and after a final shake of the limbs, I feel great and ready for some protein.

Each home work out is an individually work-out system, but it is totally flexible and discreet as you want it to be, with the added value of unveiling your new physique to friends who will never know how much work you've put in to look and feel great.

16/11/2008

Sports & Recreation
Who is to more to blame for poor soccer team performances: Players or managers?

Who's to blame for poor team performances: Players or Manager?

After watching the recent football comings and goings among English Premiership managers, especially with the team I support, Tottenham Hotspur, and with other sports teams, I have now decided that it is the manager who has the ultimate responsibility when teams break down and start losing. There are many reasons for this.

First, take my team Tottenham Hotspur. We've had so many managerial changes in recent years it boggles the mind, but the dramatic difference between Juande Ramos and Harry Redknapp is there for all to see. Ramos was definitely not a bad manager; he is one of the best in Europe, which is why Spurs 'stole' him from Sevilla in the first place. He inherited a strong team and won the Carling Cup in his first few months. However, the Cup hangover lasted too long as he lost quite a few games after that, which continued into the current season. Many will blame the Board, the Director of Football and the selling of key players, but Spurs had done well under that regime for two years under Martin Jol, Ramos' predecessor. Ramos' managerial style didn't suit the system and he had a steep learning curve in English football. He lost the support of the players and fans, and he too was summarily axed along with his assistants and the Director of Football.

Then in came Harry Redknapp, the well known wheeler-dealer East London boy, who has all but worked miracles and put a spring back in the step of Spurs, all with the same players. So what has happened? Yes, the Director of Football has gone, giving Redknapp control over transfers and players, but it is the confidence he has instilled within the team. He knows the English game intimately, knows that players need the love and respect to perform, and he can communicate that effectively. I believe that is where Ramos failed, and not just with the players.

Ramos had to learn English while managing, so there were bound to be a few misinterpretations. But he was also known as a disciplinarian, which the players complained about. There had to be some give and take between players and manager, which Ramos didn't seem to take to. This is illustrated in another one of my favourite teams, the NFL's New York Giants.

When Tom Coughlin came to the New York Giants, he was also known to be a disciplinarian, 'a martinet' as one media pundit put it, and the Giants were on a losing streak. But the players recognised there was room for change and had a long talk with Coughlin. The players and coach had regular meetings about what was working and what wasn't; they sorted out their season and actually won the Super Bowl, which no one expected. Now in the current season, even with the loss of key players, the Giants are now considered one of the best teams and likely to reach the Super Bowl again. And this is directly attributable to Tom Coughlin changing his managerial style, in his 60s, for the sake of the team.

There are also parallels in the workplace. If you have a bad boss, then morale and productivity goes down, no matter how good the workers are. Weak and ineffectual management is the downfall of many a company and it's the workers that suffer. The same is true for football, which nowadays is a hard-nosed financial commodity. The task of the manager is to keep productivity high to generate a quality product, for maximum earnings.

Football players need to be loved, respected, and feel confident. Talent can only get you so far; a player has to be honed and matured, deployed properly and supervised on and off the pitch, which is the manager's job. Money is not the issue since it doesn't seem to be incentive enough for players to win under a bad manager, plus if you look at smaller teams doing better than bigger teams, then it suggests that the manager is getting the best out of his team through other incentives, rather than just money. This could be a good case for salary caps, performance pay, and/or lower salaries, but that's for another debate. If you're a talented and well-paid star playing for a bad manager and the team keeps losing, the manager will get the blame. Conversely, if you're a bad player earning an average salary and the team is losing, then it's the manager's responsibility to pick the team up and motivate them and instil loyalty and pride in results. But if the manager is an unresponsive and/or inept motivator, then his job will be at risk.

This doesn't mean that the manager isn't a scapegoat sometimes. Sometimes his players aren't good enough, but again that comes down to the manager's choice in transfers, style of play, and even his relationship to the players. Managers are hired for their man management skills, to train, set an example, and make the players understand their roles in the team. If the players do not respond then it is up to the manager to change the system or the players.

The manager is in the middle; he's the lynchpin in the synergy of players, the Board, fans and even the media. The manager is on the front line, the most visible and most responsible for the team's performance. The players have to respect the manager, feel confident in their ability and be loyal to the team. The Board also has to feel that, which emanates to the fans, who will support the manager to the hilt. The British media is well known for 'hiring and firing' managers everyday in the back pages of newspapers and if they sniff weakness, they will hound the manager until his position is untenable, no matter the performance of the players. The media recognises where the buck stops: fail to deliver and the manager is gone –simple.

AFTERWORD

I have always endeavoured to be creative, a little non-conformist, and a free-thinker outside of the echo-chamber surrounding me. Times have changed and some topics have become outdated in our 24/7 news culture. But some will always be eternal subjects cycling through our minds ready to be pondered over and reinterpreted.

The four years of intense creativity (2007-11) which took up a central part of my life were but reflections of my past and a beacon to my future. I was moulded into an Infovore, always seeking more information, distilling data until it became a part of my soul. That creative impulse is still pent up in me, now distributed into various streams, diluted by social media, but undeniable.

But I hope my words have given you pause to reflect, rage and revel; to write, blog or vlog in the future, bringing your own creative forces to bear

And who knows, maybe this old Infovore will write once again. At this moment in time, the world could use a little more knowledge and creativity.

Lightning Source UK Ltd.
Milton Keynes UK
UKHW022020110822
407199UK00003B/77